ASPEDEN HALL

AN OPEN ELITE?
ENGLAND 1540–1880

AN OPEN ELITE?
ENGLAND 1540-1880

BY

LAWRENCE STONE

AND

JEANNE C. FAWTIER STONE

OXFORD · CLARENDON PRESS

1984

Oxford University Press, Walton Street, Oxford OX2 6DP
London New York Toronto
Delhi Bombay Calcutta Madras Karachi
Kuala Lumpur Singapore Hong Kong Tokyo
Nairobi Dar es Salaam Cape Town
Melbourne Auckland
and associated companies in
Beirut Berlin Ibadan Mexico City Nicosia

Published in the United States
by Oxford University Press, New York

OXFORD *is a trademark of Oxford University Press*

BRITISH LIBRARY CATALOGUING IN PUBLICATION DATA

Stone, Lawrence
An open elite? England, 1540-1880
1. Great Britain—Gentry—History
I. Title   II. Stone, Jeanne C. Fawtier
305.5'23   HT657
ISBN 0-19-822645-4

LIBRARY OF CONGRESS CATALOGING IN PUBLICATION DATA

Stone, Lawrence.
An open elite? England, 1540-1880
Bibliography: p.
Includes index.
1. Elite (Social sciences)—England—Case studies.
2. England—Social conditions. 3. Architecture, Domestic
—England. 4. Country homes—England—History.
I. Stone, Jeanne C. Fawtier. II. Title.
HN400.E4S76   1984   305.5'232'0942   83-8221
ISBN 0-19-822645-4   Rev.

Printed in the United States of America
by
Princeton University Press

IN MEMORY OF

ROBERT FAWTIER	&	JULIA READ STONE
who remembered		indefatigable
July 1914		visitor
spent at Taplow Court		of country houses
the country seat		open to
of the Grenfells		the public

CONTENTS

Part I
INTRODUCTION

Part II
OWNERS

Part III
HOUSES

FIGURES IN THE TEXT

PLANS IN THE TEXT

LIST OF PLATES

PHOTOGRAPHIC SOURCES

Photographs have been supplied by owners, with the exception of the
following:

Country Life: XI A & B
Courtauld Institute of Art: XII B
Paul Mellon Centre for Studies in British Art (London) Ltd.: XIII B,
XIV
Yale Center for British Art: I

LIST OF TABLES

(following page 458)

GENEALOGICAL CHARTS

PREFACE

The division of responsibilities between the two authors has been as follows: Lawrence Stone conceived the project, prepared the proposal for funding, worked out the concept of "units" of living-space, and was responsible for all conversion of known measurements into these units and for all estimates of house size; he devised the original format of the questions to be asked of the computer, collected the literary evidence about contemporary attitudes, and wrote the book. Working on and off for over a dozen years, Jeanne C. Fawtier Stone was responsible for the initial exploration of secondary sources to find out what information was available for statistical manipulation; the recruiting, training, and supervision of research assistants to assemble these data, and for re-evaluation of the latter when they conflicted. The general aspects of the code-book and the nature of the questions to be asked of the data and the computer were worked out collaboratively, Jeanne Stone acting as interpreter between Lawrence Stone and the programmers. It was she who devised the code-book, personally encoded the data, negotiated with the programmers over the details of data storage and retrieval, and dealt with the problem of predigesting the results of the programs, where necessary reassembling these in tabular summaries with evaluative conclusions. Many of the major findings of the book emerged as a result of suggestions made by her about what questions to ask and how to manipulate the data to find the answers. Every page was subjected to her constructive criticism and frequently incorporates material added by her. She wrote Appendix II, 2 and drew up the Bibliography and the Index. Although neither of us would wish to repeat the experience, the task was nonetheless one which could only have been carried out on a collaborative basis.

The publisher is the Clarendon Press, Oxford, but responsibility for printing was subcontracted to the Princeton University Press.

If the intellectual production of this book failed to make full use of the most up-to-date computer technology, the same cannot be said about its physical production. We are very grateful to the Directors of the two Presses for having made possible this collaboration; to Dr Charles Cullen who first introduced us to the possibilities of such a procedure; and to Ms Carolyn Kappes and Mr Phil Leclerc of the Princeton Press for making so relatively painless our introduction to this new printing technology. We are also extremely grateful to Ms Judith Waterman, who guided the book

through the final difficult stages of production with calm efficiency.

We are indebted to the National Science Foundation, Grants
GS28832X and GS1559X for financial support of the project over
a number of years. Without this support to pay for research assistants, coders, programmers, computer time, and sabbatical leave,
this study could never have been accomplished. We are also grateful to the Mathematical Social Science Board, which first encouraged and supported this project and under whose auspices an original pilot exploration of methodology was carried out and some
tentative results were first published.[1] Princeton University contributed sabbatical leave, summer travel grants, and a grant for
typing the final product. Thanks to the generosity of the Rocke-
feller Foundation, we were provided with a month of peace and
leisure in country-house surroundings at the Villa Serbelloni, during which much progress was made in writing drafts of several
chapters.

For prompt and courteous attention and advice, thanks are due
to the staffs of the British Library, the Bodleian Library, the National Monuments Record, the County Record Offices of Hertfordshire, Northamptonshire, and Northumberland, the Northampton City Library, the Society of Antiquaries of Newcastle-
upon-Tyne, and the Newcastle Central Library.

Jennifer Clark, Virginia Finney, Patrick O'Hern, Barbara Roth-
blatt, and Dean Tjösvold provided invaluable research assistance
over the years. For essential guidance in coming to terms with the
computer, we are deeply indebted to my colleague, Theodore K.
Rabb, to Judith Rowe of the Princeton Computer Center, and also
to Andrea Smith and Nita Rome, who designed the programming
of the data. Finally, I am deeply grateful to my secretary, Joan
Daviduk, for her patience and paleographic skill in deciphering my
now all but illegible handwriting, and turning it into a typed first
draft with her usual brisk efficiency.

A book such as this covering so wide a span of time and so many
problems, obviously depends heavily on monographic studies by
other scholars. So many friends and colleagues have contributed,
in one way or another, by helping us to formulate our conclusions
and by supplying specific information, that it is impossible to
mention them all. But we are well aware that we are standing
upon the shoulders of a multitude. Particular acknowledgments

[1] L. Stone and J. C. Fawtier Stone, 'Country Houses and Their Owners in Hertfordshire
1540-1879', in *The Dimensions of Quantitative Research*, ed. W. O. Aydelotte, A. G. Bogue,
and R. W. Fogel, Princeton, 1972.

should be made of the help given by H. M. Colvin, Wilfrid Prest, Dame Elsie Thom, and the late Joan Wake.

For some helpful general suggestions I have to thank the audience at the Social Science Seminar at the Institute for Advanced Study at Princeton, to whom I presented some of my findings. I am particularly grateful for suggestions from my friends Clifford Geertz, Felix Gilbert and Jerrold Seigel. I am also grateful to Peter Lindert for permission to quote from an unpublished working paper.

Throughout this book, spelling, capitalization, and punctuation have been modernized, and all dates are New Style.

L. S.

J. C. F. S.

Part I

INTRODUCTION

I

THE PROBLEM

'Society, like each of ourselves, is perpetually renovating itself' [J. A. Froude, On the Uses of a Landed Gentry', in his *Short Studies on Great Subjects*, London, 1907, iv, p. 304.]

I. DEFINITIONS

i. The Hypothesis

Twenty years ago Professor Hexter looked with amazement at the astonishingly successful tenure of power of the English landed elite over a period of seven centuries. He identified as one of the great unanswered problems about English history, one which itself would solve many others, the single question 'How . . . did they do it?'[1] This book sets out to test and challenge one of the most common answers given to this question.

Ever since the fifteenth century it has been generally held, among foreigners and natives alike, that one feature which has distinguished English society from that of the rest of Europe has been the easy access of self-made men to power and status: the harmonious intermingling with the landed interest not only of successful public officials and lawyers, but also of men enriched by trade, speculation, what was called high, and sometimes dubious, finance, and even industrial entrepreneurship. In England, we are told, these new rich have been more eager to enter into the ranks of the landed squirearchy, and more rapidly and more readily accepted when they got there, than anywhere else in Europe. England, that is, has long been 'an open elite' (the word aristocracy in its broader definition, comprising all the greater landowners, regardless of their titular rank, has been avoided to prevent confusion with its narrower definition, comprising only members of the peerage).[2] This is a paradigm readily accepted both by liberal and by Marxist social historians, even if they have drawn different

[1] J. H. Hexter, *Reappraisals in History*, London, 1961, p. 19.
[2] This use of a phrase such as 'elite' avoids the pitfalls of confining attention to the titular peerage, which probably never comprised more than two-thirds of the greater landowners of England. See F. M. L. Thompson, 'The Social Distribution of Landed Property in England since the Sixteenth Century', *Economic History Review*, 2nd Series, xix, 1966, pp. 506-7. This looser terminology does, however, raise very difficult problems of definition.

moral conclusions from it. I myself have been as guilty as others of making this assumption.[3]

Four profound consequences have been held to follow from this alleged social pattern of frequent and easy upward mobility by successful men of business into the ranks of the landed elite. One is the creation of the most productive agricultural system in Europe, with the possible exception of Holland. It has been argued—for example by Adam Smith in the eighteenth century, and R. H. Tawney in the twentieth—that these thrusting, calculating, profit-oriented, self-made men turned their entrepreneurial skills into reorganizing agricultural practices and introducing new crops and new rotations, and were the leaders of the agricultural revolution, whenever it may have occurred. It is an accepted fact that this revolution enabled England to escape from the Malthusian trap some two hundred years before most of the rest of Europe, with critical demographic and economic consequences.

The second major alleged consequence is the primacy of England in the race to modernity and industrialization. It has been argued that the ease of upward mobility into the landed elite provided ambitious business men with an incentive to make money, since glittering rewards of social prestige were within their grasp, and that after 1650 the landed elite itself was willing to adopt economic and foreign policies designed to protect domestic industry and commerce and open up foreign markets by direct naval action around the globe.

The third major alleged consequence is the creation of a stable yet flexible political system, which defused potentially threatening attacks by its readiness to co-opt newcomers into the ranks of the ruling class. It has been argued that there is an inverse correlation between the rate and ease of upward mobility and the intensity of class conflict: when mobility channels are blocked, social tensions rise, and vice versa. Thus it was due to the willingness of the ruling elites to absorb newcomers into their midst that England transformed itself from an agricultural nation into an industrial one with a huge urban proletariat, and also slowly shifted from an

[3] The number of historical commentators who have made these claims about the fluidity of the upper reaches of English society are legion. Among the more widely read of recent works are C. Hill, *Reformation to Industrial Revolution*, London, 1967, p. 184; R. H. Tawney, 'The Rise of the Gentry 1558-1640', in *Essays in Economic History*, ed. E. N. Carus-Wilson, London, 1954, i, p. 188; L. Stone, *The Crisis of the Aristocracy 1558-1641*, Oxford, 1965, pp. 38-9; H. J. Perkin, *The Origins of Modern English Society 1780-1880*, London, 1969, pp. 61-2; and P. Laslett, *The World We Have Lost*, 1965, pp. 47-50. The latter's concept of a 'one-class society' is based on this theory of fluidity of movement in and out of the landed elite.

oligarchy to a participatory democracy, both without revolutionary outbreaks of violence and destruction.

The fourth and last major alleged consequence is Britain's relentless economic decline over the last hundred years. It has recently been argued that this has largely been caused by physical assimilation of the successful entrepreneurs of Victorian England into the landed elite through the purchase of a country house and the adoption of a gentrified life style, and by cultural assimilation through the public schools and admittance to the House of Lords. As a result, the heirs of these upwardly mobile families have been made ashamed of their fathers' profit-maximizing activities, and have lost their enthusiasm and aptitude for industrial capitalist innovation.[4] Thus a great deal of English social, economic, cultural, and political history over the last 400 years is riding on the truth of a single paradigm, the alleged fact of the ease of upward mobility by successful men of business into the higher levels of landed society. It is of no small importance, therefore, to know whether this supposedly unique social pattern actually existed, and if so when, and to what extent and in what ways it varied over time.

It is a curious historiographical phenomenon that up till now the facts of the case have never been satisfactorily demonstrated. There are two ways in which the hypothesis might be tested, one of which would be to trace the careers of successful men of business. The object would be to determine how many of these new men used their wealth (and if so, how much) not for reinvestment in the enterprise whence it originated, but for purchase of a landed estate, a country house, and a genteel education for their children in order to establish a family of respectable country squires.

Another approach, which is the one primarily adopted in this book, is to look at the problem from the point of view of the county elite itself, to analyse, and whenever possible to quantify, its composition and the degree and methods of infiltration of new wealth into its ranks from generation to generation. In one sense, of course, the question of whether or not the English landed elite can be described as open can be answered with an unqualified affirmative. It was indeed open in the sense that there was little to prevent most of the male children sliding out of it. Generation after generation, younger sons were left to trickle downwards through the social system, with only some education, some money,

---

[4] M. J. Wiener, *English Culture and the Decline of the Industrial Spirit, 1850-1980*, Cambridge, 1981. The argument is couched in cultural terms, but the author also uses as a basis of his case 'English history's normal pattern of ready absorption of new into old wealth' (pp. 12, 14).

and influential patronage to give them a head start in life. This situation is in striking contrast to that in most European countries, where economic primogeniture was not so rigidly practised, where younger sons retained titles of nobility and the legal privileges that went with them, and where status-enhancing offices in government service, and especially in the army, were more numerous and more easy to come by. But this incessant downward drift of younger sons answers only part of the question. If the two-way valve was left open to allow these unfortunates to fall out of the status group into which they were born, was it also left open to allow access from below for men of humbler origin (and also for younger sons), who by their own exertions had acquired new wealth and power? The first question, the downward mobility from above of younger sons in England, cries out for a book of its own, for it is one of the most important and most obscure aspects of English social history from the sixteenth to the twentieth centuries. It is, however, to the second and even more important issue of the ease of upward mobility from below and the consequent degree of turnover among the old landed elite, that this book primarily addresses itself.

ii. The Landed Elite

By the 1580s the gentry were drawing apart into two groups, definable in terms of economic resources, life-style, occupation, and range of cultural interests and activities. The first, known to modern historians as the 'parish gentry', were men whose interest and powers were limited to the boundaries of one or at most two villages, most of whom had had no education beyond that at the local grammar school, and who were rarely eligible for any administrative post above that of JP. These were the butt of the London wits, poets, and playwrights from Shakespeare to Sheridan and beyond. They are *not* the subject of this study.

The second are known as the 'county gentry', men of greater wealth, power, and sophistication, who automatically laid claim to local political leadership, including membership of parliament, who enjoyed the benefits of higher education, often finished off by the Grand Tour of Europe, and whose intellectual and political horizons began with the county but spread out to include the capital city of London.

These two groups lived in houses of different size and function, since they necessarily pursued different styles of life. The parish gentry entertained on a small scale, for short periods of time. The county gentry had a position to keep up and so needed a seat of suitable grandeur; they had a political connection to maintain, and so needed space for generous entertaining. Their sociability led them to fill their houses with guests, regularly entertaining company at dinner several times a week in season, and welcoming relatives and friends on extended visits of days or weeks on end. All this required space, both above and below stairs.

The dichotomy between county gentry and parish gentry is of course based on a Weberian model of ideal types, and reality does not always conform to theory. Some wealthy county gentry lived like pigs; some modest parish gentry obtained significant political influence, and there was movement in both directions between the two. The cut-off point is inevitably a somewhat arbitrary one. But the social historian is obliged to formulate his categories as best he can, knowing full well that there will always be borderline cases and anomalies, whatever choice he makes. The distinction between the county elite and the parish gentry is a real one to us looking back on the past today, and it was also a real one to contemporaries. It was and is based not merely on subjective perceptions but also on objective criteria of life-style, reflected in education, housing, taxation, political power, and office-holding. It cannot be denied, however, that the obsessive anxiety about rank and status in the late sixteenth and seventeenth centuries, as witnessed by the many attempts at ranking and classification, were caused by a genuine weakening of old lines of division, as men began attributing to themselves coats of arms and titles such as esquire and gentleman by virtue merely of office or income. This devaluation of titular ranks in no way softened the distinction between parish gentry and county squires, but the division was now seen at least as much in terms of life-style as of status. By the late seventeenth century, for example, the word gentleman no longer meant a landed proprietor and the word esquire could include a mere urban office-holder like Samuel Pepys. But even if the assumptions had become devalued, the concept of a ruling landed elite was preserved, as nearly all commentators were prepared to concede.

The subject of this study is therefore the changes which occurred in the composition of the upper reaches of the English landed classes over the 340 years from 1540 to 1879. It was from this elite group that were drawn most of the political rulers of England during this period, and those few who were not born into it, like Lionel Cranfield in the early seventeenth century or Disraeli in the late nineteenth, were soon established in a country seat and assimilated to it. This last point needs to be emphasized, since the justification of the myth of an exclusively landed ruling class in England resides in the fact that those rulers who were not drawn *from* the landed classes were automatically drawn *into* them by virtue of their office. The last relic of this tradition is the provision in the early twentieth century of Chequers as the ex officio country house of the Prime Minister, who nowadays rarely possesses one of his or her own.

The section of the landed classes under study consists of those members of the aristocracy, baronetage, knightage, and squirearchy whose main territorial base took the form of at least one large country house and a substantial landed estate. By the eighteenth century, most of them also owned or rented a town house in London. These men formed what we shall call the county elite, whose characteristics were a combination of great power (at some point in the family's history), participation in local administration, substantial landed wealth, broad but not deep education, a generous style of life, and high status, the minimum status attribute being the nominal title of squire. Before the mid-seventeenth century the key division of society was between those who styled themselves gentlemen or above, and those who did not. But this line had become hopelessly blurred by the late seventeenth century, because increasing numbers of bourgeois men of business in the cities and towns, possessing no land, little or no classical education, and few aspirations to cultural gentility, were nevertheless styling themselves gentlemen. In the late seventeenth century, however, the word 'squire' came into general use to establish a new social division, this time confined to those who owned a substantial landed estate and a country seat. After 1660 a highly placed bureaucrat with court connections but of humble origin and possessing no land, like Samuel Pepys, might sign himself 'esq.' on the basis of his office as Secretary of the Admiralty. But no one addressed him or referred to him as 'Squire Pepys', the way people addressed and referred to Fielding's archetypal wealthy country gentleman as 'Squire Allworthy'.

Since access to this elite of squires is the chief concern of this study, it includes not only the established county families but also all those who by their way of life appeared to be trying to gain admission into their ranks. Entry was possible either through purchase of an already established country seat whose previous owner had sold out, or through inheritance or purchase of a smaller house (and estate) which was then enlarged as a visible token of increasing substance and aspiring status. The successful integration of these newcomers might be immediate, it might be spread over several generations, or it might abort for lack of staying-power. But since different modes of recruitment to the elite are a central question, the inclusion of at least some of these ultimately unsuccessful aspirants is as essential as is that of those on their way towards decline from former elite status into the ranks of the mere parish gentry.

Power is a difficult concept to handle. It is fairly easy to define, as the capacity to exercise one's will over the majority of others in the community. It is usually associated with some institutional structure, such as local government or national office. Access to these offices tended to be restricted to persons who possessed certain physical objects, a country seat and estate, certain psychological attributes, good manners and a genteel education, and up to a point a certain socio-biological attribute, of birth within this status group, at any rate for one generation. Those among this group who had the talents, the interest, and the energy would and did become the rulers of England, the key decision-makers in government, Court, Parliament, and the county. These people thus formed an economic and status elite, a pool of talent from whose ranks emerged the ruling class that ran both the counties and the country.

It has long been known that the composition of this group has never been static.[5] But hitherto no attempt has been made to demonstrate statistically the main cause of this mobility, nor to chart the different rates of change at different periods of time. It is well known that families have constantly been dying out in the direct male line. When this happened, their county seats and their estates might either be passed on more or less intact to a near or distant male relative, or descend to a single heiress and so to her husband, or else be dispersed among several heiresses and male relatives. They might also be sold by any of these along the way.

Other families were ruined, either by financial imprudence or by association with unsuccessful political causes. More common, though much less dramatic, was the fate of those families whose slow decline was mirrored in that of their houses. They sank, as it were, by omission, by maintaining their traditional ways and failing to move with the times. As a result their income failed to provide them with sufficient resources to maintain the standard of living appropriate to their status. In a period of steadily rising standards of comfort and luxury, failure actively to 'improve' land,

---

[5] A masterly overview of current knowledge is to be found in H. J. Habakkuk, 'The Rise and Fall of English Landed Families 1600-1800', *Transactions of the Royal Historical Society*, 5th Series, 29-31, 1979-81.

house, and fortune spelt ultimate decline. Conversely there were those who, through shrewd investment and entrepreneurial management of land, and judicious marriages with heiresses, managed to elevate their standards of housing and display expenditure to match those of the times. If they combined this with playing their political cards astutely and cultivating the right court patrons, they stood a very good chance of picking up a title on their way up.

Century after century, the balance within the landed class was maintained by the injection of outsiders. A few, who were the artificial products of sudden royal favour and unscrupulous exploitation of the fruits of office, amassed so much wealth that they were able within one generation to acquire very extensive estates, build or enlarge a 'prodigy' house, and establish one of England's great aristocratic families. Others, whose takings from law, office, or trade were more modest, were sometimes obliged to leave it to their heirs to obtain admission to full membership of the county elite.

So far, however, we have had no hard facts about what proportion of a local elite was made up by newcomers at any given time, how exceptional they were, how they made their money, and to what extent they succeeded in establishing new landed families rather than grafting themselves on to old ones or merely buying in for one or at most two generations and then selling again. There have been a few studies of county societies over a short period of time, very many family histories (of the successful) over a long period, and several studies of urban elites over short periods. But there has never before been attempted a survey in depth over three and a half centuries of three county elites, geographically scattered so as to provide a reasonable sample of variations in experience.

The use of a very large body of evidence in a variety of different ways makes it possible to answer a series of critical questions about such matters as the degree of social homogeneity of this landed elite; how much this homogeneity has varied from century to century, and also from county to county; how this landed elite has renewed itself, whether from its own ranks or by absorbing outsiders; how far this process of renewal has been affected by changes in demographic patterns or marriage strategies; where these outsiders came from and how they made their money; and what was the role both of women and younger sons in the transmission of property.

iii. The Seat

A critical problem which arose at an early stage of this enquiry concerned the selection of an appropriate set of criteria by which to define membership of the elite. Since ownership of a country house was a *sine qua non* of elite membership, and since this would provide a coherent framework within which to operate, it was decided to try to formulate a meaningful definition in terms of ownership of (and residence in) a country house of a certain minimum size, standing in pleasure-grounds of a certain minimum acreage. It cannot be emphasized too often that this is a study of owners of country houses, not of landed property. Owners of seats as here defined may have bought and sold estates on a considerable scale, but this is only taken into account if increasing landed wealth induced a parish gentleman to build himself a lavish country seat and so enter the elite, or if, conversely, a member of the elite dissipated so much of his estates that he was either forced to sell his seat or was unable to live in it in the appropriate life-style and so fell out of the sample. This book is thus concerned exclusively with the country-house market, not the real-estate market, and only pays attention to movements in the latter when they affected the former.

The justification for adopting this methodology is that it was found that ownership of a house of a certain size was a suitably reliable status indicator for membership, or aspirations to membership, of the county squirearchy.[6] The identification of country-house ownership as one key test of membership of the elite also made it possible to use this study to answer another set of questions about how their owners treated the houses themselves, how they changed the size, layout, and aesthetic appearance over three and a half centuries. Since this building activity can be correlated with changes of ownership, the evolving social configuration can to some extent be linked to its appropriate architectural setting. Consequently, although this book is primarily a study of changes in the social composition of the owners of country houses, its last section is concerned with the changing appearance of the houses themselves as symbols of elite status.

2. VALUES: LAND AND A COUNTRY SEAT

From the sixteenth to the nineteenth centuries, land had one principal economic advantage as an investment, and that was security. Overseas trade or business was always risky, and bankruptcy at all times very common. Moreover these risks were vastly increased if the management was left in the hands of a dishonest agent, an

---

[6] L. Stone and J. C. Fawtier Stone, 'Country Houses and their Owners in Hertfordshire, 1540-1879', in *The Dimensions of Quantitative Research in History*, ed. W. O. Aydelotte, *et al.*, Princeton, 1972, pp. 88-101.

inexperienced widow, or a lazy and good-for-nothing heir. Thus
it was the prospect of having to hand his great brewing enterprise
over to a daughter which drove Henry Thrale and his wife to such
extreme despair at the death of their only surviving son and heir.[7]
Land, on the other hand, could be made very safe indeed. A tolerable land agent, a sense of family responsibility, the convention
of primogeniture, the legal safeguards of the strict settlement, and
a readiness to use surrogate heirs if the direct male line failed, all
made a large landed estate relatively immune to erosion over time.
Ownership of land was almost the only way in which the rights
of posterity could be properly safeguarded, to make sure not only
that the family name and fortune would endure, but also that the
widow would get her jointure, the daughters their marriage portions, and the younger sons their cash grants or life annuities. Nor
was land always an altogether unprofitable investment in itself. In
periods of rapidly rising land values, such as 1590 to 1640, 1770
to 1815, and 1850 to 1880, there were also large capital gains to
be made by shrewd speculation in land purchase. Thanks to legal
changes after the Restoration, it became very much easier and safer
to raise capital sums in a hurry through a mortgage for a period
of years. The fall in the rate of interest from 10 per cent in the
sixteenth century to 5 per cent in the nineteenth, together with
the development of a legally enforcible equity of redemption, made
borrowing on mortgage both safe and attractive.

Against these advantages, however, there had to be set the normal low rate of net return on investment in land—usually less than
from lending money on mortgages or taking shares in ships or
trading corporations. There were long periods when profits from
agriculture were stagnant or declining, and could only be increased by capital-intensive and risky ventures, such as enclosure,
drainage, and the planting of new crops. Moreover land was difficult to liquidate in a hurry, so that a man threatened with bankruptcy who had a considerable share of his assets tied up in land
would find it hard to avert disaster. When all is said, it is therefore
hard to avoid the conclusion that the principal economic advantage
of land was not profit but security.

By the eighteenth century, however, this security could be
matched by government funds, which now became readily available. Dr Johnson was drawing attention to a major shift of financial opportunity when he observed that 'it is better to have five
per cent out of land than out of money, because it is more secure.

7 M. Hyde, *The Thrales of Streatham Park*, Cambridge, Mass., 1977, pp. 156, 160, 162.

But the readiness of transference and the promptness of interest make many people prefer the funds.' By the mid-eighteenth century, the two were in direct competition for capital, so that by 1747 it could be said that 'as this is a time when so much money is turning on government securities, it is not easy to raise any immediately on land'. There is indeed statistical evidence to show that the price of land fluctuated inversely with that of the funds in the eighteenth century, being dominated by the factor of demand. As a result, land which could be bought for eighteen years' purchase in the late seventeenth century, rose to twenty-seven years' purchase in the late eighteenth.[8]

Land and a country seat, however, did not merely mean a secure if small economic return. It also signified power and status. The role of the greater landlords in the power structure of the nation was a commonplace of political theorists like James Harrington in the seventeenth century. It was this conception of landed property as a source of power which was the basis for Lockeian political theory, according to which it was perfectly logical and proper to withhold the vote from large numbers of the English population, especially those without property. The forty-shilling freeholder franchise in the countryside was defended on the grounds that a stake in the land was a necessary qualification for political rights. 'Persons ought not to have voices unless they contribute to the public charge', that is by way of taxes, observed Sir William Jones in 1680. 'There is no such security of any man's loyalty as a good estate', agreed Mr Coningsby in 1685. As for MPs 'the Commons . . . think themselves safest in the hands of men of great estates', complacently asserted Sir Henry Capel in 1689. All these remarks, casually made in the course of parliamentary debates, reveal by their unstudied assurance of revealed truth how widespread was the view that only the possession of some landed property gave legitimate access to the vote and thus to the political process, and that the greater the property the greater the claim to political power. In 1782 Lord Kames agreed with Boswell that 'if property was the principle, a man should have a number of votes in proportion to it; and he thought men of large property less liable to be bribed'.[9]

[8] *Private Papers of James Boswell*, ed. G. Scott and F. A. Pottle, New York, 15, 1932, p. 173; E. Hughes, *North Country Life in the Eighteenth Century*, Oxford, 1952, i, p. 158; C. Clay, 'The Price of Freehold Land in the later Seventeenth and Eighteenth Centuries', *Economic History Review*, 2nd Series, xxvii, 1974, p. 174.

[9] A. Grey, *Debates of the House of Commons 1667-1694*, London, 1763, viii, pp. 127, 365; ix, p. 469; *Boswell: The Applause of the Jury, 1782-1785*, ed. I. S. Lustig and F. A. Pottle, New York, 1981, p. 21.

Landowners consequently felt it perfectly proper to ensure their own political monopoly by limiting MPs for the county to men owning land worth a minimum of £600 a year, besides giving themselves and their farmers a monopoly over game by forbidding shooting by anyone with less than £100 a year. After the stabilization of the political system in 1721, they drastically reduced the number of both electors and contested elections. The parliamentary candidates were selected from among the elite by prior arrangement, hammered out over the dinner-tables at their country seats, and contested elections became a relative rarity—necessarily so because of their inordinate expense. Thus the county seats of Nottinghamshire were not contested at all between 1722 and the early nineteenth century.

The ownership of land continued to carry with it political power long after the passage of the First Reform Bill in 1832. The latter enfranchised the middle classes but isolated them from the rural voters, who remained under the influence of their landlords, whose power only really began to wane after the Second Reform Bill of 1867. Trollope made Archdeacon Grantley observe in the mid-nineteenth century 'land gives so much more than the rent. It gives position and influence and political power, to say nothing about the game'. In 1867 *The Economist* was a little more precise about what a landed estate and a seat could offer to the aspiring newcomer: 'The sherrifalty [*sic*], a squeeze of the hand from the Lord Lieutenant, the County balls for his wife and daughters, and perhaps an opening to the House of Commons'. Put that way, it does not sound like a very worthwhile return in terms of social advancement for the investment of several hundred thousand pounds. But the fact remains that as late as 1867 over 500 of the 658 MPs were still members of the landed elite.[10]

Ownership of land did not only confer power and prestige, it also carried corollary obligations. As William Marshall observed in 1804, 'a tenanted estate differs widely from any other species of property . . . It has . . . a dignity, and a set of duties, attached to it which are peculiar to itself '. It was just this combination of residential rural living and a paternalist responsibility for estate management and the direction of local affairs which conferred on the county elite the great prestige and political authority it continued to enjoy at least up until the end of the nineteenth century.

[10] J. D. Chambers, *Nottinghamshire in the Eighteenth Century*, London, 1966, p. 31; A. Trollope, *The Last Chronicle of Barset*, [1867], World's Classics, London, 1946, ii, p. 178; *The Economist* quoted by F. M. L. Thompson, 'Britain', in *European Landed Elites in the Nineteenth Century*, ed. D. Spring, Baltimore, 1977, p. 29; *Essays on Reform*, 1867, p. 16.

If men strove to enlarge the size of their estates and to use the income to build larger and more elegant seats, it was because at bottom they were prestige-maximizers rather than profit-maximizers. In 1823 Lord Calthorpe was prepared to sell his [potentially enormously lucrative] suburban properties around Birmingham in order to extend his holdings around his seat in Norfolk by the purchase of some 11,000 acres of poor-quality soil. His reason was that 'it affords an opportunity of acquiring space at a comparatively small expense'. By doing so he could create 'one of the finest residential estates in the country' and so greatly extend his prestige and political influence. It was this, not the potential profit of urban development, which really counted in his mind. Indeed many landowners deliberately traded rent in return for political influence over their tenants and their votes. As late as 1842 Alexander Somerville observed that 'landlords to maintain a political control over their tenants, sacrifice a large pecuniary interest'. It is therefore not so surprising that when in 1881 the Earl of Derby listed 'the objects which men aim at when they become possessed of land', he put rental income last. Before it came political influence, social importance, power over the tenantry, and residential enjoyment and sport, in that order.[11]

The heyday of the country squire lasted from about 1660 to about 1880. Before 1660 the members of the group were still busy acquiring their estates, establishing their position in local society, and building their seats. They were also struggling to work out a viable relationship with the local magnate on the one hand and the central government on the other, both of whom had threatened their independence at one time or another in the sixteenth and early seventeenth centuries. By 1660, however, they were fully settled into their economic and social niche as the semi-independent rulers of the countryside, in harmonious but wary relationship with both influential local noblemen and powerful officials in London. Moreover, after 1660 the economic strength of the greater squires relative to the parish gentry tended to increase, thanks to their activity in enclosure, drainage, fertilizing, the introduction of new crops, the sinking of coal-mines, and urban development. They were an energetic entrepreneurial elite, many of whose political actions incidentally served the economic interests of themselves and their tenants. They limited the import of cattle from

---

[11] W. Marshall, *On the Landed Property of England*, London, 1804, p. 335; I owe the Calthorpe reference to Dr David Cannadine; *Land and Industry*, ed. J. T. Ward and R. G. Wilson, Newton Abbot, 1971, p. 9. H. A. Clemenson, *English Country Houses and Landed Estates*, New York, 1982, p. 96.

Ireland, so as to keep up the price of domestic livestock, and they
restricted foreign trade in corn, so as to keep up the price of domestic wheat.[12] They also improved communications by sponsor-
ing canal and turnpike Acts in order to get their produce to market. As will be seen later, however, these men were very far from
being an irresponsible plutocracy, which was the secret of the extraordinary duration of their social and political hegemony.

3. PERCEPTIONS: UPWARD SOCIAL MOBILITY

As early as the fifteenth century, foreigners were commenting upon
the openness to new wealth of the entrenched landed elite in England, and the reluctance of the nobility to live in cities. These two
themes were associated, since it was this relative rejection of urban
life and urban values by the arbiters of opinion which encouraged
wealthy merchants to turn their liquid capital into land purchase
and to set themselves up as country gentlemen. In the early fifteenth century the Italian Poggio Bracciolini reported that

the English think it ignominious for noblemen to stay in cities. They live
in the country, cut off by woods and fields. They devote themselves to
country pursuits, selling wool and cattle, and they think it no shame to
make money from agriculture. I have seen a man who has given up trade,
bought an expensive estate, and left the town to go there with his family,
turn his sons into noblemen, and himself be accepted by the noble class.

Here is perhaps the first clear statement of the perception of the
English social paradigm, to be repeated *ad nauseum* for the next
four centuries. In the late sixteenth century an anonymous observer remarked that rich Londoners 'do for the most part . . .
convey themselves after Cicero's counsel, *veluti ex portu in agros et
possessiones*'. In 1565 Sir Thomas Smith declared that gentlemen 'be
made good cheap in England', in other words that money from
any source could purchase status.[13] In 1559 an agitated conservative actually drafted legislation to prevent merchants buying land,
a proposal also vaguely contemplated earlier by Thomas Cromwell
in the 1530s and Edward VI in 1548.[14] Thereafter, the alleged

[12] 12 Ch. II Cap. 4; 22 Ch. II Cap. 13; 1 W. & M., Cap. 12; N. S. B. Gras, *Evolution
of the English Corn Market from the Twelfth to the Eighteenth Century*, Cambridge, Mass., 1926.
[13] P. Bracciolini, *Opera*, p. 69 (quoted by G. Holmes, *Florentine Enlightenment*, London,
1969, p. 146); J. Stow, *Survey of London*, ed. C. L. Kingsford, Oxford, 1908, ii, p. 208;
T. Smith, *De Republica Anglorum*, ed. L. Alston, London, 1906, p. 39.
[14] *Letters and Papers of Henry VIII*, ix, p. 725; xiv, pt. i, p. 330; 'Discourse concerning the
Reformation of many Abuses', in *Literary Remains of Edward VI*, ed. J. G. Nichols, Roxburghe Club, 1857; *Historical Manuscripts Commission, Salisbury MSS*, i, p. 163.

infiltration of the elite by men of low birth but large fortune was a subject of animated and continuous debate and comment. Both the English themselves and foreign observers continued to be fascinated by the question, and many could talk of little else. It was the staple of the plays by Marston and Massinger in the early seventeenth century, running on through Wycherley to Sheridan in the eighteenth. James Harrington constructed a whole political theory around it in the mid-seventeenth century. Daniel Defoe returned again and again to the subject in his voluminous writings. Novelists from Samuel Richardson to Jane Austen also made it one of the two basic themes in the English novel, the second being the closely related issue of love versus money and status as the decisive factor in the business of marriage.

The first crescendo of allegations about the decline and disappearance of the established families of the county and their replacement by self-made newcomers from the City occurred in the early seventeenth century, when it became a stock theme of social commentators as well as playwrights. Marston, for example, remarked '. . . tradesmen well 'tis known, Get with more ease than gentry keeps his own'. In 1614 it was said of Northamptonshire that 'most of the ancientest gentlemen's houses in the country are either divided, diminished or decayed'. This was the theory of the decline of the gentry, one which totally neglected the flood of new building which was replacing these tumbledown old houses. The second theme was that the replacements for these older families were men from outside the county and of dubious background: 'There hath been within these three or four years many good lordships sold within the county, and not [one] gentleman of the county hath bought any, but strangers, and they no inhabitants'.[15]

The desire of merchants to buy land was a stock-in-trade of early seventeenth-century playwrights. 'Oh, that sweet, neat, comely, proper, delicate, parcel of land', exclaims the merchant Quomodo in Middleton's play *Michaelmas Term*. Many believed that by withdrawing capital from trade at each generation to put it into land and a country house, English commerce was thereby being starved of necessary capital. As early as 1621 Sir Dudley Digges complained that 'the City of London is a place that seeks only to enrich themselves, and then away they go to the country in the second descent'. He alleged that 'when they grow rich, they purchase lands and go live in the country; or else give over their

---

[15] G. Chapman, B. Jonson and J. Marston, *Eastward Ho*, II, i; *Montagu Musters Book, 1602-1623*, ed. J. Wake, *Northamptonshire Record Series*, vii, 1935, p. 235.

trade and turn usurers, as most of the Aldermen of the City do'. Forty years later MPs were still voicing the same complaint about the withdrawal of risk capital from trade. They contrasted English practice unfavourably with that of the Dutch. In 1667 Sir William Coventry observed that 'merchants in Holland, not having much land to purchase there, employ their money generally in trade. 'Tis otherwise in England, for as soon as a merchant has a good stock of money, he presently buys an estate'. Three years later the crusty Colonel Birch snarled 'now, if your trade be worse, it is because the merchant must have his London and country house and his wife must go as fine as his neighbour John's'.[16]

In 1693, the great merchant prince Sir Josiah Child asserted that 'if a merchant in England arrives at any considerable estate, he commonly withdraws his estate from trade before he comes to the confines of old age'. Child was indeed one who successfully did just that. His motives, however, were curious, since he offered a unique twist to the standard argument that capital in land is safer than in trade, even if it brings in a far lower annual return. According to Child, one of the main reasons for investment in land was the poor economic education of English wives, unlike those of Holland. As a result, 'if God should call him [a merchant] out of the world while the mass of his estate is engaged abroad in trade, he must lose one third of it through the unexperience and unaptness of his wife to such affairs, and so it usually turns out'. English mercantile wives seem to have been withdrawing at this time from the counting house to become genteel ladies, as Colonel Birch, as well as Defoe, complained, so there may be some grain of truth in Child's argument.[17] How many merchants actually withdrew the bulk of their capital from trade in order to set themselves up as country squires, however, is another matter.

Defoe was confident that substantial numbers of merchants were displacing the gentry, at any rate near London. From what he saw on his tour of England, he deduced 'how the present encrease of wealth in the City of London spreads itself into the country, and plants families and fortunes, who in another age will equal the families of the ancient gentry, who perhaps were bought out'. In Essex he found 'several very considerable estates purchased and now enjoyed by citizens of London, merchants and tradesmen'.

---

[16] T. Middleton, *Michaelmas Term*, II, iii; *Commons Debates, 1621*, ed. W. Notestein, F. H. Relf, and H. Simpson, New Haven, 1935, iii, p. 394; A. Grey, *Debates of the House of Commons 1667-1694*, i, pp. 116, 360. The same argument was used to criticize the investment of merchant capital in the national debt in the early eighteenth century (P. M. G. Dickson, *The Financial Revolution in England 1688-1756*, London, 1967, p. 29).

[17] J. Child, *A New Discourse of Trade*, London, 1693, p. 5; D. Defoe, *Complete English Tradesman*, [1729], London, 1890, pp. 352, 355.

The west of Epping Forest was 'filled with five seats, most of them
built by the citizens of London', the finest of all being the home
of Sir Josiah Child. In Surrey, the ground under the Downs near
Carshalton was 'crowded with fine houses of the citizens of London; some of which are built with such a profusion of expence that
they look rather like the seats of the nobility than the country
houses of citizens and merchants'. (Plate VIB.) Guessing wildly,
he reckoned that 500 large estates within a hundred miles of London had been bought up by merchants and tradesmen in the previous eighty years. In 1733 an indignant pamphleteer complained
bitterly about the rise of 'a set of brocaded tradesmen, clothed in
purple and fine linen, and faring sumptuously every day, raising
to themselves immense wealth, so as to marry their daughters to
the first rank, and leave their sons such estates as to enable them
to live to the same degree'.[18] Defoe's conclusion was twofold, that
'the rising tradesman swells into the gentry, and the declining gentry sinks into trade'. He pictured how, on the one hand, an immensely wealthy merchant 'marries his daughter to a gentleman
of the first quality, perhaps a coronet; then he leaves the bulk of
his estate of his heir, and he [the heir] gets into the ranks of the
peerage. Does the next age make any scruple of their blood being
thus mixed in with the ancient race?' He clearly assumed that the
answer was no.[19] He also described the rise of the modestly successful businessman.

The estate [of £1800 per annum] is purchased by a citizen, who having
got the money by honest industry, and pursuing a prosperous trade, has
left his books and his warehouse to his two younger sons, is retired from
the world, lives upon his estate, is a justice of the peace, and makes a
complete gentleman. His eldest son, bred at the university, and thoroughly accomplished, is as well received among the gentry in the county
and upon the valuable fund of his true merit, as if he had been a gentleman by blood for a hundred generations before the Conquest.[20]

Defoe's description of how merchants entered the gentry is entirely accurate, and could be supported by numerous examples in
real life—just how numerous, however, is yet to be determined.
Defoe also describes how gentry in financial straits often saved
themselves by commerce. 'The declining gentry in the ebb of their

[18] D. Defoe, *Tour Through England and Wales* (Everyman ed.), London, 1928, i, pp. 15,
89, 158; *A Plan of the English Commerce*, [1728], in *Defoe's Writings*, xiii, Oxford, 1927, p. 38;
P. M. G. Dickson, op. cit., p. 29.
[19] D. Defoe, op. cit., p. 9.
[20] Op. cit., p. 62.

fortunes frequently push their sons into trade and they . . . often restore the fortunes of their families. Thus tradesmen become gentlemen, by gentlemen becoming tradesmen'. His description matches, although with a different emphasis, the one given by Edward Chamberlayn as early as 1669, when he observed that among the squires and gentry 'younger brothers . . . have small estates in land, but are commonly bred up to divinity, law, physick, to Court and military employments, but of late too many of them to shop-keeping'. In 1710 Steele also claimed, as did many others before and after him, that 'the best of our peers have often joined themselves to the daughters of very ordinary tradesmen, upon . . . valuable considerations.'[21]

There were clearly three distinct parts to the paradigm advanced by these social commentators. The first was the alleged fact, that merchants were busy buying landed estates, building seats, and turning themselves into squires or nobles. The second was another alleged fact, that the declining gentry often restored their fortunes by putting their sons, especially their younger sons, into trade. The third was an alleged social attitude, the relatively easy acceptance of self-made men, as companions or marriage partners, by persons of genteel birth and elite status.

The facts will be examined later, but even the perceptions were far from being as straightforward as Defoe asserted. He was pushing his argument of the ease of social entry far too far when he alleged that the only thing that mattered in England was money, from whatever source, and that birth and breeding were irrelevant:

> Wealth, howsoever got, in England makes
> Lords of mechanics, gentlemen of rakes.
> Antiquity and birth are needless here,
> 'Tis impudence and money makes a peer.[22]

This was mere fanciful rhodomontade. Indeed, sometimes Defoe took the reverse position, complaining that the elite 'would divide the world into two parts only . . . This family jargon [gentility by birth], for it is no more, they oppose to the trading part of the whole world, which they divest of all dignity as well as degree, and blend together under one general or rather common denominator of mechanics'. His more sober conclusion was that this division was a false one, because of the rapid interchange he believed

---

[21] Op. cit., p. 9; E. Chamberlayn, *Angliae Notitia*, London, 1669, pp. 486-7; *The Tatler*, ed. G. A. Aitken, London, 1899, iv, p. 168.

[22] D. Defoe, *The Trueborn Englishman*, [1701], in Defoe's *Writings*, xiv, Oxford, 1927, p. 45.

existed in practice between the two groups. He consequently regarded it as 'a scandal upon the understanding of the gentry to
think contemptibly of the trading part of the nation'.[23]

The fact is, however, that throughout the seventeenth century
a vigorous debate raged amongst the heralds and antiquaries as to
whether the apprenticeship of sons of squires to a trade or a
profession meant the loss of gentility, and conversely whether the
acquisition by a monied man of an estate and a country seat meant
that he automatically acquired gentlemanly status. The critical issue was the servile nature of apprenticeship. From Ben Jonson's
Volpone onwards, moreover, the stock attitude of the dramatists
towards the wealthy city man was one of contempt and ridicule.
Marston, Massinger, and the rest insinuated that his wealth was
obtained by fraud and extortion and that his manners were not
those of a gentleman.

This psychological tension between the world of gentility and
the world of business was at its most acute from about the 1670s
to the 1710s, when there was widespread suspicion among members of the landed interest that their coffers were being drained in
extravagant foreign wars to benefit a new monied interest of stock-
jobbers, bankers, and government contractors. The phrase 'monied interest' was loosely used at the time to mean both this restricted group of new financial manipulators who sprang up between
the foundation of the Bank of England and the South Sea Bubble,
and also all holders and beneficiaries of liquid as opposed to landed
wealth. In this book the phrase is used in the broader sense, to
embrace all who acquired a fortune through business, whether
trade, banking, stockjobbing, or manufacture.

Some contemporaries defended bankers on the grounds that 'they
have been useful for gentlemen to place their money', but the more
general 'country' view, brilliantly and savagely stated by Swift,
was that they were dangerous parasites. Anything which adversely
affected the banker 'will make money come again into the country'
for 'as interest goes up, land goes down like a pair of scales'. As
late as 1728 an embittered country gentleman could still see merchants as merely a gang of conspirators aspiring to displace the
ancient gentry. 'Trade is the game of the politic public, who screen
its industrious arts from the idle nobility and gentry by glaring,
dazzling notions, and starve 'em even in lace and grandeur, and
make them administer to their riches and plenty; and are only
gilded blocks to mount them and their families upon'. The Tory

[23] D. Defoe, *A Plan of the English Commerce*, pp. 4, 9, 63, 60.

Bolingbroke argued stubbornly that 'the landed men are the true owners of our political vessell; the monied men, as such, are no more than the passengers'.[24]

Behind these somewhat incoherent expressions of fear and resentment lay a vision of a clash of cultures. On the one side was the entrepreneur. He was an upwardly mobile capitalist, combining a spirit of adventure with rational organization to minimize risk. He was self-disciplined, abstemious, hard-working, and utilitarian. He lacked culture, sophistication, and any sense of values other than the maximization of profit. On the other side was the country squire. His chief characteristics were education in the classics, and the pursuit of a life of elegant ease and leisure based primarily in the countryside. But there was more to him than that. He was also a virtuoso, an admirer of aesthetic beauty in art, architecture, and gardens, a defender of tradition and the rights of birth, and (in theory) a conscientious paternalist ruler of the countryside. He was interested in spending rather than getting and he was constantly exposed to the wiles of the crafty entrepreneur, merchant, or banker. Such were the stereotypes of fiction, the theatre, and popular imagination.

As the century wore on, however, the two interests began to be perceived as less antagonistic and mutually incompatible. Despite savage polemics over specific tax issues which favoured one group at the expense of the other, such as the land-tax or the stamp duties, there was grudging but growing recognition that they were inextricably bound up with one another. As Sir Thomas Clarges put it in the House of Commons as early as 1693, 'the land will be worth nothing if trade be not supported. By trade, London makes up your rents'. 'Trade is to land as the soul to the body', remarked another commentator. Only a minority, especially Bolingbroke and his circle and the minority of Tory squires, took a diametrically different view, and remained obstinately hostile to and resentful of the monied interest.[25]

Over the fifty years from 1690 to 1740, there was a significant shift of opinion and a modification of the previous stark clash of values. Since this was a time when the monied interest was achieving new heights of affluence and power, with the foundation of

[24] J. Loftis, *Comedy and Society from Congreve to Fielding*, Stanford, 1959, passim and especially pp. 1, 81-3, 94-5, 122, 127, 133; A. Grey, *Debates* . . ., i, pp. 146, 188, 273, 351-3; E. Hughes, op. cit., i, p. 68; J. Swift, *The Examiner*, London, 1710-11, passim; H. St John, Viscount Bolingbroke, 'Reflections on the State of the Nation', in *Works*, London, 1844, p. 458.

[25] A. Grey, *Debates*.., x, p. 313; P. M. G. Dickson, op. cit., pp. 25, 27-9, 477.

the Bank of England and the financing of the wars with France, evidence of a quiet shifting of opinion is most significant. One hint of this shift comes from the contents of the standard work of reference of the age, Edward Chamberlayn's *Angliae Notitia*. Editions from 1669 to 1692 denounced the recent practice of the landed elite to 'seek their children's support by shopkeeping . . . , much less to subject their children to an apprentissage, a perfect servitude . . . , which marks of slavery considered, heralds are of the opinion that a gentleman thereby loses his gentility forever, till he can otherwise recover it'. But the 1700 edition quietly dropped this passage. All editions had conceded that 'in England as well as Italy to become a merchant of foreign commerce, without serving any apprenticeship, hath been allowed as no disparagement for a gentleman born, especially to a younger brother'. Domestic wholesale and retail trade was for Chamberlayn beyond the pale, but sons of gentry who were active in the East India Company or the Levant Company were recognized by late seventeenth-century society as still gentlemen.[26]

Richard Steele offered the way out of the dilemma by going back to the Renaissance and defining a gentleman not by his birth or his occupation but by his manners: 'The appellation of a gentleman is never to be affixed to a man's circumstances, but to his behaviour in them'. This allowed him to define a merchant as 'a man that does business with the candour of a gentleman and performs his engagements with the exactness of a citizen', thus blurring the distinction between the two by uniting their separate qualities in one person. Defoe was an immoderate and extreme proponent of the importance of the commercial interest and he was grossly exaggerating when he claimed that England's 'best families owe their wealth and rise, first and last to the opulence and profits of trade'. A few certainly did, but far more owed their rise to office, war, or the law. Defoe was on safer ground when he said that 'colonels come to be lords and generals, though they were bastards at first'.[27] Thus the Fitzroys, the bastard children of Charles II, had no difficulty in being accepted in the highest circles of the land, both socially and in marriage.

In fact it was the rise of the professions which confused the status hierarchy more than any influx of low-born merchants. The 'middling sort' in the eighteenth and nineteenth centuries took up

[26] M. Shinagel, *Daniel Defoe and Middle Class Gentility*, Cambridge, Mass., 1968, pp. 109-10. Dr Shinagel's account of the shift is not entirely accurate.

[27] R. Steele, *The Tatler*, 207, 1710, ed. G. A. Aitken, London, 1899, iv, p. 72; M. Shinagel, op. cit., pp. 96, 114-5, 162.

semi-genteel occupations, like clerks, doctors, apothecaries, or schoolmaster, and called themselves gentlemen. At the higher levels, however, it was still very hard for a low-born man to rise to a colonelcy in the army, the governorship of a colony, or a key office in the central administration.

Merchants were another matter. The anxious insecurity that is so obvious in the alternate bragging and complaining that run together through the writings of Defoe are in striking contrast to the comments made half a century later towards the end of the eighteenth century. By then the argument in their favour depended on ideas about national superiority. It was argued first that it was commerce which had 'caused England to rise so high in the political scale of Europe', and second that English merchants were different from, and superior to, those of foreign countries, since they had adopted the gentlemanly values of elite society. The first argument was given a new twist by Adam Smith in 1776 when he observed that 'merchants are commonly ambitious to become country gentlemen, and when they do, they are the best of all improvers'. The Scottish professor found an additional advantage to the economy in an alleged stimulus to agricultural development.[28]

The second argument about the social difference between England and abroad was made by James Lackington in 1775. He asserted that while many English merchants still 'have not an idea but what they have acquired behind the counter, . . . you may also find many thousands of the same class of life who are possessed of very liberal sentiments, and who would not commit an action that would disgrace a title'. He argued that on the Continent they were despised by the gentry and nobility, and behaved accordingly, 'whilst in England the merchants and respectable tradesmen, being held in higher estimation, and often admitted to the company, conversation, and honours of higher classes, the sordid mind by degrees imbibes more liberal sentiments, and the rough manners receive a degree of polish'. By then, what in the early eighteenth century Defoe had called 'this land-water thing called a gentleman tradesman' had allegedly become an acceptable social type.[29]

This view from below was supported from above by Topham Beauclerk, who told Boswell in 1775 that 'now in England being of an old family [is] of no consequence. . . . People did not enquire far back. If a man [is] rich and well educated, he [is] equally well

[28] A. Smith, *Wealth of Nations*, ed. E. Cannon, London, 1904, i, p. 382.
[29] *Memoirs . . . of J. Lackington*, London, 1794, pp. 301-2; D. Defoe, *Moll Flanders*, ed. G. A. Aitken, 1895, i, p. 58; see also below Ch. VIII, 4, iii.

received as the most ancient gentleman.' Even Doctor Johnson thought that 'an English tradesman is a new species of gentleman'. The same position was taken by James Nelson in his well-known didactic handbook of 1768. He thought that England was 'a trading nation, connects more closely with the whole body of the people; links them, as it were, in one continued chain, and brings them nearer to a level'. This allowed him to speak of 'the genteel trades', seeing no contradiction in such a definition.[30]

One can document this melding with concrete examples. When in 1790 the King's brewer was made a member of the Royal Staghounds at Windsor, George III himself gave his approval. James Brasbridge, a silversmith, remarked proudly, 'I hope you do not consider me as a common shopkeeper, but as a gentleman and a man of honour'.[31] Admittedly there continued to be snobs who considered such large-scale manufacture as brewing to be a degrading occupation. Mrs Thrale always thought she had married down in uniting a Salusbury like herself, with claims on Offley Place, to a brewer like Henry Thrale, although she had to admit that her husband was a true gentleman with his own country seat. On the other hand she continued to look down on the other great genteel brewing families, also well established in their country seats, the Whitbreads and Calverts, men, she somewhat implausibly alleged,—'whose acquaintance he [Thrale] was ashamed of, and whose persons he shrank from if he met them in a public place'.[32] This sort of snobbery persisted amongst children, always the most conservative of creatures, and Thomas Gisborne in 1797 described how in boarding-schools girls cross-questioned each other about the opulence and social exclusiveness of their home life. They

triumph or repine according to the answers which they receive concerning the number of servants kept in the house, the magnificence of their liveries, the number of courses habitually served up at table, the number of routs given at their town residence in winter, the extent of the gardens and of the park at the family mansion in the country, the intercourse maintained with nobility and people of fashion, and the connections subsisting with the sordid occupations and degrading profits of trade.[33]

[30] *Boswell: The Ominous Years, 1775-76*, ed. C. Ryscamp and F. A. Pottle, New York, 1963, p. 103; J. Boswell, *The Life of Samuel Johnson, LL.D.* (Everyman edition), London, 1906, i, p. 307, n. 1; J. Nelson, *An Essay on the Government of Children*, London, 1768, pp. 273, 317.

[31] J. Brasbridge, *The Fruits of Experience*, London, 1824, p. 144.

[32] M. Hyde, op. cit., p. 206. The fact that Thrale was a Tory and the Calverts and Whitbreads were Whigs may have influenced the former's judgement.

[33] T. Gisborne, *An Enquiry into the Duties of the Female Sex*, London, 1797, pp. 87-8. Such conversations were not unknown in mid-twentieth century elite Public Schools.

The very nature of the interrogations of the girls, however, reveals
unmistakeably that some intermingling of the children of the landed
elite and those of the elite of business was taking place in the
exclusive boarding-schools of England at the end of the eighteenth
century.

The most delicate question of perception naturally concerned
the propriety of intermarriage between ancient lineage and new
wealth. The issue was savagely depicted in Hogarth's *Marriage à
la mode* of 1745, a very popular set of prints showing the disastrous
consequences of the forced marriage of the rakish heir of an extravagant and indebted earl to the only daughter and heiress of a
rich City merchant. (Plate 1.) The two dislike each other at first
sight and go their separate ways. While she surrounds herself with
fops and parasites, he sleeps with other women. As a result, when
he tries to beget an heir, he causes his wife to give birth to a
syphilitic child. Meanwhile she takes a lover of her own, and is
caught in bed with him by her husband, which provokes a duel
in the bedroom in which the lover kills the husband. The lover is
arrested, tried, and hanged for murder, on hearing the news of
which the wife—now a widow—poisons herself. As she dies, her
old father, disappointed in his hopes of having a countess as a
daughter, grimly pulls the wedding-ring from her finger before the
breath is out of her body. In 1727 Defoe made much the same
point, stressing the contempt and shame felt by the daughter of a
nobleman forcibly married to a rich City magnate. She refuses to
sleep with him and 'was it not for some convenience of her way
of living, equipages, the mansion house which is new and fine and
costs £50,000 building, and the like, she would feign another quarrel and step out of the house too'.[34]

Defoe thought that these marriages were a common occurrence,
and in 1768 James Nelson regarded them not only as normal but
natural. 'The man of trade marries the daughter of the gentleman;
the gentleman the tradesman's daughter; and again the gentleman
makes his son (the younger at least) a man of trade'. He thus considered the economic and cultural symbiosis of land and money to
be already complete.[35] What both he and Defoe missed was the
widely held view among the gentry that it was permissible to trade
status for money and marry your son to the heiress of a tradesman,
but not to marry your daughter to the tradesman or even to his

[34] R. Paulson, *Hogarth: His Life, Art and Times*, New Haven, 1971, i, pp. 479-89;
D. Defoe, *A Treatise Concerning the Use and Abuse of the Marriage Bed*, London, 1727, p. 254.
[35] D. Defoe, *A Plan of the English Commerce*, London, 1728, p. 61; J. Nelson, op. cit., p.
317.

heir. Despite some dissident voices, it is clear that the open elite, meaning one open to access from below and lacking in social prejudice against those of inferior birth, was widely believed to be already an accomplished fact of English life by the late eighteenth century.

In 1818, however, there were new complaints, undoubtedly exaggerated, about the invasion of the elite by wealthy cotton-spinners 'without education or address. . . . But to counter that deficiency they give you enough of appearances by an ostentatious display of elegant mansions, equipages, liveries, parks, hunters, hounds, etc.'[36] Note that the external attributes of the life-style here identified are the seat, the grounds, the servants, and the equipment for fox-hunting. A quarter of a century later the whole idea behind the reformed public schools of the Victorian era was to inculcate the sons of the newly enriched middle-class professional man, merchant, or banker with the same moral values, religious beliefs, sense of duty, good breeding, and classical education as the sons of the gentry. The end-product was to be an homogenized gentleman by education, whose background was not detectable in his accent, behaviour, or culture, and who was thus clearly distinct from the vulgar cotton-spinner industrialists.

To the radicals, who failed to perceive this critical social distinction, the homogenizing of land, the professions, money, and commerce was a major obstacle to social change. As late as the mid-nineteenth century, Richard Cobden could see little hope of improvement. 'We have the spirit of feudalism rife and rampant in the midst of the antagonistic development of the age of Watt, Arkwright and Stephenson', he complained in 1863. 'Manufacturers and merchants as a rule seem only to desire riches that they may be able to prostrate themselves at the feet of feudalism'. 'See how every successful trader buys an estate and tries to perpetuate his name in connexion with "that ilk" by creating an eldest son'. Cobden thought he observed both a psychological assimilation of feudal values by the mercantile classes, and also constant upward mobility by self-made men by the purchase of land and a seat and the creation of a county family. At times his exasperation exploded. 'We are', he concluded in 1849, 'a servile aristocracy-loving, lord-ridden people, who regard the land with as much reverence as we still do the peerage and baronetage'. He despaired about

[36] Quoted by E. P. Thompson, *The Making of the English Working Class*, London, 1964, p. 218.

the values of merchants and manufacturers, 'toadies of a clodpole aristocracy, only less enlightened than themselves'.[37]

The perceptions of the English observers from the late sixteenth to the mid-nineteenth centuries are thus clear enough. At all times they believed that the psychological subservience of trade to land and the steady withdrawal of mercantile capital to set up a landed estate were exceptionally marked in England by comparison with the rest of Europe. They thought that mercantile infiltration was growing particularly fast in the early seventeenth century, and they strongly deplored it. They judged it to be even more frequent in the late seventeenth and early eighteenth centuries and they fought it bitterly, only Defoe welcoming the trend. By the middle of the eighteenth century, however, social tensions had eased off, and they regarded it as an acceptable commonplace. They had begun in the seventeenth century by thinking that any infusion of new men into the old elite would corrupt its manners and morals, and some of them—not Cobbett or Cobden—ended in the late eighteenth century by seeing it as a biologically rejuvenating process which presented no serious cultural threat and indeed promoted social stability. This theory found institutional expression in the reformed public schools of the nineteenth century, where the sons of old and new wealth rubbed shoulders and absorbed an identical, elitist, culture.

The English landed elite retained their power, privileges, and prestige for so long, so the theory goes, because of the stunning success of the technique of 'the aristocratic embrace'.[38] Generation after generation, the landed elite picked out the richest of the new rich and clasped them to their bosom, either marrying their daughters to them and so absorbing much of their ready cash, or else swallowing them whole like a boa constrictor. The self-made man was made dizzy by the lure of charm, grace, favour, and an entrée into the company of the elite. He hastened to abandon the counting-house for the country house, the making of money for the spending of it. His son, if not himself, was indistinguishable from other members of the squirearchy in education and values, besides being furnished by an accommodating herald with an imposing genealogy to fit his new station in life. According to accepted wisdom, this was how the landed elite of England perpetuated their political and social hegemony and their economic

[37] J. Morley, *The Life of Richard Cobden*, London, 1903, pp. 945-6, 561, 518, 134.
[38] F. M. L. Thompson, 'Britain', loc. cit., p. 23.

property rights through and beyond the great transformations of the industrial revolution and the advent of participatory democracy. Such were the perceptions of contemporaries, and such are the conclusions of most modern historians. But what were the facts?

II

THE SAMPLE AND THE
SOURCES OF EVIDENCE

1. THE LIMITS OF THE SAMPLE

i. The Temporal Limits: 1540-1880

The terminal dates, 1540 and 1880, were in many ways self-selecting. The year 1540 is the moment when the impact of the Dissolution of the Monasteries first began to make itself felt. The transfer during the 1540s and early 1550s of perhaps a quarter of the land of England from institutional to private hands, and the throwing of it upon the private real-estate market, profoundly affected the whole evolution of English landed society until the end of the nineteenth century and later. The year 1540 is also about the time when the Tudor state had reached the point when it could provide reasonable physical security from armed conflict in the countryside, at any rate in the Lowland Zone, although it took another seventy years to pacify the Scottish border. As a result, it was now at last possible to live in safety in country houses rather than castles, and local government could begin to function without fear that its authority would be flouted by open military defiance from great magnates. Although these conditions were not achieved in the far north until about 1610, for the south and midlands 1540 seems an appropriate date to begin a study of county elites. Moreover because of the immense turnover of property generated by the sale of Crown and Church lands, and the consequent lawsuits over title, this is also the moment when documentation suddenly becomes much more abundant. Henceforward more legal and administrative records were made and kept, while growing literacy among the secular elite also meant that more private correspondence was written and preserved.

The terminal date of 1880 was chosen because the 1880s mark a major turning-point in the political authority of the landed elite. In the first place it was then that, for the first time, they lost their predominance in the House of Commons to men whose fortunes had been made in industry and business. Landed men were elected to three-quarters of all seats in the House in 1840, two-thirds in 1868, but less than one-half in 1886, and probably only about one-tenth in 1906.[1] Secondly, the establishment of County Councils in 1888 struck a deadly blow at the hegemony over local politics and administration hitherto exercised by the landed elite. Thirdly, there occurred the first serious erosion of their persistent economic pre-eminence, which may have been at an all-time peak at just this moment. In 1882 the Settled Land Act, by allowing life tenants to sell, undermined the power of the strict settlement to keep great estates intact from generation to generation. Even more important was the beginning in 1873 of the great agricultural depression, which in areas of primarily cereal cultivation spelt ruin for many landed families, who suddenly fell upon very hard times. Income tax, death duties, and the holocaust of World War I further con- tributed to the economic crisis in landed society, and by 1925 many of the familiar names which had been prominent in the country for generations were gone. The political and economic débâcle between 1880 and 1925 was of lasting importance, even if the great magnates managed to cling on to office in Tory cabinets until after the Second World War.

By sheer coincidence the year 1880 also more or less coincides with a remarkable burst of documentation, particularly the great twenty-five-inches-to-one-mile Ordnance Survey carried out be- tween 1867 and 1882, and the 'New Domesday' or *Return of Own- ers of Land*, the massive and unique parliamentary inquiry into the distribution of rural landed property and landed income through- out the country, made in 1873. To this can now be added a de- tailed survey of property ownership in London in the 1890s.[2] This is therefore a rare moment when it is possible to measure both the landed income and the acreage of the elite and also the approxi- mate ground-plan of their houses.

In terms of status, Walter Bagehot had seen the writing on the wall as early as the 1860s. He observed that the great landowners 'have less means of standing out than they used to have. Their power is in their theatrical exhibition, in their state. But society is every day becoming less stately.'[3] Although this might have been true of society at large, the stately features of English high society,

[1] F. M. L. Thompson, 'Britain', in *European Landed Elites in the Nineteenth Century*, ed. D. Spring, Baltimore, 1977, p. 25.
[2] *The Returns of Owners of Land in Ireland and Wales, 1873*, London, 1875; J. Bateman, *The Great Landowners of Great Britain and Ireland*, London, 1879; G. C. Brodrick, *English Land and English Landlords*, London, 1881; R. Hyde, 'Mapping London's Landlords: the Ground Plan of London 1892-1915', *Guildhall Studies in London History*, i, 1973.
[3] W. Bagehot, *The English Constitution* (World's Classics), London, 1958, p. 83, quoted by D. Spring in *Land and Industry*, ed. J. T. Ward and R. G. Wilson, Newton Abbot, 1971, p. 53.

including the formality of noblemen's dress, etiquette, and way of life, actually became more marked rather than less up to the First World War. But Bagehot was right in pointing to the widening gap between the solemn state maintained by dukes and earls, and the prosaic world of smoking factories and mills which formed the underpinning of their—and England's—position in the world. So gigantic and obtrusive was the sheer size and value of the land owned by this tiny elite minority that the 1870s saw a rising tide of criticism and demands for social and economic redistribution, led by liberals like John Stuart Mill. The 1880s also coincided with the long-delayed beginning of an infiltration into the peerage of self-made men of business who did not possess any landed estate at all. Only seven such men were elevated before 1885, but about fifty between 1885 and 1911. All the ancient barriers to social change among the elite thus began to crumble in about 1880.[4]

Moreover after 1880 the distinctive feature of a country house and its owner, that is the universal acceptance of the former as the symbol of the latter's status and responsibilities to society, tended to become blurred. The quantity of land and old houses up for sale or rent as old families went under, the amount of new wealth generated in industry and commerce, and the growth of a speedy railway network around London, all had striking consequences. They caused genuinely new self-made men to replace old families on a hitherto unprecedented scale; they stimulated the spread of the suburban villa far out into the countryside; they encouraged the adoption of the 'weekend' among both the country-house set and the London mercantile community; and they led to the development of the concept of the house in the country, as opposed to the country house. The former differs from the latter not so much in size as in function. It has no surrounding estate, merely gardens and a paddock or two, and serves as no more than a weekend or summer retreat for a business-man or professional and his family and friends, a place devoted to pleasure and leisure activities, free of responsibilities to tenants or parish or local government. The country house, on the other hand, remained the focus of its owner's loyalties and responsibilities, even if he might absent himself for long recreational visits to London or Bath.

ii. The Geographical Limits: the County

One of the prime foci around which landed society in the past concentrated its loyalties was the county. When a man in the six-

---

[4] R. E. Pumphret, 'The Introduction of Industrialists into the British Peerage: a Study in Adaptation of a Social Institution', *American Historical Review*, 65, 1959.

teenth or seventeenth or even eighteenth centuries said 'my country' he usually did not mean England, but his county. During this
period there was an intensification of this local patriotism and a
growth of a strong sense of county community. This found concrete expression in the development of county institutions, particularly the quarter sessions which by the seventeenth century had
developed almost into local parliaments, formulating and forward-
ing up to London petitions concerning local grievances. The JPs
had also been encouraged or obliged to shoulder a larger and larger
burden of local administration. This process culminated in the
County Committees of the civil-war period of the 1640s, which
assessed and raised taxes, and spent them on the conscripting of
local levies of troops, control over which they guarded very jeal-
ously. After the war was over, first the Rump Parliament and then
Lord Protector Cromwell had a good deal of difficulty in re-estab-
lishing the sovereignty of the central government. Although the
degree of local particularism varied inversely with status and wealth,
during the first half of the seventeenth century the county had
become, even for the elite of the local squirearchy, a major arena
for administrative action, political conflict, social intercourse, economic investment, and marriage connections. It was this new sense
of local identity which stimulated the writing of the first great
county histories in the late seventeenth century which were in
essence the histories of the local county families, many of which
had patronized and paid for their publication.[5]

Although the feeling climaxed in the mid-seventeenth century,
for a long while the county remained the strongest focal point of
loyalty and affection among many squires, and as a result it also
became the unit around which both manuscript collections and
printed records have been arranged. The first dictionary of national biography, Thomas Fuller's *The History of the Worthies of
England*, published in 1662, was arranged neither alphabetically
nor chronologically, but by counties, because, as he explained,
'*where* is as essential as *when* to a man's being'. Nor did this sense
of belonging to a county community quickly die away, despite the
attraction of the metropolis.

When he toured England in the early eighteenth century, Defoe
remarked on the persistence of close-knit county communities of
squires. In Cornwall, according to a local proverb, 'all the Cornish
gentlemen are cousins'; in Dorset, 'they seem to have a mutual

[5] W. Dugdale, *Antiquities of Warwickshire*, London, 1656; R. Thoroton, *Antiquities of Nottinghamshire*, London, 1677; H. Chauncy, *The Historical Antiquities of Hertfordshire*, London,
1700.

confidence in, and friendship with one another, as if they were all relations'. As late as the mid-eighteenth century, gentry from the same county who were in London for the season or for Parliament would meet regularly for dinner. In 1765, for example, 'many gentlemen of rank and fortune of the county of Nottingham' dined together at a 'county club' once a week at the Star and Garter Tavern in Pall Mall—a sign of local solidarity even if the meetings did once result in a fatal duel! In the early seventeenth century, at the height of county community feeling, even the merchants and tradesmen of London born in the same county would dine together periodically to plan the support of charitable causes back home. Advertisements in the newspapers of the eighteenth century show that there were regular fortnightly meetings during the season of the gentlemen of Westmoreland, Wiltshire, and Lancashire, and dinners, apparently annually, of the Hereford Society and the Cumberland Society. By 1788, there was also a Buckinghamshire Society and a Gloucestershire Society.[6] Thus there is little doubt that residual loyalty to their county of origin persisted amongst the elite even while resident in London. Those who assembled twice a month were clearly closely tied to the elite from their own county, those who merely attended an annual dinner far less so. Some vestigial sense of county identity persisted into the late twentieth century, as evidenced by the strong—but in the end ineffectual—recent efforts of little Rutland to preserve its existence during the first drastic alteration of English county names and boundaries to take place since their establishment in Anglo-Saxon times. As a result of this administrative revolution, psychological attachment to one's county has at last all but disappeared from English life.

On the other hand, the significance of this concept of a county community has been exaggerated in recent years. No county was an island unto itself, even in the sixteenth and early seventeenth centuries, and marriage, education, litigation, politics, and pleasure all created wider connections among the elite of the nation. It would therefore be a serious mistake to exaggerate the strength of this sense of county community even in the early seventeenth century, since it grew in parallel with one major and one minor wider

[6] T. Fuller, *The History of the Worthies of England* [1662], ed. P. A. Nuttall, London, 1840, i, p. 73; *The Trial of William Lord Byron for the Murder of William Chaworth*, London, 1765, p. 6; *Yorkshire Diaries and Autobiographies*, Surtees Soc., 63, 1877, p. 126; D. Defoe, *A Tour through England and Wales* (Everyman ed.), i, pp. 234, 216; *Daily Advertiser*, 31 Jan., 28 and 30 Nov., 1747; 30 Jan., 21 March 1748, 30 Jan., 1749; *St James's Chronicle*, 8 Feb., 29 April, 25 Nov. 1788.

focus of loyalty.[7] The main rival was the growing influence of London and the national interest, especially strong after 1660 but already visible by the late sixteenth century, and the second and minor one was a growing regionalism, which also increased significantly after 1660. The first was reflected in a rising interest in national politics, as shown in a striking expansion of the franchise, more frequent contested elections, and increased competition among squires for a seat in the House of Commons. This trend was stimulated by a growing social involvement in the great national clearing-house of London. More and longer visits were paid to the city during the seventeenth century, and when Parliament at last became an annual affair from November to May, as it did in the 1690s, the London winter season began to exercise an irresistable attraction to all who could afford such luxuries. Moreover, after about 1700 the expansion of places in the patronage of the Crown, because of bureaucratic growth to manage the wars with France, decisively shifted the focus of political allegiance from the local magnate to the London politician who controlled this patronage. Localism consequently declined.

In the course of the eighteenth century, improved communications, with sprung coaches and much-better-surfaced turnpike roads, greatly eased communications with London, and it seems likely that this is the period in which the county elite spent the maximum time away from home, most of it in London. In the late eighteenth century, Thomas Gisborne summed up the role played by the capital city for English elite society:

London is the centre to which almost all individuals who fill the upper and middle ranks of society are successively attracted. The country pays its tribute to the supreme city. Business, interest, curiosity, the love of pleasure, the desire for knowledge, the thirst for change, ambition to be deemed polite, occasion a continual influx into the metropolis from every corner of the Kingdom.

The truth of Gisborne's observations is fully proven by the massive extension of substantial residential housing in the West End of London during this century.[8]

The second development of the late seventeenth and eighteenth centuries was regionalism, admittedly a weaker competitor for loyalty than the ties to the county on the one hand and to the nation-

[7] For a cogent criticism of the 'county community' school of historians, see C. Holmes, 'The County Community in Stuart Historiography', *Journal of British Studies*, xix, 1980.

[8] L. Stone, 'The Residential Development of the West End of London in the Seventeenth Century', in *After the Reformation*, ed. B. C. Malament, Philadelphia, 1980, pp. 167-212.

state and capital city on the other. Though local politics remained centred on the county, some of the provincial towns which grew in this period tended to be the foci of economic regions straddling several counties.[9] Some, such as Newcastle, York, or Norwich, might also be county towns; others such as Birmingham, Manchester, or Liverpool, were not. The common economic and cultural interests which linked those who frequented them ensured a large enough population, both of residents and of visitors from within the region, to sustain such hitherto exclusively metropolitan institutions as circulating libraries, coffee-houses, theatres, assembly rooms, and literary and philosophical clubs. As these towns developed, so did the middling sort who engaged in the commerce of the region, for whom these towns became increasingly what London was to the landed elite. As they emerged from their obscurity, the middling sort now provided for the first time a growing provincial market for reading matter, toys, theatrical entertainments, and other luxuries hitherto obtainable only in London, and thus contributed to the expansion of the 'commercialisation of leisure' so characteristic of the eighteenth century. This was a development which also benefited the landed classes, and the Assemblies or race-meetings held in some of the cities turned into major marriage markets for the elite from the counties of the region. This regionalism, however, was mainly of a pragmatic nature and never overrode either loyalty to the county, as expressed in similar, though minor, cultural activity in purely county towns like Ipswich or Durham or Buckingham, or the growing cultural hegemony of the great metropolis of London. Even in the eighteenth century, therefore, the county remains a meaningful unit of elite study, so long as it is treated with flexibility as part of a wider regional area of common interests and sociability, and one subject to the increasing dominance of metropolitan culture and to increasing political patronage by national figures like Walpole or Newcastle.

An excellent test of the relative significance of these three foci of loyalty and social intercourse, the county, the region, and the nation, is the geographical range within which the landed classes chose their brides. At one point in time, in 1640, there is data covering several counties both for the parish gentry and for the elite.[10] To take the parish gentry first, in Kent, Suffolk, Norfolk, and Cheshire in 1640, the proportions who had married wives

    [9] A. McInnes, *The English Town 1660-1760*, London, 1980, p. 6.
    [10] C. A. Holmes, 'The Eastern Association' (Cambridge Univ., unpublished Ph.D. thesis, 1969), App. I, p. 492; A. Everitt, *The Community of Kent and the Great Rebellion 1640-60*, London, 1966, p. 328; J. S. Morrill, *Cheshire 1630-1660*, Oxford, 1974, p. 4, n. 2.

from within the county were all between 70 per cent and 80 per cent. Only in the Home Counties of Hertfordshire and Essex, more subject to the pull of London, did the proportions fall as low as about 35 per cent to 45 per cent. Because of the high cost of London life, however, there developed an inverse correlation between status and wealth on the one hand and county particularism on the other.

Except in the counties bordering on London, it was the small parish gentry who were narrowly locked into their county by their relative poverty and the restricted nature of their education, property-holding, marriages, and aspirations for office. The baronets and knights had more contacts outside the county, were more involved in national affairs, stayed for longer periods and more frequently in London, and were more inclined to find their partners in a regional rather than a county marriage market. The proportion of them who married within the county in 1640 was much smaller than that of the parish gentry, ranging from a high of about 60 per cent for Kent to a more normal range of 40 per cent to 50 per cent for Suffolk, Norfolk, and Cheshire, and dropping to 30 per cent in the Home Counties of Essex and Hertfordshire (Table 2.1). Even so, it says a lot for county cohesiveness among men with such wide social contacts that nearly half of them should have married inside the county in 1640 in all areas except near London, where the proportion fell to one-third.

This glimpse of the geographical range of choice of brides in 1640 offers no indication of change over time, for which it is necessary to turn to the data generated by this study. As has been observed, 1640 represented the high point of county localism. By the end of the seventeenth century, however, many members of the elite were spending six months away from their county seat in London. This development, and the social contacts outside the county that it bred, fostered the growth of a national marriage market. London became a central matrimonial clearing-house, with scriveners, attorneys, solicitors, and clergy acting as sources of information on likely prospects, while the many balls, parties, and assemblies served as supervised meeting-places for the young. The development of Bath as a summer watering-place for the elite in the early eighteenth century provided a second national marriage market. Simultaneously with these developments in the late seventeenth and eighteenth centuries, a series of regional marriage markets also developed, centred around assemblies, balls, horse-races, and other gatherings held in major regional centres such as Norwich for East Anglia, or York for the North. At an assembly in York in 1710, for example, Lady Mary Pierrepont counted some 'two hundred pieces of women's flesh (fat and lean)' that were on display for prospective suitors.[11]

As a result of these various trends, one would expect to find a fairly high rate of county endogamy among the elite in the sample in the sixteenth and early seventeenth centuries, declining there-after as regional and national networks expanded horizons; that local endogamy would nevertheless remain substantial, since pro-pinquity breeds familiarity, and families had an interest in making marriage alliances with one another within the political arena of the county; and that the more distant a county was from London the higher the level of county and regional endogamy was likely to be. All three predictions are largely substantiated by the facts (Table 2.2, Figs. 2.1 and 2.2).

To take the last point first, the Hertfordshire-born elite began

FIG. 2.1   County Endogamy (First Wives from within the same County) [Table 2.2]

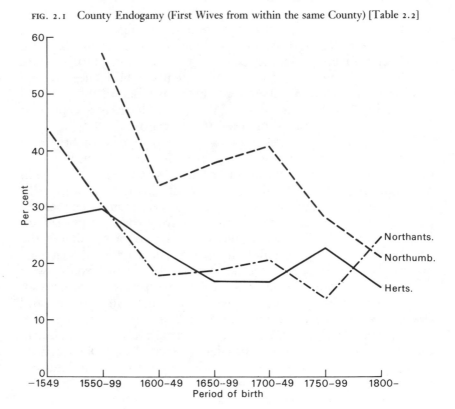

[11] A. McInnes, op. cit., p. 21.

FIG. 2.2   Regional Endogamy (First Wives from within the same Region) [Table 2.2]

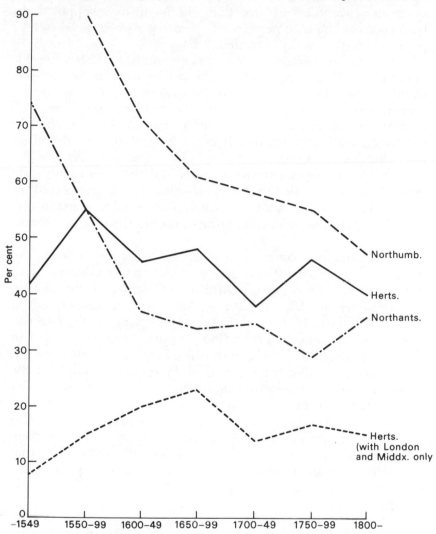

with a substantially lower rate of county endogamy than that of Northamptonshire, and that of Northamptonshire than that of Northumberland. Presumably because of its straggly geography, the local-born elite of Northamptonshire were quick to extend their marriage network outside the county, and even the region. The cohort born in the late sixteenth century was already marrying out as frequently as that of Hertfordshire, and thereafter there was no significant difference between them. The Northamptonshire-born elite were clearly less isolated than one might have supposed. In both counties about 20 per cent of all marriages continued to take place within the county, but that is all.

With Northumberland, however, one enters a different world. One-half of all marriages among the cohort born in the late sixteenth century took place within the county, and the proportion remained at about 40 per cent until the middle of the eighteenth century. It was only as communications improved during the late eighteenth and early nineteenth centuries that the Northumberland elite began to join the nation. Only after the arrival of the railway in the mid-nineteenth century did their endogamy rate become the same as that of everybody else. These figures confirm what other evidence indicates, namely that Northumberland was not fully opened up to outside influences until the nineteenth century.

If one turns from county endogamy to regional endogamy, the most striking feature is the degree to which the local-born elite in Northumberland remained faithful to the northern connection to a surprisingly late date (Table 2.2, Fig. 2.2). Over 90 per cent of all their brides came from the north of England in the late sixteenth century, and the proportion was still about 50 per cent in the early nineteenth. Northamptonshire-born owners also married predominantly within the regional Midlands area throughout the sixteenth century, though declining from 75 per cent to 55 per cent. After 1600 the proportion stabilized at about 35 per cent. Hertfordshire was a special case, since the metropolis of London was within its regional area. As a result, although the proportion of regional marriages was at all times after 1550 higher than that of Northamptonshire, hovering around 40 per cent to 45 per cent, in fact about 15 per cent to 20 per cent of them were with London brides.

One may therefore conclude that intra-county marriage ties between elite families declined as communications improved and regional and national marriage markets developed, until by the nineteenth century, they amounted to no more than about one in five in the south and Midlands and one in four in the north. Regional ties remained particularly strong in Northumberland but declined very quickly in Northamptonshire to about one in three by the mid-seventeenth century. In a home county like Hertfordshire, the presence of London makes the whole concept of regionalism largely meaningless.

2. THE THREE COUNTIES

i. Introduction

To study the county elites and their houses in all the counties of England would be far beyond the capacity of a single scholar in a single lifetime working with limited resources—and in any case it would be unnecessary. It was not thought possible even to cover as many as four counties, although this has meant that no sample could be taken of the West Country, which may upon investigation show a distinctive regional pattern. For reasons of economy of time, the choice was therefore limited to three counties, selected so as to offer the greatest possible diversity of social experiences. If, as was assumed from the start, proximity to London was a key element in determining the degree of mobility within a local elite, it was essential to choose one county very close to London, one some distance away and with no big city within or near it, and one as far away as possible. A number of counties would have fulfilled each of these requirements, but those actually selected were chosen for pragmatic reasons of convenience and accessibility. They needed to be especially well documented, including a modern local history, parish by parish and manor by manor, and also one or more good seventeenth- to nineteenth-century county histories. In addition they had to be counties with good sets of local record publications, good collections of seventeenth-, eighteenth-, and nineteenth-century prints or drawings of houses, good maps, and particularly active and well-organized local record offices. The counties which seemed best to fulfil these requirements were Hertfordshire, adjacent to London; Northamptonshire, in the depths of the country some sixty miles away; and Northumberland, up on the Scottish border and containing the industrial city of Newcastle. Hertfordshire is close enough to London to have felt its pull as early as the mid-sixteenth century. Northamptonshire is further away, but was brought within London's orbit with the improvement of turnpike roads in the eighteenth century, and was close enough for weekending after the building of the railway by the middle of the nineteenth. Northumberland is so far away that it remained more accessible to London by sea than by land until the advent of the railways. After that, however, it rapidly became fashionable for the shooting. Together, the three counties include agricultural counties, both arable and pasture; and counties with no industry, light industry, and heavy industry. The classic socio-political dichotomies of Puritan and Catholic, Court and Country, Royalist and Parliamentarian, monied and landed,

Whig and Tory, can all be found in varying degrees in all three counties. Change, moreover, is well illuminated by comparison between the three counties, since Northamptonshire provides a valuable yardstick of exceptional stability, both in the longevity of its families of owners and the durability of its stone-built houses.

ii. Northamptonshire

The most difficult choice was of a predominantly rural county some way from London and without any significant urban agglomeration within its borders, a county where change might be expected to have been slow, and infiltration by outsiders limited. The choice fell on Northamptonshire, in the heart of the Midlands, and far from any large industrial or commercial city. The county was known to possess an excellently run and well-stocked record office, and a long series of record publications. On the other hand, only one of the three large-scale county histories was ever finished, which turned out to be something of a handicap. However, owing to the largely uninterrupted rise of its elite into the ranks of the titular aristocracy, many gaps in the data could be filled by consulting standard works of reference about the peerage and baronetage.

Until the very recent development of opencast mining of iron ore, Northamptonshire was one of England's most rural counties, its only light industry being the manufacture of boots which goes back to the seventeenth century. It lies some sixty to seventy miles from London, and before the end of the nineteenth century it possessed no town of any size. The nearest large city or even thriving town was Birmingham, which in fact hardly affected it at all. Not a single Birmingham business man bought his way into the county elite in all the 340 years from 1540 to 1880. But the county was by no means totally isolated from London, for it was bisected by the great arterial highway of Watling Street, that ran from London to Chester, and thence connected by sea to Dublin. In 1722 Defoe described it as 'that most travelled of English highways', but its well-engineered Roman roadbed had long since been plundered, and the traffic was apparently now more than it could stand. In the 1748 edition of Defoe's *Tour* it is described as 'not passible but just in the middle of summer, after the coal carriages have beaten the way. For as the ground is stiff clay, so, after rain, the water stands as in a dish, and horses sink into it up to their bellies.' It was not long, however, before the turnpike system vastly improved the situation. By 1804 the main roads in the county were turnpiked and well surfaced, even if the parish roads were still single track and very poorly maintained.[12]

The third feature of Northamptonshire, after the absence of a big city or even substantial town and its position astride a major highway to London, was its heavy dependence on cattle and sheep-grazing and the consequent early and extensive enclosure of the common fields for pasture. By 1809, 227 of its 316 parishes were enclosed. This did not only mean that most of the great landlords were large-scale cattle and sheep masters, producing wool, mutton, and beef for the London market. It also meant that its pastures and hedges made it excellent hunting country, especially since parts of it were still wooded, remnants of the extensive old royal forest of Rockingham. As such, it was peculiarly attractive as a place of residence to the hunting squirearchy and nobility, even if, as Repton declared bluntly in 1791, 'the face of the county . . . is certainly not picturesque'. In 1809 it was remarked that 'by far the greatest part of the landed property is in the possession of noblemen and gentlemen, who reside at least some part of the year in the county'. By then it contained 'a great many magnificent and elegant seats of nobility and gentry', allegedly more than any other county of its size in the kingdom.[13] Certainly, in about 1670 there had been a rather large number for its size of big houses with more than forty-five hearths (Fig. 2.3). Moreover, this pattern persisted, as is suggested by the high proportion of estates over 10,000 acres in 1873, and the high proportion of houses in this county which have been the subject of articles in *Country Life* (Fig. 2.4). Northamptonshire is thus very well suited for a study of a local elite situated some way from London and under no pressure from a nearby city, but still in the lowland zone and with relatively good communications with the metropolis.

iii. Hertfordshire

Among the home counties within a dozen miles of London, Hertfordshire was easy to choose, because of the extreme richness of its documentation, being the subject of no less than five large county histories. It was also chosen partly because it was thought likely to provide one of the most extreme cases of mobility between land and trade, since it was already known that through all periods it,

---

[12] D. Defoe, *A Tour of Great Britain*, London, 1748, ii, p. 425; W. Pitt, *General View of the Agriculture of the County of Northampton*, London, 1809, pp. 230-1.

[13] D. Stroud, *Humphrey Repton*, London, 1962, p. 64; W. Pitt, op. cit., pp. 21-5. In 1670 Northamptonshire had been outstripped by Surrey (see Fig. 2.3), but the claim may have been true by 1800.

FIG. 2.3 Density of Houses by Size in Seven Counties c.1662-1673 [Table 2.3]

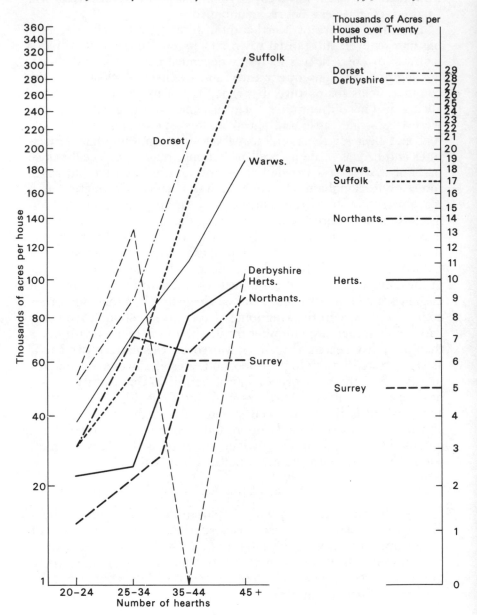

FIG. 2.4 Distribution of Private Estates by Size in 1873 [Table 2.4]

Surrey, and Essex had been favourite areas for the purchase of a landed estate by successful London merchants. Although it is situated so close to the capital, with good road communications, even today much of it is rolling country of woods and fields of great natural beauty and offering an extraordinary sense of rural peace. The special quality of Hertfordshire was recognized at the time, and in 1704 Robert Morden wrote with pardonable hyperbole— 'this county has an incredible number of palaces and fair structures of the gentry and nobility. From Totteridge where the county begins and East Barnet to Ware, are so many beautiful houses, that one may look upon it almost as a continual street. The rich soil and wholesome air, and the excellency of the county, have drawn hither the wealthiest citizens of London'. A century later an official report for the Board of Agriculture remarked how 'a considerable addition is made to the beauty of this county by the villas and seats of rich proprietors presenting themselves to our view in every direction'.[14] It was the combination of proximity, accessibility, and rusticity that made Hertfordshire so attractive to generation after generation of rich Londoners. It is no coincidence that as early as the 1630s the only regular coach service in the whole country ran through Hertfordshire from London to Cambridge, and the only three wagon-cum-coach services ran between London and the Hertfordshire towns of St Albans, Hertford, and Hatfield; and that there were also regular carrier delivery services several times a week to four other Hertfordshire towns.[15] The ties that bound the county to the city were thus exceptionally close even before the middle of the seventeenth century.

It is not surprising, therefore, to find that Hertfordshire was unusual in the number of substantial country houses of which it could boast. This is demonstrated by comparing thousands of acres per house assessed at twenty hearths or more in this and other counties in the Hearth Taxes of 1662 to 1673, which reveal a direct relationship between density of houses and proximity to London. Surrey, which is adjacent to London on the south bank of the Thames and also up-river toward Richmond, had the highest density of houses, but Hertfordshire came next. Calculated in terms of thousands of acres per house, the density in Hertfordshire is nearly twice as great as in Suffolk or Warwickshire and about three times as great as in Dorset and Derbyshire (Table 2.3, Fig. 2.3). Seventeenth-century Hertfordshire was thus a demonstrably atypical county in the extraordinarily large number of big houses which it contained relative to its size.

A different but related comparison between our three counties can be made 200 years later, in 1873. Hertfordshire was then second only to Essex in the proportion of acreage (excluding waste) owned by small to medium-sized landowners. No less than 18 per cent was owned by men holding between 300 and 1,000 acres each. In counties farther from London those in the 300 to 1,000 acre bracket would probably only count as yeomen, but in Hertfordshire they were usually small gentry living gentlemanly lives in gentlemanly houses, on the strength of an income derived partly from the high rental per acre in the county, but more from investments in business companies and in the Funds. The social

---

[14] R. Morden, *New Description of England*, London, 1704, p. 36; *General View of Agriculture in the County of Hertfordshire*, London, 1804, p. 2.
[15] J. Taylor, *The Carriers' Cosmography*, London, 1637.

structure of mid-Victorian Hertfordshire thus forms a striking contrast with Northamptonshire, with its higher concentration of large landowners, and even more with Northumberland, half of which was in the hands of great magnates with over 10,000 acres (Table 2.4, Fig. 2.4).

Despite these unusual features, it would be a mistake to imagine that most of the landowners of Hertfordshire did not possess a sense of community. Although the degree of mobility and of access to non-landed sources of income may have been exceptionally great, the majority of landowners in the county were at all times resident at least periodically on their estates, and owned property exclusively within its boundaries. An examination of all the manors in the county in 1640 shows that 86 per cent of them were owned by residents within the county, and only 14 per cent by residents elsewhere.[16] This figure is much the same as those for Essex, Suffolk, and Norfolk, although it is likely that the causes are somewhat different in the more remote counties of Norfolk and Suffolk than in counties close to London like Hertfordshire and Essex. In the former the non-residents were probably mostly landowners with estates elsewhere; in Hertfordshire, and to some extent in Essex, very many of them were Londoners buying into the county either temporarily or with a view to later retirement.

This situation did not change significantly before the middle of the nineteenth century when the railways opened up the southwestern parts of the county as easily accessible weekend dormitories for London business and professional men, and when the suburbs of London began encroaching upon the southernmost edges of the county. But as late as 1873, of the 146 inhabitants of Hertfordshire houses who also owned over 2,000 acres of property and a rent-roll of over £2,000 a year in or out of the county, only 13 per cent held a seat elsewhere, and only 25 per cent held more than 1,000 acres elsewhere (and this was usually in an adjacent county).[17]

iv. Northumberland

The county remotest from London was also an easy choice: Northumberland enjoys the best modern multivolume survey in the whole of England, a work entirely conceived, planned, financed, and executed by local initiative. It is England's northernmost county, covering over 2,000 square miles of often very rough

[16] C. A. Holmes, op. cit., App. II, p. 494.
[17] J. Bateman, op. cit.

country between the Scottish border on the river Tweed to the north and the river Tyne to the South. At its northernmost tip, guarding the border, lies the town of Berwick, which in the early sixteenth century had been provided with the most elaborate and up-to-date defence works of any city north of the Alps. Despite this enormous fortress, Northumberland continued to be exposed to Scottish cattle-raiding or even invasion, since it was unprotected by any mountain barrier. The area was not pacified until James VI of Scotland became James I of England in 1603, which at last put an end to endemic border warfare between English and Scottish cattle-raiding parties. Consequently it was not until the beginning of the seventeenth century that the Northumberland county elite began to feel safe enough to live in unfortified country houses, a whole century after these had appeared around London. Before then, the rich lived in strongly walled castles, and the mere gentry in 'bastle houses' consisting of a lean-to dwelling space attached to a tall three-storey tower into which the family retreated during the night for security. 'There is not a man amongst them of the better sort that hath not his little tower or pile', remarked William Camden in the late sixteenth century. Nearly a century later, in 1662, Thomas Fuller confirmed that 'here it was the rule with ancient architects what was firm, that was fair; so that it may be said of all houses of gentry herein *quot mansiones, tot munitiones* [so many houses, so many forts], as either being all castles or castle-like, able to resist, though no solemn siege, a tumultuary incursion'. (Plate III B.) In consequence, it is not possible to begin to speak of country squires or country houses in Northumberland before about 1610, some seventy years later than in Northamptonshire and Hertfordshire; and our sample therefore does not begin until then. Even so, the squirearchy remained remarkably violence-prone as late as the mid-seventeenth century, two of them (Thomas Carr of Ford Castle and John Swinburne of Capheaton) meeting their deaths by murder.

The level of culture was correspondingly low, and in 1595 there was no grammar school and only four preaching clergymen in the county. As late as the 1590s only two-thirds of those describing themselves as gentlemen were able to sign their names, and it was not until the 1620s that literacy became universal among the gentry.[18] In Northumberland, therefore, the story of the elite and their seats cannot begin before 1610, and even after that the growth

[18] W. Camden, *Britannia*, London, 1610, p. 799; T. Fuller, op. cit., ii, p. x; D. Cressy, 'Social Status and Literacy in North East England 1560-1630', *Local Population Studies*, 21, 1978, p. 20; D. L. W. Tough, *The Last Years of a Frontier*, Oxford, 1928, pp. 26-48, 71.

in numbers was very slow, since much of the county was thinly populated and impoverished moorland, with few or no roads. The county economy was badly damaged by the Civil Wars of the mid-seventeenth century, suffering from occupation by a rapacious Scottish army and from sequestration and fines imposed on the many royalist delinquents. So undeveloped was the area that in the late seventeenth century land was selling at only fourteen years purchase of the rental, as against the more usual twenty-one years in the south. Thereafter agricultural improvement and the creation and settlement of estates and county seats proceeded very slowly, producing a pattern of steady numerical growth over three centuries, rather than a sudden spurt up to 1660 followed by a levelling-off, as in the southern counties. Even as late as 1733, land in Northumberland was still much cheaper than that in the south, selling at twenty-two years purchase of the rental instead of thirty, while the rent per acre was also much lower than in the south.[19]

For a long while, therefore, Northumberland remained a very backward area, one reason for this backwardness being the extreme difficulty of land communications. In 1771 Arthur Young said of the turnpike to Newcastle that 'a more dreadful road cannot be imagined', being full of pot-holes, some of them 2 feet deep. 'Let me persuade all travellers', he continued, 'to avoid this terrible country, which must either dislocate their bones with broken pavements, or bury them in muddy sand'. 'I must in general advise all who travel on any business but absolute necessity to avoid any journey further north than Newcastle'. As late as the beginning of the nineteenth century, the roads in the northern part of the county 'were little more than tracks following along the sides of fields with a gate at every boundary fence'. When they reached open common the tracks stopped altogether, leaving 'roadless heatherland, swampy in parts and treacherous underfoot, so that horses plunged through as best they could'. When in the early nineteenth century the Charltons of Hesleyside on the North Tyne river took their coach to go to and from Newcastle, their tenant farmers had to bring oxen to drag it up and down a boggy hill between the towns of Bellingham and Wark further down-river.[20] Given these difficulties of communication, as well as the harsh cold and rain of the long winters, it is hardly surprising that elite landowners were slow to set up residences in these remote areas. It is also not surprising that much of this undeveloped and under-

[19] E. Hughes, *North Country Life in the Eighteenth Century*, London, 1952, i, pp. xvi, 81.
[20] B. Charlton, *The Recollections of a Northumbrian Lady, 1815-1866*, ed. L. E. U. Charlton, London, 1949, p. 134.

populated area fell into the hands of very large landlords. By 1873 over 50 per cent of the acreage of the county was in the hands of men with over 10,000 acres, and over 70 per cent in those of men with over 3,000 acres, which were much higher proportions than in any other county in England except Rutland (Table 2.1, Fig. 2.1).

A second peculiarity of Northumberland was that so many of its landed families remained attached to Roman Catholicism, thanks to a massive reconversion effort by seminary priests from 1580 to 1595. By 1600 the pattern was set which was to last for centuries, and was to cause the downfall of many lesser gentry families which became involved in the first Jacobite rebellion of 1715. In the early seventeenth century Catholic families included such prominent names as Radcliffe of Dilston, Swinburne of Capheaton, and Grey of Chillingham, even if in many cases a husband or brother nominally conformed in order to preserve the family estates. This loyalty meant that many leading families were semi-permanently excluded from public office, and their activities confined to hunting, the managing of their families and estates, and entrepreneurial activities. They were an inward-turned and inbred coterie of internal exiles for their faith.[21]

The third feature which distinguished the squirearchy of Northumberland from those of southern counties was their involvement with the coal industry. Many of the county elite felt the pull of Newcastle, which as late as 1750 was still the fourth largest city in England outside London, deriving its wealth from coal and shipping. Many landowners developed coal-mines on their own estates and profited from the lease of way-leaves for coal-wagons across their property.

To sum up, the Northumberland elite were physically and psychologically very isolated from the mainstream of English life, while at the same time many of them were being brought in direct personal touch with the world of business.

3. THE COUNTY ELITE

The county elite with which this book is concerned was composed of three overlapping groups. The first was the local power elite which ran the affairs of the county and was mostly recruited from

---

[21] F. M. L. Thompson, *English Landed Society in the Nineteenth Century*, London, 1963, p. 32; E. Hughes, op. cit., p. xvii; J. A. Hilton, 'Catholicism in Elizabethan Northumberland', *Northern History*, xiii, 1977. For a vivid description of the restricted life they led even in the early nineteenth century, see B. Charlton, op. cit., passim.

the much larger ranks of the second, which was the local status elite. The latter consisted mainly of the surviving descendants by primogeniture of former power elites. The third was the local elite of wealth, which included most members of the other two, and also such newcomers to the landed classes as were both resident in suitable houses and prepared to spend lavishly in order to obtain either status or local power or both.

The county elite is therefore not limited only to active participants in the running of county affairs, but also includes all those from whose ranks such persons might be drawn. This covers all members of the titular aristocracy who not only owned land in the county but also a seat of a certain minimum size in which they resided regularly for at least part of the year, and also all squires resident in such houses. The use of ownership of houses of a particular size or above as a criterion for putative membership of this elite is based on two considerations. One is that muster books and other tax assessments in all three counties surveyed show that those who made up the county elite stood out from the rest by being assessed for the charge of at least one horse, and also lived in country houses of a certain minimum size. The other is the observation that those with, or thought to have, elite aspirations also lived in such houses, though not necessarily owning very large estates. That this should have been so makes perfectly good sense, since the possession of the financial and physical resources with which to entertain on a generous scale was the visible proof of 'port', the assumption of which distinguished the elite from the ruck of parish gentry and below.

In terms of their involvement in local politics, the county elite fell roughly into three groups: the active, the nominally active, and the inactive. The active consisted of those who ran the affairs of the county, mostly in their capacity as magistrates, deputy-lieutenants, or as Knights of the Shire in Parliament. The nominally active might hold the same offices, but treated these positions as sinecure honours rather than as serious responsibilities. They numbered in their ranks members of the peerage who served as *Custos Rotulorum*, which was mainly an honorific function. It was not unusual for such men to be quite active in their youth before succeeding their father in his honours.

The inactive are more difficult to identify, since they included men who, for one reason or another, were not competitors for political office. Most did so by personal choice, others were deliberately excluded for one reason or another. Between 1680 and 1720 the ferocious struggle between Whigs and Tories, and the see-saw swings of power from one to the other and back again, resulted in a series of political purges of the Bench and other offices by the current ruling junta. Others were excluded because of their religion, either as Dissenters, or more likely as Catholics (legally until 1825). Most of the inactive were drawn from the ranks of the descendants of once active members of the local elite.

For newcomers with little save their wealth and the grandeur of their houses to recommend them, one of the most common modes of entry into the lower ranks of the local power elite was a willingness to serve for one year in the onerous and expensive office of sheriff, which nearly everyone else tried to avoid. This was often accompanied by promotion to the Bench. The sons and grandsons of newcomers, however, seem to have met with no great obstacles to their social acceptance, so long as they had the proper credentials of a substantial income, at least some of it in land, ownership of a sizeable country seat, genteel education and manners, and a suitable style of living. To use an eighteenth-century phrase, they were all 'persons of quality at their seats in the country'.[22] In Hertfordshire, where the turnover was high and the proximity of London overpowering, a number of elite members continued to remain active in that area of politics or the professions in which their ancestors had first made the family fortunes. Two groups in particular, brewers, from the late seventeenth century, and bankers, from the late eighteenth, continued to practice their avocations without any noticeable loss of status.

All the members of the elite thus had four things in common. The first was the sheer size of their wealth. The majority were owners of vast tracts of land whose income supported the expense of living in luxury in a great seat, such as the 1,700 landlords who in 1873 owned about 40 per cent of all the real estate in England and Wales.[23] The second was their style of life, which included a superior education, often at one of the two elite schools, Eton and Westminster, a knowledge of the world not infrequently acquired on the Grand Tour, and the maintenance of a generous level of hospitality. The third was the possession of a house of a certain size with decorative public rooms for entertaining, elaborate pleasure-grounds, and possibly also a park. The fourth, even if they chose not to exercise it, was an inherited right to compete for access to offices involving administrative duties and public serv-

[22] Lambeth Palace, Court of Arches, Process Book D 1017, f. 237.
[23] G. C. Brodrick, op. cit., pp. 173, 87. Only a handful of these, all of them in Hertfordshire, did not own the freehold of their houses, but held on ninety-nine year or three-life leases, mostly granted by the Church and conventionally renewable in perpetuity.

ice—in other words the exercise of authority. They were thus an elite of wealth, status, and power.[24] After the Restoration, these men went by the courtesy title of 'Squire', if they did not possess a legal title as knight, baronet, or peer. They were bound together by a common culture and sociability, and by ties of patronage and marriage, by an intricate network of personal, family and official relationships.

This book is constructed around two basic assumptions. The first is that, although other elements are important, an indispensable criterion for defining men of landed elite status is ownership of a country seat of a certain minimum size and aesthetic elegance. If this is correct, the key question in deciding upon the composition of the sample of elites, is how to measure house size.[25]

The second proposition is that the only way to test the traditional beliefs about the degree of mobility in and out of the English landed elite is by rigorous use of quantification. In view of the size of the sample, 2,246 owners of 362 houses over 340 years with up to 160 pieces of information available about each of them (Table 2.5), the only way to process the data was by the use of the computer.[26]

4. THE SOURCES OF EVIDENCE

There is a certain poetic justice in the fact that much of the evidence upon which this study is based is drawn from compilations, many of which owe their existence to both the longevity of ancient families and the possibilities of upward social mobility from below which lie at the heart of this study.

England is extraordinarily, perhaps uniquely, rich in the records of its upper landed class, partly because its archives, and particularly its private archives, have never suffered the dispersal and destruction of a social revolution, and partly because family pride and anxiety to stress or invent an ancestry has encouraged the collection of genealogies and family histories. This widespread passion for the minutiae of genealogy is bound up with the fear and the reality of infiltration from below. At first, in the days of

[24] For a more extended discussion of the criteria of choice of the universe, see L. Stone and J. C. Fawtier Stone, 'Country Houses and Their Owners in Hertfordshire, 1540-1879', in *The Dimensions of Quantitative Research in History*, ed. W. O. Aydelotte *et al.*, Princeton, 1972, pp. 73-105.

[25] For a detailed explanation of how house size in units is calculated, see Appendix II, 1.

[26] Precisely how this was done, and the not too happy confrontation with the computer, is described in detail in Appendix II, 2.

heraldic visitations, it was prompted by the need to establish degrees of antiquity of family origins both for those already established and for those seeking to join their ranks, many of whom
were laying dubious claims to remote gentry descent. Later, in the
nineteenth century, it was a means of recording the admission of
new members of the landed classes, whose pedigrees now often
went no further back than to the self-made man whose fortune
provided the only family passport to upward social mobility.

i. County Histories

It was this passion for historical and antiquarian research into the
landed families of the country which was the main stimulus for
the production, from the late seventeenth century onward, of a
series of stately folio volumes of local histories, which tell the history of a county, parish by parish, manor by manor, and family
by family. This obsession with elite family history, genealogy,
seats, and monumental inscriptions, which in other respects is a
serious drawback to these works, is for our purposes an enormous
blessing. For each of the three counties, these volumes provide
much of the basic information. Since these were enormously lengthy
and expensive undertakings, the research and publication costs could
only be paid for by prior subscription, often made decades before
the volumes finally appeared. Only the local elite were willing to
support such enterprises, and they naturally expected the histories
of their families and houses to figure prominently. Nor were they
disappointed.

It is no accident that the illustrations mostly consisted of engravings of seats of the county gentry, since the latter paid directly
for them, each for his own house. (Plates II, IIIA and B, V, VIA
and B, VIIB, VIIIA, XA and B.) 'I find gentlemen are only intent
upon plates of their seats', complained John Hutchins, the historian of Dorset, in 1769. Hasted, the historian of Kent, explained
that plates of seats 'are done in a more elegant and expensive style,
where the donors have shown a more than ordinary liberality'.
Similarly gentry patronized local historians in the expectation that
they would write at appropriate length about their families. As
one commented—probably unfairly—of Hasted, 'those families who
present him highest are the most favourably inserted'.[27]

A detailed account of how these things were managed has sur-

---

[27] J. Simmons, *English County Historians*, East Ardsley, 1978, pp. 149, 203, 201. For
prospectuses by publishers for subscriptions to county histories, see *Catalogue of Publishers'
Prospectuses in the John Johnson Collection*, ed. J. Feather, Oxford Microfilm Publications,
1978.

vived regarding an abortive attempt to launch a history of Wiltshire. In 1659 there was a meeting of the gentlemen of the county
at Devizes to choose a Knight of the Shire for Parliament—a normal method at that time of avoiding the hazards and expense of
rival candidates submitting themselves to the electorate. At the
meeting, the gentlemen discussed other matters as well, including
a desire to emulate Dugdale's great work on Warwickshire. A local
lawyer offered to collect data for the middle half of the county,
and a gentleman-antiquary, John Aubrey, for the north. Three
other local squires offered to help, and there were already collections of copies of local deeds in the hands of Judge Nicholas and
a Mr Yorke. But as Aubrey commented tersely: 'both now dead.
'Tis pity that those papers should fall into the merciless hands of
women, and be put under pies'. Partly as a result of this destruction by the widows of antiquaries, and partly because Aubrey by
his own admission 'set down things tumultuously, as if tumbled
out of a sack, as they come to hand', nothing ever came of the
project.[28]

The authors of these monumentally learned volumes produced
in the seventeenth and eighteenth centuries came from a variety of
social backgrounds. John Norden, one of the earliest topographers,
was a surveyor and map-maker and a minor government official.
Sir Simon Archer, Sir Robert Atkyns, Robert Thoroton, Richard
Carew, Thomas Habington, Sir Henry Chauncy, and John Aubrey were themselves country squires. Richard Carew and Sir
William Dugdale were heralds by profession, as was Augustine
Vincent, author of an abortive history of Northamptonshire. James
Wright and Sir Henry Chauncy were lawyers, George Lipscomb
and Robert Thoroton physicians, and Francis Drake a surgeon.
From the early eighteenth century, many of them were clergymen, like Nathaniel Salmon, William Borlase, John Collinson, John
Hodgson, John Hutchins, and Thomas Nash. One way or another, they all performed their prodigious labours as an obsessive,
passionate, and often ruinous hobby, and drew their livelihood
from other sources. Salmon was an impoverished non-juring cu-
rate, whose book on Essex, published in 1740, was 'his last shift
to live', and as usual a financial failure. Thomas Nash was a wealthy
absentee parson, who lived like a country squire and could afford
to subsidize his researches from the tithes extracted from his neglected parishioners. Those without such resources often came to

[28] J. Aubrey, *Collections for the Natural and Topographical History of Wiltshire*, ed. J. E.
Jackson, Devizes, 1862, pp. 3, vi.

disaster. The first three volumes of Edward Hasted's *History of Kent* ran him into debt, for which he spent the next seven years in the King's Bench prison. While there, he not only completed and published the fourth and last volume, but also a new and heavily revised twelve-volume second edition. Nothing, not even prison, could dampen his enthusiasm or stop his pen.[29]

No fewer than three successive revisions, two of them major, of Sir Henry Chauncy's *Historical Antiquities of Hertfordshire*, first published in 1700, were brought out in 1728, 1827, and 1881, which gives some indication of the speed with which Hertfordshire county society was observed to be changing.[30] This issue of edition after edition was designed to keep pace with the rate of turnover in elite society in the county. The old elite felt threatened and wished to record their claims to antiquity, and the newcomers wished to record their arrival at social eminence. Both were willing to pay to have their genealogies and histories published to the world at large.

In stable counties like Northamptonshire and Northumberland, on the other hand, the old elite must have felt perfectly secure. They therefore saw no pressing social need to subscribe to such lavish projects in order to get their family histories recorded for posterity, nor were there many newcomers anxious to pay in order to establish their identity. As a result, nearly all local-history projects in these counties before the twentieth century ultimately proved abortive for lack of financial support.

The difficulties encountered in publishing the two early multi-

[29] J. Norden, *Speculum Britanniae*, London, 1593-8; *Speculi Britanniae Pars Altera, or a Delineation of Northamptonshire in the Year 1610*, London, 1720; descriptions of Cornwall and Essex were also published from his manuscripts long after his death; P. Styles, *Sir Simon Archer, Dugdale Society Occasional Papers*, 6, 1946; R. Thoroton, *Antiquities of Nottinghamshire*, London, 1677; T. Habington, *Survey of Worcester*, ed. J. Amphlett, *Worcestershire Historical Society*, V (2 vols.), 1895-9; W. Dugdale, *Antiquities of Warwickshire*, London, 1656; J. Wright, *History and Antiquities of the County of Rutland*, London, 1684; R. Atkyns, *Ancient and Present State of Glostershire*, London, 1712; J. Aubrey, op. cit.; A. N. Salmon, *History of Hertfordshire*, London, 1728; *History and Antiquities of Essex*, London, 1740; F. Drake, *Eboracum*, London, 1736; W. Borlase, *Antiquities of the County of Cornwall*, Oxford, 1754; J. Hutchins, *History and Antiquities of the County of Dorset*, London, 1774; J. Collinson, *History and Antiquities of Somersetshire*, Bath, 1791; E. Hasted, *A History of the County of Kent*, Canterbury, 1778-99, 2nd ed., 1797-1801; G. Lipscomb, *The History and Antiquities of the County of Buckingham*, London, 1831-47; [T. R. Nash] *The Index to Dr Nash's Collections for the History of Worcestershire*, ed. J. Amphlett, *Worcestershire Historical Society*, iii, 1894-5; for a survey of county historians, see J. Simmons, op. cit., ch. 1.

[30] For subsequent references to material concerning the three counties, see below, Bibliography.

In view of the fact that most of the information on which this book is based is derived from the standard reference works listed in the Bibliography, it has not been thought necessary to clutter up the book with further references to them, except in the case of direct quotations.

volume histories of Northamptonshire illustrate the way these massive enterprises were financed, and the risks run by their authors because of it. John Bridges, whose father purchased and enlarged Barton Seagrave Hall into an elite residence, was a successful lawyer and government financial official, who only turned his attention to the project of a county history in 1718, at the age of fifty-eight. He personally visited every parish, and spent several thousand pounds of his own money in hiring copyists of documents, researchers, and artists. But he died prematurely in 1725, leaving behind him thirty folio and nine quarto volumes of manuscripts. An initial attempt to edit and publish the material by raising subscriptions from local gentry foundered for lack of support, and the entrepreneur—a Londoner—went bankrupt. The manuscripts were then acquired by a local county squire, William Cartwright of Aynho. A committee of wealthy squires was founded to promote the publication, an editor was hired, and two parts appeared in 1762 and 1769. But the committee became inactive when the chairman died, the editor was incompetent and lazy, and final publication was delayed until 1791. It is clear that only a minority of the county elite was sufficiently enthusiastic about the publication of a local history of themselves and their county to see the project through to completion. The lack of financial and psychological support by many landowners was a serious obstacle, and although the support of a sufficient number of subscribers finally saw the massive survey into print, no attempt was made to bring the seventy-year-old manuscript up to date.

The next venture, by George Baker in the early nineteenth century, fared even worse. Baker was a middle-class bachelor and JP, who devoted his life to this project for a new county history, the financing of which was, as usual, to be supported by private subscriptions. Over a period of nineteen years, between 1822 and 1841, Baker produced five exquisitely printed parts, covering only eight hundreds out of twenty. But by then many of his subscribers had become exasperated by this slow rate of production, and 220 of them failed to pay the subscriptions they had promised. Baker was forced to abandon his undertaking and sell his books and manuscripts to stave off bankruptcy.

Even the *Victoria County History* of Northamptonshire, begun in the early years of this century, remains unfinished, the reason for this being probably the near collapse between 1880 and 1925 of the old elite of the county, many of whom sold their ancestral seats and moved elsewhere, often abroad to southern Africa. Their *nouveau-riche* successors had nothing to record, and so a solid basis of local squirearchy support was lacking. Nor did Northamptonshire

possess a university or other centre of learning which might have
provided the necessary intellectual stimulus, nor a great city with
prosperous manufacturers, merchants, lawyers, and doctors to take
up the burden of historical responsibility abandoned by the squirearchy. As a result of this unhappy history of delays, false starts,
and failures to complete the task, only Bridges managed to cover
the whole county, and he wrote as long ago as 1720. However,
Baker and the VCH complement each other, leaving only three
hundreds, or about a quarter of the county, uncovered by one or
the other.

In Northumberland, no large-scale scholarly work was done on
the history of the county before the early nineteenth century. John
Hodgson began publication of a multivolume project in 1820, but
was obliged to halt it far short of completion in 1841. The reason
was the usual one, a lack of subscribers, although a seventh volume was brought out after his death by J. Hodgson Hinde in
1858. Plans to complete Hodgson's project contributed to the decision of the county in the 1890s to opt out of the proposed coun-
try-wide *Victoria County History* and embark on the publication of
a sixteen-volume *History of Northumberland* (1893-1940). This is
perhaps the best planned, the most detailed, and the most wide-
ranging study of a county ever compiled, and it is no accident that
it was planned, researched, written, financed, and published entirely by the combined local initiative of noblemen and squires,
city magnates, professional men, and antiquaries. The driving force
behind this great undertaking were the thrusting entrepreneurs of
Newcastle, bursting with local pride and self-confidence.

ii. Genealogies

These county histories can be amplified and supplemented from a
wide variety of sources. Most valuable are the many national genealogical compendia of peers, baronets, and gentry, and the more
specialized genealogies often available for each county. Membership of the Bench of Justices can be discovered from the manuscript *Libri Pacis* in the Public Record Office, which cover the late
sixteenth and seventeenth centuries, and from the original quarter-
sessions papers, which are either in print, as in Hertfordshire, or
in other cases, survive in manuscript in the local record offices.
Equally helpful are the numerous large-scale county maps, which
were issued fairly regularly every twenty years or so from the
early eighteenth century onward.[31] Since they were aimed at a

---

[31] Detailed maps showing country houses, parks and often the names of the owners, are
to be found in the county histories already separately discussed, and also in maps, usually

local gentry market, they were careful to identify the county seats, and sometimes actually name their owners as well. Parks were nearly always prominently displayed, which helps to identify the houses with large pleasure grounds. It will come as no surprise that country houses should feature so prominently on these county maps when one considers that that of Northamptonshire, by Thomas Eyre, published in 1780, was 'corrected by the gentlemen of the respective hundreds, before whom it was laid by the late Sir Thomas Cave, bart.'[32]

iii. Tax Assessments

Evidence about the size, appearance, construction, and alteration of the houses themselves is less comprehensive and less easy to get at than that about their owners. Owing to the perennial weakness and inefficiency of the central government, and its inability to make accurate tax assessments, it is only at two widely separated points in time that comprehensive government surveys become of real value. These are the assessments for the Hearth Tax of 1662 to 1673 and the Survey of Landowners of 1873. By combining and collating the various returns, the Hearth Tax of 1662-73 can be made to provide coverage of all but six of the 135 parishes in Hertfordshire, and virtually all in Northamptonshire. The records for Northumberland, however, are not usable for this purpose, since most houses cannot be identified.

A comparison of the number of hearths listed in the Hearth Tax assessments for Hertfordshire and Northamptonshire with wholly independent calculations of house size in terms of units of liveable space, based on extant buildings, old drawings, etc. shows a comfortingly high degree of correlation, with only a few unexplained anomalies on either side of the mean (Tables 2.6 and 2.7, Figs. 2.5 and 2.6). It is noticeable that the really huge houses with over 200 units are clearly underassessed, especially so in Northamptonshire, so that the mean line is dog-legged. This should be no cause of surprise, since one would assume that in the seventeenth century, just as in the twentieth, the tax machinery favoured the super-rich. This rough correlation gives one confidence that the unit

---

on a scale of 1' to the mile, published separately. For Hertfordshire there are: J. Oliver, *Map of Hertfordshire*, 1695; J. Warburton, J. Bland, and P. Smyth, *A New and Corrected Map of Middlesex, Essex and Hertfordshire*, 1726; A. Dury and J. Andrews, *Map of Hertfordshire*, 1766. For Northamptonshire there are: T. Eyre and J. Jeffereys, *Map of Northamptonshire*, 1779; A. Bryant, *Map of Northamptonshire*, 1827. For Northumberland there are: A. Armstrong and Son, *Map of Northumberland*, 1769; J. Fryer and Son, *Map of Northumberland*, 1820; C. and J. Greenwood, *Map of Northumberland*, 1828. For the whole country there are the magnificent Ordnance Survey 25" to a mile maps of 1867-82.

[32] R. Gough, *British Topography*, London, 1780, ii, p. 52.

FIG. 2.5   Correlation of Hearth Tax Assessments and Estimated House Size in 'Units',
c.1662-1673: Hertfordshire [Table 2.6]

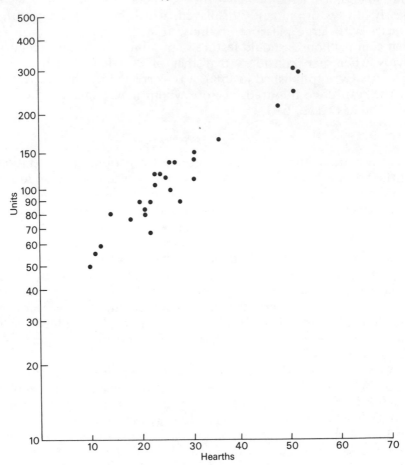

measuring system is meaningful, and also that in the lack of any other evidence, the Hearth Tax can provide an approximate indication of unit size in cases (about a fifth of the whole in Hertfordshire and Northamptonshire) where no other evidence is available for this period.

iv. New Domesday Book, 1873

The great 'New Domesday Book' of 1873 was compiled by Parliament in response to growing concern about the alleged concentration of landed property in relatively few hands, caused, it was argued, by the system of primogeniture and the great agricultural

FIG. 2.6   Correlation of Hearth Tax Assessments and Estimated House Size in 'Units', c.1662–1673: Northamptonshire [Table 2.7]

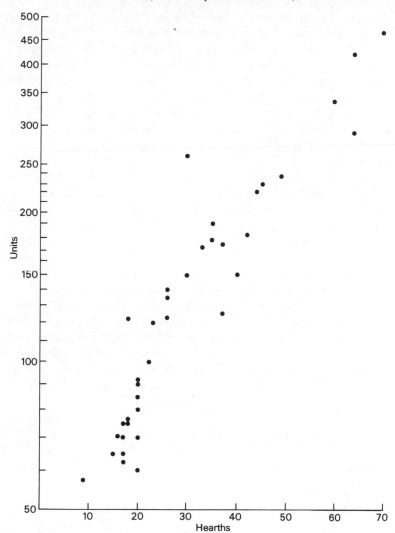

boom of the mid-Victorian period. As a comprehensive survey it left much to be desired, as critics were swift to point out, one of the most serious omissions being of all property in the metropolis of London.[33] Moreover it was compiled geographically by coun-

[33] This gap has recently been filled by the discovery of a set of large-scale maps of London landownership made between 1892 and 1915, R. Hyde, op. cit.

ties, rather than by owners, and it was left to private researchers to reassemble the data to discover the true degree of concentration of property in private ownership. The best results from many years of work were compiled in two forms by Mr John Bateman. One was an alphabetical list of owners, another a statistical compilation of ownership county by county, the owners being allocated to the county of their main seat. Recently, the whole survey has been analysed by counties for the distribution of properties by size, regardless of holdings by owners in other counties (Table 2.4). The two produce very similar results. Those owners in 1873 with their main seat in the county and owning 3,000-acres or more bringing in a rent of at least £3,000 amounted to 64 persons in Hertfordshire, 67 in Northamptonshire, and no fewer than 146 in Northumberland. The numbers for the two southern counties are rather below those who are counted amongst our 'owners in sample', a category which clearly dips slightly lower in the social scale. The massive discrepancy in the Northumberland figures is presumably explained by the large number of landowners drawing substantial incomes from coal-mines, but who failed to play a significant role in county affairs, and whose status was basically that of parish gentry, despite the large acreage of wasteland they owned. The peers and greater landowners owned about 40 per cent of the acreage in private hands in the county of Hertfordshire, 50 per cent in Northamptonshire, and over 70 per cent in Northumberland, which conforms very closely to the figures for 3,000-plus acre estates in Table 2.4. Concentration of ownership at the top was thus at its greatest in Northumberland, largely because of the gigantic holdings of the dukes of Northumberland. Together, these two sources of informative data about the relative wealth of the greater landowners in the three counties permit analyses at two points in time of the relative distribution of all private property between large, medium, and small landholdings.

v. Maps and Illustrations

For the size and shape of many houses, the most reliable evidence comes from the Ordnance Survey maps of 1867-82, drawn on the gigantic scale of twenty-five inches to the mile. The scale of these maps is such that they provide an outline plan of every house and therefore make possible a rough estimate of the square footage that each house covered at that time. Evaluating this evidence, however, is fraught with difficulties, since the map does not distinguish the lowly, often one-storey, offices from the main block. This vital information has to be obtained from other sources, usually illustrations of the houses, although even where these are lacking in most cases it is not too difficult to establish strong probabilities. For a minority of houses there are scale plans and even some elevations, but these cover only the more important structures. Except in Northumberland, scale plans of medium-sized houses of the seventeenth, eighteenth, and nineteenth centuries are largely non-existent. On the other hand, exact measurements of the main reception rooms of a number of houses which have now vanished were included in the many 'Books of Seats' and topographical works which were published in great profusion from about 1790 onward. Auction catalogues, which can be found in most local record offices or libraries, are a valuable source since they describe every room, and often its contents. A very small number of houses have the full record of their architectural history preserved in private account books and drawings, either still in private hands or deposited in the local record office. The detailed histories of most of the larger houses have been written up in *Country Life*, and more briefly in Sir Nikolaus Pevsner's invaluable county guides.

Some of the most illuminating visual material comes from sets of drawings executed at different times, but all dating from before so many houses were changed almost beyond recognition by Victorian additions and alterations. The value of these sets is greatly enhanced by the fact that each is the work of one man. This makes possible comparisons between one house and another at a given date, whereas individual stylistic peculiarities make it more hazardous to compare contemporary illustrations by different artists. For example, for Hertfordshire, Chauncy in 1700 inserted in his county history very elaborate engravings of thirty-two houses and gardens, all but five by J. Drapentier. (Plates VIA and B, VIIB, and endpaper.) These are of exceptionally high quality and are a mine of information about the life led in the country houses themselves and in the mass of ancillary domestic and farm buildings which at that time clustered around them. There were eighty-five houses in our sample at that date, twenty-nine of which are illustrated in Chauncy. Eleven of the twenty-nine belonged to purchasers or their sons, and since the engravings were paid for by the owners, this is an indication of both the pride of ownership, and the anxiety to do the right thing, of newcomers to the county elite.

Nearly a century later, between about 1790 and 1799, a draughtsman called H. G. Oldfield plodded around Hertfordshire making drawing after drawing of over a hundred houses. Although not very skillfully executed, and largely devoid of any sense of perspective, they are unimaginatively faithful to the original and provide the only coverage for many houses of that date. Altogether, Oldfield made some 250 sketches of houses and churches in the hope of making up twenty duplicate sets of the hundred best, and then selling them to the nobility and leading gentry at a handsome profit. But his plans went awry, and he landed in Hertford gaol for debt in 1799, with the drawings as his only asset and thus his only lifeline to freedom. Fortunately both for Oldfield and for posterity, one set was ultimately purchased by Lord Dimsdale and has been preserved. Some thirty years later, in the 1830s, an infinitely more talented artist, William Buckler, followed in Oldfield's footsteps and recorded from many angles some sixty houses. Buckler showed meticulous attention to architectural details, a firm grasp of perspective, and a fine sense of composition (Plates VIIA and VIIIB). His drawings, like the Drapentier engravings in Chauncy, are a pleasure to look at.

For Northamptonshire, the coverage of houses in sets of drawings is almost as extensive. Bridges had planned to illustrate his early eighteenth-century history with engravings of houses as fine as those in Chauncy's *Hertfordshire*, and in 1718 he had taken a first class artist, Peter Tillemans (1684-1734), down into the country with him to do some sketches. As already noted, publication was delayed until 1791, by which time the drawings had parted company from the manuscripts, but fortunately twenty-seven of them found their way into the British Library (Plates IIIA and VIIIA). The few illustrations eventually published in Bridges are both aesthetically undistinguished and architecturally unhelpful.

The next set of drawings, much larger in number but aesthetically unattractive, was provided by a local schoolmaster named George Clarke. His work, and his ambitions for a career, are very similar to those of Oldfield in Hertfordshire. He began in 1819 by combining his schoolmastering with sketching houses, but he retired from the former occupation in 1832 and tried to make a living out of selling collections of topographical drawings to local gentry. Every summer he would walk the roads and lanes of the county, making his sketches, and every winter he would convert them into finished drawings for sale to prospective clients. He continued this mode of life for thirty-six years until his death in 1868. By then he was senile and so absent-minded that he frequently lost his way. That winter he lost his way once too often and spent all night in a ditch in frosty weather, an experience from which he never recovered. Like that of Oldfield before him, Clarke's attempt to make a living out of rather low-quality topographical sketches for sale to the gentry was not a great success. But, like Oldfield, he was a faithful recorder of architectural detail, and his collection provides an invaluable record of forty-three of the seventy country houses in our sample in the early nineteenth century before the great wave of Victorian restorations and additions. Buckler contributed little to this form of documentation in Northamptonshire, since there survive only seven sketches of well-known large houses, done by him in the 1840s.

These groups of drawings may be supplemented by large numbers of individual engravings and drawings, most of which date from between 1680 and 1840. They were commissioned by individual owners presumably to give to their friends, and in 1697 the Duke of Newcastle ordered from L. Knyff 400 copies of engravings of his three seats.[34] Finally, there are photographs of the buildings as they are today. Many houses were photographed in the 1950s, some of them often only weeks ahead of the hammer of a demolition contractor, and many more of those which still survive were recorded by the authors in 1967-73.

Northumberland lacks the sets of drawings available for Hertfordshire and Northamptonshire, but this is compensated for by the very large number of old prints and drawings reproduced in the twentieth-century county history, by the numerous photographs of the houses as they are today, and by the fact that plans are available for no fewer than seventy-five of the eighty-eight houses in the sample. What makes this wealth of visual material so important is the way in which each item supports the other, so that it is frequently possible to trace the changing appearance of an individual house in all its vicissitudes between 1700 and the present day.

The life histories of the local antiquaries, who wrote the great county histories, the compilers of national genealogies of the elite such as Arthur Collins, the makers of large-scale county maps, and the illustrators of country houses prove that they all depended almost entirely upon subscriptions from the landed elite to raise the capital to finance their lengthy researches and pay for the printing of their expensive products. Almost all the evidence available today about the histories of the leading county families and of the houses they lived in comes from materials which they themselves had sponsored and paid for in the first place. It was the interest many of them took in their own family histories which induced

[34] J. Harris, *The Artist and the Country House*, London, 1979, p. 92.

them to finance, however inadequately, the publications which have proved so invaluable to the modern researcher. This interest was most stimulated, it appears, precisely by that perceived threat to old landed families by the new monied interest which is the central subject of this book.

Part II

OWNERS

III

STRATEGIES: SOCIAL IDEALS AND DEMOGRAPHIC CONSTRAINTS

1. INTRODUCTION

For the landed elite, the tenure and preservation of a country seat was of paramount importance, since it represented the outward and visible symbol of family continuity. Transfer of seats by inheritance could take two forms: the first was direct male inheritance from father to son or grandson; and the second was indirect inheritance within the family, passing through the male or female lines to close or distant kin. In addition, there were a handful of minor anomalies, which can safely be ignored. These include temporary or nominal transfers to lessees or trustees for a term of years, grants to a widow for her lifetime, nominal transfers within a family, and a variety of other ambiguous transactions (Table 3.1). The only other way in which seats could be transferred was by sale and purchase, which involved a drastic break in continuity, and thus a failure of family strategy.

Inheritance, the transmission at death of material property including seats, is usually controlled by laws, customs, or general principles concerning the respective rights of one male child, all male children, female children, and the widow of the deceased. The seat almost always changed hands only at death, although parts of the real or personal estate were often distributed earlier, on the marriage of the son and heir, or possibly that of other children. The patrimony was therefore constantly being reduced by minor fission as bits of it were parcelled out to the children, or enlarged by major fusion, as fresh estates were incorporated into it by marriage with the heiresses of other families, or by inheritance because of the failure of branch lines.

2. SOCIAL IDEALS: PRIMOGENITURE AND PATRILINEAL DESCENT

i. Objectives

The prime preoccupation of a wealthy English landed squire was somehow to contrive to preserve his family inheritance intact and to pass it on to the next generation according to the principle of primogeniture in tail male.[1] If possible he would like to pass it on in an improved condition, financially, socially, and aesthetically. On the other hand, he also wished to be free to raise capital to pay marriage portions to his daughters and to provide money or possibly land for his younger sons, in order to give them a gentlemanly start in life. He also needed some mechanism by which he could borrow money and raise capital to pay off debts. Since the estate was finite these two objectives of preserving the patrimony, and at the same time providing for younger sons and daughters and paying off debts, were necessarily to some extent in conflict with one another. The solution, which is technically known as 'preferential partibility', was first to keep the seat and the bulk of the estates tied up more or less in perpetuity for transmission by male primogeniture; but second, to leave some small properties, or new properties recently acquired, at the free disposal of the current owner; and also, if only once in a lifetime, to allow him to raise mortgages, cut down woods, or convey property to trustees for a term of years, in order to pay off debts or provide cash sums for daughters or younger sons.

Whatever dispositions of property were made, the one central objective, which was rarely lost sight of, was to preserve the link between the house, the estates to support it financially, and the family name. The contemporary word for a country house was a 'seat', that is a place where one is seated; 'house' tended to mean lineage and kin, the vertical chain of ancestors, the living kinsmen, and the future descendants. Thus clients spoke of their loyalty to 'the house of Percy' or 'the house of Dacre'. When the word house was applied not to a family line but to a building, it meant an urban residence. The rich owned a town *house* and a country *seat*.

In a very few cases, where the families were of considerable antiquity, they even bore the same name as that of the seat they lived in, both being derived from the name of the manor. In our three sample counties, this phenomenon is entirely confined to a few cases in Northumberland, such as the Crasters of Craster, the Haggerstons of Haggerston, the Mitfords of Mitford, the Whitfields of Whitfield, and the Widdringtons of Widdrington. There are, however, a few other cases where the identification of the

[1] J. P. Cooper, 'Patterns of Inheritance and Settlement by great Landowners from the Fifteenth to the Eighteenth Centuries', *Family and Inheritance*, ed. J. Goody, Joan Thirsk, and E. P. Thompson, Cambridge, 1976; C. S. Kenny, *The History of the Law of Primogeniture in England and Its Effect upon Landed Property*, Cambridge, 1878; A. W. B. Simpson, *An Introduction to the History of the Land Law*, Oxford, 1961, pp. 54-9.

family with the seat was publicized by the name given to houses newly-built on virgin sites. When in about 1500 the first Hertfordshire Brocket built himself a house, he called it Brocket Hall. Soon after her father's death in 1756, Frances St John, coheiress of a baronet, built herself a house in Hertfordshire which she called St John's Lodge. When in 1770 the Earl of Marchmont built himself a suburban retreat in Hertfordshire, he called it Marchmont House.

In the eighteenth century, upwardly mobile purchasers might change the old name of a seat, because they found it insufficiently genteel or imposing to suit their aspirations. In Hertfordshire, Pricketts became Greenhill Grove, Tillers End became Coles Park, and Cokenhatch, at least for a time, became Earlsbury Park. Such name-changing of houses is an indication of the very real degree of identification between an owner and his seat: the latter's name was meant to enhance the status of the former, which is why so many houses in the eighteenth century were called 'Park' instead of the older, less grandiose, 'Hall'. By the nineteenth century, the close identification of the *nouveau-riche* with his small villa was an aping, lower down the social scale, of this form of proprietorial imperialism.

The seat did not only have close connections with the family history and family name, and provide the physical embodiment of its ancestral traditions. It was also often adjacent to the family place of burial, which not infrequently, at least amongst old and distinguished families, was in a church sited in the park close by the house and miles from the village. This could be either because the village had been moved in the eighteenth century to give more privacy, or because the Anglo-Saxon lord of the manor had built the church in the first place close by his house to suit his own convenience. Prime examples of such lonely churches beside the house in the great park which serve as little more than family mausoleums are Lydiard Tregoze in Wiltshire (the St John family), Melbury Sampford in Dorset (the Strangways family), Fawsley in Northamptonshire (the Knightley family), and Stapleford in Leicestershire (the Sherrard family). Even when the church was in the middle of the village, it was sometimes virtually appropriated by the family for its private use as a place of burial. Examples of churches so crammed with family monuments that there is scarcely any room left for the congregation are Belton in Rutland (the Manners family), Tong in Shropshire (the Vernon family), and Bisham in Surrey (the Hoby family). Thomas Fuller summed up the ideal in 1662 when he wrote: 'many families, time out of mind, have been certainly fixed in eminent seats in their respective counties, where the ashes of their ancestors sleep in quiet, and their names are known with honour'.[2]

Since continuity of the 'house'—meaning the patrilinear family line—was the fundamental organizing principle to which these families subscribed, the prime object was to keep together the five component elements which made it up. The first was the seat, the family residence itself; the second was the land, which provided the income without which a seat could not even be lived in, much less maintained, repaired, and embellished. If at all possible the main estates and the seat had therefore somehow to be kept together. The third was the family heirlooms which the seat contained, especially valuable relics such as the family archives, including the deeds and patents of nobility, portraits of ancestors, family plate and jewels, and personal gifts from kings or queens. A house gutted of its contents lost a good deal of its character as a symbol of continuity. The fourth was the family name, which was liable to disappear if there was any failure in the male line and the house passed in tail general to or through a female. In this case, the husband or son of the female in question was often made to adopt her maiden name if he wished to succeed to her property. He thus kept the family name associated with the family seat, by allowing himself to be transformed into a surrogate heir. The fifth and last element which it was desirable, but not essential, to keep attached to the seat, was the hereditary title, if the owner happened to have one. This might be difficult to achieve, since titles did not pass exactly like property. According to their letters patent, they normally descended in tail male from the first creation, while the seats might pass by will or settlement to a different male relative whose claims predated the title, or in tail general through a daughter or to another family altogether. Some medieval titles could pass through tail general, but nearly all post-sixteenth-century titles were exclusively restricted to male descent of the first creation.

ii. Methods

If the basic principle of inheritance was strongly preferential partibility with a bias towards primogeniture, the basic mechanism to enforce it was the entail, a deed which settled the succession of an estate inalienably upon the descendants of an individual owner, in a specifically described order of precedence. The legal instru-

[2] T. Fuller, *The History of the Worthies of England*, ed. P. A. Nuttall, London, 1840, i, p. 74.

ments for implementing this arrangement varied over time, but in some way or another all turned the current owner into a tenant for life, a trustee for the transmission of the patrimony to ensuing generations.[3] By 1540, when this study opens, a series of judicial decisions against perpetuities, and the two Statutes of Uses and of Wills, had undermined the late medieval structure of entails by uses. For just over a hundred years, from 1540 to the 1650s, current owners among the English landed elite enjoyed exceptional discretion in the disposal of their property. Although they used this power to enhance their patriarchal authority to favour one child over another, the effect on the principle and practice of primogeniture seems to have been slight.

After 1650 lawyers developed a new device, called the 'strict settlement', which enabled a landowner to tie the hands of his heir and turn him into a tenant for life. This was achieved by settling property upon trustees for contingent remainders, including those for children as yet unborn. The terms of the settlement preserved the patrimony for the eldest son of the marriage, or failing a son for the next or closest male relative; safeguarded the bride's jointure or pension if she became a widow; and guaranteed adequate financial provisions for any daughters or younger sons. Flexibility was also achieved by provisions allowing the current owner to raise capital, and by the use of private Acts of Parliament in exceptional cases to change the settlement in order to remedy any gross injustices which might have arisen. The device was thus in principle satisfactory to all parties. As Lord St John put it in the eighteenth century, when he made his settlement: 'Where the bulk of the estates and honours descend, there all helps should be given. I am for putting the head of a family as clear and independent as possible'. On the other hand, '. . . What I design to settle on the children will make them quite independent of me'.[4] What this last meant in practical terms was that the widow was guaranteed a life annuity from the estate (and probably also a dower house, if one

---

[3] For the sixteenth-century situation, see L. Stone, *The Crisis of the Aristocracy, 1558-1641*, Oxford, 1965, pp. 175-83, 635-7; J. P. Cooper, op. cit., pp. 200-27. For the seventeenth- and eighteenth-century situation, see B. English and J. Saville, *Strict Settlement: A Guide for Historians*, University of Hull Occasional Papers in Economic and Social History, no. 10, 1981; L. Bonfield, *Marriage Settlements, 1601-1740*, Cambridge, 1983, ch. 6; H. J. Habakkuk, 'Marriage Settlements in the Eighteenth Century', *Transactions of the Royal Historical Society*, 4th Series, xxxii, 1950; C. Clay, 'Marriage, Inheritance and the Rise of Large Estates in England 1660-1815', *Economic History Review*, 2nd Series, xxi, 1968; B. A. Holderness, 'The English Land Market in the Eighteenth Century: the Case of Lincolnshire', ibid., xxvii, 1974; J. P. Cooper, op. cit., pp. 227-33; R. Trumbach, *The Rise of the Egalitarian Family*, New York, 1978, pp. 69-82.

[4] R. Trumbach, op. cit., p. 70.

was available) which amounted to the rate of interest on the capital portion she had brought with her on her marriage. Daughters were guaranteed substantial cash sums to enable them to marry. Younger sons were also given a guaranteed share, at first outlying parts of the estate (usually only for the lives of themselves and their wives), in the seventeenth century life annuities, or by the eighteenth century the same cash sums as their sisters.

The strict settlement thus involved three generations. It was normally drawn up either by will on the death of the father, or when the heir reached twenty-one, or a little later at the time of his marriage as a result of negotiations between the fathers and/or guardians of the bride and groom, and it made provision for children as yet unborn. If renewed regularly, generation after generation, the strict settlement offered fair protection for the practice of primogeniture, and the smooth passage of seat and main estate in the direct male line, relatively immune from dissipation or waste or sale by the owner for the time being. The convention behind the arrangement deliberately sacrificed the power of the individual owner to dispose of his property as he wished to the long-term interest of family continuity. It was not so much the legal documents themselves as the spirit that inspired them which ensured this continuity.

The strict settlement had wider implications. By endowing younger sons with assured cash sums, it in theory made it rather easier for more of them to marry, although in practice this advantage was more than offset by the rising cost of education and launching on a career, especially when posts in the army (which had to be purchased) became fashionable. If younger sons were able to marry and produce children, one of their elder sons or grandsons might one day turn out to be the essential link in the hereditary chain, which would preserve in the family the title, name, seat, and estates in case there was a failure of the direct male line. More important was the elaborate contingency planning built into settlements by the early eighteenth century, in which every possible eventuality was considered and an appropriate solution specified. As a result everyone knew where he stood, family litigation over inheritance was reduced to a minimum, and seat and estates tended to be kept largely intact. For since an elder son had to agree to such a settlement at his marriage, long before he knew whether or not he would produce a surviving male heir, this was a major insurance against property dispersal among heiresses.

The principles applied in ranking the various branches of the genealogical tree in terms of their claims to succession were as follows. First, males had priority over females. Second, descent, as its name implies, means that property always passed downwards to the next generation in preference to upwards or laterally. For example, nephews had priority over uncles. Third, status, and with it claims to inheritance, diminished inversely with the antiquity of the branch: this means that the male representative of the branch which had most recently separated itself from the main stem had prior claims over members of branches which had separated themselves further back in time, and the ranking of claims was in reverse chronological order. There was, of course, room for minor variations and adjustments to this pattern, but these were the general principles adopted by both lawyers and their clients in setting out claims to the property under settlement. These documents tried to envisage every possible demographic contingency, and to establish beyond dispute who was, and who was not, the heir in each particular case. Although disputed successions were not uncommon thereafter, if properly drawn up by a skilful conveyancer, these settlements must have done much to reduce family quarrels over inheritance.

The question of how much protection the strict settlement really provided to property held in primogeniture has recently come under question.[5] In the first place it is by no means certain how many families regularly made use of the device. It seems to have been normal among the aristocracy and greater landowners, but less frequent as one moves down the social scale. Secondly, it is clear that it was by no means unbreakable, given the demographic pattern of the time. It has been shown that, as applied to the Northamptonshire and Kentish aristocracy between 1600 and 1740, high child and adult mortality and a fairly late age of marriage resulted in a situation in which only about a third of all fathers both produced a surviving adult son and were also still alive to make a settlement when he married. This meant that in two cases out of three the entail might be broken for a while, and the current owner might be left temporarily free to dispose of his property as he wished. It has been argued that this means that the strict settlement can have had no significant effect upon the preservation and enlargement of great estates in the late seventeenth and eighteenth centuries.

The demographic data produced to support this argument are confirmed by those for our three-county sample of owners. During

[5] L. Bonfield, 'Marriage Settlements and the Rise of the Great Estates: the Demographic Aspect', *Economic History Review*, 2nd Series, xxxii, 1979; Comment by B. English and J. Saville, and Rejoinder by L. Bonfield in ibid., xxxiii, 1980.

the demographic slump of 1650-1740 about a half of all landowners failed to produce an adult male heir to succeed them (Table 3.7, Fig. 3.8). Moreover at that period less than half of those fathers who did produce an adult male heir lived to see them married (Table 3.9, Fig. 3.10). The weakness of the argument lies not in the demographic facts but in the practical consequences alleged. It is assumed first that the strict settlement was normally drawn up at marriage; and second that it only lasted as long as the original bridegroom and putative father remained alive. This was, however, not always the case, since a number of settlements were made by will and arranged to last for the lifetime of the groom *plus twenty-one years*.[6] Moreover, settlements also made the most elaborate provisions for remaindermen whenever there was no male heir, so that those 45 per cent of all transfers where there was no son were fully taken care of. It is certainly true, however, that the entail could be broken in cases when the settlement was only for the life of the son and the unborn children, and not for a further twenty-one years; when there was a surviving male heir aged over twenty-one; and when the father died before his heir married and made a new settlement. In such cases, which were probably not a majority, the heir was legally free to alienate what property he wished between the time he reached his majority at twenty-one and the time when he married, usually at about twenty-six. During these five years or so he could legally do as he pleased, and, if he could persuade his prospective father-in-law to agree, the new settlement made at his marriage could exclude certain properties, which would remain at his disposal to be sold or otherwise disposed of. This happened, for example, in the early nineteenth century to the ex-Bennett estates which had been acquired by marriage by the Cecils of Hatfield about a century earlier.[7]

The central significance of the strict settlement was that it was in practice not very strict. Effective controls lay not in legal documents but in states of mind. The fact that once every generation it was possible to clear off debts or pay daughters' portions by sale of outlying properties gave the system the necessary flexibility that was its ultimate strength. Thus there were occasions when the sale of the pictures and other valuable family heirlooms was averted only by the sale of land, made possible by this flexibility. Consol-

---

[6] R. Trumbach, op. cit., p. 73. Professor Trumbach is unable to tell me how many of the settlements made by the aristocracy in the eighteenth century which he has examined were drawn up to last twenty-one years beyond the death of the tenant for life.

[7] H. J. Habakkuk, 'The Rise and Fall of English Landed Families 1600-1800', *Transactions of the Royal Historical Society*, 5th Series, 29, 1979, pp. 205-6.

idation of properties in geographically tight locations also depended on the ability on occasion to sell in order to buy. Thus
the growing concentration of property in the hands of this elite
landowning class was aided not only by the strictness of the legal
settlements but also by the frequency with which these provisions
could be circumvented. The long-term interests of family continuity were best served by intermittent legal flexibility and permanent psychological strictness, which is exactly what these arrangements provided.[8]

The test of the system came usually once every generation when
an heir reached twenty-one and his father was still alive. Under
these conditions, the father, the tenant for life, and the son, the
tenant in tail, had each a strong interest to combine to break the
settlement and make a new one, which is what they almost invariably did. The father wished to pay off debts and make provision
for his younger children; the son wanted a present annuity for his
maintenance, which would enable him to marry and support a
family in the years before his father died. The settlement was thus
broken every generation, new debts were charged upon the estate,
and some land was sold or mortgaged or conveyed to trustees to
pay off debts and obligations. Thus it was not the strict settlement
which preserved family properties intact, but the mind-set which
allowed father and son to act in collusion to break it, and in most
cases kept them working in the best long-term interests of the
family.

Writing in 1881, G. C. Brodrick observed that the practical effect of the strict settlement in keeping property together was probably not considerable. On the other hand, 'it has been a most
powerful agent in moulding the sentiment of the class by which
the custom of primogeniture is maintained'. The principle of primogeniture, he went on, was accepted by the great landowners,
'almost as a fundamental law of nature, to which the practice of
entail only gives a convenient and effectual expression'. In other
words, what really mattered was not the legal possibilities of dis-
inheritance, which were nearly always present at least once a generation despite the strict settlement, but the attitude of mind of
the proprietors who made the system work.[9]

Consequently, it is very unlikely that even if the heir was in a
position legally to break the entail, he would in practice commonly
wish to take advantage of the opportunity to sell his inheritance.

[8] C. Clay, 'Property Settlements, Financial Provision for the Family, and the Sale of
Land by the Greater Landowners, 1660-1790', *Journal of British Studies*, 21, 1981.
[9] G. C. Brodrick, *English Land and English Landowners*, London, 1881, pp. 130-4, 96, 99.

The strict settlement was an ingenious legal device, but it was invented by conveyancers to meet the wishes of their clients. There was a strong sense of moral obligation felt by most greater landowners, first that they were no more than trustees for the transmission intact of their patrimony according to the rule of primogeniture and, second, that all their children were entitled to a fixed and guaranteed monetary share. The fatherless heir's freedom of action was circumscribed first by the potential demands of his prospective father-in-law and second by the full force of social convention and family custom brought to bear by his kindred, 'friends', trustees, and advisers such as the family clergyman, solicitor, and conveyancer. Even when he did find himself legally free to break the entail, it was only an unusually independent or unusually irresponsible young man who would be able to stand up to such psychological pressures.

A potentially more dangerous situation arose when there was no male heir to carry on the line. This is where the elaborate contingency provisions of the strict settlement came into play, and in such cases a critical factor was sheer family longevity: the longer a family had lasted, the better became its chances for survival in the future, since somewhere in the remote branches of its genealogical tree there was bound to be a remote cousin, several times removed, who was entitled to inherit at least the seat and some part of the family estates. The fastest turnover was therefore among relative newcomers, who had not had time to develop these spreading branches ready to replace the main stem if it happened to die off. The genealogical tree was thus more than merely a symbol of pride in family ancestry. It was essential to the elaboration, generation after generation, of the incredibly complex contingency plans which were so carefully incorporated into the strict settlements. These latter laid out what was to happen in case of every possible permutation of nuptiality, fertility, and mortality, not only among the generations already alive but also among those not yet born. These bulky documents were essential insurance policies guaranteeing the future of every family, securely locked away in the family archives, or housed in the vaults of the family solicitor. After their institution in the mid-seventeenth century, it seems certain that among the elite much less property and many fewer seats could be transmitted merely at the whim of the current owner. On the other hand, the success of the elite in weathering the post-1650 demographic crisis suggests that it was the spirit behind the settlements, rather than the legal documents themselves, which provided the real safeguard. When the premature deaths of their fathers left young men free to do as they pleased, few of them took the opportunity to sacrifice long-term family interests to short-term personal advantage.

Those parts of the estate which were not governed by an entail, use, or strict settlement, as well as all the personal estate, including most of the household goods, plate, money, jewels, livestock, and leases, could be disposed of by will at the free choice of the testator. The latter could use this freedom to augment the jointure of his widow, increase the portion of a favourite child, or provide for the children of a second marriage. In cases where there was no son to inherit, frequent transmissions to cousins might still hold seat and estates and family name together, but they were likely to cause the family heirlooms and the title to pass into other hands. Thus Oswald Barron remarked of the Knightleys of Fawsley, Northants., 'again and again the direct line has failed, but a cousin of a younger generation has never been wanting to carry on the succession at Fawsley, a house which such changes have swept clean of all heirlooms save a few family portraits'.[10] As an incidental result, what must have been the very extensive family papers of the Knightleys seem to have vanished without trace.

In cases where the settlement had been broken by premature death, or where one had never been made, the owner was free to dispose by will of the whole estate, seat and all, just as he pleased. But such was the strength of tradition that there is hardly a single example over the whole 350 years of our three-county sample in which an owner left the family seat away from the direct heir male, if there was one. This potential power existed only in a minority of cases, and even then was very rarely used arbitrarily to disinherit a clearly defined heir male. But such things could certainly happen from time to time. If there was no legal settlement at all, and if the individual owner chose to put his personal inclinations above his duty to his family, the results might indeed spell the end of the line.

This is shown by the early eighteenth-century story of Edward, son and heir of the 2nd Lord Griffin of Dingley, Northants. The first Protestant in a raffish family of fanatical Catholics and Jacobites, Edward at the age of eighteen fell in love with the daughter of a small Derbyshire squire, and went through a clandestine marriage with her in the Rules of the Fleet. When they got to hear of this act of bravado and folly, the two fathers were unable to come to financial terms. Edward's father, therefore, first ordered him

[10] O. Barron, *Northamptonshire Families*, London, 1906, p. 169.

abroad for a while, and then, some eighteen months later, bullied him into a second, loveless, marriage to the daughter of a wealthy ex-governor of Madras. There was a lawsuit to try to validate the first marriage, but it failed. The second marriage, however, was a biological as well as a psychological disaster, since the pair were childless. Edward, by then 3rd Lord Griffin, took a mistress, and on his death left Dingley and all his property to trustees for the use of his illegitimate son by her.[11] This later led to the only sale of the seat in the 350 years of its existence in the sample. In this exceptional case, the personal whim of Lord Griffin triumphed over family responsibility, thanks to the absence of the constraints of a strict settlement, the exceptional circumstances of the forced marriage, and the lack of a legitimate son and heir, or indeed a legitimate heir of any kind except perhaps a distant cousin in the female line.

Another example of an arbitrary act of will, unrestrained by any feelings for family continuity, this time outside our sample, is provided by Sir John Knightley of Offchurch Bury, Warwickshire. In 1688 Sir John, the second baronet, died childless. A staunch Anglican, he decided not to leave the seat and estate to his nearest relative, his uncle, who had Dissenting leanings, and first planned to bequeath them to a distant cousin Richard Knightley of Charwelton. But, as he explained in his will, 'reflecting upon the unkindness of my relations, and particularly cousin Knightley of Charwelton, who refused living with me to be a comforter and assistant to me', he changed his mind and settled all his property on the grandson of his late wife by her first marriage, a child called John Whightwick. The Knightleys were thus totally shut out of Offchurch by the whim of one cantankerous old gentleman.[12]

There are two cases in the sample of a will being used to endow a cadet branch with sufficient estates to maintain a new great family, to take the place of a senior branch which had merged with another or otherwise become extinct. On her death in 1744, Sarah Duchess of Marlborough left in her will a considerable fortune to her grandson John Spencer, the younger brother of Charles, 5th Earl of Sunderland, who on the death in 1733 of their aunt, Sarah's only surviving daughter, had become 3rd Duke of Marlborough (the title by the grace of Queen Anne having been permitted to descend through women). On inheriting the gigantic palace of Blenheim, Duke Charles had given his brother John his former

---

[11] Lambeth Palace, Court of Arches, Process Book D.875.
[12] O. Barron, op. cit., p. 203.

main seat of Althorp, Northants. The bequest of a great fortune from his grandmother Sarah, together with possession of Althorp, turned John Spencer into a magnate in his own right, and his son was elevated to an earldom. This special provision by Duchess Sarah for a cadet branch thus saved the Spencers of Althorp from being swallowed up by the Spencer Churchills of Blenheim.

Another exception to the rule of primogeniture, carried out by will, took place in Hertfordshire. At his death in 1803 the bachelor 3rd Duke of Bridgwater was obliged to leave his seat of Ashridge and his entailed estates to his heir male, a very remote cousin, John Egerton, who also succeeded to the title of their last common forebear and became 7th Earl of Bridgwater. The Duke, however, had been a coal entrepreneur and had amassed a huge personal fortune, which was entirely at his own disposal. This fortune, which included pictures which alone were estimated to be worth £50,000, he left not to his heir John Egerton, but to his sister's son and his nephew, George Granville, Marquis of Stafford and first Duke of Sutherland, the reversion being settled not on the latter's son and heir, but on his second son Francis, who was created Earl of Ellesmere in 1833. This is a good example of the vagaries of entail and primogeniture, which could lead to the passage of seat, estate, and a very old title to a remote relative in whom the owner had no interest, at the expense of a closer relative in the female line for whom only the personal estate could be saved. In both these cases a strong-willed testator possessed of a huge personal fortune used it to endow a cadet branch to replace a main line which had either died out or merged with another, an action confirmed by the Crown through the creation of a suitable title.

There was a third mechanism which might upset the basic primogenitural principles embodied in the entail, settlement, or will: and this was the law. It was possible, though difficult, for a landowner to overthrow an entail or settlement by private Act of Parliament. If he could persuade the judges in the House of Lords that he had a reasonable case, they would recommend passage of an Act either to enable him to sell land to pay off his debts, or to give portions to his younger children. But when family disputes arose or when a man died intestate, the matter would end up in the Court of Chancery, which tended to favour the principle of equal partible inheritance, and therefore a division of the patrimony. This might well leave the inheritor of the seat with an income inadequate to maintain it, and the family would consequently drop in the social scale.

In most cases, however, the principle of modified primogeniture, inevitably subject to the accidents of demography, governed the transmission of the five elements of the inheritance. The seat, the household furniture, the estates, the name, and usually the title (if any) all tended to descend together. Occasionally the widow was left by will the personal estate, which meant that she was entitled to strip the seat of its furniture and equipment. But in these cases the heir usually bought them back from the widow and so kept the seat and its contents together. Sometimes a devoted husband would leave the seat and its contents to his widow for her life, only devising it to the main heir at her death. But this did not happen very often—in only about 5 per cent of all transfers by inheritance in our sample. Three-quarters of these occurred after 1700, when affectionate marriages became increasingly the norm. The wealthier families in the sample owned substantial dower houses which were available for widows, and did not need to resort to this awkward device to ensure that their widows could pass their declining years in the comfort to which they were accustomed.

Sometimes the seat and estates passed through an heiress by marriage to another family, which already possessed its own seat. In this case, the title (if any) would normally die out or go to a distant male cousin, and, unless some special provision had been made in the marriage contract, the heiress's country house would pass to her husband's family. It would then either become a secondary residence, visited only very occasionally by the family, or would be abandoned altogether and allowed to fall into ruins. Sometimes the seat might pass in tail male to a distant cousin while the estates or most of them went in tail general to daughters. If this happened and if the owner of the seat lacked the resources to maintain it, he and it would drop below our sample level. Unless he sold it to some wealthier man, the seat might well degenerate into a farmhouse. (Plate XVIB.)

iii. Problems

The great weakness of the system was the absence of a clear understanding about the descent of property between tail male and tail general. In other words, if there were no son and heir, how much property, if any, was it proper for the nearest surviving female, say a daughter, to inherit? Most families seem to have left about a third of the estate to the heirs general and the bulk of it, including the seat, to the heir male. A failure in the direct male line therefore might involve a significant loss of property hitherto attached to the family seat. Alternatively the seat itself might pass by tail general through a daughter or niece to her husband. As we shall see, after about 1690, the latter was often obliged to adopt his wife's maiden name in order to keep the family name attached to the seat. He thus became a fictive tail male.

Another problem was how to provide for younger sons. In the late Middle Ages it was common practice, especially in the north, to allocate to them quite substantial estates in tail male.[13] This meant that branch families of the same name would establish themselves in the county, but if they died out in the male line, as they often did, the estates would revert once more to the main stem of the family. By the eighteenth century, younger sons were usually accorded equal treatment with daughters, an identical capital sum, specified in the strict settlement drawn up before they were born, being allocated to them when they came of age. Very often, of course, these sums were not paid in cash, and the sons instead drew the interest in the form of an annuity. After about 1600 there were only four cases in our sample in which younger sons were endowed with large estates, including that of John Spencer, aforementioned. The first concerned the son of a purchaser, who was free to dispose of his property at will. Robert Cecil, the younger son of Lord Burghley, inherited Theobalds and the estates in Hertfordshire, while Thomas, the eldest son, inherited the vastly enlarged family estates in Northamptonshire which his father had built up round his prodigy house at Burghley. Theobalds was so impressive a palace that it took the fancy of King James, with whom it was exchanged for the old Bishop's Palace at Hatfield, beside which Cecil, now Earl of Salisbury, built the present family seat.

The second case in which a younger son might inherit large estates was when a wealthy owner married an heiress whose father, by a previous settlement, had conveyed the property to trustees for her, and so kept it out of her husband's control. In such a case her estates would often pass to her second son to found a new county family. Thus in 1800 George Bowes, younger son of the eighteenth Earl of Strathmore, inherited from his mother her estates and seat at St Paul's Waldenbury, Herts. But in this case since George died without heirs soon after, the seat became a secondary house of the earls of Strathmore after all, and the plan to found a new family was frustrated.

Very occasionally the accumulated inheritance was so vast that

[13] J. P. Cooper, op. cit., p. 214.

its subdivision between the heir and the second son was the only rational solution. This occurred in the late eighteenth century as a result of the inheritance by the Fitzwilliams of Milton in Northamptonshire of the great house of Wentworth Woodhouse in Yorkshire and huge estates both in that county and in Ireland. The next Earl Fitzwilliam gave Milton and the Northamptonshire estates to his second son and withdrew to Wentworth Woodhouse, and the two houses and estates were only reunited by a failure of the male line of the elder branch in the middle of the twentieth century.

The Montagus had been seated at Boughton House, Northants. for over a century, when the first Duke greatly extended and altered it in the late seventeenth century. He added a huge Frenchified north front with two projecting wings, and remodelled much of the interior, although one wing of the new front was never floored inside. When the Montagus died out in the male line in the mid-eighteenth century, the daughter and heiress married a Brudenell and moved to her husband's seat at Deene nearby. In the early nineteenth century, a second heiress carried the ex-Montagu estate and Boughton to a Duke of Buccleuch, who inherited such an accumulation of huge seats from Scotland to southern England that he hardly knew what to do with them. But the Buccleuchs never abandoned a presence in Northamptonshire, and the house was kept in good order throughout, although only actually visited for a few days or weeks in the year. When they took a liking to the place in the 1880s and carried out extensive remodelling, they still did not finish the late seventeenth-century wing: it was just too large for even their opulent needs. And so the wing remains unfinished today, frozen in time, the bare floor-beams and rafters a monument to seventeenth-century extravagance, and to the waste involved in the casual accumulation by inheritance of seat after seat in the hands of a diminishing number of great families.

To sum up, different rules of inheritance applied to all five elements of the inheritance. Seat and estate passed by entail or settlement through either sons or daughters, and failing them through close members of the patrilinear line, whether male or female. By partition between a distant male heir and a direct heiress, the seat could get separated from a good deal of the property. The personal estate, including all chattels not designated as heirlooms in the entail, could be disposed of by will by each successive owner at his death, being sold to pay debts, or to provide portions for daughters, or else given to widows or dispersed among relatives.

The surname passed through the male line only, although after about 1690 husbands of heiresses were often obliged to adopt their wife's maiden name. The title (if any) normally passed downward in tail male from the first holder.

Under these conditions all these five elements—seat, estates, furniture, name, and title—would descend together only so long as a male heir was produced every generation and survived to inherit. But very often no such continuity could be preserved. If the current owner had no surviving children but a younger brother, all might pass together to the latter, excluding only the title if it was a new one, since, unless specified otherwise in the original royal grant, a fresh title could only pass to a descendant of the original grantee. If there was an heiress, a part of the estate might pass to her and so become separated from the rest if the latter went to a nephew, uncle, or male cousin. If there was no male relative and everything descended to an heiress, only the title and name were lost, but the latter could still be preserved by the adoption of fictive kin, and the former might be revived by the Crown.

The desire to keep these five elements together and to hand them down to posterity was constantly threatened, primarily by the hazards of biological failure. In theory, another factor which might have threatened the unified descent of all five parts of the inheritance was the element of personal whim. The affection of a father for a particular child, perhaps a younger son rather than the son and heir; the desire to endow the children of a second marriage; the doting affection of an old man for a new young wife— all these might have been supposed to have disturbed the normal flow of inheritance by inducing an owner to divide up the estates. This could lead to a severing of name, title, and seat from some part of the property, and give rise to endless litigation between competing heirs. In practice, however, the progressive introduction among the elite of the strict settlement after 1650 was remarkably effective in blocking any such ambitions by a current owner, who was usually largely powerless to act in an arbitrary manner. In any case there is no reason to believe that more than a small minority might ever have wanted to do so. Those who were entirely free to leave the seat and property as they wished were mostly newcomers who had made the purchase themselves, and thus were the first generation of owners in their family, not bound by any earlier moral or legal obligations. But since the supreme desire of these newcomers was to found a secure county family, they were perhaps the most unlikely of all to deviate far from the primogenitural norm. They might have the power to do so, but not at all the inclination.

The only case in the sample where the seat and estate were left by will to a more remote relative in preference to a closer one is the exception which proves the rule. The first and only Lord Wallace inherited from his purchaser father Featherstone Castle in Northumberland. He married the daughter of a Scottish nobleman, by whom he had no children. Instead of leaving the castle to his nearest relatives on his father's side, who were distinctly middle class and based in London, he chose instead to leave the estate to his nephew by marriage, who was a Northerner like himself and cut a far more gentlemanly figure. One can speculate that had he been able to pass his title on as well, he would perhaps not have felt so free to ignore the claims of his cousins. It is, however, a good example of the greater freedom of newcomers in such matters.

3. DEMOGRAPHIC CONSTRAINTS

The prime factor which so regularly strained the principles of preferential primogeniture and patrilineage was not personal whim: it was demography. In practice the accidents of birth, marriage, and death largely determined who got what, when, and how. Despite a high birth-rate, an equally high mortality-rate very frequently interrupted the continuity of the male line. On the average, families were unable to transfer their inheritance from father to son in regular sequence for more than about 100 years. This did not matter too much so long as there were available close male relatives such as younger brothers or the sons of younger sons of an earlier generation. But it became more serious if the seat had to pass to a remote cousin while some of the estate stayed with daughters, or if the seat had to pass through females to another family; and it became disastrous if the line died out altogether and the executors had to sell both seat and estate and so liquidate the whole family enterprise.

The demographic parameters which determined the success or failure of families to continue in the direct male line remained far from constant over time, a surprising fact which can be demonstrated by a study of the life chances of the members of the sample. The sample itself is composed of the elite in three widely separated counties, and therefore should comprise a reasonably random universe of elite landowners. It consists of families whose genealogies have been particularly well recorded, owing to family piety and the devotion of local antiquaries over the centuries to the history of just this class. But the data is by no means perfect. It has been collected from many different sources, and the coverage is undoubtedly much better for some families than for others. As always, many infants who died in the first few weeks and months did not get recorded, especially in the sixteenth and early seventeenth centuries. To sum up, the size of the sample is large enough, the data are at least as good as those for any other groups, and the conclusions may therefore provide a valuable check on the only demographic statistics for the elite so far available, those provided by Dr Hollingsworth for the British peerage as a whole.[14] Furthermore, more questions can be asked and answered than those he posed, for example by distinguishing heirs from younger sons in terms of nuptiality and age of marriage.

i. Nuptiality

The probability of direct descent to a male heir depended on the nuptiality-rate among owners, on the fertility of those who married, and on the mortality of their young children. Fertility in turn depended on the age of the female at marriage, whether she breastfed her child, her general health and nutrition, and the term of life of both spouses. Much turned on whether or not they both remained alive—and together—until the wife's menopause, thus forming what demographers call a completed family, and whether or not they practiced some form of birth control. The number of children who survived infancy depended on whether or not it was the mother who breast-fed the child rather than a nurse, a practice which certainly improved its expectation of life; on the prevalence of great scourges like bubonic plague or smallpox; on the level of hygiene practiced; on the supply of pure water; and on the degree to which the child was exposed to the (often harmful) ministrations of the medical profession. These are known to be the causal variables, but they cannot be isolated and identified from the data assembled for this project.

The proportion of owners of seats who remained unmarried starts at a very low figure of only about 5 per cent for the cohorts born in the late sixteenth and early seventeenth centuries, but rises sharply to about 15 per cent for the cohorts born between 1650 and 1750, and then falls back slightly (Table 3.2, Fig. 3.1). These are surprisingly high proportions of bachelors to find among a group of

[14] T. H. Hollingsworth, *The Demography of the British Peerage*, Supplement to *Population Studies*, xviii, 1964.

FIG. 3.1   Male Nuptiality [Table 3.2]

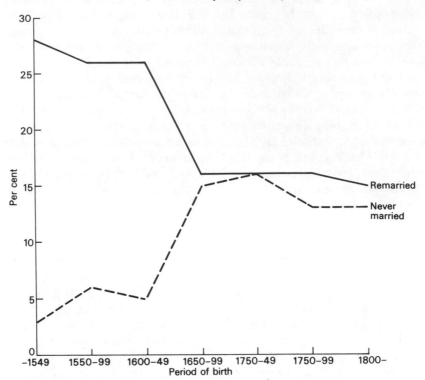

men unconstrained by financial considerations and upon whom rested the heavy responsibility to the family to marry and beget a legitimate son and heir. Some of them, those who died under the age of twenty-six, may be written off as accidental bachelors, which accounts for twenty of the 229 unmarried owners in the sample. Another twenty-four were purchasers who acquired the seat and estate at a mature age (some of whom may have been poorly documented childless widowers). Another ten were the sons of purchasers who showed their disinterest in their fathers' ambitions to found a county family by selling the seat and estate soon after they inherited it.

This leaves 174 bachelors, all but seventeen born after 1649, whose motives for defying the normal rules of family strategy have somehow to be explained. What is so striking is the sudden three-fold jump in the proportion who remained single in the cohort born after 1650, just at a time when the landed classes were running very short of heirs for other demographic reasons. The only explanation that makes any sense is that the trend to bachelordom is one of the consequences of that preference shift from social obligation to personal choice which is so striking a feature of all aspects of family life among this class in the late seventeenth and early eighteenth centuries. It would thus seem to be one more effect of the rise of affective individualism and the consequent decline of the sense of prime responsibility to any larger collective unit than the self. It is also possible that less pressure was being brought to bear on heirs to marry and beget children once it was realized that a break in the direct line did not necessarily mean the end of family continuity. But there is no evidence to support this tenuous hypothesis.

The precise reasons why each of these 174 individuals decided not to marry are largely lost in obscurity. No doubt some were impotent, and others had a very low libido. Others were almost certainly homosexuals who found themselves able to follow their sexual preferences without scandal in the more relaxed moral atmosphere of the eighteenth century. One may speculate that some who inherited at an advanced age saw no reason why they should disturb their lives and undertake the psychologically risky enterprise of finding a nubile young wife upon whom to beget heirs. Others were no doubt deeply attached to lower-class mistresses whom they felt unable to marry for social reasons. At least one had been rejected by the woman he loved. About one-third of all the bachelors inherited indirectly, which is about average. Their refusal to marry therefore seems to have had little to do with whether they were the heir apparent from birth or whether they unexpectedly became the heir because of one or more deaths in the family. More significant is the fact that about a third of the post-1650 bachelors continued to pursue an active career in business or the professions after they inherited the seat and estates. They remained busy lawyers, soldiers, office-holders, overseas merchants, and bankers. None of these were occupations which precluded marriage, but they must have absorbed much of the time and energy that could otherwise have been diverted into estate management, hunting, and the cares of a wife and children.

The results of the decision not to marry varied from family to family. In most cases, the careful provisions for contingent remainders in the strict settlement, and the availability of other kin to inherit, took care of the problem of descent, and the fact that there were no heiresses meant that there was little danger of a partition of the estates. Apart from purchasers and sons of purchasers, who were a special group with little or no family stake in the seat, only a handful of the remainder caused the end of a family dynasty by their refusal to marry. But no rational explanation can be offered for the lifelong bachelordom of a man like Ralph 4th Lord Grey of Warke, whose property went to a niece on his death at the age of forty-five, and through her to another family.

Relatively few of these bachelors caused titles to die out altogether. Twenty-seven—all born after 1700—were holders of heritable titles of peer or baronet, half of whom allowed their title to die with them—a betrayal of one's duty to one's family second only to that of allowing the line to become extinct. However, the consequences did not always turn out to be as serious as might have been expected. In some cases the Crown came to the rescue by recreating a title for the heir to the estate: when Ralph 4th Lord Grey of Warke died unmarried in 1706 and his seat and estate went to his niece, her husband was made Lord Tankerville. In other cases, it was known that the seat and property would descend to a relative who already held a title, although admittedly not the same one. This occurred with the Jocelyns of Hyde Hall, Herts. The Jocelyns had been at Hyde Hall since the thirteenth century, but did not acquire a baronetcy until 1668. Sir Robert, the 1st baronet, produced no fewer than ten sons, which was ample to perpetuate line and title. His eldest son succeeded him as 2nd baronet in 1712 and had two sons. Both, for reasons unknown, remained lifelong bachelors, succeeding one another as 3rd and 4th baronets. On the death of the latter in 1770, the baronetcy passed to his cousin, the 2nd Viscount Jocelyn, who had pursued a successful career as auditor general of Ireland, and was raised to the peerage as Earl of Roden in 1771. The two successive bachelorhoods did not cause the end of the line of the Jocelyns or of the baronetcy, but allowed them to merge with a more vigorous cadet branch which possessed a peerage and a grander seat in Ireland.

Some of these fourteen bachelors whose titles ended with them died fairly young and may simply have postponed until too late the accepted obligation to marry and beget an heir. Sir William Norwich, 4th baronet of Brampton, died at thirty-one. Thomas Watson, 5th Lord Rockingham of Rockingham, also died at thirty-one, within a year of succeeding his brother. Four others died in their thirties, and may have intended to marry. One, Charles Sackville, 5th Duke of Dorset, only succeeded a remote cousin when he was forty-eight, and refused so late in life to embark upon the hazards of matrimony. Francis Egerton was twelve years old when the death without heirs of his elder brothers suddenly translated him into the 3rd Duke of Bridgwater. Till then, as a younger son he had been allowed to run wild, and his guardians now attempted to make up for the years of neglect. On his return from the Grand Tour, though still something of a rough diamond, he became engaged to be married. The engagement was, however, soon broken off, when the lady declined to take an oath never again to see her sister, to whom some hint of scandal was attached. The Duke thereupon withdrew from society, and went off in a sulk to his Lancashire estates, where he proceeded to exploit his coal-mines and build the canal which bears his name. When he died in 1803, at the age of sixty-seven, the dukedom died with him. As has been seen, a distant cousin succeeded to Ashridge and to the former title as 7th Earl of Bridgwater. Though married, he too died childless in 1823, and was succeeded by his brother, an elderly, eccentric, bachelor, clerical don. When he died in 1829 Ashridge descended to his nephew, Viscount Alford, son and heir of Earl Brownlow, whose wife was the sister of the last two earls of Bridgwater. Thanks to two bachelors, the Egertons of Ashridge finally died out, leaving their Hertfordshire estates to be absorbed by the Brownlows. On the other hand, the bachelor Duke partially made amends by willing his vast Lancashire estates and fortune to his nephew, who was elevated to the peerage in consequence of his wealth and breeding.

In the last resort, however, these elite landowning bachelors remain a puzzle, a freakish anomaly of personal choice in a world where marriage and the procreation of children were an accepted duty. Since none of them have left diaries or letters to explain their motives, we are blocked from penetrating the secret of their behaviour. All that can be said with confidence is that it must have been the result of purely personal choice unaffected by, or even in defiance of, the social conventions of the day. Even when catastrophic family consequences did not follow, a refusal by the owner to marry always meant an increase in the number of indirect as opposed to direct inheritances, with all that this involved in complicated readjustments and possible name-changing.

Not only did more owners remain unmarried in the eighteenth and nineteenth centuries, but also fewer remarried when their wives died. The proportion who remarried a second or third time starts high, at about 25 per cent for the sixteenth- and early seventeenth-century cohorts, but falls to about 15 per cent in the late seventeenth-, eighteenth-, and nineteenth-century cohorts (Table 3.2, Fig. 3.1). A decline in remarriages would not affect total fertility of males if it merely reflected a longer duration of first marriages due to a decline in wives' mortality. But this was not the case, for remarriages declined in the late seventeenth century just as the median duration of first marriages was falling sharply from about twenty-five years to below twenty years. Only in the late eighteenth and nineteenth centuries does the duration of a first marriage rise again to nearly thirty years (Table 3.3, Fig. 3.2). These changes in the duration of first marriages were directly linked to the fall and then recovery in the expectation of life at twenty-one. The late seventeenth and early eighteenth centuries form a period of uniquely high mortality and low life expectancy, even for adults (Table 3.4, Fig. 3.3). As a result, over 25 per cent of all first marriages were broken by death within nine years among the cohorts from the late seventeenth century, falling to 20 per cent and then to 10 per cent in the eighteenth century.

This makes the decline in the number of second and third marriages all the more mysterious. One possible explanation may be that the new practice of drawing up a strict settlement, with its tight provisions for descent of property and for provision for chil-

FIG. 3.2   Median Duration of First Marriages (Heirs only) [Table 3.3]

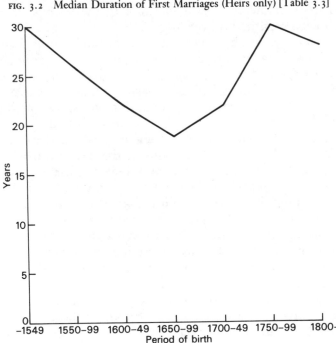

FIG. 3.3   Male Life Expectation at 21 (Heirs only) [Table 3.4]

dren by the first marriage, may have been an inducement to forgo
the luxury of a second. Certainly when a second marriage took
place there was often considerable family tension and rivalry between the kinship groups and the children of the two wives.[15]

ii. Mortality

At the same time as nuptiality and remarriages declined, mortality, especially of infants and children, rose. The cause is still obscure, but it may well be a result of the 'microbian unification of
the world'.[16] In the sixteenth century, mortality seems to have
been exceptionally low, but the opening-up to Western travellers
and shipping of the Americas, West Africa, India, and Asia meant
that whole populations suddenly found themselves attacked by
diseases which their immunity systems were entirely unprepared
to handle. This had happened already once in Europe, when the
importation from Asia of the bubonic plague in 1348-9 probably
halved the population and kept it there for a century.

No such catastrophies happened in Europe in the seventeenth
century, but the importation of new bacteria and viruses by ship
from hitherto isolated areas may well explain the mysterious rise
in mortality in England, just at the time when bubonic plague at
last disappeared forever. One possible leading culprit is the small-

[15] R. Trumbach, op. cit. pp. 50-1.
[16] E. Le Roy Ladurie, 'Un Concept: l'unification microbienne du Monde (XIVe-XVIIe
siècles)', *Le Territoire de l'Historien*, ii, Paris, 1978.

pox virus, which increased in its virulence and its diffusion throughout the population at just this time. For example, three successive heads of the Caesar family of Bennington Place, Herts., died of the disease between 1642 and 1667. If this was indeed the cause of the mortality increase in the late seventeenth century, it seems quite possible that a major factor in the mortality decline in the late eighteenth century was the success of smallpox inoculation in reducing the death-rate from this horrible disease.[17] This hypothesis of the significance of smallpox in causing the rise in mortality is supported by recent evidence which shows that among much the same class nation-wide—namely the children of the British peerage—the rise in mortality was concentrated particularly upon the under-twenty-five age-group. This was the one most seriously affected by smallpox, since it was an almost universal childhood disease by the late seventeenth century, and the survivors had gained immunity from further attacks.[18]

Death in, or resulting from, childbirth was another important factor affecting mortality, although its effects were limited to women. In this case fertility acted upon mortality by drastically lowering the life expectation of women in their child-bearing years. Wives were four times more likely than husbands to die within the first

FIG. 3.4   Termination of First Marriages by Death of Husband or Wife
(Heirs only) [Table 3.5]

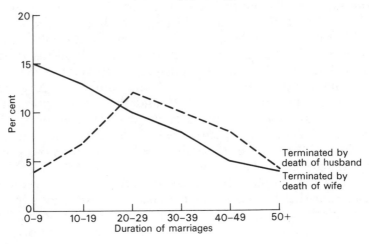

[17] P. Razzell, *The Conquest of Smallpox*, Firle, 1977.
[18] T. H. Hollingsworth, 'Mortality Among Peerage Families since 1600', *Population Studies*, 32, 1977, Tables 5, 6.

ten years of marriage and twice as likely within the second. Thereafter the balance of life tipped the other way in favour of wives
over husbands (Table 3.5, Fig. 3.4).[19] There seems no doubt whatever that women had good reason to be as fearful as they were of
the perils of childbirth. Nor do their chances seem to have improved after 1750 when men began to enter the obstetrical profession, to supplement female midwives. The numbers are too small
for any firm conclusions to be based upon them, but if anything
after 1750 the ratio of wives' deaths to those of husbands during
the first ten years of marriage seems to have deteriorated rather
than improved. All this evidence about the dangers of childbirth
is in conflict with the mortality data for both sexes provided by
Dr Hollingsworth for the peerage. But the explanation probably
lies in the fact that he does not distinguish between married and
unmarried women.[20]

FIG. 3.5   Mean Number of Recorded Children born [Table 3.6]

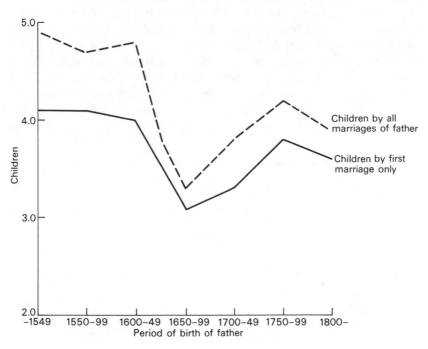

[19] L. Stone, op. cit., p. 619.
[20] T. H. Hollingsworth, pp. 56-9; T. H. Hollingsworth, 'Mortality . . .', Table 3, p.
328.

iii. Fertility

Between 1650 and 1740, just as nuptiality was declining and mortality, especially among children, was rising, marital fertility was falling to an all-time low, to judge from the mean number of children born per married couple (Table 3.6, Fig. 3.5).[21] One reason may be that women were marrying later, and therefore the period of exposure to insemination between the menarche and the menopause was reduced. The evidence for median age of first marriage supplied by our sample only covers men, who were certainly marrying at a progressively later age. Those born in the sixteenth century married at twenty-one, and in the seventeenth century at twenty-four, rising in the late eighteenth century to a peak of twenty-nine and then falling slightly (Table 3.6, Fig. 3.6). The movement of ages of first marriage of all the sons of peers, both elder and younger, are very similar, so that it can reasonably be assumed that the movement of wives of owners is also fairly similar to those of daughters of peers. These latter show a rather similar but slower rise from twenty for the cohort born in the late sixteenth century to twenty-three in the early eighteenth century and twenty-four in the late eighteenth and early nineteenth, only beginning to fall in the late nineteenth century.[22] Since the dates of these tables are those of the birth of the cohort, they should all be pushed on by about a quarter of a century to arrive at the dates of marriage.

The probable rise in the age of first marriage of wives in our sample would have reduced their reproductive period by about

FIG. 3.6   Mean Age of Husbands at First Marriage (Heirs only) [Table 3.3]

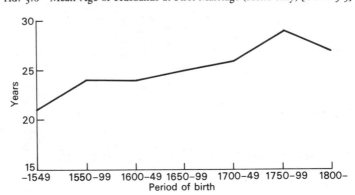

[21] The figures for marital fertility in our sample move in a very similar S curve to those of Hollingsworth for the English peerage (T. H. Hollingsworth, *Demography*, Table 19).

[22] T. H. Hollingsworth, op. cit., p. 25.

four years and thus their potential fertility by about two births. This, coupled with increased mortality among both spouses, and the decline in the rate of remarriage by widowers, might suffice to explain the reduction in fertility in the period 1650 to 1750. On the other hand, the figures do not preclude the possibility of a slow introduction of birth control for all cohorts born after 1650. The sharp fall in births from 1650 to 1750 might be the result both of a combination of the demographic factors already described, and the beginning of family-limitation measures. The decline in child and adult mortality after about 1750 would suffice to cause the late eighteenth-century rise in fertility by prolonging the duration of marriages, even if family limitation continued to spread. All this is conjectural, but the sustained slow fall of fertility throughout the nineteenth century can without much reasonable doubt be ascribed to contraception.

It cannot therefore be *proved* that the English elite, like their counterparts in Europe, were definitely practicing family limitation in the late seventeenth and eighteenth centuries, since the statistical evidence is concealed under a much more serious century-long decline in fertility, due to involuntary causes which mysteriously passed away in about 1740. On the other hand, there is every reason on theoretical grounds to believe that the English elite would be likely to be in the lead of Europe in such practices, and no reason whatever why they should have been the exception to a European norm.[23] There is no literary evidence to suggest that the elite in the seventeenth and eighteenth centuries were deliberately trying to control the number of their children. The decision presumably did not lie with the wife, but with the husband. It was he who decided, both for himself and his wife, when they should marry. If births were to be restricted within marriage, it was he who had to exercise self-restraint involving either sexual abstinence or coitus interruptus, and presumably he who would be likely to suggest some other form of non-procreative sex.

It was also the husband who was responsible for the overall planning of 'heirship strategy'.[24] On the one hand he needed to

[23] For theoretical reasons to believe that the English landed elite might be expected to be practicing birth control, see L. Stone, *The Family, Sex and Marriage in England 1500-1800*, London, 1977, pp. 415-22. For evidence that the European nobility were actually practicing contraception in the eighteenth century, see S. Peller, 'Births and Deaths among Europe's Ruling Families since 1500', and L. Henry, 'The Population of France in the Eighteenth Century', in D. V. Glass and D. E. C. Eversley, *Population in History*, London, 1965, pp. 89-90, 451-2.

[24] There is now a considerable literature on 'heirship strategy' among various social groups. See: P. Bourdieu, 'Les stratégies matrimoniales dans le systême de reproduction', *Annales*

procreate a sufficient number of boys to be reasonably certain that
one of them would survive to maturity, while on the other hand
he needed to avoid an excess of expensive younger sons and daughters to be taken care of. By now younger sons were costly to educate and launch into the world, and their fathers were unable to
economize at their expense, thanks to the conditions of the strict
settlement, since by the eighteenth century it was customary to
give them as much money as daughters.

Financially, daughters were apt to be a burden, since they were
expensive to maintain in clothes and finery and to equip with fashionable educational polish like dancing and French, and were even
more expensive to marry. On the other hand, provided that their
spouses were equal to or above their own status, the marriages of
daughters could be helpful in a family's political and social strategy, by cementing useful alliances or uniting contiguous estates.
Moreover, if all their brothers unexpectedly died, they might in
the last resort come in useful, by providing fictive male heirs in
the form of their husbands or their sons.

Between the Middle Ages, when some could be bundled off to
nunneries, and the eighteenth century, when spinster females became increasingly common residents in the houses of relatives,
fathers believed that they had a moral obligation to find suitable
husbands for all daughters. To do this required the provision of a
suitable dowry, which by the late seventeenth century often
amounted to one and a half years' gross income. It is hardly surprising that by the eighteenth century an increasing number were
left as spinsters, and many girls were made to feel unwanted. Barbara Tasburgh (later Charlton) of Burghwallis Hall, Northumberland, who was born in 1815, recalled in later life that 'though I
was my mother's favorite I certainly was not my father's, who . . .
thought a third daughter a superfluous addition to his family'.[25]

Altogether, it was a very difficult balance of choices that had to
be made, and it is hardly surprising if the upshot was that many
families had too many children and almost ruined themselves in
getting them launched into the world, and many had too few, and
also almost ruined themselves for the lack of a direct heir or heiress
to carry on the line.

In view of these hazards, it may seem odd that prominent land-

E.C.S., 27, 1972; J. Goody, 'Strategies of Heirship', *Comparative Studies in Society and History*, 15, 1973; H. Le Bras, 'Parents, Grandparents, Bisaieux', *Population*, 28, 1973; E. A.
Wrigley, 'Fertility Strategy for the Individual and the Group', in *Historical Studies in Changing Fertility*, ed. C. Tilly, Princeton, 1978.
   [25] B. Charlton, *The Recollections of a Northumbrian Lady 1815-66*, London, 1949, p. 29.

owners should have practiced family limitation, when their main purpose in life was to ensure the continuity of the family line. At least part of the explanation may therefore lie elsewhere than in family strategy. It is now generally agreed that during the eighteenth century courtship, marriage, and marital fidelity tended to pass from social to individual control. Marriage based on prior affection between spouses, and at the free choice of the spouses, tended to replace marriage determined by the 'interest'—whether economic, social, or political—of the family as a whole, spouses being selected by parents, 'friends', and kin. Secondly, there was growing concern for the well-being of children.[26] The first led to a delay in marriage until both parties were of an age to be able to make a mature choice, and also to a desire by husbands to spare their wives the tedious, painful, and dangerous chore of indefinitely repeated childbirths every two years or so until menopause. The second led to a desire to limit the number of children so that more time, effort, and money could be devoted to their upbringing. Improvement in the quality of children's upbringing demanded a reduction in the number of children born. One may speculate that increased familiarity with animal husbandry and stock-breeding may have taught many members of the class some useful lessons in eugenics.

Even more striking than the decline of total births after 1800, which was presumably caused by contraception, is the apparent rapid rise in the recorded number of wholly childless first marriages—from 10 per cent to 22 per cent in the early eighteenth

FIG. 3.7   Proportion of Childless First Marriages (Heirs only) [Table 3.3]

[26] L. Stone, *The Family, Sex and Marriage in England 1500-1800*, Ch. 6; R. H. Trumbach, op. cit., passim.

century—despite the certain improvement in baptismal and burial records (Table 3.3, Fig. 3.7). A detailed case by case examination of this phenomenon of childlessness shows that it does not correlate with the duration of marriage (Table 3.3, Fig. 3.2). It must therefore be attributed to some other, presumably biological, factor, a possible explanation being the widespread and apparently growing prevalence of gonorrhoea among the English upper classes in the eighteenth century, which may have caused increased sterility in both sexes.[27]

Owners without sons to succeed them thus fall into four categories: those who did not marry; those who married but whose marriage was sterile (so far as the records go); those who married but died young before they or their wives had had time to procreate; and those who begot one or more sons who were removed by death in infancy and childhood before they reached maturity. It is this last group who were most affected by the practice of birth control: they were the men who miscalculated the odds on their children's survival.

iv. The Social Consequences of the Demographic Crisis 1650-1740

The conclusion is inescapable that there was a major demographic crisis among the English landed elite in the late seventeenth and early eighteenth century. It is now known that this crisis was a generalized phenomenon throughout the population as a whole, as Professor Wrigley and Dr Schofield have demonstrated. The only differences between the demographic behaviour of the elite and that of the lower classes is in nuptiality and age of marriage, but the results in terms of a failure to reproduce were very similar.[28]

Wrigley and Schofield attribute the crisis to a delayed Malthusian response to a decline in real wages some forty years earlier. But this cannot possibly be the cause of an identical crisis among men of wealth and property. As we have seen, the causes among this elevated group are very complex, involving a combination of declining nuptiality, rising mortality, and declining marital fertility. The crisis was first observed by Dr Hollingsworth as long ago as 1964, when he established that during that period the children of the British aristocracy were not even reproducing themselves (meaning producing two children of either sex who lived to the age of fifteen). Recently the same phenomenon has been observed among the gentry of Lancashire, where the number of failures in

---

[27] L. Stone, op. cit., pp. 599-600.

[28] E. A. Wrigley and R. S. Schofield, *The Population History of England 1541-1871*, London, 1981, pp. 162-70, 418.

the male line increased sharply, and among the Glamorgan gentry, where childless heads of families rose to one-third of the whole, and the average number of children fell by half.[29] But none of these authors has attempted to explore the social consequences of this crisis, nor those of the steady decline in overall fertility after 1800.

Between the cohort of owners born in the last half of the sixteenth century and that born in the first half of the eighteenth, the proportion who died leaving no sons to succeed them rose from 26 per cent to the extraordinary figure of 52 per cent (Table 3.7, Fig. 3.8). Among married men only, the figures come very close to the theoretical prediction that in a stationary population 20 per cent of married men will have no surviving children at all, 20 per cent only daughters, and only 60 per cent at least one son to succeed them when they die.[30] If one examines all transfers of property over twenty-year spans, it becomes apparent that this demographic crisis had the most serious consequences upon the descent of property and seats from generation to generation (Table 3.8, Fig. 3.9). The proportion of direct transfer from father to son or

FIG. 3.8   Proportion of Owners who died without a Surviving Son [Table 3.7]

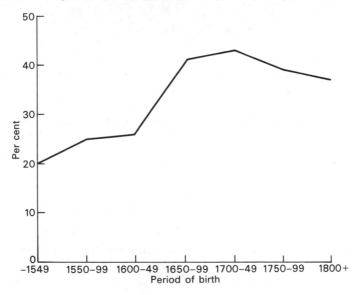

[29] Hollingsworth, op. cit., Table 23; J. S. Morrill, 'The Gentry and the Great Rebellion', *Northern History*, 15, 1979, p. 87 (quoting B. G. Blackwood and J. P. Jenkins).
[30] E. A. Wrigley, 'Fertility Strategy for the Individual and the Group'.

FIG. 3.9 Inheritances by Children as a Proportion of all Transfers by Inheritance
[Table 3.8]

grandson or heiress, or from mother to child, started at about 80 per cent to 85 per cent of all transfers by inheritance in the six-teenth century and remained at this high plateau until 1700. The proportion, which reflects demographic conditions twenty years before, dropped precipitously after 1700 and remained below 60 per cent from 1740 to 1780. It then began to recover, but never got back much above 65 per cent until the late nineteenth century. This was presumably due to the reduction in the number of children born through family-limitation methods, before the decline in infant mortality began to offset this reduction after 1860.

Increased mortality among adults during the demographic crisis also had a number of important social consequences. One was a reduction of the proportion of fathers who lived to see their sons married, to less than half of those who left sons to survive them (Table 3.9, Fig. 3.10). For unknown reasons, this contrasts unfavourably with the situation among the peasantry at Shepshed, Lancs., between 1538 and 1799, where three-quarters of all sons married before their father's death, despite a significantly later me-

FIG. 3.10   Proportion of First Marriages of Heirs after the Death of their Father
[Table 3.9]

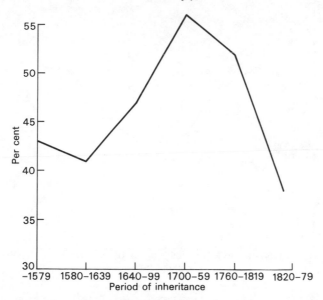

dian age of marriage.[31] This meant that many more eldest sons
were left free to choose their own brides without interference from
their fathers. Another effect was to reduce the median age at which
a son and heir—if there was one—could expect his father to die
and thus for himself to inherit the estate, from twenty-nine years
in the late sixteenth century to about nineteen in the late seventeenth, climbing back up again slowly over the next 150 years
(Table 3.10, Fig. 3.11). The result was an exceptionally youthful
society in the eighteenth century, in which men often inherited
power and estates as soon as they reached their majority.

   It is clear that the primogenitural principle of direct male descent was in practice severely threatened by worsening demographic conditions in the late seventeenth and early eighteenth
centuries, and that for one reason or another the favourable circumstances of the sixteenth century were never again to be repeated. By the early nineteenth century the period of high mortality was over, but the new birth-control strategy practised by
the elite to comfort their wives, improve the quality of their children, and ease the pressure on their purses was proving self-de-

[31] D. Levine, ' "For their own Reasons": individual Marriage Decisions and Family Life',
Journal of Family History, 7, 1982, p. 257.

FIG. 3.11 Median Age of Heirs at their Father's Death [Table 3.10]

feating. The numbers of children were now being limited, but infant and child mortality were still sufficiently high to make this a risky gamble. The result was certainly to reduce the number of unwanted children, but it also tended to reduce the chances of having a living son to succeed to the seat and the estates and to carry on the family line. As will be seen in the next chapter, however, a failure in the male line did not necessarily result in partition of the inheritance, transfer to a new family, or outright sale. Strategies of indirect inheritance were evolved to deal with this problem and to save the principle of family continuity.

IV

TRANSITIONS: INTRA-FAMILIAL INHERITANCE

1. INTRODUCTION

By far the commonest way a man gained membership of the landed elite was by inheritance from a relative of seat, estates, status, and title. He could obtain this inheritance in three basic ways, the most common and most straightforward being directly from his father or grandfather in his capacity as the eldest living son or grandson. This was the ideal model of inheritance according to patrilineal and primogenitural principles. Failing such direct descent, the inheritance tended to pass indirectly to the nearest male relative, priority being given to a younger brother or nephew. Failing them it would pass up the genealogical tree to an uncle, or across to a patrilineal male cousin. In a number of cases, however, no patrilineal male descendant was available, and the inheritance had perforce to pass in a third way through a woman, either to a daughter and her husband, or to a sister, aunt, or matrilineal cousin. If this happened, the family name would inevitably die out, thus causing an apparent rupture. To avoid this, heroic measures of name-changing were adopted as a mode of concealment, so as to perpetuate through surrogate heirs the impression of unbroken descent in the male line. The appearance of patrilineal descent was thus preserved by the adoption of fictive kin.

2. DIRECT INHERITANCE: FATHER TO SON

The theoretically normal pattern of inheritance from father to son was constantly at the mercy of demographic failure, to an extent which it is difficult today to comprehend. It is one thing to examine statistical curves of demographic aggregates, which governed median probabilities, but quite another to discover how demographic accident affected the fortunes of individual families or individuals. At this personal level, meaningless random chance appears to reign supreme. Changes in the legal provisions and in the wisdom or folly with which different families planned their strategy were both critical factors in softening or accentuating the impact of biological chance. But it cannot be denied that some families were extraordinarily lucky and others extraordinarily unlucky in the production of live male heirs. It is no coincidence that most of the former families survived, and a good many of the latter eventually disappeared.

The fortunate families were those whose property passed uninterruptedly century after century from father or grandfather to a direct male heir. That heir was not necessarily the first born, who often died before he could come into his own, but in each generation there had to be at least one younger brother ready and waiting to take his place. One such lucky family was that of the Robinsons of Cranford, Northants. Between 1599 and 1813 it experienced eleven descents, nine of them direct from father to son, and two indirect from the heir to his brother. The line never wavered for over 200 years. The Thorntons of Brockhall, Northants., were almost as lucky. Between 1625 and 1931 they had nine descents, seven from father to eldest surviving son, one to a younger brother, and one to a nephew. The Palmers of East Carlton, Northants., did still better. Out of fourteen descents between 1451 and 1892, eleven were from father to eldest surviving son, one to a nephew, one to an uncle, and one to a younger brother. One of the most remarkable of all in their good fortune were the Sebrights of Beechwood, Herts. Between 1690 and 1880 there were only two occasions when the current owner died childless, and on both he had a younger brother ready to take over. This was especially fortunate, since this was a family which hardly ever produced a crop of fertile younger sons, so that there were no collateral branches to fall back on if the main line had run out.

More typical, however, was the experience of the Ishams of Lamport, Northants.: out of ten descents, only five were from father to son, although none strayed further from the direct line than nephews. Only seven out of twelve Langhams of Cottesbrooke, Northants., died leaving a son and heir, but again the line (and title) ran on unbroken through younger brothers, uncles, and nephews. Much more devious was the descent of the Knightleys of Fawsley, Northants., one of the oldest families in the county: between 1534 and 1900, only ten out of twenty-one left a son and heir to succeed them, but the line always just managed to struggle on in the male line through younger brothers, nephews, or cousins. In so ancient a family the genealogical tree had many branches, so that if the main stem died out, there were always others to take its place.

Up to 1700, by which time the demographic crisis which began forty years before was beginning to take effect, the proportion in our three counties of direct inheritances to all disposals by inheritance was consistently running at over 80 per cent. For the next eighty years, however, from 1700-79, there was a slow but inexorable slide to a mere 60 per cent, recovering slightly thereafter and stabilizing throughout the late eighteenth and nineteenth centuries at about 66 per cent, or two-thirds of all disposals (Table 4.1, Fig. 4.1). The persistence of this relatively low proportion of direct inheritances long after the demographic crisis was passed is hard to explain. Dr Hollingsworth's data about the children of the peerage indicates a very high generation replacement rate for the cohorts born between 1750 and 1850, which should have led to a striking increase of direct inheritances some twenty-five years later, from 1775 to 1875.[1] Our data for the landed elite fails to indicate any such trend, but rather a permanent, irreversible, lowering of

FIG. 4.1   Disposals by Direct and Indirect Inheritance [Table 4.1]

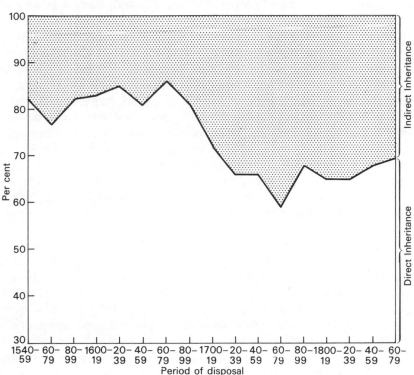

[1] T. H. Hollingsworth, *The Demography of the British Peerage*, Supplement to *Population Studies*, xviii, 1964, Table 23.

the proportion of direct descents from father to son after 1700. This being so, it becomes imperative to explore with care the complex legal mechanics which determined the social consequences of that third of all descents which were indirect and passed to a relative or through a female.

3. INDIRECT PATRILINEAL INHERITANCE BY MALES

The English elite never fully made up its mind whether to follow the patrilineal or the cognitive principle in organizing the transmission of title and property. By the sixteenth century, they were fairly clear that the patrilineal principle took precedence: their genealogical trees were organized on this basis, and connections were rarely traced very far back through the mother. On the other hand, it was recognized that the claims of cousinhood could survive transmission through several women. When it came to the critical matter of the descent of property in cases where there was no son to inherit, daughters were admitted to have strong claims to a substantial, and occasionally a major, share of the inheritance. Given a free hand, fathers were naturally likely to favour daughters over cousins in such circumstances. The long-term interest of the family, however, as expressed in legal documents such as entails and settlements, demanded passage of the property more or less intact to the nearest male relative. Finally, everyone was more or less agreed that the bulk of the estate should be passed intact to a single individual on the principle of primogeniture, the other children, both male and female, being looked after by annuities or cash gifts when they reached twenty-one or at their marriage, whichever came first. These sums were usually raised out of income, by assigning part of the estate to trustees for a period of years to pay the annuities or raise the capital.

So much for the theory, but what of the practice? As we have seen, existing conditions of high infant and child mortality meant that the proportion of direct descents by inheritance from father to child varied from 85 per cent to 60 per cent, the remainder going to close or remote kin. Indirect inheritance by kin inevitably became much more common during the great demographic crisis among cohorts born between 1650 and 1740. But what is truly remarkable is that the potentially disruptive consequences of this crisis in causing the dispersal of estates and the breaking-up of families were generally mitigated, partly by a fortuitous—if it was fortuitous—legal invention just as the crisis was beginning, namely the strict settlement with contingent remainders, and partly by

devices to provide surrogate heirs from distant kin. Indirect inheritance filled the gap created by the decline in the numbers of sons
and heirs, so that the proportion of all disposals which passed by
some form of inheritance, direct or indirect, did not change at all
throughout the period of demographic crisis (Table 4.1, Fig. 4.2).

In terms of family continuity, the least disturbing substitute for
direct inheritance was the death without heirs of an owner who
left a younger brother to take his place. If there were no younger
brother to take on the inheritance, the rules of primogeniture and
patrilinear descent dictated that the estate and seat should pass
downward to the senior paternal nephew or great-nephew, or, if
one was not available, sideways or upward to a paternal uncle. By
legal convention, however, descents—as their name implies—
whenever possible passed downward, or failing that sideways rather
than upwards. Close male relatives had a reasonable chance of
picking up an inheritance—a chance which increased markedly after
1680 when the number of direct heirs declined. After 1700 about
a fifth of all transfers of seats were to younger brothers, nephews,
great-nephews, or uncles.

FIG. 4.2   Disposals by Inheritance as a Proportion of all Disposals [Table 4.1]

If no close male relative was available, the genealogical tree would be traced one stage further back to the paternal grandfather, and a search would be made for a male cousin, the eldest grandson of a younger son of an older generation. In very many cases, especially in well-established families, one was indeed found, which explains why so few families died out altogether and were forced to sell as a result of biological failure during the century of demographic crisis.

This ample supply of male kin waiting in the wings was the product of relatively high nuptiality rates among daughters and younger sons, compared with those of other European elites. The English were willing to make possible the marriage of both daughters and younger sons. This was a process undoubtedly encouraged by the strict settlement, which made monetary provisions for all children before their birth. But more important still was probably the habit of encouraging younger sons to seek a career in some profession, which eventually enabled them to afford to marry, even if rather late. As for women, the absence of nunneries in Protestant England undoubtedly encouraged marriage. Dr Hollingsworth found that the proportion of both male and female children of peers who never married rose from about ten per cent in the late sixteenth century to about 25 per cent in the early eighteenth century. For males the proportion declined again to nearer 15 per cent in the nineteenth century as job prospects in the army and the law improved, although it remained high for women.[2] But this means that some 75 to 85 per cent or more of all sons did get married, which is in striking contrast to parts of Europe such as Sweden or Florence where a majority remained unmarried. Thus relatively high nuptiality rates by younger sons and daughters provided the English elite with a reservoir of nephews and cousins who were essential for the maintenance of family continuity, on the frequent occasions when there was a failure of the direct male line.

The effect of the inheritance by distant relatives upon the long-term future of family and seat might be negligible or serious according to circumstances. Regardless of the relationship, the essential question was whether the man who inherited the estate was or was not a wealthy property-owner in his own right. If not, then he stepped smoothly into the family succession. But if the inheritor already had a distinguished name and seat of his own, either in the same county or elsewhere, unless his new inheritance was

[2] Op. cit., Table 11.

grander than his own, or came in useful as a subsidiary residence, he might well treat it with indifference. This could eventually cause the decline or sale of the seat and the disappearance of the family name from the locality. Whether or not this would happen depended on a wide variety of contingencies. It was, however, made more probable by certain customs. It was normal to try to marry an heiress not to an impoverished younger son—though this was the dream of all young men in that position—but to an heir with equivalent or near equivalent property to hers. Similarly if there was no heir or heiress, settlements almost always were drawn up on primogenitural principles, so that if there was no younger brother to take over, the next in line would be the nearest male on the father's side, starting with the eldest patrilineal nephew, and working out to distant cousins. The chances were consequently quite high that the man who inherited the seat and property would be a wealthy property-owner in his own right. The fact that this could endanger the continuity of the ties of family to ancestral seat was something of which contemporaries became increasingly aware during the demographic crisis, but this consideration still weighed less than the overriding need to follow the rules and contract wealthy marriage alliances.

Inheritance by a remote relative, such as a male cousin, might also cause a partition of the family patrimony between him and the heiress. The chances of inheritance by cousins had been almost negligible in the high demographic boom of the sixteenth and seventeenth centuries, but after 1700 they could expect to pick up about 8 to 10 per cent of all transfers of seats by inheritance. In some of these cases the seat, estates, and title were somehow kept together, even if the family archives and heirlooms were dispersed and lost, as with the Knightleys of Fawsley. In other cases, descent to a remote cousin caused seat and property to fly apart. Thus when Sir Henry Page-Turner of Battlesden, Northants., died in 1874, his title passed to his cousin Sir Henry Edward Leigh-Dryden. But the former had settled all his estates by will on the eldest son of his eldest daughter, so the seat and title parted company. Far worse was the disintegration in the eighteenth century of the family of Elwes of Stoke College, Suff. The second baronet died without heirs and the empty title passed to a nephew. The seat and estate went to the son of his sister, John Meggott (who changed his name to Elwes). He was a miser and accumulated a huge personal estate which he left to two illegitimate children by his housekeeper. The run-down entailed estates, however, went to his sister's husband, John Timms (who also changed his name to Elwes). Thus the title, the money, and the seat and estates passed to three different persons, two of whom changed their names in consequence.

When a seat inherited indirectly was superior to the old family residence, the latter might be displaced for a while, or forever. When in Hertfordshire Nicolson Calvert of Furneaux Pelham Hall inherited Hunsdon House in 1746 from his maternal grandfather, the Calverts moved their base to the latter until 1856, when the family brewery failed. They then sold Hunsdon House and re- turned to Furneaux Pelham Hall, which in the meantime had been lived in by a succession of younger sons.

In some long-lived families which owned one seat and inherited another, both equal in aesthetic attraction and comfort, it was cus- tomary for fathers to give their sons and heirs the other seat to live in until they died. In such cases the main family seat might switch back and forth each generation from one to the other, since each new owner was reluctant to move on the death of his father be- cause he had become attached to the house in which he and his wife had first been settled. Thus in Northamptonshire the Vaux alternated back and forth between Harrowden and Boughton Hall every generation, and the family never became identified with any one house.

A similar ambivalence was shown in the eighteenth century by the Freemans, who had been seated at Aspenden in Hertfordshire since the beginning of the seventeenth century. (Endpaper.) In 1712, in his father's lifetime, Ralph Freeman IV bought the estate and seat of Hamels, in the same part of the county. (Plate V.) He had already shown himself to be a compulsive improver by the additions and landscaping which he had carried out at Ecton, Nor- thants., which he had acquired by marriage. Over the next few years he totally transformed the fine Elizabethan house which Sir John Brograve had built for himself at Hamels into a much larger plain classical pile, with elaborate pleasure-grounds. His father had died in 1714 and at first he lived at Aspenden, while supervising the work at Hamels. When this was finished, he moved to Hamels and proceeded to pare down and classicize the old family mansion at Aspenden, where he installed his heir. When he died, the latter moved to Hamels and let his younger brother live at Aspenden, where he was the incumbent rector. When in due course, the lat- ter, who was a bachelor, inherited from his brother, he thus found himself with two houses on his hands. However, they came in quite useful since between them they spanned the Puckeridge Hunt country. Being a devoted rider to hounds, he used whichever house was most convenient for the next day's hunting, presumably spending his weekends at Aspenden. On his death, Aspenden was sold, and Hamels went to his niece. But her husband eventually inherited two other houses, so that Hamels was finally sold in 1796.

This kind of behaviour, an unwillingness to make a final choice between two seats, can be traced in about twenty families in the three counties, although it was almost entirely confined to the wealthier families and rarely lasted longer than a century before the family settled down permanently at one or the other. At a lower level of the economic scale, declining families were likely to sell the large house and move into the smaller one, as happened to the Calverts after the collapse of their brewery. In Northumberland, families who owned one house in the suburbs of Newcastle and inherited another in the country, or vice versa, tended to retain both, using the Newcastle one for winter and the country one for summer residence. This was how the Blacketts lived at Wallington and Anderson Place (Plate II), the Ords at Whitfield and Fenham, the Ridleys at Blagdon and Heaton.

Similarly, some houses in the south of Hertfordshire were kept as suburban homes close to London for use in Parliament time by landowners from remoter parts of the country. Thus the Scottish representative peers, Lords Marchmont and Napier, were seated respectively at Marchmont and Buckskin Halls in Hertfordshire when Parliament was in session. Even one or two Hertfordshire families with seats in the northern part of the county retained another in the south since it was handier for commuting to and from London. This seems to have been the case with Thomas Brand of The Hoo (later 22nd Lord Dacre) who retained Buckskin (later Dacre) Hall for this purpose in the late eighteenth century. It was especially members of Parliament who found this a convenience, and this was probably the reason why John Cust, Viscount Alford, who inherited Ashridge in 1824 and Wormleybury in 1838, held on to the latter and used it frequently when the House was sitting.

Finally, at least one inherited house on the edge of a town, Holywell in St Albans, was retained largely for its political use as a base from which to influence elections in the borough, although it also came in useful as a dower house for elderly widows of the Spencer family.

It is clear from these examples that houses accumulated by inheritance could be used for various purposes by successive owners, and a good example of this is provided by the chequered history

of Aldenham Hall (formerly Penn's Place) and Aldenham House
(formerly Wigbournes). In 1485, Humphrey Coningsby, the
younger son of a Shropshire gentleman and himself a prospering
London lawyer, acted as executor to the will of Ralph Penn of
Aldenham, Herts., from whose estate he purchased the moated
capital messuage for his own use. He later rose to be Chief Justice
of the King's Bench and died in 1535. He left a much larger seat
and estate in Herefordshire to his eldest son Thomas, and his original purchase of Penn's Place to his grandson Humphrey, younger
son of a younger son, who had married the heiress of North Mimms
Place nearby. This enabled Humphrey to set himself up as a country gentleman in considerably greater style than his father. On the
death without heirs of his son and heir Edward, Penn's Place went
to his younger brother Thomas who, meanwhile, had inherited
their grandfather's Herefordshire estates, including the seat of
Hampton Court, on the death without heirs of his great-uncle
Thomas. Neither he nor his son Fitzwilliam appear to have used
Penn's Place, which in 1626 they let to Henry Coghill, a second-
generation London merchant. (Genealogical Chart 1.)

Henry Coghill was then in his early thirties, the son of another
London merchant, John Coghill, younger son of a parish gentleman, Marmaduke Coghill of Coghill Hall, Knaresborough, in
Yorkshire. In 1621, Henry's wife Faith, coheiress of a London
merchant tailor, had brought him in marriage a small estate known
as Wigbournes, which was contiguous to Penn's Place and no doubt
explains the choice of the latter as his home. He seemed to have
renewed the internal panelling at Penn's Place to improve the look
of the house for entertaining the county during his year as sheriff
in 1632, and finally purchased it from the Coningsbys in 1640. In
about 1664 he left the old moated courtyard house, giving it to his
son and heir Henry II, and moved into a more modest, compact,
and very elegant house nearby which he had built on his wife's
land at Wigbournes, where they spent their declining years. Henry
II, who had married a Yorkshire woman, seems to have gone on
living at the big old house, using the smaller one of Wigbournes
as a secondary seat. At all events, on his death in 1709, he left
Penn's Place, now upgraded in name to Aldenham Hall, to his son
and heir Henry III, and his parents' house at Wigbournes to his
younger son Thomas, who four years later also inherited Bentley
Priory in Middlesex from his uncle John. In 1716, Aldenham Hall
descended to a fourth Henry Coghill, who died unmarried twelve
years later, while still in his twenties.

From him it went to his sister Sarah, who two years later married Robert Hucks, a wealthy young London brewer, a son and grandson of brewers and MP for Abingdon. (Gen. Chart 2.) His younger brother had married a Yorkshire heiress, which may explain the connection with the Coghills. In 1734, Sarah's uncle Thomas died, leaving her Wigbournes, which she thereupon enlarged and improved, incorporating in the process the panelling which her great-grandfather had put up in the old house at Aldenham Hall, which was now abandoned. Six years later, Robert Hucks inherited his father's country seat at Clifton Hampden, in Oxfordshire. Five years later still, in 1745, Robert died, leaving Sarah a widow with four young children. Some time between then and her death in 1772, Sarah moved back to Wigbournes (now Aldenham House) where she died. In the 1770s, her son Robert threw out a bow window in the library and installed new stables and seems to have used the house occasionally. When he died, unmarried in 1814, the Coghills' estates in Hertfordshire and the Hucks' estates in Oxfordshire descended respectively to his two nieces, the daughters of his sister Sarah and the only grandchildren of Sarah Coghill and Robert Hucks. However, they both remained spinsters, and lived and died at their father's house in Reading.

On their deaths in 1841 and 1842, both estates went to George Gibbs, a London merchant, grandson of William Hucks of Knaresborough, brother of the first Robert. When George died later the same year, his son Henry Hucks Gibbs, on inheriting, *inter alia*, Aldenham House, had it renovated after all the years of neglect, and added a billiard-room. His mother lived here till her death in 1850, when it was again let. It was not till 1869 that the old house finally came into its own again, as the suburban residence of Henry Gibbs, by now a wealthy merchant banker, and was further enlarged, including a campanile. The climax came in 1882, three years after this study ends, when the house was almost doubled in size with, among other improvements, the addition of a chapel for Victorian family prayers, and a 'court room' for the dispensing of justice by the resident JP. Ten years later, shortly before he became Lord Aldenham, Henry Gibbs let the house to his younger son Vicary, who lived here for the next forty years, dividing his time between attendance at the House of Commons, the scholarly revision of a volume of G. E. Cockayne's *Complete Peerage*, and the landscaping and planting of an arboretum which was to become the largest privately owned collection in the world.

Thus over a period of 400 years Aldenham Hall was first the only seat, then the suburban seat, of a Chief Justice. Subsequently it became his grandson's seat; went into abeyance for over fifty years until for a century it became the seat (briefly the secondary seat) of the Coghills, a London merchant family originating in the gentry; and finally it was abandoned. Aldenham House began as the main retirement seat of the first Coghill. Subsequently it became a secondary seat; then the main and later the secondary seat of Thomas Coghill; then the suburban seat of a brewing family, the Huckses. It was then used as a dower house, then a suburban seat, then left in abeyance for thirty years, then reverted to a dower house. Then a major rebuilding transformed it into a rather grand suburban seat of a magnate, and finally the main seat of a wealthy younger son of a peer. Despite these multiple changes in use of these two houses, only one of them ever changed hands by sale in the more than three centuries since 1540.

It is interesting to note how this story provides examples both of bequests to namesakes (to Humphrey Coningsby II and Thomas Coningsby II) and from younger son to elder brother's younger son (to Thomas Coghill of Wigbournes and Bentley Priory), and of the complex hunt through the genealogical tree to find a remote cousin to whom to leave an estate in cases of failure of the direct male line (to the Noyes sisters and to George Gibbs). In both these cases no change of name was involved, but George's son had prudently been christened Henry Hucks.

The story also shows the way the humble personal names of fifteenth- and early sixteenth-century houses, like Penn's Place and Wigbournes, ceased to be grand enough for the elevated social aspirations of their owners in the seventeenth and eighteenth centuries, and were therefore transformed into Aldenham Hall and Aldenham House, named not after persons but the name of the village. The rising living standards of the seventeenth and eighteenth centuries are shown by the many improvements carried out in first one house and then another, in order to provide the environment for an appropriately genteel style of life—improvements carried out by owners of varying social backgrounds and sources of income. The houses themselves were changed to reflect changing taste and fashion, from the rambling sixteenth-century moated courtyard house of Penn's Place to the compact 'double pile' (two rooms deep) of Henry Coghill's new house at Wigbournes of 1664, to the added music-room, library, and stables needed to meet the aesthetic and sporting tastes of the eighteenth century, to the opulent display house of the Victorian period, with its proliferation of specialized functional rooms like the billiard-room, the chapel, and the court room, the whole edifice dominated by a towering campanile.

Other stories confirm that the passage of an inheritance to a cousin always carried with it the possibility of the relegation of the seat to a secondary residence, its abandonment, or its sale, besides the disappearance of the family name and title. Two examples of indirect transfers will serve to show how complicated the process might be, and how variously they affected family fortunes. The Willes family were minor landed gentry settled in Warwickshire since the early sixteenth century, 'taking rank below the squireship' in their genealogist's phrase. (Gen. Chart 3.) In the early years of the eighteenth century the family emerged from this provincial obscurity by the efforts of the two sons of the Revd John Willes, a younger son who had married the daughter of a Mayor of Oxford and risen to be Rector of Bishop's Itchington in Warwickshire and Prebendary of Lichfield. The younger son, Edward, also married the daughter of an Oxford merchant and rose to be Bishop of Bath and Wells. Sir John, the eldest son, was knighted as he rose through the law to be Chief Justice of the Court of Common Pleas, and purchased in 1735 the manor of Astrop in Northants., where he proceeded to build himself a fine new house in the Palladian style. He married the daughter and heiress of a Lancashire merchant, and had four sons, the third of whom, Edward, followed in his father's legal footsteps and rose to be Solicitor-General, when he owned a seat in Hertfordshire, Little Grove. He later rose to be Judge of the King's Bench, when he acquired a larger seat in Berkshire, Hungerford Park.

On his death without heirs in 1802, the Chief Justice's grandson left Astrop to his cousin the Revd William, youngest son of his uncle Edward. This was because he wanted to divide the inheritance, and his eldest cousin John already owned Hungerford Park. When some years later John died without heirs male, he took a leaf out of his cousin's book, and in turn left Hungerford, not to his younger brother the Revd William of Astrop, but to the latter's youngest son George. As a result, Astrop and Hungerford remained in separate Willes hands.

On William's death, Astrop went to his heir John, and on John's death without heirs to his brother, William, who was about to enter the East India Company having recently graduated from Haileybury, and whose prospects were thus changed overnight. Five years later, his marriage to a daughter of William Cartwright of Aynho established beyond any doubt the elite credentials of the Willes family. Seventy years later, however, in 1902, their son John sold Astrop and emigrated to New Zealand. One of the most interesting aspects of this tangled story is the way the family did

not hesitate to use the practice of ultimogeniture so as to create
two family lines, and so prevent the absorption, and probable loss,
of the supernumerary seat if left to an existing owner.

All these complicated stories illustrated one thing above all, and
that is the extraordinary tenacity with which families clung to seats,
whether ancestral or inherited or acquired, even through periods
when they were clearly superfluous to needs. Sale was an option
only rarely adopted among these families, and was much less common than abandonment.

4. INDIRECT INHERITANCE BY OR THROUGH FEMALES

If sons, brothers, and patrilineal nephews and male cousins were
lacking, the inheritance would perforce have to pass to women or
through the female line. At first the proportion of transfers of seats
directly to heiresses was fairly low, about 7 per cent of all transfer
by inheritance throughout the sixteenth and most of the seventeenth centuries (Table 4.2, Fig. 4.3). During the demographic
crisis after 1680, however, it rose to reach a peak of 17 per cent in
1760-79 and then declined again to about 10 per cent and below.
This rise and fall of heiresses faithfully reflects the changes in the

FIG. 4.3   Transfers to or through Women as a Proportion of all Transfers by Inheritance
[Table 4.2]

number of male heirs who were born and lived to inherit their father's property. This is why there were more heiresses available in the first half of the eighteenth century than before or after, although the marked peak in the 1760s and 1770s is not so easily explicable.

Apart from direct inheritance, the second way in which women played a decisive role was by transmission of seats and property to their male heirs. For example, the eldest son of a sister or the son of a mother's brother might be the nearest male relative, and therefore the heir. This form of indirect inheritance through the female line was infrequent throughout the sixteenth, seventeenth, and early eighteenth centuries, rarely rising above 5 per cent of all transfers by inheritance before 1740. After 1740, however, there was a marked increase, peaking at 12 per cent in the 1760s and 1770s and then falling back to about 5 per cent (Table 4.2). The reasons for this post-1740 rise of inheritance through females are not easy to determine, and one can only speculate. This was certainly a period in which the position of women in society was improving, and their rights to property were being increasingly protected by legal devices and by the courts. It may be that this had the consequence of encouraging great landowners to draw up the contingent remainder in their strict settlements in such a way as to give precedence to close cognitive kin, such as a sister's son, over a remote patrilineal cousin only tenuously linked by male blood some two or three generations back. But this is something which only lengthy research into the contents of eighteenth-century strict settlements will confirm or disprove.[3] Another possibility is that once the practice of enforcing a change of name and arms upon fictive kin became common, owners of seats were more willing than they had been before to settle their estates on females, or on the children of females in tail general, since they could now ensure that the family surname would remain attached to the seat.

If one takes all transfers to women and through women and adds them together, it becomes clear how extraordinarily important a role women played in the transmission of property and seats. Hovering at about 10 per cent of all transfers by inheritance up to 1700, the proportion thereafter rose rapidly to a peak of nearly a third in 1760-79, and never fell below a sixth until after 1840 (Ta-

[3] The only discussions of the rules governing eighteenth-century settlements are by B. English and J. Saville, *Strict Settlement: a Guide for Historians*, University of Hull Occasional Papers in Economic and Social History no. 10, 1982; L. Bonfield, *Marriage Settlements, 1601-1740*, Cambridge, 1983, ch. 6; R. Trumbach, *The Rise of the Egalitarian Family*, New York, 1978, pp. 41-50. Unfortunately none of them makes any mention of this problem.

ble 4.2, Fig. 4.3). The initial rise can be explained in terms of the demographic crisis, but its persistence as late as 1840 remains a puzzle.

The social and economic consequences of inheritance by or through a female varied very widely, depending on the circumstances. If there was only one heiress and she married prudently and modestly, family continuity could still be preserved. If she married a respectable but unendowed younger son who was willing both to take up residence in the seat and to change his surname to that of his wife's family, then to all outward appearances, and indeed for all practical purposes, the family line continued unbroken. This was a very common procedure in the late eighteenth and nineteenth centuries and will be discussed at length below. Here it is merely necessary to stress the crucial importance of name-changing by fictive kin to the survival of the link between family and seat.

On the other hand, if the heiress married a man who was himself the heir to a seat and great estate commensurate with or superior to her own, the estate and seat of the heiress was liable to be swallowed up by those of her husband, who also had every incentive to keep his own name and not to change it for the equal or inferior one of his wife. A good example of this situation is the case of Cassiobury, Herts. In the 1630s the heir to the Capels of Hadham Hall married the heiress of the Morisons of Cassiobury, thus acquiring two great seats in the same county. During his lifetime, Arthur Capel kept both of them going, adding to and embellishing the old house of Hadham Hall. (Plate IV.) But during the Interregnum, Hadham was sequestered, certainly looted, and probably badly damaged. After the Restoration, therefore, Arthur Capel's heir switched his allegiance to Cassiobury, which was further enlarged, and Hadham Hall slowly sank first into a neglected secondary residence and then to a farmhouse out on lease. By the end of the seventeenth century, Cassiobury had thus become the family seat of the Capels. (Plate IXA.)

It has been seen how the Willes family practised ultimogeniture in order to avoid the amalgamation of two estates and seats. This was a variant of a more common practice by which, when a man married a great heiress, the marriage contract and settlement specified that her inheritance should not pass to the son and heir but to the second son, who would thus restart his mother's family line all over again. This second son generally bore his mother's family name as a first name, further to identify his rights and inheritance. Thus when Sir Strange Jocelyn married an heiress Mary Conyers, his second son was called Conyers Jocelyn. This was not uncommon in the seventeenth and eighteenth centuries, especially in ancient families. If, on the other hand the second son died without heirs, leaving his mother's estate to his elder brother, or if his elder brother died leaving him his father's estate, then the whole plan collapsed. One son would then inherit both estates, his mother's seat would probably degenerate into a secondary residence, and her name would certainly be lost.

The most dangerous situation of all for a seat was when an equal share was left to two heiresses. The only solution was to put the house on the market and divide the proceeds, unless one heiress was willing to buy the other out. This did occasionally happen, as at Finedon in 1690, which was left to two heiresses who were married to two brothers called Dolben. The elder managed to persuade the younger to sell him his wife's share of Finedon, thus reuniting the estate around the seat, which he then doubled in size. As a result (with the further help of two name-changes), a Dolben was still residing at Finedon in 1912.

Passage of a seat through a woman, therefore, could have a wide variety of outcomes. Only if the husband took a fancy to it and moved house to make it his main seat, or if the wife and heiress made careful arrangements for it to descend to a younger son so as to recreate the family under another name, did a seat have a good chance of surviving passage through a female. And even in the latter case its future depended on the second son not inheriting the main estate on the death of his elder brother without children.

Everything depended, therefore, upon the degree to which heiresses were snapped up by the heirs of established elite families, a question which was governed both by the number of heiresses available, and by the willingness of heirs to marry them. It may be taken for granted that landed heirs married within their own social class, or if they married down it was only for the sake of large quantities of money. Whether marriages are determined by parents or by children, both opportunity—the chance of meeting at a reception, a ball, or in the hunting-field—and inclination—the affinity of cultural like to like—will always make social endogamy the norm. The heir of a squire who marries a milkmaid may occur in fiction, but very rarely in real life, where he is, if carried away by sexual passion, more like to become entrapped by a singer or actress. One of the first such *mésalliances* by an English nobleman of which there is record is the second marriage of the third earl of Peterborough to a singer. He lived with her for nearly twenty years before his death in 1735, but it was only as he was dying that he acknowledged that he had actually performed a clandestine marriage with her. The date—and even the fact—of the marriage remain obscure.

Since such social *mésalliances* were on the whole so rare, the radical transformation in the way marriages were arranged from the sixteenth to the nineteenth centuries had little effect on the social range within which the brides of heirs were chosen. In the sixteenth century the choice was made by parents, kin, and influential patrons, the 'friends' who bulked so large in this weighty business, and the children had little say in the matter. The choice was made primarily on economic or political grounds, collectively known as 'interest', and prior affection was not an important consideration. It was thought that this could safely be left to develop later on, as a result of the sexual bond. By 1600, however, it was considered immoral for parents to force children to tie themselves for life to someone for whom they had a positive dislike. This was all very well in theory, but uncertainty rather than clear attraction or aversion was the most likely response to a few brief encounters with a prospective spouse. During the seventeenth century, opinion shifted still further, and by the mid-eighteenth century it was common and perhaps normal for the children to select their own spouses. The children now decided and the parents retained a right of veto rather than the other way around. Courting procedures took many months, and the choice was based, far more than before, on prior mutual affection. Both romantic love and physical lust, however, continued to be regarded as ephemeral passions, and therefore as inadequate bases for the choice of a spouse.[4]

There is one obvious way in which these radical changes in both the way marriages were arranged and the motives behind them should reveal themselves statistically: one would expect to find a decline in the number of wealthy squires and above who pursued and captured widows or heiresses. Marriage with a widow or an heiress is always fraught with the not unjustified suspicion that the motive is mercenary rather than emotional. There was indeed a sharp decline in the number of heiresses married to the heirs of peers born after 1700, which seems to confirm this hypothesis. In these elevated circles the proportion fell from an astonishing 40 per cent in 1700-19 to a mere 10 per cent in 1780-99.[5] The data from our sample of squires and peers shows a similar decline from a peak of 36 per cent in the early eighteenth century to 13 per

4 L. Stone, *The Family, Sex and Marriage in England 1500-1800*, London, 1977, chs. 5, 7.
5 L. Stone, op. cit., p. 319, Graph 14.

cent in the early nineteenth. But it also shows that the 36 per cent was an all-time high, the culmination of a rising trend since the early seventeenth century. This determined pursuit of heiresses was thus not at all a traditional norm going back to the Middle Ages (Table 4.3, Fig. 4.4).

The decline of marriages with heiresses after 1750 can be explained easily enough by the factors which have already been mentioned, the shift of decision-making from parents to children and the partial shift of motives from 'interest' to affection. But why the rise from the early seventeenth century to the early eighteenth from 15 to 36 per cent? This would indicate that there was indeed, as Sir John Habakkuk suggested long ago, a growing pursuit of heiresses among the elite after 1680, in order to unite one great estate to another and to expand the economic and political resources of the family.[6] He argued that the rise of the 'Venetian

FIG. 4.4   Marriages by Inheritors to Heiresses or Widows as a Proportion of all their Marriages [Table 4.3]

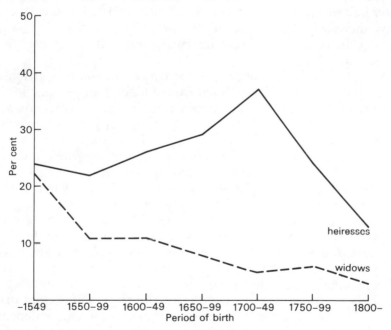

[6] H. J. Habakkuk, 'English Landownership 1680-1740', *Economic History Review*, x, 1940; 'Marriage Settlements in the Eighteenth Century', *Transactions of the Royal Historical Society*, 4th Series, xxiii, 1950; 'The Rise and Fall of English Landed Families 1600-1800', loc. cit., 5th Series, 29, 1979.

oligarchy' of the eighteenth century, when England was dominated by great landowners, and the concurrent decline of the small
gentry were in some measure products of this increasingly obsessive hunt for heiresses. The thesis has recently been challenged,
but the curves of the graph bear him out.

Besides inclination there was also opportunity: there were more
heiresses on the marriage market among the cohorts born between
1650 and 1740 than either before or after, since so many of their
brothers died in infancy or early childhood during this period.
This is proven by the rise in inheritance through women (Table
4.2, Fig. 4.3). The more numerous opportunities of marrying heiresses, combined with a reluctance to allow them to be captured
either by impoverished younger sons or by aspiring members of
the monied interest, acted at this level as a brake upon any growth
of affective individualism in the sphere of mate selection. The family interest of the elite in the choice of a spouse remained paramount for another half century, until sapped from within by the
spread of new attitudes towards love and freedom of choice in the
latter half of the eighteenth century. Until the late eighteenth century, therefore, a good deal of elite property was changing hands
through heiresses, who were intermarrying with other members
of the elite.

A second striking change was the decline in the proportion of
widows among brides, which fell from a high of 20 per cent in the
sixteenth century to about 10 per cent in the seventeenth and
eighteenth century, and was down to a mere 3 per cent amongst
those marrying after 1800 (Table 4.3, Fig. 4.4). This must presumably be attributed to the growth of marriage by personal choice
and for affection rather than for money, and also, perhaps, by a
growing reluctance to take on a woman already burdened with a
crop of children. Another factor may have been the growing sophistication of the trustee system, which gave a widow greater
ability to protect her property from being squandered by her second husband for his own benefit. Widows were thus not financially as attractive as they had been, and so were less sought-after.
This may help to account for the general decline in the number of
remarriages, since widows were often the targets of second marriages. If this is correct, widows gained more economic independence but at the price of reducing their attractiveness on the marriage market. It also meant that remarriages no longer brought
great financial benefits to the husband, and therefore were less
influential in causing the concentration of property into the hands
of the few. The decline in the proportion of widows married by

the elite in the eighteenth and nineteenth centuries thus reinforced the identical trend in the proportion of heiresses.

As a result of these marriages by the elite with heiresses, and also to some extent with widows, seats tended to accumulate through female inheritance into a few hands. Some noblemen acquired an astonishing collection of houses by this means, far too many for functional use. In 1680, in England alone, the Duke of Norfolk, for example, owned Arundel Castle, Sussex, Albury and Weybridge, Surrey, Worksop, Notts., Sheffield Manor, Yorks., and two town houses, Duke's Place in Norwich and Norfolk House in London. Another great accumulator via heiresses was the Duke of Newcastle, who owned Welbeck Abbey, Notts., Bolsover Castle, Derby., Blore Hall, Staffs., and two houses in Nottingham and London. These older families contrast with newcomers who had not had time to specialize in heiresses, and therefore had only one seat, like the Duke of Grafton (a bastard son of Charles II) at Wakefield Lodge, Northants. Yet other families of an older vintage had not acquired seats by marriage or inheritance and also owned only a single country seat. The Earl of Clare owned no more than Houghton House, Notts., and town houses in Nottingham and London; the Earl of Northampton, Castle Ashby, Northants., Compton Winyates, Warws., and a town house in London; Lord Montagu, Boughton and Barnwell, Northants.; Lord Hatton, Kirby Hall, Northants., and nothing else.[7] Everything depended upon the fortunes of marriage and demographic extinction, but the trend, for those families which endured in the male line, and who did not sell, was for houses and estates to accumulate almost indefinitely. A century later, in 1779, the Duke of Bolton owned no fewer than six seats in five counties.[8] Some of these secondary houses were enormous white elephants. Others, however, were quite small, and never used by the owner himself. They were suitable only as a hunting-lodge, a dower house for a widowed mother, a residence for a son and heir until he succeeded to the main seat, or for a younger son during his lifetime. Some were either rented to tenants or left empty to decay. This last option, which was far from uncommon, tended to embitter younger sons, especially when they saw an elder brother allowing his secondary houses to go to rack and ruin rather than giving one to them to live in. In 1825 Lord William Russell, himself a younger son, commented savagely:

[7] J. Adams, *Index Villaris*, London, 1680, pp. 409-12.
[8] A. Collins, *The Peerage of England*, London, 1779, i, p. 234.

Selfishness is the ruling passion of the nobles of this island; to possess several houses and to keep them empty is their great delight, and a feeling peculiar to this country. In my daily and wearisome rides to Hounslow, I pass by the villas and palaces of my dearest friends, the wet streaming down the walls for want of fire.[9]

Indirect inheritance thus had very varied consequences. Although its main tendency was somehow or other to keep the family seat from being sold, it often resulted in the seat being relegated to the status of a secondary residence, inhabited only very occasionally, or used as temporary accommodation for heirs, widows, or younger sons. It also often led to the division of the estates between the patrilineal heir and the cognatic heiress, which reduced the economic foundations of the family. And until the development of the device of name-changing, transmission to or through a female led inevitably to a separation of the seat and the family surname.

5. SURROGATE HEIRS AND CHANGES OF NAME

As one pores over the genealogies of the ancient landed families of England, it soon becomes clear that the apparent stability of inheritance from generation to generation by males of the same name is something of an illusion. In 1906 it was said that 'it is doubtful if there are fifty authentic male pedigrees today which can be taken back to the Conquest', and that there were only 300 families which had held the same property in male succession over the 400 years since the reign of Henry VIII.[10]

There were two ways in which an ancient family name might die out. The first was by amalgamation, carried out through marriage with an heiress, in which case the surname of the husband would become the new family surname. The second was by indirect transfer in case of a lack of any children, the inheritance passing to a male relative linked only through the female line and thus bearing a different surname. In either case, the family surname would disappear unless something was done artificially to save it. The main reason for this total disappearance of the family name was the peculiar English habit of wholly obliterating the wife's maiden name at marriage. This was almost unique to Eng-

[9] *Lord William Russell and his Wife 1815-1846*, ed. G. Blakiston, London, 1972, p. 135.
[10] A. C. Fox Davies and P. W. Poole Carlyon Britton, *A Treatise on the Law Concerning Names and Changes of Names, London*, 1906, pp. 43-4; W. P. H. Phillimore, *The Law and Practice of Change of Name*, London, 1905, pp. 8-12.

land in Western Europe, not being practised in Scotland, France, or Spain, for example, and is remarkable evidence of English stress on patrilinear descent. The English today seem to be scarcely aware of this national oddity, although they were certainly conscious of it in the late seventeenth century. Edward Chamberlayn pointed out in his much read and reissued handbook on England that 'the woman upon marriage loseth not only the power over her person and her will and the property of her goods, but her very name; for ever after she useth her husband's surname, and her own is wholly laid aside; which is not observed in France and other countries where the wife subscribes herself by her paternal name'.[11] This gave rise to serious difficulties when the family property and seat did indeed pass through the female. Hence the peculiarly urgent need in England for a system of name-changing to cope with this situation and adjust to the realities of family descent. Again and again the ancient and venerated surname of the family could be preserved only by a series of pious fictions. If a line seemed about to die out, surrogate heirs were provided, and then obliged or persuaded to change their names to those of their wives or benefactors.

These devices only came into common use in the eighteenth century, apparently for three very different reasons. The prime stimulus was the demographic crisis of the late seventeenth and early eighteenth centuries, which caused a substantial increase in the probability of family extinction in the direct male line, and of inheritance by someone bearing a different name. Name-changes were therefore introduced by the landed classes in the eighteenth-century primarily in order to perpetuate the name of a forebear on the distaff side. In this case there was still a blood linkage and the purpose was to make it obvious by creating a nominal linkage also. Once introduced, the device was also used to perpetuate the name of a childless testator, whose relationship to the beneficiary might well be very remote. Thirdly, the device was exploited by the *nouveaux-riches*, who when they married their daughters and heiresses into an impoverished elite family, now demanded the minimal psychic satisfactions of having their name attached by hyphenation to that of the ancient family they were rescuing. If they married their daughters and left their hard-earned money to a member of the landed elite, they were no longer content to allow

[11] R. A. McKinley, *The Surnames of Oxfordshire*, Chichester, 1982; E. Chamberlayn, *Angliae Notitia*, London, 1669, p. 501.

the origin of the new family affluence to be buried in the decent obscurity of a genealogical tree.

The first and second purposes solved the problems of members of the landed interest, the third primarily satisfied the monied interest. In the first case, the inheritors themselves were often only too anxious to adopt and preserve an ancient and famous surname; in the second and third, the name was forced down the throat of the beneficiary, whether he liked it or not, as one of the conditions laid down in a will or a marriage contract. Since it was and is the custom in England to bear only a single family name, the problem of how to carry out the desired name-change was not easy, and it took some 400 years, from 1500-1900, to work out a satisfactory solution.[12] Three options were successively adopted one after the other, although they all, and especially the last two, overlapped and ran concurrently for decades or even centuries. The first was the use of a surname as the first name, the second was surname substitution, and the third was surname hyphenation.

i. Surname as First Name

The earliest practice, which was common in the sixteenth and seventeenth centuries, was to give the son and heir of an heiress his mother's surname as a first name, in order to provide witness to the amalgamation of two seats and estates through marriage. It was, however, impossible to guarantee that the practice would be repeated indefinitely, and that the son and heir in every succeeding generation would continue to perpetuate the name. For one thing, even if the son of the first generation was given the name and passed it on to his eldest son, the latter might well die young, in which case the inheritance would pass to his younger brother, who normally bore a different first name. In any case, in some early seventeenth-century cases only minimal efforts were made by the family to preserve the tradition. Thus in 1629 the Fanes acquired the great seat and estate of Apethorpe in Northamptonshire by a marriage with the Mildmay heiress. Despite the fact that this new acquisition became the main family seat and raised the family to a wholly new level of affluence and prestige, the only acknowledgement made was to give the eldest son and heir the name of Mildmay. But Mildmay's son and heir was not given the name, although it was given to the eldest son of a second marriage who died young and did not inherit. By the eighteenth century

---

[12] W. P. W. Phillimore and E. A. Fry, *An Index to Changes of Names 1760 to 1901*, London, 1905, introduction.

this kind of casual elimination of another important family name was limited to cases in which the heiress did not come from an old landed family and did not bring a seat with her. When in 1726 Sir John Robinson of Cranford, Northants., 4th Bt., married an heiress, Mary Morgan, one generation of the use of Morgan as a first name was thought sufficient. The same happened in 1797 when the 2nd Lord Lilford of Lilford, Northants., married an heiress, Anne Marie Atherton; the eldest son and heir and 3rd lord was called Thomas Atherton Powys, but thereafter the name Atherton disappeared from the family genealogy. A more complicated case in which a mercantile name was kept, but only intermittently, is that of the Rokebys of Arthingworth, Northants. Benjamin Rokeby was a fifth son, who only entered the ranks of the gentry (though not our sample) by marrying in about 1680 the co-heiress of a wealthy apothecary Thomas Langham, who brought with her the newly acquired seat of Arthingworth. The son and heir was duly named Langham Rokeby and the name Langham persisted in the family tree, but not consistently. A Henry Langham Rokeby was certainly still owner of Arthingworth in 1931, but the first name Langham had not been held by an owner for two generations. These are examples of short, long, or intermittent survival as first names of the surnames of non-gentry families originally representing the monied interest.

By the eighteenth century, if the family inheritance was a large one, it was now customary for the heiress's maiden name to be preserved in the family as the first name of the eldest son. When in 1687 Sir Edward Sebright, 3rd baronet, married a Saunders heiress, they gave their eldest son as his last Christian name that of Saunders. The fourth baronet did the same, but on the death of the fifth in 1736 without heirs, the title, seat and estates went to his brother John, who had not been named Saunders. Sir John, however, improved on and consolidated the family tradition, not only by naming his eldest son Saunders, but also by giving the name to both his sons. From that time on, all Sebright sons have been so named, and right up to the death of the twelfth baronet in 1933 there was still no break in the Saunders Sebright continuity. It became a hereditary name for all sons, but left the family name as Sebright.

ii. Surname Substitution

The second, more radical, option was a change of surname by the husband or relative, who abandoned not only his own name but also his coat of arms, and took those of his wife or mother or other

benefactor instead. This is similar to a process of adoption, and
turned the inheritor into fictive kin. In some ways the change of
coat of arms is symbolically even more significant than the change
of surname. The trouble was that if an heiress should marry the
heir to an equally distinguished family, which she often did, or if
the distant cousin who inherited bore an equally respected name,
this solution obviously caused great difficulties, and might be altogether impossible. This practice of full surname change began
after the Restoration, coinciding with the demographic crisis, but
it did not become common until the 1730 and reached an initial
peak between 1790 and 1820, despite the fact that in 1766 Lord
Chief Justice Mansfield had already denounced it as 'silly'. (Table
4.4, Fig. 4.5.) Normally, the name-change was made compulsory
in the will of the heirless testator. Few took such elaborate precautions as John 3rd Duke of Montagu, who procured an Act of Parliament in the 1740s to declare that any husband of a woman succeeding to the Montagu estates was obliged to drop altogether his
own name and arms and adopt those of Montagu if he wished to
possess his share of the vast inheritance.[13] This must have been a
bitter blow to George Brudenell of Deene, 4th Earl of Cardigan,
who had married the principal Montagu heiress, but he complied,
as indeed he had to.

Full surname and arms change was more easily accepted when
a man of distinctly inferior status and income, usually a younger
son, either inherited a vast estate including a seat or was left one
by a distant relative. Thus when in 1767 a fifth son of the Drakes
of Shardeloes inherited the seat and estate at Lamer, Herts., from
a remote cousin, Benet Garrard, he simply assumed the name of
his benefactor and became Charles Garrard. When in 1791 Sir
John Dryden, 7th baronet of Canons Ashby, Northants., died
without heirs, his seat and estate passed to his niece. She had
married Sir John Turner who promptly changed his name to Dryden and took up residence at the old family seat of Canons Ashby.
In 1795 the baronetcy of Dryden was revived for him—probably
for hard cash—thus enabling the Drydens to continue the family
name, arms, and title by a process that was very close indeed to
the Chinese practice of adoption. In this case, all traces of the
Turner name and connection were obliterated. This total name
substitution in order to inherit properties could result in some very
bewildering genealogical trees. For example, in the late eighteenth
century, William Constable (who had been born a Haggerston) of

[13] J. Wake, *The Brudenells of Deene*, London, 1953, p. 261.

FIG. 4.5   Surname Changes in Britain, 1760-1899 [Table 4.4]

Everingham Park, Yorks, had three sons who, because of various inheritances, changed their surnames respectively to Maxwell, Middleton and Stanley. On other occasions the habit of christening the younger son of an heiress with his mother's maiden name, when coupled with subsequent surname changing to register an inheritance, could lead to ludicrous results. Thus in the early years

of the nineteenth century Edward Loveden Loveden of Buscot
Park, Berks., had a son called Pryse Loveden, who on inheriting
his mother's estates changed his name to Pryse Pryse. When his
son Pryse inherited the Loveden estate of Buscot Park, he hur-
riedly changed his name back again to Pryse Loveden.

Some ancient surnames were only preserved by the most heroic
measures of adoptive name-changing by fictive kin. The classic
example of this process is the case of the Lyttons of Knebworth,
Herts. (Gen. Chart 4.) This was a family well established by the
early fifteenth century, and for 200 years everything proceeded
smoothly. Thereafter, however, they were plagued by a succession of either no heirs at all, or only heiresses. Despite two marriages, Sir William Lytton died without heirs in 1705 and the seat
and estates passed to his younger sister's grandson, Lytton Strode,
who obligingly changed his last name to Lytton. But he too died
without heirs, and left the estate and seat to a maternal cousin
William Robinson, who also changed his name to Lytton. His son
in turn died without heirs, and the estate and seat passed to the
husband of his niece, Richard Warburton, who also changed his
name to Lytton. He had an only daughter, who married William
Earle Bulwer. On her father's death, when she was already a widow,
she inherited Knebworth, which she proceeded to pull down and
rebuild in the Gothic style. On her death, she left it to her younger
son Edward, the politician and novelist, who changed his name to
Bulwer-Lytton, later Lord Lytton. All this frantic name-changing
could effectively conceal, but not alter, the fact that ever since the
Robinsons the so-called 'Lyttons' did not have a drop of Lytton
blood in their veins.

This case is by no means unusual, except for the frequency of
the use of the adoption procedure. The ancient Northumberland
family of Widdrington of Widdrington only kept the surname
through the nineteenth century by converting a Cook and later a
Jacson into Widdringtons. Other ancient families turn out on close
inspection to have survived by a similar process of forcible adoption. The Crasters of Craster, Northumberland, lasted through
the nineteenth century by adopting a Wood; the Collingwoods of
Dissington, Northumberland, by adopting a Stanhope. Even the
Percys, Earls of Northumberland, only kept their surname by
adopting a Smithson son-in-law and changing his name and arms
to Percy by Act of Parliament.

This was all very well when it was the case of an ancient family
swallowing up and obliterating the name of an obscure or common
one. But when the reverse was the case, when an ancient family,

in order to lay hands on a mercantile fortune, was obliged to drop its famous surname in favour of that of some obscure nouveau-riche, the deed was done but the experience was painful. It was, however, one aspect of that process of wary interaction between the landed and the monied interest which is so central to our story.

One of the more remarkable cases of the abandonment and re-covery of an ancient surname concerns the Wakes of Courteenhall, Northants. (Gen. Chart 5.)[14] The Wakes are a very ancient family indeed—one of the very few which can definitely be traced back in a continuous line to the twelfth century. They were never very distinguished or wealthy, and were more or less wiped out for having sided with Richard III instead of Henry VII on Bosworth field. The family struggled through the sixteenth century, often renovated through a line of younger sons, but the first to achieve distinction again was Sir Baldwin Wake, a successful courtier and diplomat under James I, who was made a baronet in 1621. The next generation, however, was severely impoverished once more by over-enthusiastic military support of Charles I in the Civil War, and subsequent fining as a Royalist delinquent.

In about 1660 Sir William Wake, 3rd baronet, made a fairly inconspicuous marriage with Diana, daughter of Sir Dru Drury, Bt. of Riddlesworth. There was no reason at the time to think that anything would come of such an alliance. Sir Dru had a healthy son to succeed him and Diana had no expectations, although she was the niece of an ambitious London merchant, Samuel Jones. But here chance stepped in. Samuel Jones made a great fortune, bought the seat and estate of Courteenhall, Northants., and died without heirs. He picked on the fifth son of Sir William Wake and his niece Diana to be the heir to his great estate, which now included not only Courteenhall but also another seat at Waltham Abbey in Essex. The boy was chosen, partly because he bore Jones's name of Samuel, and partly, no doubt, since he seemed very unlikely to inherit the Wake estates, and would therefore preserve the Jones estates as a single entity.

On receiving this vast inheritance, sometime in about 1700, Samuel Wake changed his name to Samuel Wake Jones, presum-ably in accordance with his great-uncle's will. But he too had no heirs, and so adopted the younger son of his elder brother the fifth baronet, a boy called Charles Wake, whom he removed into his care and educated at his own expense. Charles, who was born in

[14] The following illustrations of name-changes are all drawn from O. Barron, *Northamp-tonshire Families*, London, 1906, and J. B. Burke, *Genealogical and Heraldic History of the Landed Gentry*, London, 1937.

1701, inherited his uncle's estate on the latter's death in 1713, duly changed his name to Charles Wake Jones in 1718, and took up residence at Waltham Abbey. But he too left no heirs and on his death in 1740 he passed the Jones inheritance on to his nephew the sixth baronet, who in turn found himself obliged to take the name of Charles Wake Jones. In 1740 the Wakes had at last established themselves at a major seat at Courteenhall, endowed with an estate sufficient to support their dignity, but at the cost of the loss of a surname that went back to the twelfth century.

But demographic fortune once more came to the rescue. Diana Drury, whose uncle was Sir Samuel Jones and who had married Sir William Wake was, it will be remembered, the daughter of Sir Dru Drury. Despite three marriages, her brother Robert, the second baronet, was unable to produce an heir. When he died in 1712 he therefore left his whole estate to his widow and after her death to a great-nephew, the third but eldest surviving son of the fourth son of his brother-in-law, the third Wake baronet. This William Wake was a mere London attorney when he inherited Riddlesworth from his great-uncle Drury. In 1755, however, Sir Charles Wake Jones, 6th baronet, died without heirs, and the title of baronet and the whole Wake and Jones estates of Courteenhall and Waltham Abbey passed to his cousin and next male heir William Wake of Riddlesworth. The latter thus became the sole heir of the Wake title of baronet, and the family seats of the Wakes, the Drurys, and the Joneses, while managing to preserve the surname of Wake owing to an oversight in Sir Samuel Jones's will. As a modern genealogist of the family disdainfully observed, the name of Wake 'has three times been in peril of merging in the commonplace name of Jones', a point of view which no doubt closely reflects that of the eighteenth-century Wakes themselves. It was Samuel Jones, however, who—quite contrary to his intentions—supplied the seat and inheritance upon which a succession of Wakes have lived happily ever since.

The Wakes were by no means the only family to endure the humiliation of the loss of an ancient surname and the assumption of a new one as the condition for inheriting a great estate. Sometimes the names were of equal ancestry and distinction, but one of them had to go. This could occur either when two families merged through the marriage of an heiress, or when a remote nephew and younger son was picked out as surrogate heir to inherit from a maternal uncle so as to keep a family artificially alive. Examples in our sample of the former are when Calverley became Blackett, Reynardson became Coppin, Newman became Toll,

Watson became Samwell, Holdrich became Hungerford, Hodgson became Hinde, Englefield became Silvertop, and Darling became Culley. An example of the latter is when Grimston became Bucknall.

Very occasionally the same individual changed his surname back and forth in conformity with fortuitous accidents of inheritance. Thus a younger son of the Delavals, Francis Delaval, changed his name to Francis Delaval Blake in 1718 when he inherited through his mother the great Blake seat of Ford Castle in Northumberland. But five years later he quite unexpectedly, thanks to a series of deaths, also inherited the family seat of Seaton Delaval. In this predicament he partly changed himself back again, and became Francis Delaval Blake-Delaval.

By the end of the seventeenth century there are signs that this practice of changing surnames was becoming offensive to some persons of quality, who were naturally reluctant to abandon altogether their own family name. On the other hand the earlier practice of using the old surname as a last first name for elder sons had been proved inadequate since it offered no guarantee of permanence. This first solution had offered too little, and the second, name-changing, had granted too much.

iii. Surname Hyphenation

The third solution, increasingly adopted whenever the testators would allow it, was to modify the surname by tacking on by hyphenation the name of the benefactor, whether distant relative, mother, or heiress. This was a compromise between the two previous alternatives, and one which had the additional advantage that it normally included an addition to the coat of arms rather than a substitution. There were only two drawbacks to the new scheme. The first was that there was a limit to the number of times it could be employed by a single family, determined by the number of names which could reasonably be hyphenated without making the bearer of them a laughing-stock. Four was the absolute maximum.[15] The second was that there was some uncertainty as to whether the prefix or the suffix was the more important and significant of the two or more names. Families were therefore

---

[15] Four names linked by hyphens seem to have been the maximum that any family could tolerate, however boastful it might be of its ancestry. Some examples (all nineteenth century) are:
   Burdett-Coutts-Bartlett-Couts; Howell-Thurlow-Cumming-Bruce; Bateman-Hanbury-Kincaid-Lennox; Borlase-Warren-Venables-Vernon; Pleydell-Bouverie-Campbell-Wyndham; Butler-Clarke-Southwell-Wandesford.

sometimes uncertain how to struggle for precedence in the hyphenating process.

J. B. Burke in his classic work on the genealogies of *The Landed Gentry* arranged families alphabetically according to the last of the hyphenated names and not the first, but Marshall in his *Genealogical Guide* adopted the opposite arrangement. W. P. W. Phillimore, however, stated firmly in 1905 that 'the last name to all practical purposes becomes the surname'. Families do indeed seem to have regarded the last name as the critical one and in fact the coat of arms of the last name was always placed first. This explains why, as the practice grew more and more common in the late nineteenth century, the proportion of prefixes over suffixes rose very rapidly indeed (Table 4.3). More and more of these combinations were cosmetic rather than concerned with property and status, and the additions were therefore increasingly used as prefixes, leaving the more important surnames unaffected as the suffixes.

It is no accident that the practice of hyphenation first began just at the time when many blocks of real estate and family seats were passing from hand to hand through heiresses of ancient families as the male lines failed during the demographic crisis of the late seventeenth and early eighteenth centuries.

One of the earliest examples of hyphenation is that of the Leveson-Gowers. In the late seventeenth century Sir Thomas Gower, Bt., married the coheiress of Sir John Leveson, and named his second son William Leveson-Gower, the intention clearly being to establish a new family line distinct from the senior line of Gowers, and founded on the Leveson inheritance. But when his eldest brother's only son unexpectedly died childless, William succeeded to the Gower baronetcy, which has been associated ever since with the hyphenated name of Leveson-Gower.[16]

Another early example is provided by the Cavendish family. Henry Cavendish, 2nd Duke of Newcastle and owner of Welbeck, died in 1691 leaving three daughters. The eldest married John Holles, Earl of Clare, and their only daughter Henrietta, the heiress of Welbeck and the Cavendish estates, took the name Cavendish-Holles. She married Robert Harley, Earl of Oxford, and their only daughter and heiress was named Margaret Cavendish-Harley. Since she brought the seat and estate with her when she married her second husband, William Bentinck, the latter duly changed his name to Cavendish-Bentinck. Thus it was contrived that the

---

[16] A. Collins, *The Peerage of England*, London, 1779, v, p. 141.

seat of Welbeck remained linked, if very artificially, to the surname Cavendish.

By the mid-eighteenth century men of great new wealth but low
birth were insisting that if their daughters and heiresses were to
marry a nobleman, the occasion should be marked in perpetuity
by the addition of their names as prefixes. Early in the eighteenth
century Sir Edward Turner, Bt., married Mary Page, and in 1775
his grandson, Sir Gregory Turner, inherited the huge fortune of
his great-uncle on his grandmother's side, Sir Gregory Page, who
had been a Director of the East India Company. Under the terms
of the will, he obediently changed his name to Page-Turner. Even
the Cecils, marquises of Salisbury and owners of Hatfield House,
had to submit to this humiliating blackmail. When in 1821 they
received an urgently needed infusion of new wealth and new blood
from marriage with the daughter of a Liverpool business tycoon,
they were obliged to change the family name to Gascoigne-Cecil—
and Gascoigne-Cecil it remains to this day.

This sort of thing became more and more frequent in the first
half of the nineteenth century, the procedure being not so much
controlled as legitimated by the issue of royal licences. Thus when
in 1861 Henry Powys, fifth son of Lord Lilford, inherited Staugh-
ton Grange from his uncle by marriage, George Legh-Keck, he
changed his name and arms by royal license to Powys-Keck. From
there it was a short step to multiple surnames. In 1831 John Ward,
a younger son of William Zouche Lucas-Ward, married a woman
who was both the daughter and heiress of Sir Edward Leigh, Bt.,
of Brownsover Hall, and the heiress of her mother, the sister and
heiress of Sir Thomas Boughton, Bt., of Lawford Hall. Through
his wife, Ward inherited both Brownsover and Lawford Halls,
and changed his name by sign manual to Ward-Boughton-Leigh,
since each of the new names carried with it a seat and an estate.

It was only at the end of the nineteenth century, however, that
this buildup of multiple surnames reached its apogee, families accumulating surnames like hunting trophies, sometimes reaching as
many as four strung together by the tenuous link of hyphens. In
1845 a younger son of James Smith of Ashlyns, Herts., married
Mary Drever, whose mother had been the last of the Dorriens of
Haresfoot. Since Haresfoot came to him with her, he thereupon
changed his name by royal licence to Smith-Dorrien (ignoring her
family name of Drever). In 1872, his son Thomas Algernon Smith-
Dorrien inherited the Ashlyns estate from his uncle, Augustus
Smith, and, to mark the acquisition of yet another seat, he changed
his name to Smith-Dorrien-Smith. It is noticeable that both the

names were added on at the end, the suffix clearly being regarded as taking precedence.

Perhaps the most complex case of name substitution and hyphenation concerns the descendants of the two families of Drax, who made their fortune in sugar in the seventeenth century and then died out, and of Ernle, a cadet branch of a very ancient family going back to the Middle Ages, which died out in the eighteenth century. (Gen. Chart 6.) The story begins with the marriage, shortly after the Restoration, of Thomas Shatterden of Popes in Hertfordshire, to Elizabeth Drax, eventual co-heiress of her brother Henry, a Royalist colonel who made a fortune in Barbados. Their son Thomas changed his name from Shatterden to Drax on inheriting his uncle's estates in the West Indies, and married Elizabeth Ernle, grand-daughter of the first baronet of that name. Her brother, the third baronet, married the heiress of General Thomas Erle of Charborough, but left no son so that on his death his estates went to his only surviving daughter, another Elizabeth Ernle. She married her first cousin, Henry Drax, thus uniting the estates of the Ernles, the Tookers of Maddington, and the Erles of Charborough with those of the Draxes, now seated at Ellerton Abbey. Elizabeth and Henry had two sons, but the first died unmarried and the second left an only daughter, who married a nephew of Earl Grosvenor, who became Richard 'Erle Drax' Grosvenor. Their son, who called himself Richard Edward Erle Drax, died unmarried and his sister and heiress married John Sawbridge, who changed his name to Sawbridge Erle-Drax, which marks the first appearance of the hyphen. They had only two daughters, the eldest of whom, Maria Sawbridge-Erle-Drax, was her mother's heiress but did not marry. Her sister and eventual heiress, Sarah, married first Francis Plunkett Burton, by whom she had an only daughter, and after his death, John Egginton, with whom, seventeen years later, she changed her name, first to Ernle, and then assumed the further names of Erle and Drax, all hyphenated. Why the name Ernle re-surfaces after five generations, and a whole century after the death without heirs of the last Ernle baronet, remains a mystery. Mrs Ernle-Erle-Drax's only child, Ernle Elizabeth Louisa Maria Grosvenor Plunkett, married her cousin the 17th Lord Dunsany, and on inheriting her mother's estates in 1905 changed her name to Plunkett-Ernle-Erle-Drax. On her death in 1916, her second son Reginald Aylmer Ranfurly Plunkett, on becoming her heir, also changed his name to Plunkett-Ernle-Erle-Drax. A full admiral in the Royal Navy in the 1930s, he had as many surnames as he had gold stripes upon his sleeve.

iv. Procedures

The procedures for changing surnames varied over time. When a change of surname, either by substitution or addition, was prescribed in a will as a condition for inheriting seat and property, the change could only legally be carried out in one of two ways. The first was by a private Act of Parliament. Thus when in 1706 Ralph Lord Grey of Warke left his property to a devisee contingent upon his changing his name, the change was carried out by Act of Parliament. This method was commonly used in the early eighteenth century, but it was a complicated and expensive procedure, only worth doing when huge estates were involved. By the 1730s, a 'name and arms' clause in a will usually demanded no more than petition for a royal licence for the change. The first recorded change by royal licence was in 1679, and it became increasingly common after 1770, as a result of which the use of a private Act of Parliament thereafter became very rare (Table 4.4). Since changes in coats of arms were involved, and the argument was based on genealogy, after 1783 it became standard procedure for the Crown to refer all requests for a royal licence to the College of Arms for its approval, which in practice was never denied.

v. Conclusion

The volume of both types of name-changing, by substitution and by hyphenation, varied over time (Table 4.4, Fig. 4.5). Both practices began in the 1680s, but hyphenation did not become important until the early nineteenth century, whereas substitution reached an initial peak in 1800. Thereafter substitution mysteriously declined for half a century, with the result that the total volume of name-changes remained stable at about 360 a year for nearly half a century, ending with an inexplicable drop in the 1840s. Thereafter the volume of both methods increased dramatically, tripling in numbers to reach an all-time peak in the 1880s.

The total number of both kinds of name-changes on record between 1760 to 1879 amounted to over 4,000.[17] To discover the true significance of this figure, however, it is necessary to have some fixed population with which to compare it. This can be done by examining the proportion of name-changing which took place among our sample of elite families in three counties (Table 4.5). Whereas the proportion of owners who changed their surnames had been negligible before 1700, in the early eighteenth century it rose to 5 per cent, and from 1760 onwards to 10 per cent. Among North-

[17] A 25 per cent sample gave a total of over 1,000 names.

umberland owners, the proportion of surname substitution and addition at the height of the Victorian period, from 1850 to 1879, reached the astonishing figure of 19 per cent. During this thirty-year period one-fifth of all elite landowners in Northumberland changed their surnames. Before 1820 the names substituted or added were divided between those of the mother and those of some other, more remote, relative. Unexpected windfalls, whether of seats, estates, or money, usually came indirectly, from relatives of the mother, and this was always the commonest mode of acquisition of a new seat that involved taking a new name. Very few name-changes were to those of a wife. After 1820, however, this pattern altered, largely because hyphenation was becoming more common, and thereafter it was the surname of the wife which was adopted in over one-third of all cases.

By the late nineteenth century, when name substitution and name addition became a mania, several other motives became involved other than a necessary condition for inheritance under a will, or decent respect for an ancestor, or recognition of a great fortune acquired by marriage to a monied heiress. Self-made men with common names like Smith hastened to change them or add to them. In the whole country between 1760 and 1899, 73 wealthy Smiths discarded their surname altogether and 93 hyphenated it, 57 of them with a prefix. By the late nineteenth century there also began to appear newly enriched men with vulgar names, foreign names, or Jewish names which they wished to conceal in order to ease the process of assimilation into the English upper classes. Yet others were motivated by vanity or Gothic antiquarianism. In 1764 Charles Reed Dower chose to change his name to Charles Reed de La Bere, while a number of Fords changed to fforde, and Smiths to Smythe. These vanity changes, as opposed to those involving seats and property, were often carried out by deed poll or even by a mere announcement in the newspapers. Both in purpose and in method, therefore, a number of these late nineteenth- and early twentieth-century name-changes were quite different from those with which we are here concerned.[18] They do, however, represent symbolic ways by which some members of the late Victorian and Edwardian monied interest were trying to achieve respectability.

In the main, however, the cause of the astonishing growth of name-changing seems to have been an increasing desire in English high landed society to preserve an ancient surname. At first this

---

[18] W. P. W. Phillimore and E. A. Fry, op. cit., pp. xii-xv; A. C. Fox Davies and P. W. Poole Carlyon Britton, op. cit., pp. 87-90.

was handled very simply by turning the surname of the heiress or testator who brought the seat to the family into a first name. But this was very impermanent and in the seventeenth century wealthy men or trustees began inserting a clause in their wills making the substitution of their own surname and arms a condition of the inheritance of their seat and estate, especially in cases where their family was older, their seat grander, and their estate larger than that of the legatee.

The abandonment of a family surname was often a painful process, however, and in the eighteenth century the intentions of the trustees of the testator could sometimes be fulfilled, while still retaining the old family name, by joining the two names by hyphenation and incorporating both sets of arms on a coat of arms. This procedure became increasingly common in the mid- and late nineteenth century. From 1880 to 1920 this became more than a device to fulfil conditions to acquire new property and seats. It became a kind of status symbol to have two or more linked surnames. As a result there was a rush for surname accumulation by hyphenation, a few families acquiring as many as four names, some three, and very many two. This evolution seems to reflect a growing pride of ancestry and a growing concern to keep on record an ancient surname which would otherwise have disappeared from the records of history by extinction in the male line. The extraordinary passion for surname accumulation during the late Victorian and Edwardian period is presumably a reaction to the economic collapse of the class, caused by the agricultural depression, death duties, and demographic decimation in the trenches of the First World War. It was a desperate attempt to distinguish old families from the flood of newcomers, who of course themselves immediately tried to adopt the same procedures as protective colouration.

Another reason for this evolution was perhaps a growing attachment to the family seat and a growing reluctance to see it parted from the surname of the family who had lived in it for generations. With the growth of fox-hunting, and the advent of swift transportation by railway, county families seem to have lived more in the country in the nineteenth century than they had done in the eighteenth. There was a consequent increase in their attachment to their country seat. The popularity of Gothic architecture in the late eighteenth and nineteenth centuries is further evidence of the influence of a romantic pseudo-feudal antiquarianism, both cause and effect of greater emotional attachment to the family seat—and consequently of reluctance to see it totally detached from the family surname.

There were several results of the numerous surname changes by adoption or addition. The most obvious was that the relationship of blood-lines to surnames became more and more remote. Many heads of ancient families, who in 1900 bore the old family surnames and lived in the old family seats, did so by virtue of artificial name-changes in the past, and often carried hardly a drop of the blood of the family they purported to represent. The second was a growing fluidity of names. Despite the growing pride of ancestry, the very desire to keep family surname and seat attached to each other resulted in a striking degree of impermanency about personal surnames among the landed elite after 1750. No fewer than 10 per cent of them changed their names, even if in some cases the change only took the form of hyphenation. It is significant of the values prevalent in this social class that it was thought preferable to alter the personal identity tag of the individual—his surname—than to separate the seat from the family name.

Name-changing by hyphenation continued between the wars, and it was only changing social values during the period of the first Labour government after the Second World War which caused the legal collapse of the system. Adopting the principle of following what they conceived to be the national interest, judges now refused to validate clauses in devises which made an inheritance conditional upon a change of surname. In 1945 a wife who inherited an estate on this condition petitioned that she should not be obliged to change her name to one different from that of her husband, and was upheld on those grounds. Next, in 1952, a husband and wife petitioned that they should not both be obliged to change their surnames in order to receive an inheritance, and the judge again struck down the name-clause in the devise but allowed the devisees to inherit the estate. Name-changes in order to preserve fictitious family continuity were declared 'inconsistent with the spirit of the time'.[19] Thus ended a convenient and flexible system of adoption of fictive kin much practiced by the English landed elite for two and a half centuries—and without which Sir Winston Churchill would have travelled through life as Winston Spencer.

6. CONCLUSION

The changing significance over time of intra-familial transmission of seats and estates can be gauged by comparing them with all

[19] C. D. Squibb, 'The End of the Name and Arms Clause', *Law Quarterly Review*, 69, 1953, p. 224.

disposals, including sales, over twenty-year periods (Table 4.1, Fig. 4.2). Any change in the proportion indicates a corresponding but inverse change in the proportion of sales of seats. A rise must be caused by fewer extinctions of families by demographic attrition or economic catastrophe, or just possibly by a growing reluctance to sell superfluous secondary homes. A fall must be caused by more families having to sell for demographic or financial reasons, or just possibly by a greater willingness to sell off superfluous houses.

A comparison of transfers in the three counties shows very much what one would expect (Table 4.6, Fig. 4.6). Stable Northumberland had the highest proportion of transfers by inheritance, consistently over 80 per cent, with Northamptonshire running very close until a fall after 1840. The proportion in Hertfordshire was always lower and much more irregular. The two low periods in the mid-seventeenth century and the early nineteenth are explicable by sudden jumps in sales, as we shall see, corresponding to two great waves of commercial wealth flooding into the county. The most striking feature of the trends in all three counties is that none of them reflect the late seventeenth- and early eighteenth-century demographic crisis, which is quite invisible on the graph.

If one turns from examining transfers by both types of inherit-

FIG. 4.6   Transfers by Inheritance as a Proportion of all Transfers [Table 4.6]

ance, and looks instead at the relative proportions of indirect transfers to kin or through women to direct transfers to heirs, the explanation becomes very clear (Table 4.1, Fig. 4.1). Families survived
the crisis without having to sell by sharply increasing the proportion of indirect inheritances in order to make up for the decline in
direct inheritances. Between 1540 and 1700 the proportion of direct inheritances from the father remained high, at about 80 per
cent of total inheritances. The proportion then slid, in a delayed
response to the demographic crisis affecting births and deaths
twenty-five years earlier, to under 55 per cent from 1740 to 1780.
As mortality declined and as fertility picked up again in the late
eighteenth century, the proportion rose again to 60 per cent where
it remained until a further decline in mortality in the mid-nineteenth drew it up to 70 per cent. The demographic crisis thus
affected the composition of the county elite not by diluting it with
new men to replace extinct families, but by including more and
more men of genteel stock who had not been brought up from
infancy in the expectation of a great inheritance, but were younger
sons or more distant relatives upon whom the inheritance unexpectedly fell thanks to a spin of the roulette wheel of biological
chance. The psychological results upon prospective heirs of this
condition of prolonged uncertainty about inheritance could be very
severe. When the unexpected inheritor was a younger son, his
sudden change of fortune might put the family assets in jeopardy
if it went to his head. This was especially likely to be the case if
he had been a mere idle annuitant hanging around the gambling
clubs in London, or nominally acting as bailiff or agent on one of
the estates but in practice spending most of his time in the village
alehouse or the hunting-field. Although brought up and always
living with the possibility of this contingency, its realization might
find him unprepared to put the family interest first and his own
second. The behaviour of the third baronet Brograve of Hamels,
Herts., is a classic example.[20] His reaction was likely to be affected
by several factors, his own age and his relationship to his brother,
whether the death was sudden or expected, whether his brother
was married and had had children who had died. But his conduct
perhaps chiefly depended upon how well he himself had come to
terms with the dilemma facing all younger sons of the landed classes:
whether to face up squarely to the downward social mobility in-
herent in his situation and make the best of it by the successful
pursuit of an interesting occupation, or whether to settle for the

[20] See below, Ch. VI, p. 199.

trappings of gentility and a life of waiting, dominated by hopes of stepping into a dead man's shoes.

Some of these younger sons lived on tenterhooks for years, depressed by news of the pregnancy of their brother's wife and then elated by her miscarriage or still birth; depressed by a successful birth and then elated again by the early death of the infant in the cradle; elated at the death of a childless sister-in-law, and then depressed by their brother's remarriage with a nubile young girl. To others, on the other hand, it must long have been obvious that their elder brother was very unlikely to produce a male heir because he was unmarried, or sickly, or his children had died before him and his wife had reached the menopause. In these latter cases the younger brother had had his expectations as heir presumptive whetted for a long time, and the inheritance came as no great surprise.

Whichever was the case, in terms of character the new owner was likely to be a rather colourless version of his elder brother. If the family fortunes did not benefit by the change, they were unlikely to suffer from it. But the accidental succession of a younger son who had struggled successfully to carve out a career in the outside world could bring a whiff of fresh air—and better still an injection of fresh capital—which could transform the family situation. This was particularly apt to be the case where the family was an old one and, for one reason or another, had not recently been much involved in the activities of the ruling class. A new owner who had had to make his own way in the world would be better able than his father or older brother had been to reach long overdue decisions with regard to consolidation of estates by sale of outlying properties and purchase of others closer at hand, new investments, major improvements in agricultural practice on the estates, and architectural and decorative remodelling of the family seat. Examples of this last activity will be found in Chapters X and XI.

Not surprisingly, the whole of this elite society lived breathlessly upon every rumour of sickness or death, marriage or pregnancy, miscarriage or still birth, for the lives of others might be transformed overnight by the outcome. Since almost everyone was sick so much of the time, since death even among adults of all ages was still so common that it was taken for granted, since the ministrations of doctors were so often positively lethal, everyone could plausibly dream of the possibilities that might come his way by the hazards of biological chance. It was a situation which inevitably induced pipe-dreams, plots, jealousies, and a great deal of Mi-

cawberism; everyone was waiting for something to turn up, usually dependent on the death of one or more relatives, not
infrequently one's own parents or siblings. Totally unexpected inheritance was never a very high probability, but the chances were
sufficiently large, especially during the demographic crisis, to colour the daydreams of many otherwise level-headed men. At a conservative estimate, about 10 per cent of all indirect inheritances
within the sample between 1710 and 1750 seem to have been unexpected, while even in more stable times they amounted to at
least 5 per cent.

Anthony Trollope was very much aware of this situation, which
is touched on in so many of his novels and is in part the subject
of *Ralph the Heir* and *Mr Scarborough's Family*. He had watched his
own father waste the best part of his life waiting hopefully for his
great-uncle Adolphus Meetkerke to die and leave him his seat of
Julians, Herts., and the estate which went with it. The prospect
seemed secure enough, since the old man was married to a sterile
wife. But she died in 1817 and Adolphus, then sixty-four, remarried a young girl, produced several children, and only died at the
advanced age of ninety-one. Trollope's father was forty-three when
the first Mrs Meetkerke died and his hopes of the inheritance began to collapse. By then he was too old to recover from the blow.

Things were not easy even for the eldest son, the automatic heir
to his father, who was carefully groomed for the succession; far
more care was taken over his education and far more control was
kept over his choice of a bride than was the case with his siblings.
He remained dependent upon the goodwill of his father to provide
an adequate allowance while he was young, and an adequate settlement to support him and his wife and children until his father
died. The only time this situation of dependency might be reversed was on the occasion when his father wished to break the
settlement, in order to sell property to pay off some of his debts
or alter the arrangements for the younger children. This could be
done if the heir was over twenty-one but still unmarried, and would
agree to co-operate.

The heir was also dependent on his father for a place of residence. In the sixteenth and early seventeenth centuries, some fathers kept their son and his young bride and children under their
close scrutiny in the family seat for years on end, a situation that
inevitably created a good deal of friction. Others provided the heir
with a secondary house somewhere on the estates. But however
generous the arrangements, the heir could not help, subcon-
sciously or consciously, wishing that his father would die and al-

low him to step into his inheritance before he became too old to enjoy it. This was a state of mind which could only be exacerbated by the decline in adult mortality in the nineteenth century, which caused heirs to wait longer and longer before coming into their own (Table 3.10, Fig. 3.11).

This prolonged delay before inheritance is probably the explanation of why as time went by more and more heirs tended to have careers, mostly in the army or politics. These were men whose period of activity was limited to their fathers' lifetime, and who on succeeding led a much more ceremonial existence of leisure and pleasure. Many sons of peers, for example, exchanged the busy life of an MP for the stately rituals of the House of Lords on succeeding to their fathers' title.

The principal conclusion of this chapter, however, is the extraordinary degree of family continuity. Thanks to the skilful shift from direct inheritance by heirs to indirect inheritance by relatives, families contrived to survive the demographic crisis of 1650-1740. It took a secure economic base, good will, good lawyers, and a lot of juggling with indirect heirs and name-changing by surrogate heirs to keep the seat and main estate unsold for centuries. But it could be done, and usually it was done. The principle of preferential male primogeniture, the legal instrument of the strict settlement, and the practice of the adoption of surrogate heirs were the devices adopted to enable property and seats to be passed on from generation to generation within the extended family tree. Once in-laws and legatees were obliged to change their surnames, the surrogate principle achieved perfection, and discontinuities in the line were scarcely even visible any more to the casual observer. Only close inspection of genealogical trees reveals the degree of forethought, planning, and artifice involved in the maintenance of so elaborate a social fiction—a fiction that was a necessity if the ideal of family endurance was to be realized in practice. Some families were obliged to pass their seats on through heiresses to other families in order to preserve continuity. For example Offley Place passed from Spencer to Penrice to Salusbury to Hughes; Tyttenhanger went from Pope to Blount to Yorke. Others had better luck. Deene never left the Brudenells for 350 years, nor Althorp the Spencers for 300 years. Easton Neston got by with a hyphenated name, passing from Fermor to Fermor-Hesketh; Lamer from Garrard to Drake-Garrard. One way or another, family continuity was usually somehow preserved, and the ultimate catastrophe of the sale of an old family seat was a rare event, to be talked about and lamented for years thereafter.

V

RUPTURES: SELLERS AND DROP-OUTS

'Families have their fate and periods as well as particular persons—and no marvel, since families are made up of particulars' [R. Gough, *History and Antiquities of the Parish of Myddle, County of Salop*, London, 1875 (written *c.*1700), p. 138].

1. INTRODUCTION

The previous chapter explored how the landed elite ensured continuity of family ownership of seat, name, estate, and title through emphasis upon primogeniture, bolstered if necessary by such devices as the use of surrogate heirs and name-changes. Such efforts attest to the high esteem in which was held the social system of the county family and country house, and to its basic internal stability despite fissiparous tendencies caused by economic or demographic attrition. Thus in the seventeenth century, it was a reaction against the sale or subdivision of estates by an irresponsible minority, facilitated by the freedom of owners to dispose at will of some or all of their property, which stimulated the invention and widespread adoption of the strict settlement. Similarly, in the late seventeenth and early eighteenth centuries, it was the demographic crisis which gave rise to devices for transferring property through women while keeping the family name, through the use of surrogate heirs and name-changing. It was the attitude that lay behind the devices rather than the devices themselves which succeeded in staving off what otherwise might well have been a serious diminution in the ratio of old-established to new families among the ruling classes. Even so, sales did happen, and the problems tackled in this chapter are the scale upon which they occurred, and the possible motives of the sellers. Besides sellers, there were also owners who dropped out of the sample. These were persons who retained their seats but were financially and socially unable or unwilling to maintain the 'port' necessary to keep their status as members of the elite. They are fairly simple to deal with, and in any case not very common. The transfer of a seat by sale, however, is more complex. It is the result of the convergence of two independent acts of will, one by the seller and the other by the buyer. The bargain and all that it involves have therefore to be considered from these two quite distinct points of view, which will be discussed consecutively in this chapter and the next.

It should be noted that sales could and did affect the size of the county elite in several different ways. The transfer of a house from a seller not in sample to a socially ambitious and wealthy buyer would cause both the new owner and his seat to enter respectively the two samples of owners and houses. Sale and purchase between two members of the sample would merely transfer ownership from one elite family to another, although the house might decline from a major to a secondary seat, if it was not one already. The sale of a seat to a socially unsuitable purchaser would cause it to drop out of the sample. A sale might thus increase, leave unaffected, or decrease the number of both seats and owners, depending upon the particular circumstances of each of the two parties involved.

Close inspection shows that sales of seats were rarely simple matters, and were often merely one option among several. The extreme complexity and wide range of motives which could lead to a sale are illustrated by an examination of the interlocked history of the ownership of two Hertfordshire seats, Blakesware and New Place. The story provides a good example of the wide range of demographic hazards which threatened both a smooth descent by inheritance and a family strategy for survival and improvement; and also of the problem of the disposal of surplus houses accumulated by inheritance and how this was met, whether by abandonment, pulling down, conversion into a farm, use as a secondary seat, or outright sale.

The Leventhorpes—originally from Leventhorpe Hall in Yorkshire—had been seated at Shingle Hall, Herts., since the fifteenth century. Nothing is known about the latter house, except that it was assessed at twenty-three to twenty-five hearths in 1662, which suggests that it was a large rambling old courtyard house. Successive generations of Leventhorpes served as sheriff, in the days when that office counted, in 1510, 1526, and in both 1593 and 1607 in the person of Sir John Leventhorpe, later 1st baronet. Since his eldest son predeceased him while on the Grand Tour, he was succeeded by his eldest surviving son. In 1649 the latter's son, the 3rd baronet, died unmarried of smallpox at the age of twenty, and was succeeded by his younger brother Thomas, who became 4th baronet. He married an heiress and soon after purchased the nearby seat of Blakesware from an Essex Royalist who had bought it and lived in it during the Interregnum. Sir Thomas Leventhorpe much enlarged and improved the house, adding a marble hall decorated with busts of the Caesars and a mosaic pavement, and turned it into his main seat, moving out of the old family seat of Shingle Hall, over a third of which appears to have been pulled down by 1673.[1] Ten years later, however, Sir Thomas sold Blakesware and retired to live in Derbyshire, presumably in order to be close to his only daughter and heiress, who had recently married and settled there. The following year he was killed by a kick from a horse. What was left of Shingle Hall descended to his daughter, whose son sold it in the early eighteenth century. The baronetcy went to Sir Thomas's uncle, who died unmarried the next year, when it became extinct.

The new purchaser of Blakesware was Sir Thomas Clutterbuck, who had made a fortune while consul at Leghorn as Commissioner for victualling the Mediterranean fleet. He had a son and three daughters, but the boy died at the age of eighteen within a year of the move to Blakesware and was buried in the family mausoleum which his father had just completed. This lack of a son no doubt explains why on Clutterbuck's death in 1683, five years after the purchase, Blakesware was once more put up for sale.

The new purchaser was John Plumer of Ware, a brewer who had married a daughter of the Hales of King's Waldenbury, and who served as sheriff in 1689. (Gen. Chart 7.) In 1697 he became universal legatee to his father's first cousin, Sir Walter Plumer, on the latter's death without heirs. Sir Walter had been a successful Lincoln's Inn lawyer, who had been made a baronet in 1661, served as sheriff of Surrey in 1663, and remained a bachelor. This windfall enabled John Plumer to set up more than one of his sons as country gentlemen.

It was presumably with this object in view, as well as to round off his Hertfordshire holdings, that in 1701 he purchased the nearby estate and seat of New Place, a large courtyard house dating back to the 1580s. This had come on the market soon after the death in 1699 of Humphrey Gore, who came from a wealthy and distinguished London aldermanic family, several members of which settled in Hertfordshire in the course of the seventeenth century. He was himself a younger son, who had become his father's heir on the death of his elder brother while on the Grand Tour. Humphrey's eldest son had died in 1691, shortly after New Place had been settled on him, and when he died his younger brother Henry

[1] Public Record Office, E179/375/30 and 31; description by Charles Lamb, quoted in J. Cussans, *History of Hertfordshire*, i (i), p. 43.

(now his heir), who had started a career in the army, was already living at New Place and serving as sheriff. As well as owning New Place, Henry was also the heir to his seventy-year-old bachelor uncle, William Gore of Tewin House nearby, a compact double-pile house of about 1630 which the latter had recently much enlarged.

Henry and his wife had no children, and this lack of heirs, combined with the prospective inheritance of a more modern and convenient residence, may explain his sale of New Place. It is also possible that Henry Gore did not much care for life as a country gentleman, since he also sold Tewin House six years after his wife's death.

To return to the Plumers of Blakesware and New Place, it seems probable that Sir Walter Plumer, Bt., had originally intended to leave his fortune to John Plumer's second son, who had been named after him. But the eldest son John had meanwhile died unmarried, so that Walter now became his father's heir, which is presumably why it was left to John Plumer to decide which son, Walter or one of his two younger brothers, William or Richard, should succeed to their cousin's estate.

Walter the heir married the daughter of an established landed family and settled at Chedeston Hall in Suffolk, where he served as MP for Aldborough and Appleby; but he died childless in 1746, when his estates went to his younger brother William. The youngest brother Richard served as MP and Commissioner for Trade and Plantations until his death unmarried in 1750, when once again his brother William inherited.

William Plumer, who had previously lived at New Place moved into Blakesware on his father's death in 1719. He was thrice elected to Parliament, where he served for a total of fifteen years—leaving no record of either vote or speech. He spent much of his time managing the Puckeridge Hounds, which were kennelled at Blakesware. In 1731, at the late age of forty-four, he incestuously married his niece Elizabeth, daughter of his sister Catherine and Thomas Byde of Ware Park. In 1767 he died and all his property devolved on his only son William, on whom he had settled New Place on the latter's marriage in 1760.

According to the *English Chronicle*, William Plumer the younger was reckoned in 1781 to have an income of £15,000 a year from lands in the four counties of Hertfordshire (where he was said to be the largest landowner), Essex, Middlesex, and Suffolk. He served forty-one years as Knight of the Shire for Hertfordshire, and altogether spent forty-seven years as a Whig in Parliament, where he never once made a speech.[2] He married twice, first the daughter of a viscount, then the granddaughter of an Earl, but he died childless at the age of eighty-six in 1822. Contrary to normal practice, he chose to leave everything to his widow rather than to one of his nephews.

This formidable lady was his first cousin once removed, whom he had married as his second wife when he was fifty-six, and who must have been at least thirty years his junior. As soon as she inherited, she proceeded to pull down the old seat at Blakesware, which had only been lived in by a housekeeper since 1767 and was consequently in decay. Four years later, she also pulled down half the venerable Lordship at Standon, which Sir Ralph Sadleir had built in 1746 and had remained in the hands of his descendants until bought by William Plumer the elder in 1761 from the heiresses of the last of the family to own it. (Plate XVIB.) After serving first as a clubhouse for the Puckeridge Hounds and then as their kennels, it had since degenerated into an agricultural slum.

Mrs Plumer remarried, first in 1825 a naval Captain, who died soon after, then in 1828 Robert Ward, a successful novelist and politician who had been a protégé of the younger Pitt. She made him assume the surname of her first husband, and he duly became Robert 'Plumer-Ward'. Together, they built a massive neo-Elizabethan addition to New Place. Cussans noted in 1870 that

the feudal state maintained by Mrs Plumer-Ward is still remembered in the neighbourhood. She never 'took the air' but in the family chariot—a huge, lumbering affair, drawn by four horses—preceded by two outriders in livery. So wide and cumbrous was her carriage, that when driving through the lanes in the vicinity, it was impossible for any other vehicle to pass; to obviate which difficulty she caused bays or 'turn-outs' to be cut in the hedges, which still remain as mementoes of her grandeur.[3]

On her death in 1831, she in turn left everything to her widowed husband. Two years later Robert Plumer-Ward took as his third wife yet another immensely rich widow, and removed the Gothic decoration of New Place put up in the eighteenth century by his predecessor, William Plumer; shortly after, he left Hertfordshire to go and live in his new wife's seat. Soon after his death in 1846, his only son by his first marriage, Henry George Ward,

[2] L. B. Namier and J. Brooke, *History of Parliament. The House of Commons 1754-1790*, London, 1964, *sub* Plumer.
[3] Cussans, op. cit., i (*i*), p. 63.

who had a distinguished career in Parliament and in the colonial administration, seems to have opted very firmly against life as a country gentleman, and sold off all the Plumer landed estates which he had inherited from his father.

In the 1850s the new purchaser of New Place, a wealthy north countryman, razed it to the ground and had Philip Hardwick build him a new neo-Elizabethan house close by, which he called Gilston Place. In 1878 another formidable widow, Mrs Gosselin, had Devey build a new, also neo-Elizabethan, mansion close to the long-abandoned site of the old Blakesware. In both cases, descendants of the purchasers were still living in the houses in the early 1900s.

This account of devious inheritances, untimely deaths, semi-incestuous marriages, multiple remarriages, and name-changes, many accompanied by house accumulations, destructions, and new constructions, gives an idea of the variety of factors which might lead directly or indirectly to the sale of a seat and estate.

The first step in the classification of sellers according to motive is to make a clear separation between two groups according to their mode of acquisition (Table 5.1, Fig. 5.1). The first are owners who had inherited their seats from other inheritors and whose families had thus been in possession for at least three generations. They represent established landed families of the county who sold a seat their family had occupied for at least half a century. The second group consists of purchasers, men who had bought their seats and resold in their own lifetime, as well as the immediate heirs of purchasers. These two groups—heirs of inheritors, and purchasers and purchasers' heirs—had very different bonds of attachment to

FIG. 5.1   Sales by Sellers' Mode of Acquisition [Table 5.1]

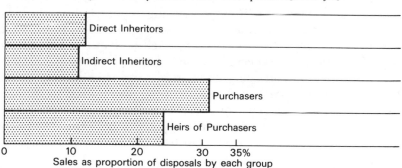

their seats and behaved towards them in very different ways, as shown by the greater propensity of the latter to sell.

2. HEIRS OF INHERITORS

There can be no more traumatic and decisive event in the life of a landed family than the sale of the ancestral family seat and the dispersal of its contents, archives, family portraits, furniture, and the rest. This is the typical nightmare catastrophe of legend and fiction. 'How many noble families have there been whose memory is utterly abolished', lamented one commentator in 1603; 'How many flourishing houses have we seen which oblivion has now obfuscated. . . . Time doth diminish and consume all'. But, as Professor Tawney remarked over forty years ago, 'lamentations that the oaks are shedding their leaves are a piece of sentimental, common form, too fashionable in all ages to throw much light on any of them'.[4] The question that must be asked, therefore, is what relation, if any, there was between reality and this picture of large numbers of ancient families reduced to penury and forced to sell the old family seat to some thrusting *nouveau riche*. How frequent were such shattering events? It is the argument of this chapter that they were, in fact, fairly rare. Many representatives of established families who sold were often merely getting rid of seats inherited from relatives or through marriage that were superfluous to their needs. Others were totally lacking in heirs. Sales by purchasers and their heirs, neither of whom had much hereditary or emotional stake in the property, and whose departure was scarcely noticed by county society, are a different matter altogether, and are dealt with separately.

i. Sale of Supernumerary Houses

A quarter of all inheritor sellers were merely disposing of houses superfluous to their needs (Table 5.1, Fig. 5.2). One would have supposed that an indirect inheritor, who obtained a house from his wife or cousin, was more likely to sell it than the heir of the body, who might be expected to have more of a personal attachment to it since he had spent at least part of his childhood there. The most frequent sales amongst indirect inheritors were indeed of seats recently acquired from wives or distant relatives. These houses were often white elephants, expensive to maintain and of no interest to the new owner, who had his own seat elsewhere.

---

[4] R. H. Tawney, 'The Rise of the Gentry', in *Essays in Economic History*, ed. E. M. Carus-Wilson, i, 1954, pp. 179, 191.

FIG. 5.2   Sales by Inheritors by Motivation to Sell [Table 5.2]

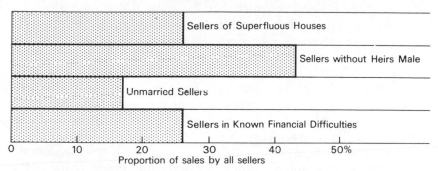

Proportion of sales by all sellers

Though constituting only 16 per cent of all sellers, indirect inheritors were responsible for no less than 38 per cent of all sales of
supernumerary houses.

A number of houses sold by direct inheritors quite often also
turn out on close inspection to be supernumerary seats which had
been indirectly inherited by the owner's father or grandfather. The
family often kept such seats for a while as unentailed assets, which
could be sold at a later date whenever capital was needed for rebuilding the main seat or marrying a daughter, or when the houses
had outlived their usefulness to the family for the placing of widows or children. Thus 17 per cent of all sales by direct inheritors
were of supernumerary seats. Two such sales took place in seventeenth-century Northamptonshire. The first concerns the Lanes
of Horton and Glendon, originally the Lanes of Orlingbury. In
1617, on the death of his paternal grandfather, William Lane inherited several manors, including that of Horton, where he was
seated. About ten years later William Lane sold Horton to Henry
Montagu, Earl of Manchester, and moved his seat to Glendon.
This was a small house which had been in the family even longer
than Horton, and which Lane had recently modernized and more
than doubled in size, turning it into a substantial, compact manor
house. Glendon was now very different in appearance from the
old, rambling, castellated courtyard house at Horton, although the
latter must have been well maintained to warrant purchase by
Montagu. The sale of Horton is therefore open to two interpreta-
tions: it can be seen as retrenchment, possibly brought about by
overspending on William's part on the expansion of Glendon. Or
it could have been part of a young man's scheme of estate consolidation and modernization following the death of his grandfather.

A more clear-cut case of retrenchment concerns William Tresham, who died unmarried in about 1660, leaving Newton-in-the-Willows, his main seat which had been in the family since acquired by marriage in the late fifteenth century, to be sold to Alderman James Langham, later baronet. Until the Treshams died out a couple of generations later, the main and only seat of the declining family was the more modest Pilton Manor-House, where William's heir and nephew Maurice had been living. In both these cases, the seats sold were grander than the seats kept, but their sales no doubt helped to keep the families going until demographic attrition took its final toll.

Among the rich, who were relatively immune to such economic pressures, seats acquired from the distaff side might remain in a family for a generation or more. But even at this elevated economic level these seats were often superfluous, and many found their way on to the land market sooner or later. Two good examples of such delayed sales are provided by Hertfordshire. The first concerned Broxbournebury, the sixteenth-century seat of the Cocks. In 1612 it passed to the only daughter and heiress, who married three times. On her death in 1645 she left it to her third husband for his lifetime and then on his death in 1667 to her only daughter and heiress by her second husband. The latter had married a Lincolnshire squire, Sir John Monson, 2nd Bt., who thereupon moved south to Broxbournebury, where he created a park and otherwise improved the old house. It remained in the Monson family until sold in 1789, and was in fairly consistent use as a convenient suburban residence until near the end, when the 3rd Lord Monson disparked the park to turn it into pasture for the grazing of cattle, presumably to supply the London market.

In this case the convenient location of the house close to London, unlike the main seat in Lincolnshire, combined with filial piety to keep it in the family of adoption for over a century. It was a further advantage that the Monsons could easily afford to keep it up for occasional visits. That it, and the similar house of North Mimms which passed by marriage to the Osbornes (later dukes of Leeds) in 1682, were well looked after during these years of secondary use is attested to by the fact that both houses are still standing to this day. Although modified by succeeding owners, the old cores were in good enough condition to be incorporated in the succeeding houses rather than being razed to the ground. Indeed North Mimms Place is one of the few extant Elizabethan houses in Hertfordshire, since it did not change hands until the late eighteenth century when its purchaser was able superficially to Gothicize it at very small expense.

The second case concerns Brickendonbury, which passed in 1754 from Sir Thomas Clarke to his niece, the wife of Thomas Morgan of Ruperra, younger son of a wealthy Welsh squire, all of whose estates he was to inherit nine years later on the death without heirs of his nephew. Morgan was active in Parliament and lived at Brickendonbury whenever his business brought him to London. To this day there survives a great avenue of trees known as 'Morgan's Walk', which he planted on acquiring the house. It remained in use by the family until it was let in 1845, and finally sold in 1881. It was probably the victim partly of the family's lessened interest in London and partly of the development of the railways which brought South Wales so much closer to the metropolis.

ii. Lack of Male Heirs

Apart from the disposal of a house superfluous to needs, the second clear reason for the sale of a seat was partial or complete demographic failure, the lack of a son to whom to leave it. This could be the explanation of 43 per cent of all sales by inheritors— some of whom were also selling supernumerary seats (Table 5.1, Fig. 5.2). As we have seen, the majority of childless owners contrived to keep the seat in the family by passing it on to a surrogate heir, but some either had no distant relatives, or disliked or despised them, or did not care about the future of their family, or wanted the money. No fewer than 20 per cent of all direct inheritors who sold remained unmarried, and thus deliberately deprived themselves of all hope of legitimate posterity. The reasons for this unusual behaviour remain mysterious. Some of them had remote relatives to whom to leave their estates, but these bachelors who sold were wilfully ending a family line.

iii. Financial Ruin

The proportion of inheritors who sold at least partly because of known financial difficulties is surprisingly small, amounting to only forty-two persons (or a quarter of all inheritor-sellers), ten of whom may have got into trouble by over-ambitious building (Table 5.1, Fig. 5.2). Indeed there are only seven cases in three counties in 340 years in which the sale of a seat by an inheritor can definitely be proved to have been caused by nothing other than total financial ruin. The fact that the number of clear-cut cases of disaster is so small is convincing evidence that the phenomenon was a rarity, which perhaps accounts for its high publicity value as a morality play on the stage of real life. Very few families at this relatively exalted level fell into ruin between 1540 and 1879, and when they did they were the talk of the town and country alike for many years to come. Moreover, as will be examined in Chapter XI, only a very small proportion of those who sold can have been forced to do so by excessive building, despite the common beliefs to the contrary.

One of the few established families to go to the wall was the Hertfordshire family of Caesar. In the elegiac prose of John Burke: 'Charles Adelmare Caesar esq. of Bennington Place inherited the most part of his father's splendid possessions in the twenty-first year of his age, in all the pride of youth, health and ancestry; and died at the age of 67, insolvent and broken-hearted, a melancholy memorial to the ruin of a once highly flourishing family'. On succeeding his father in 1694, Charles at once tore down the old mansion and built a sumptuous new one. But before he had time to move into it, it burnt to the ground as a result of a fire started by workmen melting lead for the weights of sash-windows—a not uncommon hazard at that time. Presumably he could not afford to build it all over again, since it remained in ruins until it was sold after his death (when it was rebuilt, only to burn down again!). Meanwhile he lived in a smaller house on the estate, Bennington Lordship, which he enlarged. The rest of his life he spent fighting contested elections. He was a Tory, indeed a moderate Jacobite, so that he derived no rewards from his politics. Unfortunately for his pocket, he lived at a time both of frequent elections and of soaring electioneering costs. In 1701 he first stood for Hertford borough, where he fought another six elections, losing two, before contesting and winning two enormously expensive elections for the county seat in 1728 and 1736. As a result, 'after his death in 1741, he was so deeply involved in debt that all he possessed was forced to be sold'.[5]

This was not, however, quite the end of the Caesars. His two daughters never married—presumably because their father could not afford to give them dowries—but his son, clearly in an attempt to shore up the family fortunes, married the daughter and only heiress of one Henry Long, about whom we know nothing save that he bought Bayford Place in 1713, was sheriff in 1714—at a time when the prestige of that office had reached possibly its lowest point—and died soon after. Charles Caesar the younger was therefore saved by his wife's fortune from sharing in the wreckage of his father's affairs. However, he left no son, and soon after his

[5] J. Burke, *The Commoners of Great Britain*, 1835, ii, p. 21; J. E. Cussans, op. cit., ii (*iii*), p. 128.

death in 1758 his daughters joined in selling Bayford Place to a former Lord Mayor of London. The story of the Caesars thus illustrates two types of sale, the more usual one brought on by demographic attrition as well as the far less common one caused by overspending.

Not all who sold plummeted as dramatically as Charles Caesar. Unfortunately bankruptcy, though less frequent, is better documented than gradual decline, since perception of the various stages of the latter will usually depend on the survival of more than one document. Moreover, this study, being concerned with the ownership of seats and only marginally with the buying and selling of land, does not deal with the piecemeal dismemberment of estates. The story of the dispersal of the estate of Thundridgebury, Hertfordshire, in the late eighteenth century, however, may serve to shed some light on modes of slow decline. The Gardiners had been settled at Thundridgebury since the first John Gardiner, merchant and fishmonger of London, purchased the manor in 1543 and built himself a seat there, which descended by inheritance through eleven successive owners. In the course of the seventeenth century the house was embellished and enlarged, thanks to several judicious marriages with City wives. The last John Gardiner was born in 1760, the same year his father died. His mother came from a well-to-do Derbyshire family and one would have expected the ensuing long minority to have helped to boost the family finances. But such does not seem to have been the case. In 1780, the old family seat of Thundridgebury was let on long lease. On coming of age a year later, the first act of John Gardiner IV was to sell off two portions of the family estates to the trustees of Sampson Hanbury, then aged twelve, the younger son of a family of Staffordshire bankers and brewers. In the 1790s, John Gardiner was said to have borrowed money from William Cunliffe Shawe, the then owner of Youngsbury, a new seat nearby. The latter was reported to have 'behaved very ill to [him] lending him money on his estates at 4½ per cent' and then demanding 5 per cent.[6] At about this time, John Gardiner inherited a windfall through his mother, who had died in 1793; but whether this was enough to restore his fortunes is not clear. In any event in 1811, when the lease had run out, he finally sold the seat, manor, and remaining estates of Thundridgebury. Three years later he died, still unmarried. The new purchaser was Daniel Giles II, whose father, a

[6] Bodleian Library, interleaved N. Salmon, *Hertfordshire* (Gough, Herts., 18), *marginalia* on p. 242.

Director of the Bank of England, had bought Youngsbury from Shawe in 1796. Giles's razing of all but one chimney of the old house (left in order to preserve his right to the pew in the chancel) effectively symbolized the substitution of Youngsbury for Thundridgebury and the change of ownership from Gardiner to Giles.

These stories of financial shipwreck are the exceptions, and most often, if the estate was substantial and debts not too extensive, a period of retrenchment was all that was needed to halt the decline. This retrenchment could take various forms. Thus in late eighteenth-century Hertfordshire, Thomas Brand, having overspent on improvements to his seat at the Hoo, went and lived abroad for a time, while his wife stayed at home and retrenched. Similarly his neighbour Robert Heysham let his seat at Stagenhoe and went to live in France for a while, for the same reason.[7] In 1822, when John Bennet Lawes of Rothamsted died leaving an only son under age and an estate much encumbered with debt, his widow let the main seat and went to live in a smaller house nearby, while the boy went to Eton and Oxford. By the time he came into his inheritance in 1832, the financial crisis had been averted.

The possibilities of a successful period of retrenchment were very much a matter of chance: of the availability of a good overseer during the absence of the owner abroad, such as the Hon. Mrs Brand; of the opportunity to minimize expense offered by a long minority; of the accident of a timely inheritance or a wealthy marriage to buttress the family fortunes. Any or all of these might or might not occur, and family name, seat, and inheritance consequently be preserved or finally dissipated. It is important to regard all sales as the tip of a far larger iceberg of financial difficulties which were somehow overcome by luck and good management.

3. PURCHASERS AND HEIRS OF PURCHASERS

i. Purchaser-Sellers

So far, this discussion has been concerned exclusively with men who had inherited their seats and estates from other inheritors, and has ignored new purchasers and their heirs. One would have supposed that since the latter were ambitious men on the make, they were anxious to establish a permanent niche for their families in county society, as well as possessing the financial resources to do so, and therefore very unlikely to sell. The reverse turns out to be the case. It is astonishing to find that purchasers and purchasers' heirs were more than twice as likely to sell as inheritors

[7] Op. cit., *marginalia* on p. 152.

of inheritors (Table 5.1, Fig. 5.1). About one in three of all purchasers and one in four of all purchasers' heirs resold, as compared
to one in eight of all inheritors. This occurred despite the fact that
they were almost equally likely to remain bachelors, equally likely
to have no heirs, and far less likely to have supernumerary houses.
However, if the figures are broken up into counties, it immediately becomes clear that the phenomenon of a seller who was a
purchaser or purchaser's heir was mainly confined to Hertfordshire, where they constituted two-thirds of all sellers, as opposed
to one-third in Northamptonshire and less than a sixth in Northumberland (Table 5.2). No less than 86 per cent of all sales in the
three counties by purchasers and the heirs of purchasers took place
in Hertfordshire (172 out of 200).

Who were these transient members of the Hertfordshire elite?
One would naturally assume that they were all men of business,
but a closer look reveals that the situation was more complicated
(Table 5.3). Most of these purchaser-sellers were certainly busy
men of affairs whose base of action was London, but their origins
varied considerably over time, both in their ultimate provenance
and in their social rank.

In the late sixteenth and early seventeenth centuries when purchaser-sellers first manifested themselves, the main influence was
proximity to the Court, the bulk of them being landowners from
elsewhere who were courtiers and office-holders. Only three of
them were merchants. By the mid-seventeenth century, total numbers nearly doubled, and the sources of wealth changed. There
were now a few lawyers, while the number of merchants rose
steeply to become the largest group. The next sixty years however, 1700-59, witnessed a very sharp drop in numbers of these
transients. This is all the more remarkable since this was also a
period when the number of suitable houses began to increase, as
houses were rebuilt, or new houses were constructed on new estates made up from dispersed fragments of older ones. Landed
magnates, now mainly active politicians, once more formed the
largest group, and the office-holders were now all military or naval
men. Between 1760 and 1819 Hertfordshire transients reached their
greatest number. Landed magnates and business men bulked equally
large, with twenty-four each, and the number of lawyers went up
again. This 1760-1819 peak is not linked to any great land boom
and its cause is mysterious.[8] There is circumstantial evidence to

---

[8] 'A Century of Land Values: England and Wales', in *Essays in Economic History*, ed.
E. M. Carus-Wilson, London, iii, 1962, p. 129.

suggest that a few of the business men who entered the sample at this time were sometimes buying merely to sell again for profit.

Thus in 1790 John Spurrier, variously described as a solicitor and an auctioneer, bought leases of Little Court and Ardleybury, two houses which belonged to the Dean and Chapter of St Paul's and had been out on long lease but in the sample since the late sixteenth century. He bought the freehold of Little Court in 1791, selling it again the next year, and that of Ardleybury in 1808, selling it again in 1810. The buying and selling of Little Court would appear to be straightforward speculation, were it not for the fact that his son Richard was already living there and employing Repton to improve the grounds in 1790. It looks as though Richard died soon after, causing the sale of Little Court in 1792. His father, however, lived on at Ardleybury until the sale in 1810.[9] This seems to be a mixed case of business speculation and thwarted family aggrandisement.

Not much more straightforward is the story of John Kingston, a wealthy London wine-merchant, active in the anti-slave-trade movement, a founder of the Sierra Leone Colony and an MP, who bought Oakhill in 1790 for £7,000, enlarged it by the addition to two wings, and sold it again for £18,900 in 1810. Soon after 1805 he also bought the neighbouring estate of Belmont (presumably as a speculation since he let it), which his executors sold in 1813.[10] One gets the impression that these were purchasers with an eye to the main chance, who bought for their own convenience, but were equally ready to sell if given the opportunity to make a financial profit. Certainly neither Kingston, who was elderly and whose heir was settled in another county, nor Spurrier after his son's death, can have been interested in long-term settlement in the county. But they were shrewd men of business who improved their investment and did well out of it.

After 1840, the Hertfordshire picture changes once more with the development of the railways. The magnates were now mainly busy politicians whose main seats were beyond easy reach of London by train. Only the business men remained as numerous as in the preceding period, but they were mainly crowded into the extreme southern part of the county which was in imminent danger of being overrun by suburbia. It is among their ranks that residences of the kind that would later be described as 'houses in the

[9] *Victoria County History, Herts.*, iii, p. 195 and iv, p. 80; D. Stroud, *Humphrey Repton*, London, 1962, p. 53.

[10] J. Wilson, *Biographical Index to the House of Commons*, London, 1806, *sub* Kingston; F. Cass, *East Barnet, London and Middlesex Archaeological Society*, London, 1885-92.

country' to distinguish them from 'country houses' began to make their appearance during the last two and a half decades of the sample. It is, however, an indication on the part of their owners of a lack of awareness of any such distinction that they went to the trouble of having them drawn and engraved as 'seats' to illustrate Cussan's *History of Hertfordshire* as late as the 1870s.[11]

It is very suitable that such a development should have started in Hertfordshire, since in many respects these purchaser-sellers right from the start were pioneers in a new conception of the country house, not so much a symbol of status and power as a convenient residence, comfortable and agreeable to live in during brief intervals between the pressures of business or public life. If these houses remained on the whole so stately in appearance and in the life that was led within their walls, it was because the first houses to be used in this way were existing 'country houses'. It was only in the eighteenth century that the villa was developed.

. Analysed in terms of social and occupational background, purchaser-sellers in Hertfordshire were at all times drawn from three distinct but overlapping groups (Table 5.3). First, there were distinguished members of the landed classes with main seats elsewhere, who were active in London political and sometimes administrative life. Second, there were lesser rootless members of the same social and occupational categories, including members of the armed forces, as well as men, often of middle-class background, who had risen in the armed forces or the law. The third category consisted mainly of middle-class Londoners, who might be bankers or merchants in the luxury trades who, though middle class in origin, often adopted the life-style of the upper classes with whom they rubbed shoulders in their business dealings; or overseas merchants, including nabobs, who retired to live the life of a country gentleman after half a lifetime abroad. It is among the latter that are to be found the greatest number of purchaser-sellers some of whom were thwarted purchaser-settlers, such as Clutterbuck of Blakesware, and others with no desire to establish a county family.

The first group, the magnates, had already been acquiring such houses in Hertfordshire in the sixteenth century: Ambrose Earl of Warwick had a suburban seat at Nyn House. The famous gardens of Lucy Countess of Bedford in the early seventeenth century were at the Moor in Hertfordshire, not at Woburn. When she and her husband died in 1627, the Moor was sold to the courtier William Herbert Earl of Pembroke, and when he died three years later, it

---

[11] J. Cussans, op. cit., iii (*ii*), opposite p. 186, and (*iii*), opposite p. 215.

was bought by an office-holder at Court, Sir Charles Harbord. It seems reasonable to assume that those magnates who owned a main seat further afield and who bought another in Hertfordshire did so as a short-term measure, and therefore that the eventual resale of the latter was implicit from the moment of purchase. As a new acquisition, it was not part of the entailed family estates, and therefore could be sold at any time.

The second group, the officials in the royal administration, the armed forces, or the law, were of two sorts. Some were essentially a rootless subcategory of the landed classes, namely career-oriented younger sons from families which had a hereditary connection with service to the Crown. These were people who pursued more or less distinguished careers, usually in the armed forces, but were always aware of the possibility of a windfall through one of their many rich and influential relatives, whether it be an inheritance or a sinecure office. Meanwhile, they tended to live where their careers took them, which might occasionally afford them the possibility of spending a few years in a country seat similar to the one in which they were born and raised. Officers in the armed services needed a house in which to live in the intervals between wars, sited close to London so as to enable them to keep in touch with their patrons and political superiors in the Admiralty or War Office, as well as their friends. Another group pursued similar occupational careers, but came from middle-class backgrounds. They too needed a temporary base near London so long as they were actively employed, but they may also have been buying land in other counties with an eye to establishing a new county family elsewhere.

The third group of purchaser-sellers were middle-aged London business men whose children were often grown-up and established either in a trade or profession, or as country gentlemen elsewhere. They bought a Hertfordshire country house merely because of its rural charms and its closeness to London, which made it unnecessary for them to break their ties to their business. Others may have moved into the country to please their wives. But whatever the reason for the move, the distinguishing characteristic about these men is that their purchase of a seat was an act of purely personal self-gratification, largely devoid of overtones of long-term social climbing. It is at least possible that some of them might have rented rather than purchased their seat if they had had the choice.

Many of these purchaser-sellers from London remained active in their business or profession, thus distinguishing them from the local squirearchy. They failed to conform to Dr Johnson's definition of a gentleman as a man who did not visibly work for his living.

They were a social hybrid, half office-holder, lawyer, banker, or city merchant, and half owner of a county seat. It was the proximity of the seat to the place of work which made it possible for a successful man of affairs to have a taste of country-house living while still keeping in touch with his business in Westminster, the Inns of Court, or the City.

Another way of looking at these purchaser-sellers is to place them in categories according to aspirations rather than origins or occupations. There were those who intended to put down roots as purchaser-settlers but were thwarted in their design either by demographic failure or by financial difficulties, and therefore were obliged to sell; there were those who had intended and could afford to put down roots in county society, but changed their minds for whatever reason, possibly because they found the life tedious or the rural society unfriendly or boring; there were those who may have bought as a speculative investment in a rising land market (largely confined to the 1760-1820 period); and there were those who never intended to do anything more than buy a large and pleasant rural retreat for occasional or periodic use, in some cases for retirement after a life of exertion in the City or abroad. The majority, at least in Hertfordshire, seem to have fallen into this last category.

On the whole the only ones among these purchaser-sellers who abstained from much involvement in local affairs were the magnates from other counties whose political interest was focused on the county of their main seat. On the other hand, they quite often turn out to have been bound by ties of kinship or sociability to the local elite. For example, it was from his brother-in-law that in 1780 Lord Fairford, future Earl of Downshire, bought the lease of Hertford Castle. He considerably improved and Gothicized the house and lived there in great style until he succeeded his father in 1794, when he let it. The Londoners and nabobs were more likely to allow themselves to be pricked for sheriff, and more willing and perhaps anxious to serve as JP. One may suspect, however, that their behaviour by now probably reflected more what they believed was expected of them than what they felt to be an obligation to society arising from ownership of a country house. It is doubtful whether they had internalized the elite values which purchaser-settlers elsewhere were so anxious to absorb.

ii. Examples

After analysing in various ways the chronology and typology of these transient purchaser-sellers, the next step is to flesh out the picture by some concrete examples of how houses were passed rapidly from hand to hand among such men. The story of the successive owners of Wormleybury in Hertfordshire between 1733 and 1851 offers a fairly typical view of the variety of types of such country-house owners. In 1728, John Deane, who had already made two fortunes and lost one in India, purchased Little Grove, an elegant Hertfordshire seat recently built by a successful London lawyer on a small estate. In 1733 Deane went on to buy the manor and seat of nearby Wormleybury. The old Tudor house had been in the sample since 1541, and immediately after purchase Deane pulled it down and started a new building. The style was conventional Georgian, and the public rooms were on a substantial scale, the smallest being 20 feet square. He must have built at a furious pace, if the house was finished in time to entertain the county in the year he was sheriff in 1734. Deane was also JP, and by his purchasing, building, and office-holding was clearly trying to force his way into the local elite as fast as possible. But by all this activity, and possibly unlucky speculation, he seriously over-extended himself, and in order to pay his creditors he had to sell Little Grove in 1734, and a year later to mortgage his newly built Wormleybury for £12,500. By 1739, he was bankrupt and had to sell the freehold to his creditor for £13,000. The last that is heard of John Deane, once the opulent nabob and open-handed host at Wormleybury, is of him working as a tapster in a London public house.

In startling contrast is the steady upward progress of his creditor and successor at Wormleybury, Alexander Hume, who had started life as a surgeon on an East Indiaman. He had broken the Company rules by privately engaging in trade with Ostend, and so was obliged to flee abroad. A man of infinite resource and few scruples, he wangled a warrant from the Emperor to establish a colonial settlement at Bancaban in India, and obtained a trade treaty with England. He then returned to England, insinuated himself into the good graces of the Duke of Newcastle, and was appointed Commissary for the supply of the English troops in Flanders just before the battle of Dettingen. It was from this office that he made the money which enabled him to buy Wormleybury from the bankrupt John Deane. Thus established, he went on to achieve respectability as an MP and Director of the East India Company. He also obtained a Commissary's place for his younger brother and heir, Abraham, to whom he left the estate on his death in 1765. Four years later Abraham acquired the respectable title of baronet, after having spent £11,000 enlarging the house. His son, the 2nd baronet, had the seat lavishly decorated by the Adam brothers in 1777-9, and constructed a large lake in the grounds.

This time, however, appropriately enough for his status as a country gentleman, the money came not from government contracting but from the winnings of a racehorse, whose burial place in the park he gratefully marked with a large and elegant stone vase. He himself married the granddaughter of a peer and his two daughters and coheiresses married peers. When he died, the house descended to his grandson, John Viscount Alford, son and heir of the 1st Earl Brownlow. He was an active member of Parliament, who used the house merely as a convenient residence when the House was in session. The owners of the house thus varied from John Deane, an unwilling purchaser-seller, to Alexander Hume, a successful purchaser-settler, to Lord Alford, a magnate based elsewhere.[12]

Colney Chapel House, which is also in Hertfordshire, was successively bought and sold by a wide variety of owners, the great majority of whom were purchaser-sellers. The first house on the site was begun around 1770 by the King's Proctor, Philip Champion de Crespigny, a successful ecclesiastical lawyer of French Huguenot extraction, whose father had been King's Proctor before him. In 1773, however, his wife died, and work on the house was interrupted. Next year he married again and in 1778, perhaps because his new wife did not like living in the country, he sold the 150-acre estate and unfinished shell of the building at a knock-down price of £6,500. Charles Bourchier, the new purchaser of Colney Chapel House, burst upon the Hertfordshire scene in a blaze of glory, having recently returned from India where he had been Governor of Madras. He had married the daughter of the Knight of the Shire, and proceeded to spend an alleged £53,000 on pulling down and rebuilding the house, with no expense spared. In 1788 he served as sheriff, and in 1789 he bought Marshallswick, a more modest seat a little further north at Sandridge, which he enlarged and called Sandridgebury. He seemed desirous of putting down roots into county society. But this did not happen, although he certainly had at least one son, who became a parson, and possibly another, who was an army general. In 1795 he sold Colney Chapel House and in 1802 he also sold Marshallswick. When he died in 1810, he had disappeared from the public eye some years before, and it seems possible that the exorbitant cost of rebuilding Colney Chapel House had broken him financially and that he never

---

[12] Bodleian Library, interleaved N. Salmon, *Hertfordshire* (Gough, Herts., 16), between pp. 14 and 15; D. Buckley and W. Le Hardy, *Wormley in Hertfordshire*, London, 1954, pp. 104-35.

fully recovered.[13] Like so many nabobs he may also have suffered from ill health. But a third possible explanation may lie in the fact that he never bought a large estate, but only houses with small grounds. He was certainly putting down roots, if his acceptance of the office of sheriff is anything to go by, but they were shallow ones.

After only four years, the Margrave of Anspach, the new magnate purchaser of Colney Chapel House, sold it in 1799 to another magnate, George King, son and heir of the 2nd Earl of Kingston, who lived here for the next five years until he succeeded his father. King then sold it to George Anderson, about whom little is known except that he sold it about four years later to Patrick Haddow of the East India Company, who lived here for several years, served as sheriff in 1824, and sold the seat in his lifetime in 1832. The next owner was Henry Oddie, a London lawyer who had married a Shropshire heiress. He clearly took an interest in his new suburban seat, almost doubling the size of the Park, and serving on the Bench as JP. He passed the seat on to his son, and between them they held it for nearly forty years until 1871, when on the latter's death it was sold once more. The new purchaser, Andrew Lusk, was a London grocer and Lord Mayor of London in 1873-4. He was made a baronet for his pains, but went bankrupt in 1879, when the house was sold again to a Mr Kingham, about whom nothing at all is known. In its final transmogrification, Colney Chapel House was bought by a community of nuns.

These successive owners of Colney Chapel House provide some idea of the strange birds of passage who sought shelter for a while in large houses in small grounds in South Hertfordshire. One further example will suffice. This is a house called Woolmers, close to Hertford, which first appears in the sample in the 1780s when it belonged to Samuel Whitbread, the brewer, whose main seat was at Bedwell Park nearby. In 1801, his son, Samuel Whitbread Jun., sold it to a magnate, the Duke of Bridgwater, who wanted a temporary residence nearby while he was busy tearing down and rebuilding his seat at Ashridge. The Duke paid £15,100 for the house, fully furnished. Gough's comment to the effect that 'Mr Simpson from Bombay with a large family bid within £50 of the Duke' is interesting since it encapsulates the wide variety of needs and backgrounds of these short-term owners of largish houses with small estates.[14] On the death of the Duke in 1803, Woolmers went

[13] Bodleian Library, Gough, Herts., 13, iii, f. 64.
[14] Bodleian Library, interleaved N. Salmon, *Hertfordshire* (Gough, Herts., 16), between pp. 212 and 213.

to his nephew the Marquis of Stafford, who sold it to another magnate, Sir John St Aubyn, 5th Bt., of Cornwall. He was an active Whig who probably used it mainly when the House was sitting during the time when he was MP between 1807 and 1812. In 1821 he sold it for £35,000 to Sir Gore Ouseley, a former Levant merchant, oriental scholar, and ambassador to Persia. Ousely hired the architect C. R. Cockerel to enlarge and improve the house to the tune of a further £35,000, which might lead one to suppose that he had a mind to settle here. In 1832, however, he purchased an even larger house in Buckinghamshire and sold Woolmers in 1836 to Rear-Admiral George Hotham, who sold it again six years later to William Wodehouse, who left it in 1903 to his son. Of these seven successive owners, three (Bridgwater, Stafford, and St Aubyn) were short-term purchaser-sellers; one (Whitbread) a purchaser's heir who sold; and only one (Wodehouse), a purchaser-settler. In the cases of Ouseley and Hotham, their original intentions are unknown. The former eventually became a purchaser-settler in another county, and may well originally have intended to settle in Hertfordshire. It seems unlikely, however, that Rear-Admiral Hotham bought Woolmers with any intention of settling down. He was probably merely waiting for a new naval appointment.

The sample deliberately excludes short-term leases for a year or so, unless they led to purchase of the seat. With very few exceptions, such leasehold houses as figure in the sample are mainly confined to a few out on long lease: two that belonged to the Dean and Chapter of St Paul's (Ardeleybury and Little Court) and two that belonged to the Earl of Salisbury (Popes and Hertford Castle). To judge, however, by the small group of late eighteenth and early nineteenth century houses purchased only to be sold again within a lifetime, all in Hertfordshire, it is possible that the cycle of their purchase and sale may have been initiated by the pressure of demand at the time of the first such sale, and that in other circumstances at least some of them might have been let rather than sold.

The letting of houses is not a very well-documented subject, but it appears to have been very common both in Hertfordshire and, mainly for the hunting, in Northamptonshire. What is certain is that a great deal of short-term—mainly furnished, or at least partly furnished—leasing was taking place. The reader of late eighteenth and early nineteenth century diaries and memoirs of this class cannot but be struck by the peripathetic nature of the existence they led. Before the development of luxury hotels—on the whole a nineteenth-century phenomenon—this depended on a

plentiful supply of suitable houses to let, and none were more
suitable to the needs of the lessees than large houses with small
estates. Advertisements in the newspapers for houses needed by
these deliberate transients reveal the qualities for which they were
looking. One in 1748 for a house in Buckinghamshire, twenty-four
miles from London, describes it as follows: 'A new-built commo-
dious house, fit for a large family, genteelly fitted up, sashed and
wainscotted, and exceeding good chimney pieces, with all convenient offices, stabling for 10 or 12 horses, coach house for four
carriages, and a big but not expensive garden'. Another, forty years
later, set out the needs of a rather grander prospective lessee: 'For
a nobleman's family. Wanted to rent on lease for 7 years about 70
to 80 miles from London, a modern mansion house, furnished or
partly furnished', plus about sixty acres of grassland, a manor, and
a fishery.[15] Here were two large country houses offered and being
sought for a limited period of residence, both of them without any
agricultural property attached to them except what was needed for
pleasure grounds. Both advertisements, it is interesting to observe,
stressed the need for modernity. Both also specified the exact distance from London, one near, one rather further afield.

4. HOUSES LIABLE TO SALE OR RETENTION

What was it that made certain houses so very attractive to transient
purchaser-sellers from such very different backgrounds? It is clear
that there was no specialization in the type of house sought by the
different kinds of purchaser-sellers, for the same house passed in-
discriminately from magnate to official to lawyer to City merchant
and back. They all seemed to want the same set of houses, which
were in consequence constantly passing from hand to hand. Just
as there were certain special features about people which made
them particularly likely to sell, so in Hertfordshire, but not elsewhere, there were special features about houses which made them
peculiarly liable to be sold.

In his play *The Country House*, Vanbrugh depicts the luckless
purchaser of such a house, a Mr Barnard, who complains to his
brother that the cost of living in the house is ruining him. The
latter's first suggestion is to abandon the house altogether, and
move back to London. This is rejected as impracticable due to
opposition from Mrs Barnard. His next suggestion is to sell the
house, but Mr Barnard explains that 'nobody will buy it. It has
got as ill a name as if it had the plague; it has been sold over and

[15] *Daily Advertiser*, 30 Jan., 1748; *St James's Chronicle*, 17 Jan., 1788.

over, and every family that has lived in it has been ruined.' Since
it was hospitality that was the chief expense, his brother then suggests that Mr Barnard 'send away all your beds and furniture . . . ,
for then your guests can't stay with you all night'. The final, and
only really practical, suggestion is a drastic one: 'you must e'en do
what's done when a town is afire; blow up your house, that the
mischief may run no further'.[16]

The best way to explain these houses which changed hands so
regularly and rapidly is to begin with their opposite, houses which
were very rarely put up for sale. In 1879 there were forty-one seats
out of a total of 362 in all three counties which had never been
sold for a period of over 250 years. None of them had come on
the market since 1639, and many of them not since the reign of
Henry VIII. There were another six which had lasted for 250
years before being pulled down, and there were another forty seats
which had also never been sold for about 300 years, but which
had only become large enough for the sample after 1650. Thus
about a quarter of all houses in sample were almost never sold.
These long-lived houses had three features in common. Almost all
of them were very large, comprising over 120 units; with five exceptions they were all attached to large estates of over 3,000 acres;
and half of them were owned by the peerage. Of particular importance was the size of the estate. In 1879 40 per cent of houses
attached to estates of 3,000 acres or more in 1873 had not been
put on the market for over 180 years, as opposed to only 13 per
cent of houses with less than 3,000 acres (Table 5.5A). If one confines the agricultural estate to that within the same county as the
seat, the correlation of estate size with durability is even more
remarkable. In Hertfordshire in 1879, 50 per cent of all seats with
estates in the county over 3,000 acres, but only 8 per cent of those
under 1,000 acres, had never been sold for 180 years. Conversely,
69 per cent of those with estates under 1,000 acres but only 22
per cent of those over 3,000 acres had been sold in the last eighty
years (Table 5.5B, Fig. 5.3). The conclusion is inescapable that a
seat with a large consolidated agricultural estate in the same county
was largely indestructible, tending to pass from generation to generation by inheritance without ever once being put on the market.
It was no doubt an awareness of this which drove landowners to
consolidate property whenever the opportunity arose.

In contrast with these seats which were hardly ever sold, there
were twenty-three—a significant number of seats in fact—which
were constantly changing hands by sale and purchase almost every

---

[16] *The Complete Works of Sir John Vanbrugh*, ed. B. Dobrée and G. Webb, London, 1927,
ii, p. 216.

FIG. 5.3   Frequency of Sales relative to the Size of Estates in 1873: Hertfordshire
[Table 5.5]

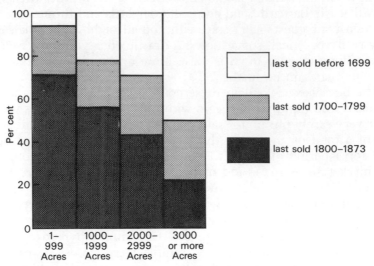

generation (Table 5.6). Often quite large houses, most of them had very small estates attached to them, far too small for the size of the house, and all but one of them were located in Hertfordshire. Of the eight of them which were frequently sold after 1800, six had estates in the county in 1873 which were less than 300 acres. From the start, the houses of many of these purchaser-sellers had surrounding estates not large enough to make them self-sufficient, a factor which was of small concern to magnates from elsewhere and was a positive attraction to men whose wealth did not depend on their landholdings. This is why all but one of these frequently-sold houses were in Hertfordshire, close to London.

There were two principal ways in which a large house with insufficient estates to support it could come into being. Either it was an old house which had somehow become separated from its estate, or it was a new house built by a man who did not want a large estate in the first place. Along with piecemeal sale of land to pay off debts, the commonest way in which a house could lose part of its attached estates was as a by-product of indirect inheritance, in turn caused by demographic failure in the direct male line. In these cases the seat and the entailed part of the estates often went to an indirect male heir, while the rest of it was split off and passed to one or more heiresses. This fragmentation could induce the indirect heir to break the entail and sell or otherwise dispose of his unwanted and/or economically draining inheritance.

The ultimate destiny of such a seat depended on the state of the local land market. It is instructive in this respect to compare what happened in Northamptonshire and in Hertfordshire in the seventeenth century. Beginning in the 1630s and gathering momentum right up to 1700, a number of such houses started to come on the market in both counties. There were, however, marked differences. In the first place, the Northamptonshire houses tended to be older than the Hertfordshire ones, because the first Northamptonshire building boom went back to the late fifteenth and early sixteenth centuries. Because they were old, and were mainly built of stone, they were sometimes not so large but mostly far more solid than houses in a similar situation in Hertfordshire, where building was mostly in brick but had not begun on a substantial scale before the late 1530s. This in turn meant that in Hertfordshire, where demand for seats exceeded supply, these old brick houses lent themselves easily to conversion and modernization. In Northamptonshire, on the other hand, where supply exceeded demand, the older stone houses could still make perfectly good minor seats or farmhouses without having much done to them, although their attractions as residential seats in terms of their capacity to be brought up to date were by now minimal. As a result, a great many of them simply fade out of the sample in the late seventeenth and early eighteenth centuries, as families dwindled socially, died out, or moved to new quarters. They were classic drop-outs. Without indulging in an exercise in counter-factual history, it seems at least not implausible that, had fox-hunting developed some fifty to a hundred years earlier, these old houses might have survived as hunting-boxes. But at the time there was no ready market for them, and in the eighteenth century a number of them were snapped up and razed to the ground by magnates eager to increase their landholdings.

By the late eighteenth century in counties close to London like Hertfordshire, large new country houses were being built on small estates, whether on the site of an older house with shrunken land attached, or on a new site altogether. The following description, taken from the 1800 sale catalogue of High Cannons, Herts., conveys the importance attached to the appearance of luxury and spaciousness in such houses: 'The house is a modern regular square brick building, painted and sanded to imitate stone, seated in the centre of its own grounds, which wear the appearance of a neat park, with a double entrance from the roads by handsome lodges and extensive drives through the grounds to the mansion'. There were stabling facilities for fourteen horses and four coach-houses. The park, which included a home farm, at that time was only 315 acres.[17] High Cannons was a small seventeenth-century manor house bought and enormously enlarged in 1771-3 by Robert Trefusis, a Cornish magnate who died soon after. In 1778 it was bought by Justinian Casamajor, a nabob from Antigua, who later inherited and moved to the old seat of Potterells, nearby. After him, High Cannons belonged successively and briefly to two MPs before being acquired as a suburban seat in 1812 by Enoch Durant, whose descendants sold it in 1888 to Mr Burdett Coutts. During the nineteenth century, the park was enlarged to 800 acres, so that High Cannons, despite the rapid turnover of owners, was still very much a country house.

On the other hand, one in six of all the architecturally prominent houses (not all of them large) newly built in England between 1855 and 1874 had less than 150 acres attached to them.[18] These were now houses in the country, not country houses in the sense in which the term had been used for the previous 400 years. They were architecturally prominent features in the landscape, but no longer elements of an integrated network of social, economic, and power relationships in the county. For centuries confined to the area close to London, the advent of the railways meant that such houses began to spread well beyond the Home Counties. The objectives of their purchasers were well described in his novel *C* by Maurice Baring in 1924. His hypothetical London business man 'wanted a large house, but not *too* large a house, in which he could entertain 14 or 15 people if he wanted to . . . He didn't want the house to be too far from London, yet he didn't want anything *suburban*. An hour and a quarter's journey would be about the limit; it must not be longer'.[19]

5. DROP-OUTS

Between 1540 and 1879, 131 houses dropped out of the sample. This means either that their owners were so rich that they had more seats than they needed and let some go to ruin, or that they

[17] Bodleian Library, interleaved N. Salmon, *Hertfordshire* (Gough, Herts., 18), between pp. 60 and 61.

[18] J. Franklin, *The Gentleman's Country house and its Plan 1835-1914*, London, 1981, pp. 35-6. After 1895, the proportion rose to 90 per cent. These figures have to be used with care, since Mrs Franklin has included in her sample many small houses which happened to find their way into the architectural journals of the day.

[19] Op. cit., p. 4.

were so poor that they were themselves downwardly mobile (Table 5.7). Fifteen seats were inherited by men who did not qualify for the sample because they were unable to maintain the status of a member of the elite. Twenty-nine were sold out of sample, twenty-four being bought by individuals who did not qualify as members of the elite and five by institutions. Three in Hertfordshire became schools (Hertford Castle, Totteridge Park, and Aspenden Hall); another (Bushey Hall) became a 'hydropathic establishment', the Victorian equivalent of a modern 'health spa'; and one in Northamptonshire (Abington Abbey) became a lunatic asylum. Four reverted to or were exchanged with the Crown: Nyn and Theobalds were exchanged for other properties, Holdenby was taken back for debt, and Dilston seized under an attainder.

Another eighty-three remained in the hands of the elite but were no longer used as country houses. The majority had already sunk in status to be at best secondary houses only very occasionally used. It was thus not poverty but excessive wealth and a surplus of houses in a few hands that led to their abandonment. In addition to being superfluous to need, many of them were too old or too neglected to be worth refurbishing. Some seventy of them were physically diminished or razed to the ground, and five were let. Two, Pytchley Hall in Northamptonshire and the Lordship, Standon, in Hertfordshire, were used as Hunt Club houses for a time. Nine remained for a while in abeyance owing to their ownership by single women. The most anomalous group in this somewhat artificial category are houses which remained in the hands of the elite, being bought up by nearby magnates not to use as seats but for purposes of aggrandizement and consolidation. Since the main interest of these transactions is not the motives of the sellers but the buyers, a detailed examination of this phenomenon will be postponed until the next chapter. But the important conclusion is that only in a minority of cases does the dropping-out of a house mean the disappearance of a family from the elite.

6. CONCLUSION

i. The Scale of Sales and Drop-outs

On what scale were seats put up for sale, and how did the scale vary over time and from county to county? The simplest and most meaningful measure of the scale of selling and variations in it is the number of sales proportionate to the number of all disposals through either inheritance or sale over twenty-year periods (Table

5.8). This is a formula which measures the scale of selling relative to the number of houses in sample at any given period.

Taking all three counties together, the results are much what one would expect (Fig. 5.4). Sales relative to total disposals were very few in the sixteenth century, when the class was in the process of formation, and jumped after 1600 to a plateau of about 15 per cent every twenty years, where they remained until the 1780s. After an all-time peak created by the huge turnover in Hertfordshire alone from 1780 to 1820, the causes of which have already been explained, the total ratio fell back again from 1820 to 1879.

It has recently been argued that the period between about 1670 and 1720 was financially a particularly difficult one for the landed elite, and that in consequence there was an unusually high level of sales of land, often resulting in the financial ruin of families.[20] It is said that this situation was caused by a combination of lagging rental income, a sharp rise in taxation upon land, and a diversion of capital away from loans to landowners on mortgages and into the public funds. The main evidence offered, apart from some individual examples, is a striking increase in the number of private Acts of Parliament passed to permit sales of land in order to reduce burdens of debt which had become intolerable. But no significant rise in sales of seats can be detected in any of the three counties

FIG. 5.4   Sales as a Proportion of all Disposals [Table 5.8]

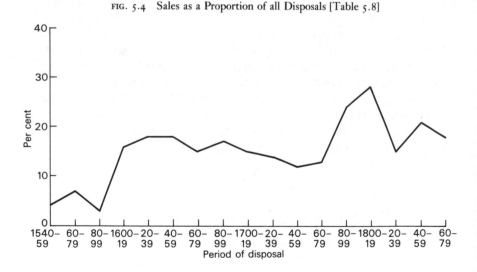

[20] H. J. Habakkuk, 'The Rise and Fall of English Landed Families 1600-1800', ii, *Transactions of the Royal Historical Society*, 5th Series, 30, 1980.

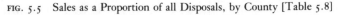

FIG. 5.5   Sales as a Proportion of all Disposals, by County [Table 5.8]

in our sample (Fig. 5.5). It seems likely that sales of land made possible by the Acts were confined to some outlying estates, and that these sales, together with windfalls from marriages and indirect inheritances, enabled most families to survive or recover. In other words, the crisis is illusory, and the Acts of Parliament strengthened rather than weakened family continuity by providing necessary financial flexibility. There is certainly no sign whatever of a major turnover at that time among the elite families in our three-county sample. On the other hand, this is the period in which large houses with truncated estates first began to make their appearance, and this, as well as sales and purchases of estates for purposes of consolidation, may have been the most significant consequence of the rise in private Acts of Parliament to alter settlements so as to permit land sales.

Comparing the three counties, it is clear that Hertfordshire always had a rate of sales about twice those of the other two (Table 5.8, Fig. 5.5). As a result, in the course of 340 years from 1540 to 1879 the number of houses ever sold proportionate to all houses ever in the sample varies from 60 per cent in Hertfordshire to 39 per cent in Northamptonshire to 19 per cent in Northumberland (Table 5.6). There was thus a direct correlation between propinquity to London and the turnover of seats by sale: geography mattered.

The social significance of sales can only be revealed if sellers are divided into two groups, those who inherited their seats from members of established elite families either directly or indirectly, and those who were relative newcomers, that is purchasers and the heirs of purchasers. If the latter group is removed and sales are compared with all disposing, it is possible to obtain a picture of attrition among the older established families. The scale of selling by older families turns out to be fairly small, no more than about 6 to 10 per cent of all disposals every sixty years. Moreover the extraordinary peak of sales in Hertfordshire between 1780 and 1820 is greatly reduced, although still prominent (Table 5.3, Fig. 5.6).

It is noticeable that in Northumberland the Victorian period saw some increase in the level of sales by older families. Many of these, however, may have been sales of supernumerary seats, and in any case the numbers are too small to allow any firm conclusions to be drawn. More puzzling is the discovery that in Hertfordshire sales actually declined in the Victorian period. So far from selling out to the *nouveaux riches*, the older families dug themselves in ever more deeply, fortified perhaps by participation in

FIG. 5.6   Sales by Heirs of Inheritors as a Proportion of all Disposals [Table 5.3]

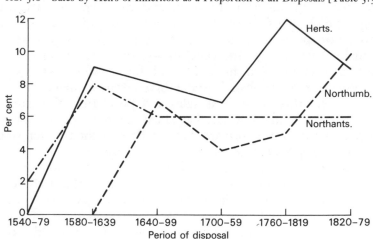

the new sources of wealth, and certainly benefiting from the agricultural prosperity of the years 1850-79.

The final conclusion is that although the rate of extinction of established families in Hertfordshire before 1820 was consistently higher than that in the other two counties (Fig. 5.6), it was by no means as dramatically higher as the figure for total sales would have led one to believe (Table 5.2). In all three counties there was a very large, very stable core of well-established families who continued to retain their hereditary seats from generation to generation. What makes Hertfordshire exceptional was not the attrition of this core, but the rapid coming and going of new men from London or elsewhere, as they set up temporary bases in the county and then moved away again.

ii. The Significance of Sales and Drop-outs

Finally there are the questions of motivation and significance. Of the total 362 sellers, only 160 had inherited their seat and estates directly or indirectly from relatives who had themselves inherited, and were therefore at least the third member of the family to own the seat (Table 5.1). The other 200 sellers were transients, purchasers, or their heirs.

Why did these 160 inheritor sellers part with their ancestral seats? To establish the maximum number who may have sold for financial reasons, the safest way to proceed is to make a series of worst-case assumptions. There were 42 inheritor sellers who are definitely known to have been in financial difficulties, 13 of whom also had other reasons to induce them to sell which may have been more compelling. Then there are the 29 who sold for unknown reasons. To the extent that it is in the nature of historical documentation that people who decline economically and socially tend to disappear from the records, it is likely that many of these were financially hard-pressed. But others may easily have evaded classification because of moving to another county and/or changing their name. To be on the safe side, it is best to assume that two-thirds of these 29, or about 20, were under financial pressure. One may therefore conclude that at most 62 out of the 160 sales by inheritors, or rather more than one in three, may have been caused by economic decay.

To this group of 62 inheritors who may have sold under financial duress must be added the drop-outs. There were 15 inheritors who lost membership of the sample since they were unable to maintain the status of a member of the elite, another 29 who sold out of sample, and 2 whose seats were returned to the Crown,

making a total of 46. Adding these to the 62 makes a grand total
of 108 out of 1,377 inheritor owners who may conceivably have
lost seat or status for financial reasons in three counties over 340
years. This means that at most there was on the average only one
sale or drop-out by an established family because of financial duress in each county every decade. More significant is the fact that
at most only 8 per cent of all inheritor owners over a 340-year
period were forced out of their status position in the county elite
by financial difficulties causing sale or status decline. This is certainly not a negligible proportion, but neither is it large enough
significantly to alter the composition of the group, except very
slowly over a very long period of time.

This reinforces the conclusion of the previous chapter, that established families were extremely tenacious in clinging to their
seats. Thanks to the flexibility built into the strict settlement, they
were able to sell outlying estates fairly freely to meet changing
needs, an option which did much to enable them to avoid the final
disaster of the sale of the family seat. It is important to realize,
therefore, that the very stability of families in their seats depended
on this ability to sell estates (and also to buy them) as the need or
opportunity arose. The argument here made is not that great landowners rarely sold off portions of their estates but rather that,
partly because of the availability of these options, they were rarely
wiped out altogether. Most of them were thus protected by legal,
institutional, and, above all, psychological barriers against the most
catastrophic effects not only of demographic attrition but also of
financial misfortune or mismanagement. But the full impact upon
the composition of the landed elite as a whole of such attrition as
there was can only be assessed after this examination of the scale
on which established families were being forced out has been combined with a study of the scale on which new families were thrusting their way in.

VI

INTRUSIONS: NEWCOMERS

1. INTRODUCTION

Although established elite families were very successful at adopting survival strategies that insured continuity, they were constantly being nudged by newcomers anxious to make their way into the elite. The extent of the pressure applied, the origins of those who exercised it, the degree of resistance to intrusion, all vary considerably over time and space. Most of the newcomers were purchasers of established seats already in sample, who merely substituted for the sellers, but a few, whom we shall call 'entrants', were responsible for introducing a house into the sample. Some were purchaser-entrants, who either bought a small house and enlarged and remodelled it to bring it into the sample, or assembled an estate on which they built an altogether new seat. Others were inheritor-entrants, who were parish gentry who inherited a minor seat, which they then suitably enlarged. In order to identify all the genuinely new men, and to separate them clearly from this last category of rising parish gentry, one must include with purchaser-entrants those entrants who had inherited the house from a purchaser or purchaser's heir. These men will be described as 'near purchaser-entrants'. Those few entrants whose mode of acquisition is unknown are assumed—not unreasonably—to have been purchasers. If they had been parish gentry slowly working their way up the social ladder they almost certainly would have been recorded in one of the county histories. Purchaser-entrants, near purchaser-entrants, and undocumented entrants, together with purchasers of houses in sample, were all men relatively or completely new to the county. Confirmation that the significant line of cleavage lay between these new men and the rising parish gentry is provided by the very sharp difference between them in their propensity to sell, similar to that observed in the last chapter between inheritor-sellers and purchaser-sellers. This group of men who were all relatively new to landed society were almost three times more likely to sell than inheritor-entrants who rose up out of the parish gentry (Table 6.1). The latter had a clearer perception of the hazards of living beyond their means, and were more determined in their social aspirations. They were therefore more

cautious about adopting an expensive life-style, and more tenacious once they had done so. Representing as it usually did the
culmination of several generations of struggle for upward mobility,
entry into the elite by members of the parish gentry was neither
lightly embarked upon nor lightly abandoned.

2. ENTRANTS

i. Numbers

When the sample begins there were only forty-nine owners in it.
Over the next 340 years to 1879 another 300 persons were entrants
through a combination of suitable house size, life-style, and local
political influence. In addition, there were another nineteen existing owners in the sample, most of them magnates, who also introduced new houses to the sample, mostly by building on land they
already owned, but sometimes through purchase of another house
or rebuilding it. This might be because their original house had
become dilapidated through age or neglect, for example the 5th
Earl Cowper at Panshanger, the Danvers at Culworth House, or
the Mitfords at Mitford Hall; or because they wanted something
less formal than the house they had inherited, for example Lord
Bacon at Verulam House or the Earl of Exeter at Wothorpe; or
simply because they had a passion for building and the means of
assuaging it, for example Sir Thomas Tresham in Northamptonshire, or Lord Burghley and Ralph Freeman IV. These are not
included as entrants, since they themselves already belonged to
the sample. Nor did purchasers of houses already in sample add
to the number of members of the elite, since they merely replaced
one family by another. Increase in numbers, therefore, was exclusively caused by entrants.

The first question to ask about the 300 entrants into the sample
is how they distributed themselves between the counties and over
time (Table 6.1, Fig. 6.1). The graphs of entrants into Hertfordshire and Northamptonshire follow very similar trajectories between 1540 and 1640. Although some families went to the wall for
demographic or more rarely economic reasons, on the whole this
period of unprecedented upheaval in the social scale witnessed more
rise than fall, resulting in the formation and consolidation of the
landed elite of England. The proportion of entrants during this
century was at an all-time high, never to be reached again.

Thereafter, entrants into Northamptonshire remained consistently at a very low level, due partly to the isolation of the county,
remote from any major wealth-producing city, and partly to the

FIG. 6.1   Entrants into the Sample [Table 6.1]

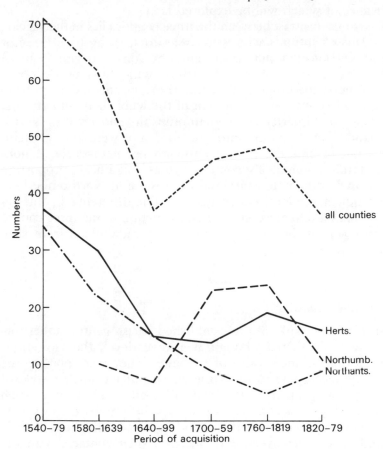

entrenched conservatism of its established elite. After 1700 there was on an average never more than one entrant every five years. In Hertfordshire, however, which was exposed to a persistent flood of rich newcomers, some of them Londoners and others magnates from further afield seeking a residence near the Court and Parliament, the proportion of entrants remained high, rising to a peak in the period 1760 to 1820 when there was a rush of transient purchaser-sellers.

In the eighteenth century, Northumberland was far more open to entrants than the two southern counties. It was then still in an active period of squirearchy formation, having missed out on the great 1540-1640 boom because of its physical insecurity and economic backwardness. More surprising is the fact that in Hertfordshire, and more specially in Northumberland, there was a sharp decline in the number of entrants during the Victorian period, the significance of which will be explored later.

The greatest contrast between the three counties lies in the varying proportions of entrants who were inheritors, going back three or more generations, or purchasers and the sons and grandsons of purchasers (Table 6.1). In Hertfordshire, which was most exposed to newcomers, the proportion of inheritor-entrants rising up from the local gentry was only 7 per cent of the whole body of entrants, whereas it was a quarter in Northamptonshire and a half in Northumberland. Thus entrants into Hertfordshire were almost exclusively from outside the county although not necessarily of non-gentry status or source of income, whereas a significant proportion of those in Northamptonshire and even more in Northumberland rose up out of the local parish gentry. The difference in this respect signifies a difference in the basic structure of the three county elites in terms of their relative openness to new blood from elsewhere.

ii. Types

a. Inheritor-Entrants

Drawn from the ranks of the established parish gentry, inheritor-entrants already shared, though at a lower level, the aspirations for office, status, and wealth of the elite. They were playing the same game, according to the same rules, but for smaller stakes.[1] Climbing slowly up from the ruck of small parish gentry, such families bit by bit accumulated property by purchase and inheritance; they improved their flocks and herds and the yield of their soil; and they never overspent. Socially, their contacts with the world outside their own class and county were minimal. This does not mean, however, that they were exclusively 'mere gentry', with no non-landed injections of wealth. A younger son, who had been bred to the law or apprenticed to a merchant and was reasonably successful in his calling, might on the death of his elder brother inherit the family estate and invest his profits in the acquisition of further land; an heir might occasionally marry the daughter of a lawyer, an office-holder, or even very occasionally, a merchant. Over a hundred years or so, several such small accretions to the family fortune could combine to raise it from obscurity to relative affluence and hence eventually into the elite.

[1] L. Stone and J. C. Fawtier Stone, 'Country Houses and their Owners in Hertfordshire 1540-1879', in *The Dimensions of Quantitative Research in History*, ed. W. O. Aydelotte *et al.*, Princeton, 1972, pp. 98-9.

The member of the family who in the end made the decisive move was sometimes given the necessary final boost by marriage with an heiress or a windfall inheritance from a relative. He would then proceed to demonstrate his claim to elevated social status by enlarging the old manor house, and then expanding the scope and range of his hospitality. To be pricked as sheriff—the latest in a succession of more lowly local offices faithfully executed—might help to certify his arrival.

Membership of the elite carried with it the implication of 'port', as it was referred to in the sixteenth and seventeenth centuries. This meant the obligation to spend generously, even lavishly on occasion, as part of one's duty to society, in return for the privileges of wealth and membership of the ruling class. When and how a man should assume the port of a squire must have been for every putative entrant his most delicate and risky decision. Especially in the case of inheritor entrants from the parish gentry, it implied a radical break with the habits of frugality which had played an essential part in the family's upward climb, and it is surprising that only a trivial number seem to have miscalculated the financial consequences of their enhanced status and been forced to sell.

It would be hard to find a better example of the exclusively landed rising 'mere gentry' than the family of Danvers of Culworth, Northants.[2] The first Danvers who settled in the village in the early sixteenth century was the younger son of an old gentry family based elsewhere. He inherited the three manors in the village, amounting to about 1,500 acres; he married well, to a daughter of the Fiennes of Broughton Castle; and took advantage of the Dissolution of the Monasteries to buy from the Crown the rectory and advowson of Culworth, which completed his stranglehold on the village. Probably in about 1550 he built himself a smallish manor-house on the site of an older medieval hall, and then set about improving his estate in the usual ruthless sixteenth-century manner. As lay rector, he was responsible for the upkeep of the chancel of the church, and when the aisle of the chancel fell into decay, he simply pulled it down to save himself the cost of repairs. That was annoying enough to the villagers, but he compounded their grievances by enclosing some of the common fields for his own use, for which they sued him. He may have had Puritan inclinations, for he named his four daughters Justice, Temperance, Prudence, and Fortitude. He presumably admired all four virtues

[2] F. N. MacNamara, *Memorials of the Danvers Family*, London, 1895, pp. 306-8, 335-6, 346-62, 471-81.

and may well have practiced three, but the first appears from the record to have eluded him.

His son succeeded him in the late sixteenth century, and continued to live the same quiet frugal life of a parish gentleman, adding yet another nearby manor to the family patrimony by purchase in the late 1580s. His heir died within four years of succeeding, and was himself succeeded by his younger brother John, with whom the Danvers enter the sample. In 1609 John further advanced the work of enclosing the village, taking in for himself more of the common fields. The villagers protested and sued once more, but John bought them off with a donation of £100 for relief of the village poor, and safeguarded himself by obtaining—presumably for a fee—a royal pardon under the great seal for his illegal actions. Displaying characteristic Danvers parsimony and calculation, he bought himself a knighthood at the very bottom of the market in 1624 when they were being sold wholesale by the Duke of Buckingham and his cronies, for a mere £100 each.[3] Emboldened by this advancement in rank, he served as sheriff in 1627, not a good year to do so since the Crown was still busy raising an illegal forced loan in the face of considerable gentry opposition. About this time he modestly enlarged his house and thus entered the sample.

Sir John died in 1642, leaving his son Samuel to steer the family through the perils of the Civil War. Already in 1640 Samuel had defied the king and refused to pay coat and conduct money to send a soldier to fight the Scots, for which he spent three months in confinement. Although his younger brother took an army commission under the king, Samuel seems thereafter to have equivocated. In 1643 he followed the family tradition and bought a baronetcy, once more at the bottom of the market when Charles I was selling them fairly freely to raise money for the war. But this royalism did not last, for in 1649 he was pricked for sheriff of the county (although legend has it that he rode to the Assizes dressed all in black in mourning for the execution of the king). He certainly escaped having to compound for royalist delinquency, and must somehow have managed to stay on the winning side, which no doubt is where he intended to be. But Northamptonshire was a border area that saw a lot of fighting, and his equivocation did not prevent his manor house from being damaged by a raiding party from one side or the other. He therefore bought another manor with a small house upon it, and retired there for a time to

---

[3] L. Stone, *The Crisis of the Aristocracy 1558-1641*, p. 80.

recuperate. He dutifully supported the Restoration, and was appointed Deputy Lieutenant for his pains, dying at last in 1683.

He was succeeded by his son Sir Pope Danvers who died in
1712. His one claim to notoriety had occurred in 1678, when he
engaged in a heavy drinking contest with a friend in an alehouse,
challenging him to drink two flagons of ale at one go. In his cups,
he claimed that his friend's flagons were not as full as his. When
his friend gave him the lie, they staggered outside and started
fighting one another with their bare hands. Next day, there was a
duel in the fields, in which Pope ran his friend through the body
and killed him. The coroner's inquest brought in a verdict of wil-
ful murder against him, but he escaped prosecution by obtaining,
presumably for money, a royal pardon.

It was Sir Pope's son Sir John, the 3rd baronet, who at last built
a new house suitable to his status and so brought the family into
the elite. He seems to have been as disagreeable as his ancestors,
quarrelling violently with the last two of his three wives. He died
in 1744, and was followed by two bachelor and therefore childless
sons, the second of whom left the estate of his sister. She was a
very pious lady, who gave away to the church most of the family
estate so carefully accumulated over generations of single-minded
acquisitiveness.

So ended the Danvers of Culworth. They were cautious, thrifty,
canny, and grasping, creeping slowly, generation after generation,
up the ladder of social and economic progress, and even at the end
only barely indulging in a life-style and housing suitable to their
dignity and income. They were an unlovable family, but their
history typifies the self-sustaining durability of a mere gentry family on the make, as it moved slowly up with almost no extraneous
aid from any quarter from a mere parish gentleman in a small and
unpretentious manor house to a baronet in a seat, however modest.

Nothing could be more different from the slow and cautious
strategy of the Danvers of Culworth than the enterprising and
risky gambles of the Smiths of Haughton Castle, Northumberland.[4] In 1642 two local men, Robert Smith and his brother, bought
for £2,500 from Sir William Widdrington the thirteenth- and four-
teenth-century castle and the estates that went with it. The old
castle was far too big for the relatively impoverished Smiths to
handle, so they lived in a small part of the old *camera* and let the

[4] *Northumberland County History*, xv, pp. 207-14.

great hall fall into decay. By 1715 the castle was described as 'something ruinous'.

To improve their finances, the Smiths turned to business. William Smith, who died in 1795, spent his life as a sea captain but did not make much out of it. It was his son William, also a sea captain, who at last put the family fortunes on a firm footing. He seems to have led an adventurous life at sea, for he was known in the family as 'the Buccaneer'. In 1788 he withdrew from the sea, and used the profits from his dubious activities to build a paper-mill near the castle, which at first he directly managed himself. The mill prospered, making, amongst other things, forged assignats to help depreciate the currency of France's revolutionary government. William used his profits to carry out a modest modernization of the more habitable parts of the castle, but it was only in 1816 that the income from the paper-mill was large enough to enable the Smiths to convert the old castle into an up-to-date gentleman's seat, and so hoist themselves up into the ranks of the local elite. They did the job on a grand scale, shifting the entrance, remodelling the interior, and building a castellated terrace overlooking the river. They also enclosed the large park, which involved diverting the road and moving the whole of the village. Thanks to the buccaneer's paper-mill, the Smiths had finally arrived. Even so, it was not until 1845 that they finally reoccupied and renovated the whole of the medieval castle they had so rashly bought two centuries before.

The Crasters of Craster, Northumberland, provide an example of an intermediary type of small gentry family, who worked their way up neither by exploitation of land like the Danvers, nor by entrepreneurial activities like the Smiths, but by combining land management with the fruits of respectable professional occupations.[5] The Crasters had been living at Craster Tower since before 1415, and they passed the inheritance down, sometimes through remote affines, into the twentieth century. Craster Tower began as a tiny medieval fortified place, with only four hearths according to the 1665 Hearth Tax. By 1675 Edmund Craster had added a small house to the tower, so as to bring it up to eight hearths, and he served as sheriff in 1683. But all this activity was too much for him, especially at a time of depressed rents, and he over-extended his resources in the process and had to retrench. In 1688 he let the tower rent-free for twenty-one years in return for the paying-

[5] Op. cit., ii, pp. 177-80; W. Hutchinson, *A View of Northumberland*, Newcastle, 1778, ii, p. 192.

off of his debts incurred as sheriff, and withdrew to live in Durham. His son and grandson never lived in the house at all, and it was let to tenants, being described in 1757 as ruinous. Meanwhile, the Crasters set out to recoup their fortunes by other means than as landed gentry. John, who was the head of the family from 1722 to 1764, made a career as a London lawyer, becoming a bencher of Gray's Inn and MP for Weobley in far-off Herefordshire. There is nothing to suggest that he did anything more than draw rents from Craster Tower and its estate. His heir George was a professional officer in the Grenadier Guards, but he retired to Craster and there built himself 'a neat little mansion', as it was described in 1778. An initial attempt to live in the appropriate style on the land alone had brought disaster a century before, but now at long last the Crasters just qualified themselves to enter the elite, thanks to profits drawn from the law and the army.

b. Purchaser- and Near-Purchaser-Entrants

The second group of entrants derived their wealth not from slow accumulation of land, with occasional help from elsewhere, but entirely from the profits of law, office, or business. They used these profits to put together an estate, perhaps with a small parish gentry house upon it, and built or rebuilt a large seat, an operation which could take anything from one generation (purchaser-entrants) to two or three (near-purchaser-entrants). Both shared certain features with inheritor-entrants, *qua* entrants, and with purchasers of houses already in sample, *qua* purchasers. To the extent that they perceived themselves as entrants, they were staking a claim to status. Those who merely purchased a house of suitable size whose previous owner had failed (or not tried) to make his mark, were not so very different from those who bought a seat from an owner in sample. On the other hand, those who enlarged a more modest house and/or estate were closer in some ways to inheritor-entrants, in as much as they brought to fruition their immediate forebears' efforts. But when the whole enterprise was started from scratch, from the acquisition of scattered fragments of land through their consolidation into a compact estate, to the erection of a new seat on virgin soil with all that that entailed, it represented a conscious departure from precedent, an accumulation that among inheritors was customarily spread over several generations being squeezed into a few years.

Some examples will serve to chart the acquisitive process from initial investment to rise into the sample. The sixteenth century was the period when the longest time was likely to elapse between the former event and the latter. This was largely due to the glut of church property put on the market at the time of the Dissolution of the Monasteries. There were clearly many who bought land then while the buying was good, and had to wait until they had accumulated more funds before building. Some were merely speculators who later sold to others at a profit. Some may have been thwarted in their social ambitions, some must have feared a restoration of Catholicism and a loss of their lands; others just took their time.

Thomas Fanshawe was a purchaser-entrant in the sixteenth century, who broke into the elite in a single generation. Thomas was the second of four generations of Fanshawes—originally gentry from Derbyshire—who nepotically succeeded each other in the lucrative financial office of Queen's Remembrancer in the Exchequer. In about 1570 he used his accumulated official profits to buy Ware Park, Herts, which had been a royal manor and no doubt was obtained at a very low price, since he was both agent for the seller (the Queen) and also the buyer. He took his time, and only in the late 1580s built himself a substantial house in the park, and so entered the sample. Interestingly enough, it was the Fanshawe's close connection with government which in the end was their undoing, for the third Fanshawe in office ruined himself in the royal cause during the Civil War. He received a viscountcy for his pains after the Restoration in 1661, but his son was obliged to sell Ware Park in 1668, only three years after inheriting it. This is one of several cases of ruin because of allegiance to the king during the Interregnum.

The Hydes provide a simple example of a near-purchaser entrant. Between 1542 and 1544 John Hyde, a minor office-holder in royal service, bought the dispersed fragments of the manor of Aldbury, Herts., of which he already held the lease. He died in 1545, and it was his heir Thomas, an office-holder like his father, who built a substantial manor-house in the 1560s and thus qualified for entry into the sample.

In one rare seventeenth-century case it is possible to observe a more complicated acquisitive process from its inception, by the piecemeal acquisition of dispersed fragments of property, through the process of consolidation, to the building of not one but two seats on newly formed estates. Joshua Lomax was born in Bolton, Lancs., early in the seventeenth century, became an attorney, and settled in St Albans, Herts., where during the Interregnum and early years of the Restoration, he 'dealt much in buying and selling of lands, by which . . . [he] obtained a fair estate'. Lomax was 'always accounted a friend and assistant to the fanatical party' and originally did his buying and selling in conjunction with a local Presbyterian attorney.[6] Between 1664 and 1674 Lomax bought and then resold three manors, one half-manor, and one rectory, besides buying and keeping four manors, so that he was clearly speculating heavily in real estate. On the largest of the properties, a 900-acre estate at Childwickbury near St Albans, he built himself a substantial seat, the original restrained elegance of which is still attested to by the old stable block, and qualified himself for entry into the sample. When he died in 1686, he left Childwickbury and the bulk of the surrounding property to his heir Joshua. He also left another smaller estate, made up of lands he had acquired around Bovingdon across the valley, to his younger son Thomas, for whom he built a smaller house at Westbrook Hay. Both sons were bred to the law, but only Thomas appears to have practised it. His heiress married a nonconformist London merchant, and their descendants numbered several distinguished lawyers and politicians, one of whom acquired a barony in 1776. Westbrook Hay, which remains in the hands of a cadet branch to this day, was suitably enlarged in the nineteenth century.

The story illustrates the ambivalence of some of these self-made men towards the value system of the world they sought—in this case successfully—to penetrate. On the one hand, there is the strong whiff of puritanical non-conformity about the first purchaser, Joshua, as well as a denial of primogeniture in the division of his inheritance, and the similar education in preparation for professional careers he gave to both his sons. On the other hand, he displayed social aspirations by serving as sheriff, and hiring Grinling Gibbons to decorate Childwickbury. His sons served as JPs and MPs and his great-grandsons attended Eton.

Joshua Lomax started assembling his estates and building his two houses at a relatively early age, but most purchasers did not have the capital for such investments until near the end of their careers. For them the problem was that the odds against the builder living to enjoy residing in his completed seat were high.

As it was pointed out in about 1680: 'A man must be twenty or thirty years in raising a fortune: the business is hardly done till he be growing up to sixty; when he is an old man he begins to build a fine house, and just when he finishes it, drops away'. A century later, Lord Torrington independently came to the same conclusion. 'Men do not make their fortunes before they are fifty years of age, when they are harassed and worn out; and then should buy

[6] H. Chauncy, *The Historical Antiquities of Hertfordshire*, London, 1700, p. 536; *Historical Manuscripts Commission, Verulam MSS*, p. 102.

a place ready cut and dried. Now my grandfather admiral and my uncle admiral would, from folly and pride, rear places, and they both died ere they were finished'.[7] This explains why so many newcomers were eager to buy existing seats in order to have time to enjoy some of the fruits of their labours before they died. But such a seat was not always available on the market, or its price was too high, in which case the prospective purchaser was obliged to buy a smaller parish gentry house and enlarge it to suit his new station. In at least one case it is possible to follow the fortunes of such a seat making its way slowly through the market in search of a buyer rich enough to transform it into a seat worthy of a member of the elite.

In the early sixteenth century, John More, Justice of the Common Pleas and father of Sir Thomas, built himself a small house at Gubbins in South Hertfordshire. On Sir Thomas's attainder it reverted to the Crown and it was not till the seventeenth century that it came back to his great-grandson Cressacre More who enlarged it slightly and died in 1640. The house was still no more than a modest parish gentry manor-house and in 1693 Cressacre's grandson Basil, who had ruined himself in the royalist cause, was obliged to sell to a French Huguenot Turkey merchant, Sir Edward Desbouveries. It is possible that the sale represented the foreclosure of a mortgage. Sir Edward's main country base was in Kent, but he seems to have summered in Hertfordshire, where the year before he had purchased from the Earl of Salisbury the old seat of the Dacres at Cheshunt Great House, which he sold again in 1694. After his death in 1695 his son William seems to have used Gubbins briefly as a suburban retreat, but sold it in 1697 to Robert Beachcroft, a London cloth merchant and a packer at Blackwell Hall. Beachcroft was knighted in 1700, became Lord Mayor of London in 1711, dabbled in the South Sea Bubble, and at some point before his death without heirs in 1721, hired Bridgman to lay out an elaborate set of formal gardens around the old manor-house. On his death the house was sold to Jeremiah Sambrooke, the younger brother of a recent Kentish baronet, and a man with City connections. He had James Gibbs enlarge and modernize the house, thus completing the scheme begun by Beachcroft when he laid out the gardens ten or fifteen years before. It thus took a succession of two ambitious purchasers to complete the construction of seat and grounds at Gubbins on a suitably grandiose scale.

[7] The first reference is mislaid; J. Byng, *The Torrington Diaries*, London, 1934-8, iii, pp. 318-19.

Ayot House, Herts., had a similar history. It began as a small Elizabethan house which for 150 years remained unaltered in the hands of the same obscure family. Modestly enlarged in the early years of the eighteenth century, in 1723 it was bought by a merchant of Bristol, on whose death in 1747 it descended to his two daughters and coheiresses. In the same year the eldest married her cousin Lionel Lyde, who bought out his sister-in-law's share. He was 'an eminent tobacco merchant', the eldest son, by his second marriage to an heiress, of a Virginia merchant and former Mayor of Bristol. In 1765 Lionel doubled the size and modernized the interior of the house, building a dining-room decorated in the Adam style. In 1778 he used his wealth and demonstrated his good taste by building an exquisite little avant-garde Greek Revival Chapel in the park. He remained active in business, and ended as a baronet and Governor of the Bank of England. He was thus a social hybrid, a cultivated elite squire banker, and his descendants (still bearing his name, but only because of two name-changes) were still living in the house in the early twentieth century.

By contrast to these successful purchaser- and near-purchaser-entrants into the elite, one may look at one last family, who lacked both similar aspirations to social climbing and the resources to bring it off. John Wilby was a wirepuller, who made a lot of money from the monopoly of gold braid for epaulettes during the Napoleonic Wars. He and his wife personally ran and expanded their shop in the East End of London, and in due course they bought an unmodernized Elizabethan gentry house on the outskirts of Bishop's Stortford. Their son and grandson lived lives of leisure mainly in London, devoting their time to charitable pursuits and the collection of stuffed birds.[8] The Wilbys thus exemplify an upwardly mobile family whose heirs adopted a genteel style of life, but who remained London-based and never attempted to break into county society.

3. PURCHASERS' AND PURCHASER-ENTRANTS' SOURCES OF PERSONAL WEALTH

To analyse the sources of wealth of newcomers, purchasers of existing seats in sample and purchaser-entrants must be examined together, to provide a comprehensive profile of all those who entered the sample in their own lifetime by purchase. They represent the quintessential new men, who gained access to member-

---

[8] [F. Skeet], *History of the Families of Skeet, Somerscales, Widdrington, Wilby, Murray, Blake, Grimshaw and Others*, privately printed, 1906.

ship of the county elite by the use of their wealth. How did they acquire it?

The purchase of a landed estate and the enlargement or refurbishing of a country house could only be undertaken if backed by substantial capital. Furthermore, the maintenance of such an establishment and the way of life that it implied both involved considerable annual expenditure. If the agricultural estate was large and in good running order, the seat might financially be largely self-supporting, at least in the long run. But the chances were that the initial costs would be high, especially if the seller had been in financial difficulties for some time before selling, and the house and estate needed extensive renovations. Because of the costs involved, there were only a limited number of fields of activity in the pursuit of which a man might hope to make a fortune sufficient for him to be able to crown his career by establishing himself as a member of a county elite.

The first step is to examine the sources of personal wealth of purchasers and purchaser-entrants (Table 6.2). This is to some extent an artificial exercise, since close examination shows that many purchasers derived their wealth from a variety of sources, accumulated over more than one generation. For the moment, however, only the wealth of the purchaser himself is under analysis.

As one would expect, the three counties differ widely in their newcomers' sources of personal wealth. In Hertfordshire, land and nothing else supplied less than one-third, compared with nearly one-half in the other two counties. Office-holders were quite prominent in the two southern counties, but hardly at all in Northumberland, which missed out on the great dispersal of Church and Crown lands to government officials in the sixteenth century. All three counties had their fair quota of lawyers. The principal contrast is in the role of the monied interest, or business. This supplied the wealth of 40 per cent of all newcomers in Hertfordshire, 24 per cent in Northumberland, and 14 per cent in Northamptonshire. Propinquity to a centre of business in the first case London, and in the second case Newcastle and the coal-mining areas, was clearly crucial.

i. Landed Sources

a. Parish Gentry

Land was always an important source of personal wealth for purchasers, some 30 per cent to 45 per cent of whom were themselves gentry.

The requirements for successful upward mobility among the

mere gentry are now familiar: just the right number of children to carry on the line, but not too many to be burdensome to educate, marry, or launch on a career; the fortunate extinction of collateral branches which allowed entailed property to return to the main trunk; enforced saving through a long minority; the speedy demise of a succession of widows soon after the deaths of their husbands, which avoided the burden of long jointures. Surprisingly few of these gentry purchasers and purchaser-entrants had become rich by the time-honoured way of marriage. In Northamptonshire, twelve purchasers had either themselves or through their fathers acquired a landed estate by marriage, and three of them had increased their fortunes by marriage to merchant heiresses.

Even so, luck was not everything and long-term economic factors and shrewdness in exploiting them both played an important part. The favourable periods for landlords were those of agricultural prosperity when food prices, and therefore rents, were rising rapidly. Landed newcomers in all three counties were thus most common in the boom period 1580 to 1639 and again in the second boom period after 1760 (Table 6.2). The post-Waterloo agricultural depression does not seem to have had much effect, for reasons which are not at all clear. In Northamptonshire, it is possible that the development of fox-hunting at this period, bringing as it did considerable employment and prosperity to this area, including opportunities of letting surplus minor seats as hunting-boxes, may have contributed to muting the effects of agricultural depression upon the local landlords.

b. Magnates

In addition to these newcomers from the rising parish gentry, there is a small but special group of purchasers operating in the period 1720 to 1820 in Hertfordshire and Northamptonshire. They were local magnates, leading members of the county elite, who were actively buying up the houses of their neighbours in order to consolidate or enlarge the property around their own seats. In Northamptonshire, Newton-in-the-Willows was bought in 1715 by the Duke of Montagu, Upton Manor house in 1750 by Earl Fitzwilliam, Easton Maudit in 1799 by the Earl of Northampton. In all three cases the purpose was to round off the estates of the purchaser, and all three seats were therefore shortly thereafter pulled down or allowed to decay into farmhouses. That this behaviour was typical of one period rather than another is shown by the different treatment meted out by the Spencers of Althorp to Steane manor-house, which they bought in 1774 and largely pulled down, and Harlestone House, which they bought in 1831 and then let.

In both cases, the houses were lost to the sample, but the period of wholesale destruction was largely confined to the century between 1720 and 1820. Thereafter, these old sixteenth- and early seventeenth-century houses became quite fashionable again, which insured their preservation.

A classic example of consolidation for the purpose of aggrandizement, leading to the total obliteration of earlier seats, is provided by Peter 5th Earl Cowper, who, on the unexpected death in 1799 of his elder brother, suddenly found himself at the age of twenty-one the master of a large estate. Capital had accumulated over a long period, thanks to two marriages with wealthy heiresses whose large dowries had to be invested in land according to the marriage contracts. Large-scale land purchases had begun in 1785, while more recently the estate had been administered by trustees, first during the last years of Earl Peter's father, which had been spent abroad, and then during his brother's minority. They had invested the surplus money in land purchase to round out and expand the estate originally established by his great-grandfather, the 1st Earl, around the seat the latter had built himself in 1710 at Cole Green, on the southern flank of the Mimram valley. These purchases included the old Tudor mansion of Digswell, and the more modest Elizabethan manor house of Panshanger, directly across the river from Cole Green. In 1804 Earl Peter rounded out the collection by acquiring Tewin House from the son of a wealthy furrier, Charles Schreiber, who had acquired it and lived there during the last decade of the eighteenth century. (The house dated back to the early seventeenth century, but had been enlarged in the 1690s, and completely redecorated inside and out in the Baroque manner some twenty-five years later by one of Marlborough's generals, Joseph Sabine.) With the exception of the seat and estate of Marden Hill, which somehow eluded him, Earl Peter now owned the whole sweep of the Mimram valley, which he proceeded to redesign on a grand scale with the advice of the great landscape gardener, Repton. They decided to abandon Cole Green, which had suffered from not being lived in for many years and in any case was aligned East-West and thus faced the wrong way, and instead to build a large new seat in the fashionable Gothic style at Panshanger, where it would have a commanding view over the whole newly landscaped valley.[9] (Plate XVB and Plan 1.) With

[9] L. Stone, 'Cole Green Park, Hertfordshire', in *The Country Seat*, ed. H. M. Colvin and J. Harris, London, 1970; J. Brushe, 'Further Light on Cole Green House', *Architectural History*, 24, 1981, p. 57; I owe much of this information about the Cowpers to Dr Christopher Clay.

this object in mind, they proceeded to pull down first Panshanger in order to clear the ground for the new house, then Cole Green, Tewin House, and Digswell to open up the view from the terrace and enlarge the park. Some years later an elegant villa was built at Digswell as a secondary seat for a younger brother, but Cole Green and Tewin House vanished without trace, barely a century after they were built.

Almost as destructive of seats were the activities of James Cecil, 7th Earl and 1st Marquess of Salisbury, who succeeded his father at the age of thirty-two in 1780. Over the next forty years he ruthlessly enlarged the already very large park at Hatfield through the annexation and destruction of two of his own secondary seats, and the purchase and destruction of a third. Quixwood, a secondary seat which had been in the family since 1618, was the first to be pulled down and have its park annexed. In 1792 he bought and destroyed Hatfield Woodhall, the ancient seat of a cadet branch of the Botelers of Watton Woodhall. Then in 1817 he recovered control of Popes, which had been out on a ninety-nine year lease, and which he now destroyed to expand the size of Hatfield Park.

ii. Non-Landed Sources

The principal means of acquiring great wealth leading to swift upward mobility varied strikingly over time. Office-holding predominated in the sixteenth and early seventeenth century, legal office in the early eighteenth century, the army and navy in times of war after the end of the seventeenth century. Overseas trade was important at all periods before the nineteenth century, brewing from the late seventeenth century, Indian administration and banking from the eighteenth century, and big business from the mid-nineteenth century (Table 6.2).

These variations require both illustration and explanation. Before 1579 nearly half of all purchasers in Hertfordshire and Northamptonshire were government officials and courtiers, the recipients of Crown grants of ex-Church lands, and beneficiaries either of the rampant corruption of the 1540s and 1550s or of the favour of Queen Elizabeth. Many of these officials were great political figures who instantly became some of the most prominent and influential notables in the county. In Northamptonshire, there were men like Sir Walter Mildmay, Chancellor of the Exchequer, who was given Apethorpe, or Sir Christopher Hatton, Courtier and Lord Chancellor, who built Holdenby and enlarged Kirby Hall, or smaller fry like Sir Miles Fleetwood, Receiver of the Court of Wards, who bought Aldwinkle.

In Hertfordshire there were men like Sir Anthony Denny, Privy Councillor and favourite of Henry VIII, who was showered with gifts, including no fewer than three houses in Hertfordshire, Bedwell Park, Camfield Place, and Cheshunt Nunnery. Henry Carey, later Lord Hunsdon, Queen Elizabeth's first cousin on the Boleyn side and Lord Chamberlain of the Household, was given the old royal palace at Hunsdon in 1559. Lord Burghley, the Lord Treasurer, acquired Theobalds and built a prodigy house upon it which surpassed in size even the one he had already built at Burghley House on the Church lands his father had acquired in his native Northamptonshire. Sir Philip Boteler of Watton Woodhall was a local magnate who was also Receiver-General of the Duchy of Lancaster, which explains how he was able to buy Sacombe for his second son in 1593. There were also mere courtiers like Sir Edward Cary, who was granted the lease of Berkhamstead Place, which he rebuilt, before purchasing Aldenham Manor House, which he also rebuilt; or Sir William Harrington who was granted Hertford Castle and Hertingfordbury by Charles I, also both rebuilt.

By 1640, in both Northamptonshire and Hertfordshire, a number of these courtiers and office-holders, such as the two Cecils at Burghley and Hatfield, and the Comptons at Castle Ashby, had firmly established great county families of peerage rank, which have endured until the present day. After 1640, however, the numbers of office-holders among purchasers dropped off sharply. With the exception of four diplomats in the eighteenth century and two overseas administrators in the nineteenth, the only post-1700 office-holding purchaser was John Rooper, who purchased the lease of Berkhamstead Place, in 1720. The last such purchaser-entrant of any note was Henry Guy, for whom Sir Christopher Wren built Tring, on land obtained by royal favour, in order that he might entertain William III in it. He was the last office-holder in the three counties to be able to rise to such heights.

The reasons for this sharp decline in purchases of seats by rich office-holders are not hard to find. By 1630, the Crown had largely dissipated the huge windfall of Church lands which had fallen into its hands a century before, and it had little more to give away. Corruption, having reached a peak from 1540 to 1553 and again from 1590 to 1630, thereafter declined, which severely reduced the profits of office. After the Restoration, election costs grew more and more expensive, which raised the overheads of political office, while the growth of political parties and the cabinet, and the transfer of financial control from Crown to Parliament, shifted the focus of power. Walpole was the last leading minister of the Crown

to make a fortune out of politics, and the Duke of Newcastle actually ended up poorer for a lifetime of high governmental office.

The decline in civilian office-holders was in some small part
compensated for by the rise of admirals and generals. War had
brought small pickings to senior officers in the sixteenth and seventeenth centuries—which anyway was not a glorious period for
English military forces—and it was only the wars of Louis XIV
which again made the fortune of well-placed admirals and generals. The navy was particularly lucrative, due to the profits of prize-
money. In Hertfordshire Admiral Sir David Mitchell bought the
lease of Popes in 1700, Rear-Admiral Sir John Jennings bought
Newsells in 1726, Admiral Lord Anson bought Moor Park in 1740,
Admiral Viscount Howe bought Porters in 1772, and Sir Charles
Pole bought Aldenham Abbey in 1812. Among army officers, Ma-
jor-General Joseph Sabine bought and rebuilt Tewin House in
1715, the loyalist American general Cornelius Cuyler, later Sir
Cornelius Cuyler, Bt., bought and enlarged St John's Lodge (later
Danesbury) in 1794, and General Sir David Baird bought Ardeleybury in 1810. On the other hand, three of these Hertfordshire-
based naval and military purchasers were also sellers, two of them
for lack of heirs.

Rewards from the law have always been very unevenly distributed, and in the sixteenth and seventeenth centuries in particular
it was mainly holders of the major legal offices who were purchasers. One example of a successful Elizabethan lawyer is Sir
John Brograve, who for thirty-three years till his death in 1613
served as Attorney-General of the Duchy of Lancaster. During
this time, 'he bought several parcels of land of divers men which
lay contiguous together and built a neat and uniform pile of brick,
near a pleasant grove, with four turrets in the four corners thereof
which do adorn the house, situated upon a dry hill where is a
pleasant prospect to the East'. To judge by the looks of the house,
Hamels was built fairly early on in his career, though no doubt
he went on enlarging the estate as opportunity offered and more
capital accumulated. The family endured at Hamels for over a
century, rose to a baronetcy in 1662, but crashed and had to sell
all in 1712 to pay off extravagant debts run up by the third baronet, described as 'a poor silly man'. He had been a younger son,
who in sixteen years of reckless dissipation managed to destroy his
inheritance.[10] He provides, therefore, one of the rare examples of

[10] H. Chauncy, op. cit., p. 226; G. E. Cokayne, *Complete Baronetage*, iii, London, 1909,
p. 272.

ruin by an indirect inheritor, and indeed of financial collapse of any major elite family.

In the late sixteenth and early seventeenth century both in Northamptonshire and in Hertfordshire, there were several legal office-holders who founded long-lasting families. In Northamptonshire Sir Edward Montagu, successively Chief Justice of the King's Bench and of the Common Pleas, bought Boughton House; his grandson Henry, Earl of Manchester, Chief Justice of the King's Bench was seated at Horton; and Sir Christopher Yelverton, Justice of the Queen's Bench, bought Easton Maudit and vastly enlarged it. In Hertfordshire Lord Ellesmere, Lord Keeper, purchased the old monastery of Ashridge in 1605 which he, and his son after him, turned into one of the largest seats in the county. There was also Sir Charles Caesar, whose father Sir Julius, Master of the Rolls, bought him first Bennington Place and later the Mastership of the Rolls; and Sir Harbottle Grimston, the Speaker of the House, who bought Gorhambury, the old palace first bought and built by Lord Keeper Sir Nicholas Bacon and further enlarged by his son the Lord Chancellor. The 1st Earl Cowper, Lord Keeper, purchased and built Cole Green in 1701-4; John 1st Lord Somers, Lord Chancellor, bought Brookmans in 1701.

By the early eighteenth century the number of lawyers buying seats reached their peak, forming a third of all purchasers in all three counties though the scale of their purchases was on the whole more modest. The reason for this peak seems to be that by now lawyers who did not rise to high legal office sometimes made sufficient money in legal practice to establish themselves as country gentlemen. Such a one was Joshua Lomax whose career has already been described. Matthew Lamb operated on a loftier social level but made much the same use of his opportunities in legal practice. The younger son of a North Country attorney, he became legal advisor to the Cokes of Melbourne Hall, one of whom he eventually married. In 1734, at the age of thirty-one, he inherited a fortune from an uncle who had been a successful barrister. He 'extended his business' to include advice to Lords Salisbury and Egmont, entered Parliament soon after his marriage, and in 1746 purchased the seat of Brocket Hall, Herts., from an old family that had died out. Five years later his wife unexpectedly inherited Melbourne Hall on her brother's death and in 1755 he was made a baronet. In 1760 he hired James Paine to pull down Brocket Hall and rebuild it. In 1768 he died 'leaving property estimated at nearly half-a-million, besides half a million in ready money'.[11] His

[11] *Dictionary of National Biography*, *sub* Matthew Lamb.

son Peniston Lamb (named after the barrister uncle) was created Viscount Melbourne, whose son William was Queen Victoria's Prime Minister. It is careers like this which may explain why, despite the fact that the number of barristers was declining in the mid-eighteenth century, lawyers were then at the peak of their success as purchasers of seats and landed estates.[12]

For reasons which are not at all clear the number of lawyer purchasers dropped off in the nineteenth century, and there were only eight in all three counties for the period 1820-79, down from a high of thirty-one in 1700-59 (Table 6.2c). It is possible that as towns became more salubrious, lawyers chose to settle where they worked. Instead of playing a relatively minor role in the country, they became leading members of a sophisticated and cultivated urban society, especially in London.

Before 1640, the only business men to join the sample were overseas merchants, a majority of them members of the great London trading companies. The process of assimilation into the elite tended to be gradual, often spread over more than one generation. A good example is the slow rise of the Garrards of Lamer, in Hertfordshire. Sir William Garrard of Dorney, Bucks., Haberdasher and Lord Mayor of London, bought Lamer in 1555 and built himself a house there, which he presumably used in the summer when London was most unhealthy. On his death in 1571 he left it to his third son John who followed in his footsteps, rising to Lord Mayor in 1601. His son and heir John was made a Justice of the Peace for Hertfordshire in 1621, a baronet in 1622 shortly before his father's death in 1625, and became sheriff and later Deputy-Lieutenant of the county. He was the first of the family to reside mainly at Lamer, to which he added a chapel in 1631, and to loosen the family ties with London, although he married the daughter of Sir Edward Barkham, later Lord Mayor of London.

An interesting example of the way these county families of mercantile origin maintained their links to the City through their younger sons is provided by Samuel Garrard, the younger brother of the 3rd baronet. Because of his elder brother's death without heirs, he succeeded to Lamer and the baronetcy in 1700, but these did not stop him from becoming Lord Mayor of London in 1710. The possibilities of part-time landowning in the Home Counties, while engaged in actively furthering a career in London, put both Surrey and Hertfordshire in a very special category. Many of these

---

[12] H. Phillips, *The Grandeur of the Law*, London, 1684; G. Holmes, *Augustan England: Professions, State and Society, 1680-1730*, London, 1982, ch. 5.

wealthy Londoners bought a house in the country nearby while still maintaining their City connections. Hardly any, however, bought a large landed estate to go with the house.

Other Company merchant purchasers before the Restoration numbered Sir William Leman, who bought Nyn House from the 4th Earl of Bedford in 1632, Sir Job Harby, Bt., who bought Aldenham Manor House from the Second Viscount Falkland in 1642, and John Ellis, a merchant tailor who bought some former Church property at St Julians near St Albans and built a house there in 1649. The first Levant Company merchants to purchase a Hertfordshire seat were the Freeman brothers, who bought the modest parish gentry house of Aspenden in 1608 and considerably enlarged and embellished it subsequently. (Endpaper.) They were soon joined by Henry Coghill, who purchased the lease of Penn's Place at Aldenham in 1626, which he later bought outright, Francis Floyer who bought Brent Pelham in 1627, Thomas (later Sir Thomas) Soame who bought nearby Throcking Park in 1631, and by Sir Thomas Keightley who bought Hertingfordbury. (Plate VIB.) All of these belonged either to the East India or the Levant Companies and with the exception of Coghill lived within easy reach of each other.

One gets the impression that groups of friends and business associates from a single company were buying seats so as to maintain in the countryside the same ties of sociability which they had formed in the City. Thus in the sixty years between 1760 and 1819 no fewer than eleven members of the East India Company (six of them Directors), bought seats in Hertfordshire. Perhaps the richest of them all was Thomas Rumbold, who in 1778 at the early age of forty-two bought for £85,000 Watton Woodhall, the large Elizabethan seat of the Botelers which had burned down seven years before, together with the whole estate. Rumbold had made his vast fortune in India between 1760, when he left military service under Clive to become a member of the Council in Bengal, Chief of Patna and Governor of Fort St George, and 1770 when he returned to England loaded with riches. In the next seven years he used his wealth to become an MP and marry the daughter of a bishop. In 1777 he returned once more to India as Governor of Madras, a post he held for the next three years. Foreseeing trouble, he prudently resigned in 1780 on the grounds of ill health, and returned to England with replenished coffers, allegedly the fruits of rampant corruption. He then proceeded to tear down the ruins of old Walton Woodhall and build himself a large new seat. His wealth enabled him to fight off a parliamentary investigation into his finances and administration in India, and he died a baronet in 1791. He was one of the more colorful newcomers in the late eighteenth century Hertfordshire, but he was only one of several.[13] Indeed Levant and East India Company merchants between them amounted to nearly half of all Hertfordshire merchant purchasers. This probably explains why, when in 1801 the East India Company decided to set up its own training school, it did so in Hertfordshire at Haileybury.

Other eighteenth-century nabobs came to Hertfordshire from the West Indies. Mention has already been made of Justinian Casamajor. Such another was James Gordon who in 1749 purchased Moor Place, a reasonably large late Elizabethan manor house which had changed hands seven times in the last 129 years. A former Chief Justice of St Kitts and a member of the Council of Antigua since 1741, he died childless in 1768, when the property descended to his nephew James Brebner, who took the name of Gordon. His career followed closely that of his uncle: he joined the Council of Antigua in 1761 and was Chief Justice of the Ceded Islands in 1767. It was his son James who, in his father's lifetime, pulled down the old house at Moor Place and had Robert Mitchell design an elegant new one which went up between 1776 and 1779. In about 1790 he secured his position in local society by marrying the only daughter and heiress of Samuel Whitbread Jun., the Bedfordshire and Hertfordshire squire, brewer, and Whig politician.

In the mid-seventeenth century overseas merchants were being joined by government contractors and the early members of the monied interest. Government contracting for the supply of goods for military forces in war-time has always been a lucrative, if shady, way to make a great deal of money. Contractors do not begin to enter the sample until the wars of the seventeenth century, eight of them appearing among purchasers thereafter (seven in Hertfordshire, one in Northumberland), starting with Sir John Harrison who bought and built Balls Park in 1640, and going on down to Commissary General Adolphus Murray, the purchaser and rebuilder of Ardleybury after the Napoleonic wars in 1820. Two extremely wealthy late eighteenth century government contractors were Lawrence Dundas, who bought Moor Park in 1763 out of the profits of the Seven Years War, and Paul Benfield, who bought Watton Woodhall from Sir Thomas Rumbold for £150,000 in 1794, also out of the profits of war.

The first monied men to enter the sample were scriveners, who

---

[13] Op. cit., *sub* Thomas Rumbold.

were then acting as primitive bankers. Such were Philip Holman, who purchased Warkworth Castle in Northamptonshire for £14,000 from the last of the Chetwodes in 1629, and Humphrey Shalcrosse who bought Digswell in Hertfordshire in about 1650. Among purchasers and/or builders of country houses in Hertfordshire, the first financiers to have made a fortune by lending to the government were Sir Jonathan Keate who built the Hoo in 1655 (Plate VIIB), the two brewer financiers, Sir William Bucknall who bought Oxhey Place in 1668 and Felix Calvert of Furneux Pelham Hall, as well as Sir John Shaw who purchased Cheshunt Great House in 1694. It is worth noting that these were very rich men who lived in appropriately opulent houses.

In Hertfordshire, the banker Jeremiah Snow bought and largely pulled down the large old courtyard house of Salisbury Hall and replaced it with a compact double pile. The South Sea Bubble also contributed to the fortunes of Sir Robert Beachcroft who bought Gubbins, Sir Benjamin Styles who bought and did over the Duke of Monmouth's house at Moor Park, and Robert Chester who bought and built Briggens. With the exception of Snow nearly a century before, it was not till the 1760s that bankers make their appearance on the Hertfordshire scene. In the next 120 years from 1760 to 1879, however, no fewer than twenty London bankers and one local banker bought country houses in Hertfordshire, and another two in Northamptonshire. Of these over half were buying or enlarging houses of over 100 units (five of them houses of 200 units and more).

For a long time the only manufacturers to force their way into any county elite were Hertfordshire brewers. The county had long been famous for its beer, allegedly because of the sweetness of its water. The industry was mainly centred around Ware, in the southeast of the county where it seems that a great deal of the barley for malting was grown. Brewing was a capital-intensive and very large-scale industry, perhaps the largest in the country except for coal-mining or ship-building, and the leading manufacturers, if they were both lucky and shrewd, could amass very large fortunes. The first brewers to buy themselves country seats in Hertfordshire were not Londoners but local brewers: Thomas Byde, who acquired Ware Park from the Fanshawes in 1668, John Plumer who bought Blakesware in 1683 and New Place for his second son in 1701, and Felix Calvert, the brewer turned financier who bought Albury Hall in 1675 and Furneux Pelham two years later. He later sold Albury to his first cousin, also a brewer of the same names, so that for the next 150 years there were two Calvert families in the sample, both deriving their income mainly from the family brewery. In 1743 Josiah Nicolson, a distiller from Clapham, bought Hunsdon House. His only daughter married a Calvert from Furneux Pelham, so in due course this family, who meanwhile had mainly lived in temporary residences on lease, became the Calverts of Hunsdon, which they rebuilt in 1805. In 1745 Benjamin Truman seems to have bought the lease of Popes, and when the old house burnt down the next year he rebuilt it most handsomely and laid out elaborate gardens which figure in the background of his portrait which hangs to this day in the brewery that bears his name. Soon afterwards, John Mason, a distiller of Greenwich and Deptford, purchased Porter's Park in Shenley. In 1751 Samuel Whitbread I, a London brewer from the neighbouring county of Bedfordshire, bought Bedwell Park and, some years later, Woolmers. In 1790 Sampson Hanbury built Poles, which had been bought for him when a minor. In 1820 Henry Meux, soon to become a baronet, purchased Theobalds, which he enlarged. This is another case of a local man settling in the county from which he sprang. The last brewer/distiller to enter the sample was Sir Charles Booth who purchased Netherfield House in 1844 and later rebuilt it. It is not clear whether these Hertfordshire brewers blazed a trail which was followed by others from less accommodating counties, or whether this was a common phenomenon in all counties where beer was brewed on an industrial scale.

What is clear, however, is that brewing was accepted as a perfectly respectable source of income among the landed elite of eighteenth- and nineteenth-century Hertfordshire. Whether it was acceptable as an actual occupation is more questionable. The genealogical table of the Hucks's (Gen. Chart 2) is instructive in this matter. Of three brothers, Thomas, the youngest one, was in charge of the actual running of the brewery, near which he lived in Southwark; Joseph, the middle brother, lived in Great Russell Street and was presumably in charge of distribution; and William, the elder brother lived in a seat at Clifton Hampden in Oxfordshire, was MP for Abingdon, and also member of the Brewers' Company. The various branches of the Calvert family, the Calverts of Albury, Hunsdon and Nine Ashes (the last not in sample) were similarly more or less closely connected with the actual process of manufacturing beer.

This grudging and partial social acceptance of brewers sets them apart from other manufacturers, who did not enter the sample by purchase until much later, and their numbers even then were surprisingly small. All told, they do not amount to more than twelve in all three counties, the earliest being an ironmaster from a neighbouring county who purchased Norton in Northamptonshire in 1800. But he was altogether unique. All the others bought after 1835, six in Hertfordshire and five in Northumberland. The latter were all local men involved in shipping, mining, and metallurgy. By contrast, in Hertfordshire only one paper manufacturer was a local man, the other five being from further afield, including two North Country textile manufacturers. These manufacturer purchasers were rich men who lived in style, and only four of them (three in Hertfordshire and one in Northumberland) lived in houses of under 100 units.

Even in a county like Hertfordshire, so close to London, the industrial revolution thus had minimal effects upon the composition of the county elite. Few manufacturers tried to enter, and three of them, all in Hertfordshire, soon sold again, whether for lack of interest or social ostracism we do not know.

This relative absence of manufacturers among the new rural elite in the nineteenth century was a nation-wide phenomenon. In the whole country in the forty years between 1840 and 1879, less than fifty self-made men worth half a million pounds and upwards died owning 2,000 acres of land or more. This represents only one-third of the new men who had acquired such gigantic riches, and these fifty were virtually invisible—a mere 1.5 per cent—among the 3,200 other landowners with property of this size. One has to conclude that before 1879, the majority of the very wealthy business men in England were either landless or owners of very small estates indeed. Less than 10 per cent of all major landowners in 1873 were newcomers since 1780, and only a tiny fraction of them were industrialists. Most of these millionaires did, however, either rent country seats or buy ones with small estates attached to them, so that the appearances are a little less devastating to received wisdom than they seem at first sight.[14] Wealthy manufacturers were present in the countryside in the Victorian period, but not as full and accepted participants in elite landed society, except perhaps in the north-west, where they were thickest on the ground.

There are many possible causes for this reticence on the part of new men of the Victorian age to put money into land and the status that went with it. Land was expensive and a very large-scale investment beyond the reach of all but the super-rich. Moreover

[14] W. D. Rubinstein, 'New Men of Wealth and the Purchase of Land in Nineteenth Century England', *Past and Present*, 92, 1981.

so much land was tied up in marriage settlements—one estimate is about two-thirds of England—that large compact estates were hard to find at a time when few older families were going to the wall and being forced to sell. More compelling, however, is the question of status. No amount of land purchase, no amount of house-building would confer social respectability upon a man whose wealth was obtained in sordid ways, whose origins were obscure, whose manners and accent were demonstrably vulgar, and whose religion might well be nonconformist. Only after 1880 did titles and seats in the House of Lords begin to be conferred in substantial numbers upon (mainly elderly and childless) low-born and landless manufacturers.[15] Between 1800 and 1880, therefore, there was an unprecedented disassociation between the world of modern industrial business and the world of land, at a time when the social connections between the latter and both the professional classes and the banking community seem to have been drawing ever closer. A nation-wide survey of prominent and well-documented Victorian country houses built or wholly rebuilt between 1835 and 1914 has produced evidence which supports this conclusion. The sample is admittedly an odd one, dependent as it is primarily upon descriptions in architectural journals and the preservation of a plan, and varying from prodigious palaces costing £200,000 or more to modest villas costing as little as £6,000. None the less, it probably covers a majority of the larger country-house buildings of the time as well as many small ones unsuitable for residence by the elite. For what it is worth, during the period 1835 to 1879 landed families were responsible for rather less than half of all these buildings. New men who had acquired their wealth in traditionally respectable careers as bankers, lawyers, and professionals, including such new professionals as publishers, stockbrokers, engineers, and even an eye surgeon and two artists, accounted for another third. Five per cent had made their fortunes in overseas trade, leaving a mere 17 per cent of the total, or twenty-seven men, who had risen to affluence as a result of the industrial revolution: wool, cotton, and alpaca manufacturers, railway and building contractors, South African gold-mining entrepreneurs, coal and iron magnates, heavy engineering company directors, even a wholesale grocer. But twenty-seven individuals, building their country seats scattered across the length and breadth of England over a forty-five year period, can hardly be regarded as an invading army of

[15] R. E. Pumphret, 'The Introduction of Industrialists into the British Peerage', *American Historical Review*, lxv, 1959.

vulgarian industrialists descending upon the countryside and displacing the old elite, or even the more traditional and respectable
forms of new wealth. Many of these houses were quite small, so
their owners were not even displacing the parish gentry.

The real change came quite suddenly after 1880, when new
industrialists began pushing down the class barriers. They began
at last to force their way into the peerage, high society, and the
county elite, and to build themselves country seats on a much
larger scale than ever before. Only after 1880 were there substantial numbers of men enriched in vulgar ways, now living in great
new country houses. There was 'the King of Nitrate', a travel
agent, a soap manufacturer, a wholesale druggist, a shipbuilder, a
chemical manufacturer, an oil magnate, a mustard magnate, a tea
magnate, a malted-milk magnate, a linoleum magnate, a glove-
making magnate, an insurance magnate, a bleaching magnate, and
so on and so on.[16] By 1914 both the House of Lords and the
county elite were substantially transformed from what they had
been in 1879, being heavily infiltrated by self-made men of dubious origins and manners, who had made vast fortunes in hitherto
unheard-of ways in hitherto unheard-of industries.

4. PURCHASERS' AND PURCHASER-ENTRANTS' SOURCES OF FAMILY WEALTH

Hitherto, purchasers and purchaser-entrants have been examined
according to the personal wealth of the individual concerned, and
the results have suggested that about one-fifth of entrants were
upwardly mobile landed parish gentry. But if these parish gentry
are examined more closely, to see whether or not there had been
any mixture of non-landed wealth in their family up to two generations back, then a significantly different picture emerges. Many
of these apparently mere gentry had benefitted from injections of
money from office, the law, or business via wives, parents, or
grandparents.

A few examples from Northamptonshire will serve to demonstrate the slow process of capital accumulation from several different sources over several generations, which eventually led to the
purchase of a seat. Bartholomew Tate, the purchaser of Delapré
Abbey in 1548, had a father who held government office and a
grandfather in trade, both successful men and knights. The pater-

---

[16] Jill Franklin, *The Gentleman's Country House and its Plan 1835-1914*, London, 1981, Ch.
II and Appendix.

nal grandfather of James Langham, the purchaser of Newton-in-the-Willows in 1660, had been no more than the younger son of a yeoman. James's father made a fortune in trade in London, married the daughter of another London merchant and bought Cottesbrooke, which James later inherited. Sidney Wortley Montagu, who bought Walcot in 1684, was the younger son of a court office-holder and nobleman, and the grandson of a lawyer. These various combinations of occupations through two or three generations form a recurrent pattern among purchasers and purchaser-entrants at all times. Office and the law and to a lesser extent business provided repeated injections of new wealth which eventually enabled a family to buy its way into the elite.

In Hertfordshire, hardly any purchaser or purchaser-entrant family turns out to have been mere gentry for three generations without any contribution whatever from a non-landed source of wealth. Only sixteen of the 104 gentry purchasers and purchaser-entrants in that county had been exclusively mere gentry for three generations, which reduces the total proportion of exclusively landed wealth among these groups from 32 to 5 per cent (Table 6.3). In Northamptonshire, the decline in the proportion of gentry by shifting from personal to family wealth is rather less dramatic, from 49 to 23 per cent—a reduction by about a half. In Northumberland, however, only two gentry families had obtained any influx of wealth from a non-landed source for three generations, so that the proportion of mere gentry purchasers and purchaser-entrants in that county remains virtually unchanged at 47 per cent. It must be admitted, however, that many of these Northumberland mere gentry must have derived some of their income from coal-mines on their estates, and to that extent were involved in non-agricultural pursuits.

Four conclusions stand out from this new computation based on family wealth. The first is that Hertfordshire, with only 5 per cent mere gentry purchasers and purchaser-entrants, and Northumberland, with 47 per cent, were two utterly different societies. The one was inextricably involved in the world of office, law, and business, the other was largely isolated from it. Northamptonshire stands somewhere in between. The second conclusion is that, except in the far north, the concept of mere gentry is somewhat fictitious, since even in Northamptonshire a half of all rising gentry families derived some of their wealth from non-landed sources. Even as early as the sixteenth century, there was a good deal of interpenetration of land with office, law, and business.

The third conclusion is that this interpenetration was at its most intense in the period 1640 to 1760, when hardly any apparently gentry families on the move were without some assistance from other sources of income. This was as true of Northamptonshire, where only 1 out of 15 personally landed purchasers came from a mere gentry family, as it was in Hertfordshire where the proportion was 2 out of 25. This suggests that the infiltration of non-landed wealth into the parish gentry was considerably greater than it was into the county elite.

The last conclusion is that if these strict three generation criteria have any social or psychological validity, the degree of mere gentry penetration up into the elite was far smaller than the earlier calculations would indicate. Taking all entrants together, the proportion of mere gentry for three generations cannot have exceeded an eighth in Hertfordshire, a half in Northamptonshire and three-quarters in Northumberland. Only in the latter county were new-comers from generations of mere gentry families in a clear majority.

VII

INTERACTIONS: LAND AND MONEY

'. . . England, modern to the last degree
Borrows or makes her own nobility,
And yet she boldly boasts of pedigree.'

[D. Defoe, *The True-born Englishman* (1701),
in Defoe's *Writings*, London, 1927, vol. 14, p. 44.]

1. INTRODUCTION

The previous chapters have examined mobility patterns in general, including old families who sold up or dropped out, and new families who used wealth derived from a variety of sources to buy up existing seats or build new ones and so enter the ranks of the landed elite from below. The time has now come to tackle the two central questions concerning the interaction between the landed elite and business. The first is the degree to which there was physical mobility between the two groups, by successful men of business entering into the landed elite, and by younger sons of the elite making a career in business. The second is the degree to which social and cultural symbiosis was achieved between the two groups. This last is a question of values and attitudes, and need not bear a very close relationship to the facts of social mobility.

2. SOCIAL MOBILITY

i. *The Questions*

No one denies that at all times and in all countries, merchants have put some of their wealth into the purchase of land, since it was a secure, if not particularly rewarding, investment. But the issue here is how far they aspired to the trappings of gentility that went with establishment in a rural seat. In other words, to what extent did the commercial classes plough most of the profits of their business into those essential attributes of social climbing, a substantial landed estate and a country seat, and to what extent did they adopt a suitable style of life? There are two ways in which this question might be answered. The first is by examining samples of the urban patriciate to see what proportion of them withdrew their capital from trade and settled themselves and their children into a country seat. The second is by calculating the proportion of the landed elite who were former business men or sons of business men. The traditional hypothesis being tested is that there was a fairly rapid but homoeostatic circulation of elites, with junior members of the landed classes dropping down into the bourgeoisie as frequently as the latter were moving up. Some attention must therefore also be given to the degree to which younger sons of the squirearchy infiltrated into the commercial classes by apprenticeship to a career in trade. That younger sons of gentlemen in England were downwardly mobile to a degree unknown abroad is beyond dispute. Less certain, however, is whether the sons of the landed elite were apprenticed in the City, or whether they mainly used their influential connections to promote their careers in the army, the Church, or government office.

ii. The Urban Patriciates and the Land

Successful merchants have always been urban-based, either in a provincial city or in London. Of the former, York will serve as well as any, being one of the five largest and most prosperous in the kingdom before the eighteenth century. During the whole of the seventeenth century, from 1603 to 1702, only ten aldermen of York were knighted, only three owned a country house, only four married into the gentry, and only five moved out of the town altogether to set up minor gentry families. The vast majority of the patriciate of the city stayed put, intermarried, and carried on trade until the family line ran out, which was usually within two or three generations thanks to the high mortality rate in the overcrowded and polluted cities of the period. The identical pattern of behaviour is also found amongst the seventeenth-century merchant patriciate of the great bustling city of Bristol, only a minority of whose members bought a country house.[1] The same story is true of a small county town like Worcester, where between 1560 and 1600 only twelve of the seventy-eight members of the ruling oligarchy bought land and moved back into the countryside, and only two of those twelve founded an upper-gentry family.[2] Everything suggests, therefore, that infiltration into the squirearchy by provincial merchants before 1700 was negligible.

The links between landed and monied society in the eighteenth and nineteenth centuries have been explored for the great trading families of two prominent provincial cities, Leeds and Hull, with

---

[1] Victoria County History: the City of York; P. McGrath, Merchants and Merchandise in Seventeenth Century Bristol, Bristol Record Society, xix, 1955, p. xxxi.
[2] A. D. Dyer, The City of Worcester in the Sixteenth Century, Leicester, 1973, p. 187.

not dissimilar results. The Leeds merchant elite came from the yeomanry or lesser gentry, and when they had made their fortunes they hastened to adopt the values and life-style of the landed elite.[3] They became urbanized gentry, 'gentlemen-merchants', and developed their own parallel set of cultural amenities. They founded the Leeds Hunt in 1740, built a theatre in 1771, and an assembly room in 1774. As a result 'many of the merchants divide the week between their pleasures and their business'. In this they were merely aping some of their wealthier London colleagues in the Levant Company, described as 'gentlemen-merchants, who trade as it were, by rote', one of whom went gaily off on the Grand Tour for two years, leaving his factor in Aleppo to handle the business.[4]

Very few of these gentlemen-merchants of Leeds enjoyed incomes comparable with those of the landed elite, although they were fully equivalent to those of the local parish gentry or clergy, with whom indeed they mixed on terms of social equality. After 1780 their education more and more focused on genteel manners and attributes and less and less upon vocational apprenticeships. Their wives studied the latest fashions, and they themselves patronized the most fashionable architects to build their villas and suburban residences. They symbolized the closure of ranks against the manufacturing newcomers by seeing to it that when the great local history, Ralph Thoresby's *Ducatus Leodensis*, first published in 1715, ran to a second updated edition in 1816, it was only their own older families which were mentioned.

Although this merchant elite of one of the most prosperous towns in eighteenth-century England aimed at, and often succeeded in, living 'a country life in business', in fact remarkably few of them settled in a large seat surrounded with a park or founded a major county family. The forty or so who did establish themselves in the country were nearly all small gentry. Of the thirteen great merchant dynasties of the period from 1700 to 1780, only six moved out into a major country seat, and in one case this was the ultimate cause of family bankruptcy. William Medhurst, the younger son of a physician, settled in Leeds in 1708, worked his way up to great prosperity in the cloth trade, and bought Kippax Hall, to which he withdrew in 1741. He was, however, snubbed by the county elite, being defeated in an effort to become sheriff in 1744. On his death a year later, his two sons took over the firm and the country seat, but spent most of their time in rural pleasures at the

---

[3] R. G. Wilson, *Gentlemen Merchants 1730-1830*, Manchester, 1971.
[4] R. Davis, *Aleppo and Devonshire Square*, London, 1967, pp. 71-2.

latter. The elder became both mayor of Leeds twice and JP of the West Riding, so he seems to have spanned both worlds. But in 1780 the firm of Medhurst failed, due partly to the American war and partly to diversion of attention from business management to life as a country gentleman. One may conclude that in psychological terms the gentleman-merchants of Leeds in the eighteenth century became culturally assimilated with the landed gentry. On the other hand the amount of physical interpenetration by purchase of estates or marriage was very limited, and what there was was mostly confined to the level of the lesser gentry.

A similar picture emerges from a study of the merchant elite of the trading seaport of Hull in the eighteenth century. Here, as at Leeds, the life of the city was dominated by a handful of big family firms, about twenty in all. Very few of the heads of these firms, however, put their money into a large country seat, the majority buying land piecemeal merely for investment. Not one withdrew all his money from trade, and very few abandoned trade for life as a country gentleman. Even the bankers rarely bought a seat. On the other hand, just as in Leeds, the merchant and banking elite of Hull constructed a social and cultural life within the town that was all but indistinguishable from that of the smaller country gentry in the area. They commuted to work from rented or recently purchased villas in the neighbouring villages, and spent much of their time in gentlemanly pursuits, such as hunting, shooting, fishing, card-playing, horse-racing, and wenching. In the late eighteenth century, it could be said that Hull was 'as gay a place as could be found out of London. The theatre, balls, great suppers and card parties were the delight of the principal families in the town'.[5]

The merchant patriciate of Exeter between 1680 and 1760, when it was the third largest city in the country, followed an identical pattern: strong family continuity in trade; a good deal of purchase of small parcels of land as a safe investment; partible inheritance policies; virtually no desire to withdraw from trade to set up as country gentry; and signs in the mid-eighteenth century of assimilation to genteel culture, and the building of comfortable suburban villas a few miles out of town.[6]

Another study of an eighteenth-century provincial urban patri-

[5] G. Jackson, *Hull in the Eighteenth Century*, Oxford, 1972, p. 267; K. J. Allison, ' "Hull Gent. seeks a Country Residence" 1750-1850', *East Yorkshire Local History Society*, 36, 1981.
[6] F. Wood, 'Merchant and Class: The Social Identification of Merchants in Exeter, 1680-1760' (MA Thesis, Monash University, 1977). I am indebted to Mrs. Wood for permission to quote from her unpublished work.

ciate and its land purchases concerns the great colonial tobacco merchants of Glasgow between 1770 and 1815.[7] This was a period in which, according to our own evidence, country house purchases by merchants were at their height in the area around London, and the same seems to have been true at any rate of land purchases around Glasgow. Since Glasgow merchants were both buying and selling again, one may reasonably hypothesize that a buying spree in hopes of making quick capital gains out of rising food prices after 1790 was at least one causal factor. It should be pointed out that this increase in activity in the land market in the late eighteenth century, around both Glasgow and London, directly contradicts conventional wisdom, which has it that the market was actually closing down during this period, that 'the inflow of new families into the ranks of landowners was much lower between the 1730s and the end of the eighteenth century than in the previous 200 years'.[8]

Of the 140 Glasgow colonial merchants between 1770 and 1815, ninety comprised an elite of the very wealthy. Of these ninety, 80 per cent owned at least 500 acres of land, one-third of it acquired by inheritance or marriage, and two-thirds by purchase. These are impressive figures, but the Glasgow merchants were a peculiar group, since about half were younger sons of gentry in the first place. They too, like their counterparts in Leeds, can be described as 'gentlemen-merchants' possessing their own urban cultural institutions which mirrored those of the landed classes. Most of them remained in business after they had purchased their land. On the other hand, they adopted the values and trappings of the elite, buying themselves bogus coats of arms, and insisting that all heirs to the property must bear their own name, even if this involved a name-change. And yet at least one, Andrew Thompson, made no bones about where his money came from, inscribing upon his coat of arms, granted in 1760, the defiant inscription *Industriae Munus*.

The conclusion is that there was an unusual degree of involvement on the part of an elite of Glasgow merchants in Scottish lowland agriculture at this particular period. They were, however, only a successful minority, and 'almost by definition they were

[7] T. M. Devine, 'Glasgow Colonial Merchants and Land, 1770-1815', in *Land and Industry*, ed. J. T. Ward and R. G. Wilson, Newton Abbot, 1971, pp. 203-65.
[8] G. E. Mingay, *English Landed Society in the Eighteenth Century*, London, 1963, p. 39. Professor Mingay was relying on the conclusions of Sir John Habakkuk, 'The English Landmarket in the Eighteenth Century', in *Britain and the Netherlands*, ed. J. S. Bromley and E. H. Kossmann, London, 1960. The error seems to have arisen since Sir John was using data primarily for Northamptonshire, which may not have been typical. It certainly does not fit the evidence for the Leeds, Glasgow, or London merchant elites.

atypical of their fellow merchants'. Moreover, they were unusual
in the degree to which they came out of the gentry in the first
place, and inherited or married landed property. Finally, the degree to which they cut their ties to business and set themselves up
as pure country squires is very uncertain. The impression given is
that the majority did not take this final, sociologically decisive,
step.

Information about the eighteenth-century merchant elite of a
small but flourishing brewing and North Sea port town, King's
Lynn, indicates much the same. Most of the families of the elite
continued for three to five generations as merchants and civic leaders in the town, many getting richer and richer and some ending
up as baronets. One family of brewers and overseas merchants,
the Bagges, produced no fewer than eighteen mayors between 1711
and 1911 and acquired a baronetcy on the way, but never moved
out of town to set up as country squires. Only one family of the
ten described, the Turners of Warham Hall, acquired a country
seat, but even so its members remained actively engaged in trade,
served as mayors and MPs, and mostly resided in the town.[9]

These published studies about eighteenth-century provincial patriciates, and two recent doctoral theses on Norwich and Bristol,
all tell the same story.[10] They indicate that there was plenty of
land purchase but little movement out of the town into the ranks
of the landed squirearchy. But they also show that there was a
very high degree of cultural assimilation, and a striking development of provincial cultural amenities patronized by both merchant
elites and neighbouring parish gentry.[11] As early as the beginning
of the eighteenth century, for example, the small county and market town of Shrewsbury had developed an astonishing range of
ancillary services for leisure. It could boast of an assembly room,
a racecourse, and some fine parks and gardens in which to take a
stroll. In 1698, Celia Fiennes noted that 'every Wednesday most
of the town ladies and gentlemen walk there as in St James's Park,
and there are abundance of people of quality lives [sic] in Shrewsbury'. These people of quality could find in town the services of

[9] H. F. Bradfer-Lawrence, 'The Merchants of Lynn', in *A Supplement to Blomefield's Norfolk*, ed. C. Ingleby, London, 1929, pp. 155-203.
[10] P. J. Corfield, 'Social and Economic History of Norwich 1650-1850: A Study in Urban
Growth', London Ph.D. thesis, 1976, i, pp. 236-7; R. H. Quilici, 'Turmoil in City and
Empire: Bristol Factions 1700-1775', University of New Hampshire Ph.D. thesis, 1976,
pp. 142-4; both quoted by N. Rogers, 'Money, Land and Lineage: the Big Bourgeoisie in
Hanoverian London', *Social History*, iv, 1979, p. 453 note.
[11] P. Borsay, 'The English Urban Renaissance: the Development of English Provincial
Urban Culture, *c*.1680-*c*.1760', *Social History*, ii, 1977.

six watchmakers, two booksellers, a bookbinder, a stationer, several musicians, and two dancing masters, quite apart from three surgeons and ten apothecaries, a number of coffee-houses, and two small private boarding-schools for 'the daughters of gentlemen'. By now these 'gentlemen' and 'persons of quality' included both local parish gentry and members of the urban patriciate.[12]

In the late eighteenth and early nineteenth centuries, the political and cultural hegemony of these merchant patriciates for the first time came under challenge by the rising tide of self-made lower-class manufacturers. The Leeds merchants despised and treated as social parvenus these vulgar, ruthless entrepreneurs of industry who appeared upon the scene towards the end of the century. The old mercantile elite would have little or nothing to do with the new industrial activities, preserved their genteel way of life, and finally either were replaced in control of their cities or else withdrew in disgust to the country. Thus the closing of social ranks against newcomers, which seems to have been so marked among the landed elite of the Victorian period before 1880, was also shared by the old 'gentlemen-merchant' urban patriciates. In Leeds, the latter finally lost out to the new men and withdrew, in Wakefield they successfully kept industry at bay, and in so doing ruined the economy of the town. The business world thus split in two under the stress of industrialization: one group, the old commercial and monied elite, was acceptable in polite society; the other, the new industrial entrepreneurs, by and large were not.[13]

The acid test of the hypothesis of merchant infiltration into the squirearchy has to be London, which was twenty times larger and richer than any other city in the country in 1600 and still in 1800. And yet there were at all times relatively few rich merchants of this uniquely opulent and populous city who founded new families among the landed elite. For the fifteenth century, Professor Thrupp concluded that in 1436 'there could scarcely have been enough new immigrants from London in that generation to make much impression on the character of the landed gentry of any one county . . . Even in the home counties one could not expect to find more than a small proportion of London names at the higher social levels'. In about 1500, out of 183 gentry families in Kent there were only six who bore London names. In Hertfordshire in about 1480 there were fifty-four gentry families, only five of whom bore Lon-

[12] A. McInnes, *The English Town 1660-1760*, Historical Association, London, 1980, pp. 17-21.
[13] R. G. Wilson, 'Denisons and Milneses: eighteenth century Merchant Landowners', in *Land and Industry*, ed. J. T. Ward and R. G. Wilson, pp. 158, 165-6.

don names, and only two may possibly have been recent immigrants.[14]

Even in the late sixteenth and early seventeenth centuries far
fewer successful London merchants transformed themselves into
country squires than one would have expected from the shrill complaints of playwrights and social commentators. Among the merchants of the Muscovy Company in 1555, one of the richest corporations in London, it has been shown that 'the very few who
not only bought landed estates . . . but also abandoned trade and
London itself appear to be quite exceptional'.[15]

This evidence from the mid-sixteenth century is confirmed by
that about men elected aldermen of London between 1600 and
1624. Admittedly, a few very rich men refused this honour in
order to concentrate on making money, but by and large the aldermen comprised the wealthiest and most successful merchants of
London. The theory of a substantial circulation of elites, from
land into trade and back into land, is not borne out by the evidence for London in this period. Only a few London aldermen
came from the land into trade, and only a few moved from trade
into land. Only twenty-four of the 140—or 17 per cent—were
sons of gentlemen and only one was the son of a knight. The
fathers of these twenty-four possessed very modest economic resources, and were clearly at the very bottom of their status group,
parish gentry who bordered upon the yeomanry. Most of these
wealthy merchants invested in land, usually buying substantial
manorial estates. But only eighteen of the 140 actually retired from
the City and set themselves up in their own lifetime as country
gentry, and only seven were buried in the country. Only sixteen
became JPs in the country and only seven sheriffs. Only two, Sir
John Spencer or Sir Baptist Hicks, acquired such vast holdings
that they earned promotion into the peerage.[16]

One may therefore conclude that the recruitment of London
merchants from the sons of the gentry was rare in the early seventeenth century and was anyway confined to very minor gentry,
and that acquisition of a great estate and retirement to it to adopt
the life-style and obligations of a country gentleman was even rarer.
Eighteen out of 140 in twenty-four years is not a very impressive
figure. The phenomenon certainly existed, but the scale upon which

[14] S. Thrupp, *The Merchant Class of Medieval London, 1300-1500*, London, 1948, pp. 284-6.

[15] T. S. Willan, *Muscovy Merchants of 1555*, Manchester, 1973, p. 73.

[16] R. G. Lang, 'Social Origins and Social Aspirations of Jacobean London Merchants', *Economic History Review*, 2nd Series, xxvii, 1974.

it occurred in the Jacobean period was relatively small, and quite out of proportion to the outraged comment and criticism to which it gave rise. The enormous economic success, and the spectacular titular rewards showered upon a handful of tycoons like Spencer, Hicks, Cranfield, and Craven, drew public attention to a statistically minor trend, whose significance was blown out of all proportion by contemporary commentators.

Some less detailed data are also available about the Aldermen and members of the Common Council of London from 1660 to 1689. Only forty-two of 386 leading London merchants over this thirty-year period were the sons of squires or above. Another 133 were the sons of 'gentlemen', but by now this was a term loosely applied to the urban bourgeoisie as well as small landed gentry. How many ended their life as owners of country seats is unknown, although most of them had some sort of suburban retreat, mostly in Middlesex, Surrey, or Essex. Of their daughters, only three married into the peerage. Neither their social origins nor their daughters' marriages suggest that more than a handful of members of this wealthy London patriciate had direct personal ties to the landed elite. By and large they neither came from the landed elite in the first place, nor retired into it at the end of their careers.[17]

This relative lack of movement is all the more remarkable since the late seventeenth century was not only a period when London merchants were making fortunes on an unprecedented scale. It was also one in which they were gaining status recognition from the Crown by the granting of baronetcies and knighthoods on a scale wholly unparalleled before or since. In 1675 and in 1715 there were respectively twenty-four and twenty-six knights and baronets on the Court of Aldermen.[18] It is easy to be so impressed by the financial and social successes of men like Sir Josiah Child, Sir James Bateman, or Sir Robert Clayton in the late seventeenth century as to forget that they were the exceptions and not the rule. César de Saussure was exaggerating in the 1720s when he remarked that 'some merchants are certainly far wealthier than many sovereign princes in Germany or Italy. They live in great state, their houses are richly furnished, their tables spread with delicacies.' Saussure neglects to make it clear whether this high living was taking place in the City or in a seat in the country. The example he has in mind seems to be James Brydges, 1st Duke of

---

[17] J. R. Woodhead, 'The Rulers of London: the Composition of the Courts of Aldermen and of Common Council of the City of London 1660-1689' (London M.A. thesis, 1961, p. 24 and Appendix III).
[18] A. B. Beaven, *The Aldermen of the City of London*, London, 1913, ii, p. xliv.

Chandos, who made an enormous fortune in a very short time in his capacity as Paymaster of the Forces Abroad from 1707 to 1712, built the immense palace of Cannons, and lived there in what was indeed a princely style. In 1732 John Macky observed that 'few German sovereign Princes live with that magnificence, grandeur and good order'. But Brydges was enriched by corruption in office, not commerce; his seat was close to the suburbs at Edgeware, not fully in the country; and he was a unique figure in his day.[19]

By the middle of the eighteenth century, the picture of a largely self-sufficient merchant and banking patriciate flourishing in London is even clearer. A study of the seventy-four aldermen of London between 1738 and 1763 reveals how previous trends had evolved a stage further.[20] More were now recruited from the City and business and fewer claimed to be gentlemen, whatever that might mean by 1750. Only six of these seventy-four very wealthy tycoons—that is 8 per cent—bought a large estate and a seat and tried to enter the county elite (one of whom was Sir William Baker of Bayfordbury, Herts.). The others bought no more than a suburban villa and less than 300 acres of ground to go with it, and 'there is little evidence of a major diversion of wealth from commerce and high finance to landed property'. Many of those who bought these villas ordered them to be sold again at their death. One may conclude that only a tiny handful of the very richest men in mid-eighteenth century London were seeking permanent entry into the ranks of the landed elite.

The last piece of evidence about the movement of the bourgeoisie into land is a study of the very richest men in England in the nineteenth century.[21] Most of the wealthy business or professional men in 1880 either possessed no land at all, or else an estate of very small size indeed, consisting almost entirely of the pleasure-grounds around a villa or seat. Nine-tenths of the richest land-owners in England in 1880 were men whose wealth antedated the industrial revolution, and Lord Overstone of Overstone, Northants., a banker who spent over £1½ million on buying 30,000 acres of land, was the exception to the rule. This suggests what the evidence of the sample also indicates, that the landed elite in the nineteenth century before 1880 was an increasingly isolated

[19] C. de Saussure, *A Foreign View of England in the Reigns of George I and George II*, London, 1902, p. 217; J. Macky, *A Journey through England*, London, 1732, ii, p. 5; R. S. Neale, *Bath 1680-1850*, London, 1981, pp. 119-315; C. H. Collins Baker and M. Baker, *The Life and Circumstances of James Brydges, first Duke of Chandos*, Oxford, 1949.
[20] N. Rogers, op. cit., pp. 438-43.
[21] W. D. Rubinstein, *Men of Property*, New Brunswick, 1981, pp. 195-6, 215-20.

caste, far more cut off from the vulgar world of industry than their eighteenth-century predecessors had been from the more genteel world of overseas commerce and banking.

This scattered evidence about rich merchants and bankers in both London and provincial cities from the sixteenth to the nineteenth century is sufficient to indicate four things: first, that at all times there was a substantial investment by rich merchants in land purchase, as the only secure form of property available; second, that, despite persistent beliefs to the contrary, no more than a thin trickle of merchants were buying country seats and attempting to acquire the accompanying status and prestige as landed squires; third, that during the eighteenth century there was a high degree of cultural assimilation between land and trade.

iii. The Landed Elite and Business

The only other way to test the scale of the shift of money into land is to reverse the procedure, and to study the degree to which local landed elites, including both inheritors and purchasers, were composed of men enriched in any way by business activities (Table 7.1, Fig. 7.1). The results set out in the last chapter show that

FIG. 7.1   Owners in Business as a Proportion of all Owners [Table 7.1]

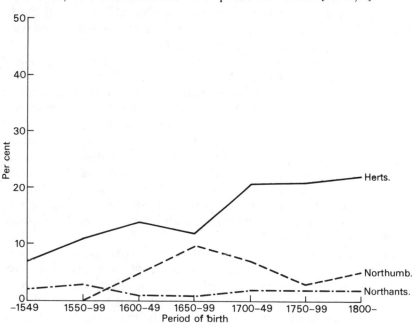

in the two counties of Northamptonshire and Northumberland, away from the vicinity of London, the proportions were always negligible, never rising above 3 per cent in the former and 10 per cent (due largely to coal) in the latter. In Hertfordshire conditions were different, with the proportion hovering about the 10 to 15 per cent mark up to 1760, after which it jumped to a little over 20 per cent. In this county very close to London, there was a substantial influx of monied men, sufficient after 1760 seriously to affect the composition of the county elite. On close inspection, however, the true number of permanent migrants from the City to the countryside turns out to have been very much smaller. Over one-third of these business newcomers were transients who bought and sold again in their own lifetime or at their death, and another third sold up within the next generation (Table 5.2). Thus two-thirds of these new business families in Hertfordshire had vanished from the scene within fifty years or less. Either they never had any intention of founding a county family, or for some reason or other they quickly abandoned the attempt. These calculations therefore tend to reinforce the conclusion from the data about merchant patriciates, that only very small numbers pulled their capital out of business and invested it all in the establishment of a major county family. The only possible exception to this generalization is the semi-suburban southern parts of Hertfordshire after 1790, while no doubt similar suburban areas of eastern Surrey and south-western Essex had the same experience. But even here the vast majority of buyers were merely transients.

If the purpose of this investigation is to probe for all possible interactions between the landed and the monied interest, it is not enough to study the proportion of all owners of seats at any given time who were or had been engaged in business. This figure is obviously powerfully influenced by the proportion of self-made men who were buying their way into the landed elite. The question must therefore be sophisticated. First one needs to know what proportion of all hereditary owners of seats, excluding all newcomers, had some personal involvement in business activity. Second one needs to know how many owners of any kind had fathers or fathers-in-law with such experience, and therefore had had some family contact with business.

Most inheritor owners were little more than passive *rentiers*, making renewable leases to large tenants, who took the initiative and bore most of the cost of agricultural innovation. It is clear, however, that a minority, although perhaps not a substantial one, was keenly interested in agronomy and the exploitation of the resources of their lands, going frequently so far as to invest considerable time and money in experiments of one sort or another. Only a handful of these, however, seem to have had the combination of time, energy, and capital to turn these enterprises to profitable advantage. Such were the third duke of Bridgwater, the profits of whose canal and coal-mines in Lancashire financed the massive rebuilding of his seat in Ashridge in Hertfordshire; or Sir John Bennet Lawes of Rothamsted, also in Hertfordshire, whose agricultural interests combined with a natural curiosity regarding chemistry led him to found not only the first experimental agricultural station in England, but also the English fertilizer industry, the profits of the latter helping to finance the former. Both Bridgwater and Lawes, however, lived very untypical lives. For decades they both existed in relative penury, ploughing every penny they could lay hands on into their speculations. These speculations eventually paid off, and they ended up extremely rich men, but very few of their peers were prepared to make similar sacrifices.

Northumberland in the early eighteenth century seems to have numbered amongst its elite a high concentration of entrepreneurs owing to the presence of coal upon their lands, from which some of them derived considerable fortunes, such as the three successive Matthew Ridleys of Blagdon and Heaton Hall in the second half of the eighteenth century. So close was the dependence of the local squirearchy on the profits of coal that Sir Henry Riddell, Bt., could ask in 1729 'What signifies all your balls, ridottos, etc., unless navigation and the coal trade flourish?'[22] In Northamptonshire, inheritor entrepreneurs were very rare indeed. In the sixteenth century, there was the great sheep-master family of the Spencers, which has risen in 400 years from haggling over the price of wool to marriage with the heir apparent to the English throne. In the early nineteenth century, Lord Althorp, future third Earl Spencer, spent a great deal of money and most of his life (amongst a host of other occupations) perfecting his herd of pedigree cattle; but although a very successful venture, it is doubtful that it was a very profitable one.

Confining oneself entirely to what is known, owners who inherited their estates and were active in business were negligible in numbers in all three counties before 1700 (Table 7.2). They remained negligible in Northamptonshire, but rose to 10 per cent in Northumberland between 1700 and 1759, thanks to coal. In Hertfordshire from 1700 to 1879 the proportion hovered around 12 per

[22] E. Hughes, *North Country Life in the Eighteenth Century*, i, 1952, p. 151.

cent, so here there was clearly an innovative and active minority
of hereditary landlords. These men would have been horrified to
find themselves described as business men, but they were applying
capitalist market principles to estate management.

To complete the picture, some account has to be taken not only
of the owners themselves but also of their families, going back one
generation to fathers and father-in-law to see how many had had
any family contacts with business or derived any benefit from it.
This is the extreme limit of any reasonable calculation of the links
of business to the landed elite. It provides a measure of the source
of family wealth, although hardly of social status, since in England
few cared too much about social origins even one generation back
(Table 7.3, Fig. 7.2). The picture revealed more closely approxi-
mates to the traditional paradigm about the English landed elite,
and if, as seems likely, a fair number of the 'Unknowns' also had
business ties, then the family connection of land and money would
be closer still. In Hertfordshire the proportion of family connections with business grew rapidly up to the early seventeenth century and thereafter levelled off at the astonishingly high level of
40 per cent. Things were very different in the other two counties.

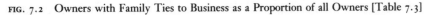

FIG. 7.2   Owners with Family Ties to Business as a Proportion of all Owners [Table 7.3]

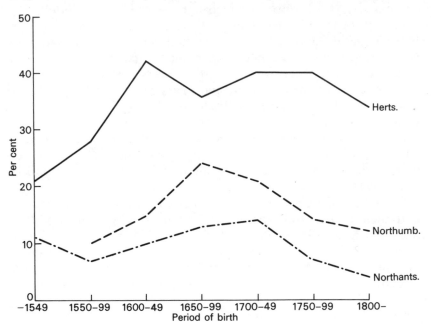

Coal drove Northumberland family business connections up to a temporary peak of 25 per cent in the late seventeenth century, but in Northamptonshire they never even reached 15 per cent.

What is very noticeable is the marked decline of those ties in all three counties in the cohort born in the nineteenth century, which confirms previous evidence that there was a social distancing of land from money in the early and mid-Victorian period. These figures support all of the other data in suggesting that only in Hertfordshire did business make a serious impact upon the composition, personal experience, or even family source of wealth of the landed elite. Only in an almost suburban county on the fringes of the metropolis does the stereotype of a relatively free interchange between land and money amongst members of the English elite society appear to be justified by the facts. If Northamptonshire was more typical of England, as seems very likely, then the degree of penetration of business interest into the landed elite was certainly persistent but at all times relatively small.

The conclusion has to be that the contemporary perceptions and conventional historical wisdom about the exceptional freedom of interchange between land and money amongst the English elite are not borne out by the statistical facts, either about land and seats purchased by the urban patriciate, or about personal, marital, or family ties back one generation among owners of landed estates and seats, or even—as we shall see—about the entry of younger sons into business.

iv. The Landed Elite and the Professions

Far more important than the ties of the landed elite to business were those which connected them at all levels to government service and the professions, mostly law and the army. These occupations were not only critically important as sources of new wealth for purchasers and new entrants into the sample; they also provided work and income for inheritors.

Taking this last point first, in the seventeenth century these occupations were pursued by about 20 per cent of all inheritors in Hertfordshire, 10 per cent in Northamptonshire, and 5 per cent in remote Northumberland (Table 7.2, Fig. 7.3). No social stigma had ever been attached to any of these entirely genteel pursuits, which active and ambitious landowners had always found attractive. After 1700, however, there was a striking increase in the level of involvement in these occupations, less marked in Hertfordshire, many of whose hereditary elite had always pursued office or the law, but very dramatic in the other two counties. By the nine-

FIG. 7.3   Inheritors with an Office or Profession as a Proportion of all Inheritors
[Table 7.2]

teenth century at least a quarter of all three elites were involved in government office or a profession.

If one turns from hereditary members of the elite to the whole body of owners, and includes both inheritors and newcomers, and if one extends the data to include connections with office or a profession by a father or father-in-law, then the degree of family involvement was substantial (Table 7.3, Fig. 7.4). In the sixteenth century new families enriched by government office or the law poured into Hertfordshire and Northamptonshire, so that a half and a third of all owners respectively had such connections. The proportion dropped in both counties to about 30 per cent during the seventeenth and early eighteenth centuries, and then shot up again after 1750. In Hertfordshire the proportion was running at over 40 per cent and in the other two counties at around 60 per cent. In terms of family connections, the Victorian elite was well on the way to being a service aristocracy. Partly, of course, the increasing pursuit of professional careers was a by-product of demographic change. Heirs were now having to wait much longer to step into their fathers' shoes, and while waiting it was natural to

FIG. 7.4   Owners with Family Ties to an Office or Profession as a Proportion of all
Owners [Table 7.3]

spend the time as an officer in a guards regiment or some other
congenial pursuit, but these were temporary occupations which
are not included in these calculations of an increase in owners with
professional jobs. But many clearly retained their jobs after inheritance, which indicates that in the Victorian period significant
numbers of the established landed elite no longer contented themselves with local administration, but were shifting into a new pattern of life as a service elite in the army, government office, or the
professions. This transformation of the old way of life was undoubtedly stimulated by the ideal of service to the state inculcated
by the reformed Victorian public schools. It was also encouraged
by the increase during the French Revolutionary Wars of 'Old

Corruption'—the number of jobs and offices at the disposal of the elite.

The drift of the landed elite into the professions in the late eighteenth and early nineteenth centuries, however, was also stimulated by the reviving moral concerns of the age. Parents were now anxious to protect their children from the temptations of idleness. This function as an aid to character formation in driving the sons of the elite into professional careers was well recognized by the early nineteenth century. In *Northanger Abbey* Jane Austen makes the wealthy landowner General Tilney explain why he thought 'it expedient to give every young man some employment. The money is nothing, it is not an object, but employment is the thing. Even . . . my eldest son . . . who will perhaps inherit as considerable a landed property as any private man in the county has his profession' (in the army, of course).[23]

To the extent that the elite continued to serve in various military, administrative, political, or legal positions after inheritance, their duties drew them out of the countryside to London or abroad, and tended to weaken ties with the local tenantry and to interfere with their ability to maintain their local political power-base. The move toward an occupation was itself perhaps in part a response to the recognition that that power-base was being eroded by changing social conditions, thanks to the long-delayed decline of deference, the shift to rack-renting, and the creation of County Councils. If pursued after inheritance, however, a professional career must have stimulated this very trend, by taking more and more of the landed elite away from their country seats for longer and longer periods of the year. On the other hand, the development of the railways made it much easier than ever before to live quite deep in the country and still pursue an occupation in London. This was especially true if the occupation only demanded a few days' work a month, such as the membership of a guards regiment in peacetime, or the holding of one of the many sinecure offices in government and the law.

v. Younger Sons

Besides the trickle of business men into the ranks of the elite, there was also a reverse current that carried some elite younger sons into trade or banking.[24] The mere accident of birth-order debarred a younger son from a stable niche in society, although this was a

[23] J. Austen, *Northanger Abbey*, ed. R. W. Chapman, Oxford, 1933, p. 176.
[24] The only study of younger sons is a brief but suggestive article by Joan Thirsk, 'Younger sons in the Seventeenth Century', *History*, 54, 1969.

situation which could at any moment be reversed, if his elder brother or brothers died without heirs. His fortune in the main had to be of his own making, and his only status was that of a gentleman, although a gentleman with connections. His early experience would have habituated him to handling differences of status and made him particularly aware of them. He was a man whose potential for success depended either on exploiting his family ties by making himself indispensable to more fortunate relatives and connections, or on his making his way by his own exertions, either by marriage to an heiress, or in a trade or profession (in all of which his status might be a help, or occasionally a hindrance).

Like other European landed elites, that of England was preferentially primogenitural, and after 1650 a younger son could expect little more than an annuity or a cash sum to launch him into the world. He was, however, peculiarly disadvantaged in a number of respects, the first being his lack of an hereditary title. The younger sons of dukes and marquesses are admittedly accorded the purely courtesy title of 'lord' but they are unable to pass the privilege on to their heirs. An anomaly is that the daughters, not only of dukes and marquesses but also of earls, are accorded the courtesy title of 'lady'. The younger or female children of barons, however, do not enjoy even these purely courtesy and non-inheritable titular symbols of status. This means that younger sons had no legal protection against arrest by creditors, so that there was therefore almost no bottom to the pit of indigence into which a younger son of an English peer could fall. It is hardly surprising that in the eighteenth century it was widely believed—rightly or wrongly—that many highwaymen were younger sons with no alternative employment for their martial skills, and no aptitude or taste for more arduous occupations.

Another English peculiarity was that sons of the landed elite had no legal claim to any particular offices, for example in the army, although it must be admitted that de facto they contrived to do very well out of Old Corruption in the late eighteenth and early nineteenth centuries. Worse still there were relatively few respectable jobs open to the crowd of aspirants. For one and one-half centuries after the Reformation, the clerical profession was poorly paid and socially contemptible, and so offered few opportunities for men of this class. As late as about 1730 Walpole observed with annoyance—since it diminished the political value of controlling ecclesiastical patronage—that 'it has not been customary for persons either of birth or fortune to breed up their children to the church'. This observation is confirmed by the fact that in the first

half of the eighteenth century only 6 to 7 per cent of the Leicestershire parish clergy were son of esquires and above. There were
plenty of sons of gentry, and even more of clergy, but very few
from the ranks of the landed elite.[25] In the late eighteenth and
early nineteenth centuries, however, thanks to pluralism and rising
incomes, coupled with the powerful stranglehold held by the landed
elite on the patronage network of clerical livings, many younger
sons found comfortable sinecures in Georgian or Victorian parson-
ages, often in the same village where lay their elder brother's seat.
Yet even then the numbers of rich Church livings were insufficient
to cope with the demand.

The second option was a commission in the armed services, but
many naval officers were promoted from the lower deck, and the
standing army remained small except in time of war. There was
not much satisfaction to be gained from living obscurely on half-
pay in a provincial town, waiting for another war to come along.
Moreover, in order to rise into the higher ranks of the army, it
was necessary to have the substantial capital needed to buy the
office, something many younger sons lacked. Thirdly, England,
unlike Europe, had no large and expanding institutionalized bureaucracy, openly supported by the sale of offices to members of
the elite. Admittedly, the *Black Book* of the early nineteenth century revealed an extraordinary proliferation of sinecure offices and
pensions held by relatives of noblemen and influential landed squires,
but even so the numbers and rewards were small compared with
those available in France or elsewhere. Finally, the gentlemanly
profession of barrister was actually contracting in the late seventeenth and eighteenth centuries, as the work previously done by
this group shifted to lesser legal functionaries such as attorneys
and solicitors, usually men of lower birth and inferior education.

Given this situation, what was a younger son to do? The lucky
few married heiresses from their own class, and thus retrieved
their hereditary position with a single *coup*. The majority, however, had to rely upon their talents, being launched into the world
by their parents with little more than a lump sum and perhaps an
education fitting for the career which they were to follow. Future
clergymen were often sent to the university, future lawyers to the
Inns of Court, future government officials to academies to brush
up their accounting and their languages. This career orientation
was particularly marked in England, which offered relatively few

[25] J. H. Plumb, *Sir Robert Walpole: the King's Minister*, London, 1960, p. 97; J. H. Pruett, *The Parish Clergy under the Later Stuarts*, Urbana, 1978, p. 35.

opportunities for the impoverished remittance man and gentleman of leisure, other than hanging about the house dependent upon the bounty of their elder brother. Consequently, when younger sons were given a higher education, it was with a specific career in mind, and not merely as a finishing school, as was the case with their elder brothers.

In view of how important education was in preparing younger sons for at least two professions, the Church and the law, one would have expected a high proportion to have attended the university or Inns of Court, higher than that of elder sons destined to inherit the seat and estates. Some evidence can be obtained by comparing men born to be heirs, and those who at the age of twenty still expected to be younger sons but who by the accidents of mortality ended up as heirs. There is no reason to suppose that the educational experience of this lucky minority of younger sons was any different from that of the majority who in the end had to make their own way in the world.

The data shows there was indeed a significant difference between the education given to the two groups, but not in the expected direction. There is a consistent pattern of more heirs than younger sons being given higher education at the university, despite the fact that the latter needed it more to get a start in life (Table 7.4, Fig. 7.5A). The reason for this discrepancy is not clear. One possibility is that those younger sons who did attend a university stayed longer and took a degree, while the elder sons dropped in for a year or two and then dropped out again. But even this does not seem to be the case, for very few owners who started as younger sons possessed a BA degree. It looks as if after 1650 younger sons were not given much of a chance in the struggle for jobs in the Church, perhaps because the profession had been seriously glutted by an excess of candidates in the early seventeenth century, and because job opportunities were declining due to growing pluralism. But nepotism and clientage should have worked in their favour and not against them by obtaining for them through elite patronage a larger proportion of the diminishing number of now more lucrative jobs. Whatever the reason, at the university the gap between the proportions of heirs and younger sons in our sample became wider after 1650. It was 44 to 36 per cent in the first half of the seventeenth century, but 43 to 22 per cent in the first half of the eighteenth century, and still 55 to 32 per cent in the nineteenth century.

As for legal training, the proportion of educated younger sons who attended the Inns of Court was always only about the same

FIG. 7.5   Higher Education of Owners as Heirs or Younger Sons [Table 7.4]

as that of those born as heirs (Fig. 7.5B). In the legal profession, attorneys, who were trained by apprenticeship, seem by the eighteenth century to have been doing much of the work previously monopolized by barristers, and it is possible, though unlikely, that younger sons were being articled to attorneys instead of being sent to the Inns of Court. These discrepancies in the higher education of younger sons meant that, among the generations born after 1700, whereas more and more heirs were getting some form of higher education—mostly at the university—the proportion of younger sons remained absolutely static at about 30 per cent (Fig. 7.5C). The most plausible explanation for this widening educational gap must be that more and more younger sons were finding some other career which enabled them to avoid higher education altogether.

One occupation which did not require university education, but

about which very little is known at present, is that of private secretary to a statesman, politician, nobleman, or bureaucrat. Such
offices were common and becoming commoner, and they demanded persons of genteel background, high intelligence, and devotion to duty. It seems likely that this provided an outlet for
many of the brighter younger sons, while commissions in the armed
forces took care of the less intelligent and more extrovert.

Failing these gentlemanly professions like the law, the Church,
administration, or the army, there remained trade, especially overseas trade. The perception in England in the sixteenth and seventeenth centuries was certainly that an important outlet for the
younger sons of gentry was not arms or the law but trade. In the
late seventeenth century Aphra Behn put into the mouth of a dis-
gruntled younger brother the following complaint: 'I am a cadet,
that outcast of my family, and born to that curse of our old English custom. Whereas in other countries, younger brothers are
trained up to the exercise of arms, where honour and reknown
attend the brave, we basely bind our youngest out to slavery, to
lazy trades, idly confined to shops or merchants' books, debasing
of the spirit to the mean cunning, how to cheat and chaffer'. Not
all contemporaries agreed with this assertion, and some thought
that true gentlemen would do almost anything rather than put
their sons to trade. In 1711, the *Spectator* denounced elite fathers
'who had rather see their children starve like gentlemen than thrive
in a trade or profession that is beneath them'. In 1741 Samuel
Foote, referring to a knight of ancient pedigree who had sent a
younger son to sea in the 1690s, commented that he 'was determined not to adhere to that false principle which had so much
prevailed amongst the English gentry, of rather letting their younger
children starve, than derogate from the dignity of their family, by
putting any of them to trade'.[26]

Despite these assertions, there can be no doubt that some English squires were apprenticing their sons to a trade. But how many?
The statistics of apprenticeship can only be properly interpreted
if it is first decided what is meant by the word 'gentleman' in the
late seventeenth and eighteenth centuries. Scrutiny of the surviving apprenticeship records of London guilds in the seventeenth
century show that although between 1629 and 1673 14 per cent of
the 4,387 apprentices styled themselves sons of 'gentlemen', only

---

[26] A. Behn, *The Younger Brother or the Amorous Jilt*, in *Works*, ed. M. Summers, London,
1915, iv, pp. 327-8 (published posthumously in 1696); *The Spectator*, July 4, 1711; S. Foote,
The Genuine Memoirs of the Life of Sir John Dineley Goodere, Bart., London, 1741, p. 6.

a mere 139, or 3 per cent, were sons of esquires or above.[27] Some
of these self-styled 'gentlemen' may have been the younger sons
or grandsons of parish gentry. One may reasonably suspect, however, that the majority were the sons of 'pseudo-gentry', that is
modestly respectable urban tradesmen who by the mid-seventeenth century were styling themselves gentlemen by reason of
their economic position. They were men of limited means, were
actively engaged in retail buying and selling, and probably did not
own a single acre of agricultural land, certainly not a country house.
They had no knowledge of Latin. They did not dream of swaggering around town with a sword at their side, and they would
have been completely at a loss if anyone had challenged them to a
duel. By any sociological definition, they did not count as gentlemen, yet gentlemen is what they called themselves on public documents. Unless these pseudo-gentry can be filtered out, perhaps
by excluding all who gave their place of residence in a town, the
statistics of apprenticeship by social origin in the eighteenth century are almost worthless.

Only the word esquire usually meant a well-to-do landowner,
and the records show only minimal entry of the sons of this class
into apprenticeship in London guilds in the late seventeenth century. In his more sober moments, even Defoe realized that the
number of younger sons of landed squires and gentry who went
into trade was in fact small, and merely claimed of London merchants that 'some of them are, and for many ages have been true
members of the gentry by collateral branches, nay sometimes by
the chief lines of the best and most ancient families'.[28] This is a
more modest assertion, which one can perhaps accept, while dis-
counting the more extravagant claims of the interactions of land
and money through younger sons made at other times by Defoe
himself, and by some modern historians.[29]

The evidence from a random search of well-documented genealogies suggests that in fact very few younger sons entered trade
from the elevated social levels of the county elite. It looks as if the
mercantile option was largely restricted to the period 1650 to 1710,
and that for the upper landed classes the only possible opening
suitable for their sons was membership of one of the great overseas
trading companies like the Levant Company or the East India

[27] R. Grassby, 'Social Mobility and Business Enterprise in Seventeenth Century England', in *Puritans and Revolutionaries*, ed. D. Pennington and K. Thomas, Oxford, 1978, p.
356.
[28] D. Defoe, op. cit., p. 5.
[29] R. Grassby, op. cit., pp. 378-80.

Company. Access to apprenticeship in such companies was only open to the sons of rich and generous fathers. In the Levant trade, apprenticeship fees amounted to £200 to £300 in the middle of the seventeenth century, rising to £1,000 by the end, and to this has to be added another £1,000 or so for working capital once the apprenticeship was expired. These were sums far beyond the reach of younger sons of all except the very wealthiest and most open-handed of the merchant elite, rich farmers or the squirearchy and nobility. And even then some of the latter had doubts about whether it was worth the money. In 1698, Roger North wrote to his sister about his nephew Dudley Foley, whom his mother was thinking of launching into the East India or Levant trades. He commented 'the trade of staking vast sums with youths for little expectation is at such a pass that one would almost choose an annuity without a trade to buy it so dear. All crowd their sons into trade, so that the country wants and cities swarm'. He reckoned that the purchase price of an apprenticeship in one of these great London trading companies was £700 to £800, and that the boy would later on need a further £500 to £600 as working capital to set him up in business. Despite these warnings, however, Mrs Foley went ahead, and Dudley sailed for India eight months later.[30]

The degree to which elite families were willing to put their children even into these prestigious apprenticeships depended upon their status level. Squires were more amenable than baronets, and baronets than peers. The Halsey family of the Golden Parsonage, Herts., for example, who had been country squires since the mid-sixteenth century, seem to have had relatively few inhibitions. In the course of the eighteenth century two younger sons who had had prosperous careers as overseas merchants inherited the estate on the death without heirs of their elder brother. They brought with them substantial injections of new capital, permitting the building of a completely new house nearby, called Gaddesden Place, leaving the old mansion as a dower house for widows.

Families of baronet status had less tolerance for commerce, and the not particularly well-to-do Wakes of Northamptonshire seem to have deliberately shunned trade as an occupation for their younger sons. In the early seventeenth century, the two younger sons of the 1st baronet became respectively a clergyman and a naval officer. The three younger sons of the 3rd baronet in the late seven-

[30] Op. cit., pp. 365-6; R. North, *Autobiography*, ed. A. Jessup, London, 1887, p. 245; R. Davis, op. cit., p. 65.

teenth and early eighteenth centuries became respectively a clergyman, a landed gentleman (by inheritance from an uncle), and a
captain (who was hanged for murder). In the late eighteenth century one of the two sons of the 7th baronet inherited land from
his father, and the other became an army officer. In the nineteenth
century the younger son of the 9th baronet became a parson, and
of the five younger sons of the 10th baronet, four became army
officers and one a naval officer. For over 300 years, not a single
Wake younger son ever went into trade.[31]

The younger sons of the baronet Elwes family of Stoke College,
Suffolk, had at least some slight contacts with business. One younger
son of the 1st baronet, who died in 1706, was apprenticed to a
merchant, but at the first opportunity he went off to become an
army captain instead. Another became an army captain, yet another a naval officer, and only the last was a businessman of some
sort in London.

The peerage virtually never sent their sons into trade. In 1730
Voltaire alleged that in England 'le cadet d'un pair du royaume ne
dédaigne point le commerce'.[32] But he could only produce two
examples, one Horatio Townshend, who was indeed the younger
brother of Charles 2nd Viscount Townshend and a Levant Company factor in Aleppo, and the other a brother of Robert Harley,
1st Earl of Oxford, who was a governor of the Bank of England.
But banking was socially not the same as commerce, the Harley
family had long been engaged in public finance, and anyway Harley's father was not a peer.

When one examines the handful of sons of the elite who became
members of one of the great trading companies—and they certainly would not have stooped to anything lower—it often turns
out that the decision was taken against the opposition of the father,
who only put his son into trade because the boy obstinately refused to bend his mind to anything else. Take, for example, the
late seventeenth-century case of Dudley North, third surviving
son of the 4th Lord North. He was such a hopelessly recalcitrant
scholar in grammar school that he had to be removed, and any
plans for a professional career abandoned. He was then sent to
writing school, and apprenticed, at a cost of £350, to a Turkey
merchant, which is what he wanted all along. Thus he forced his
parents to send him into trade, rather than vice versa, for at that
time in the 1650s the option of a military career was hardly open.

[31] O. Barron, *Northamptonshire Families*, London, 1906, pp. 326-39.
[32] Voltaire, *Lettres sur les Anglais*, Cambridge, 1961, p. 33.

He not only succeeded in getting his own way, but also went on to make a fortune, while keeping on excellent terms with his noble father and elder brother.[33]

The career of John, younger son of Sir Ralph Verney of Clay-don, Bucks., was very similar. Sir Ralph intended him to be a lawyer, and was very unwilling to allow him any commercial training. But the boy was obstinate, urging that he be bound 'apprentice unto some very good tradesman'. He told his doubting father in 1657 that 'I do know Lord's sons which must be apprentices, and their elder brother is worth £5,000 a year'. But the only example he could think of was the not very impressive one of a younger son of an obscure Irish peer. None the less, he succeeded in his aim, and went off to Aleppo as a factor for twelve years, before coming back to London as a prosperous Turkey merchant. On his return, he was warmly welcomed by the family and kept in close touch with his father, both by visits and by correspondence.[34] In this case there was no sign that his successful overseas mercantile career was any bar to easy relations with his father the baronet, to whose title and estate he indeed eventually succeeded, on the death without heirs of his elder brother.

The few examples we have of the sons of peers entering overseas trading companies all come from the period 1650 to 1710, and thereafter the evidence is virtually non-existent. During the eighteenth and nineteenth centuries the peerage packed nearly all their younger sons off into the armed forces, with perhaps one in each generation going into the Church. The younger sons of the Fanes, Earls of Westmorland, mostly became colonels; those of the Fitzroys, Dukes of Grafton, tended to rise to generals.

The information so far available is admittedly largely impressionistic. But it strongly suggests that the interaction of the landed elite and the merchants through younger sons, at any rate in the seventeenth and eighteenth centuries, has been grossly exaggerated. The bold claim that 'baronets, knights and esquires were prepared to put their children into trade' is not supported by the evidence.[35] It is certainly possible that in counties close to London like Hertfordshire, where there were a significant number of landed families with hereditary connections to trade, more younger sons may have embarked upon business careers than was usual elsewhere. Even here, however, the evidence suggests that this was

[33] R. North, *Lives of the Norths*, London, 1826, ii, pp. 289-99.
[34] *Memoirs of the Verney Family in the Seventeenth Century*, ed. F. P. and M. M. Verney, London, 1907, ii, pp. 95, 261-73, 365-76.
[35] R. Grassby, op. cit., p. 356.

not common. One can certainly find examples in Hertfordshire of younger sons who made a career in some business—usually that which had provided the wealth which had brought about the gentrification of the family in the first place. But they were only a small minority of the whole, and most of them, although sons of elite families, belonged socially to the lower third of that elite. They were, for example, sons of brewers such as the Hucks or the Calverts, or bankers such as the Dimsdales or the Smiths. Among wealthy merchants proper, neither Sir Samuel Garrard, 4th Bt., nor Edward Radcliffe, nor Charles Halsey very much cut back on their highly successful commercial activities when, through the death of an elder brother, they inherited their family seats and estates. But they were the exceptions to the rule. Thus Edward Radcliffe's several older brothers, who like him had all started in the Levant trade, were only too happy to exchange a merchant's life for that of a country gentleman when their turn came to inherit Hitchin Priory.

Even if these merchant younger sons had been more plentiful, there would still remain the question of how closely they kept in touch with their elite relatives and *vice versa*. Sir Dudley North and John Verney in the late seventeenth century clearly did, but they were both strongly motivated and highly successful, and both came from long-established families securely enough entrenched to be indifferent to criticism from outsiders. On the other hand, if unrewarded by success and not bolstered by the self-confidence derived from a long gentry pedigree, it seems unlikely that these ties of the elite to younger sons in business were as common or as psychologically important as other linkages to the monied interests which have already been described and quantified.

This conclusion is reinforced, not merely by the smallness of the numbers of younger sons of squires who went into trade, but also by the probability that only a minority of those who tried in fact succeeded in rising to the top. This was likely to be the case, because of their lack of working capital and kin connections in the business—two problems admittedly soluble at one stroke by marrying the master's widow or daughter. The archetypal story of the roads to success through application to business was displayed in Hogarth's set of prints of *Industry and Idleness*, published in 1747. Here the industrious apprentice marries his master's daughter and rises to be sheriff, alderman, and finally Lord Mayor of London. But this was a wholly bourgeois career line, beginning as an artisan's apprentice in a workshop and ending in high civic office, nei-

ther of which offered any attractions to the younger sons of the
landed elite.

3. SOCIAL RELATIONS

i. Introduction

Economic penetration is one thing, but social interaction is another. How easy was it for the first generation of new men, that
trickle of purchasers and purchaser-settlers, to win acceptance among
the elite of the county into which they inserted themselves? Everything suggests that this is the critical test, since by the second
generation few would challenge a family's social respectability. In
England, unlike in France, where three generations were necessary
to purify a man of his lowly origins, one generation of landed
property and a seat, together with a genteel education, was sufficient to create a gentleman.

One significant piece of evidence for this contention is provided
by the famous quarrel of 1621 between the 2nd Earl of Arundel
and the 1st Lord Spencer in the House of Lords. When the latter
said of the Earl of Arundel that two of his noble ancestors had
been sentenced by the House for treason, the Earl retorted that
when his ancestors had been doing great and honourable service
for their Prince and country the Spencers had been shepherds.
Both statements were correct, but the House took such exception
to Arundel's slur upon Lord Spencer's ancestry that he was ordered to apologize, and when he refused to do so was committed
to the Tower.[36] The English elite were certainly sensitive about
admitting a self-made man of obscure origin into their midst. But
they seem to have had relatively little objection to the son or
grandson of such a man, provided that he had had a suitable education and consequently had the manners, graces, and values of
a gentleman, and conducted himself accordingly.

Men who rose through the professions or office naturally found
social assimilation much easier than did the monied interest. But
even the former had sometimes to move cautiously. The career of
Thomas Anderson illustrates how the few professional men who
bought into Northumberland slowly edged their way into this very
closed and archaic society. His grandfather was not even a gentleman, but he himself was educated at Cambridge and the Inns of
Court, and became a successful lawyer. In 1831 he inherited a
windfall of Newcastle urban property from a cousin. Two years

[36] *Letters of John Chamberlain*, ed. N. E. McClure, Philadelphia, 1939, ii, pp. 374-5.

later, he sold it and bought a very small country house, and three years later still a much larger house next door. He became a JP and Deputy Lieutenant, and was given the expensive but now honorific office of sheriff in 1843. Towards the end of his life, in 1861, he finally took the plunge, pulled down the larger of the two houses, and enlarged the smaller one into a really very grand Gothic seat (150 units in size) which he called Little Harle Tower. Slowly, over a period of thirty years, he had successfully inserted himself into county society and founded a lasting elite family. His son qualified as a barrister, but spent his time on local affairs, following the footsteps of his father as JP, Deputy Lieutenant, and sheriff, and marrying a daughter of the Cadogans of Brinkburn Priory— also newcomers. His grandson, who was educated in grand style at Eton, Christ Church, Oxford, and the Inner Temple, was also a barrister, JP, and sheriff. He was still in residence in Little Harle Tower on the outbreak of the Second World War in 1939. This was a family which joined the landed elite, but which never severed its ties with the professional world of the law, and whose marriage alliances were not with the older families.

Although the evidence is ambiguous, it is tempting to suggest that what distinguished English society from that of Europe was not the volume of mobility so much as the relative lack of legal, cultural, or psychological obstacles to the assimilation of newcomers. As the examples of Sir Dudley North and John Verney indicate, younger sons who made fortunes in one of the great trading companies were socially made welcome by their landed and titled families. Nor is this the only evidence of symbiosis between land and money in the late seventeenth century. One may ask in what other capital city in Europe could one have witnessed a scene like that of the funeral of a great London goldsmith, Alderman Sir Thomas Fowke, in 1698, which was attended by members of the peerage walking humbly on foot?[37] Men like Fowke, however, and occasions like his funeral were few and far between. Narcissus Luttrell, who clearly kept a close eye on London millionaires, only recorded the deaths of about one man a year worth over £40,000. Men worth £100,000 or more ranged from well-known figures like Sir Charles Duncombe or Sir Josiah Child the banker, or Sir Joseph Hern, the East India Company tycoon, down to nonentities like Mr Western an ironmonger, or Mr Boulter a grocer. There is nothing to suggest that Mr Western or Mr Boulter either aspired to or succeeded in founding a landed family.[38]

[37] N. Luttrell, *Brief Relation of State Affairs*, Oxford, 1857, ii, p. 623.
[38] Op. cit., iv, pp. 346, 488, 530; vi, pp. 130, 408.

There are four tests which can be applied to determine the degree to which newcomers to the elite, that is purchasers and purchaser-entrants, were socially assimilated. The first is how easy it was for them to obtain titles of honour; the second how many of them had experienced the same educational training as the elite; the third how many were elected MPs, especially within the county where they were seated, and particularly as Knights of the Shire; and the fourth how many of them married wives from the ranks of the elite. These will not provide direct indicators of how the landed classes regarded the monied interest, since many purchasers had obtained their wealth in such respectable pursuits as the law or government office. But they do provide an indication of the relative ease of access to titles and local offices for older families and those who bought them out. The significance of these four indicators varies considerably. Titles of honour were awarded by the Crown for its own purposes. Birth and landed wealth were always critical considerations, but political prominence, family connections, and downright corruption also played important roles. Borough MPs could often buy their seats or intimidate the electorate. The position of Knight of the Shire, on the other hand, was at the choice of the leading squires and nobility of the county, either unanimously, in which case there was no contest, or divided, in which case there was an election. The two most reliable tests of social acceptance are therefore nomination as Knight of the Shire, and intermarriage.

ii. Titles of Honour

One way to test the degree of social integration is to compare the success of purchasers of country seats as opposed to inheritors in acquiring (or inheriting) titles of honour (Table 7.5, Fig. 7.6). Only in competition for the non-hereditary title of Knight were purchasers markedly more successful than inheritors, and then only in the period after the title had been devalued on the accession of James I. Thereafter it was put up for sale to the highest bidder, and eventually was neither sought for by, nor conferred upon, members of the hereditary landed elite. After the Restoration it was largely confined to the merchant patriciates of the big cities, especially to lord mayors and similar functionaries. It is therefore hardly surprising that there were relatively more knights among purchasers than among inheritors, especially in the seventeenth century. It was by now a title without social distinction, and therefore meant nothing in terms of social integration.

Ownership of the two hereditary titles of baronet and peer show

FIG. 7.6   Proportions of Inheritors and Purchasers with Titles of Honour [Table 7.5]

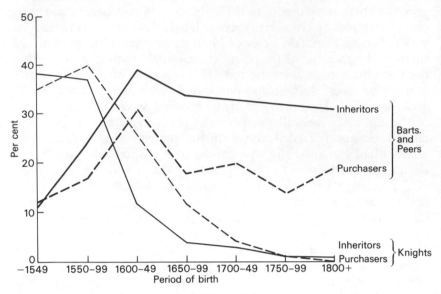

a markedly different pattern, with inheritors always well ahead of purchasers. For the period of peak creation of baronets, it is possible to be more specific, and to take a nation-wide sample and examine the degree to which this new title was open to men of mercantile origin in the decades immediately after its institution in 1611. Of the 417 new baronets created between 1611 and 1649, only nine were themselves merchants. But fifty-five were either sons of merchants or married the daughters of merchants, while another twenty-four had links at a third generation. Only 2 per cent of baronets at this period were self-made men in trade, although as many as 21 per cent had ties with trade two or three generations back.[39] This suggests that the major breakthrough into titular status by the business elite had yet to take place. It was only later, in the late seventeenth century, that a few baronetcies began to be granted to elderly childless business men whose titles thus died with them.

   Thereafter hereditary titles had social significance, and in some periods inheritors were twice as likely as purchasers to enjoy them. Even so, about a fifth of all purchasers already had, or later acquired, a hereditary title. But this was usually because of their

[39] G. E. Cockayne, *Complete Baronetage*, Exeter, i-ii, 1900-3.

service to the state in government office, law, or war, and the business men were noticeable by their relative absence in these ranks. Hereditary titles thus served to integrate purchasers from the professions into elite society, but only rarely were they much help to members of the status-seeking monied interest. The role of titles in easing the acceptance of the monied interest therefore remains uncertain, although it is clear that purchasers generally in the nineteenth century before 1880 could no longer so freely obtain access to them. Whether or not this impeded their acceptance into local society is a matter for further research into the intricacies of Victorian social etiquette.

iii. Higher Education

Another test of social integration is whether or not the sons of landed and business families underwent a similar process of higher education in the same institutions, and followed the same curriculum. Some interesting differences emerge if one categorizes owners according to their fathers' occupations under the three broad rubrics of land, office or profession, and business. These figures have to be treated with some reserve, since they include both inheritors and purchasers, and owners who had been brought up with the expectation of being younger sons, as well as those raised as heirs. However the proportions between both groups and their distribution between fathers according to occupation, do not differ sufficiently to cast doubt on the trends that are revealed. Fathers practicing an office or profession gave more of their heirs some form of higher education than those purely concerned with their estates; and those in some form of business gave fewest of all. These differences were clear and marked right up to the early nineteenth century, when they began to get blurred. For the cohort born after 1800, fewer heirs of office-holders and professions were undergoing higher education, presumably because more and more of them were going straight from school into the army (Table 7.6, Fig. 7.7).

Business men followed in the footsteps of the hereditary landed elite in the way they educated their sons, but at all times before 1800 they had significantly less enthusiasm about the merits of a university education. No doubt they wanted to give their sons the same genteel education as their social superiors, but were more afraid of moral corruption by the habits of idleness, gambling, and sexual promiscuity for which university students were notorious from 1670 to 1820. They also presumably regarded training in the classics as an irrelevant waste of time, particularly since they lacked

FIG. 7.7   Higher Education of Owners by Father's Occupation [Table 7.6]

the contacts and patronage to get their graduated children into good positions in the Church. It seems likely that they much preferred the more closely supervised and less narrowly classical or mathematical education offered by the private academies. Until the early nineteenth-century reforms in discipline and curriculum, therefore, the men of business were distinctly more dubious about the value of a university education than were the traditional landed elite. From 1600 to 1750 only about 25 per cent of their heirs are recorded as attending a university, compared with about 40 per cent of those of the hereditary landed elite.

Business men behaved quite differently from either of the other two groups in their attitude to legal education for their heirs. They were unaffected by the great boom in popularity of the Inns of Court in the early seventeenth century, but equally unaffected by the collapse of that boom in the late seventeenth and eighteenth centuries. Some 20 to 15 per cent of owners who were sons of business men attended the Inns of Court fairly consistently right through the 340-year period. There were none of those great swings of popularity which affected the education of the sons of the landed and professional classes, and as a result business men were sending more of their heirs to the Inns of Court after 1700 than were land-owners.

How one should interpret the discrepancy between landed and business parents in their attitudes to higher education is not clear. Since at the best of times only about half of all eventual heirs of established squire families were sent to the university, the lack of such an experience cannot be said to have been a bar to genteel status. The key test was rather a knowledge of Latin, which could be acquired at one of the greater public schools such as Eton or Westminister, or at a grammar school, or at one of the many academies. The test of educational integration of land and money through higher education is consequently inconclusive.

The last major educational experience for many sons of the very wealthiest members of the elite was the Grand Tour, which often lasted two years or more. It was intended to give young men a familiarity with foreign languages, foreign art, and foreign customs, and to improve their manner and deportment, without, if possible, debauching their morals. It was very expensive and not always an unmitigated success: although many returned as sophisticated connoisseurs and men of the world, others came back as syphilitic rakes and/or pretentious and boring xenophiles. But it was undoubtedly an important aristocratic *rite de passage*, especially in the late seventeenth and eighteenth centuries, and it would be interesting to know how often the sons of wealthy business men purchasers were dispatched on these risky missions. Unfortunately the data are too fragmentary to be able to offer any firm conclusions on this matter, although it is certain that some business fathers who had bought a seat and an estate were sending their heirs on the Grand Tour. Known examples are largely concentrated in the late seventeenth century, which may or may not be purely accidental. Two merchants and one scrivener who were purchasers of seats in seventeenth-century Northamptonshire sent their sons on the Tour. In Hertfordshire John Wittewronge, the heir to a wealthy Flemish cloth-merchant purchaser, was carefully groomed by his mother to conform to English elite social-behaviour patterns, a grooming which included the Grand Tour. The same happened in the late eighteenth century both to John Fiott Lee, a merchant's son and prospective heir to a distant landed relative, and to Samuel Whitbread Jun., the son of a wealthy brewer.

iv. Membership of Parliament

A much more promising test of social integration of purchasers into county society is their success in getting themselves elected members of Parliament (Table 7.7). In the sixteenth and seventeenth centuries the surprising number of seventeen, all but one of them in the two southern counties, succeeded in getting either nominated by their fellow squires or elected by the voters as Knights of the Shire, which was always one of the most coveted of elite positions. The significance of this is considerably reduced, however, when it is discovered that most of them were government office-holders with prior family connections with the local gentry. During the same period another thirteen were elected MPs for a borough in the county, which indicates local influence, but not necessarily popularity. After 1700, however, only one or two purchasers became Knights of the Shire, and only six became MPs for county boroughs. This evidence, coupled with the relative decline of titles, suggests that after 1700 it was becoming significantly more difficult rather than less for newcomers to obtain prestigious local positions. The success of purchasers in the post-1700 era in getting themselves elected MPs in other counties does not mean much, for many of these men were squires from elsewhere who for various reasons had bought an additional seat in Hertfordshire. It is also possible that the post-1700 purchasers were more likely to be active in business or a profession, and simply did not have the time to spare to sit in the House of Commons. But at the very least, the evidence does not contradict the hypothesis of growing resistance to the full acceptance of business newcomers in county society in the nineteenth century.

v. Local Office-holding

Local offices like sheriff or JP are indicators of local status, but also ambiguous ones (Table 7.8). After about 1680 few wanted to be sheriff, since it was too expensive and too time-consuming, and the old elite tended to shift the burden as far as possible on to others, of whom rich purchasers were prime targets. In Hertfordshire, purchasers after 1700 were consistently much more likely to be pricked for sheriff than inheritors, despite the fact that the median age of sheriffs was low, in the late thirties to early forties. But in Northamptonshire this grossly disproportionate involvement was only true for the late seventeenth century, and thereafter sheriffs continued to be chosen fairly equally from inheritors and purchasers in proportion to their numbers.

In the sixteenth and seventeenth centuries considerable prestige
was also attached to the office of JP. It is interesting to observe
that while in Hertfordshire the old elite packed the Bench at the
expense of newcomers, some of whom were self-made business
men, this was not true of Northamptonshire, where from the sixteenth century purchasers were as likely as inheritors to be put on
the Bench, despite their advanced age. In this respect, social integration in Northamptonshire seems to have been complete from
an early stage, the reason being that nearly all the purchasers were
respectable office-holders or lawyers, and hardly any were city
merchants. There was therefore no sense in which they could be
regarded as socially inferior and unworthy of local office. Thus
the two groups, inheritors and purchasers, continued to act together in this county, both of them deserting the Bench in the
eighteenth century because it was too much trouble. Only in the
nineteenth century does a sharp divergence appear, with the inheritors resuming their responsibilities for office and the purchasers being either largely excluded or unwilling to share the burden.

vi. Intermarriage

A more reliable test of social integration than a title of honour,
membership of the House of Commons, pricking for sheriff, or a
seat on the Bench is likely to be the degree to which inheritors of
landed estates and seats married the daughters of men with monied or commercial interests, thus trading status for hard cash. Although there are a considerable number of unknowns—about a
fifth—of whom a proportion must certainly have been daughters
of business men, the data are none the less suggestive. The impression of a relatively modest impact of the monied interest upon the
landed elite outside of Hertfordshire is reinforced by an examination of first marriages made by inheritors (Table 7.9, Fig. 7.8).
The proportion in all three counties who are definitely known to
have married the daughters of business men began at 7 per cent
in the early sixteenth century, rose to a peak of 11 per cent in the
early eighteenth century, and then fell to 3 per cent after 1800. In
Hertfordshire, which was usually the county most closely linked
to the monied interest, marriage by inheritors with the daughters
of business men also rose and then fell in the same slow secular
movement, but the proportions were all almost always twice as
high, and the peak was reached a century earlier, in the first half
of the seventeenth century (Table 7.9A). All three counties, how-

FIG. 7.8   Occupational Origins of Wives of Inheritors [Table 7.9]

ever, register the same rise beginning in the early seventeenth century, and the same marked fall beginning in the late eighteenth.

The rise causes no surprise, since it coincides precisely with contemporary comment, such as Hogarth's prints of *Marriage à la Mode*, and with evidence of substantial new wealth being made in the great London monopoly companies and in government contracting. What is far more surprising, however, is the decline of intermarriage between the landed elite and the monied interest after 1750, a decline which accelerated sharply in the nineteenth century. One may therefore conclude with some assurance that there was a constant but small-scale mingling of men of elite status with the daughters of men of business, which rose to a peak in the early eighteenth century and then fell off. At its height it undoubtedly signified a fairly common readiness among the elite to trade status for money on the marriage market. The subsequent decline probably indicates not only a rise of social snobbery, but also a decline in the willingness of young men to sacrifice personal happiness for family economic ties.

One way to test the degree to which purchasers from the monied interest were accepted into landed society is to see how many of their heirs married the daughters of landed families in the sample. Although the numbers are far too small to follow trends over time, they indicate that these heirs of monied purchasers always had much more difficulty in finding elite landed brides than did those of inheritors. Between 55 and 65 per cent of all inheritors married brides from elite families, but this was only achieved by a mere 17 per cent of heirs of monied purchasers (twenty-nine out of 174). There was clearly a strong tendency for the children of the latter to marry their own kind.

This figure of 55 to 65 per cent for marriage of inheritors with members of their own class is surprisingly low. The second largest category is unfortunately 'unknown', who fairly consistently comprised about 20 per cent of all marriages. The largest known occupational group with whom inheritors married were the office-holders and professionals. Previously well below 10 per cent of all marriages, the proportion began to rise sharply after 1750 to reach more than a quarter of all marriages among those born in the nineteenth century. If the mingling of land and money on this personal level was low in the Victorian period, that between land and the professions was equally high. This finding reinforces the suggestion that in social terms the nineteenth century saw the rise of the professional classes rather than the rise of the commercial or industrial bourgeoisie.

The ambiguous complexity of attitudes on both sides in the seventeenth century is well illustrated by the story of Stephen Fox. He came from borderline gentry stock, his father drawing an exiguous living from rental income. He was given a good basic education, including Latin, by the help of an uncle, and in 1640, at the age of thirteen, went off to Court in London to make his way in the world. Half a century and one revolution later, he was one of the richest commoners in England, the indispensable financial agent and adviser of the government, and a friend and associate of nobles, courtiers, and high officials. Although he used some of his vast wealth to buy land and a country house as a safe investment, he was not in the least interested in becoming a country squire, and never went near his seat for thirty years. The furthest that he went to copy the life-style of the elite was to build himself an elegant villa just outside London at Chiswick, in which to entertain his friends. Nor did he seek a peerage for himself, and indeed there were well-informed reports that he rejected several offers of one.

He did, however, have high social ambitions for his children. His only surviving son by his first marriage was childless, and it soon became clear that Sir Stephen would have no male heirs to inherit his fortune. All his attention was therefore concentrated upon providing socially distinguished husbands for his two surviving daughters, both of whom married peers. On the other hand, one of these sons-in-law was a disreputable compulsive gambler, while the other made Fox pay dearly for his consent: the ratio between his wife's cash portion and her jointure, the annuity promised in her widowhood in return, was twice that normal in socially equal marriages.

In 1698, Fox was given a brutal lesson in what his aristocratic friends really thought about him. After the death of his elder daughter, his son-in-law, Lord Cornwallis, had remarried the Duchess of Buccleuch, and died soon after. The Duchess had been a friend of Fox's for over thirty years, he had spent much time and effort in sorting out her tangled affairs, and he was even paying for the funeral of her husband—his former son-in-law. In accordance with the custom of the day, he put a funeral escutcheon over his front door, bearing the arms of Lord Cornwallis and his two wives, the first his own daughter Elizabeth Fox, and the second the Duchess of Buccleuch. On learning of this, the Duchess 'grew so far enraged . . . that she . . . caused it immediately to be torn down, and the arms of the first lady to be razed out, and set it up again without her arms'. This was the unforgivable insult, a reminder that despite his urbanity, culture, and social graces, despite his great services to the government, despite his immense wealth, despite his lifelong association at Court with nobles and men of fashion, his relatively humble origins had never been forgotten.

And yet, when a late second marriage unexpectedly provided Sir Stephen with two sons to succeed him, both of them made dazzlingly successful social careers. They were carefully educated at Eton, Christ Church and on the Grand Tour. The elder married the great Strangways heiress and was made Earl of Ilchester, while the second married a daughter of the Duke of Richmond and was made Lord Holland.[40]

The story indicates that in England there were enduring, al-

[40] C. Clay, *Public Finance and Private Wealth: the Career of Sir Stephen Fox 1627-1716*, Oxford, 1978, pp. 1-3, 175-6, 196, 246, 269, 276-7, 283, 296-7, 305, 329.

though usually latent, barriers to full social acceptance among the elite of the first generation of self-made men, even ones, like Stephen Fox, who had made their money in government finance rather than in trade or private usury. It seems likely that Fox's firm rejection of offers of a peerage were based on a fear that he might expose himself to ridicule, a fear which the episode of the funeral escutcheon can only have reinforced. On the other hand, his ambitions for his children were unlimited, and he was able to buy, at a price, peerage titles for his daughters, while his sons had no trouble in gaining full acceptance in the highest ranks of society, particularly since they had been educated as gentlemen.

vii. Social Mingling: London

One more aspect of the interaction of land and money is at the purely social level of personal face-to-face sociability at clubs, parties, assemblies, race-tracks, and private engagements. In the late Elizabethan and Jacobean period, when the London merchant tycoons first became prominent enough to arouse comment, the relationship between the monied interest and the landed interest appears to have been largely confined to a simple matter of money-lending. In the sixteenth and early seventeenth centuries, the contacts of the great capitalist merchants and financiers of London with the landed elite were like those of Shylock and the aristocracy of Venice; the former acted as the money-lenders—at a price—to sustain the extravagance of a spendthrift class of courtiers and fops, which is no guarantee of social esteem and mutual respect. To give but one example among many, in 1620 James Anton's widow declared that her late husband 'had great dealings with many of the chief nobility and gentry of this realm'. Indeed he did, but it is very doubtful whether his noble clients such as the Earls of Leicester, Essex, Cumberland, or Oxford ever invited him to dinner, or thought any the better of him because of their indebtedness to him.[41]

Despite the attendance on foot of several peers at the funeral of the goldsmith banker Sir Thomas Fowke, there is good reason to believe that Court and City lived apart.[42] For one thing, during the seventeenth century, housing segregation in London actually increased. The landed nobility and squirearchy moved out of the old walled city into the West End, but the monied interest did not follow them. Of the thirty-seven aldermen of London elected be-

[41] Public Record Office, Chancery Proceedings, Series I, James I, A1/62.
[42] For Fowke's funeral, see above, p. x.

tween 1687 and 1701 and alive in 1695, thirty-one then lived within the walls and six just outside. A directory of 1667 showed that of some 2,000 London merchants and bankers, only 4 per cent lived in the West End, and even they were confined to the by then unfashionable part of it. As a result, in the early eighteenth century the nobility and gentry lived isolated lives in the rapidly expanding western suburbs around St James's Square and Mayfair, and the monied men still kept largely within the walls of the old city to the east. The first Lord Mayor of London to live in the fashionable West End was Sir James Bateman, father of a future Viscount, who in 1717 took up residence in St James's Square.

Nor did the clubs act as bridges between the landed and the monied interest, and as late as 1814 Captain Gronow observed that 'the members of the clubs of London, many years since, were without exception belonging to the aristocratic world'. London was still, in Addison's words a century earlier, 'an aggregate of various nations [i.e. classes], distinguished from each other by their respective customs, manners and interest'. As late as 1780 von Archenholz could remark 'two towns many miles apart could not be more different from each other than the City and the West End. . . . The West Londoners are derided by the inhabitants of the City for their idleness, their love of luxury and their fondness for French manners; but the West Londoners amply repay this derision by depicting the City Englishman as an impotent uncouth animal who only sees merit in money'.[43]

What is not in doubt, however, is the huge influx of country squires and noblemen into London, at least for part of the year, which began with the revival of court life and the social season at the Restoration, and continued thereafter. In 1665, a conservative commentator like Edward Waterhouse was lamenting the social effects of such a migration with a passion which wrought havoc with his style:

immoderate flocking to, and residing in, London and Westminster and the precincts thereof, from the several quarters of the country and nation, where the nobility and gentry reside, and their seats are, is . . . a great danger to destroy persons of worth in their virtue and fortune, by drawing them from their retirements, where they may live thriftily and usefully to the king, country, and themselves, into the public, where they are taken off their local service, and assaulted by delicacies and vices of cost, effeminacy, and inconsistence with all abode of virtue.

[43] L. Stone, 'The Residential Development of the West End of London in the Seventeenth Century', in *After the Reformation*, ed. B. C. Malament, Philadelphia, 1980, pp. 186-8; J. W. von Archenholz, *England und Italien*, quoted in R. and E. Forster, *European Society in the Eighteenth Century*, New York, 1969, pp. 16-17.

Waterhouse was obliged to admit, however, that the attractions of London life in the fashionable West End were now all but irresistible. It was there—and only there—that there were to be found in abundance 'rich wives, spruce mistresses, pleasant houses, good diet, rare wines, neat servants, fashionable furniture, pleasures and profits the best of all sorts'.[44]

Nor was this all. The fact that Parliament now sat annually rather than intermittently meant that most of the peers and up to 500 squires were drawn to London on business from late November to early April. The London 'season' also began about the same time, in November, and was at its height from February to April. The date of the season in the 1740s and 1750s can be documented quite closely. In October, Horace Walpole used to lament that there was no one yet in town, but by November he was rejoicing that it was full of people. In April he began complaining again that 'everybody is going out of town', and by May 'the country gentlemen are all gone'. From May until October the town was 'notoriously empty' and Walpole was bored with 'the usual deadness of the summer'. In August the place was empty, 'there is not a coach to be seen, the streets are new paving, and the houses new painting, just as it always is at this season'.[45]

The tide of squires and nobles flowing annually into London was thus highly seasonal, limited first to four and then six winter months, growing longer and longer as the century progressed. It also grew in scale, sucking in more and more of the county elite, as evidenced by the steady expansion of the elegant squares and residential streets to the north and west of Hyde Park. As Walpole remarked in 1776, 'rows of houses shoot out every way like a polypus'.[46] In the early nineteenth century the season developed an elaborate ritual of exclusiveness, designed to keep out all but the social elite.[47] Outside London the growth of spas like Bath, Tunbridge Wells, and later of seaside watering-places like Brighton, Lowestoft, and Scarborough, meant that the nobles and squires spent less and less time in their country seats, and more and more time in fashionable places of assembly. In 1778 it was said that the Duke of Devonshire's grandfather used to spend nine months at Chatsworth, his father six months, and himself three months. In the same year Dr Johnson offered his explanation for the trend: 'there was not now the same temptation to live in the country as

[44] E. Waterhouse, *The Gentleman's Monitor*, London, 1665, pp. 292, 295.

[45] *Horace Walpole's Correspondence*, ed. W. A. Lewis, New Haven, 1937-80, 17, pp. 165, 183, 398, 450, 503; 18, pp. 88-9, 211, 311, 496; 19, p. 39; 20, pp. 50, 89, 315, 438; 21, p. 427; 22, pp. 508, 520; 24, p. 149.

[46] Op. cit., 24, p. 238. See J. Summerson, *Georgian London*, London, 1945.

[47] L. Davidoff, *The Best Circles: Society Etiquette and the Season*, London, 1973.

formerly. The pleasures of social life were much better enjoyed in the town, and there was not now in the country that power and influence in proprietors of land which they had in olden times, and made the country so agreeable to them'. Johnson was seriously exaggerating the decline of rural political power and prestige attached to ownership of and residence in a larger country seat and estate, but he was correct in evaluating the importance of the improved amenities for social life in London.[48] This influx of landowners into London, which seems to have been at its height in the eighteenth century, must certainly have had some effect in increasing contact between the landed and monied interest, even if the two did live in separate areas of this sprawling metropolis. In the nineteenth century, however, there seems to have been a drift of the elite back to country living, stimulated partly by the growing obsession with the rural sports of fox-hunting and shooting, and partly by a renewed sense of social responsibility for the maintenance of law and good order in the increasingly turbulent countryside.

Another aspect of the process of assimilation was the suburbanization of growing areas around London, caused by monied men building weekend or commuting villas in the nearby countryside. The southern parts of Hertfordshire, for example, were by the early eighteenth century thickly sprinkled with villas owned by city merchants, alongside seats owned by noblemen and squires. This intermingling was even more evident on the banks of the Thames about London, and in 1740 it was said that: 'The river on both sides down to London is full of villages, as Isleworth, Twickenham, Petersham, Richmond, Chiswick, Mortlake, Barn Elms, Fulham, Putney, Hammersmith, Battersea, and Chelsea, and many more, and all these villages are full of beautiful buildings, being country houses of noblemen, gentlemen, and indeed tradesmen of the city of London'.[49] John Roque's map of London and its suburbs of 1746 confirms this description, showing both banks of the river full of elegant houses set in elaborate symmetrical gardens, often with rectilinear canals. Some belonged to the high court aristocracy such as the Duke and Duchess of Argyll and the Earl of Harrington, and others to humbler men like Sir Matthew Decker, 'Justice Salwyn', and 'Mr Jeffries'.

The statistical evidence of social mobility, which seems to sug-

[48] *Boswell in Extremes 1776-1778*, ed. C. McC. Weiss and F. A. Pottle, New Haven, 1970, pp. 169, 184; see also *Private Papers of James Boswell*, ed. G. Scott and F. A. Pottle, New York, 1932, 15, p. 173.
[49] *The Foreigner's Guide to London*, London, 1752, p. 162.

gest a positive hardening of class barriers in the nineteenth century, is supported by a similar change in the relations of the owners of seats with the respectable bourgeoisie of the localities. In the late seventeenth and eighteenth centuries, most great houses were open for inspection by tourists of the respectable middle classes. In the nineteenth century, however, this privilege was curtailed, partly because the numbers of visitors was becoming unmanageable, partly because the owners were spending more and more time in their country seats, and partly because of a social withdrawal of the landed interest in the face of growing competition from bourgeois and industrial wealth. Thus in 1846, an anonymous author recalled that two generations before, the local castle, owned by an earl and countess, had been open once a week to all respectable neighbours, from borough magistrates to minor gentry to curates. Now, however, the park gates were shut upon the locals and 'the castle was filled with the fashionable denizens of St James and Grosvenor Square. It seemed but an offshoot from London— London hours, London habits, London morals'.[50] Court and Country were at last united in a common world of fashion to the exclusion of both the City and the local parish gentry.

The extent to which these connections through shared titles, education, membership of Parliament, local office-holding, marriage, and social intercourse in London added up to psychological assimilation will be discussed in the next chapter.

[50] Anon., *The English Matron*, London, 1846, pp. 225-6.

VIII

PROFILE OF A LANDED ELITE

1. BASIC PATTERNS

i. Composition

Based on materials supplied in the previous chapters, it is now possible to stand back and draw a profile of the landed elite in three counties over a 340-year span. In many aspects the counties diverged so widely from one another that they might be in different countries rather than different regions in one small and politically very centralized island nation-state. Usually, therefore, the profile has to be broken into three parts to bring out these very real differences.

The composition and structure of the English upper classes differed from those of other European countries in several ways. One is that its titular aristocracy did not form a *noblesse d'épée*, clearly distinct from and superior to a *noblesse de robe*. The reasons for this were that the former had lost most of its credibility during the Wars of the Roses, was considerably pruned by Henry VII, and for 150 years lacked an outlet for martial activity, since there was no standing army before the late seventeenth century. There was therefore no functional difference between the old aristocracy and the new, and no snobbish esprit de corps of a warrior class which would exclude lawyers or government officials from full membership.

Another difference is that in England there was only one elite, the landed class, with no powerful and self-confident urban patriciate to act as a counterweight. For reasons which are still not clear, successful merchants in England did not form a parallel, hereditary, town-based elite, like those of Amsterdam, Lyons, or Genoa. In England, only a handful of the very richest sought to buy landed estates and merge into the landed class, so that cannot be the explanation. But the fact is that few English bourgeois families lasted more than three generations in a city, partly, it seems, because of the disintegrating effects of partible inheritance, and partly because of a very high level of demographic attrition, not compensated for by the elaborate fictive kin devices for name-changing developed by the landed elite.

A third distinctive feature of the English landed elite was the fact that their younger sons were downwardly mobile, with few career options except the church, the army or at worst unpaid bailiffs on their fathers' or elder brothers' estates, unless they should have the good fortune to marry an heiress. Because there were no special legal privileges or hereditary titles attached to them, younger sons had to make their own way in the world.

In the Tudor and early Stuart periods, the rise of the nation-state gave birth to a new *noblesse de robe*, rewarded from the loot of Church property, who moved in to fill the vacuum in the old aristocracy created by the deliberate destruction of their 'over-mighty subjects' by the Crown. This new Henrician nobility were almost to a man people who, like the Cecils or the Russells, had risen through office-holding. Meanwhile, the expansion of trade provided opportunities for the building of great fortunes and the consequent return to the ranks of the landed gentry of a few of the descendants of gentry younger sons, who in the fifteenth century had often sought their fortunes in the wool trade. Such were the Fitzwilliams of Milton or the Ishams of Lamport in North-amptonshire. The gentry had long also numbered among its new recruits a handful of former gentry younger sons who had been able to buy themselves an estate from the profits of the law: such were Sir Edward Montagu of Boughton in Northamptonshire or the first Sir John Cutts of Salisbury Hall in Hertfordshire. At the same time, the gentry *in situ* waxed richer in the sixteenth century as agricultural prices outstripped all others. As these minor gentry rose, they enlarged their estates and their manor houses and (as part of the wing-clipping operation against the old aristocracy) were encouraged by the Crown to help in running the counties and thus to join the ruling elite. Such were the Brudenells of Deene, Nor-thants.

These numerous groups all competing for land would have driven up its price to prohibitive levels if the market had not been flooded by the Dissolution of the Monasteries and the dispersal of their lands in gifts to buy political support and in sales to pay for war. Thus a century after the battle of Bosworth, the social situation had fundamentally changed, as the boundaries between for-merly distinct social groups became permeable to the strongest elements of those below. The result was the development of a cohesive and united ruling class made up of three former groups: the survivors of the old *noblesse d'épée*, the new *noblesse de robe*, and the powerful country squires whose ranks were not exclusively landed but included, as did those of the aristocracy, some success-ful lawyers and office-holders, a few descendants of gentry younger sons who had made good in trade, and a handful of rich merchants turned gentry.

All the members of this unified elite had some or all of four things in common. The first was their landed wealth. They were owners of substantial tracts of land whose income supported the expense of living idly in luxury in a great seat. They were the 1,700 landlords who in 1873 owned about 40 per cent of all the rural real estate in England and Wales. The second was their style of life, which included a superior education, often at one of the two elite schools, Eton and Westminster, a knowledge of the world not infrequently acquired on the Grand Tour, and the maintenance of a generous level of hospitality. The third was their possession of a house of a certain size with decorative public rooms for entertaining, elaborate pleasure-grounds, and possibly also a park. The fourth was their potential access to power. Even if they chose not to exercise it, men with such credentials had an inherited right to compete for offices involving administrative duties and public service. These are the features which made them an elite of wealth, status, and power.

ii. Numbers

The numerical expansion of the squirearchy in the sixteenth and early seventeenth centuries varied from county to county (Table 8.1, Fig. 8.1). Hertfordshire and Northamptonshire were regions pacified by the Tudors early in the sixteenth century, which made it possible for the squires to live in unfortified houses, and allowed local politics and administration to be carried on without the use of physical force and bloodshed. In both counties the number of the elite rose steadily to a peak of about eighty around the middle of the seventeenth century, which is perhaps one of the most convincing proofs of the rise of the gentry that can be offered. After about 1670 a hardening of social attitudes tended to keep out new entrants, and the exhaustion of the sources of lavish royal bounty meant a tailing-off of large fortunes made in national politics or administration. In Hertfordshire, numerical stability was maintained, as the inflow of newcomers matched the outflow of families that died out or decayed. In Northamptonshire, however, there was a net numerical decline as replacements failed to keep pace with normal attrition. Only in the latter half of the nineteenth century did numbers in both counties begin to rise again, as *nouveaux riches* from banking, trade, and the professions—but not from industry—began to trickle into the countryside and build themselves huge houses to match their affluence.

FIG. 8.1   Frequency Count of Owners in Sample [Table 8.1]

In Northumberland the evolution was entirely different. Country house building could not begin until after the pacification of
the Scottish borders in about 1610, and numbers grew slowly but
steadily thereafter for the next 270 years, as communications improved and as more and more of the countryside was opened up
to agriculture and coal-mining. As a result, whereas in the south
elite numbers rose rapidly before the mid-seventeenth century and
levelled off thereafter, in the north they continued to rise right up
to the great agricultural depression that began in 1873.

iii. Demography

The demographic characteristics of this elite were in many ways
very unlike those of both the English poor and the Continental
elite. Nearly all of those who reached adulthood married, although
the proportion of lifelong bachelors tended to rise, from a negligible 2 per cent in the sixteenth century to 12 per cent in the
nineteenth—for reasons which probably lie in greater freedom of
personal choice, less family pressure, and increased involvement
in military and overseas administrative careers. They began in the
sixteenth century by marrying early, at about twenty-one, but
postponed the decision later and later to twenty-six or twenty-

seven when in the eighteenth century they acquired freedom of choice to select their own spouses. By the standards of the age, they were a fairly healthy group of adults, with an expectation at twenty-one of living to about sixty-three, except for the cohort born in the bad period of the late seventeenth century. Even so, only about half lived to see the marriage of their son and heir. But because of their relative longevity, only the cohort born between 1650 and 1700 could expect to succeed their fathers before the age of twenty-five.

They married wives only two or three years younger than themselves, thus avoiding the large age gap between spouses that occurred in some places on the Continent like Italy where grooms of thirty or more married young girls in their late teens. For most of the period, owners could expect a married life of around twenty-two years before the death of one or other spouse, but their chances improved considerably to around twenty-nine years as mortality declined in the late nineteenth century. On the average, they produced five recorded children each up to 1650 (the true figure was certainly higher), dropping to four thereafter. This decline was due at first to the rise in mortality and later to family limitation practiced in order to reduce the cost of launching younger sons and daughters into the world and to reduce strain and stress on the wives caused by multiple childbirths; it is also possible that fertility itself may have declined, for reasons which are obscure but may be related to the wider diffusion of gonorrhoea.

iv. Titular Ranks

The degree to which the elite possessed titles of honour does not signify very much since numbers fluctuated more according to the whims of royal policy in granting them than to the merits or status of the recipients (Table 8.2, Fig. 8.2). The non-heritable title of knight was originally conferred on the field of battle, and the proportion of the elite who were knights hovered between 24 per cent during the generous days of Henry VIII and 15 per cent during the parsimonious days of Queen Elizabeth. Immediately upon his accession, James I made knighthoods saleable commodities, and inflated numbers to such a degree that over a third of all owners in our three counties were knights in 1619. Between 1603 and 1605 no fewer than twenty-two London aldermen were knighted in a wholly unprecedented burst of generosity.[1] Subsequent monarchs

[1] A. B. Beaven, *Aldermen of the City of London*, London, 1908, i, pp. 147, 158, 208, 256; ii, p. 222.

FIG. 8.2   Proportion of Owners with Titles of Honour [Table 8.2]

were far less generous on or off the field of battle. In the late
seventeenth century knighthood became a suitable reward not only
for Lord Mayors of London, as it had been since 1522, but also
for other civic dignitaries and for successful business men or judges.
It was hardly appropriate for members of the county elite. After
about 1740 very few knighthoods were conferred at all, and from
then until 1880 the proportion of owners who were knights drops
to negligible proportions. Indeed after 1860 there were none at all.
The title was now reserved as a reward for meritorious work in
public service such as diplomacy, war, Indian and colonial administration, local government, and the home civil service.[2]

    The new title of baronet was invented in 1611, partly to make
money, and partly as a status substitute for the now badly dis-
credited knighthood. Numbers rose fairly steadily to a peak in
1680 of about 20 per cent of all owners, and then slowly declined
over the next hundred years to below 10 per cent, as old titles died
out and the Crown failed to create new ones on a comparable
scale. Peerage titles, the most prestigious of all, were carefully
husbanded by the Tudors, and the proportion of the landed elite
who were peers remained fairly stable at about 5 to 8 per cent.

    [2] F. M. L. Thompson, 'Britain' in *European Landed Elites in the Nineteenth Century*, ed.
D. Spring, Baltimore, 1977, p. 40.

Under the Stuarts, however, the inflation of honours took off, and
the proportion grew steadily for a century until it reached 15 per
cent by 1700, after which it levelled off for eighty years. Thereafter the proportion fell steadily throughout the nineteenth century, ending up at 11 per cent of the sample of owners. The reason
for this fall is not difficult to discover. Hard-pressed by their supporters, politicians found it difficult to refuse titles for notable
public service in war or peace, with the result that after 1800 large
numbers of men were being made peers who had little or no landed
estates to support their titles. George III protested, but to no avail,
and between 1802 and 1830 thirty of the ninety-two new peers
were virtually landless, like Lord Nelson for example.[3] Although
the landed elite itself was increasingly becoming oriented to public
service, this stress on political merit rather than birth or wealth
told against it in the long run. Throughout the nineteenth century
there was consequently an increasing divergence between possession of a title of honour and the holding of a large estate and
membership of the landed elite of the counties.

v. Higher Education

The shift of elite responsibilities from military performance on the
battlefield to administrative talents as a bureaucrat and verbal dex-
terity as a counsellor or orator led to a widespread concern over
the proper training and education for the efficient fulfilment of
these new obligations. It was no longer enough to absorb gentlemanly values and martial skills by service in a noble household.
Not only the body, character, and behaviour, but also the mind
now needed training. The elite therefore turned to the University
to provide a gentlemanly knowledge of Latin, training in rhetoric
and the powers of logical reasoning, and knowledge about the world
and politics. The University also helped to create a network of
nation-wide friendships through shared adolescent residence in
College, the value of which in a society that ran on patronage and
clientage can hardly be exaggerated.

University admission figures, however, need to be treated with
caution. Those for this early period are extremely patchy and incomplete and only comprise a proportion of those attending the
university.[4] Unfortunately, it was precisely the eldest sons of the

[3] M. W. McCahill, 'Peerage Creations and the Changing Character of the British Nobility, 1750-1830', *English Historical Review*, 1981, p. 274.
[4] For a discussion of the accuracy of matriculation records, see L. Stone, 'The Size and
Composition of the Oxford Student Body', in *The University in Society*, ed. L. Stone, Princeton, 1974, i, pp. 82-8, 91-2, 109. Further work on the Cambridge data shows that the
corrections applied to Cambridge matriculation figures in the eighteenth century to obtain

social elite, who hardly ever took degrees, who most commonly omitted to matriculate and so were not recorded. A further problem is that there is a serious discrepancy in the degree of error in the records of the two universities, which almost certainly creates a discrepancy in the completeness of the recording of students from Northamptonshire and Hertfordshire. Since geographical propinquity was always a very important factor in the selection of a university, most Northamptonshire men went to Oxford, and most Hertfordshire men to Cambridge. Since Oxford students are not as well documented as those at Cambridge, this may mean that the number of Northamptonshire gentry recorded as attending the university is artificially low, at least before 1700. It must also be borne in mind that the figures for the education of heirs and of younger sons are not necessarily the same. Since it is owners, not owners' sons, who have been counted, heirs are fully covered, but younger sons only when they happened by chance eventually to make their way into the sample. Furthermore, the educational significance of the data is limited by the fact that an elder son, who attended a fashionable college for one term and then moved on, rates the same as the younger son who completed his four years of study and took a degree. But there is not sufficient data on enough owners for it to be possible to produce more refined statistics: we are obliged to work with what we have.

The second problem, quite apart from that of the incompleteness of the records, is that there were great changes over time in the importance which was attached by the landed elite to attendance at a university or Inn of Court, and what they hoped to get out of them. Before about 1560, this elevated social class was not much concerned with higher education but thereafter interest increased rapidly, and especially from 1620 to 1640 it became extremely fashionable to attend a college or an Inn of Court. For this brief period, there was a consensus that a smattering of academic and legal education was a very valuable component of gentility. After 1670, however, disillusionment set in. Fewer of the sons of the landed elite attended the Inns of Court, and for a while many fewer of them attended the university. When they came, they tended to bunch up in one or two socially prestigious colleges, notably Christ Church at Oxford and Trinity at Cambridge.

Variations in the degree of importance elite parents attached to an education at Oxbridge or an Inn of Court is revealed by the

---

estimated total admission figures were in fact far too low. It is likely that in fact Cambridge numbers fell at about the same rate as those at Oxford, not faster and further as indicated in op. cit., Graph 1, p. 6.

graphs of the proportion of heirs at these institutions. Even without making adjustments to allow for serious under-registration in
the sixteenth century and some in the seventeenth, the trend is
clear enough, and is supported by everything that is already known
about these institutions (Table 8.3, Fig. 8.3). Attendance by the
landed elite shot up to a peak in the mid-seventeenth century and
then fell back amid widespread disillusionment with the value of
an academic education, and extensive fears of moral corruption
and debauchery. At its peak, over 40 per cent of the elite attended
a university, usually for only a couple of years and without taking
a degree. The proportion then fell to 30 per cent for those born in
the last half of the seventeenth century, but thereafter it picked

FIG. 8.3   Proportion of Owners with Higher Education [Table 8.3]

up again, equalling the early seventeenth-century peak by the late eighteenth century, and soaring beyond it to nearly 50 per cent of those born after 1800. The flight of the elite from the universities in the late seventeenth century, although serious, was thus less long-lasting and less dramatic than the flight of men of lesser rank and wealth. Even so, at no time before 1880 do we have evidence that as many as half the elite of the three counties attended the university, even in the early seventeenth and late nineteenth centuries.

As for the Inns of Court, attendance by the elite boomed in the late sixteenth and early seventeenth centuries, since the Inns acted not only as a training ground for professional barristers but also as a finishing school for wealthy amateurs. After 1660, the profession of barrister contracted, and the future squires went elsewhere, probably mostly on the Grand Tour. By the nineteenth century, the Inns of Court played an insignificant role in the education of the landed elite (Fig. 8.3).

Taking both sets of institutions of higher education together, it was only in the first half of the seventeenth century that the proportion of the elite attending one or the other rose above 50 per cent. This does not necessarily mean that the elite were generally less well educated during the late seventeenth and eighteenth and nineteenth centuries than they had been in the peak period of attendance in the early seventeenth century. The probability is that they were merely being educated in other places. Those who went to a boarding grammar school, and also the many others who attended the numerous private academies, remained at school until much the same age as that at which they had left the university a century before. Thus secondary educational institutions as well as private tutoring in large measure offered the same curriculum to boys of the same age as had earlier been acquired at the university. Many of the private tutors and the schoolmasters of these schools and academies were of the same background and calibre as the college tutors of the earlier period.

The important change is the increasingly exclusive social segregation of the educational experience. Not only were the poor now virtually excluded from the university, but the sons of the elite were either taught at home by private tutors, or were largely congregated in two schools, Westminster and Eton, and also in two colleges, Christ Church at Oxford and Trinity at Cambridge. The hardening of class lines, which has been observed throughout this study during the eighteenth and nineteenth centuries was replicated and reinforced by social segregation in the educational institutions. The success of the colleges in inventing and maintaining the highly privileged undergraduate status of Fellow-commoner is proof of this segregation, even within the same college.

2. OBLIGATIONS

i. Fiscal Prudence

The minimum duties of an owner were first to pass on to his successor the inheritance of seat and estates in as good a condition as he himself had found them, and second to provide a responsible, appropriately educated son, who would live to adulthood and so be able to carry on the line, to succeed him. If he left both estate and seat in more flourishing shape than he found them, so much the better. There were four ways to achieve this end, three positive and one negative, all being complementary to each other. One was to improve the revenue of the estates by agricultural innovation, enclosure, introduction of better drainage or new crops, efficient surveying and rent collection. Where applicable, the encouragement of urban development and mining of coal and other ores provided enormously lucrative new sources of income. All this needed capital, but the returns could be high. The owner could also increase family wealth by obtaining high political or military office, or a sinecure place or pension, or by marrying an heiress. The second positive action was to secure the succession by fathering a legitimate heir, together with a small reserve of younger sons to be drawn upon to take over the succession if necessary. The third positive contribution was to maintain in good repair, and possibly to renovate the seat and grounds and bring them up to the latest fashion in architecture and landscape gardening.

The negative action was the exercise of prudence in expenditure by the avoidance of gambling and extravagant building projects, and by the practice of family limitation to avoid an excess of younger sons who had to be launched into the world and of daughters who had to be expensively trained in the necessary graces to catch a husband, and even more expensively married off.

Given these ideals and constraints imposed by the imperious demands of family continuity, what sort of lives did these landed elite live in their large country houses? It is important to establish that, despite appearances, they were not free agents, at liberty to behave as they pleased. In return for the wealth and power and prestige which they inherited, certain codes of conduct were expected of them. There were at all times cultural constraints, derived both from their upbringing, and from the views of their peers and inferiors.

The prime obligation was neither to dissipate the inheritance by wanton extravagance, nor to bring discredit upon the family name by notorious parsimony and avarice. George Payne provides an object-lesson of the first. In 1790, George's grandfather, René Payne, a Lothbury banker whose father had been Chairman of the East India Company, bought a great estate with a rent-roll of £17,000 a year on the Northamptonshire-Leicestershire border. Here in 1793 he had Soane build him a modest but extremely elegant country house, Sulby Hall. On his death six years later, he left this to his younger son George, who was killed in a duel in 1810, leaving as son and heir a boy of the same name, then aged seven. Young George went to Eton and Oxford, where he managed the difficult feat of getting himself sent down from Christ Church for his sporting excesses. Upon coming of age, he spent the next forty-four years in consistently extravagant living. In the process, he not only worked his way through the £300,000 accumulated during his minority, but also 'two other large fortunes which he successively inherited from relatives'. He enlarged Sulby Hall, whence he served as sheriff 'in unparalleled state', but soon had to sell it to recoup himself. In its place he bought Pitsford Hall, a more workaday country house which had served as a base for successive Masters of the Pytchley Hunt, an office which he held not once but twice, and which he filled with 'unwonted splendour'. He owned racehorses and was a reckless gambler on both cards and horses—he thought nothing of losing £32,000 on one race. He also speculated—usually unsuccessfully—in everything from 3 per cent stocks to Russian tallow. When he died unmarried in London in 1878— of a stroke at a race-meeting—the Prince of Wales attended his funeral.[5] He remained a popular figure in the county, but not one whose career anyone would hold up for emulation.

At the other extreme lies the behaviour of Sir Hervey Elwes, Bt., of Stoke College, Suffolk, in the early eighteenth century. On the death of his grandfather, he inherited a large but vastly encumbered estate, in the process of salvaging which he carried fiscal prudence so far as to turn into a miser, 'the most perfect picture of human penury that ever existed'. When his nephew and heir came on a visit to his uncle, he would first stop at the local inn to change his clothes into rags in order not to offend the old gentle-

---

[5] *Dictionary of National Biography*, *sub* George Payne.

man by his decent appearance. 'Shy, diffident and timid in the extreme', 'the hoarding up, and the counting his money was his greatest joy'. He kept only one man and two maidservants in the huge house, and in season they all fed on nothing but partridges from the estate. As a result, Sir Hervey spent a mere £110 a year, and died in 1763 worth a quarter of a million pounds.[6] This was a manner of life far more heartily condemned by contemporaries than the reckless dissipation of George Payne, although both provided paradigms of how a gentleman should not conduct himself.

Anything in between, however, was generally acceptable, and views about the proper way in which time and money ought to be spent allowed a great deal of latitude for variety and indeed eccentricity. Above all, a country-house owner was expected to give the appearance of being leisured. As we have seen, quite a number, especially in the nineteenth century, had some professional occupation, but even so Dr Johnson's aphorism holds good, that it is 'the essence of a gentleman's character to bear the visible mark of no profession whatsoever'. This enforced idleness was itself a serious test of character for its practitioners, as contemporaries realized only too well. In 1706 Sir Nicholas L'Estrange of Norfolk warned his son: 'Of all degrees of mankind, the fate of your nobility and gentry seems the hardest; who are generally persuaded and too apt to think themselves born only to ease and pleasure, and the time that thus lies upon their hands too often proves their ruin'.[7] It was careers such as that of George Payne that Sir Nicholas clearly had in mind.

Even if one chose to ignore this principle that a gentleman was by definition a man of leisure, one of the main constraints upon combining country-house living with the active pursuit of a professional career was the slowness of communications. The great improvements of the eighteenth century, notably macadamized, turnpike road surfaces and sprung coaches, revolutionized transportation along the main roads. Even so, travel with wife, children and servants from a country house in the north Midlands to London could easily take several days. Only the advent of the railways in the 1840s and 1850s at last made communications so fast that an owner could combine a job in London with living in the country. Before that time, the busy MP or professional lawyer or man of business was tied to his office, and only in a county like Hert-

    [6] E. Topham, *The Life of the Late John Elwes Esq.*, London, 1790, pp. 4, 8, 13.
    [7] D. Cherry, 'Sir Nicholas L'Estrange, Non-Juror', *Norfolk Archaeology*, 34, 1968, p. 328; H. L. Piozzi, *Anecdotes of the Late Samuel Johnson*, ed. S. C. Roberts, Cambridge, 1925, p. 102.

fordshire within a few hours drive from London could he conveniently establish himself before retirement. Examples of commuter business men in Hertfordshire in the late nineteenth century were Sir John Bennet Lawes of Rothamstead and Henry Gibbs, later Lord Aldenham, of Aldenham House. In the main, therefore, the country seat was a place for leisure and entertainment and the fulfilment of paternalist obligations to local society. Only rarely was it used for the recharging of energies strained by the bustle and stress of city life.

ii. Holding of Office

What, then, did the majority do with their time? Owners of seats were, and were expected to be, a power elite, holding such offices as sheriff, JP, Deputy Lieutenant, Commissioner for Taxes, and local MP. In terms of their involvement in local politics, owners fall roughly into three groups: the active, the nominally active, and the inactive. The active consisted of those who actually ran the affairs of the county. The nominally active might hold the same offices, but treated these positions as sinecure honours rather than as serious responsibilities. They are men who, in the words of the 1st Earl Cowper, 'enjoy the credit and title in their country, without giving themselves the trouble of doing the duty'. Their numbers increased enormously in the early eighteenth century with the doubling of the size of the Bench of justices for political reasons between 1675 and 1720. In Northamptonshire, for example, the number of JPs jumped from 47 to 94. Not all of these new men took their duties seriously, or indeed needed to. 'If they can gain the title of Right Worshipful, and have their neighbours stand bareheaded to them, they have their designs' observed an indignant commentator in 1693.[8]

Except during the Interregnum period, qualifications for appointment as JP before 1675 had been social and personal, not political. Dismissals on political grounds had been rare, although there had been mild purges of men too obviously identified as retainers of great nobles. Between 1675 and 1720, however, substantial purges and mass new appointments were made by both Whigs and Tories as the ferocious power struggle swung back and forth. In 1711, for example, the Tories dismissed 183 and added 919 to the lists. The ideal may have been to appoint 'men of the best quality and estates' but the reality was modified to fit party

[8] L. K. J. Glassey, *Politics and the Appointment of Justices of the Peace 1675-1720*, Oxford, 1979, pp. 24, 15, 31.

interests. On the other hand, too severe purges were counter-pro-
ductive. They alienated large numbers of influential county squires
from government, for 'the honour of being in is not so great as the
disgrace of being turned out'. After 1721, however, with the triumph
of the Whigs, things settled down and these political purges ceased.[9]

Apart from these political victims between 1675 and 1720 the
only groups who were more or less permanently excluded from
the Bench were the Dissenters and the Catholics, but the latter
were only significant among the elite in Northumberland. Participation in local political and administrative activity, therefore, remains one of the tests for the inclusion into the sample of newcomers to the landed classes. It must be remembered, however, that
the mere holding of the office of JP was ambiguous in its meaning,
since the power it carried with it depended upon the voluntary
zeal of the office-holder. Some were the work-horses of the county,
others enjoyed the prestige but did little to earn it.

Because of the rapid turnover and the pull of London, one would
expect the elite of Hertfordshire to have been less involved with
local office-holding than in more stable counties further removed
from London such as Northamptonshire[10] (Table 8.4, Fig. 8.4). In
all counties in the eighteenth century, the elite increasingly tended
to leave the office of JP to the parish gentry and the clergy, in
order to allow themselves the leisure to hunt, travel, and make
lengthy visits to London. Thus despite the increase in numbers,
the proportion of Hertfordshire owners in sample who had been
JPs fell from nearly a half, as it had been under Elizabeth, to a
third or less in the eighteenth century, the difference being made
up by clergymen, who by 1800 comprised another third. In the
nineteenth century, however, under the inspiration of evangelical
religion and a sense of social threat from below, the elite resumed
their positions on the Bench, and the proportion of Hertfordshire
owners who were JPs rose to 60 per cent and the proportion of
clergymen again collapsed.

The same general trends were repeated in Northamptonshire,
but there the abandonment of the responsibility for local govern-

    [9] J. H. Gleason, *The Justices of the Peace in England 1558-1640*, Oxford, 1969, pp. 63-6,
72-82; L. K. J. Glassey, op. cit., p. 7.
    [10] Manuscript JP lists (*libri pacis*) exist for all counties up to about 1680 in the Public
Record Office or the British Museum, and the printed quarter-sessions records for Hertfordshire provided names thereafter. For Northamptonshire, the manuscript quarter-sessions records in the local Record Office were combed for lists of names. For 1830-45 there
are published lists by R. W. Shorthouse in *Northamptonshire Past and Present*, v, nos. 2 and
3, 1974 and 1975. The record for Hertfordshire is therefore complete, and that for Northamptonshire is quite good but not complete; L. K. J. Glassey, op. cit., p. 7.

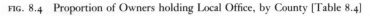

FIG. 8.4   Proportion of Owners holding Local Office, by County [Table 8.4]

ment in the eighteenth century was almost complete and the Victorian revival was weaker. One reason for this may have been that newcomers were much fewer and of higher social status, so that the elite did not feel themselves threatened. They were content to let local power slip into the hands of gentrified clergy—'squarsons'—and parish gentry, because the lines of social cleavage were still so clearly demarcated. The clergy became available as reliable substitutes because the enclosure movement turned many of them from nagging tithe-collectors into independent landed proprietors.[11]

[11] L. Stone and J. C. Fawtier Stone, 'Country Houses and their Owners in Hertfordshire 1540-1879', in *Dimensions of Quantitative Research in History*, ed. W. O. Aydelotte *et al.*, Princeton, 1972, p. 86, Fig. 8. These were nation-wide trends in the late eighteenth and

The functions and status of the office of sheriff changed considerably over time. At first, it carried considerable privileges and responsibilities and prestige, but on the other hand it always involved heavy expenses not covered by the income of office, as well as tedious account-keeping and possible legal harassment from the Exchequer to collect delinquent arrears of taxes. By the late seventeenth century, the days were gone when the sheriff, in his capacity as election overseer, could blatantly manipulate electoral proceedings to the advantage of one side or another. Its status declined with its power, and the office came to be regarded not as an honour but as a very expensive chore. Strenuous efforts were now made by those members of the landed elite who thought themselves potentially eligible to avoid being picked as sheriff. Only newcomers stood to gain prestige from serving in the office. Consequently, the government began using its patronage of the office not as a reward for its friends but as a punishment for its enemies. For example, Israel Mayo of Bayfordbury was arrested for attending a dissenting conventicle in 1666 and was pricked as sheriff of Hertfordshire two years later. Both actions were part of a single programme of persecution, launched by the zealous Anglican Lord Fanshawe with the support of the Earl of Clarendon in London.[12]

This change in the prestige of the office of sheriff is reflected in the substantial and permanent decline after 1700 in the number of Hertfordshire owners who served in that office from about 25 to 30 per cent down to a mere 10 to 15 per cent (Table 8.4, Fig. 8.4). The Northamptonshire figures show an identical fall, but the proportions went up again at the end of the eighteenth century. These changes do not seem to reflect changing total numbers or numbers of newcomers, since the decline in the eighteenth century occurred in two such different counties. This suggests that what was involved was a nation-wide fall in the prestige of the office.

In the nineteenth century the office revived in prestige and was once again filled by heads of ancient and prominent families. It was an honour, although an expensive one, which was now recorded with pride in family histories and memoirs. Mrs Charlton recorded that 'my father-in-law was pricked as High Sheriff for

early nineteenth centuries. See E. J. Evans, 'Some Reasons for the Growth of English Rural Anti-clericalism c.1750-1830', *Past and Present*, 66, 1975, p. 101; C. H. E. Zangerl, 'The Social Composition of County Magistrates in England and Wales 1831-1887', *Journal of British Studies*, xi, 1971.

[12] *Historical Manuscripts Commission, Verulam MSS*, p. 62; after the Glorious Revolution of 1688 and the passage of the Act of Toleration, Israel Mayo was at last rehabilitated. He was put on the Bench, and he registered his seat of Bayfordbury as a licensed meeting-place for Dissenters.

Northumberland in 1837, the extra expense of the office, what with outriders, trumpeters and robes of state, coming to at least £800'. Clearly the office in the nineteenth century had recovered a good deal of its ancient ceremonial splendour, the greatest expense and display being at the assizes. But if the office recovered in prestige in the nineteenth century, it none the less remained almost entirely empty of function or power. Moreover in Hertfordshire, close to London, it never even recovered its prestige, being largely left to new men like the paper-manufacturer John (later Sir John) Evans in 1881-2, who was happy to take on 'the honourable and expensive office'.[13]

The proportion of owners who had served their county as MPs, either as Knights of the Shire or representatives of a local borough, was highest in the mid-sixteenth century, before carpet-bagging finally became the norm. Thereafter, about a tenth of all owners at any given time served at some point in Parliament. Those families did best who were close to one of the boroughs which enjoyed parliamentary representation, and upon which they could therefore exercise influence. Hertford town, for example, sent two representatives to Parliament after 1624. Between 1624 and 1774 there were forty-three general and by-elections, in twenty-one of which one member of the families owning either Balls Park or Ware Park were returned, and in twenty of them a member of the family residing at Hertford Castle was returned. Generation after generation a Cowper of Hertford Castle or a Fanshawe or Byde of Ware Park were elected MPs. The hold of the Cowpers was only broken for a generation in 1700 after the scandal of the trial of Spencer Cowper for the murder of a young girl, Sarah Stout, which broke the previous alliance of convenience between the Cowpers and the local Quakers. After 1700, however, the Whig Cowpers were replaced by the Tory Charles Caesar of Bennington Place. Caesar ran for nine general elections and one by-election, winning eight, losing two, and being unseated twice on appeal, the high cost of all of which contributed to his undoing. In 1722, however, the political tide turned, and the Whig Harrisons of Balls Park replaced Caesar, who then ran for Knight of the Shire.

This close connection between local landed influence, dependent upon possession of a country seat nearby, and political factions within the town itself, dominated the political history of the borough of Hertford for the first two centuries after its enfranchise-

[13] B. Charlton, *The Recollections of a Northumbrian Lady*, ed. L. E. O. Charlton, London, 1949, p. 148; J. Evans, *Time and Chance*, London, 1943, p. 151.

ment in 1624. In 1826, however, a radical carpet-bagger, a wealthy Yorkshire manufacturer with no local connections whatsoever, ran on a platform of opposition to 'the county gentry and the old family interests'. He promised to rescue the borough at last from 'the fangs of the aristocracy', and he won. This was far from the end of elite influence in Hertford elections, but it was a portent of the future. Up to that time, however, members of the landed elite had not merely monopolized the seats of the Knights of the Shire, which was only to be expected, but also both seats in the county town.[14] Similarly, it was first the Jennings' and then the Spencers' ownership of the country house of Holywell on the outskirts of St Albans which gave these families a stranglehold for generations on the patronage of at least one seat for this other Hertfordshire borough.

At all times some elite landowners worked tirelessly in many forms of local administration, from justice of the peace to commissioner for the highways or the land tax, to Captain or Colonel in the militia. Such men were clearly driven by a passion for the power that accompanied the holding of office, but they also enjoyed the satisfaction of seeing justice done, and public affairs run efficiently. Theirs was what Colonel George Liddell of Ravensworth called 'a country life in business'.[15]

Taken altogether, the record of owners of seats as a power elite is quite impressive. With one striking exception, that of Northamptonshire in the eighteenth century, they continued for century after century to keep their hands upon the levers of local power, and also virtually to monopolize representation of the county in Parliament. Those who did administer the county did it without pay, at some considerable trouble and inconvenience to themselves. The reward was power, but only a modest addition of prestige, except for those who got themselves elected members of Parliament. Public service provided them with a justification for their privileged existence, reinforced their sense of paternalist authority, and gave them something to do, with which to stave off the torments of boredom.

What remains disturbing, however, is the virtual abdication of responsibility for local government by the elite in Northamptonshire, and to a lesser degree in Hertfordshire, in the eighteenth century. If this trend is typical of the nation as a whole, which incomplete data for Northumberland seem to suggest, there oc-

---

[14] L. M. Munby, 'Politics and Religion in Hertfordshire 1660-1740', in his *East Anglian Studies*, Cambridge, 1968.

[15] E. Hughes, *North Country Life in the Eighteenth Century*, London, 1952, p. 71.

curred a century-long diversion of interest to sport and pleasure, which the nineteenth-century revival of a conception of public service was too late and too small to remedy. This abdication is something which has hitherto gone virtually unnoticed by social historians, and yet its effect in weakening deference patterns and paternalist values in the rural areas must in the long run have been considerable. It was folly for the elite to think that they could indefinitely continue to enjoy great wealth and elicit great deference, without taking on some administrative responsibilities in return. It took the French Revolution and Evangelical religion finally to jolt them out of this bland self-confidence.

The chronology of an eighteenth-century withdrawal and nineteenth-century partial return to the duties and responsibilities of local governance does not fit either the neo-Marxist or the liberal-progressive models of English social development over the last three hundred years. The main exponent of the neo-Marxist model, Mr E. P. Thompson, fails to notice the withdrawal, and treats the trappings and display of eighteenth-century 'patrician' life as a theatrical facade, a kind of puppet-show capable of preserving authority only so long as the audience of the 'plebs' believed that it mirrored reality. Professor Harold Perkin, on the other hand, observes an abdication on the part of the governors, but attributes it to the early nineteenth century, and sees evidence of it in the abandonment of support for the traditional paternalist, old poor-relief system, and the tightening of the screws of social repression during the 1790s in response to the French Revolution. But most qualified contemporary observers agreed that the old poor-relief system had become an inordinately expensive scandal which did not even solve the social problem it had been designed to cope with. Consequently, support for Poor-Law reform can hardly be described as an 'abdication' of paternalist ideology. Moreover the return by the elite to active administration of local government in the nineteenth century helps to explain the relative success of the elite for another century in riding out the storms of participatory democracy and parliamentary, legal, and administrative reform, and in isolating and ignoring the new wealth generated by the industrial revolution. The conclusions of this book are therefore at variance with both the neo-Marxist and the liberal-democratic paradigms about the evolution of English elite society in the eighteenth and nineteenth centuries.[16]

[16] E. P. Thompson, 'Patrician Society, Plebeian Culture', *Journal of Social History*, 7, 1974; H. Perkin, *Origins of Modern English Society, 1780-1880*, London, 1969, pp. 183-95.

3. SOCIAL COMPOSITION

i. Social and Geographical Variety

Before summing up, there are two important caveats that must be made. The first is that any conclusions drawn about the county elite may well not apply to the parish gentry. For the latter, the scale of economic decline of old families was probably greater, and the scale of influx of self-made men almost certainly greater. Upward and downward mobility among the parish gentry was very probably considerably larger than among the county elite. Moreover the two were different in culture, the former being more strictly local in their interests. They had different income, education, values, and aspirations; they inhabited houses of a different size, and they pursued a different life-style. The findings of this book may well not apply to them.

The second caveat is that generalizations at a national level are often made almost meaningless by the enormous differences from county to county. A county very close to London, like Hertfordshire, had a relatively high rate of turnover; a county only a hundred miles from London, like Northamptonshire, was fairly stable; and a county in the far north, like Northumberland, was largely immune to change altogether. Although these differences became rather less marked in the eighteenth and nineteenth centuries, they persisted right up to the end of the period under study. Consequently, conclusions have to be stated in terms of this variety of experience before any attempt can be made at nation-wide generalizations.

ii. The Scale of Social Mobility

How seriously was the overall composition of the county elite affected by the outflow of sellers and drop-outs and the inflow of purchasers and entrants? At any given moment, how many seats had changed hands recently? Was elite society in universal flux, or was there a firm central core surrounded by a periphery of families which came and went with great rapidity?

By looking at the way old families passed on their inheritance, it becomes clear that the mid-seventeenth century was a watershed. Until that time, direct descent from father to son or grandson was the norm, running at over 80 per cent of all transfers. Later, the proportion slipped to 70 per cent and then to 50 per cent. The cause of this decline in the proportion of direct father-son descents was the demographic crisis of the period 1650-1750, during which century the elite were not reproducing themselves in sufficient numbers to maintain equilibrium. They responded to the crisis, however, not by sales but by transfers of property, seats, and, whenever possible, titles to distant relatives, often surrogate heirs given protective colouration by a change of name. Thereafter, fertility was deliberately restricted by the practice of family limitation. This meant that until mortality also declined, the proportion of fathers who died with heirs male to succeed them remained at only 50 per cent throughout the nineteenth century.

Despite these precautions, sales and drop-outs, purchases and entrances were undoubtedly taking place. But with what general consequences? Regardless of perceptions, what were the facts? The best test of the relative stability of the landed class in each county is to calculate the proportion of seats in sample at any given moment which were in the hands either of newcomers by purchase, including purchasers and purchaser-entrants, or of families which had been in possession of their seats for two to five generations; or of families which had endured for six generations or more (Table 8.5, Fig. 8.6). The first, and probably the second, may be regarded as families not yet established, and the last as a very stable core. For the purpose of this calculation, it has seemed best to ignore the period of rapid numerical expansion of the elite before 1660, when new entrants were acquiring land, building houses, and establishing themselves as members of the sample of owners. This numerical expansion distorts the picture.

Genuinely new men who had purchased their seats turn out to have formed a relatively small proportion of owners at any given time (Table 8.5, Fig. 8.5). As might be expected, they were most numerous in Hertfordshire, amounting to a third or more of all owners in the mid-seventeenth century, when successful office-holders, merchants, and lawyers were buying into the county, and again in the very early nineteenth century. In the other two counties the proportions were much smaller, hardly ever rising above 10 per cent or 15 per cent at any time. Only Northamptonshire saw a significant rise in purchasers in the county in the Victorian period, while the other two actually saw a fall. This is an unexpected finding, the significance of which will be discussed later.

At first sight, the proportion of new men in Hertfordshire looks remarkably high, as indeed it is. But it has to be remembered that one-third of all these purchasers sold in their own lifetime, and another third also sold within the next two generations (Table 8.6). These large numbers of short-lived families represent a rapid turnover among only a proportion of the elite, while leaving wholly

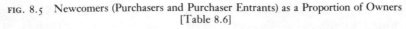

FIG. 8.5   Newcomers (Purchasers and Purchaser Entrants) as a Proportion of Owners
[Table 8.6]

unaffected considerable numbers of older families, which lasted
for many generations. In Northamptonshire and Northumberland, the proportion of purchaser families was much lower. Indeed
in the latter county there were three moments, in 1659, 1669, and
1779, when there was not a single purchaser family among the
elite. In these two counties, however, the number of transients
was also much lower.

More significant, perhaps, is the size of the hard core of durable
families which had lasted for six generations or more in the same
seat (Fig. 8.6). In Hertfordshire their numbers were at first quite
small, a mere 15 per cent or less, but they rose to a quarter or
more after 1700, reaching an all-time peak in 1779. Northamptonshire followed the same trend but at a higher level, beginning at
about a third and rising to a peak of 60 per cent in the late eighteenth century before falling back to about a half. Both counties
thus show maximum stability of the core—in Northamptonshire
at an astonishing high level—in the eighteenth century. This was
clearly the time when the elite sectors of English landed society
were at their most stable, for reasons which have already been
exhaustively analysed. In Northumberland, the proportion of very
old families progressively diminished, beginning at two-thirds and

FIG. 8.6   Old Families (6 + Generations from Purchase) as a Proportion of Owners
[Table 8.6]

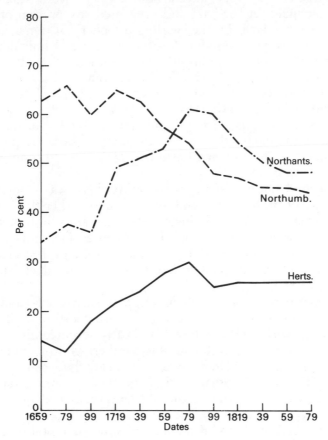

falling to under a half in the nineteenth century. This is a somewhat illusory trend, the statistical by-product of the fact that the
size of the elite was constantly growing, and thus diluting the
number of very old families.

These calculations show two things. The first is that the numbers of purchasers and purchaser-entrants were never large enough
to swamp the older elite families. Even in Hertfordshire they never
rose above a third, and elsewhere they were more like a fifth or a
sixth. Since many of these newcomers were of gentry stock, and
others, especially in Hertfordshire, were mere transients who came
and went rapidly, the proportion of genuinely new men to be
absorbed was always so small that it never represented a serious

threat to the values of the elite. In every county there was a persistent large core of very ancient families, who were usually also
the richest, who set the pace and prevented any erosion of traditional social standards by the swirling periphery of transient newcomers. The system was thus flexible enough to admit newcomers, but stable enough to absorb them without discomfort. Not
even Hertfordshire ever became a mere transit camp or landing
pad for London tycoons, and the other two counties were substantially impervious to new wealth. If most Midland and southern
counties some distance from London resembled Northamptonshire, as seems likely, the figures suggest a remarkable degree of
family stability in most of England, reaching an all-time peak in
the eighteenth century.[17]

The second finding is that what influx there was of new men
was mainly of professionals and office-holders rather than of merchants or bankers. As for industrialists, they are simply not present, except for some brewers in Hertfordshire. The unity of English elite society was a unity of the land and the professions, only
marginally of the land and business, and not at all of land and
industry.

Whatever perceptions of change may have existed—and there
were undoubtedly fears of excessive upward social mobility from
the business world in the sixteenth and early seventeenth centuries
and again in the nineteenth—in practice there is little evidence of
a massive threat to the landed elite from below between their consolidation in the early Stuart period and their collapse after 1879.
By 1925, however, many of the old landmarks had been swept
away, and that durable core had been seriously eroded.

Whether or not the total amount of upward mobility of new
groups into the landed elite in England was greater than that abroad
is at present impossible to say, since there is no comparable study
for any part of the Continent. It looks however, as if the differences, especially with regard to monied men, were greatly exaggerated by contemporaries for polemical purposes, and that the
contrast in reality with countries such as France was much less
striking than has hitherto been supposed.

Nor can the paradigm of an open elite be saved by invocation
of the peculiarly English phenomenon of the downward mobility
of younger sons. They certainly had the opportunity of making
large fortunes and buying their way back into the society into

---

[17] This point was made for the seventeenth century by Professor A. Everitt as long ago
as 1969, in justified criticism of rash claims about mobility by myself (A. Everitt: *Change
in the Provinces: the Seventeenth Century*, Leicester, 1969, p. 13).

which they had been born, perhaps indeed at a higher level. But few of them seem to have made it. In our three counties over the full 340 years from 1540 to 1879 only forty-two younger sons of landed gentry bought their way into the sample. Only fifteen of these forty-two had made their fortunes in business, the others being either lawyers or office-holders. Landed younger sons who had made a fortune in business thus comprised a mere 4 per cent of all purchasers. They were virtually invisible in the landscape at this elevated social level, whatever may have been the case among the parish gentry. The evidence of the higher education—or lack of it—of the younger sons of the elite strongly indicates that by far the most popular career choices for them were the armed forces, India, or the colonies, followed at a considerable distance by the Church or the law. The numbers at this elevated social level who went into business would seem to have been very small, although it is true that one rarely knows about the failures. So far as the evidence goes, there appears to have been more successes in the late seventeenth century than at any other time. Thereafter better opportunities were provided by the growth of more attractive professional careers, primarily catering to the needs of a vastly expanded and more militarized state, and a much more affluent upper class. After 1690, the professional officer corps in the army and navy, the large permanent bureaucracy to pay for them, the administration of the colonial empire in America and India, all offered attractive openings for younger sons, even if the rewards of the first were skimpy in (the relatively rare) times of peace.[18] Once these career openings had become available to them, hardly any younger sons of the landed elite went into business, and hardly any younger sons from any level of the landed classes were sufficiently successful in business to be able to purchase a substantial seat. Instead they and their descendants went to swell the ranks of the upper middle classes with gentry connections, who ran the Empire and upon retirement turned into parish gentry.

4. PSYCHOLOGICAL INTEGRATION

The next question is whether the model of an open elite in England can be rescued by involving a special ease of psychological integration, assimilation and aculturation between the landed elite and the bourgeoisie. This has to be tackled from several angles:

[18] G. Holmes, 'The Professions and Social Change in England 1680-1730', *Proceedings of the British Academy*, lxv, 1979.

the degree to which the old landed elite adopted an individualistic, capitalist, and entrepreneurial attitude to land and investment; the degree to which the bourgeoisie themselves developed a conscious sense of their own worth, independent of that of the landed elite; and the degree to which the landed elite were prepared to accept as social equals newcomers into the county whose wealth derived from non-landed sources.

i. The Landed Elite and Possessive Individualism

By the seventeenth century the greater landowners of England had to a considerable extent adopted a market view of land and labour, although not of their own society, which was still based on ancient concepts of honour and deference. They enclosed their land, consolidated it, and leased it out as large farms to heavily capitalized tenant farmers on twenty-one-year or three-life leases. In practice, the latter had virtual security of tenure from generation to generation, and therefore had every incentive to improve productivity. They in turn worked the soil with a labour force of cottagers or landless labourers, whom they could hire or fire almost at will. Thus there evolved the unique three-tiered system of English agriculture, composed of wealthy rentier landlords, large tenant farmers, and landless labourers. Whatever its defects as a social organization, this arrangement was dramatically successful in improving crop yields and thus in feeding the rapidly rising population of the periods 1520-1630 and 1740 onwards. It also made the greater English landlords the richest in Europe. Admittedly, most of the capital, and much of the innovation, was supplied by the wealthy tenant farmers and not by the landlords, but it was the former (or their agents) who decided upon the consolidation of the estates, arranged for the passage of the enclosure Acts, and supervised the maximization of yield and profits. Even if their role has been exaggerated, not a few of them were agricultural innovators and improvers in their own right, experimenting in stock-breeding, new crops, new rotations, and new fertilizers and systems of drainage. Their attitude towards their estates in many ways closely approximated that of merchants towards their ships, investments, and inventories.

On the other hand, after the period of ruthless enclosures during the sixteenth and early seventeenth centuries, relatively few elite landowners displayed a calculating and insensitive brutality in trampling upon the common rights of the villagers—except, of course, in Ireland, where local agents were acting for absentee landlords. Parliamentary enclosures are now thought to have been much more equitable in their intention, if not in their results, than was once assumed to be the case. It is interesting to note that perhaps the most celebrated act of arbitrary violence perpetrated by a landlord on English soil in the Victorian period was aimed at preserving the rights of the villagers, not at suppressing them. In 1866 Augustus Smith of Ashlyns, Herts., hired from London 150 navvies to come and tear down the iron railings which his fellow-magnate Lord Brownlow had recently erected around part of Berkhampstead Common. This sensational act was designed to protect the common rights of the villagers against encroachment by a nearby magnate anxious to extend the area of his park.[19]

To sum up, the greater English landlords were certainly profit-maximizers, but after about the mid-seventeenth century, they abandoned strong-arm tactics. They used large-scale tenant farmers to extract the maximum economic surplus from the soil, but acted with commendable restraint when it came to eviction or rack-renting. This was a system which did much to stimulate agricultural improvement in England, while erecting a convenient social buffer between seemingly paternalist landlords and seemingly deferential agricultural labourers.

It is now generally admitted that the concept of 'possessive individualism' and the attitudes derived from the market were unique to the English landlords, and are hard to find so well developed in any other European aristocracy of the time. Their impact must not be exaggerated, however, as some historians have tended to do. Right up to the nineteenth century, land ownership meant a good deal more than a profitable investment. It always carried with it political status and control of votes, as well as a claim to share in the political, administrative, and judicial government of the county and the country. Land ownership always carried overtones of power and status, and this must never be forgotten in the rush to trace the rise of more modern and more market-oriented attitudes. Moreover the delegation of major responsibilities for administration and innovation to the tenant farmers freed the idle noblemen and squires, of whom there were plenty, to devote themselves almost exclusively to the arts of spending time and money rather than to the science of saving the one and acquiring the other.

English landowners had for centuries been involved indirectly in overseas commercial policy. As large-scale sheep-masters, they

[19] J. A. Froude, 'On the Uses of a Landed Family', in his *Short Studies on Great Subjects*, London 1907, iv, pp. 294-5.

were wool-producers whose income depended upon the export of England's staple product, namely cloth. From the fourteenth century onward, therefore, they had a direct interest, along with the merchant community, in the expansion of England's overseas trade, which is why they refused to allow the development of a merchant estate within Parliament, with which the King could negotiate separately for taxes on the export of wool and cloth.

Yet another connection was forged in the great debate over banking and the rate of interest in the late seventeenth century, which directed the attention of landlords to the effect of interest rates upon the price of land, and therefore upon rents. The Tories were stimulated by this debate to plan a 'land bank', as a rival to the Bank of England, but it came to nothing. What emerged from this debate was an increasingly sophisticated awareness by the landed classes that their own fortunes were somehow inextricably connected with those of the monied men. There was certainly a conflict of interest, perceived especially clearly during the interminable wars with Louis XIV, for which the landed interest believed that it paid through the land tax, and from which it suspected—with some reason—that the monied interest benefited through government contracts, financing, and privateering. Thereafter, however, this conflict was dampened down by peace, by a reduction of taxation on land, and by a growing recognition of common benefits to be derived from an aggressive policy of opening up foreign markets by military force. By the time of the Seven Years War in the 1750s, therefore, there was a clear vision of the national interest, which overrode the older antagonism between the landed and the monied interest. Psychologically, the two groups had drawn closer together than ever before in a joint endeavour to conquer the markets of the world by the use of naval power.

Their attitudes to the exploitation of land and to overseas commerce and war were not the only ways in which the landed elite displayed their psychological penetration by capitalist ideas and practices. By 1750 there were few great landlords who did not have some money—often a great deal—in the public funds of the Bank of England, the great trading companies, and government debentures. In this sense they were themselves becoming inextricably involved with the monied interest, and their mental attitudes to banking and stock speculation changed accordingly. In 1760, for example, the Earl of Derby had invested all his savings 'more than my own occasions may soon require, upon a good security at 4 per cent'.[20] Others poured surplus cash into canal companies and

[20] T. S. Willan, *Navigation of the River Weaver*, Manchester, 1951, pp. 78-80.

turnpike trusts in the eighteenth century, and into railroad companies and dockyards in the nineteenth. From the early seventeenth century onward many were deeply involved in urban development of London. By the nineteenth century a few were even
more actively concerned with developing residential areas in expanding new towns, as were the Calthorpes in Edgebaston near
Birmingham, and the Cavendishes in Eastbourne, and many noblemen were profiting from the expanding suburbs to the west and
north-west of London.[21]

In a few special areas, it can be argued that by the eighteenth
century the conflation of landed and monied interests was so complete that in purely economic terms—though not in status ones—
the distinction between the two had lost all meaning. In the coal-
field areas along the Tyne, for example, landowners were active
in the coal trade because so much of their income derived from
mining coal on their own property and from the receipts from
way-leaves for the transportation of the coal of others. Thus in
1727, although there were only two coal-owners among the MPs
for Durham and Northumberland, most of the society had a stake
in the prosperity of the industry. In Hertfordshire some permea-
tion of the landed interest by commercial values evidently also was
taking place.

But the same could not be said of the probably much more
typical areas of Northamptonshire and the northern part of Northumberland, where evidence of infiltration, interaction, marriage,
entrepreneurship, and other kinds of intermingling were fairly low
right up to 1879. This suggests that the alarmist or complacent
cries of social commentators, most of whom were London-based,
reflected what was going on in the home counties close to the City,
rather than to a social or a psychological transformation of the
landed elite in the country as a whole.

The full extent of elite landed investment in the late eighteenth-
and early nineteenth-century industrial infrastructure and enterprise is only just becoming apparent. Some now think that agriculture provided most of the capital for these new enterprises, and
direct participation of the larger landowners can be traced in turnpike trusts, river improvements, the construction of canals, ports,
and harbours; in developing provincial banks and markets, in mining enterprises, especially coal, and in urban development in many
cities. A significant minority of elite landowners played as important a role in industrial change after 1770 as they had in agricul-

[21] D. Cannadine, *Lords and Landlords: the Aristocracy and the Towns 1774-1967*, Leicester,
1980, Pt. iv.

tural improvement after 1700.[22] It is also true, however, that the peak of their entrepreneurial activity was before about 1820, and thereafter they increasingly withdrew from active management into the passive role of rentiers and investors.

One may safely conclude, therefore, that the English landed elite has adopted a receptive attitude to the exploitation of land and to entrepreneurship since the late sixteenth century, when they began to be affected by the principles of possessive individualism and the maximization of profit. By the seventeenth century they were familiar with entrepreneurship on their own estates, and by the eighteenth were putting their money into the funds. They were capitalists although rentiers, innovators although patricians, and, although subject to a heavy land tax, were willing to pursue an aggressive naval conquest of overseas markets. Until the late nineteenth century, they managed to have the best of all worlds: the profits of the entrepreneur and the prestige of the aristocrat; the policies of commercial expansion and the perquisites of political power; the convenience of a banking system and a monied interest and the protection of Corn Laws and Game Laws.

ii. The Self-Perception of the Bourgeoisie

The common assumption of historians is that the English bourgeoisie, despite their precocious and astonishing economic success, have always lacked a sense of civic and social pride and self-confidence. This has been put forward as the prime cause for their alleged ceaseless ambition to buy a country house, acquire a coat of arms, and become merged with the landed gentry.

This hypothesis is brought into question, not only by the relatively small influx of bourgeois into the landed elite at any period of English history, but even more by the appearance in Hertfordshire of the transient purchaser-seller, a man who made his money elsewhere, bought a country seat, lived opulently, and then sold again without even trying to establish a county family.

Some of these purchaser-sellers were magnates from elsewhere, but most were new men whose wealth had been acquired in London business or government office or a profession. They were buying or building or rebuilding very large seats on very small properties,

[22] *Land and Industry*, ed. J. T. Ward and R. G. Wilson, Newton Abbot, 1971, pp. 10-11, 45-51, and *passim*; M. W. McCahill, 'Peers, Patronage and the Industrial Revolution 1760-1800', *Journal of British Studies*, 16, 1976; W. L. Arnstein, 'The Survival of the Victorian Aristocracy', in *The Rich, the Well-born and the Powerful*, ed. F. C. Jaher, Urbana, 1973; D. Cannadine, 'The Landowner as Millionaire', *Agricultural Historical Review*, 25, 1977, pp. 77-9; D. Cannadine, 'Aristocratic Indebtedness in the Nineteenth Century: the Case Reopened', *Economic History Review*, 2nd Series, xxx, 1977.

which allowed them to enjoy the pleasures of country-house life without getting involved either in the administration of a large agricultural estate or in the responsibilities of local administration. A seat was for them a temporary showcase to display their opulence, without the burdens and responsibilities of managing rents, tithes, and tenants, and without getting involved in administering the Poor Law or the control of alehouses, or fixing the paternity of bastards. This type of elite owner clearly possessed a vision of what living in a country house meant which was very different from the traditional aristocratic ideal of paternalistic landlordism and the exercise of political patronage and administrative power. Although their life-style was identical with that of the local elite, they regarded their seat as a lavish rural retreat, a stately pleasure dome, which carried with it none of the traditional obligations or privileges. These owners were thus members of the elite, but they were transitory and non-participating ones. The mere existence in considerable numbers of numerous bourgeois purchaser-sellers of seats suggests that there were many successful business men who had no desire to become assimilated with the landed classes.

Was there, then, a quite separate bourgeois ideology, and if so, when did it develop? In the sixteenth century there are certainly hardly any signs of emerging bourgeois self-confidence and an independent system of social values. Thomas Dekker in *The Shoemakers' Holiday* certainly tries, but his failure is demonstrated by the brief but abortive attempt to evolve a bourgeois hero in literature between 1590 and 1610. William Walwyn, the medieval lord mayor of London, or Jack of Newbury, the great early sixteenth-century provincial cloth-manufacturer, were transformed into role models who displayed not bourgeois values of thrift and hard work but gentlemanly ones of courage in battle, chivalry, and generosity and hospitality in expenditure. This was an attempt at self-definition that died of its own internal contradictions and implausibility, and was crushed under the avalanche of satirical plays and pamphlets that followed for the next hundred years, in which the figure of the merchant continued to be portrayed in stereotypical terms that went back to antiquity.[23] Their very names are revealing: Aldermen Gripe, Cholerick and Nincompoop; or Sir Thrifty Gripe, Sir Worldly Fox, Sir Simon Scrape-all, Sir Anthony Thinwit, Sir Anthony Addlepate and Sir Testy Dolt. By the 1690s, however, this contempt was beginning to focus more exclusively

[23] L. S. O'Connell, 'The Elizabethan Bourgeois Hero Tale: Aspects of an Adolescent Social Consciousness' in *After the Reformation*, ed. B. Malament, Philadelphia, 1980.

upon the new parasitical monied men, the usurious scrivener-bankers, the speculative stock-jobbers and the like, rather than on the traditional overseas merchants. In the first decades of the eighteenth century the image of the City merchant changed significantly both on the stage and at the hands of men such as Addison and Steele, whose writings were reaching the whole of genteel society. He was now portrayed as a responsible and sober citizen, with respectable morals and manners, whose commercial activities were recognized as forming the basis of the nation's prosperity and greatness. This radical shift in perceptions coincided exactly with the emergence in real life of the gentleman merchant.[24]

The extent to which the landed elite were willing to accept the gentleman merchant on an equal footing remains doubtful, as we have seen, but there can be no doubt that the status of the latter was rising and that a sense of bourgeois self-consciousness was developing. No longer was it necessary to be a country gentleman in order to acquire self-respect. It is no accident that this assertion of parity or even superiority in social utility and respectability occurred precisely at the time when landed and monied men were being brought more closely together than ever before. Both were sucked into the great stock-market boom of the South Sea Bubble, and were becoming heavy investors in Bank and East India stocks. More and more of the landed elite were spending more and more time in London, even if their social contacts with the monied interest are still problematical. But at least the two were drawn together by the common bonds of political allegiance to the Whig or Tory parties. The Whig and Tory landed magnates and the city patricians had no option other than to work closely together for political victory, and the landed politicos were constantly being dined at lavish feasts by their Whig or Tory allies in the City during the period of crisis from 1682 to 1715, as Luttrell's *Diary* amply proves. So close did the temporary political alliance of nobles and civic dignitaries become that in 1708 the Lord Mayor, the immensely wealthy Sir Charles Duncombe, persuaded his niece, the Duchess of Argyll, to act as his official hostess and lady mayoress during his term of office.[25] But after the crisis was over, contacts seemed to have diminished once more, and the residents

---

[24] J. Loftis, *Comedy and Society from Congreve to Fielding*, Stanford, 1959, pp. 1, 81-3, 94-5, 101-4, 122, 127, 133.

[25] N. Luttrell, *A Brief Historical Relation of State Affairs, 1678-1714*, Oxford, 1857, passim. For example, i, pp. 176, 179, 212; vi, pp. 59, 363.

of St James Square again drew away from the residents of the City.

If there was a turning-point in bourgeois self-perception, then it came in the early eighteenth century, as expressed by Daniel Defoe and others. But it took half a century or more fully to evolve the concept and reality of the gentleman-merchant and it is striking that both squires and gentlemen-merchants shared a common contempt for the vulgar, thrusting manufacturers of the late eighteenth and early nineteenth centuries who were the driving force behind the industrial revolution.

iii. The Psychological Acceptance of Newcomers

To begin to answer the question of how easy it was for newcomers to gain acceptance in landed society, it is essential to make fine distinctions between upwardly mobile groups by occupation and source of wealth. Many non-landed sources of wealth were perfectly respectable and indeed honourable gentlemanly pursuits to which no hint of social stigma could be attached. Government office, the Court, the law, and the army were always respectable, and the Church became so in the eighteenth century. Bankers, brewers, and East India Company directors shared with the landed classes in the spoils of 'Old Corruption', the great patronage network of monopolies, sinecure fees, and offices. In this sense, therefore, if in no other, they formed a more or less homogenized elite bound together by common participation in the lucrative *ancien-régime* system of a patrimonial bureaucracy run on patronage and pay-offs.

This suggests that the warmth of the welcome offered by established members of the county elite to newcomers varied more according to the source than to the size of the latter's wealth. Parish gentry on the way up were very easily absorbed, as were men of genteel origins enriched by politics or the law. These were the groups who formed the majority of the newcomers. Only marginally less readily acceptable in the first generation were the monied interest of merchant bankers, members of the great London overseas trading and finance companies, such as the East India or the Levant Companies, and large-scale brewers. But both the country squire and the city patrician regarded a nineteenth-century industrialist as beyond the social pale, while retail tradesmen were the least acceptable of all. The appearance of successful grocers like Lipton and Lusk in country seats in the very late nineteenth century were symbols of the first serious erosion of traditional standards of status hierarchy: water was at last beginning to trickle through cracks in the ancient status dam. There was thus a fundamental division in terms of prestige and social acceptance within the ranks of men of business. A Director of the Bank of England or the East India Company had more in common with a landed squire or even a nobleman than either had with a cotton manufacturer from Manchester or a retail tradesman from London. In their attitude towards the latter, the landed and the monied interest stood shoulder to shoulder.

One key difference between England and the Continent is the fact that the stigma of the counting-house—so long as it was overseas trade or banking—was so easily erased within a generation by the assumption by the sons of new men of the behaviour, education, manners, and responsibilities of a gentleman. There were no rigid three-generation legal and cultural taboos to delay the process of assimilation. Unlike in Continental Europe, the sons and grandsons of newcomers seem to have met with no great obstacles to their social acceptance, so long as they had the proper credentials of a substantial income, at least some of it in land, genteel education and manners, ownership of a sizeable country seat, and a suitable style of living. To use an eighteenth-century phrase, they were all 'persons of quality at their seats in the country'. In a county like Hertfordshire, where the turnover was high and the proximity of London overpowering, a number of owners continued to remain active in that area of politics or the professions in which their ancestors had first made the family fortune. Two groups, brewers from the late seventeenth century, bankers from the late eighteenth, even managed to continue to practice their business avocations without much noticeable loss of status.

During the nineteenth century before 1880 there is visible a double cultural trend among the elite, on the one hand towards even easier assimilation of some newcomers, and on the other towards an intensified rejection of others. After 1820 the old landed elite mixed more readily than ever before with the professional classes and old merchant and banking families in public schools, London clubs, and army messes.[26] Moreover the landed elite itself showed signs of moving with the times by becoming increasingly a service aristocracy, at least for part of their lives. More and more heirs joined their younger brothers in career service to the state as army officers, colonial administrators, or diplomats. They were also enriched by the great rise in rents from 1780 to 1820 and again

[26] By 1830 the proportion of members of the landed classes among officers of the Home Army rose to over a half (P. E. Razzell, 'Social Origins of Officers in the Indian and the British Home Army 1758-1962', *British Journal of Sociology*, 14, 1963, p. 253).

from 1850 to 1880. Some of them were profiting from investment in the new economic infrastructure, like canals, docks, and railways; others were making stupendous fortunes from urban development in London and elsewhere. Despite the concessions of the 1832 Reform Bill, and the abolition of the Corn Laws, as a class they still maintained a firm hold on the levers of economic and political power in the countryside. They were busy enlarging their country seats, hiring more and more servants, developing foxhunting and shooting into an all-absorbing country sport, and moulding the ritual of the London 'season' to limit access from below.[27] The Victorian landed elite lived happily in a world largely of their own contriving, both in the country and in London, although they were also willing enough to rub shoulders in the House of Commons smoking-room or the London clubs with the burgeoning Victorian professional upper middle class. Whether they were also prepared to ask them down to the country for the weekend is a question which still needs investigation. Trollope certainly leaves one with the impression that they were, at least for political weekends.

On the other hand, both the old landed elites and the professional and monied upper middle classes were now distancing themselves from the increasing numbers of very wealthy but very vulgar self-made industrialists. Hardly any of the elite could see from their bedroom windows the belching smoke-stacks or slag-heaps which represented Britain's new industrial prosperity, while their own wealth was still mainly derived from land or urban rents. Before 1880, their personal contacts with the entrepreneurs of this great Victorian economic revolution seem to have been curiously remote. This may explain the failure of more than a minority of the new Victorian industrial millionaires to buy large landed estates. Instead they contented themselves with renting country seats, or in some cases buying ones with little property attached. This hypothesis that few self-made men in the late Victorian period were interested in building up a landed estate is supported by the fact that for the first thirty years of the great agricultural depression, from 1880 to 1910, there were many willing sellers among hard-pressed landed magnates, but few buyers.[28]

[27] L. Davidoff, *The Best Circles: Society, Etiquette and the Season*, London, 1973, Ch. 1, passim.

[28] N. Rubinstein, 'New Men of Wealth and the Purchase of Land in Nineteenth-Century England', *Past and Present*, 92, 1981; J. Franklin, *The Gentleman's Country House and its Plan 1835-1914*, London, 1981, Ch. II and Appendix; F. M. L. Thompson, 'The Land Market in the Nineteenth Century', *Oxford Economic Papers*, 2nd Series, 9, 1957.

Consequently, not only did there never develop a legal or customary distinction between *noblesse d'épée* and *noblesse de robe*, but the psychological absorption of such limited numbers as there were of newcomers from the monied interest was also fairly easily achieved. The absorption, however, could only be on terms, the terms being set by the landed elite themselves. Profit-maximizers they might be, but even more they were prestige-maximizers, and the condition of acceptance of newcomers was that they adopted the values and culture of the landed classes. As a result, even in Hertfordshire where infiltration by monied men was at its greatest, the values and life-style of the elite persisted virtually unchanged, since a sufficient number of families survived in each generation to maintain them, and since those newcomers who did establish themselves hastened to adopt these values as a protective colouration. It was not the amount of social mobility that made England exceptional, but the ease of cultural assimilation of the children of those relatively few who made the move into a higher social sphere.

Part III

HOUSES

'The multitude of gentlemen's houses scattered over the country is a feature quite peculiar to English landscape. The thing is unknown in France, where . . . the landed proprietors have their houses in the nearest little town'. L. Simond, *Journal of a Tour and Residence in Great Britain during the Years 1810 and 1811*, New York, 1815, i, pp. 200-01.

'Bladesover [i.e. Uppark, Sussex] . . . is the clue to almost all that is distinctively British and perplexing to the foreign inquirer in England'. H. G. Wells, *Tono-Bungay*, London, 1925, p. 17.

IX

SOCIAL FUNCTIONS

The central assumption about which this book is constructed is that from the sixteenth to the late nineteenth centuries ownership of a country seat was an essential qualification for membership of the local elites, from whose ranks the ruling class was drawn. We have seen how families were known by their seats: the Spencers of Althorp, the Leventhorpes of Shingly Hall, the Greys of Chillingham; they were thus defined both by their family name and by their place of rural residence. The latter, in consequence, became on the one hand, the embodiment of ancestral patrimony and the outward symbol of the dignity and authority of their owner, and on the other a machine for living the life of an English country gentleman. To fulfil these symbolic as well as practical functions a seat had to possess three qualities, aptly summed up by Vanbrugh as 'state, beauty and convenience'.

Before the early sixteenth century, the development of the country house as we know it was held back by the prevailing insecurity of the countryside. Before 1540 in the south and Midlands and before 1610 in the far north on the borders of Scotland, the urgent need for defence took precedence over display in a society torn apart by bastard feudalism. In the fifteenth century, the gentry mostly lived in semi-fortified houses, and were the clients of the great magnates, upon whose favour they depended for protection as well as economic, social and political patronage, in return for which they were prepared to offer their loyalty and military support, while the greater landed aristocracy, securely entrenched behind their castle walls, competed for power with the King, who was by then little more than *primus inter pares*. During the early sixteenth century, these great magnates were one by one slowly eliminated, through fines, attainders, executions and the confiscation and redistribution of their property. Some managed to survive into the new era, but only at the cost of seeing their local power base undermined by the client gentry of the Tudors, who supplanted their own retainers and dependents in positions of authority in local government. Nowhere is this process more obvious

than in the Tudor north, but it was a nation-wide development.[1]
It was only after royal authority and royal law had been re-established and the need for defence had consequently diminished, that
country gentlemen in England were able to move out of their semi-fortified dwellings defensible against attack, and build themselves
country houses.

By this is meant an unfortified dwelling, standing in its own
fairly extensive grounds, which if they included a park could be
1,000 acres or more. This development was encouraged by the
transfer between 1538 and 1553 of perhaps a quarter or more of
all English land from institutional to private hands, through the
massive redistribution of Church and royal property, either given
away by the Crown to win support, or sold to raise money to pay
for wars. These lands were either given to the new Tudor nobility, or sold to existing gentry, thus elevating the latter into men
of power and substance.

By 1580 these families now owned the land, had saved the resources with which to build, and were spurred on to do so as a
visible means of confirming their status as members of the local
elite. Many country houses were built on ex-Church or Crown
land, some of them being actually converted from the residential
quarters of former monasteries or nunneries.

Furthermore, the sixteenth century saw a concurrent technological revolution in building materials. Bricks, which had hitherto
been imported from Holland, now began to be made in England
and a native brick industry sprang up to supply a material less
strong but much cheaper than stone, and stronger and more durable than lathe and plaster. This was particularly important in a
county like Hertfordshire which possessed no local building materials, except wood and flint. At the same time there developed a
flourishing native glass industry, as well as an iron industry to
produce window bars to hold the glass in place. These made possible a major stylistic innovation, the use of huge areas of glass
instead of solid walls, in itself symptomatic of the greater security
of the countryside.

Architecturally, the country seat is particularly important in
England after 1540, since before the nineteenth century it had no
rivals in royal, ecclesiastical, or municipal public buildings. Hardly
any notable new churches were built, except the Wren churches
in London after the fire of 1666, and the Crown was too impov-

    [1] M. R. James, *Family, Lineage and Civil Society*, Oxford, 1974; L. Stone, *The Crisis of the
Aristocracy, 1558-1641*, Oxford, 1965, Chapter v.

erished to stud the landscape with palaces. Henry VIII built one great Renaissance extravaganza at Nonsuch in the 1520s and 1530s, and in an explosion of acquisitive megalomania seized or built some fifty palaces, houses, converted monasteries, and hunting-boxes. Subsequent monarchs did relatively little building, although Charles I and Inigo Jones had dreams and plans for the largest palace in Europe, exceeding even the Louvre or the Escorial. William III's major addition to Hampton Court was the only royal building of note before the Prince Regent's lavish private folly at the Brighton Pavilion. Nor was there any serious competition from town corporations, none of which before the nineteenth century built much more than rather modest town halls. Finally, London was unusual in that the town houses of the nobility were mostly very modest in scale after about 1700, by which time most of the small number of really great town houses standing in their own grounds had vanished. After 1700 the nobility lived lavishly in the country and in relatively cramped quarters around St James's Square and other fashionable squares in the West End of the city.

Thus from 1540 to at least 1840, when great public buildings such as railway stations began to offer competition, the country house dominated the English architectural scene, to a degree unprecedented before or since, or anywhere abroad. In 1789 Arthur Young was astonished to discover the vast wealth of Renaissance churches and palaces in Italy. He rightly concluded that Italy must then have possessed the sort of wealth enjoyed by England in the seventeenth and eighteenth centuries. But in England it was 'without any such effects: it is the diffusion of comfort in the houses of private people, not the concentrated magnificence in public works'.[2]

For reasons which will be explained later, the country seats of the elite grew both in number and in size before reaching a plateau in about the mid-seventeenth century (Fig. 11.1). These seats were only the largest and most impressive examples among the 5,000 or so country houses of all shapes and sizes scattered about England at any one time after the mid-seventeenth century.[3] Since there were about 9,000 parishes, and some parishes contained two country houses, one can make a rough guess that after 1660, at least in southern England, about one parish in three had a country house, and probably a landlord normally resident in it. In 1540, relatively few parishes had any influential gentlemen living in their midst,

---

[2] A. Young, *Travels in France and Italy during the Years 1787, 1788 and 1789*, (Everyman Library), 1906, p. 291.

[3] R. Strong, M. Binney, and J. Harris, *The Destruction of the Country House, 1875-1975*, London, 1974, p. 15.

298 HOUSES: SOCIAL FUNCTIONS

to arbitrate disputes, quell incipient insurrections, and distribute charity to the needy, although many had a small manor-house where resided the somewhat impoverished lord of the manor. The growth in the number of powerful resident squires between 1560 and 1660, and the concurrent expansion of the numbers and functions of the justices of the peace, resulted in the greatest revolution in social control ever to have occurred in rural England. The country house thus symbolizes a return to law and order in the countryside after a long period of social chaos and aristocratic factional violence.

2. SOCIAL FUNCTIONS

i. Administration

Country houses served several functions. During the sixteenth and seventeenth centuries, almost all of them were centres for the administration of a large landed estate of several thousand acres, the revenues of which supported the upkeep of the seats and their inhabitants. This meant that every major seat would have a 'steward's room', 'audit room', or 'business room', where rents were received and rent books kept, and a 'record room' where financial and legal archives of the estate were housed. The more responsible owners realized that efficient management depended on their personal supervision, and they would therefore spend a good deal of time in the steward's room with the lease books, or riding about the estates on tours of inspection. But the system of long leases to large tenants, automatically renewed every seven years or so, reduced the burden of administration of an agricultural estate to the minimum, and those who could not be bothered and could find an efficient and honest agent—not always an easy thing to do— were free to spend their time as they wished.

From the Middle Ages to the late seventeenth century and after, nearly all houses had home farms closely attached to them, which had to be managed and administered directly. (Endpaper.) In those farms were produced a good deal of the food and drink for consumption in the house. A formidable amount of supplies were needed by an establishment consisting of up to ten family members and a constant flow of guests, attended upon by fifteen to forty indoor servants, and as many outdoor servants and hangers-on, all of whom could expect some free meals in the kitchen.

Because in the sixteenth century most owners depended almost entirely upon the revenues of their landed properties, there was at first a close relationship between the size of the house and the size of the estate administered from it. As time went on, however, this close connection between the location and the size of a landed estate and those of a country seat was gradually loosened. In the eighteenth century, the popularity of the formal Palladian villa, coinciding as it did with the demand for wide acres of romantic rolling grass, trees, and lakes, led to a situation in which a number of quite compact houses were situated in the middle of very large areas of parkland. There thus developed a physical discrepancy between the relatively small scale of the villa and the relatively huge size of the pleasure-grounds.[4] Another possibility, as has been seen, was the appearance of large and luxurious houses with surrounding pleasure-grounds, but little or no agricultural estate attached to them, aside from a home farm.

ii. Display of Power

The country seat was a power centre, a showplace for the display of authority. As a result, it tended to be built and lived in in a manner which would impress visitors. It was here, out in the countryside, not in the town house in London, that the real extravagance took place, much to the astonishment of foreign visitors accustomed to the great *hôtels* of Paris. Edward Gibbon noticed the difference on his first visit to France and observed that 'the splendour of the French nobility is confined to their town residence, that of the English is more usefully distributed in their country seats'. The sociological consequences were drawn out by the Frenchman, de Saussure, who saw the difference as a key to national patterns of social dominance. Writing about England in the 1720s he commented:

A curious fact is that many noblemen live in town to economize, and though they are surrounded with great luxury, they declare that in their country seats they are forced to spend far more, having to keep open house and table, packs of hounds, stables full of horses, and to entertain followers of every description. When in town they do not have these same expenses, but they are not thought of as in the country, where they are like little kings, according to the good they do and to the extent of their bounty. In the country, most of them have sumptuous abodes, or rather palaces, whereas in town they are lodged like citizens.

---

[4] H. Walpole, *The History of Modern Taste in Gardening*, quoted in *Horace Walpole: gardenist*, ed. I. W. U. Chase, Princeton, 1943, p. 34; J. Bassin, 'The English Landscape Garden in the Eighteenth Century: the Cultural Importance of an English Institution', *Albion*, 11, 1979; see also K. Woodbridge, *Landscape and Antiquity: Aspects of English Culture at Stourhead 1718-1830*, Oxford, 1970.

The key phrase in this comment is that in the country the elite 'are like little kings', their authority being dependent upon their ability to display opulence, dispense bounty, and offer hospitality. For the court nobleman or busy politician, life in the country seat might invoke a great deal of obligatory display that he might well have wished to do without. For the ordinary squire, however, without a power base at the court or Westminster, the country seat provided the only means of exercising authority and making himself useful. It was an essential element of his existence, and a prime justification for his claim to deference. It was the headquarters from which, as de Saussure observed, he exercised his paternalistic authority. John Mitford, visiting Paris in 1776, stressed how central was this political factor behind the uniquely rich development of the English country house. 'As the French have little idea of a country residence, and the nature of their government makes popularity even dangerous, their *châteaux* are not the seats of elegance. They have no interest in [the country] to preserve, no voters in boroughs to treat, no inducement to display their riches to the peasantry, or to court the favour of a mob. The glare of a city residence is the only object of their ambition. Hence the magnificence of the Parisian *hôtels*'. Arthur Young agreed, remarking that 'Banishment alone will force the French to execute what the English do for pleasure—reside upon and adorn their estates.'[5]

The first requisite of a seat was therefore an imposing external appearance. From the late sixteenth century the house was consequently usually placed in a prominent position upon a hill. This not only offered a 'prospect' for those inside looking out, but also offered an imposing appearance for those outside looking in. The façade was given particular prominence, and even where the great fortified gatehouse of the late fifteenth and early sixteenth centuries became obsolete, it was replaced by the three-tiered towering sculptured Tudor 'frontispiece', as at Burghley House. Later on, the pillared and pedimented classical entrance, approached by a flight of steps rising about a high half-basement, inspired the appropriate sense of awe. Passing through the front door, one entered a lofty hall whence rose an imposing staircase, while the linked public rooms—the 'rooms of parade' as they were called—offered opportunities for formal entertainment on a generous scale,

5 E. Gibbon, *Memoirs of my Life and Writings* [1788], in *An Eighteenth Century Miscellany*, ed. L. Kronenberger, New York, 1936, p. 513; C. de Saussure, *A Foreign View of England in the Reigns of George I and George II*, London, 1902, pp. 208-9; Glos. R. O., D.2002/F1, pp. 21-2 (I owe this reference to Dr Anne Woodhouse); R. Porter, *English Society in the Eighteenth Century*, London, 1982, p. 78.

a theatrical stage for the rituals of both hospitality and deference. In appropriately low wings (Plates VIIIA and XB), or in the attics above and basement below (Plate VIIB), were housed the inferior class of servants. The very appearance of the house thus spelled out the hierarchical structure of society, with the owner at the apex of the pyramid.

In two periods in particular some gigantic houses were designed for large-scale political entertainment. From about 1570 to 1615, a number of 'prodigy houses' were built by the leading public servants of Queen Elizabeth and James I. For these great political figures, the object was to maintain favour by providing lavish hospitality on the occasion of a royal visit. Houses like Gorhambury, Theobalds, and Hatfield in Hertfordshire, and Burghley, Holdenby, and Castle Ashby in Northamptonshire, were totally impractical and unnecessary for day-to-day living, but were designed for the housing and entertainment of the monarch and his or her retinue of several hundred courtiers and servants on their annual summer 'progresses' around the countryside. In 1579, Lord Burghley wrote a letter to Sir Christopher Hatton in which he referred to his own palace at Theobalds and that of Sir Christopher at Holdenby as buildings intended for 'her for whom we both meant to exceed our purses in these'. A year later Sir Christopher referred to Holdenby—in a letter undoubtedly meant to be shown to the Queen—as a 'shrine' in which 'that holy saint may sit in . . . to whom it is dedicated'.[6]

The decline of royal progresses after 1620 spelt the end of the construction of prodigy houses, and indeed before the seventeenth century was over three of the biggest of them all, Audley End, Holdenby and Theobalds, had been surrendered to the Crown and entirely or partly demolished. By the middle of the seventeenth century, there was in any case a reaction against such extravaganzas. Looking back on the boom period, Bishop Goodman observed that 'no kingdom in the world spent so much on building as we did'—which may well have been true. Thomas Fuller sagely advised future builders to be more cautious, observing that 'a house had better be too little for a day than too great for a year . . . It is in vain, therefore, to proportion the receipt [the public rooms] to an extraordinary occasion'.[7]

A second phase of gigantism occurred from about 1680 to 1730, also caused by the need to preserve political power and prestige,

[6] H. Nicholas, *Memoirs . . . of Sir Christopher Hatton*, London, 1847, pp. 126, 155.

[7] G. Goodman, *The Court of King James the First*, London, 1839, i, pp. 319-20; T. Fuller, *The Holy State*, Cambridge, 1642, p. 167.

now under very different circumstances. In this second period, the great Whig politicians built on an extravagant scale in order to be able to keep open house for the neighbouring squires and gentry, so as to consolidate their local power base. This was true of Chatsworth, built by the earls of Devonshire, or of Houghton House. In the latter, Sir Robert Walpole held open house 'in the autumn, towards the commencement of the shooting season. It continued six weeks or two months, and was called the Congress. At this time, Houghton was filled with company from all parts. He kept a public table, to which all gentlemen in the county found a ready admission'. Walpole is merely the most extreme example of the pre-eminence of Whig politicians as patrons of the new architectural order. Two-thirds of all 120 documented new houses built between 1710 and 1740 were the work of members of the House of Lords or House of Commons. Large new houses, in short, were primarily built with a view to, or as a corollary of, success in public life. Political ambition in the eighteenth century meant the exercise of patronage, and the exercise of patronage demanded the prestige symbol of a house from which to direct it. Not infrequently, however, the house turned out to be a white elephant. A classic example is Vanbrugh's vast pile at Eastbury Park, Dorset, which was only completed in 1738. Twenty-four years later, it was inherited by Lord Temple, who had no use for it since he already possessed Stowe. Unable to bribe a tenant with £200 a year to occupy it and keep it up, in 1775 Lord Temple had it blown up with gunpowder.[8]

Even without political incentives, owners had other reasons for needing homes of an ample size and imposing appearance. As Roger North pointed out, 'an English gentleman . . . hath business and managery, and desires splendour and elbow-room as well as air within his walls'. He also needed ancillary buildings such as stables, brewhouses, laundry, dairy, dovecote, granary, barn, forge, and storehouse to supply the household and provide transport, repairs, food, and drink. Because of these services and the patriarchal way in which the whole operation was run by the owner, Roger North aptly described a seventeenth-century seat as 'a sort of village, or rather city, with monarchic government limited by law'. This constitutional concept obviously demanded a suitably

---

[8] W. Coxe, *Memoirs of the life and administration of Sir Robert Walpole Earl of Orford*, London, 1798, p. 759; J. Harris, *The Artist and the Country House*, London, 1979, p. 206; J. Summerson, 'The Classical Country House in Eighteenth Century England', *Journal of the Royal Society of Arts*, cvii, 1959, p. 544. This brilliant article has to be the starting-point for any serious study of the social history of the country house in the eighteenth century.

impressive architectural setting. Thus Vanbrugh, who knew what his clients wanted, promised them 'a noble room of parade' inside, and 'a noble and masculine show' outside. What they desired and he offered was 'a noble thing' that displayed 'manly beauty'. The swaggering *machismo* of Vanbrugh's language is striking evidence of the patriarchal significance attached to these structures. Roger North talked about 'the parade of the house' and 'the grandeur of the apartments', while John Evelyn, when describing Cassiobury in 1680, observed that when finished 'it will be a very noble palace'.[9] (Plate IXA and Plan 1.) 'Nobility' was the order of the day, especially, it would seem, in the late seventeenth century.

Lower down the social scale, the same atmosphere of status competition prevailed. Everyone built to outdo his neighbours, thereby to earn the prestige which could be translated into power. Every county elite had its own internal struggle for pre-eminence: as Sir Henry Slingsby shrewdly remarked in 1640, 'we see an emulation in the structure of our houses', as he noted a rivalry in building in Yorkshire between 'my Lord Eure's at Malton, my Lord Savile's at Howley, Sir Arthur Ingram's at Temple Newsam'.[10] As a result, the average size of seats expanded over the years as successive owners added to them. This growth tended to go in leaps, the average size of family living and entertainment quarters in country seats rising sharply in the early eighteenth century to a new plateau where it stayed until the affluence caused by the post-1770 rise in farm prices made possible another jump (Fig. 11.2).

From 1700 onwards, the fashion for classical styles of aesthetic beauty, combined with a desire for order and decency to sweep away the messy clutter of farm buildings and ancillary domestic outbuildings like dairies and brewhouses and barns that had attached themselves to sixteenth- and seventeenth-century country houses. (Endpaper.) Palladio had found the solution in the sixteenth century by organizing the stables, kitchen, and farm buildings into symmetrical formal wings linked to the main building by corridors or porticoes. Vanbrugh insisted on such an organization for Blenheim. He argued that 'nothing more than this is necessary to all houses of *much less rank than this*' (his italics) than outcourts. 'You will find hundreds that have more outbuildings a great deal. All the difference is that they are generally ill-favoured by scram-

[9] R. North, *Of Building*, ed. H. Colvin and J. Newman, Oxford, 1981, pp. 28, 94-5, 136; *The Complete Works of Sir John Vanbrugh*, ed. B. Dobrée and G. Webb, London, 1928, iv, pp. 13-15, 138; *Diary of John Evelyn*, ed. W. Bray, London, 1879, ii, p. 362.
[10] *Diary of Sir Henry Slingsby*, ed. D. Parsons, London, 1836, p. 52.

PLAN I

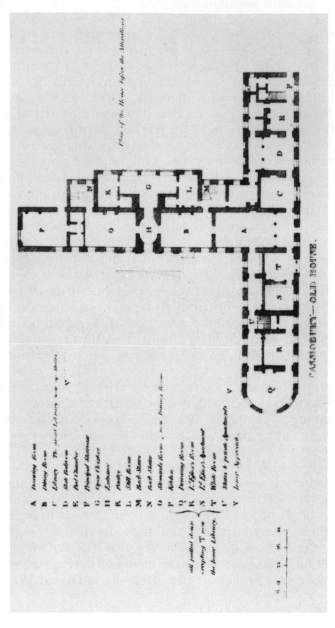

A Drawing Room
B Dining Room
C Library The great Library now up stairs   v
D State Bedroom
E   Paul Chamber
F Principal Staircase
G Open Cloister
H Entrance
K Pantry
L Still Room
M Back Stairs
N Back Stairs
O Steward's Room , now Dining Room
P Kitchen
Q Drawing Room
R L.Essex's Room
S L. Essex's Apartment
T White Room
U Stairs & private Apartments   v
V Inner Approach

all pulled down
everything down
the lower Library

CASSIOBURY.—OLD HOUSE.

Plan of the House before the Alterations

GROUND PLAN OF CASSIOBURY

bling about and looking like a ragged village'.[11] And so he built
formal courtyards surrounded by symmetrical buildings to house
the stables on one side and on the other quarters for the servants
and kitchen, dairy, dry larder, wet larder, bakehouse, wash-house,
laundry, necessary houses (privies), fuel stores, and drying-yard.
This incorporation of the service areas into the formal design of
new houses, either by putting them in the basement or in symmetrical wings, was accompanied by the removal of the home farm
away from the house altogether, and often outside the park walls.
The seat and all its services were now conceived of as a single
structure, visible from most sides and conforming to a contemporary view of architectural aesthetics. The trend that began with
rough symmetry for the main house in the 1530s was thus finally
accomplished in the early eighteenth century with a classicizing of
the exterior and the removal underground or the disguising of the
service areas and expulsion of the home farm from the grounds.
(Plates VIA and VIIA.) It was only in the Victorian age that service quarters once more were allowed to proliferate in an irregular
one-storey growth, stretching out from the seat itself, which was
now itself fashionably assymetrical once more. (Plan 3.)

The problem of imposing such symmetrical order upon the untidy clutter of an earlier house, however, was not so easy, and a
compromise usually had to be adopted. (Plate IIIB.) If the main
house was rebuilt, or given a large new wing, the offices were
either left in the old house at the back, as at Hertingfordbury, or
in one unreconstructed wing, as at Cassiobury, or in a still very
messy stable-yard at the side, as at Hamels. (Plates VIB, IXA and
V.) The elimination of outbuildings was thus a slow process, especially if, as was commonly the case, all that could be afforded
was a face-lift of the old house.

The most revealing account of the building objectives of a squire
with limited resources in the late seventeenth century, who was
anxious to tidy up and modernize his old house, is provided by
Roger North's description of what he did and why he did it at
Rougham Hall, Norfolk in 1692-3.[12] North was not a wealthy
magnate with boundless resources seeking above all nobility and
grandeur. He was, as he put it, 'a lover of elegance about an house,
but moderatedly estated out of which to supply the charge of
building'. What he was after, therefore, was external symmetry
and internal comfort and convenience, with such degree of ele-

   [11] *The Complete Works of Sir John Vanbrugh*, iv, pp. 34-5.
   [12] *Autobiography of Roger North*, London, 1887, pp. xlv-lvii; R. North, *Of Building*, pp. 77-
87.

gance as his purse could afford. 'I account it not any disgrace that I was not able to build as chancellors and admirals, and those that use it to evacuate a surfeit of the purse', he commented acidly, with a hint of the jealousy of the Tory squire for the new wealth from law, politics, and military office that was just beginning to flood into the countryside. He hoped to avoid the accusation of building for the sake of vanity 'and such is all pomp and decoration of front'.

'I found the house as ancient manor-houses usually are, of several sorts of building, and done in different ages, and for different ends'. The problem was how to reorganize the mess internally 'for habitation' and externally for modest show. Inside, the house was an inconvenient jumble of rooms either too large or too small, which he set about reorganizing. The west wing, facing the garden, he devoted to living quarters, including for himself a library and a private parlour. To tidy up the façade and bring the house up to date, he then proceeded, using the same frontal plan and symmetrical fenestration, to rebuild entirely the other wing in order to provide for a new kitchen, servants' hall, and other necessary offices. He also redid the roofs entirely. He could not afford to reface his house in stone, and refused to stucco over the brick, going so far as to build the columns of his new portico in matching brick filled with flint. Thus in two years, Roger North had converted a ramshackle, inconvenient, rambling assemblage of old-fashioned buildings into a modern-looking seat fit for a squire, both pleasing to look at and practical to live in. It was now a triple pile, rectilinear, modestly imposing block, with a symmetrical porticoed façade. To North, the ideal was summed up in the word 'elegance', which he repeatedly used and to achieve which at minimum expence he went to enormous trouble. In his own modest way, he too wanted to make a show.

iii. Hospitality

The third main function of the country seat was to act as a centre of hospitality, which was in part a function of sociability, in part a method of displaying generosity and authority, and in part a way to make useful political or matrimonial contacts. For the hosts, hospitality was a necessary, although expensive, way of enhancing prestige in the neighbourhood, and of providing themselves with people to talk to and play with. (Plates XIIA and B.) Moreover, generous hospitality was the hallmark of a gentleman, and it was a quality which was stressed with monotonous regularity in the memorial inscriptions to the deceased in the sixteenth, seventeenth, eighteenth, and even nineteenth centuries. The rich Virginia planters of the eighteenth century followed in all respects the behaviour patterns and values of their English contemporaries. It has been calculated that in the second decade of the century, William Byrd II of Virginia spent at least 80 per cent of his days throughout the year either visiting or being visited by friends, neighbours or relatives.[13]

English memoirs and diaries tell the same story, and the journals kept between 1804 and 1822 by Frances Calvert give a very good idea of the pace of elite social life both in town and country at the beginning of the nineteenth century. She was the daughter and coheiress of a wealthy Irish landowner who was raised to a Viscountcy on retiring from the Speakership of the Irish House of Commons. On her marriage in 1789 she brought with her a portion of £60,000, but only 'after a good many delays' no doubt occasioned by her family's social objections to the groom. He was Nicolson Calvert, son and heir of Felix Calvert, a brewer of Portland Place, who was shortly to inherit Hunsdon House, Herts., on the death without heirs of his elder brother. Nicolson Calvert became an active politician, Whig MP for the borough of Hertford for thirty-two years and later Knight of the Shire. During the season, when Parliament was sitting, they were both constantly on the go between their London house and Hunsdon, which was within his constituency and where their younger children lived. Very well connected on her mother's side, Mrs Calvert—accompanied by her husband when he had the time—mixed in high society at court and in the world of politics. In the country her life proceeded at a less feverish pace and on a less exalted level.

It is possible from her diaries to obtain an idea of the daily round of elite life. Visiting came essentially in two kinds: short-term, when hosts and guests were constantly together, and long-term, when life resumed its normal patterns and the guests were treated as part of the family.

Since nineteenth-century by-roads were mostly muddy and deeply rutted tracks, and visitors could only travel at the speed of a horse-drawn carriage, guests from any distance often had to be put up for the night. There was therefore need for plenty of spare bedrooms, as well as rooms for the servants of the visitors, and special space and kitchen staff to feed them all.

Short-term visiting could be for the day—usually for dinner—

[13] D. B. Smith, *Inside the Great House: Planter Family Life in Eighteenth Century Chesapeake Society*, Ithaca, 1980, pp. 200, 217.

or for one or two nights or for a week or two. The duration of the visit seems to have varied partly according to the distance travelled and the status of the guests. At Hunsdon, in the early nineteenth century, 'the Corporation of Hertford dined with us, also Mr Lamb [future Lord Melbourne], who slept here. The Corporation played at whist and seemed to like their party'. Similarly, when the Calverts and their daughter went in 1820 to the Salisburys' at Hatfield for the Assizes dinner (an annual event), they found the house crowded with over a hundred guests, only some of whom, including themselves, stayed the night. The next day, there were only nineteen for dinner before the ball at Hertford.

On the whole, visits of between five days and a fortnight were limited to close friends or associates: thus the Calverts spent five days at Firle with Lord Gage in 1807, and five days with the Cokes of Holkham in 1820.[14] As persons still alive today can remember, visits by coach for the day were limited by the range of carriage-horses, which was about nine miles each way, and then only on moonlit evenings. For this reason the dinner-hour was early: first at 2 p.m. then drifting slowly to 4 or 5 p.m. throughout the eighteenth and early nineteenth centuries. This allowed time to get home by coach before darkness fell. Despite this handicap, large houses normally entertained guests to dinner two or three times a week, partly for sociability, partly to maintain useful contacts. In the late eighteenth century Sir Alexander Dick, an eminent physician with a seat near Edinburgh, told Boswell that he used to entertain a thousand persons a year to dinner.

It is very clear from correspondence, diaries, lawsuits, and novels that it was very common indeed for relatives and friends of the family to pay extended visits, lasting from a few weeks to a few months. Dr Johnson remarked that 'a man who stays a week with another makes him a slave for a week'—but this did not prevent him from settling into the household at Streatham Park as a semi-permanent guest of Mrs Thrale. It must be remembered, however, that in these large rambling houses, guests could lead very separate lives, being waited on and even served meals by the servants in their own apartments, so that they might only meet their host and hostess for dinner, cards, or hunting.[15]

It has also to be remembered that the concept of privacy only penetrated very slowly into the mentality of owners of country

[14] *An Irish Beauty of the Regency*, ed. W. Blake, London, 1911, pp. 5, 334, 346, 85-7, 348-9.

[15] *Boswell: the Applause of the Jury, 1782-1785*, ed. I. S. Lustig and F. A. Pottle, New York, 1981, pp. 101, 142.

houses. So long as they were entirely dependent upon servants for their most trivial personal needs, and so long as the habit of open hospitality persisted, privacy was unobtainable, and indeed unheard of. Under such circumstances, the additional burden of house parties of guests was more easily borne, especially since they served to relieve the tedium of country-house life, and their creature comforts were attended to by the servants.

The economic cost of entertainment was high, however, and there were complaints from the early eighteenth century onward. In Vanbrugh's play, *The Country House*, he makes the new owner, Mr Barnard, complain 'since I bought this damned country house, I spend more in a summer than would maintain me seven years'. To which his servant retorts soothingly: 'why, if you spend money, haven't you good things for it, all the country round—come they not all to see you? Mind how you're beloved, master'. In 1710 Steele commented savagely that 'a vainglorious fox-hunter shall entertain half the county for the ostentation of his beef and beer, without the least affection for any of the crowd about him. He feeds them, because he thinks it a superiority over them that he does so, and they devour him, because they know he treats them out of insolence'.

A century later this traditional practice of keeping open house, which combined the pleasures of sociability and friendship with those of display and ostentation, had degenerated in some cases into an expensive obligatory chore. In 1826 a perceptive German visitor to England observed that:

it requires a considerable fortune here to keep up a country house; for custom demands many luxuries! . . . A handsomely fitted-up house with elegant furniture, plate, servants in new and handsome liveries, a profusion of dishes and foreign wines, rare and expensive dessert, and in all things an appearance of superfluity—'plenty' as the English call it. As long as there are visitors in the house, this way of life goes on; but many a family atones for it by meagre fare when alone: for which reason, nobody here ventures to pay a visit in the country without being invited, and these invitations usually fix the day and hour. . . . True hospitality this can hardly be called; it is rather the display of one's own possessions, for the purpose of dazzling as many as possible. After a family has thus kept open house for a month or two, they go for the remainder of the time they have to spend in the country to make visits at the houses of others; but the one hospitable month costs as much as a wealthy landed proprietor spends in a whole year with us.[16]

[16] *The Complete Works of Sir John Vanbrugh*, ii, p. 216; *The Tatler*, ed. G. A. Aitken,

iv. Sport

Life in the country involved taking part in a great deal of outdoor activities such as walking, riding, and hunting. The pursuit and killing of wild animals could take many forms, whether practised on foot or on horseback, whether unaided, such as fishing, or with the assistance of hawks, or of hounds of one kind or another. Though originally designed mainly to provide meat for the table, and to keep down vermin, these pursuits had rapidly become ends in themselves, or sports.

In the sixteenth and seventeenth centuries, hawking was still almost as important as fox-hunting was later to become, and no large country house was without its mews. Hunting on horseback—primarily stags in the sixteenth and seventeenth centuries— had always been popular with the landed classes. With the invention of fox-hunting, however, it became for many a way of life, since the greater stamina and cunning of the fox made it possible for the chase to last much longer. This in turn encouraged the breeding of horses with a suitable endurance. It was to house these very expensive, finely-bred, horses that the old dirt-floor stables were replaced by new, paved and well-aired stables, which sprang up all over the countryside in the early eighteenth century. (Plate VIIIB.) These were the centre of many a gentleman's life, and a detailed record of the daily routine of one eighteenth century squire, William Middleton of Stockeld Park in Yorkshire, shows that he and the family visited the stables at least once and usually several times a day. Both men and women spent much time watching their horses being groomed, fed, and exercised, or riding about the country on their backs. The late nineteenth-century artist Ben Marshall observed 'I discover many a man who will pay me fifty guineas for painting his horse, who thinks ten guineas too much to pay for painting his wife'. This was a discovery which had helped to make the fortune of George Stubbs.[17]

Fox-hunting became 'the only chase worth the taste or attention of a high-bred sportsman' as the *British Sportsman* put it in 1796. (Plate IXB.) It was a sport peculiar to England, since it involved a wild gallop over private property, often doing a considerable amount of damage to hedges and standing crops. It was thus only possible under two conditions, one social and the other economic.

London, 1899, iv, p. 46; [H. L. H. von Pückler Muskau], *Tour in England, Ireland and France . . .*, Philadelphia, 1833, p. 28.

[17] Lambeth Palace, Court of Arches MSS, Process Books, D 601, 1395; W. S. Sparrow, *British Sporting Artists*, London, 1922, p. 180 (quoted in R. Carr, *English Fox-Hunting: a History*, London, 1976, p. 41).

The land must be owned by a few huge landed proprietors, and managed by a small number of large tenant farmers, who are under the thumb of their landlords and usually themselves not averse to joining in the sport. The second condition is that large areas should be given over to permanent pasture, thus providing a smooth and comfortable surface for a fast gallop. Small peasant proprietors with strips under mixed farming simply would not have put up with having their crops trampled into the ground by a pack of idle gentlemen on horseback. If the pastures were divided by hedges and ditches, which had to be jumped, so much the better, for it added a spice of danger to the day's outing. Thus it was the very socio-economic system that created and sustained the landed elite and their houses, and gave them their power and prestige, which also made the sport of fox-hunting possible.

By the late eighteenth century, fox-hunting had become a major, perhaps the major, obsession of the landed classes. In *The American Senator* Trollope makes Reginald Morton, on becoming squire of Brogton on the death of his cousin, take up fox-hunting because now that he could afford it, not to do so would be 'churlish'. But fox-hunting had to do with more than good manners, or even sociability. In a county like Northamptonshire, which was superb fox-hunting country and also dominated by large landowners, it could also be a source of power. In 1888 it was said of the Pytchley country (in Northamptonshire), that 'when more than half the country was owned by a dozen keen fox-hunters, it was far easier to manage than it is today'. In other words, the power of the Master of a pack of foxhounds over the tenant farmers, across whose fields the hunters galloped, was far greater and more intimate in a county full of great landlord enthusiasts. In the hunting-field paternalism was directly and immediately visible, as an instrument of social control and co-operation. It is no surprise, therefore, to find the great noblemen of Northamptonshire acting again and again as Masters of the Pytchley Hunt for over a century. This was the case from 1752 when John Spencer—soon to be created Earl Spencer of Althorp—first founded it, through two Spencer heirs, lords Althorp, down to the 5th Earl who was Master from 1874 to 1898. In the early nineteenth century, so devoted to the sport was Lord Althorp, the future leading parliamentary reformer, that after attendance at a late sitting of the House of Commons he would gallop all night, using relays of horses, so as to be able to hunt with the Pytchley the next day. He also introduced a lighter and faster breed of fox-hound, and kept detailed

hunting journals.[18] The extraordinary tenacity through thick and
thin of the English elite is well displayed by the 5th Earl, who in
1898 was Lord Lieutenant, Chairman of the County Council, as
well as Master of the Pytchley Hunt. As such, Spencer was still
king of Northamptonshire. The sport remained in the hands of
the very rich because of its very high cost. Farmers were welcome
to trail along on their nags, but serious hunting was a different
matter. In the early nineteenth century, the cost of a good hunter,
which would keep its owner at the head of the field, was anything
between £400 and £700. Lord Althorp in his capacity as Master
kept a stable of thirty, at a cost of between £4,500 and £5,000 a
year.[19]

If Northamptonshire landowners could hunt with the Pytchley,
the Fitzwilliam, the Grafton, or the Bicester and Warden Hill,
those in Hertfordshire could hunt with the old Berkeley, the Delmé-
Radcliffe, the Puckeridge, or the Hatfield. Most of these Hunts,
it will be noted, are named either after a great landowner or after
his seat. In Hertfordshire, just as in Northamptonshire, fox-hunting was established, organized, and managed by the magnates of
the county. It was the Calverts of Albury Park, the Hales of Kings
Waldenbury, the Sebrights of Beechwood, the Delmé-Radcliffes
of Hitchin Priory, and the Hanburys of Poles who were the Masters of fox-hounds for generations. As has been seen, the Plumers
found room for the Puckeridge hounds, first at Blakesware and
then at Standon Lordship. The administration of a hunt kept these
men very busy, while hunting provided an absorbing occupation
for many of their fellow owners of seats.[20] Indeed, over fifty owners in Northamptonshire and Hertfordshire have left evidence of
their particular absorption in blood sports. Nor was this passion
limited to men, although hunting by women required considerable
skill and courage, since it is not easy to ride side-saddle at full
gallop over rough country, and it was a Countess of Salisbury who
founded the Hatfield Hunt in the late eighteenth century. Fishing
and coursing also remained popular outdoor sports century after
century, as well as shooting, a sport monopolized by the elite and
preserved for them alone by increasingly harsh and restrictive Game
Laws. (Plate VIA and Endpaper.)

The result of this obsession with field sports was an enormous

[18] A. Trollope, *The American Senator* [1877], Oxford, 1931, pp. 503-4; H. O. Nethercote,
The Pytchley Hunt, Past and Present, London, 1888, p. 7; *Dictionary of National Biography, sub*
Spencer, John Charles, Viscount Althorp, and 3rd Earl Spencer.
[19] H. O. Nethercote, op. cit., p. 18.
[20] *Victoria Country History, Hertfordshire*, i, 1902, 'Fox-Hunting'.

growth in the eighteenth century of buildings in which to house
the animals involved, especially the horses. The most important
adjunct to a country house was the stables for horses, which got
larger and more palatial in the eighteenth century until from a
distance they can not infrequently easily be mistaken for country
houses. Defoe in 1724 described the stable court at Petworth as
'equal to some noblemen's whole houses'. Many an eighteenth-
century landowner provided better accommodation for his horses
than for his servants, some of whom slept uncomfortably in the
little low attics over the large and airy stabling. (Plate VIIIB.) To
take Northamptonshire alone, truly monumental stable blocks were
built at Boughton, Easton Neston, and Althorp in the late seventeenth century and in the early eighteenth century at Milton,
Lamport and Lilford. (Plate VIIIA.) At Winchendon House, Bucks.,
the stables, which were built by Lord Wharton in the late 1670s,
had partly-gilt stuccoed ceilings for the delectation of animals and
visitors. Many of these blocks also included rooms for kennels for
hounds and mews for hawks. But occasionally the dog kennels
were a detached building, put up to look like a large and elegant
country house, such as that of the Duke of Hamilton at Chatel-
herault, in Scotland. At Nunwick, Northumb., in 1768 dog kennels were built with lancet Gothic windows.[21]

The trend towards the expenditure of more and more money,
time and energy on bloodsports culminated in the late Victorian
and Edwardian era when gigantic *battues* of slaughtered birds and
animals became a kind of symbolic preview of the human slaughter on the Somme. Thus in the season of 1914 on the eve of World
War I, some 7,000 pheasants, 1,000 partridges and 250 hares were
shot by the hosts and their guests in the woods and coverts of
Panshanger.[22]

Owners also enjoyed less strenuous outdoor sports, and by the
seventeenth century any good-sized house would own a bowling
green close by for the entertainment of both sexes. This was a
favorite sport for the family and guests, and greens figure prominently in the many commissioned pictures of country houses from
1700. Chauncy takes evident pride in describing how the Elizabethan Sir Walter Mildmay at Pishiobury, Herts. 'adorned the
front thereof with a fair bowling green raised about 5 foot high,
enclosed with a brick wall topped with stone, and balls upon it'.

[21] J. Harris, op. cit., fig. 84, p. 140; R. Strong, M. Binney, and J. Harris, op. cit., fig.
334.
[22] H. Prince, 'The Changing Landscape of Panshanger', *East Hertfordshire Archaeological
Society Transactions*, xiv, 1955-6, p. 55.

(Plate VIA.) A handful of the very largest and wealthiest houses of the sixteenth century—such as Buckhurst House, Sussex—also boasted of a tennis court, a large enclosed area for a game very different from the present-day lawn tennis.[23]

Because of the prevailing weather, indoor sports were almost as important and time-consuming as outdoor ones. In many houses an astonishing amount of time was taken up by both sexes in playing cards, and indeed one reason for all the sociability was to provide one or more foursomes for the card-table. During the seventeenth century billiards became popular, and by the nineteenth century there were few large country houses without a specialized billiard-room, which along with the small library and the gunroom were largely a male preserve.

The entertainment functions of the house thus demanded a wide variety of specialized ancillary buildings, rooms, grounds, landscaping, and interior fitments. By the eighteenth century they took up a significant amount of the total cost of house-building and the maintenance of the establishment. The pursuit of pleasure could not be achieved cheaply.

v. Pleasure

In 1751, Henry Fielding observed that 'to the upper part of mankind, time is an enemy, and (as they themselves often confess) their chief labour is to kill it'.[24] What does a leisured elite do with itself all day, year in and year out? There were, as has been mentioned, administrative responsibilities for the estate, the home farm, and the household; there were the endless parties and the flitting to and fro from house to house. There were field sports and indoor sports, particularly cards. But how else could the days be filled? Increasingly throughout the late seventeenth and eighteenth centuries one solution was escape—flight to London, to Bath, and after 1770 to one of the fashionable seaside watering-places like Brighton, or Lowestoft, or Scarborough. In the country, one of the most striking developments in the eighteenth century was the growth in the provincial capitals of elite service trades, like coffee-shops, booksellers, French teachers, dancing teachers, doctors, dentists, attorneys, etc. The county elite had always had their ritual gatherings, of which the most important were the three an-

---

[23] H. Chauncy, *The Historical Antiquities of Hertfordshire*, London, 1700, p. 178; see also, for example, Offley Place (p. 405) or the Hoo (p. 510); R. Blomfield, *History of Renaissance Architecture*, i, p. 68. The Buckhurst tennis court was sixty-five feet long.

[24] H. Fielding, *An Enquiry into the Causes of the late Increase of Robbers*, London, 1751, sect. 1.

nual meetings of the assizes in the county town, which were at
least as much social and political as judicial occasions. For those
who were on the Bench, there were also the meetings of the
Quarter Sessions. As important as the social gatherings were the
local horse-races, firmly established everywhere by the late seventeenth century, which drew large crowds from all classes of society. By the eighteenth century most country towns also had assembly rooms for dancing and conviviality. In October 1819 the
Calverts visited Bury St Edmunds for ten days, attending the annual fair and visiting friends in the neighbourhood. The expedi-
tion was such a success that it was repeated the following year.[25]

This still left a great deal of time on the hands of a class which
was in principle without a professional occupation. Many found
contentment in the paternalistic care of their tenants, the diligent
management of their estates, the duties of a JP, the pleasures of
field sports, the intimacies of family life, and the entertainment of
friends. Many women were content to please their husbands, produce and care for their young children, run an efficient household,
and act as graceful hostesses. Their leisure hours were spent in
needlework, gossip with their companions, visitors, and friends,
reading mainly but not exclusively novels, and playing endless
games of cards. Some of both sexes, however, were bored and
discontented at such a humdrum existence, and it is amongst this
minority that adultery was common. Yet others solved the problem by more frequent and extended visits to London and Bath,
and by filling the house with an endless succession of guests. There
were thus at all times widely different life-styles to be found amongst
country-house owners, ranging from that of the fox-hunting booby
squire to the man-about-town to the serious philanthropist or art
collector. Moreover, the same individual was likely to follow very
different regimes in his youth, his middle years, and his old age.
As is true at all levels of society, no two households were exactly
the same.

When not occupied with administration, hunting, travelling and
giving and receiving hospitality and pursuing sexual conquests, the
elite occupied their leisure hours in a variety of ways. Only about
one in sixty of our sample has left evidence of a special interest or
another, but they provide useful indications of changing fashions
in taste. For example, religion became an absorbing concern to
many at two periods, the early seventeenth century with the rise

---

[25] P. Borsay, 'The English Urban Renaissance: the Development of Provincial Urban
Culture c.1680–c.1760', *Social History*, ii, 1977; *An Irish Beauty . . .* , pp. 332-4, 349-50.

of Puritanism, and the early nineteenth century with the rise of Evangelical Anglicanism.

Some owners concerned themselves with improving the breed of their cattle, horses, and dogs, and the quality of their crops. Yet others experimented with horticulture and avidly imported trees, shrubs, and flowers from all over the world, a development that was already in full swing by the early seventeenth century, and the collection and supply of which made the careers of the Tradescants, father and son.

Interest in philanthropy was a constant, but only a small minority interest, not more than a dozen or so of the sample distinguishing themselves in this area in any one century. Liberal causes, such as the abolition of slavery and Catholic emancipation enlisted the enthusiasm of some in the late eighteenth and early nineteenth centuries. Paternalist values certainly encouraged many, perhaps a majority, to take the trouble to distribute minor charity to the tenantry, either in the form of free food and clothing, or remission of rent in bad times, but surviving account books suggest that none of this amounted to a significant sum in comparison with overall income and expenditures. It rarely, if ever, for example, approached the amount of money—or time—spent on gambling.

The best recorded activity of the elite after about 1700 was a variety of aesthetic and intellectual pursuits. Both squires and noblemen were more serious than the word diletante suggests in their single-minded enthusiasm for collecting, whether of great libraries, classical antiquities, or foreign paintings. Many devoted their lives to the pursuit of local antiquarian studies, and patronized local literary, philosophical, or archaeological societies. If the driving force behind such local intellectual institutions came from the professional classes, the clergy, doctors, and lawyers, the nobility and squirearchy gave the essential support and patronage, and often showed serious interest in the proceedings.

One result of this intellectual and collecting enthusiasm was the construction of specialized rooms—libraries, picture galleries, sculpture galleries, even museums, to accommodate the acquisitions. The most dramatic development was the explosive growth of libraries in the eighteenth century. One of the very first houses to be fitted with a library as such was Lord Ellesmere's seat at Ashridge in the early seventeenth century, not surprisingly since he was an eminent legal scholar and administrator. By the late seventeenth century, the installation of libraries was becoming much more widespread. But Heythrop House, designed by Archer in 1705, had no library, despite its substantial size, and in 1708 Vanbrugh was warning his patrons the Marlboroughs that in the designs for Blenheim Palace 'there is no library in the house'. Even when libraries existed in the late seventeenth century, they tended to be small, and at Ham House in 1670 the Duke of Lauderdale's books were squeezed into a confined 'library closet'. By the 1720's, however, it was unthinkable to build a house without a substantial room set aside for a library. Sir Robert Walpole's Houghton of 1721 had a whole wing—over 4,000 square feet—given over to the library, and Kedleston of 1760 had two libraries as well as a music-room and a music gallery. At Nostell Priory, Yorks., begun in 1733, James Paine's original plan included a pavilion entirely devoted to a library, and Holkham, Norfolk, begun a year later, provided a semi-detached wing for the same purpose.

Luton Hoo of 1766 had a three-room library 144 feet long and covering 3,600 square feet, which occupied a whole wing of the house, while later in the century Stowe had a library, a 'Gothic library', an ante-library, and a music-room. Even more modest houses of squires, like Peper Harow of 1765, had a library as one of the eight rooms on the main floor. At the end of the century, Lord Torrington always regretted 'the want of a good library, the first of all luxuries'. At Trentham he commented: 'nor is the library fitted up as it should be; a library is the first of rooms'. By 1792, Richardson was including a library and a music-room in all his plans for anything larger than the very modest country house, and in the 1770s even a small house like Berrington had a library. By 1806, a library was described as 'an appendage which no man of rank or fortune can now be without, if he possesses or wishes to be thought to possess taste or genius'.[26]

By now the library had often become the largest and grandest room in the house, which is evidence of the very great importance attached to it. Confining the examples to our three counties, when in the 1750s the Duke of Northumberland remodelled Alnwick Castle he created a vast library sixty-four feet by twenty-two, the biggest room in the house. That at Capheaton, Northumb., built in 1795, was fifty-five feet by thirty-three feet, and 'well stocked'. In Hertfordshire, Watton Woodhall had one smallish library in 1777, but two, 'the little library' and 'the great library', before

[26] J. Byng, *Torrington Diaries*, ed. J. B. Andrewes and J. Beresford, London, 1934, i, p. 129; iii, p. 157; Anon., *A Tour of Wales*, London, 1806, p. 155; G. Richardson, *New Designs in Architecture*, London, 1792, pl. xxxiv, fig. 2; pl. xxxvi, fig. 2; J. Summerson, *Architecture in Britain, 1530 to 1830*, London 1953, figs. 43, 49, 52, 57; C. Campbell, *Vitruvius Britannicus*, London, 1715, i, p. 6; R. Blomfield, op. cit., ii, pp. 289 (Latham Hall), 272 (Luton Hoo).

1791. The library at Woolmers, built in 1803, cost no less than £9,000 to erect and stock with books. At Cole Green in 1800, the house itself was insured for £1,000 but the contents of the library, which included Renaissance art collected in Italy by the late Earl Cowper, for £2,000. As early as 1680 John Evelyn observed that Cassiobury had 'a large rich' collection of books, and by the early nineteenth century this was housed in three libraries. (Plans 1 and 2 and Plate XIIIB.) At Althorp, Northants., Henry Holland added a library for the 2nd Earl Spencer on the ground floor in 1786, but the collection grew at such a pace that an additional wing had to be added in 1820. By the early nineteenth century they amounted to 70,000 choice volumes, which, when finally sold to the John Rylands Library in Manchester in 1892, were occupying no fewer than four ground-floor rooms. It was one of the really great collections of early printed books in the country. The huge library collected at Ashridge, Herts., by successive earls of Bridgwater was hardly less distinguished in quality. At Stoke Bruerne, one whole wing—admittedly not a very large one—was given over to the library before 1725, there was a huge law library at Easton Maudit before 1763, and at Laxton by 1810 the library was the largest room in the house, measuring fifty-five feet by thirty-three.[27] Of course the contents of these libraries were often the work of a single collector, and may have sat on the bookshelves neglected and unread by his descendants. The room itself was also a convenient social amenity, serving as a family room if there were no guests, and as a masculine preserve if there was a house party. Not all owners of large libraries were automatically book-lovers and book-collectors, but some of them certainly were.

Another special amenity fitted into many of the larger houses in the early eighteenth century, for example at Boughton House, Northants., and St Paul's Walden, Herts., was the music-room, where the family and their guests practiced their instrumental and

[27] T. Bernard, *Pleasure and Pain, 1780-1818*, ed. J. B. Baker, London, 1930, p. 6; W. W. Tomlinson, *Comprehensive Guide to Northumberland* [1888] Newton Abbot, 1969, p. 240; N. Pevsner, *Northumberland, Buildings of Britain*, 12, London, 1957, p. 112; J. Hodgson, *History of Northumberland*, Newcastle, ii, (i), 1827, pp. 213-34; G. Richardson, *New Vitruvius Britannicus*, i, London, 1802, pp. 27-8; H. A. Tipping, *English Houses*, vi, (i), p. 219; *Country Life*, lvii, 1925, p. 203; R.I.B.A., British Architecture Library, Drawings Collection; C. R. Cockerell's Diary, 22 Feb. 1822 (we owe this reference to the kindness of Mr H. M. Colvin); Herts. R. O., Cowper MSS A.18 p. 13; *Diary of John Evelyn*, ed. W. Bray, London, 1879, ii, p. 362; J. Britton, *Cassiobury Park*, London, 1837; *Country Life*, cxxvii, 1960, p. 1188; H. J. Todd, *The History of the College of Bonshommmes at Ashridge . . .* , London, 1823, pp. 62, 67; R. Kerr, *The Gentleman's House*, London, 1865, pl. 10; G. Isham, 'Easton Maudit and the Parish Church of SS. Peter and Paul', *Northants. Record Society Publications*, 1969, pp. 6, 9, 11; Northants. R. O., S. C. 544 (1921).

vocal skills. (Plate XIIB.) At least one mid-eighteenth-century house, Horton Hall, Northants., even included a private zoo, kept in a menagerie built in the grounds.

After 1620 noblemen and gentlemen began in increasing numbers to go on the Grand Tour, and to buy and ship home from Italy antique and modern sculptures and pictures. (Plate XIIIA.) The first major Italian art collections were made in the 1620s, by men like the earls of Arundel and Pembroke and the Duke of Buckingham, while in the 1630s King Charles assembled what may well have been the finest collection in Europe. In the 1650s, Wilton House, in Wiltshire, was crammed with valuable pictures from abroad, whose sale by the executors of the Earl of Pembroke was a major loss to England's aesthetic assets, second only to that of the King. These were the pioneers, but in the late seventeenth and even more in the eighteenth centuries, many noblemen spent long years in Italy, busily absorbed in the collection of works of art, some with exquisite discrimination, some with less sophisticated taste. These 'virtuosos' were described approvingly by the 3rd Earl of Shaftesbury as 'real fine gentlemen, . . . lovers of art and ingenuity'.[28] A new ideal type had been created.

Accommodation had somehow to be made for these new acquisitions. Usually they were scattered about the house, in the drawing-room, dining-room, saloon etc. But often the old sixteenth- or early seventeenth-century long gallery was converted from a place for recreation into a place for hanging pictures. One of the first such conversions was in the west wing at Althorp, Northants., in about 1682, a gallery some 115 feet long and twenty feet wide. At Aynho, Northants., the orangery was converted into a picture-gallery in 1804 when the Cartwrights inherited the pictures collected in Europe by Shovell Blackwood.

Henry Chauncy, who wrote in the 1690s and had known personally many of the late seventeenth-century owners of seats in Hertfordshire, offers us a rare glimpse of how some of them spent their time. They ranged all the way from a serious self-improver with wide intellectual interests, like Sir John Brograve of Hamels, to a frivolous and easy-going lesser gentleman like William Clerk. Sir John

studied the statutes and pleas of the Crown, was a Justice of the Peace, attended the sessions, and all public meetings to qualify himself for that

---

[28] J. Cornforth, 'Horton House, Northants.' in H. Colvin and J. Harris, *The Country Seat*, London, 1970, pp. 153-55; Hatfield House, Private and Estate MSS, Accounts 168/2; W. E. Houghton, 'The English Virtuoso in the Seventeenth Century', *Journal of the History of Ideas*, iii, 1942, p. 219.

office. He delighted much in antiquity, could read most of the old manuscripts and records, and sometimes studied the mathematics, he could
measure timber and land, and had an excellent fancy and great skill and
knowledge in building and materials necessary for the same.

William Clerk, on the other hand, 'loved the country life, delighted much in the pleasure of hawking, and would be very free,
brisk and merry in all companies'.[29] (Plate XIIA.)

A good example of the way a particularly active and energetic
family spent its time is provided by the Spencers of Althorp. In
the eighteenth century they travelled extensively in Europe assembling what is today one of the finest collections of pictures in the
country. The early nineteenth-century Lord Althorp, the son and
heir, was in his younger days a fanatical hunter, as well as a patron
of boxing. After the death of his wife in 1818, he turned his attention to the breeding of short-horn cattle, and later to politics. In
1830 to 1832 he played a key role on the national stage during the
passage of the First Reform Act. His brother, the next Earl Spencer, kept a pack of harriers, but his main interest was horse-racing.
His son and heir took a quite different tack, and became one of
England's great bibliophiles, assembling the famous Spencer collection of early printed books.

Some owners were even more remarkable in the range of their
achievements. The 2nd Marquis of Northampton in the early
nineteenth century was a member of Parliament before he succeeded his father in the House of Lords, was President of the
Geological Society, President of the Royal Society, Trustee of the
British Museum, and Trustee of the National Gallery. When his
wife's health failed in 1820, he moved for her sake to Italy, where
in ten years he proceeded to accumulate one of the finest collections of classical Greek vases ever made by a private individual, a
collection which was recently sold for three million dollars.

Of course such collections added to the prestige of their owners,
and when he was not writing about agricultural improvements and
the beauties of the parks, Arthur Young in his travels in the 1770s
was busy listing the pictures and statuary on display in country
seats. In 1771, for example, he described Castle Howard as 'much
visited by tourists on account of the great collection of antique
busts, statues, and marbles it contains'.

In 1788 Edward Gibbon noted this extraordinary assemblage of
works of art and architecture, and its wide dispersal throughout

---

[29] *Country Life*, cxxvii, 1960, p. 1124; cxiv, 1953, pp. 124-5; H. Chauncy, op. cit., pp.
226-7, 367.

the English countryside: 'We should be astonished at our own riches, if the labours of architecture, the spoils of Italy and Greece, which are now scattered from Inverary to Wilton, were accumulated in a few streets between Marylebone and Westminster'.[30]

The last phase of collecting, that of fossils, local antiquities, stuffed birds, and so on, came later in the nineteenth century, and in our three counties there are only records of two 'museums', one at Ecton Hall, Northamptonshire, extant in 1838 but gone before 1881, and one at Callaly in Northumberland in 1891.

These samples of intelligent, sophisticated, and useful contributors to the artistic and political life of the community were undoubtedly the exception rather than the rule, especially in somnolent Northamptonshire. The majority, especially in that county, seem primarily to have been interested in hunting and agricultural pursuits, when they were not gambling or philandering. (Plate IXB.) But most of them, especially in Hertfordshire and Northumberland, fulfilled the minimum duties expected of them by virtue of their position as owners of substantial country seats, and some of them devoted themselves wholeheartedly to paternalist political or administrative activities.

As we shall see, one of the major occupations among many owners and their wives was building, rebuilding, remodelling, and improving their seats, a most time-consuming occupation if it was to be closely supervised and not left to contractors. (Plate XIV.) One of the major preoccupations of many owners of seats at all times has been tinkering with the architecture and landscaping of their seats. A prime reason for all this minor activity was offered by Roger North, who pointed out that it served as a long-term diversion for a leisured class. He observed that 'it is almost indifferent how men of estates pass their time, and where they lie or abide. It is the entertainment of the mind that consummates pleasure'.[31] For him, the attractions of house alteration were that it posed an intellectual challenge, it took up a lot of time, it produced satisfyingly visible results, and it could be stopped at any moment if the money ran out. It was, he believed, the most harmless of pleasures, and he was certainly correct in thinking it to be extremely popular among country-house owners.

[30] A. Young, *A Six Month Tour through the North of England*, London, 1771, ii, p. 47; E. Gibbon, op. cit., p. 513; for the resulting collections, see C. M. Westmacott, *British Galleries of Painting and Sculpture*, London, 1824; G. F. Waagen, *Treasures of Art in Great Britain*, 4 vols., London, 1854-57; A. F. T. Michaelis, *Ancient Marbles in Great Britain*, Cambridge, 1882.

[31] R. North, *Of Building*, p. 29.

3. DURATION OF RESIDENCE

It should not be supposed that country-house owners throughout these centuries spent all or even most of their life at their rural seats. Of the four functions performed in a seat, administration, display of power and prestige, hospitality and sociability, and sheer pleasure and recreation, not even the first required continuous habitation all the year round. Throughout the whole period, the lesser landowners, the parish gentry in their small manor-houses, lacked either the money or the inclination to leave for London for long periods of the year. For the elite, however, it was different, and the proportion of time they spent at their seat varied according to personal preferences and stages of life.

Until they succeeded their fathers, elder sons of owners were often active in local politics, which meant alternating between the House of Commons in London and visits to the country, with a certain amount of electioneering involved. The groundwork for the needed local sociability would have been lain during childhood visits or extended stays in the country. If their father was still alive when they married, these elder sons tended to set up house in the family secondary seat, sometimes in another county. If this situation continued for a long time, their attitude to the main seat could remain rather distant even after they inherited, or at least until their own heir was old enough to set up on his own in the secondary seat.

If the family followed the modern nuclear mode, the period when the children were small might be one of relative withdrawal by the wife from the world of London, in order to look after her young children. This was likely to be the time when a young wife would first establish, away from her own home, close links with her social inferiors, both the servants under her orders and the recipients of her benefactions among the local villagers. But if there were no children, or the children were old enough to be off at school, the parents were more likely to stay in London or even perhaps abroad. As they became older, owners might spend more time in the country, but if they lived to a great age, unless they were physically very fit, their last few years were often mainly spent in Bath or London rather than in the country, where medical assistance was hard to come by and not of the highest standard.

The basic requirements for enjoying life in the country were good health, enjoyment of outdoor life since a great deal of riding and walking were involved, and the capacity to endure large doses of the company of one's social and cultural inferiors. These contacts might merely derive from and perpetuate a natural lack of sophistication, as was the case of seventeenth- and eighteenth-century 'booby squires' and their consorts, or they could lead to genuine efforts to better the condition of their inferiors, as often happened with women in the nineteenth century. Among those for whom such considerations mattered, and/or who cared for the responsibilities involved, a heightened sense of self-worth could be achieved through the enlightened exercise of paternalism. Thus Mrs Calvert in the early 1800s personally inoculated the Hunsdon villagers against the smallpox. In 1814, she started a Sunday school at Hunsdon where she taught eighty to ninety poor children. In the autumn of 1817 her diary reads: 'We have just set up a school for the poor, and Fanny [her daughter] and I have spent five hours each day assisting Mrs Corney, the schoolmistress. I do not mean always to do that, but I shall go often for some time to come in order to see that all goes on well'. Four years later the school was still flourishing and numbered sixty-one pupils.[32] Perhaps to any list of desiderata to make life in the country tolerable should be added a taste for independence. It was certainly possible to have greater privacy, and necessary to do more things for oneself in the country than when living in the goldfish bowl of London society. In a country house eccentricities could be quietly cultivated without causing too much outcry.

Overriding these perennial personal factors encouraging or discouraging residence in the family seat in the country there were some major alterations in English elite social behaviour which caused changes in the duration of residence of owners in their seats. Residence certainly declined from the sixteenth to the seventeenth and the eighteenth centuries and may have risen again in the nineteenth. The decline is beyond dispute, although the Victorian revival has yet to be proved conclusively. In the sixteenth and early seventeenth centuries, Parliament was a rare occurrence, and men came to London fairly infrequently and briefly, usually to deal with legal matters. Only the very rich owned town houses, and before 1630 there was not much upper-class housing available for purchase or rental. Between 1630 and 1750 all this was changed, as high-quality urban residential building spread remorselessly westward from Lincoln's Inn Fields to Covent Garden, from Covent Garden west to St James's Square and north to Bloomsbury, and from there on to Hanover Square, Cavendish Square, Gros-

[32] *An Irish Beauty* . . . , pp. 19, 23, 27, 236, 305, 356; B. Charlton, *The Recollections of a Northumbrian Lady*, ed. L. E. O. Charlton, London, 1949, p. 186.

venor Square, and Berkeley Square. Some of this housing was
occupied by courtiers and professional men, but much of it was
owned or rented by squires and noblemen up from the country.
From 1660 onward the pull of London became more and more
irresistible to all who could afford it.[33]

This change from all-the-year-round residence in the country to
residence for about six months of the year made it possible for
wealthy owners to build themselves the huge public rooms with
high ceilings and marbled floors so beloved of baroque and neo-
Palladian architects. They could put up with them since they no
longer had to live in them throughout the cold of the winter. Heating these vast halls with coal fires and charcoal braziers in the
winter months of January and February must have been all but
impossible. It was all very well for Vanbrugh to reassure the Duke
and Duchess of Marlborough as he planned his forty-foot high
saloon that heating would be no problem. He assured his anxious
clients that the owner of his other great palace, Castle Howard,
'finds that all his rooms with moderate fires are ovens', and that
there were no draughts—claims which cannot possibly have been
true.[34]

The stock theme of late seventeenth- and eighteenth-century
playwrights was the contrast between the uncouth squires, up from
the country for the first time, and the sophisticated, if corrupted,
polite society of London. The contrast was a real one and although
by the nineteenth century the county elites numbered few rustic
squires among their ranks, country sociability involved the tedium
of rubbing shoulders with them, well summed up by Mrs Calvert's *cri du cœur*: 'what dull company they are—God bless them!
They have no ideas beyond a crop of wheat, or field of potatoes'.
Over a certain income level, however, more and more of the landed
elite after 1660 were drawn regularly up to London either to participate in the social season, to attend the now annual sessions of
Parliament, or for consultation with the most skillful and famous
professional men, such as doctors, conveyancers, lawyers, architects, and painters. The growing influence of wives in the more
companionate marriages of the eighteenth century probably accelerated this process, since few women wanted to sit out the winter
in a cold and draughty country house with little to do and no one
to talk to, while their husbands were out all day hunting or shooting. The first Mrs Meetkerke who 'always came down to breakfast

[33] L. Stone, 'The Residential Development of the West End of London in the Seventeenth Century', in *After the Reformation*, ed. B. C. Malament, Philadelphia, 1980.
[34] *The Complete Works of Sir John Vanbrugh*, iv, p. 56.

clad in a green riding-habit and passed most of her life on horse-back', either visiting the poor of the parish or hunting with her husband, was exceptional in that she was sterile. Most women, even if they enjoyed riding on horseback were unable to do so much of the time owing to being pregnant. Mrs Calvert had twelve pregnancies spread over a period of twenty-one years, for a total of eight children who lived to be adults. These pregnancies do not seem to have limited her activities in town at all, but in the country it was a different matter. Small wonder that she confided to her diary: 'Living all the winter in the country is not to my taste', though there is little evidence that she was ever away from London for so long.[35]

By the early eighteenth century, the routine of the elite was to leave the country and come to London in November or December after the best of the hunting was over, to participate in the social whirl of the season, which lasted from then to April. They would perhaps spend May in Bath, and return home only in June. By the late eighteenth century, it was also becoming common to spend a week or two in the summer at a fashionable seaside resort to enjoy the benefits of sea-bathing at Brighton, Lowestoft, Margate or Scarborough. They thus spent at most seven months out of twelve in the country, and of these at least one was probably oc-cupied in sociable visits to like-minded friends and relatives in other country seats. The Calverts certainly seem to have spent much of October each year visiting in this way.[36] This change was noted, with some hyperbole, by the observant Horace Walpole: 'our ancestors . . . resided the greatest part of the year at their seats, as others did two years together or more'.[37] During the mid-dle and end of the eighteenth century, this flight from the country seems to have been at its peak, a suggestion supported by the withdrawal after about 1720 of the Northamptonshire elite from their responsibilities to run the affairs of the county as Justices of the Peace.

John Byng, Lord Torrington, who in the 1780s and 1790s toured the stately homes of England summer after summer, found many of them empty. Certainly in 1820 it was not till 5 August that the Calverts and their daughter 'took leave of London for the season'. Lord Torrington concluded, with obvious exaggeration, 'noble-

[35] *An Irish Beauty* . . ., pp. 51, 7, 168 and note, genealogical table, p. 241; T. A. Trol-lope, *What I Remember*, London, 1973, p. 30; see also above, Ch. IV, p. 146.
[36] See M. Girouard, *The English Country House*, New Haven, 1978, p. 5; *An Irish Beauty* . . ., pp. 111, 348-50.
[37] H. Walpole, op. cit., in J. Bassin, op. cit., p. 23.

men and gentlemen have almost abandoned the country, . . . yeomanry is annulled and . . . dowagers have gone away'. All that were left in the rural areas, he claimed, apart from the farmers and their labourers, were innkeepers, tax-gatherers, and stewards of absentee landlords. To prove his point he noted that Boughton House was 'verging to ruin, neglected and left to desolation'; at Belvoir 'everything [is] in neglect and ruin'; and Castle Ashby was empty. In all three cases, however, these were houses whose owners had several other seats, which they preferred. Boughton had been neglected for over half a century, for in 1726 a visitor reported that 'the gardens and house are both ill-kept, the Duke not being there above a fortnight in two or three years, and all the furniture except for family pictures taken down for other houses'.[38]

In the Victorian period, a greater sense of social threat from below, and a greater sense of moral responsibility inspired by the Evangelical revival among the elite may have driven them back once more into the country. Certainly the advent of the railways in the 1850s made it very much easier to move rapidly and frequently to and from London, while the growth of fox-hunting and shooting made country life increasingly attractive.

This hypothesis that the late eighteenth century was a period of peculiarly widespread absenteeism is supported by the fact that tourism of country houses flourished precisely in the late eighteenth century, run by the servants for profit from tips during the long absences of the owners. Some owners were less forthcoming than others, but most allowed some sort of access at least to ladies and gentlemen. Some asked for personal letters of introduction, and some required advance notice, but others were readily accessible, the more popular ones issuing tickets for admission. The actual operation was run by the servants, and it is noteworthy that in the 1770s Arthur Young should have found that Wallington, Northumb., was 'the only place I have viewed, as a stranger, where no fees were taken'. So large was the scale of this tourism that there were published, and even reprinted, guide books of the more famous houses such as Blenheim. About twenty guides for visitors of country houses were published between 1760 and 1840, and as many of private collections of pictures and statuary, especially in the 1800-40 period.[39]

In the eighteenth century, no gentleman or lady seems to have

[38] J. Byng, op. cit., ii, pp. 76, 87; iii, pp. 209, 317; iv, p. 133; *Political and Social Letters*, ed. E. F. D. Osborn, London, 1890, p. 35; *An Irish Beauty . . .* , p.346.
[39] A. Young, *A Six Month Tour . . .* , i, p. 138; iii, p. 83; J. Harris, *A Country House Index*, Shalfleet Manor, 1971.

had any difficulty in seeing over any country seat which took his or her fancy, so long as the owners were away, as they often were. In the nineteenth century, however, access to tourists was cut off, as country seats were more frequently occupied by their owners, and as the desire for privacy increased. Resident owners found visitors a nuisance, and so tourism withered away, only to revive again on a mass scale in the mid-twentieth century under wholly different social and economic circumstances.[40]

[40] I owe this suggestion to Dr Virginia Reinberg, who found it certainly true for that great eighteenth century tourist attraction, Blenheim Palace.

X

CULTURAL IDEALS AND FINANCIAL CONSTRAINTS

1. CULTURAL IDEALS

i. Location and Siting

The growth of a desire among the elite for detachment and splendid isolation in the seventeenth and eighteenth centuries was reflected in the abandonment of country houses in the proximity of towns and villages, and in new construction in isolation in the midst of huge parks surrounded by high walls. At all times country houses of a size suitable for members of the county elite had been set amidst ample pleasure-grounds. In the sixteenth century, however, they often stood on the approaches of a village and had home farm buildings abutting on or close to the offices. Some, which occupied former monastic buildings, stood on the edge of small towns, but ceased to be used as country seats in the course of the seventeenth century as a result of urban expansion. Sometimes the family would move to a more rural site, as did the Chesters of Royston Priory and Cokenhatch, who enlarged the latter in the early eighteenth century when it became their main instead of their secondary seat. Alternatively, the house might decline to a dower house, as did the Spencers' Holywell in the eighteenth century, when it was overrun by the town of St Albans. Occasionally, the family became urbanized along with their house and dropped their elite pretensions, as did the Rawdons of Hoddesdon in the late seventeenth century. On the other hand, if the houses and their grounds were large enough, former ex-monasteries on the edge of towns, such as Hitchin Priory in Hitchin or Cassiobury in Watford, could endure. So long as the landholdings of the family were large enough to enable the estate to form a barrier to development in its vicinity, and so long as the town did not grow any larger than a market town, the two could cohabit satisfactorily, as Hitchin Priory does to this day. Cassiobury, however, which had belonged to the Capels, earls of Essex, and their forebears since 1540, was overtaken by suburbia in the early twentieth century and pulled down just before World War I. All that remains today of this great house is the grand staircase—and it is in the Metropolitan Museum of Art in New York. One of the most remarkable examples of a major country house surviving to a late date on the edge of a large city is Anderson Place, which was built in 1580 actually within the walls of Newcastle on the site of a Franciscan Priory. (Plate II.) Considerably enlarged a century later, it continued as a magnate's seat within its extensive gardens for another hundred years, but was later divided into three. In the 1830s the expansion of the city led to its sale to a developer, who tore it down and turned its site into rows of suburban houses.

By the eighteenth century, isolation had become fashionable, and new seats were usually built relatively far from human habitation, or at least far enough for the latter not to encroach upon the view from the house. When in the eighteenth century the time came for refurbishing an old seat, isolation might be obtained by razing the nearby village, incorporating the resulting wilderness into an enlarged park, and moving its former inhabitants bodily to a new model village just outside the park gates, as was done at Callaly, Northumb., in 1704. A more common and less drastic operation was the relocation of a road, regardless of the inconvenience to the local inhabitants. This was carried out in Hertfordshire at Copped Hall, in the eighteenth century, at Hamels in 1808, and as late as 1906—astonishingly enough—at Lockleys, while to create seclusion at Panshanger, Earl Cowper built some six miles of new roads in 1801 to replace those he had closed off. In Northamptonshire, at Lilford and Rushton, in 1778 and 1785, the owners did not hesitate to pull down the parish churches to make space for the park, while at Apethorpe the Peterborough road, which used to run right past the front lawn, was diverted around the huge park at some time in the eighteenth century.

Second only to the problem of location, marked by a growing trend to place a country house as far away as possible from other housing, was the problem of actual siting. Owners contemplating building a country house never lacked for advice on this topic, about which a steady stream flowed from architects and social commentators from the late sixteenth century onward. Fifteenth- and sixteenth-century houses had been built either in sheltered hollows or on the flat, 'low and near water'. At that time there was no desire for a view—indeed the high garden walls and outbuildings blocked off all views in any case. But in the mid-sixteenth century, the English discovered Italy, and took from the Italians the concept of the need for a vista. For this reason Bacon therefore advised building on the top of a hill, and this remained the standard doctrine for the next three centuries. Half a century later Lord North echoed Bacon's comment, observing that the pre-

1550 method was to choose a sheltered spot and to build a house with thick walls and small windows.[1]

By the late sixteenth century, however, it became possible for the first time to see out, as the result of a technological revolution in the production of window-glass and iron window-bars. These greatly cheapened the cost, and tempted architects to fill whole walls with glass, as at Smithson's masterpiece of Hardwick Hall— making a house 'like a bird-cage, all window' as Roger North sarcastically put it in 1698.[2] This enormous expansion of the ratio of window to wall inevitably encouraged owners to provide something to look out at, and therefore to choose the top of a hill with a good view. There were, however, drawbacks, since it was not always easy to provide a reliable supply of water on the top of a hill, certainly not one with gravity feed running underneath the house, so that the standards of plumbing almost certainly deteriorated as houses were built 'upon the summit of hills, where they are intolerably exposed to the weather', according to North.[3]

Writing about Hertfordshire houses in 1700, Henry Chauncy particularly stressed the virtue of a good view. He approved of Hamels as 'situated upon a dry hill, where is a pleasant prospect to the east'. (Plate V.) He especially liked Balls Park, built in about 1650, since 'it stands towering upon an hill from whence is seen a most pleasant and delicious prospect'. But although Chauncy preferred a view, he also appreciated the older attractions of timber and streams, and level grounds for gardens and walks. He strongly approved of Watton Woodhall, also on a hill, for its timber and its streams running through the park, as well as of Wells Manor House because it 'is situated in a very dry and warm place under the brow of an hill'.[4]

In the late eighteenth century the passion for a prospect became even more strongly developed, as part of the romantic movement. In the 1780s, Lord Torrington, like Roger North, protested against this fashion because of the inconvenience. Hill-top houses were cold, he complained, exposed to the winds, and lacking convenient running water or fuel supplies. 'I am not of the present taste of clapping houses on hilltops, looking around them, in vain, for wood and water'. His satirical advice to an owner was that

[1] R. North, *Of Building*, ed. H. M. Colvin and J. Newman, Oxford, 1981, p. 89; F. Bacon, *Essays*: 'Of Building'; Dudley Lord North, *Observations and Advices Oeconomical*, London, 1669, p. 92.

[2] R. North, op. cit., p. 54.

[3] Op. cit., p. 89.

[4] H. Chauncy, *The Historical Antiquities of Hertfordshire*, London, 1700, pp. 226, 265, 332, 356, 408.

if you should have purchased a good old family hall, seated low and warm, and circled by woods, and near a running stream, pull it down and sell all the materials . . . Choose the most excellent spot in your estate, whence you may command a view of several counties. Cut down all the trees that are near your house, as they will spoil the prospect and obstruct the sun. Grub up all hedges around you, to make your grounds look parkish. Build ha-has to open up the view . . . Make the approach to your house as meandering as possible the better to discover the view.

This is what Repton had in mind at Courteenhall, Northants., in 1791. (Plate XIB.)[5]

Torrington rightly observed that the principal object was now to achieve the picturesque, and to open up the vista both of the seat from the front and from the seat at the back. It was partly for this reason that the English so readily embraced the Italian plan of putting the main floor on a raised platform above a half-basement, where the servants lived and worked, since it elevated the windows and opened up the vistas. The use of an elevated *piano nobile* over a half-basement and ground floor came in with a rush in the mid-seventeenth century, as at the Hoo (Plate VIIB), Balls Park, and Tyttenhanger, Herts. This raised the rooms of parade still higher, while the half-basements permitted the concealment of the offices below stairs and the removal of the earlier untidy clutter of ancillary office-buildings around the grounds.

There remained, however, the problem of water supply and sewage disposal. The desire to site the house on the top of a hill aggravated the first problem, but eased the second. The ideal was, of course, as Roger North pointed out, to locate a house below a reliable spring, so that gravity could feed the cisterns at all times and also drain away the sewage.[6] The introduction in the late eighteenth century of water closets, however, made it desirable to get running water to the top of the house, which was not always easy without pumps and siphons. But considerable sophistication in hydraulics had already been developed by the late eighteenth century, as some surviving plumbing maps indicate. That of Lamer House, Herts., of about the mid-eighteenth century, shows water flowing out of a hand-cranked well in the kitchen yard to supply both the offices of the house and also a newly-installed ground floor water closet in the main building. A century later, the engineering of plumbing had developed to such an extent that

---

[5] J. Byng, *The Torrington Diaries*, London, 1934-8, i, pp. 107, 333; iii, p. 10; D. Stroud, *Humphrey Repton*, London, 1962, p. 64.
[6] R. North, op. cit., pp. 89-90.

in 1881 a water and drainage plan of a country house like Ecton Hall, Northants., is a maze of wells, cisterns, siphons, suction-pipes, force-pumps, traps, soil-pipes, sewers, drains, cesspits, and sewage tanks.[7] If it worked, it was indeed a remarkable technical arrangement.

ii. Grounds

The quest for a room with a view not surprisingly coincided with a growing interest in the view itself, which consisted of two parts: the ornamental garden and the large park beyond. It is hard today to recapture the passionate enthusiasm and to appreciate the expense devoted to gardens in the sixteenth and seventeenth centuries, for the simple reason that every single one of them has today been swept away.[8] Some of the very greatest, around the royal palaces, were wantonly destroyed by the revolutionary regimes of the civil wars. The private gardens were replaced one by another as fashions changed, and were all finally destroyed by Brown and Repton and their followers as the romantic English garden and parkland became the dominant fashion. Such pre-romantic gardens as exist today are merely reconstructions of the Victorian or twentieth-century periods.

And yet there can be no doubt whatever that owners and writers in the sixteenth and seventeenth centuries devoted as much aesthetic attention to garden construction as they did to the house itself. Often, as at Wilton or Gubbins, an elaborate garden layout was the first step in modernization before the reconstruction of the house itself. Tudor gardens had hardly anything to do with plants, which anyway were a rarity, and everything to do with the artificial contrivance of man. There were geometrical walled enclosures, full of elaborate topiary work, painted wooden handrails, posts, obelisks, and fanciful heraldic animals holding banners, which celebrated the symbolic glory of the family of the owner. The ground was composed of different coloured squares of stones or sand or gravel. In the seventeenth century there arrived in England from Italy the Mannerist garden, which was more open and thus suitable for large-scale entertainment, and also replete with the bizarre contemporary mixture of science and magic and erudite symbolism. Its characteristic features now were grottoes, giant mythological statues, sophisticated hydraulic waterworks for foun-

[7] Herts. R. O., 80323b (Plan Case); Northants. R. O., maps 427, 2151.

[8] R. Strong, *The Renaissance Garden in England*, London, 1979. This magnificent piece of scholarship labouriously reconstructs this forgotten aspect of sixteenth- and seventeenth-century English life and culture.

tains and streams, and mysterious automata—moving and speaking statues operated by air and water pressure. Water was everywhere, and canals and rivulets and fountains grew in importance to dominate the whole artificial environment in the late seventeenth century.[9]

The house and garden were now a single aesthetic whole, each oriented upon the other and reflecting similar values. John Evelyn summed up the new ideal in 1657: 'Our drift is a noble, princely and universal Elysium, capable of all the amenities that can naturally be introduced into gardens of pleasure'. John Aubrey, writing at about the same time, was well aware how new these developments were: 'The pleasure and use of them were unknown to our grandfathers'.[10] Places of pleasure they were, since it was the pursuit of pleasure which was central to the moral sensibility of Renaissance man. (Plates IIIB, IV, VIIIA.)

In his eulogy of the seventeenth-century Freemans of Aspenden Hall, father and son, Chauncy in 1700 remarked of the first that, among other virtues, 'he made his house neat, his gardens pleasant, his grove delicious', and of the second that 'he has cased and adorned this manor-house with brick, beautified the gardens with delicious greens, the grove with pleasant walks, and made all things neat and curious to the spectator'. (Endpaper.) He likewise praised Sir John Brograve at Hamels for having 'enlarged his park and adorned his house with several delicious walks without', and Thomas Atkins of Bedwell Park in that he 'has much adorned and beautified this seat with pleasant gardens'. Chauncy, who set his architectural sights lower than Evelyn or Vanbrugh, was content for houses to be 'neat' but liked his gardens if possible to be 'delicious'. Even a minor gentleman like Henry Doldern, owner of Wells Manor-House, was praised since he caused it to be 'neatly adorned with walks, which shows the ingenuity of the owner and the delight he takes in his habitation'.[11] Pride of ownership demonstrated by an improvement in the grounds always met with Chauncy's approval, and the Drapentier engravings that illustrate his work give some idea of what it was that he and his contemporaries all thought so important and so pleasurable. (Plates VIA and B, VIIB, and Endpaper.)

As elsewhere in England, however, absolutely nothing of all this aesthetic activity survives today in any of our three counties. In the 1570s, Lord Burghley built at Theobalds the most influential

[9] Op. cit., pp. 15-22.
[10] Op. cit., pp. 221, 223.
[11] H. Chauncy, op. cit., pp. 125, 227, 277, 408.

of all geometric Elizabethan gardens, some seven acres in extent, with canals for boating, topiary hedges cut into animal and human shapes, arbours, cisterns, fountains, labyrinths, and other 'curiosities'. At Hatfield in 1610-12, Burghley's son Robert Earl of Salisbury built an equally famous and elaborate garden, with terraces running down to a river, a huge fountain, an artificial painted walk and statues, a stream whose bed was filled with coloured stones and shells, and artificial leaves, snakes, and fishes, all ending up in an elaborate water-garden full of live fish. At the same time Sir Henry Fanshawe was building a fanciful garden at Ware Park complete with a small artificial fortress in the middle, later altered to give prominence of place to canals and fountains. Sir Francis Bacon was also building himself an island in a lake containing an elaborate summer-house. Some fifteen years later a more 'modern' garden was being constructed by Lucy, Countess of Bedford, at the Moor, which in the 1670s Sir William Temple described as 'the perfectest figure of a garden I ever saw', the main features of which were the usual terraces, formal parterres, statuary, fountains, and summer-houses, and an elaborate grotto with hydraulically operated automata. Ten years later still, in the 1630s, Sir Arthur Capel was building a similar Italianate garden at Hadham Hall.[12] (Plate IV.) By 1640, in short, Hertfordshire could boast of perhaps the finest collection of gardens to be seen anywhere in England, not one of which survives today. But their former existence and the elaborate and enthusiastic comments of contemporary visitors, bear witness to the extraordinary significance in the sixteenth- and seventeenth-century culture of the Franco-Italianate garden, and the central place its planning played in the lives of so many country-house owners.

Nothing but some of the canals of these great seventeenth-century gardens survived the revolution in aesthetics that was begun in the early eighteenth century by William Kent and popularized later on with large-scale application of his principles first by Capability Brown and finally by Repton at the end of the century. The result was a total transformation of both the ideal and the reality of the external surroundings to a house. In 1781, Lord Torrington condemned Westwood in no uncertain terms: 'the approach to the house is bad and formal, not leading (as it ought to) through the woods. It is surrounded by gardens and walls in the old taste'. What Torrington and his contemporaries now admired was an open and pseudo-naturalistic prospect, the product of care-

[12] R. Strong, op. cit., pp. 51-6, 103-10, 123, 127, 141-4.

fully planned landscaping—often involving the destruction of whole
hills, the digging of huge lakes, and the artfully casual planting of
hundreds of trees. Lord Scarbrough instructed Brown to do his
work 'with poet's feeling and with painter's eye', which is just
what he did. He made nature bend itself to his will. Between 1790
and 1811, Repton alone totally refashioned the grounds of eleven
seats in Hertfordshire and six in Northamptonshire, so that the
scale of the revolution in garden taste was very large and very
rapid.[13] (Plates VIIA, XIA and B, XVA and B; Plan 3.)

In his *Red Book* for Antony House in Cornwall (elsewhere described as 'my *chef d'œuvre*') Repton explained the principles that
underlay this wholesale destruction of the old and replacement by
the new. Before the introduction of modern gardening, 'the importance of the mansion was supported by a display of conveniences . . . by the quantity of barns, stables and offices with which
it was surrounded. After the removal of courtyards, and kitchen-
garden walls from the front of a house, the true substitute for the
ancient magnificence destroyed is the more cheerful landscape of
modern park scenery, and though its boundary ought in no case
to be conspicuous, yet its actual dimensions should bear some proportion to the command of property by which the mansion is supported. . . . Where the house itself is so situated as not to be much
seen from the surrounding neighbourhood, it is the more necessary that some conspicuous object should mark a command of
property'. The language used by Repton, his stress on visible
'command of property', is very similar to that used by Vanbrugh
a century earlier with his emphasis on visible 'grandeur'. The object was identical and only the means of achieving it had changed.[14]

Prestige was now best displayed by a visible demonstration of
the new aesthetic of the picturesque, as illustrated by the grounds.
The importance attached to this aspect of the country seat in the
late eighteenth century is well brought out by the comments of
Arthur Young in his account of the North of England in 1771.
Again and again he commented with approval on 'a sweet landscape of the park' where 'the woods and water are sketched with
great taste'. Of Brocket Hall, Herts., he observed that the park 'is

[13] J. Byng, op. cit., i, p. 45; R. Strong, M. Binney, and J. Harris, *The Destruction of the Country House, 1875-1975*, London, 1974, p. 112. See also H. A. Clemenson, *English Country Houses and Landed Estates*, New York, 1982, Ch. IV; *The Genius of the Place: the English Landscape Garden 1620-1820*, ed. J. D. Hunt and P. Willis, London, 1975; P. Willis, *Charles Bridgeman and the English Landscape Garden*, London, 1977; D. Stroud, *Capability Brown*, London, 1957; D. Stroud, *Humphrey Repton*, London, 1962.

[14] H. Repton, *The Red Book of Antony House* [c.1794] in *The Red Books of Humphrey Repton*, London, 1976.

No VIII.

The Great Wood

and Pleasure Grounds rising behind the House.

extremely worth seeing. It contains a fine variety of ground, many hills that command noble prospects, and winding hollows very picturesque; the water is large, much of it finely traced, and of a beautiful colour'. At Grimsthorpe, Lincs., he found 'a noble piece of water, and two pretty yachts upon it', for lakes were then intended for pleasure-trips as well as aesthetics. At the Leasowes, Worcs., 'the cascade is astonishingly romantic'.[15]

In order to bring this artificially contrived nature right up to the windows of the house, the garden walls were demolished, to be replaced by invisible sunken ha-has. Beyond lay avenues of trees stretching across the countryside into the middle distance, or else the tree-studded grassland of the park, formerly stocked with deer but by the eighteenth century often turned over to sheep, since fox-hunting had largely replaced stag-hunting. (Plates VIIA and XIB.) In 1750 Horace Walpole observed with satisfaction how these innovations enlarged the view. 'The country wears a new face; everybody is improving their places, and as they don't fortify their plantations with entrenchments of walls and high hedges, one has the benefit of them even in passing by'. He went on to comment that 'the dispersed buildings, I mean temples, bridges, etc. are generally Gothic or Chinese, and give a whimsical air of novelty that is very pleasing'.[16] These eighteenth-century follies, temples, artificial ruins, grottoes, bridges, and other eye-catchers were indeed scattered as though at random among the sinuous declivities and paths of a 'natural' landscape, which shunned straight lines and flat surfaces as assiduously as the formal garden had courted them. Sixteenth- and seventeenth-century gardens had boasted of gazebos, small banqueting houses, and statues, but these had been, quite as deliberately, sited midway along, or between, or at the intersections of, straight box-lined paths. (Plates IIIB, IV, V, VIIIA.)

The prospect from inside looking out was thus radically changed by the new fashion. The ideal house was now perched upon a hill, looked south over an open garden area, across the invisible sunken ha-ha to a park beyond, dotted with trees and sloping down to a lake. Beyond, on the other side of the lake, rose a wood. Horace Walpole could not have expressed greater disapproval when in 1763 he described Easton Maudit, Northants., as having 'a small park and no view' and it is hardly surprising that it was soon afterwards abandoned when the family died out. No one wanted it.

[15] A. Young, *A Six Month Tour Through the North of England*, London, 1771, i, pp. 17, 82, 132-3, 260; ii, pp. 73, 300-12, 430-5; iii, pp. 1, 280, 286-96, 325-7.
[16] *Horace Walpole's Correspondence*, ed. W. A. Lewis, New Haven, 1937-80, 20, p. 166.

Aesthetically, the result was a doubly paradoxical evolution. The house itself conformed to Palladian taste, and its façade became formal, symmetrical, and geometrical in its proportions. But it lay amid surroundings which were conceived on exactly the opposite principle, away from the formal and the symmetrical towards the informal and the irregular. At the same time the pleasure-grounds tended to become larger, new parks were created and old ones extended. Two contradictory theories of aesthetic beauty seem to have been at work at the same time, the one affecting the house and the other its surroundings. The house became the epitome of ordered rectilinear rationality, the grounds the epitome of wild curvilinear emotion—in a word the picturesque. Thus at Twickenham, Pope built a classical villa, and a 'natural' garden to surround it.

This apparent antithesis can be explained in part by the juxtaposition of different notions drawn from different classical sources. The house derived from classical architecture, as represented by Palladio and Inigo Jones, but the garden came from classical Pompeian landscape painting, as reinterpreted by Claude and Poussin. There was, however, more to it than that. The substitution of fox-hunting for stag-hunting made necessary the replacement of forests with straight rides cut through them by grassy parkland interspersed with coverts. The irregular woodland areas were a valuable investment, which on maturity could quickly be turned into large amounts of ready cash, thus enabling the owner to get around the legal constraints on alienation of capital imposed by the strict settlement. The less formal gardens with less expensive plantings enabled the aspiring politicians 'to make a greater show at a lesser cost'. The expansion of the parkland, which often involved the removal of public highways or in a few cases whole villages, was caused by the growing desire for privacy. Parks, which very often no longer contained deer, continued nonetheless to increase in size and numbers throughout the eighteenth and early nineteenth centuries, their purpose now being to create a sense of isolation. Privacy also dictated the construction of mile upon mile of high park walls, and the deliberate planting of screens of woodland all around the periphery of the park. Total seclusion from the outside world, and a carefully controlled, artificially natural environment within the park walls were now both desired and, once the trees had grown, largely achieved.[17]

[17] J. Bassin, 'The English Landscape Garden in the Eighteenth Century: the Cultural Importance of an English Institution', *Albion*, 11, 1979, passim; for lists of parks, and evidence of an increase in their size and numbers, see E. P. Shirley, *Some Account of English*

iii. The House

If one turns from the pleasure-grounds to the house itself, a combination of changing aesthetic fashion, and the social needs already
described, determined the choice of design. From the early sixteenth century onward, one of the hallmarks of a gentleman was
the possession of a working knowledge of architectural theory. In
1607 James Cleland advised the gentry to get acquainted with 'the
principles of architecture' and by 1661 John Webb could state confidently that 'most gentry have some knowledge of the theory of
architecture'.[18] This knowledge was greatly enriched by the growing popularity of the Grand Tour, including a trip to Italy, and
by the publication of massive folio volumes of designs and plans
by Palladio, Scamozzi, Serlio, and others, as well as more detailed
pattern-books for plaster and sculptural decoration and practical
handbooks of advice, beginning with Balthazar Gerbier's *Counsel
and Advise to all Builders* of 1663. From the early eighteenth century
onward there were available huge folio volumes of plans and elevations of English houses to serve as models. From the mid-seventeenth century to the nineteenth it could confidently be assumed
that most of the landed elite knew something about architecture,
even if the personal influence of the patron upon architectural design was weakened in the eighteenth century by the rise of the
professional architect possessing sufficient prestige to have some
effect upon the views of his clients.

If the patrons were influential in determining the design of
buildings, what was it that they wanted? In the Middle Ages and
the early sixteenth century, there was little or no respect for symmetry. Function dictated design, and the external appearance of
houses was one of unstudied and casual improvisation, rambling
about as suggested by convenience and changing needs. Moreover,
houses tended to look inward on to an enclosed courtyard, where
the main ornamental features were placed, and to present a rather
bleak and forbidding face to the outside world. They did, after
all, serve a defensive purpose.

This concept of letting function dictate design died hard, and
even Bacon at the very end of the sixteenth century advised builders to 'let use be preferred before uniformity, except where both
may be had'. In 1624, however, Sir Henry Wotton was urging

Deer Parks, London, 1867; J. Whitaker, *A Descriptive List of the Deer-Parks and Paddocks of
England*, London, 1928; H. A. Clemenson, op. cit., pp. 60-2, 70-1, 78-9.
   [18] Both quoted by M. Airs, *The Making of the English Country House*, London, 1975, p.
37.

that the patron stress external appearance, and therefore insist upon seeing a large-scale model, if necessary paying up to £30 for one.[19] His general advice, if not his insistence upon a model, was already being followed, however. As Lord North remarked, in the Elizabethan period 'much uniformity is affected, after the Italian manner'. Although he disapproved of uniformity for a country house, he conceded that it was the fashion. The 'E' or 'H' or 'half H' plan, approximately but rarely fully symmetrical, was normal by 1570 for all except the gigantic palaces, where the courtyard plan, also dominated by uniformity, was the only possible solution. Thomas Fuller, who was no revolutionary, conceded in 1642 that 'uniformity also much pleaseth the eye' and that the façade should not 'look squint on a stranger, but accost him right at his entrance'. From here it was but a short step to the advice of the amateur gentleman architect Sir Roger Pratt to build a house on wholly new principles. He advocated general symmetry in the internal plan as well as the exterior, based on the aesthetic principle of the human body, as revealed by dissection, and he did not hesitate to put 'exact convenience and neat contrivance' before 'the necessity of men's affairs'. 'Uniformity is what all expect to find and blame if not observed', remarked Roger North in 1698.[20]

By the second half of the seventeenth century, the eclectic Jacobethan style and plan had completely given way to new modes of building variously derived from classical architecture. Neo-Palladianism had first been introduced into England by Inigo Jones under the auspices of Charles I. However, the only neo-Palladian house of that date in our three counties is Stoke Bruerne in Northamptonshire. It was built in 1629 with a porticoed central block and symmetrical wings on land granted by the Crown to the courtier and entrepreneur Sir Francis Crane. No other new houses were built before the outbreak of the Civil War. Thereafter, with rare exceptions, all new houses were built on variations of the 'double pile' plan, in a single solid block, rather than spread out one room deep with wings, as in the earlier style. They were extremely compact and tall (up to three and a half storeys high). This was a feature deplored by Roger North, who rightly saw it as an adaptation of the cramped urban plan imposed by city land values, 'whereby all grandeur proper to quality is laid aside'. Now

[19] H. Wotton, 'Elements of Architecture' in his *Reliquiae Wottoniae*, London, 1651, pp. 256-7.

[20] F. Bacon, op. cit.; H. Wotton, op. cit., pp. 246-7; Dudley Lord North, op. cit.; T. Fuller, *The Holy State*, Cambridge, 1642, p. 168; *Architecture of Sir Roger Pratt*, ed. R. T. Gunther, Oxford, 1928, pp. 60, 62; R. North, op. cit., p. 14.

this plan had spread to the countryside, 'to the abolishing grandeur and stateliness of that sort the former ages affected'. 'An house
is laid on an heap like a wasp's nest', he complained, 'and much
of greatness as well as conveniences lost by it'.[21] To see what he
had in mind one has only to compare the great old Elizabethan
house of Nyn, Herts., with the second Hertingfordbury Park,
built in the 1680s. (Plates XVIA and VIB.) Meanwhile the owners
of sixteenth- and early seventeenth-century houses, as the latter
grew old and in need of repair, were busy refurbishing them in a
classical mode. (Plates IIIB, V, IXA.)

The publication of the first volume of Colen Campbell's *Vitruvius Britannicus* in 1715 was a bold statement of the new national
style of triumphant Whiggery, a neo-Palladianism based on the
surviving buildings and drawings of Inigo Jones. This provided a
style which was able to dominate English country-house architecture until the end of the century, a supremacy due in no small
part to its versatility.[22] In the case of a new building from scratch,
there was almost no limit to its possible grandeur, mostly expressed in the richness of the material used, particularly in internal
decoration. On the other hand, it lent itself remarkably well to the
revamping of an old façade to give an old house a fashionable
appearance. In its purest form, neo-Palladianism did not perhaps
fare as well as it did in its more workaday form, which made due
allowance for the differences between the climates of Italy and
England, and hence for the greater need for light and warmth.
This combination of practicality and pomp made an irresistible
appeal to the eighteenth-century country gentleman. It met his
social need for an imposing external display of his authority and
the dignity of his status, as we have seen. At the same time, the
Palladian house satisfied his aesthetic desire for rural simplicity,
as opposed to the excessive and degenerate ostentation of the city
and the court. The lines were simple, the external decorations
sparse to non-existent. The Palladian home thus perfectly conformed in its aesthetic external appearance to the twin ideals of
social hierarchy and country simplicity. Within there was ample
opportunity, as we shall see, for the parade of a third ideal, individualism, shown in personal taste for interior decoration, pictures, and statuary, and even for some greater provision for its
corollary of privacy.

By the 1770s this monopoly of the Palladian style came under

[21] Op. cit., pp. 25, 63, 68-9.
[22] J. Summerson, 'The Classical Country House in Eighteenth Century England', *Journal of the Royal Society of Arts*, cvii, 1959, pp. 543, 549.

challenge from the romantic movement, slowly giving way to neo-Gothic or even neo-Jacobethan buildings, which prided themselves on their studied asymmetry, their gigantic size, and their endlessly extended servants' quarters and outbuildings. Space was now even more highly specialized, with a room for every function. Even here, however, the old ideals of hierarchy and individualism were preserved, even if by the mid-Victorian period there predominated an antiquarian revivalism which perhaps hints that elite society was no longer altogether sure of itself.

In interior planning the major change was the shift in the mid-seventeenth century from the long ranges one room thick, usually arranged around a courtyard, to the compact box-like 'double-pile' or 'triple-pile'. Sir Roger Pratt flatly declared that 'the best forms for a private man I conceive to be that which is an oblong square exactly'. In 1727 Sir John Clerk accurately summed up the dimensions of the new 'useful house' in a clumsy rhyme:

> Its front from eighty to an hundred feet
> May be extended with proportionate breadth,
> Which never under forty feet must fall.[23]

This is indeed about the median size of the compact eighteenth-century seats in our sample.

The growing desire for privacy, which became stronger as nuclear family cohesion developed in the late seventeenth and eighteenth centuries, was the principal influence on changes in the design and organization of internal space within the country house. Of the major changes, the first was the functional transformation and later the shrinkage of the great hall. In the Middle Ages and the sixteenth century, this had been by far the largest and busiest room in the house. The whole household, family, guests, and servants all ate there, and many of the servants often slept there also. It was the central space for the formal display of power and prestige. Thus when in 1549 the Earl of Arundel successfully quelled a great peasant revolt in Sussex, he did it by sitting in state on the dais at the upper end of his great hall in Arundel Castle, and dispensing instant justice to all, both rich and poor, who came before him with complaints. This was perhaps the last major occasion for the display of traditional feudal paternalistic authority.[24]

---

[23] *Sir Roger Pratt*, p. 62; he thought 120 feet the maximum length of a façade, being as much as the human eye can take in (op. cit., p. 28); H. Colvin and J. Harris, *The Country Seat*, London, 1970, p. 114.

[24] L. Stone, 'Patriarchy and Paternalism in Tudor England: the Case of the Earl of Arundel and the Peasants' Revolt of 1549', *Journal of British Studies*, xiii, 1974.

The penultimate wave of construction of gigantic halls, covering well over 1,500 square feet of floor space, took place in the 1560-1620 period, when at least thirty were built of this size or more. Their use as a communal dining-room, however, was already in full decline as the last of them were still going up. By 1660, the demand for privacy led many gentry families, even in backward Lancashire, to withdraw to eat in the great chamber or separate dining-room. The dais gradually fell into disuse, leaving the hall as an eating-place for the servants.[25] Then the hall was swung round on its axis, and made to serve as the main entrance-way into the house. This transition stage is best seen at Hardwick New Hall, where the hall is both entrance way and servants' dining-room, the now private dining-room being transferred upstairs. Although the dais has disappeared, the screens survive, and the kitchen, buttery, and pantry remain close by as usual. But by the end of the seventeenth century a servants' hall was coming into use, and since the hall had now lost all its original functions as an eating-place the kitchen no longer needed to be close beside it. By the second half of the seventeenth century the servants were eating in a special servants' hall, often in the semi-basement, the owners were eating in the dining-room, and the hall was now left functionless except as a grand entrance-way.

In the design for Hampstead Marshall, built for Lord Craven in 1664, this social segregation of eating was complete. There was indeed a large hall, but the front door opened on to its centre, and it could hardly have been used for eating except on ceremonial occasions, since it formed the only connecting link from the outside world to the two staircases and the rest of the house. On one side of the hall was the 'little parlour or ordinary room to eat in', and beyond it the 'withdrawing room or room for the lord to eat in'. On the other side was the 'room for the gentlemen to eat in', and beyond it 'the room for the servants to eat in'. A corridor linked the kitchen to all these socially segregated eating rooms, including the hall.[26]

From 1700 to 1730 there was a second and final explosion of extravagant hall construction led by Vanbrugh, this time for mere display to impress visitors with a gigantic entrance-space often filled with a towering staircase like a royal palace. This was another period when profits were flowing from political office and war

[25] D. Ashmore, 'Household Inventories of the Lancashire Gentry 1550-1700', *Lancashire and Cheshire Historical Society Transactions*, 110, 1959, pp. 61-2.

[26] See plan in O. Hill and J. Cornforth, *English Country Houses. Caroline*, London, 1966, fig. 227.

finance, much of which was quickly converted into the security of bricks and mortar. 'All the world are running mad after building, as far as they can reach', remarked Vanbrugh in 1708 with satisfaction.[27] Thereafter, however, the great hall tended to shrink in size, and by the mid-eighteenth century, the saloon or the library became the largest room in most houses.

The second major development arising out of the desire for privacy was the relegation of the servants to the half-basement, or else to a separate wing linked to the main house by a corridor that could be locked. At the same time, provision was made for several backstairs for the use of the servants to pass to and fro about their necessary business. This left the grand staircase to the exclusive use of the family and guests, who would not be troubled by meeting servants carrying coals and water up or slops and faeces down.

The third development stimulated by the desire for privacy was the transformation of the internal layout of the private rooms by the introduction of the corridor. All large sixteenth-century houses were built around a courtyard or courtyards in long connecting suites of rooms without internal communicating passages. The only means of circulation was by passing from room to room. The fundamental reorganization of internal space dictated by new social demands for privacy can be traced in the changing ground plans of the houses. Both the great Jacobean palaces such as Burghley House, Hatfield House, Theobalds, Audley End, and Buckhurst, and smaller houses such as Copped Hall had virtually no passages to link their suites of rooms together. Nor did the H-shaped houses of the period such as Charlton House, Ham House, or Wimbledon House, or even early double-piles such as Chevening or Hampstead Marshall. An important by-product of the adoption of the 'double-pile' house, however, was that it made possible the insertion of internal corridors for individual access to all rooms. Inner corridors can be found in mid- and late seventeenth-century double-pile houses like Ashdown and Coleshill, and later at Vanbrugh's huge palaces of Castle Howard and Blenheim.

Just how new this corridor concept was is shown by the fact that the very word, in its meaning as an enclosed internal passageway giving individual access to every room, was virtually unknown in the early eighteenth century. Vanbrugh had to explain to the Duchess of Marlborough that 'the word corridor, madam, is foreign, and signifies in plain English no more than a passage;

[27] *The Complete Works of Sir John Vanbrugh*, ed. B. Dobrée and G. Webb, London, iv, 1928, p. 25.

it is now, however, generally used as an English word'. The plan was a popular one, however, to judge by Vanbrugh's boast about his design for the upper storey of Kimbolton, that contained four bedrooms 'and good accommodation to them, with a corridor that runs the whole length behind 'em'.[28]

The problem of separating the private living quarters from the public state apartments was paramount in houses of this size. The latter were built for grandeur rather than comfort, and were only used for occasional large-scale public receptions. They therefore retained the suite pattern of connecting rooms without corridors, so that the guests could circulate freely. 'The parade rooms', 'the parade of the house' were central to any major house, and Roger North spoke approvingly of 'the file of rooms which is a prime beauty'.[29]

By the mid-eighteenth century, architects were boasting to their patrons of their ability to achieve such privacy, even in the grandest and most public seats. Thus in 1755 the architect John Carr reassured his client Edwin Lascelles that in his newly planned great house at Harewood, Yorkshire, 'I get into the gallery, bedchamber, dressing-room without going through any other room, which seldom can be in such a large house; and have two spacious backstairs of ten feet diameter'.[30]

When in 1728-32 the architect James Gibbs planned Kelmarsh, Northants., with every room linked to a corridor, it was thought to be something of an innovation, although thereafter it became a standard part of house plans, by Gibbs himself and others. It is, however, surprising how slow were the owners of the great old houses of the sixteenth and seventeenth centuries to adopt the obvious solution of adding thin corridor blocks around the inside walls of the old courtyards. Beechwood, Herts., was exceptional in the addition of corridors by 1700. At Wallington, Northumb., they were added inside the courtyard in 1740 and at Raby Castle, Co. Durham, in 1751, while in Northamptonshire corridors were added at Althorp in 1786-90, at Dingley probably in 1809 and at Burghley House as late as 1830-9.

Unused as they were to privacy, the owners of these great houses were slow to revolt against the inconvenience and lack of privacy that a suite-type plan dictated. They were, moreover, probably reluctant to alter the external appearance of the family seat. At

[28] Op. cit., iv, pp. 71, 22.
[29] R. North, op. cit., pp. 32, 62, 136.
[30] W. A. Eden and R. B. Wragg, 'John Carr, Stonecutter Extraordinary', *Transactions of the Ancient Monuments Society*, NS 24, 1980, p. 44.

Wilton, for example, the addition of Gothic corridors entirely obliterated the old Tudor inner façade. Other owners simply had so
many houses to choose from that they largely abandoned these
inconvenient old seats and lived elsewhere. This was true, for example, of both Deene and Boughton through much of the eighteenth century.[31]

The final step in the achievement of specialization and segregation was to concentrate all the living-rooms on the main floor and
all the bedrooms on the floors above. This was a development
which only occurred very late, towards the end of the eighteenth
century and in the early nineteenth century, and even then it was
far from uniform or complete. As late as 1823 at Tillicairn Castle,
Robert Lugar placed the master bedroom on the main floor together with two dressing-rooms and a bathroom.[32] In the sixteenth, seventeenth, and eighteenth centuries the master bedroom
or bedrooms and dressing-rooms were commonly on the main floor
along with the public rooms, and some of the public rooms were
often on a floor above together with most of the other bedrooms.[33]
At Harewood, for example, built in 1755 by John Carr with advice
from Robert Adam, two bedchambers, including that of Mr Lascelles himself, and his dressing-room and his wife's dressing-room,
were all located at one end of the main floor. The same is true of
Cassiobury in the nineteenth century. (Plans 2 and 3.)

A last technical innovation which greatly facilitated the segregation of the family from the servants, and so increased the privacy of the new affection-bonded nuclear family, was the growing
sophistication of bell-ropes. In the sixteenth and seventeenth centuries, servants had to live and sleep in adjacent rooms, within
earshot of a summons. Simple bells which hung outside the bedroom door 'to call the maids' were known to Pepys in 1663. But
bell-pulls linked by wires right through the house down to the
servants' hall seem to have been an invention of the last half of the

[31] For plans of other great houses with corridors added in the late eighteenth or early
nineteenth centuries, like Longleat, Wilton, or Woburn, see R. Blomfield,, *History of Renaissance Architecture in England, 1500-1800*, London, 1897, i, pp. 71, 83; ii, p. 291; M. Girouard,
Robert Smythson and the Architecture of the Elizabethan Era, London, 1966, pls. 108-9; J. Summerson, *The Book of Architecture of J. Thorpe in Sir John Soane's Museum*, Walpole Soc., xl,
London, 1966, pl. 49; O. Hill and J. Cornforth, op. cit., figs. 80, 132, 227; R. Kerr, *The
Gentleman's House*, London, 1865, pls. 40 and 14; for Raby Castle, see *Architectural History*,
15, 1972, p. 27; see also K. Downes, *English Baroque Architecture*, London, 1966, p. 64.
[32] W. and J. Pain, *British Palladio* [London, 1786], Farnborough, 1969, pls. i, v, xxiv;
R. Lugar, *Plans and Views of Buildings*, London, 1823, pl. 1.
[33] O. Hill and J. Cornforth, op. cit., figs. 80, 132, 248; *Sir Roger Pratt*, p. 93 (Coleshill);
R. Kerr, op. cit., pl. 40 (Longleat), 13 (Holkham).

eighteenth century. By the early nineteenth century, the system was fully functioning, with bells for each room hanging in rows in the servants' hall, each one labelled to direct the servants to the right place. Prince von Pückler-Muskau found the whole system fully developed at Penhryn in 1828.[34] This must have been one of the most important innovations in the creation of private space for the owner and his family.

The development of the corridor and of separate servants' stairs, the concentration of all bedrooms upon an upper floor, and the introduction of bell-wires, went a long way to achieve some of that privacy now so earnestly desired by the family members. They could now not only get away from one another; they could also, at least to some extent, get away from the ubiquitous, prying, eavesdropping, and gossiping servants.

By the mid-nineteenth century, this demand for privacy had reached its apex, and architects like Robert Kerr were contriving ways physically to separate the two distinct communities—the family and the servants—who co-existed under one roof. The solution was to plan the most rigid segregation of the two groups, each with separate lines of communication by stairways and corridors; by heavy sound-proofing; and by the installation of an elaborate system of bell-pulls, so that the servants need only intrude when summoned to do so. Internal planning was focused almost obsessively upon this problem of segregating the two groups from one another.

Even within the family, a certain amount of real internal segregation was achieved, the children and their nurses from the adults and the men from the women. The children were placed in day and night nurseries, easily accessible from the family rooms, but sufficiently remote that their noisy activities would not disturb the grown-ups. At Crathorne in 1911, it was observed that 'the whole of the nursery quarters are isolated, as they should be, and served by a separate corridor'. The women owned their dressing-room, the drawing-room (described as 'the ladies room'), and the boudoir, for entirely private female withdrawal. The men dominated the library ('a withdrawing-room for gentlemen, not merely a place of study'), the business room, the justice room, the billiard-room, the smoking-room, and the gunroom. The ladies often played billiards, but the smoking room and the gunroom were strictly male preserves. They were late Victorian innovations, which flourished

[34] M. Girouard, *Life in the English Country House*, New Haven, 1978, p. 264; [H. L. H. von Pückler-Muskau], *Tour in England, Ireland and France* . . . , *Philadelphia, 1833*, pp. 286-7.

during that last hurrah of the patriarchal family from 1850 to 1890, and then quite suddenly disappeared when gender relations relaxed again at the end of the century.[35]

The location of the 'rooms of parade' in the centre of the building, at the top of the main stairs, and that of the private quarters with corridor access in the wings, together with the strict separation of the servants' quarters from the family rooms by a green baize door, and of the nursery area from that used by the adults, all meant that privacy, specialization, and differentiation of function had now reached their ultimate apogee.

2. FINANCIAL CONSTRAINTS

i. Attitudes

The perennial complaint about country houses—apart from the boredom of living in them—was that they cost their owners too much, both to build and thereafter to live in. Thackeray in *Pendennis* summed up the history of such a house in his description of the fate of Clavering Park: 'Sir Richard Clavering had *commenced* the ruin of the family by building the palace; his successors had achieved that ruin by living in it'.[36]

As early as the fifteenth century, the Italian Cardano had included architecture, along with gambling, alchemy, lawsuits, and luxury, as one of the royal roads to ruin.[37] This was to be a stock theme of all social commentators for the next 500 years. Few fathers could resist the temptation to give their sons sound advice on the subject, though few in fact offered examples of prudent restraint. 'Dip not thy finger into the mortar', advised Sir Edward Coke in the early seventeenth century. 'Before thou begin, consider well how thou mayest end it, else will the stones be witness to thy folly', warned Henry Earl of Huntingdon. 'Builders seldom swim in money', observed the Elizabethan Sir Henry Lee. They all, however, had to admit that overbuilding was a well nigh irresistible temptation, 'an expenseful though bewitching delight', as the Earl of Huntingdon called it.[38] The gentleman-architect Sir Roger Pratt was one of the few who offered some practical advice

[35] J. Franklin, *The Gentleman's Country House and its Plan*, New York, 1981, pp. 81, 62.

[36] W. M. Thackeray, *Pendennis*, Chapter 11.

[37] O. Ore, *Cardano the Gambling Scholar*, Princeton, 1953, p. 122. (I owe this reference to Professor Peter Burke.)

[38] J. Smyth, *The Berkeley MSS, III*, Bristol and Glos. Arch. Soc., Gloucester, 1885, p. 28; *Historical Manuscripts Commission, Hastings MSS*, iv, p. 335; E. K. Chambers, *Sir Henry Lee*, Oxford, 1936, p. 215.

to clients about how to contract for the building. He urged them to provide the basic materials of timber, stone, and clay for bricks as far as possible from their own estates, and warned them not to be continually changing their plans, which could lead to cost-over-runs of up to 50 per cent. Others were compelled to admit that the architectural profession was at fault in deceiving clients by gross underestimates. In 1755 Robert Morris complained that 'often through the ignorance, or design, of the estimator, it [the final cost] exceeds double, sometimes treble, the sum estimated'. As a result, it became a proverb that 'building is a thief, because it makes us lay out more money than we thought on'.[39]

Overruns on building costs for a large house were one hazard, but the annual expense of maintenance in an appropriately opulent style was another, and it was the combination of the two that so often proved fatal. The 3rd Earl of Shaftesbury found himself in this dilemma when he inherited the huge family pile of Wimborne St Giles. He told himself firmly—but in fact unsuccessfully—'if I find my house at St Giles's and rank greater than I can sustain with my estate, the rather give up my family and sell all . . . than bestow all in supporting such a vast house and appurtenances, . . . striving to make an estate hold out which is not big enough'.[40]

A common solution when overheads became unbearable was to shut up the house, discharge the servants, and depart for an extended stay in London or abroad. The estate was turned over to trustees, charged with using the income partly to pay the owner a fixed allowance, and partly to pay off debts. It was a drastic remedy, but if carried out over a period of years an effective one, which allowed large sums to be accumulated at home. Thus it was in part an extended period of residence abroad, followed by a prolonged minority that enabled the Cowpers to raise the money to pull down their decayed old house at Cole Green and build a much larger new one, in more extensive grounds at Panshanger in the early nineteenth century.[41] But other families did not have such good fortune, and fell upon hard times.

A striking example of ruinous cost-overruns is the massive extensions to the old family seat of the Verneys at Claydon House, Bucks., begun by Viscount Fermanagh in 1768. His plans included a ballroom ninety feet by fifty feet in size and a spectacular

[39] *Sir Roger Pratt*, pp. 48-9, 58, 61; R. Morris, *Select Architecture*, London, 1755, introduction; *Diary of John Manningham*, Camden Soc., xcix, 1868, p. 9.

[40] Quoted in *Country Life*, xxxvii, 1915, pp. 341-2.

[41] L. Stone, 'Cole Green Park, Herts.', in H. Colvin and J. Harris, op. cit., pp. 75-80; J. Brushe, 'Further Light on Cole Green House', *Architectural History*, 24, 1981; see also above, p. 160.

saloon. His architect, Sir Thomas Robinson, egged him on with promises to make Claydon 'the noblest and most perfect piece of architecture in the kingdom'. This extravagant enterprise, the high cost of financing contested elections, and some disastrous business investments, all contributed to the final bankruptcy of Earl Verney in 1784, the collapse of the unfinished building project, the sale of the furniture and works of art, and the Earl's flight abroad to escape his creditors (according to legend smuggled out of the country in a coffin to avoid arrest).[42] The Verneys managed to hang on to Claydon, but only just.

Perhaps more typical of the majority of builders is the work carried out at Ashridge, Herts., by the Earl of Bridgwater before 1668. In a defensive memorandum drawn up for his heirs he tried to explain how he had become involved in more building than he could really afford.[43] The house had been a thirteenth-century monastery, roughly converted into a dwelling-house in the 1540s, and enlarged in 1606. There was therefore undoubtedly room for modernization. The Earl had added a riding school 'which I do not deny to have been chargeable in the building'. There was also the bowling-green 'which was indeed no slight piece of work'. Both were luxuries, but he excused the first as providing 'so innocent but so noble a recreation' and the second on the grounds that he personally never wasted money on gambling at bowls, or for that matter at any other games. The enlargement of the old deer park at Ashridge and the making of another he admitted was expensive, but he hoped that his posterity 'shall enjoy the satisfaction and content'. All these items, the riding-school, the bowling-green, and the enlarged deer park were for sport and recreation. Other work was undertaken for beauty. One of the more expensive items was the garden, but here the Earl argued that there could be no error in the eyes of 'all that have any esteem at all for accommodation and convenience'. The only things the Earl was prepared to concede were mere superfluities were the remodelling of the parlour and the rooms adjacent to it looking on to the new garden, 'but decency and convenience have ever weighed much with me, and I hope they are not quite out of other men's thoughts', despite the fact that these were 'one of my great expenses'.

The rest of the buildings were necessary items of expenditure. The kitchen and great chamber were 'things of great charge', but if they had not been torn down and rebuilt, they were in danger of collapsing, especially the former, which had long had to be

[42] M. M. Verney, *Verney Letters of the Eighteenth Century*, London, 1930, ii, Ch. xxxv.
[43] Huntington Library, Bridgwater MSS 8117.

supported with props. The same defense was offered for the re-built lodge, coach-house, and granary. Of the new walls, part was to enlarge the kitchen garden and so increased revenue, and part was to shut off the back areas of the house and so improve security. The new hay-barn, stables, and cow-house for the home farm needed no excuse, 'though it may happen that the new still-house may not be looked upon as quite so necessary', despite the fact that distilled waters were needed 'in a large family'. The new stove was justified, since it saved fuel for drying linen, and the new hall 'preserves the house both clean and quiet'.

Altogether, it was a laboured and anxious defense of many expensive repairs and improvements to the house, the garden, and the outbuildings of the home farm. Whether the document satisfied either his evidently troubled conscience or his heavily indebted posterity, history does not record. Certainly the latter did nothing whatsoever to improve the house until 140 years later, when they tore it all down and built a grotesquely huge new one in the Gothic style. The document vividly reveals the wide diversity of building operations one owner could and did perform on an old house, and the importance given to the three criteria of practical convenience, pleasure and sport, and aesthetics. The vast majority of building operations were alterations, additions, or repairs to an older structure. This meant that over-ambitious plans could be cut back and left incomplete if the money ran out or was needed for other purposes. Thus at Cassiobury, Herts., one Tudor wing was left in its original state although it ruined the symmetry of the courtyard (Plate IXA).

In the early 1800s the Calverts agonized about whether to repair and modernize Hunsdon House or tear it down and start again. They went so far as to build the foundations for a new house, before changing their minds in favour of 'adding to, and repairing the old house instead, which we fortunately as yet have not pulled down. It will cost half as much, perhaps only a quarter as much as a new house would . . . Another inducement is that Mr Leach [the architect] says we shall be able to get into it next July twelvemonth, whereas the new house would take years to finish'. A year later 'there is hardly a bit of old Hunsdon House left standing, so it is merely the name of adding to it—it will be nearly a new house'. Although the house was habitable within six years of Mr Leach's over-optimistic prognostications, it was to take another three years to complete all the decorations.[44]

44 *An Irish Beauty of the Regency*, ed. W. Blake, London, 1911, pp. 49, 66, 174.

This is an ambiguous example in which the owners drifted into a virtual rebuilding. Constructing a new house from scratch, however, was undoubtedly a more radical and more costly undertaking than remodelling an old one. As Roger North cautioned, 'the new is an engagement to go through whatever happens'.[45] Once embarked on it owners had little alternative but to go on. If they stopped, they subjected themselves to the ridicule of their friends and neighbours and were left with the uninhabitable shell of a house to live in. If they went on, they were in danger of piling up so much debt that they were ruined, although in practice few examples of this can be found.

ii. Facts

What did it cost to build a great house, to decorate and furnish it, and to construct suitable grounds and outbuildings? Enough data survives to give a rough idea. The first point to emphasize is that the bare shell of the house formed a relatively modest part of the total expenditure. The expense of erecting the stone or brick shell of a house was very small in comparison with the cost of fitments and decoration, to say nothing of gardens and grounds. The shell of Thorney Abbey, Cambs., admittedly very small, cost only £420 in 1660. The shell of Capheaton, Northumb., which measured eighty-four feet by sixty feet with half-basement, two main floors, and an attic floor, cost a mere £520. Even the rather larger Holme Lacy and Lyndon Hall only amounted to £1,645 and £1,690 respectively. In all these cases, the timber and stone were probably supplied free (at Capheaton Sir John Swinburne supplied all the stone, slates, timber, lime and sand), but even so the costs were clearly very small compared with the total price. In 1704 William Cowper paid only £1,720 for the bare shell of his new house at Cole Green Park, which was seventy-five feet by forty-three feet and two storeys high. The most dramatic example of the difference between the cost of the shell of the main building and the total cost of finishing the house, including internal decoration and furniture, outbuildings, service areas, and grounds, is provided by Erddig in Wales. In 1683, the shell, eighty-five feet by fifty feet, was built for a mere £678, but to complete the fitting-up of the house (including additional wings) cost the next purchaser some £8,000.[46]

[45] R. North, op. cit., p. 27.
[46] O. Hill and J. Cornforth, op. cit., pp. 241, 232, 174-7, 229; J. Hodgson, *History of Northumberland*, Newcastle, 1827-40, pt. 2, i, p. 220 note; L. Stone, 'Cole Green', op. cit., p. 77; M. Waterson, *The Servants' Hall*, New York, 1980, pp. 22, 55-6.

The late sixteenth- and early seventeenth-century country-house building was dominated by the great prodigy houses of the Elizabethan and Jacobean period. Longleat cost Sir John Thynne about £8,000 between 1568 and 1578, and the total must have been nearer £10,000 or £12,000. Sir Percival Willoughby spent about £8,000 on Wollaton Hall between 1580 and 1588—it was known as 'Willoughby's folly' before it was even finished. From 1607 to 1612, Robert Earl of Salisbury spent the gigantic sum of £39,000 on the house itself, its decoration and fittings, and the gardens and grounds at Hatfield, one of the largest and most magnificent buildings of its day. Apart from Audley End, alleged to have cost £80,000, it was probably the most expensive house ever built in this age of conspicuous architectural consumption. Only someone with access to the public funds, and as deeply corrupt as Salisbury, could afford such a sum. To give some idea of the extravagance of this undertaking, the main fabric (without fittings or panelling) of Wadham College, Oxford, was built at exactly the same time for a mere £11,000.[47]

By the late seventeenth century the costs of some of the next wave of gigantic house-building were equally large. The mere finishing of Nottingham Castle in the 1680s cost £14,000, Dorchester House, Surrey, cost about £10,000, Ranelagh House in London £11,000, and Kiveton Park, Yorks., £15,000. The great house of Burley-on-the-Hill cost £30,000 between 1696 and 1710, and the even larger Castle Howard by Vanbrugh, one of the largest houses ever built, cost £35,000 for the mansion, £24,000 for the extensive grounds, and £19,000 for the Mausoleum. The total cost of Blenheim from 1705 to 1715 has been estimated at a staggering £300,000, most of it paid for by the government.[48]

In the seventeenth century, the smaller houses suitable for a wealthy squire cost far less. The amounts fluctuated wildly, depending on whether the owner could supply his own materials for nothing from his estate, notably freestone, brick, and timber. In 1563-8, Sir Nicholas Bacon remodelled Gorhambury for £3,000 plus timber from his estate, and brick and stone robbed from the ruins of the abbey of St Albans. Sir Thomas Smythe spent £4,000

[47] Longleat, Bath MSS, Misc. Books, 179B, p. 18; P. E. Rossell, The building of Wollaton Hall, 1580-88 (Sheffield University MA thesis, 1957), p. 35; L. Stone, *Family and Fortune*, Oxford, 1973, p. 91; L. Stone, 'The Original Endowment of Wadham College', *Wadham College Gazette*, 146, 1959; *Camden Miscellany*, x, Camden Soc., 3rd Series, iv, 1902, p. 115.

[48] O. Hill and J. Cornforth, op. cit., p. 237; H. Colvin and J. Harris, op. cit., p. 72; *Walpole Soc.*, xii, 1923, p. 16; K. Downes, op. cit., p. 12; G. Beard, *Georgian Craftsmen*, London, 1966, pp. 184-5; D. Green, *Blenheim Palace*, London, 1951, p. 251.

to build Corsham Court, Wilts., in the years before 1582, Sir Nathaniel Bacon built Irmingland Hall, Norf., in 1609 for £3,400. Even Holland House in Kensington, which was a fairly large mansion, only cost the earl £6,600 in 1638-40, although this almost certainly excludes decoration and grounds. (Plate XIIIB.) Since a century before Hengrave Hall, Suff., a house similar in size and splendour, had cost Sir Thomas Kitson £3,000, it is clear that the cost of building itself had just about kept pace with inflation, but was not running ahead of it.[49] One can conclude that a reasonably sized house for a middling squire would cost him between £3,000 and £4,000 in the early seventeenth century, meaning at least two or three years income. A nobleman could build an appropriately lavish seat for about double, and the magnate seeking to dominate all his neighbours in the county could spend anything from £20,000 to £40,000—sums only obtainable by the grosser forms of corruption in government office or contracting.

By the end of the seventeenth century, increasing splendour of interior decoration in sculpture, plaster-work, and painting, and the increasing grandeur of the formal gardens with their canals and walks, their fountains and grottoes, their parterres and bowling-greens, was running up the cost well beyond the pace of inflation, which between 1650 and 1770 was virtually negligible. At the more modest squirearchy level, houses continued to cost £4,000 to £7,000, excluding the grounds, well into the middle of the eighteenth century, but it was precisely the interior decoration and the grounds which were costing more and more money.[50] The first escalation of decoration costs came with the practice in the late seventeenth century of covering walls and ceilings with paintings of classical or mythological scenes by the hand of a fashionable, usually a foreign, artist. Rubens began the escalation with the £4,000 he charged for the great apotheosis of James I he painted on the ceiling of the Banqueting House. At Montagu House in London after the Restoration, Rosso asked for, and got, £2,000 cash and £500 a year for two years to paint the saloon. In 1676 Verrio was paid £5,500 for the painting he did at Windsor Castle—a sum composed of piece-work payment at £3.12s.0d. a square yard, free wine and lodging, and a life pension of £200 a year on his retire-

[49] Lambeth Palace MSS 647/5; F. Blomefield, *History of Norfolk*, London, 1805-10, vi, p. 324, n. 1; *Historical Manuscripts Commission, Various MSS*, viii, p. 51; J. Gage, *History of Hengrave*, London, 1822, pp. 15-54.

[50] J. Harris, 'The Building of Denham Place', *Records of Buckinghamshire*, 16, 1953-60, pp. 193-6; F. Jenkins, *Architect and Patron*, Durham, 1961, p. 133; R. Morris, op. cit.; *Country Life*, 143, 1968, pp. 466-70; loc. cit., 47, 1920, pp. 51-4.

ment. Ricci painted three rooms for the Duke of Portland for £1,000, and Pelligrini the side of a hall for Lord Burlington for £200. Ceilings were naturally extremely awkward to get at, involving lying on one's back on slings and painting upside down, and were proportionately much more expensive than walls. Thornhill asked £5 a square yard for ceilings, and £1 for walls, but the rates he was actually paid were more like 3 to 1.[51]

These high prices charged by eminent painters greatly increased the costs of decoration. At Blenheim, Thornhill was paid nearly £1,000 for painting the hall, and Laguerre £500 for the saloon, while the bill of Grinling Gibbons for wood-carvings came to over £4,000. At Moor Park, Herts., in 1720, decoration alone cost £3,500. The later ornate work by the Adam brothers was no cheaper, for at Drayton, Northants., in 1771-2 the redecoration cost between £800 and £900 a room.[52] As a result of these escalating decorating prices, in 1865 Robert Kerr estimated that the total cost of the house alone would run to anything from £5,000 for a villa to £20,000 to £40,000 for a really large seat. These figures were confirmed in 1897, when it was said that 'one can hardly apply the term mansion to anything that can be built for less than £20,000'.[53]

If one leaves to one side for a moment the additional costs of grounds and parks, one is left with the more manageable problem of estimating the movement of costs of country-house building: one solution is to compare known costs of various buildings in terms of pounds per 100 square feet of family living-space, excluding offices and servants' quarters. This is the 'unit', according to which house size is measured in this study. About thirty houses lend themselves to this analysis, from which it is clear that in the late seventeenth century costs for a medium-size house were running at about £40 a unit, possibly up from about £25 a century earlier. Costs remained at about £40 a unit until the 1780s, when they rose rapidly to a level of about £55 to £60, a jump of nearly 50 per cent. In 1865, Robert Kerr produced estimates that ranged from about £60 a unit for a smallish house to over £80 a unit for a really large one. Because of the greater elaboration of decoration, the larger houses always cost more per unit than the smaller ones.[54]

[51] *Wren Soc.*, vi, 1929, pp. 77-9; *Vertue's Notebooks*, iv, *Walpole Soc.*, xxiv, 1936, p. 142.
[52] *Country Life*, 137, 1965, p. 1349; D. Green, op. cit., pp. 159, 247, 187; H. M. Colvin, *Biographical Dictionary of British Architects, 1660-1840*, London, 1954, p. 611.
[53] R. Kerr, op. cit., pp. 400, 407; H. Heathcote Statham, *Modern Architecture*, London, 1892, p. 183.
[54] Apart from individual houses whose size and cost are known, there are a series of useful estimates of both in R. Morris, op. cit., G. Richardson, *New Designs in Architecture*, London, 1792, and R. Kerr, op. cit., p. 392.

To these figures there have to be added the costs of grounds. No doubt the early seventeenth-century formal-garden layout with its elaborate parterres and waterworks was extremely expensive to build and maintain. But the probability is that the grandiose land-scapings by Capability Brown or Repton were more expensive still, although less expensive to keep up once they were finished. 'Who wants money when a park is to be ornamented, temples to be raised, or valleys floated with water?', asked Arthur Young rhetorically in 1771. Robert Kerr estimated that stables and grounds would amount to about a third of the cost of building the house itself.[55] For one thing, the architectural ornaments scattered about the garden were enormously expensive. A fountain by Pierce for Hampton Court in the 1690s cost £2,000, and by the 1790s Richardson was suggesting between £500 and £1,200 for a garden temple or a pavilion.[56] On a more mundane level, he also estimated that it cost between £250 and £1,100 to build a gateway and porter's lodge, £2,260 to build stabling and accommodation for twenty horses and two coaches, or £4,800 for thirty horses and four coaches. When Mr de Crespigny bought Colney Chapel House in 1775, he spent £5,000 on the purchase of the estate, £1,800 on the bare shell of the main block (without offices or internal fittings or decorations), £600 on the kitchen garden and walls, and £450 on the lake. The thirteen-acre lake at Panshanger, designed by Repton and dug out in 1799-1800, cost £2,000.[57] Once purchased, landscaped, and planted, these great parks had then to be walled, an extravagantly expensive operation which could cost as much as the building of the seat itself. At Blenheim in 1722, for example, the estimate for building the nine miles of park walls was £1,200 a mile, or £10,000 in all. This agrees with the observation of Dr Johnson in 1783 that 'we compute in England a park wall at a thousand pounds a mile'.[58]

In the case of a few exceptionally large and elaborate grounds, the costs in the eighteenth century were truly astronomical. King William III spent £88,000 on the gardens at Hampton Court between 1689 and 1699, while it has been estimated that the Dukes of Marlborough spent £200,000 on the grounds of Blenheim between 1760 and 1820. These extravagant enterprises were, however, rare and in 1865 Robert Kerr estimated that on a huge £40,000

[55] A. Young, op. cit., iv, p. 394; R. Kerr, op. cit., pp. 410-11.

[56] *Wren Soc.*, iv, 1927, p. 38; G. Richardson, op. cit., p. 25.

[57] G. Richardson, op. cit., pp. 18, 25; Bodleian Library, interleaved N. Salmon, *Hertfordshire* (Gough Herts. 13), pp. 64-5; Herts. R. O., Cowper MSS, A 18.

[58] D. Green, op. cit., p. 314; *J. Boswell: The Applause of the Jury, 1782-85*, ed. I. S. Lustig and F. A. Pottle, New York, 1981, p. 102.

mansion there would only need to be spent £12,000 on the stables and grounds, a proportion which is not so very different from that for a much smaller house.[59]

Even after all these houses, gardens, parks, lakes, plantings, and park walls had been paid for, there still remained the problem of the expense of annual maintenance which demanded the services of a small army of groundsmen, gardeners, and gamekeepers. The Cowpers found to their dismay in 1807 that the annual gardening costs at Panshanger (where the new house was still not yet built) came to £828 and the gamekeeping to £530.[60]

House-building on this scale was thus a highly capital-intensive undertaking, which could quickly absorb the savings of several lifetimes of landowners, which is why so many of the largest and architecturally most spectacular houses were built by new men with fortunes accumulated in trade, finance, politics, or the law. The result was not always regarded gratefully by the successors of the builder, who had to live in the monster. As early as the mid-seventeenth century, before the second great building boom got under way, Lord North commented that 'it hath been observed as a great unhappiness to our nobility and gentry, that generally they are over-housed'. And yet they continued to become more and more 'over-housed' all through the seventeenth, eighteenth, and nineteenth centuries, expanding, adding, and embellishing right up to the end. In 1789 John Byng commented: 'what folly it is for people to overbuild themselves, knowing as they must do that the mortgage so incurred must prevent their heirs from inhabiting their grand buildings, being only mausoleums of vanity'.[61] Mausoleums of vanity is indeed an apt description of too many of the greater English country houses.

[59] *Wren Soc.*, iv, 1927, p. 38; D. Green, op. cit., p. 199; R. Kerr, op. cit., pp. 406-7.
[60] Herts. R. O., Cowper MSS, Box 20.
[61] Dudley Lord North, op. cit., p. 88; J. Byng, op. cit., iii, p. 20.

PLATE II Anderson Place, Newcastle-upon-Tyne, Northumberland, in 1702, built within the City walls (on the right) in 1580 and much enlarged in 1680, by the purchaser Sir William Blackett Bt.

PLATE III A Astwell, Northants., in 1721, the secondary seat of an Earl, totally unmodernized, at the time of its abandonment. Built in 1492, enlarged in 1607 by the husband of an heiress, it was abandoned a century later by his descendants, who were seated in a neighbouring county.

PLATE III B Belsay Castle, Northumberland, in 1728, showing the original fortalice, with successive additions of 1614 and the early eighteenth century. It became the steward's house after Sir Charles Monck, 7th Bt., built Belsay Hall nearby in 1810-17.

PLATE V Hamels, Herts., in 1722. Sir John Brograve's c. 1580 house enveloped on all sides in a classical shell with gardens to match by its purchaser, Ralph Freeman IV, of Aspenden Hall (see endpaper). The avenue from the gate to the house is ½ mile long.

PLATE VI A Pishiobury, Herts., in 1698, built by the courtier Sir Walter Mildmay in 1585; note the bowling green and summer house. (Cf. PL. VIIA.)

PLATE VI B Hertingfordbury Park, Herts., in 1698, built in the 1680s by a London merchant, abandoned in 1815. The original house, enlarged in 1620, and which can be seen on the left demoted to offices, survives to this day as the core of yet another rebuilding in the 1890s.

PLATE VII A Pishiobury, Herts., in 1834, as landscaped by Capability Brown and gothicized by Wyatt, after a fire, in 1782. Some of the original panelling still survives.

PLATE VII B The Hoo, Herts., in 1698. Built by the financier Sir Jonathan Keate in 1656, it was demolished in 1958; note the bowling and men tending the home farm.

PLATE VIII A   Easton Neston, Northants., in 1721, almost 30 years after it was begun by Hawksmoor; the offices are in the adjoining wings. Note the topiary garden.

PLATE VIII B   Langleybury, Herts., in 1832: the entrance to the offices at the back of the house and the stables opposite, built in 1725, which are almost as grand as the house itself.

PLATE IX A Cassiobury, Herts., *c*.1802. The end of the original monastic range can be glimpsed at the back on the left. The 1670s classical house by Hugh May is undergoing Gothicization at the hands of James Wyatt (note the scaffolding at right front). The house was pulled down in 1913. (See Plan 1)

PLATE IX B   T. Rowlandson: The Return from the Hunt, 1788.

PLATE X A Kelmarsh Hall, Northants., in *c.*1730, built in 1620 on the side of a hill, with rambling offices.

PLATE X B Kelmarsh Hall, Northants., as built by Gibbs in 1727 on the brow of the hill, with formal, separate, office pavilions.

PLATE XI A   Courteenhall House, Northants., the old house, with additions, built in the valley, as seen by Repton in 1791.

PLATE XI B   Courteenhall Park, Northants., as designed by Repton in 1791.

PLATE XII A   Philippe Mercier: Sir Thomas Samwell, 2nd Bt., of Upton Hall, Northants., with friends at a Bacchanalian feast, in 1733.

PLATE XII B   J.F. ['Old'] Nollekens: the Music Party, at Wanstead House, Essex, the home of Lord Tilney, c.1737.

PLATE XIII A   R. Huskisson: the Picture Gallery at Thirlestaine House, Glos., c.1846, where Lord Northwick had over 800 paintings by old masters and modern British artists.

PLATE XIII B   C.R. Leslie: the seventeenth century Library at Holland House, Kensington, in 1838.

PLATE XV A From Humphrey Repton's *Red Book for Panshanger*, Herts.: the classical alternative (see Pl. XV B).

PLATE XV B From Humphrey Repton's *Red Book for Panshanger*, Herts.: the Gothic alternative which was the one chosen. In either case, the plan (Plan 3) remained the same.

PLATE XVI A   Nyn House, Herts., a great late medieval and Tudor house, shortly before its destruction in the mid-eighteenth century.

PLATE XVI B   The Lordship, Standon, Herts., in 1824. Built in 1546 by the successful courtier, Sir Ralph Sadleir, it was abandoned by 1800 and largely pulled down in 1828.

XI

BUILDING AND BUILDERS

'The domestic employment of a country gentleman is usually engaged in building and gardening'. *Peregrine Bertie, 11th Lord Willoughby de Eresby*, London, 1838, p. 113.

'[Building] is a sober entertainment and doth not impeach the health. Other pleasures which are less despised, as wine, women, gaming, etc. have a sting, which this hath not'. Roger North, *Of Building* [c.1698], ed. H. Colvin and J. Newman, Oxford, 1981, p. 4.

'The chief pleasure of a country house is to make improvements'. D. Garrick, *The Clandestine Marriage*, 1766, II, ii.

1. HOUSES

i. Numbers

a. Totals

The first question to be asked about the sample of houses is how many there were at different periods in each of our three counties (Table 11.1; Fig. 11.1). Hertfordshire and Northamptonshire show certain striking similarities in their developments. Both started at a low level in 1540 and built up rapidly to a peak of about seventy to eighty seats per county by 1640. Thereafter, the drop-outs in Northamptonshire exceeded the new entrants, so that numbers fell slowly over the next century from a high of about eighty in 1640 to a level of about seventy from 1740 onwards. The trajectory of the numbers of seats in Hertfordshire closely paralleled that of Northamptonshire up to 1640, but thereafter followed a rather different pattern. Instead of declining and then levelling off, numbers kept climbing slowly but steadily to a plateau of about ninety-five in 1780 and stayed there until a last influx of new entrants after 1860 pushed the total up to over 105. On the other hand, it has to be borne in mind that the Hertfordshire sample includes more marginal cases than do those of the other two counties, where a fairly clear-cut division existed at all times between houses in and out of sample.

It seems likely that Hertfordshire and Northamptonshire represent the outer limits of the basic pattern common to all counties

FIG. 11.1   Frequency Count of Houses in Sample at 20-Year Intervals [Table 11.1]

in the lowland zone of the midlands, south and east. Much of English history makes sense in the light of the initial rise of the squirearchy up to 1640 and its subsequent relative stabilization. There was a limit to the number of elite families any moderate county could support, and the figure of about eighty, reached by 1640, seems to have been it. Beyond that number, the competition for political power, prestige, places, and compact estates became too fierce. In any case, the economic climate changed after 1640, with the levelling-off or fall of agricultural prices, and the imposition of heavy land taxes. In some areas like Northamptonshire the advantage swung to the great landowners, who tended to gobble up their neighbours' estates and seats by marriage, inheritance, or purchase. These superfluous seats they then gave to relatives, leased out, left empty, allowed to decay into farmhouses, sold, or pulled down.

Some houses were thus actually destroyed or reduced in size, while others survived physically but dropped out of the sample because of the economic and status decline of their owners. This tendency towards numerical contraction could only be offset by the influx of newcomers from the ranks of rising gentry and more especially of successful government officials, lawyers, and business men. In Northamptonshire this new blood was not sufficient after 1680 to compensate for the losses, but in Hertfordshire, which was much closer to London, the influx of new money was much stronger, which kept numbers growing or stable at all periods. In the last twenty years of the study, from 1860 to 1874, these newcomers pushed the total stock of Hertfordshire seats up to an unprecedented level, and it was only because many of them were not in fact seeking local political power that this expansion did not produce intolerable tensions within the local communities.

Although the overall trends appear to be roughly similar in the two counties, what the bare figures fail to reveal is that they start off in 1540 with a very different stock of houses. By the end of the fifteenth century, Northamptonshire had a reasonable complement of country houses, admittedly most of them not very large, but solidly built of stone. In Hertfordshire, on the other hand, potential country houses were few in number, one reason being that most of the western half of the county was in the hands of the great Abbey of St Albans. Hertfordshire as a social and political unit does not emerge in its own right until the destruction of this huge holding at the Dissolution of the Monasteries, when its distribution to lay landowners made possible the creation of new private estates and seats upon it. The county did not even have its own sheriff until 1567, before which it had to share the office with Essex.

A number of the new Tudor owners were bold enough to convert ex-monastic buildings to their own secular uses. Eleven houses in Hertfordshire and seven in Northamptonshire were thus adapted. Virtually without exception, the new owners took the precaution of destroying the consecrated church itself, but the living-quarters of the monks or nuns, usually built around a quadrangle, could easily be adapted for secular purposes. As a result, a few houses in all counties preserved the name of the original religious institution: Royston and Hitchin Priories and Cheshunt Nunnery in Hertfordshire; Fineshade and Delapré Abbeys in Northamptonshire; and Alnwick Abbey in Northumberland. Few county elites can have been as heavily dependent upon the sixteenth- and early seventeenth-century dispersal of Church and Crown properties as was that of Hertfordshire. There, nearly a half of all seats extant in 1640 were built on land which had once been in institutional hands, one-third on ex-monastic land. This is hardly surprising since it has been calculated that in 1540 the Crown held 168 out of 395 recorded manors or similar estates, but only 12 a decade later.[1] The fortunes of very many of the nobility and squirearchy were here all too clearly based upon the ruins of Church and Crown, although in Northamptonshire the proportion was substantially smaller, and in Northumberland smaller still.

If the formation of the landed elites in the two southern counties marched very closely in step between 1540 and 1640, the picture is very different in Northumberland. Throughout the whole of the sixteenth century this county was a turbulent and sparsely populated upland border area, where physical insecurity made it unsafe to live in anything but medieval fortresses or fortified tower houses, called bastle houses. In any case, the shortage of labour, the lack of roads, and the backwardness of agriculture depressed the incomes of the landlords and provided no surplus for such extravagances as large-scale house-building. It was only the accession of James VI of Scotland to the English throne in 1603 which finally pacified the border, at last putting an end to raiding and banditry, and it is only then that country-house-building began. Temporarily halted by the damage caused by the Scottish occupation of the area in the 1640s, building picked up again in 1660 and the number of seats thereafter grew on a steadily rising curve to over sixty in 1840. In terms of house-building, the early eighteenth century in Northumberland was 'a Caucasian spring, the sudden blossoming of civilization with the melting away of political and social disorder under the warming influence of economic prosperity'.[2]

The pattern for Northumberland is thus radically different from that of the two counties further south. Whereas the latter reached their natural saturation point by about 1640 and then more or less levelled off, the number of houses in Northumberland increased slowly and steadily for another two centuries, only reaching that level in the middle of the nineteenth century.

b. Entrants

These alterations in total numbers reflect a shifting balance between new houses coming into the sample and others dropping out (Table 11.2). It must be stressed that entry into the sample does not necessarily mean the building of a new house on a virgin site. Entry into the sample can mean either the rebuilding of an old house on a larger scale by a man of increased wealth, power,

[1] L. Stone and J. C. Fawtier Stone, 'Country Houses and their Owners in Hertfordshire, 1540-1879' in *Dimensions of Quantitative Research in History*, ed. W. O. Aydelotte, *et al.*, Princeton, 1972, pp. 107-8; L. M. Munby, *The Hertfordshire Landscape*, London, 1977, p. 139.

[2] E. Hughes, *North Country Life in the Eighteenth Century*, Oxford, 1952, i, p. 30.

and status, passage from institutional or royal use into private hands, or acquisition of a suitable house by a suitable owner, or a completely new building on a new site. In the cases of about half of all the houses coming into the Hertfordshire sample between 1540 and 1879 there was indeed no known previous house on the site. But this figure is misleading, since it is very probable that a considerable number of these new houses were in fact constructed on the sites of farmhouses or small late medieval halls. On the other hand seventeen of these twenty-six apparently new houses appear in the nineteenth century, and it is probable that in most of these cases they were indeed built on genuinely virgin soil. The remainder of the additions to the sample were the product of the expansion of older smaller houses, and their occupation by an owner of enhanced status.

Movement into the sample was thus a combination of an influx of outside wealth buying into the local landed society, and an upward thrust of successful local gentry. Since the numbers thus reflect the levels both of official, legal, and commercial profit-taking and also of the returns from land, it is hardly surprising that no very clear trend can be detected. The great period of acquisitive money-making and influx into the elite was clearly the traditional age of the rise of the gentry, from 1540 to 1640. In Hertfordshire, however, the influx continued at full strength throughout the Interregnum, to 1660, as successful London merchants prudently shifted their assets out of trade and bought land and built a house in a militarily safe area during a period of very depressed land values.

The rapidly rising rents of the late eighteenth and early nineteenth centuries carried new entrants into both Hertfordshire and Northumberland, but for unknown reasons left Northamptonshire almost entirely unaffected. All counties were equally hard hit by the agricultural difficulties of the 1840s and 1850s, and by the reluctance of the elite to admit new wealth from outside. The 1860s and 1870s, however, was a period of influx into Hertfordshire of new men—hardly any of them manufacturers—building new houses mostly on new sites, whereas conservative Northamptonshire still remained untouched. The new wealth of the high Victorian era seems to have passed it by altogether, perhaps because of the unwelcoming posture of the entrenched elite.

c. Drop-outs

The disappearance of a house from the sample may indicate either its total destruction or its abandonment and consequent physical deterioration, or its leasing, sale to, or inheritance by institutions or owners who did not qualify for the sample. (Plates II, IIIA, XVIA and B.) The precise ways in which these things could happen to houses and the reasons for them may be examined in detail in the case of Hertfordshire (Table 11.3), where between 1540 and 1879 twenty-five were totally destroyed, thirteen leased and often later sold, two urbanized, and nine shrunken or decayed. Another eight remained intact but passed by inheritance or sale into the hands of persons who did not qualify for the sample.

Almost all of the work of destruction (twenty-one out of twenty-five) was done by men who had inherited several seats and no longer had any use for a sixteenth- or seventeenth-century house that was out of fashion and superfluous to needs. Seven of these twenty-one houses had either been inherited or deliberately bought by owners of contiguous estates and seats, who were anxious to pull down the houses and incorporate the land into an expansion of their own parks. Three of these expansionist magnates, Sir Harbottle Grimston of Gorhambury, at the time of the Restoration, and James 1st Marquis of Salisbury of Hatfield and Peter Earl Cooper of Panshanger around 1800, were responsible for eight of these demolitions or demotions into farmhouses. House destruction was at its height in Hertfordshire between 1790 and 1829, when there occurred no fewer than half of the total twenty-five recorded cases of total demolition. It should be noted that this figure only includes houses which were destroyed and not immediately rebuilt. If one were to add houses abandoned or destroyed and immediately replaced upon an adjacent site, like Gorhambury and Ashridge, concentration of demolition upon the forty years from 1790 to 1829 becomes even more striking.

One can plausibly speculate about the reasons for this brief period of destruction of old houses, virtually all of them built between 1540 and 1640. The few surviving Tudor and early Stuart houses were now very old, often built of brick, and were beginning to crumble. Only large-scale investment in restoration work, prompted by a genuine concern to save these monuments of a bygone age, would have sufficed to save many of them. The vast majority had already been refaced or remodelled to suit Georgian tastes in the late seventeenth and eighteenth centuries. This was certainly the case at Hamels, Herts., an elegant late sixteenth century house 'palladianized' and encased in stucco by its purchaser after 1713, and pulled down in the early nineteenth century to give way to a Gothic house with conscious echoes of the original (Plate V). Only two major houses, North Mimms and Hatfield, survived in Hertfordshire unaltered into the nineteenth century, and even the latter had been remodelled inside in the 1770s. The pre-1640 houses that were destroyed were therefore those to which nothing had been done, and were now so dilapidated that only a heroic act of restoration could have saved them. The great house of Nyn, Herts., just crumbled away (Plate XVIA), while in Northamptonshire Easton Maudit was pulled down, and Pytchley, after serving for a while as the leased headquarters for the hunt, followed the same path.

One reason for dilapidation and destruction in the late eighteenth century was that, as we have seen, the elite had taken to living for longer and longer periods in London, or sometimes abroad and were using their country seats less and less. Owners, especially owners of many houses, therefore tended to allow those they hardly ever used to fall into neglect, and eventually they pulled many of them down altogether, a process upon which John Byng, Lord Torrington, repeatedly commented as he rode around the country in the 1780s and 1790s.[3] Furthermore, the rising interest in Gothic did nothing to increase respect and admiration for sixteenth- and seventeenth-century houses, which failed altogether to capture the imagination of the romantics.

Destruction and abandonment only came to a halt in the 1830s, when the growth of a genuine antiquarian interest in the past began to extend the range of fashionable taste through the Gothic to embrace the architecture of the Tudors. Thus Cassiobury, a grand 1680s house, was gratuitously Gothicized by Wyatt in about 1810, and then given a mock-Jacobethan appearance in the 1830s. Finedon, Northants., began Gothic and ended up Jacobethan, while Knebworth, Herts., was elaborately re-Gothicized in imitation of its former self. As a result of this radical change in attitude, only four of the remaining older houses were destroyed between 1830 and 1879.

Some of the houses destroyed met their fate through a variety of almost accidental circumstances. Nine were too close to towns or villages to survive the encroachments of suburbia and the demand for solitude and space in the eighteenth century. Of the remaining three houses destroyed, two (Aldenham Manor House and Oxhey) had been allowed to tumble into ruins much earlier and one (Throcking) was deliberately pulled down as a result of a family quarrel between two brothers.

[3] J. Byng, *The Torrington Diaries*, ed. S. B. Andrews and J. Beresford, London, 1934, i, pp. 128, 333; ii, pp. 76, 87, 238; iii, p. 33; iv, p. 9.

Of the thirteen houses which were leased or exchanged, one 'prodigy house' (Theobalds) was early on exchanged with the Crown, and later pulled down, although a much smaller new house was built near the site in the eighteenth century. Of the rest, half of which were leased in the destructive period between 1790 and 1829, four became schools, two warehouses, two farms, one a hotel, and the remaining three became private residences of men of lesser gentlemanly status. In all but two of these cases, the family had inherited a more attractive seat elsewhere, and in these two the family had died out altogether and had no further use for the seat. Two houses became urbanized in the late seventeenth century, but survived as town houses, while two others were engulfed by urban expansion in the early nineteenth century and were either destroyed or let. Only nine dropped out of the sample because the family was the victim of shrinking financial resources or reduced social status. At this elite level, there were enough safety nets built in by society—not least the profits of government office—to prevent most families from going under.

The overall impression is that the most important factor for the survival of a house was demographic luck. When a family inherited too many houses, one or more of them was likely to be more or less uninhabited, and a period of neglect of twenty to thirty years could make a house very expensive to restore, especially if the roof had been leaking, or if it had been damaged by tenants. Seven of these destroyed or decayed seats were replaced by grander ones, built on a nearby site, and three by others in the sample, while four rose from their ashes thanks to a lavish remodelling in the 1870s, after a century or more of abandonment. Thus as many as fourteen of the forty-nine seats which were physically demolished or reduced had a successor in the sample or were ultimately restored to their original grandeur. This happened, for example, to Gorhambury and Punsborne in Hertfordshire, and to Edgecote in Northamptonshire.

Many of these demolished houses were gobbled up by great magnates anxious to extend the area of their parks, as has been shown in the cases of the earls of Salisbury and the Cowpers in the eighteenth century. Similarly, Easton Maudit, Northants., was absorbed and destroyed by the Comptons of Castle Ashby after the Yelvertons had died out.

Only the rich, usually with outside sources of income, could afford to build a wholly new house on a new site, or else completely to raze an old house and start again. This is also something which is easier to accomplish with a brick building than one built in more solid free-stone, although a completely new Kelmarsh, Northants., replaced the old one nearby in 1727-32. (Plates XA and B.) In Hertfordshire, it was relatively easy to allow the vast unreconstructed old house of Nyn to collapse after 1750, and Standon Lordship to be pulled down in 1830 (Plates XVIA and B), as well as to pull down most of old Gorhambury and Ashridge. They were too big and too old-fashioned and too decayed to be worth keeping.

In Northamptonshire, superfluous houses were more likely to be abandoned or allowed to decline into farms than to be razed altogether to the ground. The old house of Pytchley passed through various stages, first abandoned by the family in 1750, then let out to the hunt masters for their headquarters and the site of riotous hunt parties, and finally pulled down altogether in 1829. In Northumberland, the old manor-houses, bastle houses, and castles which were replaced by modern country seats were usually allowed to decay slowly into picturesque ruins, sometimes to be restored again in the Victorian period. Thus the old Mitford Manor-House was left to fall into ruins across the valley from the new Mitford Hall built by Dobson in 1823. The medieval castle at Belsay was given a fine new wing in the eighteenth century, but after Sir Charles Monck had built himself Belsay Hall in 1817, the castle was turned into a residence of the land steward. In 1897 the whole castle, including the eighteenth-century wing, was finally demolished. (Plate IIIB.)

At least some of these stone-built houses could endure quite long periods of abandonment, and still be capable of restoration. Althorp in 1772 was reported to be neglected and with the roof falling in, but it was put back into shape in 1786 after forty years of neglect, when the Spencers moved back in. Other houses were less fortunate. A dramatic example of a slow decline into ruin by neglect is the great Elizabethan mansion of Kirby Hall, Northamptonshire. In 1769 the Finch-Hattons inherited Eastwell Park in Kent, and moved their headquarters there. Twenty years later, in 1791, Kirby was still intact, although not lived in, and is said to have been suggested a decade later as a possible place of retreat for George III and the court in case of a Napoleonic invasion. But by 1810 it was plainly neglected and going to ruin, by 1828 it was partly dismantled and in full decay, and in 1857 the lead was stripped from the roof to pay for the 11th Earl of Winchelsea's gambling debts. This finally turned it from a tumbledown house into an archaeological ruin. The abandonment was probably because Kirby was just too vast to be left to relatives or other tenants. No one wanted it, or could afford to keep it up.[4]

Very different was the fate of the superfluous house of Hadham Hall, Herts., a vast rambling sixteenth-century seat. In 1675 the Capels moved from it to the much more up-to-date and convenient seat of Cassiobury Park. (Plate IXA.) But instead of letting Hadham Hall fall into ruin, in 1703 they deliberately pulled most of it down, leaving a compact and comfortably sized smaller house, which they let to a succession of tenants from 1725 to 1900, when it was reconverted to a house in the country by a Londoner.

Smaller superfluous houses often fared better, like Harrowden Hall, Northants., which in 1743 passed to the Fitzwilliams of Milton. They used it as a dower house for widows for a while, but from 1782 to 1895 it was usually let, most of the contents being removed to Milton in 1801 to 1805. Thorpe, another small house which also came to the Fitzwilliams by inheritance in 1793, was treated less well, although the story has a happy ending. From 1793 to 1850 it was totally abandoned, but before it fell completely into ruins the Fitzwilliams sold it in 1850 to an owner who lovingly restored it and so preserved it. One way or another, however, the life of a superfluous house was a precarious one.

Whatever the causes—and superfluity by accumulation, changing tastes, and sheer physical deterioration bulk large among them—there can be no doubt that the rate of decay and destruction increased markedly after 1660. Once the saturation point had been reached, as it was at that time, families began accumulating houses by intermarriage and purchase, and tearing down superfluous ones, thus inadvertently making space for newcomers. In Hertfordshire, for example, some 94 per cent of all houses in the sample in 1579 were still there a hundred years later, but only 74 per cent two hundred years later and 54 per cent three hundred years later. Only just over half of the Elizabethan houses in this county lasted for a full three hundred years. In sleepy Northamptonshire, however, which was far from the demand pressures of Londoners seeking to enter the elite, and where seats were built of solid free-stone rather than easily demolished brick, the survival rate was very much higher.

It should be observed that all houses were liable to the hazard of partial destruction by fire, and in Hertfordshire about 10 per cent of all houses are known to have suffered this fate in the course

[4] H. A. Tipping, *English Houses*, London, 1920-37, iii, (*i*), p. 69; J. Evans and J. Britton, *The Beauties of England and Wales*, London, x, 1810, p. 204; J. Nichols, *Progresses of James I*, London, 1828, ii, p. 453, n. 6; *Quarterly Review*, *101*, *1857*.

of every hundred years. The true figure is certainly very much higher, since it is only the major conflagrations in major seats that get reported. An especial hazard came from stoves used by workmen to melt lead for weights in sash windows or for roofs, and as a result houses quite often caught fire before they were even finished. So common was this that in 1750 Horace Walpole suggested the passage of an Act of Parliament, making master builders liable to pay for any damage caused by fire before the workmen had left the house.[5] Bennington Place, Herts., suffered this fate twice in fifty years, as did Stagenhoe, so that Walpole's exasperation was not altogether unjustified.

ii. Geographical Distribution

Changing tastes and changing modes of transportation affected not only the numbers but also the geographical distribution of country seats. Thus in Hertfordshire there was a marked shift of location between the sixteenth and the nineteenth centuries out of the north-east sector of the county and into the south-west. In 1609 24 per cent of all houses in the sample were situated in the north-east, as opposed to 9 per cent in 1879. In 1603 15 per cent were situated in the south-west as opposed to 24 per cent in 1879. Only one new house entered the sample in the north-east after 1700 while no fewer than nineteen were added in the south-west.

This shift away from the north-east can be explained very simply, by the fact that the countryside there was so dull and unattractive. This did not matter much in the sixteenth century, when houses were low-lying, and when the formal walled garden layout around the house effectively blotted out the natural appearance of the countryside. But after it became fashionable to build houses on the tops of hills with a view over the countryside, and after Capability Brown and the romantics had created an interest in the picturesque landscape in the middle of the eighteenth century, the aesthetic potentialities of the site became an important factor governing the choice of location. This adequately explains the seventeenth- and eighteenth-century shift into the more attractive rolling and wooded country in the centre of the county. The great popularity of the south-eastern sector did not begin until the nineteenth century, and it is almost certainly to be explained by the easy and rapid accessibility of the area from London after the building of the North-eastern Railway line.

The other significant feature about the distribution of houses is

[5] *Horace Walpole's Correspondence*, ed. W. S. Lewis, New Haven, 1937-80, xx, p. 185.

the way many of them tended to cluster along river valleys, especially after the middle of the eighteenth century. The main reason for this is that the new aesthetic of the romantic landscape demanded a southward-facing prospect over some distance, and therefore a site overlooking a valley, preferably from the north. The more ambitious owners also desired a park with a lake, which involved the damming-up of a suitable stream. These were the two considerations used by Repton in 1801 to persuade Earl Cowper to pull down Cole Green Park, which lay a mile from the river Mimram, and to build instead at Panshanger near the river to the north, facing south and overlooking a newly constructed lake. (Plates XVA and B and Plan 3.)

No such significant shifts of geographical distribution of houses occurred in Northamptonshire, where from the sixteenth to the nineteenth centuries seats were stretched broadly and evenly across the gently rolling countryside. Excellent marlstone and free-stone for building, and Stonesfield and Collyweston slates for roofing, were readily available locally, so that Northamptonshire houses were almost invariably built of stone rather than brick. This made them less easy to pull down than brick houses, and therefore encouraged adding on rather than partial destruction or remodelling.

Northumberland shows continuous settlement of the south Tyne valley, which provided physical safety as well as fertile agricultural land and extensive coal-seams beneath the ground. But as time went on, men built seats further and further to the north in the wilder and more upland country. First better security, and then faster and smoother communications, then agricultural development slowly transformed the quality of life in these remoter areas. At the same time the urban sprawl of Newcastle and the expansion along the river of coal-mining made Tyneside less and less attractive to live in. Even so, roads to the north were few even in the early nineteenth century, and transport by coach both very uncomfortable and very slow. The spread of fairly large country houses further and further north is therefore testimony as much to the endurance and resilience of the owners as to the advance of civilisation. The memoirs of Mrs Charlton testify to the fairly primitive conditions of life and the degree of isolation which prevailed in the early nineteenth century.[6] Despite all this, the shift of location of country houses in Northumberland is very striking. In 1759, the huge area north of the south Tyne basin possessed

[6] B. Charlton, *The Recollections of a Northumbrian Lady*, ed. L. E. O. Charlton, London, 1949.

only seventeen seats, while the narrow Tyne basin itself had twenty. In 1879, however, the northern area could boast of thirty-six and southern Tyneside only of twenty-eight.

If the preferred siting of houses changed over time, the one thing that was almost unalterable once the site was settled was the location of the offices, a remarkable example of such stability in the midst of radical and repeated change being the much rebuilt house of Market Cell, Herts. This stability was partly made necessary because of the high cost of resiting the huge kitchen chimneys and the heavy ovens and vats of breweries, bakeries, and laundries. Above all, however, it must have been the location of underground water-pipes and drains which explains why kitchens and breweries tended to remain in the same place century after century, even if the house itself was almost entirely rebuilt and twisted around. By the nineteenth century, the original plumbing of many houses must have been centuries old, which perhaps accounts for the trouble the Victorians had from bad drains, particularly since the system tended to become overloaded with the progressive installation of first one and then several water-closets after the 1770s.

iii. Size

The size of a country house depended on its owner's financial resources, his practical needs, and his social aspirations and on those of his forebears. Except for the gigantic 'prodigy houses' of the great sixteenth-century courtiers like Lord Burghley or Sir Christopher Hatton, the houses of the average sixteenth- and early seventeenth-century squire were limited in size, the main state room being still the medieval hall, where communal dining, entertainment, and even sleeping of servants took place. Space for fairly lavish public hospitality was always essential for a country-house owner with any aspirations to status amongst his peers, but over time the level of what was thought necessary rose in two big steps (Table 11.4, Fig. 11.2). The first jump in the median size of houses came in Hertfordshire between about 1680 and 1740, and some twenty years later in Northamptonshire. This expansion of the median house size of anyone with pretentions to elite power and status was inspired partly by fashion, first by the Baroque and then the Palladian architectural styles. Most important, at least for magnates, was the need for space in which to entertain large numbers of client gentry and others for the political purpose of electoral management during the period of intense party warfare and frequent elections that lasted from 1689 to 1721. A large formal

FIG. 11.2   Median House Size in 'Units' [Table 11.4]

entrance-hall, often half-filled with a sweeping staircase, an equally
large saloon, and a suite of public rooms—rooms of parade—often
on the floor above, were now needed for such large-scale hospitality, while a porticoed and pillared façade impressed upon visitors
the dignity and importance of the owner. (Plates IXB and XIIB.)
Rents were not buoyant at this period, but easier access to mortgage money at low rates of interest, often below 5 per cent, together with the fruits of public office and windfalls from increasing marriage portions, made it possible to finance this expansion.
As a result, the median size of houses in Hertfordshire moved
between 1680 and 1740 from ninety to over one hundred units,
while in Northamptonshire there was an even sharper, though later,
jump between 1720 and 1760 from eighty to one hundred units.
The eighteenth-century squirearchy were now in a sense over-
housed, since these public rooms, which took up so much space,
were only rarely used for the occasional large-scale party, while
the family for the most part lived in the more reasonably sized
private quarters, consisting essentially of a breakfast-room, private
dining-room, small withdrawing-room, and library. Even so, the
raising of the height of the ceilings to fourteen or fifteen feet, the
increased use of marble floors, and the insertion of loosely fitting
sash windows must have made these eighteenth-century houses
very cold and draughty.
    Expansion of what was regarded as the acceptable minimum size
of a country seat of a member of the local elite is most clearly
revealed in the decline in the proportion of the sample made up of

really modest houses ranging from fifty to seventy-nine units (Table 11.5, Fig. 11.3). The figure reveals that up to 1700 both in Hertfordshire and Northamptonshire some 40 to 50 per cent of all the elite lived in these relatively small houses, but by 1740 in the former and 1770 in the latter the proportion had dropped to 20 per cent, declining in Hertfordshire still further to a mere 10 per cent in 1830. Even in cold and backward Northumberland, where over 60 per cent of all the elite lived in these small houses up to 1760, the proportion thereafter fell steadily to 20 per cent by 1880. Thus the status and sociability constraints which impelled owners to expand the size of their houses began to operate first in about 1670 in the area most open to fashion and with easiest access to external funding, namely Hertfordshire, spread to Northampton-shire some thirty years later in 1700, and affected Northumber-land sixty years later still, in 1760.

The number of really large seats, amounting to 150 units or more, appear to have grown in two distinct bursts of activity (Table 11.6, Fig. 11.4). The first began with the arrival in the mid-sixteenth century of the Henrician and Edwardian courtiers and nobles, enriched with monastic spoils, and continued without pause until about 1620 in Hertfordshire and 1640 in Northamptonshire. The 'prodigy houses' merely set the pace for this spate of massive building. This Tudor and Jacobean building spree created a stock

FIG. 11.3   Small Houses (50-79 'Units') as a Proportion of the Sample [Table 11.5]

FIG. 11.4   Frequency Count of Large and Very Large Houses (over 150 Units)
[Table 11.6]

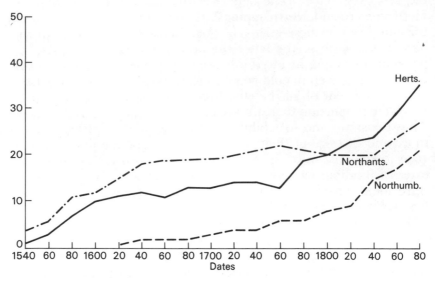

of very large houses, many of which were remodelled, refaced, and added to for the next 200 years. Some of them of course—about twenty altogether in both counties—eventually fell into disrepair and were abandoned or destroyed in the eighteenth or early nineteenth centuries. But from 1640 to 1760 the number of very large houses remained fairly stable. Additions by expansion of older houses, or to a lesser degree by wholly new building, just about matched the rate of abandonment and destruction.

The second wave of major building began in about 1780 and ran right on to 1880, accelerating in scale after 1840. It was fueled to begin with by the great boom in rental income that began in the 1770s and lasted until the end of the Napoleonic wars in 1815. What is surprising is that the depressed state of agriculture from 1815 to about 1850 does not seem to have brought the building of very large houses to a halt. The explanation must be that wealth from office, the professions, empire, and business in Victorian England was tempting more and more exceptionally wealthy men to expand their houses on a larger and larger scale, as status competition grew fiercer at this exalted level of society. This did not, however, apply to the ordinary run of landed squires.

Northumberland followed a rather different trajectory than that of the two Southern and Midland counties, since its economic backwardness caused it to miss out on the first Tudor-Stuart boom. But it compensated for this by a remarkable spurt of large-scale building in the Victorian period.

Taken altogether, this late eighteenth- and nineteenth-century period of gigantism is an extraordinary and puzzling phenomenon. There were, it seems, more servants, more guests, more weekend parties, more mass slaughter of animals, more reckless gambling, that accompanied and were provided for by this expansion of house size. It was, however, a gigantism that became wholly dysfunctional after the economic ice-age set in with the First World War. Not architecturally interesting enough or old enough to be worth preserving for their own sake, not modest enough to be habitable in an age of servant shortage, depressed rents, and high taxes, huge Victorian houses and house expansions were among the first victims of the social upheavals of the twentieth century.

It should be stressed that the number of wholly new houses built on new sites or on sites where older houses had been totally razed were only a minority of the total of these large buildings, most of which became as big as they did by piecemeal accretions and additions over the centuries (Table 11.9). Roger North noted in 1698 that great houses had mostly grown by addition and modernization, so that 'there is scarce a good palace or nobleman's house in England that is not so done'.[7] But this did not merely apply to major seats, and the bulk of all building events at all times took the form of remodelling or adding to existing houses. As a result, the proportion of wholly new building to all building events was a half in 1540-79, declining to a third in 1580-1700, to a quarter from 1700-1819, and finally to a fifth after 1820.

After 1700 very few wholly new houses were built in either Hertfordshire or Northamptonshire for the simple reason that new sites in extensive grounds were not easy to come by. Watton Woodhall and Panshanger were newly built in the 1770-1810 period, but on old sites. There are a cluster of four such wholly new houses built in the 1850s and 1860s, but that is all. In Northamptonshire, large houses on wholly new sites are virtually unknown after 1720, and it is only in Northumberland, where there was still plenty of undeveloped land in the northern part of the county, that there was a significant amount of new construction in the nineteenth century, such as Belsay, Cresswell, Matfen, Meldon, Sandhoe, and Long Ridge Towers. But many of these merely replaced older houses nearby. Thus these buildings were new, and

[7] R. North, *Of Building*, ed. H. Colvin and J. Newman, Oxford, 1981, p. 77.

often on new sites, but in locations where there had been smaller houses for centuries.

One obvious conclusion is that it is very easy to be deceived by the in fact rather small number of wholly new very large Victorian houses, mostly erected upon new sites, into believing that the nineteenth century was a period of intense activity generally in country-house building.[8] If these three counties are anything to go by, the appearance of these striking new houses conceals a generally fairly low level of activity in the mid-nineteenth century, except perhaps for the addition in house after house of extensive but dreary ranges of servants' quarters, and some much needed and ingenious innovations in plumbing and central heating.

If one narrows the focus still further to the really gigantic houses of over 250 units, the unique importance of the age of the Jacobean prodigy houses is starkly revealed. In Hertfordshire there were three of these monsters by 1630, and still only six in 1880; in Northamptonshire there were five by 1630, and still only six in 1880. Northumberland could never in its whole history boast of a single one. Thus not even the Victorian age could match the period 1570 to 1630 in the construction by private individuals of palaces fit for kings. These last are a permanent memorial to a unique period in English history, when the profits of office—first gifts from the Crown of huge tracts of ex-Church property and later the fruits of runaway corruption—were enough to finance the construction of such extraordinary edifices. At that time there were opportunities for instant wealth which were never to occur again, and also unique incentives for courtiers to overbuild, both to compete with rival courtiers in status and prestige, and also to house and entertain the still peripathetic monarch. With the accession of Charles I, these summer progresses tended to die away.

In Hertfordshire, Theobalds and Hatfield were built from scratch by the Cecils, while the monastery of Cassiobury was converted into a vast rambling country house by another official, Sir Richard Morison, and greatly enlarged at the Restoration. (Plate IXA.) At the end of the seventeenth century, Moor Park was built by Charles II's illegitimate son the Duke of Monmouth, and later refitted by a South Sea Bubble magnate, Sir Benjamin Styles. Gorhambury was built and expanded by another official family, the Bacons, in the late sixteenth and early seventeenth centuries, and then rebuilt by the Grimstons in the eighteenth century. Brocket Hall began as a sixteenth-century house, and was wholly rebuilt by the legal

---

[8] This is the view advanced by: M. Girouard, *The Victorian Country House*, Oxford, 1971; J. Franklin, *The Gentleman's Country House and its Plan*, New York, 1981.

family of the Lambs in the 1760s. Finally, Ashridge began as a monastery converted to secular uses by the great legal family of the Egertons, who two and a half centuries later in the early nineteenth century used their enormous mineral wealth to rebuild the crumbling old house in the Gothic style. They made it into the largest house in the county, and indeed one of the largest in England, although not as large as the long-vanished Elizabethan prodigy house of Theobalds.

In Northamptonshire, Burghley House, Castle Ashby, Drayton House, and Holdenby were all built from the fruits of office, while Althorp, Deene, and Kirby were the products first of office and the law and then of land and sheep. Apethorpe was doubled in size in 1623, as a result of a combination by marriage of the wealth of the Mildmays with that of the Fanes. Dingley and Boughton followed in the 1680s, the latter built from the profits of a successful political career, while Milton was enlarged in the 1750s as a result of marriage to the Wentworth heiress. Finally, Overstone was the work of a millionaire mid-Victorian banker, a unique figure who successfully broke into both the peerage and county society all at once, buying not merely a site for a vast family seat but also a very large agricultural estate to go with it.

The net result of all this building activity over three centuries was not merely to increase the number of elite houses and raise the median size, but also to alter significantly the proportions of smaller and larger houses in the stock at any given time (Table 11.8, Figs. 11.5-7). In the first century and a half, until 1679, there was little significant difference in the profile of house size, measured in units, in any of the three counties. In the century between 1680 and 1779, however, houses in the two southern counties were much more evenly spread over the middle 80- to 119-unit range. A century later by 1879 the greatest proportion of houses had shifted sharply upwards to the 120- to 159-unit range in both Hertfordshire and Northumberland, while in Northamptonshire it was higher still, in the 160+-unit range. Very big houses now predominated, and the smaller houses below sixty units had virtually disappeared from the sample in all three counties.

What these figures show is that there was a marked shift in the spectrum of houses toward the high end of the range beginning in the century from 1680 to 1780 and accelerating in the nineteenth century. The stock of English elite country houses not only got progressively larger through the centuries, but it was increasingly dominated by the really large houses. It should be remembered that below the group under study there were large numbers of small manor-houses and villas built by parish gentry and less wealthy

FIG. 11.5   House Size Profiles in Hertfordshire [Table 11.7]

office-holders, professionals, and probably merchants. But that is
another story. The most important country houses, which are today such a prime tourist attraction, were mostly the product of a
slow accumulation of building added to building for 200 years
from 1680 to 1879. The system of measurement by units of family
area of habitation in fact seriously underestimates the scale of this
progressive expansion since it necessarily wholly ignores the huge
stable-building that went on from 1680 to 1800. It also ignores the
equally huge construction of larger and larger servants' quarters,
that is so prominent a feature of Victorian houses, where the servants and their activities often took up more space than did the
owners and their guests.

iv. Appearance

Given that the initial stock of houses was predominantly constructed before 1640, it is worth asking what happened to them
thereafter. In what ways and when were they altered and de-

FIG. 11.6   House Size Profiles in Northamptonshire [Table 11.7]

stroyed? What is clear is that Jacobethan houses were warm and comfortable to live in, so that total demolition or abandonment was fairly rare except in cases where neglect had made them structurally unsafe, or where their size was too great for economical maintenance. Undoubtedly, after about 200 years, many of these houses tended to be in need of major structural repairs. Another need was for extra space for entertainment, more servants, and the display of works of art. These needs increased sharply in about 1680 to 1730, and again in the nineteenth century. The main incentive for change, however, derived from a desire to give the old house at least the external appearance of elegance and fashion. We have seen how Roger North went about modernizing his old seat at Rougham.[9] The prime need was the imposition of a symmetrical classical façade and fenestration upon the old structure, which might include a change in orientation. Sometimes, as at Milton, Nor-

[9] See above, pp. 306-7.

FIG. 11.7   House Size Profiles in Northumberland [Table 11.7]

thants., these were combined with the addition of a new string of
lofty reception rooms, or 'rooms of parade' backing up against the
old building, which had been only one room thick in the sixteenth-
century manner. Another solution was to rotate the axis of the
house so that a new front could be tacked on to the side or back,
to face the park or garden, as at Pendley, Stansteadbury, Market
Cell, and St Paul's Waldenbury in Hertfordshire. More often, all
that was done was merely a face-lifting and a tidying-up to create
a symmetrical façade, as was carried out at Ardeleybury and Little
Court., Herts., in the mid-eighteenth century. By 1830, however,
the revival of antiquarianism made such few Jacobean houses as
had survived the eighteenth century unscathed much more deserving of loving care and attention. Thus at Hatfield, the need to

rebuild a wing destroyed by fire in 1827 was made the excuse for the removal of the internal remodeling and redecoration of the 1770s in order to try to restore the Jacobean appearance of the house, both inside and out. The period of drastic modernization thus primarily lasted only from about 1720 till 1840.

A decision whether or not to build thus depended on the age and state of structural repair of the house, its convenience, and the degree of anxiety to make it conform to aesthetic fashions. An owner wishing to modernize his existing house had five main options open to him. He could pull down most of the old house and rebuild it on the old foundations, which was quite common, as at Greatworth, Northants., Brocket Hall, or Broxbournebury, Herts. He could add a block in front of or behind the old house, thus converting it into a double-pile, and giving it a new symmetrical classical façade on at least one side as at Julians, Herts. This was a very common solution, since it solved four problems in one: reorientation, exterior modernization, the addition of more rooms for entertainment, and the insertion of an internal corridor between the old block and the new. He could add a large new wing which became the main house, the old building degenerating into offices for the servants, as at Lamer, Herts. He could demolish part of the old house and restructure the remainder, keeping some of the old rooms, changing the function of others, and concealing it all behind a brand new façade in the latest fashion, as in the Gothicization of Cassiobury begun in 1805. (Plate IXA.) Or he could combine enlargement with modernization by adding new wings on either side with a new façade over the old center, as at Marston House, Northants.

Naturally enough, one of the commonest solutions for those working on limited budgets was a major face-lift combined with a certain amount of new building to create a symmetrical façade and some more internal space. Equally naturally, the bulk of the refacing took place between the triumph of classicism in about 1720 and the advent of antiquarianism in about 1840. Three-quarters of all mere refacings in the three counties took place in these 120 years. In Hertfordshire, some 15 per cent of all houses had undergone a face-lift during the previous twenty years in 1760, 1780, and 1800. Indeed most of this refacing occurred in Hertfordshire and Northamptonshire, where the pressures of fashion were more intense, but above all where the stock of substantial pre-1640 houses was very much larger than in Northumberland. Northamptonshire owners were rather slower than those in Hertfordshire to undertake the modernization of their old houses, partly because

they had less free capital, partly because more of them were owners of houses lived in by the same family for generations, rather
than newcomers with no ancestral ties and inhibitions; partly because their houses were built in stone rather than brick which
made refenestration much more difficult and expensive. The exterior walls of Althorp, for example, today consist of the original
late sixteenth-century stone walls, the red brick facing added in
the 1660s, and the present stone facing added in the 1790s. Major
remodelling of quite new houses, as opposed to older ones, was
largely carried out by purchasers, who were primarily interested
in self-advertisement.

Once antiquarianism had gained acceptance in the Victorian period, fashion was no longer a primary consideration in dealing
with an old house, but there were insistent pressures for expansion
of size. New wings sprouted in profusion, specialized rooms were
tacked on here and there, and rambling servants' quarters were
added at one side, concealed so far as possible by thick shrubbery.
In Northamptonshire twenty-seven houses underwent expansion,
often on a large scale, in the Victorian period. Ten added huge
new offices, one a billiard-room, one a library, two ballrooms, and
many conservatories. Thus in the Victorian period while major
rebuildings and face-liftings declined, the number of additions went
up.

v. Total Building Activity

To estimate total building activity in a county by decade involves
a good deal of more or less informed guesswork. As explained in
Appendix II, 1, units of building include new building, rebuilding, and additions, but exclude service areas, redecoration, and
grounds, although these may have accounted for one-third of the
total expenditure upon a house.

There is good reason to think that during the eighteenth century
a very great deal of money was poured into landscaping the grounds
and into more and more elaborate interior decoration and furnish-
ings. Once a house reached a certain size (and 120 units seems to
be about that size), competition took the form of internal and external aesthetic improvements rather than any further increase in
living-space. An extreme example of this development is Moor
Park. Built on a most lavish scale in the 1670s, it had wings added
in the 1720s. But also in the 1720s the original brick exterior was
entirely encased in stone, the interior was extensively remodelled
by Thornhill and Leoni, and a hill which obstructed the view was
physically removed. The total cost is said to have been as high as

£150,000, although this hardly seems credible.[10] Twenty years later, more work was done upon the interior, and the grounds were redesigned in the new romantic style with mounds, trees, a lake, and a temple. Twenty years later still in the 1760s still more interior decorative work was done, and the most expensive furniture was bought. The net result of all this activity was minimal in terms of building units, but enormous in terms of cost and aesthetic appearance. The statistical evidence at our disposal, therefore, can merely offer tentative support to the conclusions more reliably drawn by one's own eyes. Interior decoration is particularly poorly recorded since the latest fashion in decorative schemes successively destroyed older ones generation after generation until the money ran out. Major changes in parks and gardens, however, are better recorded, and for what they are worth show great activity in park construction and expansion in the eighteenth century, being overtaken by work on pleasure-gardens in the nineteenth, which is just as one would expect. New stable-building reached a peak in the first half of the eighteenth century, to be replaced by office-building in the nineteenth. All this merely offers tentative statistical confirmation of the visual impression presented by country houses today. Taken together, however, the statistics of work on interior decoration, stabling, and grounds suggest that in the eighteenth century an exceptional proportion of the total expenditure on country houses was being spent on these aesthetic improvements which cannot be quantified. In terms of money spent, the overall activity in the eighteenth century must have been significantly higher than indicated merely by house construction.

In the nineteenth century, concern shifted to the construction of huge rambling servants' quarters, no longer in the attic and basement as had been the eighteenth-century fashion, but now above ground, stretching endlessly out from the house along dark and dismal corridors. No fewer than thirty-one of these massive excrescences were built in Northamptonshire alone between 1800 and 1870, and about as many again in Hertfordshire. None of these activities count as units of building, which reduces the usefulness of Table 11.5, since the figures for the last two centuries are probably too low compared with those of the first two.

This bias in the data base will not, however, affect the evidence for some remarkable differences in the trends of recorded building activity over three and one-half centuries between the three counties (Table 11.9, Fig. 11.8). Hertfordshire started at an all-time

[10] E. W. Brayley, *The Beauties of England and Wales*, London, vii, 1806, p. 312.

FIG. 11.8   Total Building Activity in 'Units' per Decade (30-year Moving Averages)
[Table 11.9]

high in the 1540s, as gentry and courtiers were busy converting
ex-monastic buildings and erecting new houses on ex-Church and
ex-Crown lands. Activity dropped to a near all-time low between
1620 and 1640, for reasons that are wholly obscure, and then picked
up sharply again during the Interregnum, almost entirely because
of new building by London merchants looking for a secure investment for their money. Activity remained sluggish through the late
seventeenth and early eighteenth centuries, falling to a new low in
the 1740s and 1750s. Thereafter, however, there occurred the great
boom of the period 1760 to 1820, when rents were rocketing and
new men were moving rapidly into the area. The slump of 1820
to 1840 was presumably caused by the depressed condition of agricultural rents, and the subsequent boom to their sharp recovery
and to a fresh influx of self-made men. By and large, and with the
striking exception of the Interregnum in the seventeenth century
when exceptional conditions prevailed, the trend of building activity in Hertfordshire followed the index of rents fairly closely.

Northamptonshire marched to a different drummer. The great
building boom of 1570 to 1610 had left the squirearchy over-ex-

tended and over-housed, and it is hardly surprising that there followed a seventy-year slump lasting into the 1660s. Thereafter, activity picked up, largely stimulated by the need to adapt the old Elizabethan houses to the new Baroque and then Palladian tastes. This flurry of activity lasted to 1770 and then petered out, the county sinking into a kind of lethargic apathy that was wholly unresponsive either to changing stylistic tastes for Gothic or Victorian architecture or to rapidly rising rents during the Napoleonic wars. Only the last phase of agricultural prosperity, from 1860 to 1880, managed to generate a certain amount of renewed building. By and large, however, large-scale building or expanding of country houses petered out in Northamptonshire after 1740, which makes that county today such an extraordinary open-air museum of sixteenth-, seventeenth-, and early eighteenth-century architecture.

Northumberland is wholly different again in the evolution of its country-house building. It started late and from small beginnings in the seventeenth century, and only really took off after the opening-up of the countryside to agricultural improvement in the 1730s. It too shared with Hertfordshire the boom in building during the heady days of the Napoleonic wars, but the Victorian period saw an extraordinary slump. Astonishingly little of the profits of Newcastle coal got ploughed back into country-house building in Northumberland during the nineteenth century, although some of it probably went into building south of the river in County Durham.

It cannot be denied that there are a lot of unsolved problems in this story. Why were the Northamptonshire squirearchy so totally unenterprising in building between 1740 and 1860? What did they do with their money in the times of unparalleled prosperity for the landed classes? All that can be said is that this conservatism exactly matches their lack of enthusiasm for higher education or a professional career, and their unwillingness to admit newcomers into their company. It was for the most part a hidebound, dull, inward-turned, and stuffy society, obsessed with horses, dogs, and hunting. Their architectural lethargy matches their inactivity in other spheres of life. In Hertfordshire, the two great slumps in building activity in the 1620s and 1630s and the 1740s and 1750s are even more difficult to explain. The trend in Northumberland offers no problems, except the lack of response in country-house building to the enormous new wealth being generated on Tyneside during the Victorian period.

Despite its undeniable limitations, Figure 11.8 does suggest several things. The first is the quite exceptional character of the explosion of building, at any rate in Southern and Midlands England, during the period 1540-1620, the classic age of the rise of the gentry. The second is that except very near London, the Victorian building boom is something of a myth. The third is that there is no uniform pattern across the length and breadth of England, each region following a different path of activity. Major trends in the profits to be derived from land are all obviously important, but money flowed into the countryside from so many other sources, such as office, the professions, banking, war, marriage, and overseas trade, that there is no clear correlation between building and rents. Indeed this is hardly to be expected, since the decision to build is so highly personal a matter, dependent upon so many considerations.

2. BUILDERS

When considering the building activity of owners, it is important not to lose sight of those factors which may act as a spur to building, for example if the house has suffered a fire or a period of neglect, is old or out of fashion, too small or too large, or alternatively if the owner is temporarily out of office and needs something to occupy him, or has benefited from a financial windfall. Other factors might act as deterrents, for example if a house passes from father to elder son for several generations, or if another more desirable house is meanwhile acquired. (Plate IIIA.) Moreover, in the case of owners of more than one house, not necessarily in the same county, the seat might be used as a main or secondary residence, or in the cases of Hertfordshire and to a lesser extent Northumberland, as a suburban seat, and these uses might change over time and affect the ultimate fate of the house. Finally, when considering the financing of house-purchase or building, an important factor is potential access to non-landed sources of wealth.

i. Builders and Major Builders

The concept of 'builders' has been defined in two ways. First there are those owners who carried out any alterations or additions to house, offices, or grounds. This includes anyone who did any noticeable tinkering with the internal or external appearance of his seat or its environment, regardless of whether or not it produced units of buildings. The second definition of 'major builders' means owners who made alterations or additions which resulted in fifty or more units of additional building for family accommodation;

that is men who made significant alterations to the size, appearance, and status of their seats.

The proportion of owners in all three counties who carried out building work of some sort varied considerably over time (Table 11.10, Fig. 11.9). The proportion was highest in Hertfordshire and Northamptonshire during the great acquisitive and building boom of the late sixteenth century, and was highest in Northumberland in the early seventeenth century. Only about two-thirds as many owners built in the seventeenth century as did in the sixteenth, presumably because most of them were by now adequately housed by the standards of their age, at any rate in Hertfordshire and Northamptonshire. Between 1700 and 1820, however, about 40 per cent of all owners did something to their houses, even if it was only a classical refacing or addition. (Plate XIV.) Although the volume of building remained quite high in Victorian England, there were fewer owners who actually did anything. If one looks at the figures decade by decade the proportion fell from a high of 45 per cent of owners who built in the 1800s to a low of 25 per cent in the 1860s and 1870s. This is a not unexpected find-

FIG. 11.9   Builders and Major Builders as a Proportion of Owners [Table 11.10]

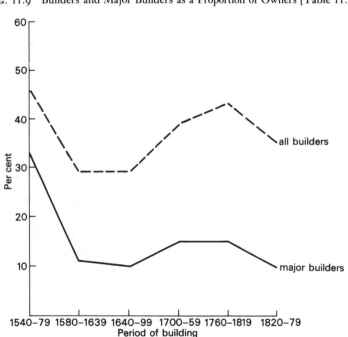

ing, which coincides with other evidence of a more conservative attitude amongst most large landowners in the nineteenth century. Fewer owners in the high Victorian period were tinkering with their houses than had their Georgian predecessors, although a few were making immense additions and alterations.

When it comes to major building, the basic trends are the same, but with significant modifications. The fall in the proportion of major builders to all owners from the sixteenth to the seventeenth century is even more dramatic, down to a third of the previous level: only 10 to 15 per cent of all owners were building on a large scale in the late seventeenth century. The recovery in the eighteenth century was also less marked but the fall-off in the Victorian period is identical, down to a mere 10 per cent of all owners. The graph thus tells us that in the sixteenth century and the eighteenth substantial numbers of owners tinkered with their houses, and that in the sixteenth substantial numbers carried out major building operations. Only about a third did anything to their houses in either the seventeenth century or the Victorian period, and only a tenth undertook major building operations. The real surprise about these findings is the fall-off in the number of builders, both large and small, in the Victorian period. They also bring out in a dramatic way the unparalleled scale of house-building activity in the 1540-1620 period.

ii. Propensities to Build

The next question is whether there were certain types of owners who either by temperament and inclination, or because they possessed larger capital resources, were more likely to build than others. So many variables enter into the calculation of what might induce an owner to build, including such entirely random factors as the age and physical condition of his house, that it would be rash to place too much emphasis on the differences that emerged. But some of those differences are both consistent over time and quite large, and therefore seem to be statistically meaningful.

As one might expect, there are no significant variations in the median age at which owners built, which varies from about thirty-seven to forty-five, with a tendency to rise as the median age of inheritance rose. This strongly indicates that building was a young man's fancy, usually undertaken quite soon after inheriting the estate and seat. Since purchasers tended to be rather older when they first acquired their prizes, they were naturally rather older when they built, being on the average in their forties.

Eventual inheritors who had been brought up with the expectation of younger sons until the age of twenty or more were rather more likely to carry out some building and considerably more likely to undertake major construction than their brothers who had grown up as heirs (Table 11.11). One may conclude that those brought up as younger sons with their way to make in the world had developed a more active and entrepreneurial attitude to life than their elder brothers who had grown up with the certain expectation of a comfortable inheritance. Psychological factors deriving from childhood expectations were therefore important.

Rather more striking is the contrast between those owners who had some professional occupation, and those who were content to cultivate the pleasures of being a country squire: 43 per cent of the former compared with 33 per cent of the latter did some building, while 20 per cent of the former compared with a mere 12 per cent of the latter undertook major operations. It seems likely that this difference is more a matter of money than of temperament since the discrepancy is so very much greater when it comes to major builders who needed the most money (Table 11.11). The most active builders with an occupation were business men, 47 per cent of whom built as compared with 40 per cent of office-holders and lawyers (Table 11.12). This could be either because they were richer, or, more likely, because they were more anxious to establish their mark in local society.

All these differences pale into insignificance when compared with those between owners who inherited and those who purchased or were granted their property. A third of the former did some building compared with a half of the latter. The discrepancy between the two groups as major builders is substantially greater, with purchasers two and a half times more likely to embark on such expensive operations as inheritors, a disproportion which becomes greater still if one includes those whose mode of acquisition is unknown, who are most likely to have been purchasers (Table 11.13). There can be no doubt, therefore, that the most active and energetic builders of all were new men who bought their estates and seats. Indeed newcomers generally, that is entrants of all kinds, whether rising up from the local gentry or buying their way into the elite with wealth acquired from outside, formed an exceptionally large proportion of both minor and major builders. Many of them were men with no ancestral feelings about the old house, were anxious to make a conspicuous bid for entry into the elite society, and all had—or thought they had—the financial resources to achieve their ambitions. Almost all of them built, and two-thirds of them built on a large scale. Consequently, entrants make up only a tenth of all owners but a third of all builders and an astonishing 58 per cent of them were major builders (Table 11.14).

Contemporaries noticed that new men were the most active builders, and some reacted with distaste and envy. 'Who are so arrogant, as builders' (i.e. builders of new houses)?, asked Roger North. 'Are they not, for the most part, citts (citizens), attorneys and such upstarts?' He claimed that the lowly origins of merchants turned gentry showed in the kind of houses they built: 'Nothing is more discernible than an upstart citizen or mechanic in his house. All fall to building, and constantly retain their native littleness, even when they aim at, and spend to obtain grandeur'. North thought that self-made courtiers like Secretary of State Arlington were as bad, and he had nothing but contempt for the latter's efforts at Euston Hall to build himself an imposing seat.[11] Be that as it may, it is undeniable that just when North was deploring (and Defoe praising) the building activities of wealthy men of business, a handful of company speculators, financiers, and merchants were erecting some of the most spectacular new buildings in England, all of them highly visible since very close to London.[12] Between 1715 and 1730 for example, Sir Richard Child, heir to Sir Josiah Child's East India Company fortune, was building Wanstead, Essex, probably the third largest house in England after Blenheim and Castle Howard; before he fell victim to the South Sea Bubble crash, Sir Theodore Janssen was building himself a huge house at Wimbledon, Surrey; Robert Knight, also a beneficiary then victim of the South Sea Company, was building Luxborough House, Essex; Sir Benjamin Styles, yet another South Sea speculator, was rebuilding Moor Park, Herts.; and Sir Gregory Page was at work on Wricklemarsh, Kent. Finally, the great government financier, James Brydges Duke of Chandos, was constructing the most lavish pleasure-palace of all at Cannons in Middlesex, and thus gaining a dubious immortality by being satirized by Pope and praised by Defoe. He too came to a bad end, according to Swift, losing in stock speculation all that he had gained in fraud in office, and on his death his house and all its contents were sold. There can be no doubt that this handful of tycoons made a marked impression upon contemporaries, and gave new life to the old belief in a massive shift of monied men into the landed elite.

[11] R. North, op. cit., pp. 30, 8-9, 142-3. For a picture of this pretentious French-style château, see J. Harris, *The Artist and the Country House*, London, 1979, fig. 52.

[12] J. Summerson, 'The Classical Country House in Eighteenth Century England', *Journal of the Royal Society of the Arts*, cvii, 1959, p. 551.

iii. Financial Ruin by Building

As has been seen in Chapter x, part 2, for centuries it was widely believed in gentry circles that excessive building was a frequent cause of family ruin. It has already been demonstrated that few established families in fact were ever forced to sell the ancestral seat for financial reasons (Table 5.2). It can also be shown that only a small proportion of those few who did sell were forced into it by personal extravagance in building. Only nineteen of all the 218 inheritors who sold and a mere seven who were not new entrants into the sample undertook major building which may have been the cause of their downfall (Table 11.15). If one confines oneself to those inheritor-sellers whose families were already in the sample there are at most only seven men from established elite families in three counties over a 340-year period who, so far as we know, can have been forced to sell the family seat at least in part because of their own recklessly extravagant building ventures. This does not preclude the probability, indeed the certainty, that there were a good many more who were forced to sell because of the imprudent building of an ancestor.

The reason for these tiny numbers of inheritor-owners who sold their seats after major building is that when costs began to get out of hand, they had many ways of recouping or retrenching. Sometimes the building was simply left unfinished until the money became available once more. In houses this large it was quite easy to leave a section unused. This was true of the new building of Broadfield Hall, Herts., which was interrupted to allow for a period of retrenchment. This is also true of Boughton House, Northants., in the late seventeenth century, one of whose wings is still unfinished today; and also in the eighteenth century of some of the rooms in the new wing at Hitchin Priory, Herts., until the heiress of the builder married the son of a banker. In any case the elite were all men with large resources and extensive lines of credit and there were many ways of retrenchment available to them. There was retirement to London or abroad, the allocation of property to trustees to liquidate debts out of income, marriage with an heiress, sale of outlying properties or woods, any of which could and usually did avoid the final humiliation of the sale of the seat. Financial decay was normally a slow process which took several generations of consistently repeated folly to force a family into bankruptcy. As a result, some of the most dramatic cases of recklessly extravagant building on record, such as those of the Verneys of Claydon House or the Temples of Stowe, caused heavy debts and an inability to keep up the house, but did not lead to actual sale.[13] At this elevated level of society, total disasters within a single generation were rare, and those attributable to building extravagance were rarer still.

The worst that might happen in the sixteenth and seventeenth centuries was a slow, multigenerational slide back or down into parish-gentry income, life-style, and status. In the eighteenth century, a more probable fate was to become a 'ghost' member of the elite, like Sir Walter Elliott, baronet, in Jane Austen's *Persuasion* who let his seat in the country and moved to Bath. In 1854, William Nelson Clarke asked, 'if family histories were known how many a decay of their worldly prosperity might be traced to its fountainhead in the vanity which prompted the erection of a stately mansion?'[14] The answer to his question seems to be perhaps a fair number of parish gentry, but very few of the county elite, certainly far fewer than those which sank because of demographic factors. It was rather lower down in the socio-economic scale, at the middling and lower gentry level, that overbuilding appears to have been at its most destructive. 'How many moderate estates had been sunk in a house and garden that have never been finished, or if they were could not have been maintained?', asked Peregrine Bertie in the 1730s. For the 'moderate estates' he was talking about the answer was probably many. But for the established elite, ruin from overbuilding was rather like the sale of the ancestral seat to an upstart merchant: it was more talked about than frequent in real life.

It has already been seen that newcomers were great builders. It was widely believed that they were also especially prone to overbuilding. They were men who had made their fortunes, bought estates, and were now anxious to make a visible display of their wealth. 'I live in an age', concluded Bertie, 'when men seem to desire to get estates, only to build fine houses and make great gardens. . . . What follies have wise men fallen into when they have got this itch'.[15] The fate of such men was disputed at length in Vanbrugh's play *The Country House*, in which a new purchaser complains that the cost of running his seat was ruining him.[16] Such over-extended purchasers probably figure among the purchaser-

[13] *Verney Letters of the Eighteenth Century*, ed. M. M. Verney, London, 1930, Chs. xxxv and xxxvi; *Country Life*, xxxv, 1914.
[14] W. N. Clarke, *Memorials of his Family*, London, 1854, p. 42.
[15] P. Bertie, 'On Oeconomie', in *A Memoir of Peregrine Bertie*, London, 1838, p. 114.
[16] *The Complete Works of Sir John Vanbrugh*, ed. B. Dobrée and G. Webb, ii, 1927, p. 218.

sellers in Hertfordshire between 1770 and 1820, when a large
number of houses changed hands rapidly. It is interesting to note
that in all three counties over 60 per cent of all purchasers and
purchaser-entrants who subsequently sold in their own lifetime
had been major builders (Table 11.15). It seems unlikely that those
who had had no intention of settling down would have put themselves to the gross inconvenience and heavy expense of major
building operations. It was thus middle-aged new men, in a hurry
to establish their claims to elite status, who were most likely to
overreach themselves and as a result be obliged to sell again. Bertie
and Vanbrugh were right: imprudent builders who came to ruin
were indeed mostly over-ambitious new men.

3. CONCLUSION

All but the last two of these conclusions about those most likely
to build or not to build were fairly predictable. Despite the importance of random variables such as chance, personality, and
fashion, the propensity to build was clearly linked to two factors:
energy and ambition, combined with at least some of the necessary
financial resources. New men on the way up had more of the first,
and sometimes of the second, than those who inherited their seats
from their fathers. Persons with some experience of an official,
professional or business career also tended to have more of the first
than mere country squires. Whether temperament or money was
the more important variable is something which mere statistics
cannot be coaxed into revealing. On the other hand, the large
number of purchasers—and especially purchaser-sellers—who were
major builders suggests that psychology was a more important
stimulus than capital. Builders were, and are, men eager for change,
ambitious to leave their distinctive mark upon their seat or grounds.
They also hoped or believed that they were in command of the
financial resources to convert their dreams into bricks and mortar.
Many left their posterity overhoused for daily needs; a number
built beyond their resources and burdened their successors with a
heavy load of debt; and a few, mostly newcomers, over-extended
themselves and sold out in their own lifetimes. Despite legend,
however, very few owners of established families miscalculated so
wildly as to be forced to sell both house and estate, thus achieving
the permanent ruin of their families. Overbuilding, excessive generosity to too many surviving children, and gambling were the
three major causes of heavy capital expenditure and a mounting

burden of debt, but of the three building seems to have been less frequently the cause of financial disaster than the other two.

Since over a third of all owners did *something* to their house or grounds and one in seven did a great deal, there are very few houses today which have survived intact over several centuries. Almost all have lost their pre-1740 gardens and grounds, which formed an essential backdrop to the houses themselves. Almost all have been redecorated and refurnished internally century after century. Many have been refaced at one stage or another. Many have been added to or reduced as fashion or fortune have dictated. With a few remarkable exceptions, English country houses are thus palimpsests, reflecting the changing tastes and ambitions of many generations of owners. Some of these owners treated their inheritance with a proper respect for its past, but many did not. As the houses stand today, they are a visual record of the aspirations of many generations of country-house owners, who demonstrated their aspirations to status or fashion, pleased themselves and occupied their time by tinkering with or radically altering the physical environment in which they lived. Comfort did not normally rank very high on their list of priorities, so that the country houses we see today are an aggregate over a long period of time of responses primarily to changing aesthetic tastes and rising status aspirations of successive owners and their wives.

Part IV

CONCLUSION

XII

THE LANDED ELITE AND
ENGLISH SOCIETY

1. THE FORMATION OF THE ELITE 1540-1660

In any hierarchically organized society based on the principle of deference to the privilege of birth, recruitment to the elite is theoretically hereditary, usually in the male line. In practice this is a demographically impossible ideal in the long run, since the male line is always failing. Consequently, a major problem confronting any hereditary elite is whence and how to recruit new members when, as it invariably does, the system of primogeniture fails to provide suitable replacements. Attrition in the direct male line may be corrected by inheritance through distant male relatives or females. In the latter case, this means the absorption of their husbands into the elite into which these women were born, in the case of England by the process of name-changing. More serious are the problems that arise from the attrition of talent among the descendants of the former power elite, whose membership of the social and economic elite is ensured by primogeniture. In classical Rome and China this was handled by adoption, a device also used in modified form in the West in early modern and modern times. In the Middle Ages, the Church could be relied on to produce men, often of very humble birth, who possessed the requisite leadership qualities. But since these men of low origins could only rise through the Church, and were therefore theoretically and legally celibate, the problem of the assimilation of their legitimate issue into a status elite did not arise.

The Renaissance and the Reformation, however, changed the picture dramatically. The small royal household was transformed into a much larger central bureaucracy, requiring capable men willing and able to serve in it in return for a salary and access to rich perquisites and rewards. At the same time the Reformation caused the regular clergy to be disbanded and the laity to replace the secular clergy in the royal service: apart from three exceptions in the 1620s and 1630s, no clergyman has held high political office in England since Cardinal Wolsey in the 1520s. Moreover, the successful efforts of the Tudor state to limit the power and influence of local magnates meant a slow shift of the loyalties of the local gentry away from the great noble households. This process was assisted by the delegation of many of the royal powers to local squires who served as unpaid Justices of the Peace, Commissioners of Taxes, and Deputy Lieutenants for the militia, thereby binding them financially, administratively, and psychologically to the Crown.

Partly as a result of these changes, two currents flowing in the same direction came together in the sixteenth century. In order to serve the nation state as members of the new bureaucracy or as Justices of the Peace, the landed classes soon found that they needed a different type of education from the one they had previously acquired as pages in great noble households. Hitherto they had managed very well with the moral qualities of endurance, courage, loyalty, and generosity, and skills in horsemanship and hand-to-hand combat. But now success in the new administrative fields of endeavour required not only the old social graces but also trained intelligence. The heirs and younger sons of gentry soon began to flock to the Universities, where till then almost the only pupils had been poor scholars aspiring to a career in the Church. It had been well enough for the latter to be learned; but in order to qualify for the new openings in the burgeoning bureaucracy, the gentry pupils at the Universities needed to possess well-trained minds rather than a body of esoteric learning. This in turn led to significant changes in the teaching practised at the Universities, and to a short-lived but intense period of intellectual enthusiasm among the landed classes, a change which is reflected in the quality and tone of the political debates of the House of Commons in the 1620s and 1640s.

It was at this point that the old landed classes became aware of the need for a reorientation of their value system, if they were to survive and prosper. Those who stuck to the old ways soon found themselves left behind. They still owned their hereditary landholdings, but often did not have the flexibility or intelligence to accommodate themselves to the new focuses of power and patronage, to shift to the new socially rewarding modes of conspicuous consumption, or to adopt the new estate-management procedures needed to keep pace with galloping monetary inflation. Worse still, they came to be regarded in fashionable circles as defective in their education and boorish in their behaviour, a favorite butt of the London playwrights, pamphleteers, and novelists. They became the archetypal mere parish gentry.

Meanwhile, new recruits to the ruling class began to include men who had succeeded by their talents, mainly in the law or the expanding royal administration. Power and wealth was being shared with new aspirants, now including a sprinkling of business men. Ever since the mid-fifteenth century when a few of the great sheep-masters began buying their way into the Midlands county gentry, the wool trade had opened the door to a few rich merchants and graziers.[1] When the Dissolution of the Monasteries threw Church land on to the market, what had hitherto been an almost invisible seepage of outsiders into the county elites turned into a temporary flood—some small gentry, some officials, some lawyers, a few merchants. By the early seventeenth century, conservatives were protesting actively against this infiltration, and especially at infil-tration by merchants.

The newcomers included many, like the Mildmays or Cecils, who had risen in the royal administration, where they had been singularly well placed to benefit from the Dissolution. The great majority of these new men were either heirs of parish gentry or younger sons of county gentry, so that they encountered no great problem of status assimilation. The process was in any case eased by marriage into the old county elite, whose surplus daughters, now that the nunneries were dissolved, had somehow to be found husbands. However, by no means all these new men were very rich, and the period 1540-1640 witnessed the rise of some, at the expense of others who sought to consolidate their fortune too soon. Some of the latter, the declining gentry, went to the wall and vanished without trace, their lands scattered to the winds, while others seem to have settled down in the social borderland between county elite and parish gentry. In a county close to London such as Hertfordshire, they begot successive generations of minor-gen-try office-holders, both office and manor-house descending more or less together.[2]

In the late sixteenth and early seventeenth centuries, newcomers to the landed classes had begun to include a handful of men like Sir Arthur Ingram, who had succeeded entirely through trade and who had no claim, or at best a very remote one, to gentle birth.[3] The social confusion brought about by the inflation of honours, which lasted from the accession of James I in 1603 to the assassi-nation of the Duke of Buckingham in 1628, for a while threw up a flimsy smoke-screen behind which took place the metamorphosis

[1] For example, the Ishams of Lamport and the Spencers of Althorp. See M. E. Finch, *The Wealth of Five Northamptonshire Families, Northants. Record Soc.*, xix, 1955.

[2] For example, the Fanshawes of Ware Park, the Tookes of Popes and Wormleybury, and the Vernons of Hertingfordbury, in Hertfordshire.

[3] A. F. Upton, *Sir Arthur Ingram*, Oxford, 1961.

of a number of self-made men, usually government officials and lawyers, into men of elite status, and sometimes even noblemen.[4]

During the political disturbances of the seventeenth century, many thoughtful commentators reflected on the significance of the major infusions of new blood into the ranks of the squirearchy. Hence James Harrington's conclusion that the great changes in landholding since the Dissolution of the Monasteries dictated a parallel shift in the *locus* of political power, which must somehow be reflected in constitutional arrangements. Hence the conclusion of Thomas Hobbes and others that in future this mobility should somehow be stopped by government fiat and a restriction of educational opportunities in order to shore up the status quo; and hence the more realistic conclusion of the late seventeenth-century Whig grandees that an accommodation must be reached in one way or another between the now revived landed elite of aristocrats and rich squires on the one hand, and the rising professional and monied interests on the other. Gradually, the necessary symbiosis between them, within a society more oriented to the principle of possessive individualism, came to be grudgingly accepted, at least within the ruling Whig elite if not among the backwoods parish gentry and Tory squires.

2. CONTINUITY AND CRISES 1590-1880

Between 1590 and 1880 the English landed elite were remarkably successful in maintaining continuity in family names, estates, and seats. This continuity is all the more impressive since the class successfully survived a series of potentially dangerous crises. The first was the crisis of the aristocracy in the late sixteenth century, which I have dealt with elsewhere.[5] Rapid price inflation found the great nobles trapped between lagging rents, rising prices, high conspicuous consumption patterns and declining rewards from the Crown. They were saved by the lavish cornucopia of grants from the crown between 1603 and 1629, and a methodical jacking up of rents which transferred the profits from rising food prices back from the tenants to themselves. This action, however, created a crisis of confidence, a threat to the principles of paternalism and deference, which was one of several component elements in setting the stage for the next crisis, the English Revolution of the mid-seventeenth century. Revolutions normally involve a massive expropriation of one elite and their replacement by another. In Eng-

---

[4] L. Stone, *The Crisis of the Aristocracy, 1558-1641*, Oxford, 1965, Ch. III.

[5] Op. cit., passim.

land a majority of the elite sided with the King and suffered accordingly by being on the losing side. Some had most of their property confiscated outright and sold on the market and large numbers were forced to pay fines for delinquency which amounted to one or more years gross income. In practice, however, hardly any suffered irreparable losses, and the pattern of landholding in 1660, after the Restoration land settlement was over, differed hardly at all from that of the pre-war period. The elite may have been more indebted than before, they had certainly gone through a very difficult period, but they had come out of it virtually unscathed. Their incomes may have gone down dramatically for twenty years, but so had their expenditures.[6]

The next two crises came almost together. One was the late seventeenth-century decline in rents and the other the rise in land taxes, which together eroded net incomes. But both these crises were successfully weathered. They may have caused the sale of some outlying properties, but at this high social and economic level there occurred hardly any sales of ancestral seats for reasons of financial ruin.

Potentially far more serious was the failure of the elite to reproduce themselves in the late seventeenth and early eighteenth centuries, which threatened the whole group with biological decline. As a result, many landowners were having the greatest difficulty in finding adult male kin to carry on the line. The end of the war with Louis XIV and the fall of the land tax eased the financial problem, and shrewd exploitation of the device of the strict settlement and the transfer of property to adoptive kin tided the elite over the demographic crisis.

The fifth crisis, which lasted for nearly half a century from 1714 to 1760, was caused by the deliberate exclusion from public life, central and local office, and the major profession of the law, of a small but vocal minority of country squires, the Tories and radical Whigs both of whom were forced to practice 'the politics of the dispossessed'. The landed elite was thus deeply fissured for two generations, although the effects of this split on the power, prestige, and wealth of the group as a whole seem to have been negligible.[7] The reason for this absence of serious consequences is that the numbers thus excluded were relatively modest, and that though

---

[6] H. J. Habukkuk, 'Landowners and the Civil War', *Economic History Review*, 2nd series, xviii, 1965; J. Thirsk, 'The Restoration Land Settlement', *Journal of Modern History*, xxvi, 1954.

[7] L. Colley, 'Eighteenth Century English Radicalism before Wilkes', *Transactions of the Royal Historical Society*, 5th Series, 31, 1981, pp. 17-18; J. Brewer, in *Three British Revolutions*, ed. J. G. A. Pocock, Princeton, 1980, pp. 326-7.

driven to adopt radical political positions, the radicalism of the proscribed Tories always remained at a relatively moderate level. They were never tempted to overthrow the system of power and hierarchy from which they still hoped one day to profit once more.

The sixth crisis was caused inadvertently by the shift in the balance of values in the late seventeenth and eighteenth centuries from the collectivity, whether kin or nuclear family, to the individual. Inspired by this shift, heirs now pleased themselves by marrying later; by marrying brides of their choice, and therefore many fewer heiresses; by staying unmarried altogether if they were so inclined and so leaving no male heirs; and by limiting births in order to ease the strain on their wives and to improve the quality of care devoted to their children. This shift in the balance of interests from the collective to the personal, from the long-term economic ambitions of the family to the self-gratification of the individual, would have had a drastic effect upon family continuity if it had not been compensated for by a continuing strong sense of family responsibility expressed in the strict settlement.

The last and most testing challenge of all came in the nineteenth century, when the landed elite was challenged by the transforming power of the Industrial Revolution and the rise of the bourgeoisie, both industrial and professional. In the long run, the tide of change this time was irresistible and irreversible. But what is so remarkable is how long the dikes and levees withstood the rising flood before they finally began to crumble. By and large, the power, wealth, and even status of the landed elite survived more or less intact until 1880.

3. THE THEORY OF AN OPEN ELITE

i. The Myth of Upward Social Mobility.

How did the elite achieve this stability? One hypothesis has long been that they defused challenges by being exceptionally open to upward movement from below. When analysed with care, however, the actual volume of social mobility has turned out to be far less than might have been expected. Moreover, those who did move up were rarely successful men of business. Most of the newcomers were rising parish gentry or office-holders or lawyers, men from backgrounds not too dissimilar to those of the existing county elite. Only a small handful of very rich merchants succeeded in buying their way into the elite, and by the second generation they were fully assimilated. Others built or bought large country seats, but failed to purchase large estates to go with them. During the whole 340-year period covered by this study there were only 137 men of business who bought their way into the elite in our three counties. They only amount to 6 per cent of all owners, and only a third of all purchasers, the bulk of the latter being men enriched by public office or the law. The real story of the English elite is not the symbiosis of land and business, but of land and the professions, just as in the rest of Europe.

Once they had bought their seats, many of these ex-merchant owners failed to take a very active part in local affairs, and they very often sold the seats again in their lifetime or at death. Many were thus transients who left no permanent imprint on county society. What emerges, therefore, is a relatively stable core of older families, some very rich but many of moderate means; a steady flow of newcomers from office and the professions, and a periphery of less obsessively family-oriented new men, mostly from business, who were buying and then selling again a limited number of large houses with small estates attached to them. It is the relatively durable and extremely tenacious core which ensured the cultural continuity and continued social preeminence of the county elite from 1540 to 1880.

Given the very small numbers of business men who bought seats, and the large proportion of them who were merely transients who came and went in a single lifetime or at most two, the idea that the fundamental cause of English political stability has been the perennial openness of its landed elite to penetration by large numbers of newly enriched bourgeoisie is clearly no more than a hoary myth, which should now be laid reverently to rest. The traditional concept of an open elite—open to large-scale infiltration by merchant wealth—is dead. What cannot be proved is whether or not the English landed elite was less, or equally, or rather more, open to upward mobility from the business classes than those of other European countries, since no comparable study has ever been attempted. All that can be established is that the degree of upward mobility in England was surprisingly small and not of great social significance. And it may well be that, thanks to the institutionalized sale of offices, carrying noble privileges, merchant upward mobility—one generation removed—was easier and more frequent in France than in England.

It is possible, of course, that further research may succeed in saving the theory of an open gentry in England. There is now no doubt that many lesser merchants, well-to-do tradesmen, and professional men bought or built small manor-houses or villas, although how many is still an open question. But all the evidence about the behaviour of urban patriciates indicates that they mostly confined themselves to aping genteel culture and building themselves villas within commuting distance of their place of work in the city. This was a very different kind of house from a country seat. This phenomenon was first noticed by Roger North in 1698, 'The country model, and that of a suburb villa, are different. The former partakes of the nature of a court, as a lord of a manor doth of regality, and should, like the court have great rooms to contain numbers. . . . A villa is quasy a lodge, for the sake of a garden, to retire to enjoy and sleep, without pretence of entertainment of many persons'. Half a century later these small houses springing up all around London attracted the attention of Horace Walpole, who commented sarcastically in 1741, 'I perceive now that there is peculiar to us middling houses: how smug they are!' Exactly forty years later, another perceptive observer, James Boswell noticed the same phenomenon on the road from Woodford in Essex to London, and tried to make a joke out of it. 'Observing many boxes on the road today, I said they should all be rented by poets, for it would require a great deal of imagination to suppose them country houses'.[8] North, Walpole, and Boswell were all snobbishly condescending, but the last two recognized the phenomenon of a very different kind of country house from those lived in by the elite. It was compact, on a much smaller scale, and used by prosperous members of the 'middling sort' as a rural retreat from the noise and stench and stress of London. North is apparently the very first to use the word villa and to remark on its development as a house in the country, as distinct from a country house with its social and administrative functions.

It was only at the end of the eighteenth century, after the villa had been in existence for a century, that it was finally given a clear sociological and architectural definition. In 1793 a London architect, Charles Middleton, described the villa in the following terms:

Villas may be considered under three different descriptions: first as the occasional and temporary retreats of the nobility and persons of fortune from what may be called their town residence, and must, of course, be in the vicinity of the metropolis; secondly as the country houses of wealthy citizens and persons in official stations, which also cannot be far removed from the capital; and thirdly, the smaller kind of provincial edifices, considered either as hunting seats or the habitations of country gentlemen

---

[8] R. North, *Of Building*, p. 62; *Horace Walpole's Correspondence*, ed. W. S. Lewis, New Haven, 1937-80, xvii, p. 142; *Private Papers of James Boswell*, xiv, p. 194.

of moderate fortune. Elegance, compactness and convenience are the characteristics of such buildings . . . , in contradistinction to the magnificence and extensive range of the country seats of our nobility and opulent gentry.[9]

There are several points to note about this remarkable passage. The first is that it comes from a book about cottages, farmhouses, and villas, in this ascending order of importance and magnitude, and regards country seats of the landed elite as something very different. It sees a clear architectural and functional distinction between the compact and unpretentious villas of the parish gentry and middle classes and the seats of the landed elite. Middleton thus lends contemporary support for the distinction between these two classes of landowners which is central to the argument of this book. He also supports Walpole and Boswell in finding villas peculiarly common around London, being used as weekend and summer country retreats for rich city merchants, officials, professional men, and members of the elite confined to London. This had been happening as early as the late seventeenth century, for example the suburban villa built by Sir Stephen Fox, and by the 1740s the banks of the Thames up-river were lined with such buildings.[10] Lord Burlington's villa and that of Pope are two of the most famous of the genre, one built by an aristocrat and the other by a professional man. The clear identification of the villa and its functions thus helps not only to reinforce the concept of a landed elite of 'nobility and opulent gentry' as distinct from the ruck of parish gentry, but also to explain the peculiar social and architectural configuration of a county like Hertfordshire so near to London.

ii. Explanations for the Myth

If the paradigm of an open elite is dead, what urgently needs explaining is why the myth has enjoyed such extraordinary longevity and ubiquity, accepted as it has been from the fifteenth to the twentieth centuries, and by Englishmen and foreigners alike. There is no easy answer to this question. It does seem to have been based partly upon a misapprehension, a mistaking of the particular for the general. Those exceptions, when they occurred, tended to be

[9] C. Middleton, *Picturesque and Architectural Views of Cottages, Farm Houses and Country Villas*, London, 1793, p. 9, quoted in J. Summerson, 'The Classical Country House in Eighteenth Century England', *Journal of the Royal Society of Arts*, cvii, 1959, p. 571.

[10] See above, p. 249. For the proliferation of suburban villas, see John Rocque's 1746 *Exact Survey of the City of London, Westminster, ye Borough of Southwark and the Country near 10 Miles round London*.

men who were lucky enough to live a very long time, long enough to accumulate great fortunes, and still have time to retire and establish themselves in the countryside. They were demographically unusual because of their longevity, as well as psychologically unusual in their willingness to withdraw large sums of capital from business in order to put it into land and country-house living. There can be no doubt that the influx of mercantile wealth into land in the late sixteenth- and early seventeenth-century and the elevation of a few very conspicuous self-made men into the titular aristocracy did much to establish the myth on a firm basis, although it certainly existed in the early sixteenth century before the seizure and dispersal of Church properties. Thereafter generation after generation of socially conservative commentators took one or two merchants like Arthur Ingram or Lionel Cranfield, Josiah Child or James Bateman, as representatives of a whole army of invading *nouveaux riches*. In literature Sir Giles Overreach was the literary model of the successful English merchant and became a stock figure on the English stage for over a century.

This suggests that one reason for the myth was the very conservatism of English elite society, its nervousness about accepting base-born *nouveaux riches* into its bosom, which led to grossly exaggerated fears of social derogation on the basis of a handful of atypical examples. These examples certainly achieved extreme prominence, by climbing into the higher ranks of the titular aristocracy like Lionel Cranfield, Earl of Middlesex, or James Brydges, Duke of Chandos, and by the often spectacular appearance of their houses, which drew exaggerated attention to their owners.

Another cause for the perpetuation of the myth may have been a confusion between the undoubted purchase of land by merchants as a secure form of investment, with a desire by them to establish an elite county family by purchasing a seat and adopting the way of life of a country squire. No doubt the construction of villas, in fact merely as comfortable country retreats around London and other big cities, added to this confusion. Whether the English bourgeoisie invested more heavily in land, or built more rural villa retreats than their equivalents on the Continent is not at all clear. It may possibly be so, since in Europe there were attractive alternative forms of secure investment, namely government *rentes* and the purchase of state offices.

Finally it seems likely that the myth perpetuated itself by dint of repetition, as myths have a way of doing. Commentators, especially foreigners, tend to repeat one another, and so the false notion is passed on from generation to generation. And yet this will not do. One is left with a feeling that if the hypothesis of frequent upward social mobility by the bourgeoisie in England is false, there must be some other explanation why the myth seemed plausible to generation after generation of intelligent observers. It is unlikely that men as astute as Arthur Young, Adam Smith and Tocqueville were wholly wrong. It is to an alternative interpretation of a basic paradigm of English social history that we must now turn.

4. THE CAUSES OF ELITE STABILITY

If massive and easy upward mobility of new commercial or industrial wealth into the landed elite is not the key to the peculiarity of English social and political history, then what is? The solution lies in psychological attitudes and cultural perceptions, many of them embodied in customary or statute law, that were generally accepted both by the English elite and by the classes below them.

i. The Absence of Legal Privileges

It is impossible to underestimate the importance in English society of the almost total absence of the complex hierarchy of legal privileges which separated status groups or geographical areas one from another in Continental Europe. Thus the only legal privileges in England were that peers were immune from arrest for debt, and could be tried for felony by their peers instead of by an ordinary jury. No other status groups, baronets, knights, squires or gentlemen, possessed any legal exemptions whatsoever. Second, noone in England could claim tax exemption by virtue of his rank, status, office, or place of residence: all were theoretically equal, whatever the reality might be. Third, the younger sons of the nobility did not inherit titles and by the rule of preferential primogeniture were likely to be downwardly mobile, unless they pulled themselves back up by their own exertions in some occupation or profession.

The causes of these differences are not clear, but they must surely be connected with the extraordinary power of the monarchy in England in the early middle ages and again in the Tudor period, which made it unnecessary to grant these manifold concessions to special interest groups; the second was the relatively light burden of war taxation due to the lack of need for a large standing army in the sixteenth and seventeenth centuries. The English government, unlike the French, therefore, was not obliged to resort to a massive programme of sale of offices, some carrying with them noble status, tax exemptions, and hereditary tenure. Consequently in England there was no need for a legal distinction between a *noblesse d'épée* and a *noblesse de robe*. Only during the period of reckless creations from 1618-28 did there even begin to develop much of a sense of difference between the old nobility of several generations and the newly elevated. One generation of nobility sufficed in England to give the heir of a new man equality of status, just as did one generation of gentility. What mattered was appropriate education and manners, not the length of a pedigree. In England the key concept of gentility was more dilute and ill-defined than on the Continent. But it certainly existed, and the failure of Victorian industrialists to break into elite society before 1880 was due in part to the fact that they were so obviously *not* gentlemen.

ii. Cultural Cohesion with the Middling Sort

English society was given a basic fluidity of status by the vigour, wealth, and numerical strength of the 'middling sort', mostly rural but also urban, whose emergence between 1660 and 1800 is perhaps the most important social feature of the age. In the first place there was a huge expansion of the professions. The armed forces and the public administration both expanded enormously in order to fight the 125-year war for world hegemony with the French from 1689 to 1814. At the same time a host of new professional men sprang up to provide services to an increasingly affluent and consumer-oriented society. Doctors, apothecaries, architects, dancing masters, musicians, schoolteachers, attorneys, secretaries, clerks, etc. all increased greatly in numbers and wealth, the only professional groups to decline in numbers (but not in wealth) being the clergy and the barristers.[11] In addition, there was a steady increase in the prosperity of merchants and tradesmen of all kinds, as both overseas commerce spread around the world, and internal exchange of goods was stimulated by improvements in the road system thanks to the turnpikes. The essential significance of this growth is that it blurred the old distinction between the gentlemen and the rest of the population. Attempts to describe eighteenth-century society as dichotomized between 'patricians' and 'plebeians' are doomed to failure since they neglect the critical significance of the rise of the middling sort.[12] In 1741 Horace Walpole wrote that

[11] G. Holmes, 'The Professions and Social Change in England, 1680-1730', *Proceedings of the British Academy*, lxv, 1979.

[12] E. P. Thompson, 'Patrician Society, Plebeian Culture', *Journal of Social History*, 7, 1974. Mr Thompson has done more than any other scholar to illuminate eighteenth-century English society. But I regard his neglect of the 'middling sort' as a very serious flaw in his work.

'there was nowhere but in England the distinction of the middling people'. In the early nineteenth century, David Robinson clumsily but shrewdly made the same point: 'with us, the space between the ploughman and the peer is crammed with circle after circle, fitted in the most admirable manner for sitting upon each other, for connecting the former with the latter, and for rendering the whole perfect in cohesion, strength and beauty'.[13]

What makes the rise of this middling sort so crucial is their attitude towards their social superiors. Instead of resenting them, they eagerly sought to imitate them, aspiring to gentility by copying the education, manners, and behaviour of the gentry. They sent their children to boarding-schools to learn social graces, they withdrew their wives from work to put them in the parlour to drink tea, they patronized the theatres, the music-rooms, the print shops, and the circulating libraries, and they read the newspapers, the magazines, and the novels. Their attitude thus provided the glue which bound together the top half or more of the nation by means of an homogenized culture of gentility that left elite hegemony unaffected.

A striking piece of evidence of the extent of this cultural mimicry of the elite by the middling sort is the story of the last phase of the code of honour of the duel, the last death caused by which occurred as late as 1852. It is surprising enough to find that almost up to the end judges and jurors were refusing to bring in a verdict of murder against a gentleman who killed his opponent in a fair fight according to the established rules. Three hundred years of fulminations by the clergy that this was an un-Christian practice had had no effect at all, since society at large continued to regard the passive acceptance of a public insult as a proof of cowardice. Far more important for the purpose of this argument is the fact that in the early nineteenth century this elite code was adopted by members of the middling sort. In 1812, Lord Chief Justice Ellenborough complained bitterly of having to spend his time on litigation arising from challenges to duels from merchants and tradesmen. He argued that 'really it was high time to stop this spurious chivalry of the counting-house and the counter'. There can be no more convincing proof of the persistence of elite cultural dominance than this aping of a peculiarly aristocratic value by middle-class people in the early nineteenth century.[14]

[13] Horace Walpole's Correspondence, ed. W. S. Lewis, xvii, p. 142; R. Porter, English Society in the Eighteenth Century, London, 1982, p. 64.
[14] D. T. Andrew, 'The Code of Honour and its Critics: the Opposition to Duelling in England, 1799-1850', Social History, 4, 1980.

This cult of gentility spread astonishingly far down the social scale, and Thomas Raybould provides a vivid example of how a prosperous, semi-educated artisan in the late eighteenth century began to aspire to the airs and graces of his superiors. Raybould was a scythe and spade manufacturer in Staffordshire, who in about 1790 was employing twenty or more workmen in his forge, and enjoying a net income of about £100 a year. His wife claimed that they lived 'in a very genteel style, and visited and were visited by genteel people of their neighbourhood'. Thomas admitted that they lived 'in a very genteel style', but the assertion is somewhat blunted by the pitiful handful of silverware which was all that he claimed to possess. His aspirations for full admission to gentlemanly status, however, are fully exposed in a poorly spelled and rather ungrammatical letter to his wife, written in 1789. 'Don't suffer Mary Mogg to sit at table with you to drink tea, as it does certainly let you down very much, as it is a very odd affair if you cannot look upon yourself as a gentlewoman, and let her sit at the ironing table. If your mother suffers such things, it is what no gentlewoman does, therefore you must not'. He goes on, 'I am determined you shall never carry a basket to market as long as you are my wife, but the way I have mentioned [sending a respectable neighbour's wife] is the proper way of doing it 'til you have a servant'.[15] Encapsulated in this letter is the ambition of a rising artisan to train his wife to practice genteel habits, to associate on an equal basis only with those of his station, and personally to withdraw from such active physical work as going to market. She was to behave as a lady of leisure, and by doing so help to raise his own status to that of a gentleman.

However it was achieved, the fact remains that the great strength of the English landed elite was its success in psychologically co-opting those below them into the status hierarchy of gentility. While in France, Arthur Young observed that 'At an English nobleman's house there would have been three or four farmers asked to meet me, who would have dined with the family. . . . It is, however, a thing that in the present manners in France would never be met with from Calais to Bayonne'. At Houghton, Sir Robert Walpole sat down to dinner with 'Lords Spiritual and Temporal, besides commoners, parsons and freeholders innumerable'. Understandably irritated at England's obstinate refusal to conform to the Marxist stage model of dialectical historical change and therefore to start a proletarian revolution, in 1858 Engels com-

[15] Lambeth Palace, Court of Arches MSS, Process Book D 1793, p. 69.

plained to Marx that 'this most bourgeois of all nations is apparently aiming ultimately at the possession of a bourgeois aristocracy and a bourgeois proletariat *as well as* a bourgeoisie'.[16] In fact, however, Engels had got it the wrong way round; England was developing an aristocratic bourgeoisie, not a bourgeois aristocracy. The perfect example of the attitude of the self-made manufacturer of the early Industrial Revolution is not that of those well-known figures Sir Richard Arkwright and Sir Robert Peel, who acquired titles, bought estates, built country houses and founded landed families. It is rather that of the great hosiery manufacturer Jebediah Strutt. In 1774 he wrote a letter to his eighteen-year-old heir which perfectly expresses his disdain for founding a county family, but his passionate desire that his son acquire all the cultural trappings of gentility. After reading Lord Chesterfield's *Letters*, he pressed the book on the young man, remarking:

I need not tell you that you are not to be a nobleman nor prime minister, but you may possibly be a tradesman of some eminence. You may be assured if you add to the little learning and improvement you have hitherto had, the manners, the air, the genteel address, and polite behaviour of a gentleman, you will abundantly find your account in it in all and every transaction of your future life—when you come to do business in the world. It is impossible for you now to think how necessary it is to have these accomplishments as well as those of a more solid or more important nature—you may believe me in this, for I now feel the want of them by dear experience.[17]

During the eighteenth century, there occurred the gentrification of the great overseas merchants of London, the bankers and the brewers, as well as the merchant elite of what at first sight might appear very unpromising cities like Hull or Leeds. In the nineteenth century, the process spread to a very large sector of the bourgeoisie, namely the professional classes, the higher civil servants, the commercial, monied and managerial classes generally, and even, as we have seen, to some of the northern captains of industry. This cultural assimilation was achieved primarily through a common education in a few exclusive and expensive reformed 'public schools'. Here boys drawn freely from all these groups were indoctrinated in the values of the classics and muscular Christianity. These values stressed the sense of imperial paternal-

[16] R. Porter, op. cit., p. 79; *Marx-Engels: Selected Correspondence 1846-95*, London, 1936, pp. 115-16. I owe this reference to Professor R. M. Hartwell.

[17] R. S. Fitton and A. P. Wadsworth, *The Strutts and the Arkwrights 1758-1830*, Manchester, 1958, p. 145.

istic destiny, and the heavy responsibilities towards the rest of the world borne by the Anglo-Saxon ruling class. With this was coupled the development of a professional imperial civil service, entry into the administrative ranks of which was virtually confined to public schoolboys, and especially those who had gone on to (by now reformed) Oxford or Cambridge, and were trained to succeed in the entrance examinations. At the same time there took place the great expansion of London club life, where members of this now culturally homogenized ruling elite could socialize and help each other in their careers.

Engels, in short, had got something else wrong. The explanation of what happened in the nineteenth century was not the rise of an industrial bourgeoisie, who in fact got little reward for their labours except money. Both status and power eluded them. Nor does the explanation lie in the emergence of a bourgeois landed elite, who in fact became more isolated and stand-offish rather than less; but rather in the rise of an imperial service elite, purified by religion of its Regency decadence, which shared the power and the glory with a newly-risen gentrified, professionalized, and bureaucratized bourgeoisie. It was only by the 1890s, when standards were slipping, that some 25 per cent of the titular nobility had accepted (largely honorific) directorships on the boards of British companies.[18] This was the first breach in the near total physical isolation of the landed elite from the new industrial base of England's greatness.

iii. Paternalism

Apart from the rise, and homogenizing aspirations for gentility, of the middling sort, the other great cultural fact which enabled the elite to remain on top for so long without serious challenge from below was their assumption of an attitude of self-conscious paternalism, which governed their relations with their social inferiors. They were certain they knew what was right and just, and this certainty guided their actions within their sphere of influence in the countryside. Paternalism presupposes an inegalitarian, unchanging, hierarchical, social order where everyone has his place and stays in it, under the protection and direction of his superiors. This imposed a number of moral obligations upon the elite, as well as providing them with a self-confident arrogance which enabled them to behave with extreme selfishness when their own interests were at stake.

[18] G. E. Cokayne, *Complete Peerage*, v, appendix C.

The sense of *noblesse oblige* manifested itself in many ways. At times of harvest failure, the landed elite were expected to sympathize with community concepts of the just price, and even with the moral economy of a mob of grain rioters. Although in the eighteenth century they transferred the greatest burden of taxation to the poor through the excise, they also voted to impose an equally severe land tax upon themselves, which in times of war amounted to four shillings in the pound, or 20 per cent of nominal gross income. This self-imposed tax amounted to at least 25 per cent of the total net income of the state.[19] In the war crisis of 1793-1815 they deliberately raised progressive taxes on luxury goods and services. They served as an unpaid local bureaucracy, which acted not only to maintain order, punish rogues, raise taxation, and repress lower-class bastardy, but also to provide necessary welfare services to the deserving poor on a scale larger, more universal, and more humane than any other in Europe, at any rate before 1834. It would be as naïve to suggest that they performed these voluntary unpaid duties primarily or exclusively from a sense of moral duty as it would be to argue that they were activated solely by a desire to enhance their prestige and local power. At work there was surely a combination of both, and when the sense of duty became slack and the prestige small, as in the eighteenth century, many neglected to serve at all.

These members of the elite also paid their share of the poor rate, carried exclusively by the richest quarter of the community, and were reasonably generous in life and in death in supporting local charities, such as schools and hospitals and almshouses. They reacted fiercely in the House of Commons to any threat to their own or others' traditional liberties, defeating Walpole's Excise Bill in 1733 for fear of a prying national police force, and struggling to limit the powers of government to control press criticism. They were, if anything, more fearful of bureaucratic and military oppression than they were of popular disorder and rebellion. So weak were their armed forces that the Jacobite rebel army of 1745 was allowed to march as far as Derby, only 130 miles from London. So legally hamstrung were the forces of order that the Gordon rioters of 1780 were allowed to burn and loot at will in the streets of London for several days until the King took the law into his own hands and ordered in the troops. Abroad, England was one of the most powerful and aggressive states in Europe, capable

---

[19] I owe this information to Professor John Brewer, calculated from the figures in B. R. Mitchell and P. Deane, *Abstract of British Historical Statistics*, Cambridge, 1962.

of dominating the sea-lanes of the world and seizing an empire, and eventually world hegemony, from the French; at home, its leaders were prepared to tolerate the rampages of an ungovernable people for the sake of preserving the liberties of gentlemen of property. But the judges extended many of these liberties to cover large segments of the population, a fact that Wilkes was quick to observe and to exploit. Foreigners like Montesquieu or Voltaire were not wrong to regard England as the most liberal country in Europe, with the possible exception of Holland. In all areas except where foreign war was involved—that is excluding the virtually unlimited intrusive powers of the excisemen to raise money and the arbitrary kidnapping powers of the press-gang to raise men—there predominated the Lockeian liberal paradigm of the contractual state, or the neo-Harringtonian anti-statist paradigm of the Country.[20]

If the elite used the law to defend property, as they did, it was property in the broader sense of life, liberty, and estate, as well as the narrower one of material possessions.[21] Moreover even when it came to the defence of material goods, most of the legislation they passed (except for the Game Laws and the Corn Laws) in fact served to protect not only their own property but also that of the expanding mass of lower-middle-class shopkeepers, artisans, small manufacturers, and smallholders. For example, the principal supporters and beneficiaries of the ostensibly absurd and cruel system of imprisonment for debt were the middling sort, whose whole livelihood depended upon the security of credit, and the ability to put pressure on delinquents. Similarly the full ferocity of capital punishment was unleashed by the elite not upon violators of property rights under the Black Act or the Game Laws, but upon those who threatened daily commercial transactions, that is the forgers of bills of exchange or banknotes. Between 1805 and 1818 almost one in two of those convicted of this latter offence were hanged, as compared with one in seven of highway robbers or one in forty-four of burglars.[22] Whatever the law might say, there was a rough consensus of moral justice among jurors, magistrates and judges, that is small tradesmen, farmers, gentry, lawyers, and members of the landed gentry, about who deserved to die for a crime against property, and who (the great majority) did not.

[20] *An Ungovernable People*, ed. J. Brewer and J. Styles, New Brunswick, 1980; J. G. A. Pocock, 'Machiavelli, Harrington and English Political Ideologies in the Eighteenth Century', *William and Mary Quarterly*, 3rd Series, 22, 1965.
[21] For the double meaning of 'property' to Locke and his contemporaries, see J. Viner, 'Possessive Individualism as Original Sin', *Canadian Journal of Economics and Political Science*, 29, 1963, pp. 552-9.
[22] J. Wade, *The Black Book*, London, 1820, p. 258.

Moreover, this passionate sense of legalism so widespread among the English landed classes, and their belief in the ultimate supremacy of the common law, placed restraints upon their own freedom of action. They themselves were bound up in a culture of legalistic obligation which not infrequently worked against their own interests, as one of their severest critics has grudgingly admitted.[23] As a result, at no period could the English landed elite as a whole be characterized as wholly irresponsible. The contrast with the situation across the Irish channel, for example, is very clear. J. A. Froude's savage description of the Irish gentry before the Famine hardly fitted the many sober, God-fearing, paternalistic, entrepreneurial squires of Victorian England. He told how a visiting Scot remarked that out of a hundred 'there may be one, or at most two, who believe that the Almighty put them into this world for any purpose but to shoot grouse, race, gamble, drink, or break their necks in the hunting-field'.[24] There were always plenty of English booby squires who fitted this description, but whether they were in the majority is very doubtful, even in the easygoing late seventeenth and eighteenth centuries.

There is, however, another side to the coin of paternalism. Such an ideology is wholly antithetical to principles of open mobility, individualism, and popular democracy, although it can and did embrace the Lockean concept of the contract state, and the common-law ideal of equality before the law. From the eighteenth century to the nineteenth, therefore, the elite was struggling to adapt to the realities of a mobile market-oriented society (at least at the lower levels), the largest and freest electorate in Europe, the spread among its own ranks of affective individualism and the nuclear family, the rise of meritocracy in the public service, and other such disturbing trends. Despite it all, the ideology of paternalism survived well into the nineteenth century, and continued to act as a major prop to maintain the old social order.

Whether such a belief system results in benevolent or oppressive behaviour depends upon the eye of the beholder. Both are clearly possible, and which motive was uppermost in the minds of the rulers is a question which is hardly worth pursuing, so inextrica-

---

[23] E. P. Thompson, *Whigs and Hunters*, New York, 1975, pp. 259-69. The paradigm of the eighteenth-century English legal system as an engine of class repression of the poor by the elite is brilliantly argued by D. Hay, 'Property, Authority and the Criminal Law', in *Albion's Fatal Tree, Crime and Society in Eighteenth Century England*, ed. D. Hay *et al.*, London, 1975. But for a devastating critique of this position, see J. Langbein, 'Albion's Fatal Flaws', *Past and Present*, 98, 1982.

[24] J. A. Froude, 'On the Uses of a Landed Gentry', in his *Short Studies on Great Subjects*, London, 1907, iv, p. 306.

bly are the two concepts confused.[25] One consequence of such a
confusion was that it was very hard for the elite to make the necessary concessions to the middling sort of a share in political authority commensurate with their education, status, and wealth.
Surrender is difficult for those who are convinced that they are
the natural rulers of society. Paternalism may be a false consciousness which conceals from those who practice it an egotistical de-
termination to rule, but it is a powerful historical force to be reckoned with, which normally affects inferiors as well as superiors.

It also carries with it a highly unequal distribution of benefits
and costs. One of the economic costs was the evolution of a financial administration and political system which in practice worked
to keep power and riches in the hands of the powerful and the
rich, and their relatives and dependants. The wholly irrational
structure of patronage in church, state, and politics, the growth of
a host of pensions, sinecures, and reversions of offices in the public
service, most of them monopolized by the elite and their families,
was the product of a general conspiracy to use the public payroll
to benefit the ruling elite. The system was described in loving
detail in the various editions of John Wade's *Black Book* published
in the early nineteenth century, and no one who reads it today
can reasonably deny that 'Old Corruption' was a central reality of
seventeenth-, eighteenth-, and early nineteenth-century English
public life. Acquiescence in so grossly inequitable a distribution
of public goods was one of the prices to be paid for a relatively
equitable legal system binding on all members of the society.

Another economic cost of paternalism was acquiescence in the
increasing concentration of gigantic quantities of landed estate and
rental income, largely unearned, in the hands of the men who
composed this landed elite. It has been argued that 'no continental
landed elite in the nineteenth century owned so large a part of its
nation's territory as did the English'. It is now possible very roughly
to estimate what proportion of the total rental value, both in the
countryside and in London, was owned by the 2,000-odd members of the landed elite in about 1880. It amounts to something
between a quarter and a third of the whole, a proportion which
must have grown as a result of the two great rises of rental values
from 1770 to 1815 and 1850 to 1873, as well as the huge increase

[25] I would not know how to demonstrate or disprove Dr Robert's assertion that 'for the
paternalist the obligation to rule firmly and to guide and superintend' took priority over
benevolence in Victorian England (D. Robert, *Paternalism in Early Victorian England*, London, 1979, p. 6.

of urban property values.[26] Being the richest landed elite in the world was alone enough to keep them afloat until 1880 in the face of the rising bourgeois and industrial tide. But the scandalous inequity of the situation finally focused public attention upon it, and by the early twentieth century it was provoking liberal legislation for a planned redistribution of national wealth through progressive taxation. Their very wealth was thus ultimately their undoing.

Nor is there any doubt that the elite were prepared to exercise careless arrogance in minor matters where their self-interest ran up against the interest of the public at large. We have already seen how eighteenth-century landowners did not hesitate to relocate roads and even whole villages that encroached on their privacy. Where such drastic measures proved inconvenient or impossible, Repton, who knew them well, clearly thought they would have no compunction about exerting moral blackmail on their tenants, to judge by one of his suggestions for improvements at Antony House in Cornwall:

The public road [from the turnpike] . . . must cross the park somewhere; . . . this road is also the nearest and the most interesting line of approach to the house, but it can only be considered as an approach by obliterating every idea of its being a public road and this will be found no very difficult task. With this view, the entrance from the Turnpike ought to be marked by such a building as may impress the mind with the full belief that the road belongs only to the proprietor and not to the public.

He therefore suggested the erection of suitably 'important' lodges. In a similar vein, F. P. Delmé Radcliffe, writing about the problem of pacifying farmers whose fields had suffered from the passage of the hunt, commended the solution adopted by the local M. F. H., 'Mr Hanbury, whose business, as head of a great brewery, enabled him at no great sacifice to keep many in entire good humour, by acceptable *cadeaux* of brown stout'.[27]

There was a strong element of humbug and self-interest in the practice of squirearchy paternalism. In 1783, Dr Johnson remarked that 'the superiority of a country gentleman over the people on his estate is very agreeable . . . For it must be agreeable to have a casual superiority over those who are by nature equal to

---

[26] D. Spring, *European Landed Elites in the Nineteenth Century*, Baltimore, 1977; P. H. Lindert, 'Who owned Victorian England?', Working Paper Series no. 12, 1983, Agricultural History Center, University of California, Davis, Appendices C1 and 2. I am grateful to Professor Lindert for permission to quote from this paper.

[27] *The Red Book of Antony House* in *The Red Books of Humphrey Repton*, London, 1976; F. P. Delmé Radcliffe, *The Noble Science*, London, 1839, p. 252.

us'. He went on to observe that 'a man is not so much afraid of
being a hard creditor as of being a hard landlord', but when Boswell enthusiastically responded 'because there is a sort of kindly
connection between the landlord and his tenants', Dr Johnson
promptly cut him down. 'No sir, many landlords here never see
their tenants. It is because if a landlord drives away his tenants,
he may not get others'.[28] Johnson was wrong in thus abruptly
dismissing the residual ideological and cultural force of squirearchy paternalism into and beyond the age of Adam Smith. It was
precisely this acute sense of limits on the free exercise of power
that enabled the English landlord to survive into the nineteenth
century.

Deference, however, could not survive the jacking up of rents
after 1770, enforced enclosure of village open fields, and the maintenance of very low wages for agricultural labourers. Overt marks
of respect were consequently on the decline in the face of the
profit-oriented market society that was coming into being in the
late eighteenth and nineteenth centuries. As early as 1790 Lord
Torrington thought that traditional patterns of behaviour were
crumbling in the countryside. He alleged that he could remember
a time when 'every gentleman then was bowed to with reverence,
and "A good morning to you, master", "Good evening", "Good
journey to you, Sir", were always presented with every old-fashioned wish and compliment of the season'.[29] Contact with London
ways thanks to turnpike roads was, he believed, destroying these
ancient habits of ostentatious deference to the quality.

Evidence of the truth of these observations comes from the tone
and content of the (relatively) free and rapidly expanding press in
eighteenth-century England. Unlike the hierarchical and pro-aris-
tocratic flavour of the French press, that of England was quick to
accuse the aristocracy of vice and luxury and was constantly praising the sterling merits of its main readership, the ever-expanding
'middling sort'.[30] In the light of this more bourgeois cultural atmosphere, the preservation of hierarchy and deference in England
is all the more remarkable. It is only explicable in terms of the
persistent adherence to a deep-rooted pattern of paternalism and
legalism. This may or may not have been adopted as a cunning

[28] *Boswell: the Applause of the Jury 1782-1785*, ed. I. Lustig and F. A. Pottle, New York, 1981, pp. 74-5.
[29] J. Byng, *The Torrington Diaries*, ed. C. B. Andrews, London, 1934-8, ii, p. 149.
[30] S. Botein, J. R. Censer, H. Ritvo, 'The Periodical Press in Eighteenth-Century English and French Society: a Cross-cultural Approach', *Comparative Studies in Society and History*, 23, 1981.

device for the perpetuation of aristocratic hegemony, but it certainly had that effect.

iv. Familiarity with Possessive Individualism

Another great strength of the English landed elite was its members' familiarity with the world of government and the professions. They rubbed shoulders with army officers, officials, and lawyers, since many of these were standard occupations for their younger sons, while they themselves increasingly had had some first hand experience of the outside world in military or colonial service, or in the professions. They were therefore prepared to accept without suspicion or resentment some of the more successful of such professional careerists into their own society with little or no legal or psychological resistance.

Moreover they themselves had early been converted to the principle of possessive market individualism in the treatment of land and agricultural improvement. As a result of entrepreneurship and judicious marriage, between the late seventeenth and the end of the eighteenth centuries this landed elite probably increased their share of English soil from about one-fifth to about one-quarter, a proportion which they still retained in 1880.[31] Slowly, over the centuries, they enclosed most of England and leased it out to a relatively small number of large tenant farmers, who in turn hired landless labourers to till the soil. The resultant tripartite social structure of the countryside was quite unlike anything to be seen elsewhere in Europe. Its weakness was the plight of the landless labourers in a bad year, but its strength was the potentiality—and reality—of substantial agricultural improvement and a progressive increase in the total output of food. This both enriched the landlords and fed the poor. Some were 'spirited improvers' in their own right. Thus in 1771 Arthur Young showered praise on the agricultural innovations of the Marquis of Rockingham, and was at pains to stress that these were 'pursuits so truly worthy of a British nobleman', and not at all 'mean and unworthy of great riches and high rank'. In addition to this singularity in agricultural entrepreneurship, the elite in the eighteenth century were investing heavily in government funds, speculative stocks like the South Sea Company, and turnpike trusts, and in the nineteenth century in canal and railroad companies and urban development. They

[31] F. M. L. Thompson, 'The Social Distribution of Landed Property in England since the Sixteenth Century', *Economic History Review*, 2nd Series, xix, 1966, p. 510.

were therefore far from ignorant of or unsympathetic towards the practices and principles of men of business.[32]

v. Commercial Foreign Policy

Another reason for the success with which the landed elite rode out crisis after crisis up to 1880, was that it was obstinate enough to continue to grasp the reins of power, but flexible enough to use that power to further the interests of the nation as a whole and the commercial bourgeoisie in particular. By the early eighteenth century its members were fully convinced that England's strength lay in its overseas commercial prosperity, and they were ready and willing to finance and build an invincible navy in order to open up the markets of the world to English enterprise. George I's Speech from the Throne to Parliament in 1721, drafted by the Whig leaders Walpole and Townshend, stated flatly that the prime aim of government policy should be 'extending our commerce, upon which the riches and grandeur of this nation chiefly depend'. But this was not merely a one-party view of the national interest, for in about 1750 Bolingbroke, the spokesman for the most unreconstructed of Tory gentry backwoodsmen expressed the same view: 'Trade gave us wealth, wealth gave us power'.[33] Napoleon was wrong to call the English a nation of shopkeepers: it had long been, and was long to remain, a nation of aristocrats and squires ruling in the interest of bankers and overseas merchants, which is a quite different matter.

Under these conditions the commercial bourgeoisie in the eighteenth century were willing to let the landed elite both run the country and pack the government and armed forces with its relatives. The only discontent was voiced by the petty bourgeoisie, now excluded from political influence and denied any share of the spoils—in a word the followers and supporters of John Wilkes. But their rumblings were muted, fears generated by the excesses of the French Revolution prevented even mild measures of reform for yet another generation, and the unreformed system success-

[32] A. Young, *A Six Month Tour through the North of England*, London, 1771, i, p. 315; see also pp. 98-143, 198-230; M. W. McCahill, 'Peers, Patronage and the Industrial Revolution 1760-1800', *Journal of British Studies*, xvi, 1976; D. Cannadine, *The Aristocracy and the Towns 1774-1967*, Leicester, 1980, Parts 1 and 4. For a comprehensive list of specialized articles about the involvement of the nineteenth-century greater landlords in various forms of industry and finance, see D. Cannadine, 'The Theory and Practice of the English Leisure Classes', *Historical Journal*, 21, 1978, Notes 5 and 6.

[33] J. H. Plumb, *Sir Robert Walpole: the Making of a Statesman*, London, 1956, p. 367; H. St John, Viscount Bolingbroke, 'Reflections on the State of the Nation', in *Works*, London, 1844, ii, p. 452.

fully waged against Napoleon what at the time was easily the greatest war in England's history.

When the demand for power-sharing by the bourgeoisie finally became irresistible in the 1820s, the landed elite brushed aside the arch-reactionaries like Lord Liverpool, and made the minimum necessary concessions, like the first Reform Act and later the abolition of the Corn Laws. Both of these measures turned out to make relatively little difference in practice, although their symbolic importance can hardly be over-estimated. Grudgingly, inch by inch, the elite also allowed Old Corruption to be whittled away by professional reform of the law courts, the administration, and the armed forces, but their members still mostly ended up on top, by competing successfully in the now allegedly meritocratic system of examinations.

vi. Successful Family Strategy

The final cause of the survival of the landed elite in positions of wealth, status, and power up to 1880 was their tenacity and resilience in seeking legal and procedural ways to retain these attributes and to keep all three more or less intact within the family from generation to generation. It was their strong sense of family responsibility which prevented owners from dissipating their family estates or charging them with an overwhelming load of personal debt on the many occasions when father and son could legally combine to defeat the provisions of the strict settlement. It was also behind the adoption of the strict settlement itself, the transmission of property to fictive kin, and the enforcement of compulsory name-changing upon these kin. All were devices which preserved continuity of the patrimony in the family and avoided the final disaster of its dispersal, symbolized by the sale of the family seat.

5. CONCLUSION

For 340 years, the elite maintained a highly stable social and political system, the result of a most delicate and precarious balancing act between several sets of opposing extremes. In their family arrangements they had had to steer between the pursuit of too many and too few heiresses; between producing too few and too many children; between allowing too little or too much individual discretion in the disposal of property; between too generous expenditures which ran up debt or too miserly expenditures which generated contempt; between overbuilding which created a seat

too expensive to live in, or underbuilding which led to status derogation. In their behaviour toward other classes they had had to
steer between too generous paternalism towards tenants which would
erode revenues, and too ruthless profiteering which would under-
mine deference; between too ready acceptance of the new rich
which would dilute numbers and values, and too rigid rejection
which would stimulate class antagonism. In their political capaci-
ties they had had to manoeuvre between too gross an exploitation
of public offices which would engender popular opprobrium and
governmental inefficiency, and too ready a welcome to reform which
would substitute merit for influence and thus might erode one
basis of their family fortunes; between the cherished ideals of popular sovereignty and the rule of law, and a practical arrangement
which preserved power in elite hands. It was a difficult balancing
act, which was fairly astutely managed throughout the sixteenth,
seventeenth, eighteenth, and even the early and mid-nineteenth
centuries.

As a result, in most respects, the relative financial resources,
background, education, and way of life of a member of the landed
elite in 1880 were not all that different from what they had been
in 1680. Many of the same families still resided in the same seats.
If the concept of 'histoire immobile' is applicable to any sector of
English society, the landed elite is the most promising candidate.
Because for centuries its members kept such a wary eye on prestige, profits, and power, and were careful to retain all three for
transmission within the family, they neither gained nor lost very
much of any. As late as 1867 the radical Bernard Cracroft gloomily
admitted the continued position of hegemony of the landed elite
over English society:

They have a common freemasonry of blood, a common education, common pursuits, common ideas, a common dialect, a common religion, and—
what more than anything else binds men together—a common prestige,
a prestige growled at occasionally, but on the whole conceded, and even,
it must be owned, secretly liked by the country at large.[34]

Once one has abandoned the hypothesis of a constant flood of
commercial and banking wealth moving generation after generation out of business and into land, much that was hitherto puzzling
about England's history begins to fall into place. One of the insol-
uble problems before was whence the working capital came with

[34] B. Cracroft, 'The Analysis of the House of Commons, or indirect Representation',
Essays on Reform, London, 1867, p. 160. I am grateful to Professor Barry Smith for drawing
my attention to this article.

which to finance the commercial conquest of the world's markets, much less to make England the workshop of the world, if so much money was so regularly being withdrawn from business to buy land and a country seat. Second, if it has always been so easy and so common for self-made men to move up into the ranks of the social elite, why was it that England is still today the most class-conscious, and yet the most violence-free and most deferential, of European societies? How did upper-class Englishmen manage so successfully to put on such airs of effortless and inherited superiority, if in fact so many of them were no more than the heirs of self-made business men a generation or so back? Once one drops the idea of upward mercantile mobility on a large scale, and reduces it to its very modest true proportions, all these questions are more easily resolved. They are parts of the pattern of a society dominated by an elite, partly landed and partly professional, but acting with the close and easy co-operation of a powerful upper bourgeoisie of overseas merchants and bankers, and with the willing acquiescence of a very large body of culturally assimilated middling sort. Both these groups, the rich merchants and bankers and the middling sort adopted genteel cultural patterns of behaviour, but only a few of the former tried to enter the landed elite by the purchase of a country seat and an agricultural estate, and the permanent establishment of a county family.

What the argument of this book boils down to, therefore, is that there has been a fundamental misperception of what an open elite means. It has been wrongly interpreted as a continuous economic process of rapid and substantial upward mobility of men of business into the landed classes. In fact, two things made England so different from Continental Europe, at least after 1700. The first was the homogeneity of cultural values and behaviour among the landed classes, the wealthier merchant and banking patriciates, and the gentrified 'middling sort'. The second was the lack of any legal barriers based on privilege clearly to demarcate the different sectors and status groups one from another, as there were elsewhere. On the other hand the whole of this genteel society was sliced and sliced again into extremely thin status layers, subtly separated from each other by the delicate but infinitely resistant lines of snobbery. These lines were all but invisible to foreigners but their brutal reality was carefully, even lovingly, delineated by the novelists, such as Fanny Burney, Jane Austen, Trollope, and of course Thackeray. The glue which held the upper and middle levels of English society together was a common bond of gentility, but the barriers which broke it down into infinite gradations of honor and

respect were those of snobbery. Then, as now, social interactions
in England tended to be fraught with status anxiety.

6. THE END: 1880-1984

Looking back on the social scene in 1880 just as this long hegemony of the landed elite was beginning to crumble before his eyes,
Lord Percy pronounced a naïve and sentimental, but not wholly
inaccurate, funerary oration upon a vanishing culture. 'That which
distinguished life in the country was what was called our county
life, under which a body of gentlemen possessed property and,
having the interests of the people at heart, took part in sports and
directed the local affairs of their district, thus showing they were
of use and influence in the world'.[35] This extraordinary statement
is redolent of a quaint out-dated paternalism, and is marked by a
failure to observe the plight of the farm labourers, an obsession
with fox-hunting and shooting, and an absolute confidence that
the landed elite are the only rightful and responsible guardians of
good order and justice in the neighbourhood. It is revealing not
only of the values of members of the Victorian landed elite, but
also of their perception that their long period of hegemony was at
last drawing to an end, with momentous social and psychological
consequences for English life. The writing was certainly on the
wall, and some of them, like Lord Percy, could read it.

Another sign of a loss of confidence came when the landed elite
wholly rejected the society of the enormously wealthy industrial
entrepreneurs. As Dr Rubinstein has observed, between 1780 and
1880 'the British landed aristocracy was increasingly becoming a
caste-like and socially isolated group, distancing itself from, and
distanced from, the newer business magnates, who found it nearly
impossible in many cases to gain full acceptance into the inner
circle of high landed society'.[36]

After 1880 the main props of elite hegemony collapsed one after
the other, opening the way to the transformation of what was
already the workshop of the world into a more openly bourgeois
society. The post-1873 agricultural depression brought financial
disaster to many ancient families in cereal areas, an economic crisis
then exacerbated by the introduction of heavy death duties coupled with the very severe elite mortality in the First World War.

---

[35] Quoted in R. Carr, *English Foxhunting: A History*, London, 1976, pp. 149-50.
[36] W. D. Rubinstein, *Men of Property*, New Brunswick, 1981, p. 219; R. E. Pumphret,
'The Introduction of Industrialists into the British Peerage', *American Historical Review*, lxv,
1959, p. 15.

Between 1880 and 1925 it appears that there was a turnover of landed property on a scale at least as great as that which followed the dissolution of the monasteries. The examination of a substantial sample of larger country houses in 1880 shows that almost two thirds had changed hands by 1980, and were no longer occupied by the original family.[37] For all but the greatest of landed families, who carried on as if nothing had changed, there was also a loss of political power and a modification of the old ways of life. The introduction of County Councils undermined the local power-base of all but a few. The influx of self-made manufacturers and business men into the countryside, the House of Commons and the House of Lords, undermined their monopoly of political power and social prestige at the centre.[38] The sensational appearance in the London season in 1881-2 of the two Tennant sisters—daughters of a Glasgow chemical manufacturer, although settled in a country seat since 1852—the dramatic rise of presentations at Court after 1882 and the inclusion of rich men of dubious social background in the Prince of Wales's set, marked the end of the exclusive monopoly of the larger landed families over London 'Society'.[39] The swan-song of country-house life in the 1930s, like the notorious Cliveden set, and the appearance of many landed aristocrats in Tory Cabinets in the 1960s, were superficial phenomena concealing the fact that the old elite were now the nominal political leaders of a country directed by quite other social groups. Mr Asquith was the first Prime Minister of England not to own a substantial country seat; and it seems likely that Sir Alec Douglas-Home will turn out to have been the last to do so.

With the outbreak of the Second World War in 1939, the whole social edifice came crashing down, for the abrupt disappearance of servants made the old style of life no longer possible, regardless of the level of affluence. In 1939, the Marquis of Bath still had forty living-in servants; forty years later his successor had to make do with two, both Spanish, a decline which almost certainly occurred abruptly, in the 1940s and 1950s. As a result, in 1945 impoverished and now socialist England found itself saddled with far more great mansions than it knew what to do with. Some were turned into Catholic seminaries or nunneries, preparatory schools, Bor-

[37] H. Clemenson, *English Country Houses and Landed Estates*, New York, 1982, pp. 119-20, 152-5.
[38] R. E. Pumphret, op. cit.; H. J. Hanham, 'The Sale of Honours in Late Victorian England', *Victorian Studies*, iii, 1960.
[39] L. Davidoff, *The Best Circles: Society, Etiquette and the Season*, London, 1973; N. W. Ellenberger, 'The Souls and London "Society" at the end of the Nineteenth Century', *Victorian Studies*, 25, 1982, pp. 138, 140, 144 note 33.

stals, orphanages, golf clubs or the prestige headquarters or conference centers of major industrial or commercial enterprises. Others were ruthlessly torn down, almost 450 of them between 1920 and 1955. Two hundred and fifty of clear architectural and historical importance have disappeared since 1945, leaving only about 1,000 more still in private hands.[40]

Some of the private owners have made over their houses to the National Trust, retaining the right to a family apartment carved out of the great mass of building open to the public; others have struggled on alone by selling off an immensely valuable picture from time to time to keep the wolf from the door, and personally showing the tourists round the house one or two days a week. Others have vested the property and the seat in a holding company, of which the owner has become a mere tenant and minor shareholder. A few others have created a brand new industry, turning their splendid houses and parks into the English equivalent of Disneylands. Yet others have survived by becoming expert manipulators of the loopholes in the British tax system.[41] The alternatives for survival are manifold, but the efforts seem doomed. Current tax laws, the virtual disappearance of residential servants, and the democratization of society make problematic in the long run the continued existence of all but a handful of seats in the hands of their ancestral families. The new capital transfer tax may well sound the death knell of the class.

This book is therefore a study of persons who pursued a special way of life, in a special location, a large country house, and enjoyed special privileges, power, status and wealth, all of which have now finally come to an end. It is an investigation into, although certainly not a requiem for, the long dead members and the physical relics of a vanished civilisation.

[40] D. Cannadine, 'The Theory and Practice of the English Leisure Class', p. 450; R. Strong, M. Binney, and J. Harris, *The Destruction of the English Country House 1875-1975*, London, 1974, pp. 8, 16; H. A. Clemenson, op. cit., pp. 124-7.

[41] J. Young, *The Country House in the 1980s*, London, 1982.

APPENDICES

I

CHRONOLOGICAL LISTING OF HOUSES IN SAMPLE

N.B.: Within a same-date grouping, houses are listed alphabetically; alternative names (or spellings) of houses figure in parentheses; the name of the parish is only given when it is not part of the house's name, square brackets supply the full name of the village; houses which go out of sample but return at a later date carry a reference to their successor's name (if there has been a change) and date of re-entry.

I . HERTFORDSHIRE

i. Houses in sample on 1 January 1540

Albury Hall: throughout
Aldenham Hall (Penn's Place): -1736
Br(o)adfield Hall, Cottered: -1768
Camfield Place (Wild Hill), Essendon: throughout
Cheshunt Great House: -1772
Digswell House: -1810
[Little] Hadham Hall: -1680
[Hemel] Hempstead Bury (Charter Tower): -1676

Knebworth House: throughout
Pendley House, Tring: -1800 (see 1874)
Pishiobury, Sawbridgeworth: throughout
Salisbury Hall, Shenley: -1813
Shingle Hall, Sawbridgeworth: -1670
Watton Woodhall: throughout

ii. Houses entering the sample 1540-1879

(listed chronologically (a) by date of acquisition by entrant who did not need to enlarge or (b) by date of building or improvement to sample size by entrant who did). Houses entering sample in a same year are listed alphabetically within that date.

Holywell House, St Albans: 1540-1783
Market (Markyate) Cell, Market Street: 1540-1879+
Royston Priory: 1540-1729
Sopwell House, St Peter's: 1540-1670
Gorhambury, St Michael's: 1541-1879+
Nyn House, Northaw: 1541-52 (see 1576 and 1864)
Wormleybury: 1541-1879+

Bayford Place: 1544-1770
Golden Parsonage, Great Gaddesden: 1544-1774 (see Gaddesden Place, 1768)
Cassiobury Park, Watford: 1545-1879+
The Grove, Watford: 1545-1879+
Thundridgebury: 1545-1811
The Lordship, Standon: 1546-1751
Bedwell Park, Essendon: 1547-1879+
Tyttenhanger, Ridge: 1547-1879+

Aldbury Hall: 1550-1665
Broxbournebury: 1550-1879+
Wyddiall Hall: 1550-1879+
Lamer House, Wheathamstead: 1555-1879+
Popes, Hatfield: 1555-1770
Hunsdon House: 1559-1879+
Cokenhatch (Earlsbury Park), Barkway: 1564-1879+
Theobalds, Cheshunt: 1564-1607 (see 1768)
New Place (Gilston Park, 1852+), Gilston: 1565-1879+
Punsborne, Hatfield: 1565-1653 (see 1727)
Brocket Hall, Hatfield: 1570-1879+
Little Court, Layston: 1570-1815
Much Hadham Hall: 1570-1730
Radwell Hall (House): 1570-1879+
Tewin Water: 1570-1879+
(Y)Ardeleybury: 1573-1760 (see 1790)
(Cheshunt) Nunnery: 1575-1804
(Hatfield) Woodhall: 1575-1792
King's Waldenbury: 1576-1879+
Nyn House, Northaw: 1576-1741 (see 1541 and 1864)
Stansteadbury, Stanstead Abbots: 1577-1879+
Hyde Hall, Sawbridgeworth: 1579-1820
Hamels Park, Braughing: 1580-1879+
Temple Dinsley, Hitchin: 1580-1715 (see 1868)
[Great] Berkhamstead Place: 1583-1823
Ware Park: 1585-1879+
Furneux Pelham Hall: 1590-1879+
Newsells Park, Barkway: 1590-1879+
Offley Place: 1590-1879+
Totteridge Park: 1592-1830
Sacombe Park: 1593-1879+
Aldenham Manor House: 1595-1700
Hitchin Priory: 1600-1879+
Mardocks (Mattocks): 1600-65
North Mimms Park: 1600-1879+
Ashridge Park: 1602-1879+
Quixwood, Clothall: 1604-1780
Beechwood, Flamstead: 1605-1879+
Hatfield House: 1607-1879+
Brent Pelham Hall: 1608-1879+
Oxhey Place (Hall), Watford: 1608-1799

Aspenden Hall: 1610-1830
The Moor, Rickmansworth: 1610-1728
Bennington Place: 1613-1700 (see 1745 and 1790)
Verulam House, St Michael's: 1617-66
Hertingfordbury Park: 1620-1816
Moor Place, Much Hadham: 1620-1879+
Rawdon House, Hoddesdon: 1622-81
Lockleys, Welwyn: 1624-1879+
Hertford Castle: 1626-1801
Rickmansworth Bury: 1630-1813 (see Rickmansworth Park, 1810)
Throcking Park: 1631-1744
Potterells, North Mimms: 1632-1879+
Tewin House: 1635-1807
Balls Park, St John's, Hertford: 1640-1879+
St Julian's, St Stephen's: 1649-1720
Bonningtons, Stanstead Abbots: 1650-65 (see 1790)
Goldings (Thompsons), Bengeo: 1650-1879+
Rothamsted, Harpenden: 1650-1879+
Stagenhoe, St Paul's Walden: 1650-1879+
Marden Hill, Tewin: 1654-1879+
Blakesware, Ware: 1655-1830
The Hoo, Kimpton: 1656-1879+
The Lordship, Much Hadham: 1660-1827
Oakhill (Monkenfrith), East Barnet: 1660-1879+
Aldenham House (Wigbournes): 1664-1879+
Tring Park: 1669-1879+
Porter's Park, Shenley: 1670-1702 (see 1740)
Childwickbury, St Albans: 1675-1879+
Brookmans, North Mimms: 1680-1879+
Westbrook Hay, Hemel Hempstead: 1682-1879+
Bennington Lordship: 1700-1879+
Julians (Rushden House), 1700-1879+
Cole Green Park: 1704-1801
Brickendonbury: 1705-1879+
[Abbots] Langleybury: 1711-1879+

Redheath, Watford: 1712-1879+

Little Grove (New Place), East Barnet: 1719-1879+

Copped Hall, Totteridge: 1720-1879+

Briggens Park, Hunsdon: 1720-1879+

Moor Park, Rickmansworth: 1720-1879+

St Paul's Waldenbury: 1725-1879+

Punsborne, Hatfield: 1727-1879+

Gubbins (Gobions), North Mimms: (1712*) 1730-1840

Porter's Park, Shenley: 1740-1879+

Bennington Place: 1745 only (see 1613 and 1790)

Youngsbury, High Cross: 1745-1879+

Preston Castle (Hunsdon House), nr. Hitchin: 1750-86

Belmont (Mount Pleasant), E. Barnet: 1758-1879+

Bayfordbury: 1759-1879+

Ayot [St Laurence] House: 1765-1879+

[Great] Gaddesden Place (Park): 1768-1879+ (see Golden Parsonage, 1544)

Theobalds Park, Cheshunt: 1768-1879+ (see 1564)

Marchmont House, Hemel Hempstead: 1770-1800

High Cannons, Shenley: 1771-1879+

Colney Chapel House, Shenley: (1770) 1775-1879+

Woolmers Park, Hertingfordbury: 1788-1879+

Marshallswick (Sandridgebury): 1789-1879+

(Y)Ardcleybury: 1790-1879+ (see 1573)

Ashlyns Park, Great Berkhampstead: 1790-1879+

Bennington Place: 1790-1879+ (see 1613 and 1745)

Bonningtons, Stanstead Abbots: 1790-1879+ (see 1650)

Coles Hall (Coleshill), Westmill: 1790-1879+

Poles, Thundridge: 1790-1879+

Buckskin Hall (Dacre Hall), East Barnet: 1794-1879+

Danesbury (St John's Lodge), Welwyn: (1775**) 1794-1879+

Aldenham Abbey (Wall Hall); St Stephen's: 1800-79+

Caddington Hall: 1804-79+

Panshanger Park, St Andrew: 1807-79+

Gadebridge Park: 1810-79+

Rickmansworth Park: 1810-79+ (see Rickmansworth Bury, 1630)

Putteridgebury, Offley: 1812-79+

Netherfield House, Stanstead Abbots: 1815-79+

Hexton Hall (House): 1824-79+

Munden (Meriden) House, Watford: 1828-79+

Newberries Park, Shenley: 1830-79+

Essendon Place: 1833-79+

Abbots [Langley] Hill: 1836-79+

Hazelwood, Abbots Langley: 1838-79+

The Frythe, Welwyn: 1841-79+

Shendish, King's Langley: 1855-79+

Carpenders' Park, Watford: 1862-79+

Shephalbury: 1862-79+

Nyn House, Northaw: 1864-79+ (see 1541 and 1576)

Bushey Hall, Watford: 1865-79

Chorley Wood Cedars, Rickmansworth: 1865-79+

Frogmore Hall: 1865-79+

Temple Dinsley, Hitchin: 1868-79+ (see 1580)

Isneye House, Stanstead Abbots: 1869-79+

Eastbury, Watford: 1870-79+

Champneys, Wigginton: 1871-79+

Batchwood, St Michael's: 1873-79+

Pendley House, Tring: 1874-79+ (see I i.)

---

* Although the house is below sample size in 1712, the owner figures in the owner sample on account of the elaborate gardening scheme which he initiated, clearly as a prelude to enlarging for rebuilding.

** Though built to sample size by a spinster in 1775, the house does not enter the sample of houses till 1794 when it was acquired by an owner in sample.

2. NORTHAMPTONSHIRE

i. Houses in sample on 1 January 1540

Abington Abbey (Hall): -1838
Astwell Castle (Manor House), nr.
  Wappenham: -1717
Blatherwycke Manor House (Park):
  throughout
Boughton Hall (Park): -1700
Boughton House, nr. Kettering:
  throughout
Catesby Priory (House): -1797
Charwelton Manor House: -1619
Deene Hall (Park): throughout
Drayton House, nr. Lowick: through-
  out
East Carlton Hall (House): throughout

Easton Neston: throughout
Fawsley Hall: throughout
[Great] Harrowden Hall: -1850
Horton Hall (House): throughout
Lilford Hall: throughout
Lyveden Old Build; -1655
Maidwell Hall: throughout
Milton Hall: throughout
Nether Heyford Manor House: -1643
Preston Capes Manor House: -1650
Rushton Hall: throughout
Southwick Hall: throughout
Stanford Hall: -1700
Steane Manor House (Park): -1740

ii. Houses entering the sample 1540-1879

Walcot House, nr. Barnack: 1540-
  1879+
Eydon Hall, 1542-1879+
Edgecote House: 1543-1879+
Upton Manor House, nr. Sutton:
  1543-1730
Delapré Abbey: 1548-1879+
Fineshade Abbey, nr. Blatherwycke:
  1548-1879+
Apethorpe Hall: 1550-1879+
Canons Ashby Priory: 1551-1879+
Burghley House, nr. Stamford: 1555-
  1879+
Great Oakley Hall: 1555-1879+
Little Oakley Manor House: 1555-
  1707
Paulerspury Manor House: 1555-1775
Brampton Ash Manor House: 1558-
  1742
Dingley Hall: 1558-1879+
Titchmarsh Manor House: 1560-1749
Winwick Manor House: 1560-1705
Thenford House: 1565-1879+
Lamport Hall: 1568-1879+
Gayton Manor House: 1570-1628
Kirby Hall: 1570-1823
Thorpe Mandeville Manor House:
  1570-1677
Castle Ashby: 1572-1879+

Althorp Park: 1573-1879+
Ecton Hall: 1575-1879+
Rockingham Castle: 1575-1879+
Easton Maudit Hall: 1578-1799
Holdenby House: 1578-1605
Adstone Manor House: 1580-1720
Barnwell Castle: 1580 1700
Pytchley Hall: 1580-1750
Sywell Hall: 1580-1744
Farthinghoe Hall: 1581-1729
Preston Deanery Hall: 1585-1879+
Thornhaugh Manor House: 1585-1613
Norton Hall: 1588-1879+
Finedon Hall: 1590-1879+
Glendon Hall: 1590-1879+
Great Billing Hall: 1590-1879+
Newton-in-the-Willows Hall: 1590-
  1715
Stoke Doyle Hall: 1590-1690
Wakerley Manor House: 1590-1643
Aynho Park: 1595-1879+
Warkworth Castle: 1595-1804
Lyveden New Build, nr. Aldwinkle:
  1596 only
Brockhall (Brockhole) Hall: 1600-
  1879+
[Great] Cransley Hall: 1600-1879+
Harrington Hall: 1600-1727

Stowe-Nine-Churches Manor House: 1600-30

Upton Hall, nr. Northampton: 1600-1840

Culworth Manor House: 1603-1776

Faxton Manor House: 1610-1717

Pilton Manor House (Rectory): 1610-84

Wothorpe, nr. Stamford: 1610-23

Aldwinkle Manor House: 1618-98

Kelmarsh Hall: 1620-1879+

Woodford Manor House: 1621-1805

Thorpe Malsor Hall: 1622-1879+

Watford Court: 1627-1879+

Stoke Bruerne Park: 1629-1879+

Cottesbrooke Hall: 1639-1879+

Thorpe Hall, Longthorpe: 1653-1879+

Courteenhall Park Hall: 1655-1879+

Wakefield Lodge, Potterspury: 1655-1660 (see 1745)

Barton Seagrave Hall: 1665-1879+

Dallington Manor House (Hall): 1665-1752

Chipping Warden Manor House: 1666-88

Greatworth Manor House: 1667-1742

Bulwick Hall: 1670-1879+

Overstone Manor House: 1672-1879+

Marston [St Lawrence] House: 1674-1879+

Walgrave Hall: 1674-1747

Harlestone House: 1675-1832

Wollaston Hall: 1675-1879+

Cranford [St Andrew] Hall: 1699-1879+

Biggin Hall, nr. Benfield: 1700-1879+

Brixworth Hall: 1700-1879+

Orlingbury Hall: 1706-1879+

Culworth House: 1712-1776

Ashby St Ledgers: 1722-1879+

Guilsborough Hall: 1730-1879+

Astrop Park, nr. King's Sutton: 1735-1879+

Evenley Hall: 1745-1879+

Wakefield Lodge, Potterspury: 1745-1879+ (see 1655)

Wicken Park: 1760-1879+

Pitsford Hall (House): 1770-1879+

Fermyn (Farming) Woods Hall, nr. Brigstock: 1788-1879+

Sulby Hall: 1793-1879+

Laxton Hall: 1805-79+

Welton Place: 1810-79+

Little Houghton House: 1820-79+

Pipewell Hall, nr. Rushton: 1820-79+

Moulton Grange: 1825-79+

Whittlebury Lodge: 1825-79+

Weston Hall: 1826-79+

Flore House: 1830-79+

Grafton Regis House: 1833-79+

Bragborough Hall, Braunston: 1841-78

Wadenhoe House: 1853-79+

Mears Ashby Hall: 1858-79+

Moreton Pinkney Manor House: 1860-79+

3. NORTHUMBERLAND

i. Houses in sample on 1 January 1610

Bamburgh Hall (Abbey/The Friars): -1701

Belsay Castle, Bolam: -1810 (see Belsay Hall, 1810)

Capheaton Hall, Whelpington: throughout

Cheeseburn Grange, Stamfordham: throughout

Chillingham Castle: throughout

Chipchase Castle, Chollerton: throughout

Ford Castle: throughout

Wallington Hall (House): throughout

Widdrington Castle, Woodhorn: -1716

ii. Houses entering the sample 1610-1879

Alnwick Abbey: 1620-85

[East] Denton Hall, Newburn: 1622-1775

Dilston Castle (Hall): 1622-1716

Benwell Tower (Hall): 1625-1780

Seaton Delaval Hall: 1626-1879+

Seaton [Delaval] Lodge: 1628-1729

Whitfield Hall: 1630-1879+

Hesleyside, nr. Bellingham: 1631-1879+

Mitford Manor House: 1637-1812 (see Mitford Hall 1820)

Holywell Old Hall: 1654-1813 (see Milborne Hall, 1807)

Close House, Heddon-on-the-Wall: 1660-1879+

Callaly Castle, Whittingham: 1676-1879+

Anderson Place, Newcastle: 1680-1777

Beaufront Castle, St John Lee: 1695-1879+

Brandon White House, Eglingham: 1695-1826

Eshott Hall: 1700-1817

Nether Witton Hall, Hartburn: 1702-1879+

Eglingham Hall: 1704-1879+

Falloden Hall, Embleton: 1710-1879+

Eslington Park (Hall), Whittingham: 1718-1879+

Kirkharle Hall: 1719-1865 (see Little Harle Tower, 1861)

Nunnykirk Hall, Hartburn: 1719-1879+

Jesmond (Manor) House: 1720-1809

Fenham Hall, St John, Newcastle: 1725-1835

Felton Park (Hall): 1732-1879+

Blagdon Hall, Stannington: 1735-1879+

Howick Hall: 1740-1879+

[Long] Benton Hall: 1745-1812

Lemmington Hall, Edlingham: 1746-1854

Etal Manor, Ford: 1748-98

Nunwick: 1749-1879+

Alnwick Castle: 1750-1879+

Gosforth House: 1755-1879+

Belford Hall, Bamburgh: 1756-1879+

Broome Park, Edlingham: 1760-1879+

Bywell [St Peter] Hall: 1760-1879+

Swinburne Castle, Chollerton: 1760-1879+

Kirkley Hall, Ponteland: 1764-1879+

Swarland (New) Hall (House / Park), Felton: 1765-1873

Craster Tower: 1769-1879+

[Long] Benton House: 1770-1849

Haggerston Castle: 1770-1879+

Pallinsburn House, Ford: 1770-1879+

Twizzell Castle: 1770-1818

Chesters, nr. Humshaugh: 1771-1879+

Shawdon Hall, Whittingham: 1779-1879+

Fowberry Tower (Hall), Chatton: 1780-1879+

Acton House, nr. Felton: 1781-1879+

Heaton Hall, Newcastle: 1783-1836

Biddlestone Hall, nr. Clennell: 1787-1879+

Ewart Park House: 1788-1879+

Minsteracres Hall, Bywell St Peter: 1790-1879+

Twizzell House, Bamburgh: 1790-1879+

Woolsington Hall, Newburn: 1794-1879+

[North] Dissington Hall: 1800-79+

Featherstone Castle, Haltwhistle: 1800-79+

Elswick Hall, St John, Newcastle: 1803-40

Blenkinsopp Hall, Haltwhistle: 1805-79+

Hartford House, Bedlington: 1807-79+

Milborne Hall/House: 1807-79+ (see Holywell Old Hall, 1654)

Belsay Hall, Bolam: 1810-79+ (see Belsay Castle, 3 i)

Linden House, Long Horsley: 1812-79+

Haughton Castle, Humshaugh: 1816-79+
Rock Hall, Embleton: 1819-79+
Coupland Castle, Kirknewton: 1820-79+
Mitford Hall, 1820-79+ (see Mitford Manor House, 1637)
Cresswell House (Hall), Woodhorn: 1821-79+
Angerton Hall (House), Hartburn: 1823-79+
Longhirst House, Bothal: 1824-79+
Brinkburn Priory: 1825-79+
Lilburn Towers, Eglinham: 1828-79+

Matfen Hall: 1828-79+
Meldon Park: 1832-79+
Sandhoe House, St John Lee: 1850-79+
Newton [-on-the-Moor] Hall, Shilbottle: 1851-79+
Little Harle Tower, nr. Kirkharle: 1861-79+ (see Kirkharle Hall, 1719)
Unthank Hall, Haltwhistle: 1862-79+
Cragside, nr. Rothbury: 1863-79+
Long Ridge Towers, nr. Rothbury: 1878-79+

II

THE METHODOLOGY OF
QUANTIFICATION

1. THE MEASUREMENT OF HOUSE SIZE

Since the group being studied is primarily a status group, as well
as an economic class and power elite, one essential criterion which
justifies inclusion is putative life-style, measured by the size and
character of the house in which the individual resided. The key
problem is to distinguish between country houses owned by small
parish gentry and those owned by members of the county elite.
The first step is therefore to devise some uniform standard of
measurement of house size, and the second is to establish the minimum cut-off point to qualify for elite membership.

In an ideal world it would be desirable to have both a measure
of building costs per cubic foot adjusted to some standard cost-of-
living index so as to make possible comparisons over long periods
of time, and also accurate measurements of size of all houses. Unfortunately, however, the number of building events for which
there are full financial records is very small, and the number for
which there are plans and elevations is certainly no larger. Moreover, even if one could measure cubic footage of the whole building in all cases, it would not mean very much, for reasons which
will be explained in a moment. Dreams of firm indices of cost and
size have therefore had to be abandoned, and attention has perforce been directed to devising some more imperfect but more
workable measure.

The most perplexing problem is how to deal with offices. In
houses of this social class, offices—meaning living-quarters for servants and rooms for laundry, food storage, food preparation, etc.—
bulk very large, since there was always a substantial retinue of
resident indoor servants, ranging from about fifteen up to fifty or
more.[1] The only crumb of comfort is that the ratio of family quarters to offices does not vary very much according to the size of the
house. The larger house certainly had a very much larger staff of
servants, but this was almost entirely offset by the fact that it also

---

[1] Robert Kerr, *The Gentleman's House*, London, 1865, p. 383, gives a table of servants
ranging from three to thirty-two and more, for whom accommodations should be provided
by the architect, dependent on the size of the house.

contained very much larger and more numerous rooms for formal
and informal entertainment. Robert Kerr's estimates for 1865 show
that, depending on the size of the house, offices then comprised
between 38 and 41 per cent of the whole in terms of square feet
of floor space, and 27 to 26 per cent in terms of costs, which is a
negligible range of variation.[2]

On the other hand, over time offices certainly changed their
location and very probably also the proportion of building space
they occupied. In the big courtyard houses of the sixteenth century, both servants' bedrooms and service areas were placed in one
or two wings off or around the main block. In the smaller houses
of the same period they might be straggling attachments, or altogether separate buildings. In the 'double-pile' rectangular house of
the late seventeenth and early eighteenth centuries, servants' bedrooms tended to be crammed into attics and the offices into semi-
basements, with the family quarters and entertainment rooms
sandwiched in between, on the two main floors. In the mid- or late
eighteenth century, both servants' bedrooms and offices were often
in semi-detached blocks, linked to the family quarters by corridors
on the Palladian model. Sometimes they were tucked away dis-
creetly on an obscure side of the house, and sometimes, in the
larger houses, they were in wings which were openly displayed as
integral parts of the architectural design. In the nineteenth century
service quarters began expanding, often on a single floor, attaching
themselves to the rear quarters of the main block and spreading
out in all directions like a monstrous fungoid growth at the base
of a tree (Plan 2). The astonishing complex of early nineteenth-
century offices at Ashridge, Hertfordshire, is an extreme example.

[2] The following table has been calculated from ibid., p. 892:

FLOOR SPACE

House Costs (in £)	Quarters	Offices	Total	Offices as per cent of total
	Size in Square Feet			
5,000	6,310	3,900	10,210	38
10,000	10,600	6,800	17,400	39
20,000	17,800	11,740	29,540	40
40,000	29,400	20,400	50,200	41
	Cost in Pounds			
5,000	3,639	1,365	5,004	47
10,000	7,314	2,686	10,000	27
20,000	14,774	5,237	20,011	26
40,000	29,800	10,200	40,000	26

Meanwhile greater and greater precautions were taken to isolate the bedrooms of the female from those of the male servants, both often in the attics, but only communicating via separate staircases to the basement.

Wherever they were sited, these offices were naturally spartan in their simplicity and cheap to put up—according to Kerr they cost about half as much per square foot as the family quarters. Since the cost was relatively so little, since they vary so greatly in their location, since they are so hard to measure accurately, and since they added nothing to the display function of the house as a social unit, they have been ignored in the calculations, which are confined to reception-rooms and family quarters. This means that a judgement has had to be made of what proportions of the floor area of a sixteenth-century courtyard house or a Victorian house was given over to offices. In the first case it has been assumed (in light of measured examples) that one-third of the floor space was taken up by offices. In the second, the proportion depends on the evidence about the appearance of the house derived from other sources, with a strong presumption that up to a half of the ground surface area and a third of the total floor-space consists of offices. Where a seventeenth- or eighteenth-century house has a semi-basement, it is assumed that the offices are there, and no deduction is made from the main floors; where there is no basement in a simple double-pile house, a deduction of one-fifth is made from the main floors, on the assumption (which is borne out by many of the known examples) that some offices were inside the main block, but that others were in a wing extending out of the back of the house, out of sight of the view of the façade.

Another difficulty is that it is virtually impossible to make allowances for the widely varying cost of internal decoration, primarily because in most cases we do not know what the cost amounted to, and also because we often do not know what the internal decorations looked like. We are therefore obliged, whether we like it or not, to ignore what in the really grand houses was admittedly a very important factor in costs.

A third difficulty is that the construction and adornment of the house is only one part of the total expenditure on a country seat. Particularly in the eighteenth century, considerable sums were spent on massive stable blocks to accommodate coaches, horses, and stable-boys, and even more went into beautifying the grounds. Park walls in brick could alone involve a very great expense if the park was large, while lakes, bridges, grottoes, fountains, temples, and so on were all heavy items of expenditure. Here again there is often no means of evaluating the cost of this type of work. All one can say is that when full documentary records are available, it appears that expenditure on grounds normally amounted to less than a third of the cost of the house. Robert Kerr estimated that for a substantial new house costing between £5,000 and £6,000 in all, there would need to be spent an extra £1,600 on stables and grounds.[3] It is only in the case of the great house situated within enormous and spectacular grounds that the ratio of cost of grounds to cost of house might be significantly higher.[4]

Accepting all these limitations and deficiencies, building has been calculated in terms of 'units', each of which consists of a hundred square feet of floor-space of living-quarters. Each main floor of the main block is counted equally as a floor area. Attic floors with dormers or mansard windows are counted at one-tenth of a unit per hundred square feet, and low third floors are counted at one-half of a unit per hundred square feet. Basements and semi-basements do not count at all, since it is assumed in all cases that they were used exclusively for offices. This computation, uncertain as is the data upon which it is often based, incomplete as it is in its omission of other important areas of expenditure, and approximate as it is in its neglect of ceiling height or building materials, nevertheless seems to give a rough evaluation of house size.

In terms of cost, it is less certain just what a unit means. In the mid-eighteenth century, plans and estimates of medium-size houses built by Robert Morris suggest a cost per unit of about £40, while prices quoted by George Richardson in the 1790s work out at more like £55 per unit. The most elaborate calculations of all were made by Robert Kerr in 1865. He reckoned 'the family department' cost (using London prices) at £58 per unit for a £5,000 house, and £83 per unit for a £20,000 house, which is roughly the range with which we are concerned. Above this level, prices per unit soar, and for a palace with 150 family rooms and 135 servants' rooms costing £80,000 the price per unit was estimated at £120.[5] The very valid point made by Kerr is that the price per unit rises directly proportionate to the size of the house, which means that the crude unit measurement is no more than a mean in terms of costs. Used as an indicator of expense, it seriously underestimates the cost of large houses and somewhat overestimates the cost of small ones.

[3] Ibid., p. 400.
[4] See above, Ch. x, pt. 1, sect. ii.
[5] R. Morris, *Select Architecture*, London, 1755; G. Richardson, *New Designs in Architecture*, London, 1792; R. Kerr, op. cit.

To sum up, therefore, the unit measurement system is riddled with imperfections, and in particular it underrepresents the real cost of the house and grounds of a great palace proportionately to that of a modest seat. A possible way to adjust for this would be to make a correction related to unit size; one could for example add 10 units to any house over 75 units, 20 units over 100 units, 30 units over 150 units, 50 units over 200 units. To do so, however, would introduce a hazardous degree of subjectivity into a statistical enquiry which is already sufficiently fraught with uncertainty, and the suggestion has been rejected.

Using this unit system of measurement, the minimum size of a house occupied by a member of the county elite has been found to be one of 50 units. The clarity of this cut-off points varies from county to county. In Northamptonshire, as far back as the 1580s there had developed a fairly sharp line of cleavage in terms of housing units between parish gentry and county gentry. The same is true of Northumberland by the middle of the seventeenth century. In both of these counties, houses tend to be either up to 30-35 units (as in Northants.) or 20-25 units (as in Northumberland), or else they are 50 units or more. The former housed the parish gentry; the latter the men who were assessed at one or more horses in the Muster Books. House size and tax assessments therefore support each other in a reassuring way. The most difficult case is Hertfordshire, where there was a smooth continuum of houses according to size, and no immediately obvious status dividing-line between those who lived in houses above and below 50 units. Even so, it is possible to confirm that the cut-off point at 50 units is not an arbitrary one but corresponded in fact with a very real division of local landed society. That this was the difference between the county elite and the parish gentry was clearly shown by comparing the assessment for a levy in c. 1663 of owners of manors in the two Hertfordshire hundreds of Cashio and Dacorum with Hearth Taxes, JP lists etc.[6] All the indicators fall into place to suggest that the economic and power elite of the county did indeed live in houses of 50 units or more.

In the sixteenth and early seventeenth centuries a 50+ unit house included a minimum of a hall and two or three public rooms, and after the Restoration an entrance-hall and four good-sized rooms. As it turns out, although the mean size of houses rose in steps from 1540 to 1870, the minimum did not alter very greatly, since

[6] *Northumberland County History*; L. Stone and J. C. Fawtier Stone, 'Country Houses and Their Owner in Hertfordshire 1540-1879' in *Dimensions of Quantitative Research in History*, ed. W. D. Aydelotte, *et al*. Princeton, 1973, pp. 88-101.

there is an irreduceable area of habitable space essential for the purpose of entertainment and display. The 50-unit cut-off effectively excludes those eighteenth- and nineteenth-century villas designed for private and domestic rather than public use.

2. THE USE OF THE COMPUTER

i. Introduction

At the outset it should be explained that, for a wide variety of reasons, several of which were unavoidable, this undertaking was spread over a far greater time-span than was originally contemplated. The project was conceived in late 1965, and preliminary research to establish the range and location of the available data and the subsequent elaboration of what turned out to be the first of two code-books were completed by 1967. Three years later, the first county had been coded, demographic and building programs had been run, and an article written based on the findings.[7] At this point difficulties were encountered owing to the inadequacy of the computer then available at Princeton.[8] It was not only in order to overcome these particular problems, but also to remedy weaknesses revealed by these preliminary runs, that the project was thoroughly restructured in 1971. Most of the programs had been worked out and tested, two counties had been coded using the revised code and the third begun, when in late 1973 the project was stalled once more. It lay in abeyance for the next seven years, while other books were written. Several generations of computers and two programmers had succeeded each other between the time when the project was embarked upon and its completion, so that it is not surprising if there is a distinctly old-fashioned look about much of the use of software. As a result of all this, the computer has been distinctly underused in cliometric terms. It was never intended, in the first place, to be more than *primus inter pares*, but undoubtedly had the initial momentum been maintained a great many things which ended up being done by hand (since there was no hurry and the numbers involved were so small) would have been handled by the computer. Whether it would have been used more extensively, over a wider range, is less certain, given the limitations set by the soon obsolete initial framework.

[7] Op. cit., pp. 56-123.
[8] At that time the Princeton Computer Center had an IBM 360/series computer.

ii. The First Plan: the House and Owner Discs

When the subject of this study was first put forward as one suitable for computerization, it was planned as a study of local elites in three English counties over three and a half centuries. Membership of the elite was defined in terms of ownership of, and residence in, a country house of, or above, a certain minimum size, since there is general agreement that the acquisition of such a country house symbolized entry into the elite. By the time the first tentative efforts were being made to plan how the computer would be used, however, the emphasis had somehow shifted, so that the project had come to be referred to as a study of 'English country-houses and their owners, 1540-1879'.

This shift away from primacy of owners over houses to parity between houses and owners was unfortunate since it clouded the issue for a time. It was due to several factors, one of which was the logical primacy of houses over owners in the arrangement of the necessary preliminary research, since data about houses and their successive owners were readily available in county histories, parish by parish, under their respective manors. This arrangement of the basic research material meant that the earliest data files grouped owners according to their houses. The tilt towards houses was further accentuated by the initial response from computer experts, which was one of enthusiastic advocacy of the use of two discs, one for houses and one for owners, which could be studied first separately and then conjointly by 'meshing' them.

The resultant parity between houses and owners, however, gave rise to a major problem of structure, about how to accommodate the data concerning two such incompatible entities as houses and owners so that they could be processed by the machine both singly and together. There are several important differences between houses and owners. The first is in life-span: whereas a man rarely lives for more than eighty years, a house can last for 340 or more; and whereas a man has only one life, a house can be resurrected many times. The second is in interrelationships: whereas one man may own two or three houses, a house can only belong to one owner at a time. Although the great majority of owners had only one house, the great majority of houses belonged to a changing succession of owners. Moreover, whereas houses are passive, men are active, and their activity sometimes takes the form of building, pulling down, or rebuilding houses. The third is in documentation: while information about transfers of property, and therefore of houses, is almost uniformly excellent, and basic biographical facts about members of the landed classes are generally fairly abundant and uniform, the same is not true of the building history of their houses, which tend to be either very well documented or hardly documented at all. The degree of documentation may depend on the period, the importance of the persons involved, on whether they left descendants and whether these stayed in the same house or county, or quite fortuitously on whether the house took the fancy of a local antiquarian at a period when more evidence was available.

These three differences, in life-span, interrelationships, and documentation result in a real difference in kind, for two reasons. A man who acquires a country house and becomes a member of the county elite is interesting not only for the period when he belongs to the elite, but also in his antecedents, which are relevant to the study of elites and their recruitment. But a house that is built from scratch has no antecedents, and those of a house that has been enlarged into a country house are irrelevant, since its previous owners and residents did not belong to the elite, although the fact that it was enlarged rather than rebuilt may be of interest in terms of the owner who did the enlarging. The one exception to this statement arises in the case of houses created from monastic dwellings seized at the Dissolution, since early acquisition of one of these tended to be restricted to a small circle of well-placed courtiers and administrators; moreover, whether rebuilt or remodelled, their siting, layout, and size were often determined by their prior use. However, they form a very small minority, and the last of them to enter the sample did so in 1650.

Moreover, there are certain milestones common to the lives of all men—descent, birth, education, marriage, career, honours, and death—which provide a natural framework for the ordering of data which are similar for all. On the other hand, when it comes to splitting up the history of a house into manageable units of time, the only item that is guaranteed to recur fairly frequently, because of the shorter life-span of men, is change of ownership. This is because, except for accidental destruction by fire, the building, rebuilding, and pulling-down of houses are governed by the whims of their owners, and their occurrence consequently follows no laws. One house may be built and torn down within a couple of generations; another may last for three centuries with only minor alterations; a third may be added to and altered every twenty years or so, if it happens to change hands frequently; the only things they all have in common is that they belonged to a succession of owners, some of whom may have built, rebuilt, or destroyed them.

With hindsight, it is quite clear that this last observation should have led logically to a reaffirmation of the primacy of owners over houses. A denial of the parity that had been allowed to develop between them would have cut the Gordian knot of disc-related problems, because the whole concept of two separate but linkable discs was rooted in this notion of parity. But this conclusion went unheeded for a while.

In the final analysis, the only milestones common to both houses and owners were changes of ownership, building and rebuilding, and partial or total demolition. On this basis, there evolved the concept of 'events' the succession of which would form the building-blocks in the history of a house.[9] Events would be grouped chronologically by 'event-year', that is years during which one or more events took place. Events fell into three possible categories: transfers of ownership, and positive and negative events, that is building and destruction of houses. The house disc therefore consisted of two cards for each house involved in any event-year; these carried descriptions of the house both before and after the event(s) of the year, and space was allowed for one change of ownership and/or up to three positive and two negative events in any one event-year.

The only common feature shared by changes of ownership and building and/or negative events was the fact that all three were concerned with both house and owner. The significance of the fact that ownership was a necessary relationship between house and owners, whereas remodelling and rebuilding were not, was not observed at the time, though this discrepancy was to prove difficult to handle.

It should be pointed out that the group under study includes owners of houses of a certain size and grandeur, but not all who owned such houses qualified for the sample. A few were what are called 'insignificant owners' who do not qualify, but whose presence needs to be acknowledged when tracing the continuity of transfer of property within a family.

These insignificant owners are non-residents (usually magnates elsewhere), males who died before the age of twenty-one, lunatics, and all females. Non-residents are excluded from the sample of owners because although they owned a seat that qualified for the sample of houses, they did not use it or maintain a presence in the county, preferring to live elsewhere. Women are excluded because

[9] This was worked out by Ms Judith Rowe of the Princeton Computer Center, who was also responsible for the formulation of the 'transfer' code.

they were shut out from political life; and even when they owned a house, if they were married, that house belonged to their husband *de jure uxoris*, a situation which was not alleviated till the late 1860s, and then only partially, when the Married Woman's Property Act was passed. Minors and lunatics are excluded for much the same reasons: like women they were non-persons in law. Insignificant owners are only counted, therefore, when dealing with questions of property and ownership. The rest of the book deals with significant owners only.

iii. Problems of Coding

It was while attempting to process these data satisfactorily that problems of coding arose. The first concerned the qualification of the information, which had originally been gleaned from a wide range of sources of varying reliability. Such qualification implied coding not only statements of fact but also statements of opinion reflecting the judgement of the researcher. The resulting 'edited data' consisted of a statement of fact accompanied by a sub-field containing one of a limited choice of explicit qualifications concerning accuracy (of dates) or reliability (of data). For example all dates are qualified:

o Accurate (i.e. as accurate as the documents allow).
1 highly probable (i.e. possible inaccurate by ± 1 year; these dates are usually arrived at by computing backwards or forwards from another, or several other 'accurate' dates).
2 estimated (i.e. possibly inaccurate by ± 2 to 5 years; these dates are mainly arrived at by computing backwards or forwards from one or more 'highly probable' dates).
3 not known.

It should be pointed out that the method employed for working out highly probable and estimated dates, often calculated in this way one from the other, proved its worth: when further data happened to be unearthed which allowed for greater precision, they all without exception confirmed the tentative dating, so that a 2 qualification could be promoted to a 1 or a 1 to a 0.

The second coding problem concerned suitable definitions which would comply with the computer's insistence on logic, without in the process distorting the truth. In particular, great difficulty was experienced in establishing suitable categories for both positive and negative events. This arose from the wide range of the documentation available, which ran the whole gamut from far more than was needed to barely enough on which to hazard a guess. Both extremes could be, and were, alleviated in one way by coding statements of opinion on the nature of the data. Nevertheless, if a house was well documented, there seemed no limit, except those imposed by the inadequacy of the code, to the number of events that might be described in any one event-year, and if it was poorly documented, the events described would consist mainly of broad generalizations. These might be arbitrarily complemented by a precise detail, if an illustration survived to document it and it happened to figure among the options offered by the code, which listed, without distinguishing between them, both general and detailed observations.

Most of these difficulties arose in connection with the house disc. The owner disc was more straightforward and was made up of three cards for each significant owner, covering information about his life and career, his marriage(s), and his forebears. In due course, the information concerning Hertfordshire owners and their houses was coded in this manner.

The first computer runs made were those dealing with demographic questions, marginal to the main study, but useful for cutting one's computer teeth on. These programs used the owner disc data arranged by date of birth, and answered such questions as age at marriage or at father's death. In handling these, full advantage was taken of the qualification code for all dates, all demographic programs being run first for all accurate and highly probable dates and then for estimated dates. As already noted, in most cases the latter merely served to reinforce the two first. Another analysis dealt with houses strictly in terms of bricks and mortar, and enumerated their size, their building, and other such events in chronological order.

When the time came, however, to deal with owners by date of acquisition and therefore to mesh the house and owner discs together, it emerged that the computer's memory could not handle the volume of data, and that a third file dealing with both owners and houses would have to be created by the computer. The project was consequently halted, pending reorganization.

iv. The Second Plan: The Transfer and Owner Files

The changes involved were radical, involving a major restructuring, an abandonment of parity between houses and owners, and a reassertion of the primacy of owners over houses. Discs, which by then had gone out of favour—temporarily as it turned out—were abandoned; the old house disc was renamed Transfer File, confined to the succession of changes of ownership, and curtailed to one card per house per year in which a house changed hands, thus acknowledging the difference between the abstract concept of ownership and the practical, physical facts of building and pulling down houses. These latter matters were now handled on two extra cards which were added to the new Owner File. This therefore now included the personal data from the old Owner Dics's three cards, as well as all relevant information concerning an owner and his house formerly listed in the old House Disc. The opportunity was taken to revise the code in order to eliminate futile categories and expand inadequate ones.

In its final form, therefore, the data bank consists of two files. The first is the Transfer File, which provides the main armature of the survey and lists in date order all changes of ownership between both significant and insignificant owners, that is whether or not they belong to the sample of owners. There is one card for each change of ownership. This contains the date of transfer, and qualification of date, the ID numbers of the house and the two owners involved in the transaction, the mode of transfer (inheritance or sale), the type of relationship, if any, existing between them, their respective gender (institution, male, male in right of female, female, and unknown), and whether they were significant or insignificant owners. It lists all transfers between all owners while a house remains in the sample of houses, i.e. not only during active ownership by significant owners but also when a house was in abeyance and belonged to an insignificant owner—for example a woman or minor. The file for each house carries its dates of entry into, and (where relevant) its exit from, the sample of houses. This Transfer File therefore holds the key to both samples, since it lists the members of the sample of houses, as well as that of owners. It is used for programs recording houses passing into and out of the sample, and for analyses of modes of transfer from owner to owner, as well as those concerned with the minutiae of intra-familial transactions.

Primacy, however, is now accorded to significant owners, who make up the second, Owner File, with a minimum of five cards for each owner, the first three listing his personal, marriage, and family data, and the last two carrying information about his house. Owners who own more than one house have as many sets of cards as they own houses, which are banked in a Supplementary File, the fourth and fifth cards being different for each house owned.

The first owner card gives his county of origin, dates of birth and death, with qualifications, birth order, and the date at which he became his father's heir (which will be different from his birthdate in the case of an eldest surviving son); whether he changed his name, the nature of the data concerning him, his titles of honour with dates; a summary of the number of wives and heiresses he married, the number of sons and daughters who survived age fifteen, and whether at his death he left a male heir; his expectations at age twenty (heir or not), and a very rough assessment of his career and wealth; the known sources of his wealth, allowing for up to three out of seventy career options; the date of known windfalls and how acquired; the highest civic dignity held; local office, and dates when he first served as sheriff, JP, MP, including the type of seat held in Parliament and the degree of his political involvement; his education at the University and the Inns of Court; and known interests, allowing for three out of a possible nine rough fields.

The second owner card covers his marriage(s), allowing for up to three, with date and qualification, the wife's connection to the sample, if any, her family background (including former husband, if any), number of children born of the marriage, and date of death.

The third card covers information concerning the heir status, local origin, status, and occupation of the owner's father and grandfathers, the dates of his father's death and promotion (if any) to honours, and the number of his own sons, sons-in-law, and grandsons who figure in the sample.

The fourth owner card carries the dates and modes of acquisition and disposal of his house, as well as the ID numbers of the previous and subsequent owners and their status; a description of the house and its age on acquisition, its ID number, and its size in terms of units both on acquisition and disposal; the number of owners since the last purchase, both in and out of sample, and a summary of the documentation regarding the house.

The fifth owner card which, in the case of non-builders, is mainly blank, contains an account of such positive (building) and negative (destructive) events as occurred during his ownership. These events may consist either of one event or a group of related events which occurred to the house or grounds. There is space to record in sequential order three negative and two positive events or groups of related events, covering major building, additions, decorative architectural effects, office and grounds, combinations of all of which successfully cover all contingencies, however superficially. The fact of the matter is that these superficial notations are all that can be claimed for the vast majority of building events, so that for counting purposes, which is all the computer can do, this is all that is necessary.

v. Uses of the Files

As already mentioned, the coded data are not limited to statements of fact but also include statements of opinion, such as the 'edited' data used to deal with the problem of qualification of dates and reliability of data. 'Selected' data are also resorted to in order to simplify both coding and programming. These are another type of statement of opinion and may consist of either a summary of one or more items of raw information already coded as such, or a summary of such information qualified by other information not already coded. Thus an owner's children appear in different guises so that answers to different questions are easier of access: they are expressed in terms of the total children borne by each wife, as well as of an owner's total sons and daughters who survived to the age when they became expensive to educate, endow with marriage portions, and launch into the world, and whether, at his death, he left a male heir to carry on the line. With imperfect data, such simple 'selection' of the raw data by the researcher instead of the computer makes programming simpler and therefore less liable to error.

Similarly an owner's heir status is assessed at birth (his birth order), again at age twenty (when if he was a younger son he might embark on a career), and again if and when he became heir presumptive to his father, through the death without heirs of one or more elder brothers. As a result, although in the case of eldest sons, who inevitably make up the majority of the sample, all these slots are in the main redundant, these assessments make it possible to follow closely the turns and twists by which one who started as a younger son might end up an heir to seat or title or both. This serves to shed some light, if not on younger sons in general, at least on those successful or lucky ones who ended up in the sample of owners.

The revision of the code for positive and negative building events relied heavily on the coding of such statements of opinion. Thus when describing building additions and alterations, these are no longer, as before, assessed in terms of the minutiae of their architectural detail, which signify nothing when lumped together with others, but in terms of the effect achieved, and therefore presumably intended. At all events the new code justified itself by successfully accommodating all contingencies that arose to challenge its response in the three counties, regardless of the amount of documentation available.

Whenever possible, data were coded in such a way that they

could be grouped and regrouped in different ways, so that programs operate like the sluices of a dam, releasing facts in greater or lesser detail as the situation warrants. Thus when dealing with the problem of owners' sources of wealth, programs were designed which considered these in a variety of ways, ranging from a simple dichotomy between 'other than land' and 'only landed', through subdivisions into four large groups (office, law, business, and landed), to a more detailed breakdown into fourteen career categories made up from the seventy sub-categories according to which an owner's occupation or source of wealth was coded. One of the more satisfactory computer runs, which shed considerable light on a number of questions relating to social mobility, both in its dramatic, upward, and more humdrum, downward, forms, was based on a program designed to cross-tabulate the occupations or sources of wealth of all owners with those of their fathers. These occupations were divided into rough categories: land, office, law, and business, with an extra slot for 'unknown' in the case of fathers. The program consisted of two successive runs for each fifty-year birth cohort, once for those who, at age twenty *expected* to inherit and once for those who did not. This was done because twenty was a critical point in the life of a young man of the landed classes, the age at which he had to decide on whether to embark on a career, and if so which one, both decisions being based on his expectations at that moment. The whole program was then run a second and a third time, both for those who did inherit their country house and for those who purchased it.

The computer having thus divided the population into these several elements, it was then necessary to interpret the results. The sons of landed fathers were the first to be considered, since they both made up the bulk of the population and essentially needed to be put to one side. The first were the landed sons of landed fathers, those who purchased as well as those who inherited. Then there were the 'occupied' sons of landed fathers, once more according to whether they purchased or inherited. The purchasers tended to be those who had succeeded well enough in their avocation to make their way back into the class in which they were born, whereas the inheritors' success in life derived mainly from the death of elder brothers and had little or nothing to do with their success or lack of it in the career of their choice.

Turning next to the sons of 'occupied' fathers, the same process of subdivision according to their mode of acquisition served to separate those whose successful career enabled them to buy their way into the landed classes from those, not necessarily successful, lawyers, etc. with gentry connections, who were rescued from the middle-class way of life of their fathers by inheritance brought about by the demographic attrition of a senior branch of their family.

A prime target of the enquiry, throughout, had been the occupations, before inheriting, of indirect inheritors and of younger sons of landed fathers, which is all that could have been attempted had there been no computer. With it, however, it was no more difficult to run the program for the whole population and then make it divide that population into its various subgroups, some of which at least were known to be meaningful. As a result, new insights and confirmation of hunches sharpened awareness of the sample as a whole, and therefore of the significance of odd fluctuations. This analysis made it possible to assess which, at different periods, were the occupations, success in which might lead to entry into the landed classes, as well as those which were deemed sufficiently genteel for younger sons and their descendants. It was possible, as a result, to see whether there existed any connection between the two, that is whether or not a career became genteel following the influx into the landed classes of some of its practitioners. This problem could be explored further by comparison with a similar program in which owners' education at the Universities and Inns of Court was cross-tabulated with their father's source of wealth. In many respects these programs provided the essential structural scaffolding for the ensuing case-by-case examination of those individual owners who were newcomers to the landed classes, and for the whole discussion of social mobility. Further light was shed by another program which cross-tabulated the particular forms of office-holding or business activity of owners over time, whether they built or not, how they acquired their property, and whether they sold it.

vi. Sample Size

A total of 2,246 'significant' owners (about each of whom up to 160 pieces of information were recorded) owned and lived in 362 country houses between the years 1540 and 1879 in Northamptonshire and Hertfordshire and between 1610 and 1879 in Northumberland. These 2,246 owners and 362 houses constitute respectively the two samples of owners and houses. If these 2,246 owners are included as many times as they owned houses, their numbers swell to 2,434. Transfers between all owners, significant and insignificant (the latter made up of 86 males—1 idiot, 27 minors, and 58 magnates elsewhere—and 129 females), amount to 2,520.

If Crown grants and nominal transfers of houses between spouses on marriage, widowhood, or remarriage are put to one side, one is left with 2,312 transfers, the distribution of which over time and space is recorded in Tables 3.1 and .8, and 4.2 and .6.

When the 2,246 significant owners who make up the sample of owners are considered simply as individuals, they are classified chronologically by date of birth (forty-five missing observations): Table 2.5 gives their breakdown according to the reliability of their date of birth. It is very noticeable how high is the proportion of correct and nearly correct dates for those born from 1600 to 1800 (with Northumberland ahead in the late eighteenth century). By the nineteenth century, the proportion is uniformly very high. Other tables in the same birth order, the totals of which vary according to the reliability of other dates used, are Tables 2.2; 3.2-.7, .10; 7.1-6; 8.3.

Data were arranged chronologically in three different ways: by owner's date of birth for demographic problems and for dealing with most questions about personal life such as education, marriages, or careers; by owner's date of acquisition of his house, for all matters relating to the acquisition, use, and building of the latter; and by date of disposal for all sales. Chronologically the first was divided into seven fifty-year birth cohorts, the other two into six sixty-year periods. Owners sorted by date of acquisition were also examined at twenty-year intervals to build up a picture of how the composition of the group appeared to contemporaries. Building activities were charted by thirty-year moving averages to smooth out the curve and to compensate for the wide margin of error.

vii. Categories of Owners

In order to obtain the answers to different questions, the sample of owners also had to be divided in different ways, each appropriate to the problem under review. We have already seen how they could be divided according to their expectations at age twenty or their occupation or source of wealth. The most frequently used method of subdividing owners, in dealing with a wide range of topics from building to social mobility, was according to their mode of acquisition of their houses; that is whether they were inheritors or purchasers.

Inheritors fell into different groups according to their mode of inheritance, whether following the rules of primogeniture or by bequest. It could be "direct" from father to son or grandson, or "indirect" to or through siblings, that is to brothers, nephews, uncles, or cousins; when primogeniture broke down, it could be by bequest through the female line or by marriage to an heiress whose husband acquired his wife's property *de jure uxoris*, or to a non-relative. Except for the last two, all these were intra-familial transfers. In terms of blood relationship, husbands of heiresses and non-relatives were outsiders.

Purchasers were split along different lines. In order to find out to what extent they were successful in establishing new families, they were divided into purchaser-settlers, who left their property to heirs in sample and thus started new county families, however short-lived; and purchaser-sellers, who either sold in their lifetime or left instructions to sell in their wills.

In order to probe more deeply into the question of social mobility, it was necessary to analyse carefully those who brought a house into the sample of houses and thereby themselves into the sample of owners. These are known as 'entrants'. Like everybody else, entrants either inherited or purchased their houses, which makes them either 'inheritor-entrants' or 'purchaser-entrants'. Similarly, non-entrants, who inherited or purchased from an owner in sample, are called 'sample inheritors' or 'sample purchasers'. If these four groups are considered in terms of upward social mobility, only sample inheritors go back one or more generations; both types of entrants and also sample purchasers being first generation in sample, or 'newcomers'.

In order to study the effect of these entrants on the overall size of the sample, owners were divided in yet another way: 'entrants' as already defined, who increased the size of the sample; 'non-entrants', who left it unchanged, that is who both acquired their house from, and disposed of it to, another owner in sample; and 'drop-outs' who diminished the sample. They might accomplish this either by the physical destruction or neglect of their house, or by their own social derogation, or by 'selling out of sample' either to an institution or a socially unsuitable owner.

viii. Programs

The smallness and changing composition of the sample caused several difficulties in programming. The first was that, since this study is essentially concerned with change, and consequently the samples of owners and of houses are constantly in flux, the framework had to be designed in such a way that various categories of owners and houses could move freely into and out of their respective samples as circumstances might dictate without bringing down the whole edifice. Arrangements had to be made to accommodate extraneous categories such as supernumerary houses. These only qualify for the sample of houses during such times as they are used as a main or an occasional seat, and not if used exclusively as residences for members of an owner's immediate family.

In the second place, the samples are not only constantly changing, they are also small: for most of the 340 years covered, none of the three county samples had more than seventy houses at any one time, while total owners are fewer still, since some owned more than one house. Moreover, two factors made it all but impossible to use global figures. The first, which was obvious from the beginning, was the long time-span from 1540 to 1879 which had to be divided up into periods. Only seven tables (5.1 and 2 and 11.11-.15) lack chronological subdivisions. With few exceptions, all counts therefore have to be repeated: subdivisions by date of birth are in seven fifty-year cohorts, as in Table 2.2; subdivisions by date of acquisition are usually in six sixty-year periods, as in Table 6.1. Subdivisions by date of disposal also use the same six sixty-year periods, so as to allow comparisons between purchases and sales, as in Table 5.3. However the first period, during which hardly any sales took place, is only forty years. Very occasionally, however, the subdivisions are as small as twenty years, as in Table 4.1.

The second factor was the very great differences between the three counties which emerged from the preliminary runs for each county. For demographic purposes, most results were the same for all three and could safely be added together. In dealing with the main question of social mobility, however, the extreme differences from one county to another made it impossible to add them together without grave distortion. This was due to the fact that the differences observed were both structural, generating quite different patterns, and temporal, involving differences of periodicity of similar developments. The consequent impossibility of using global totals meant that in some cases the numbers became too small to be usefully handled by machine. However, since the data were all stored on tape, it was possible to devise special data print-outs which ensured that the more detailed hand work at the individual level used the same data as the computer runs.

Furthermore, although the total population is small, and the long time-span makes it smaller still, the number of variables is high: there are about twenty-five variables for houses and over eighty for owners, between any number of which cross-tabulations may be tried.

All the initial programs were specially designed for the project in FORTRAN. Later, after restructuring had taken place, SPSS programs were increasingly used. The majority of these early programs were concerned with the erection of a factual scaffolding, the computer being used to count and recount the samples over time and lay them out for inspection by grouping them into various categories and subgroups.

In order to widen the scope of correlations, which always had to include time as one of the variables, various devices had to be resorted to. Only where time is known or suspected to have been an important dimension are programs run with the population divided horizontally according to time-periods, as well as vertically according to the different categories of the other variable under consideration. The program can then be run once for all owners and then, if mode of acquisition is thought to be important, once for all direct inheritors, once for all indirect inheritors, and once for all purchasers, or perhaps once for all builders, if that matters. The resultant tables, because of the horizontal layout, present change over time in clearly visible terms. On the other hand, if time is not thought to be of major importance, two variables can be cross-tabulated and the program run six times, once for each sixty-year period.

Computer print-outs in special format were used all along as reference tools. Owners were available both by date of birth and acquisition. On these print-outs, the first owner card, in which all eighty columns were filled, was extended with blanks between fields to make it legible. Houses were available in a particularly useful format: the Transfer file and the last two cards of the Owner file (including the Supplementary file) were both printed out in house order according to the sequence of ownership, thus encapsulating the whole history of the individual houses. An unexpected benefit was that thanks to these print-outs it was possible to continue working on the project even when cut off from books and files.

The first print-out in special format which was more than a straightforward data print-out was made in response to a suggestion that it might be feasible to attempt a regression analysis of the factors involved in a successful career (which, if it is possible to define success in a foolproof way, may yet prove to be the case). At all events, those fields which were thought relevant were printed out in order to explore the situation. It soon became clear that the data as coded were inadequate for such a venture, which would have required the inclusion of far more detailed data than was available for all those under review. Since the subject in any case was marginal to the main problem, it was put to one side. The only positive result was the discovery that, especially during the earlier periods, longevity was a very important factor, no doubt because it allowed the successful further time in which to consolidate the gains acquired during their original rise to power.

Other possibilities were tried but proved useless. Thus the women, who make up the bulk of the insignificant owners, were given ID numbers which linked them to their nearest male relative in the sample, with the idea that this might be useful. But it soon became clear that all that would be demonstrated thereby was either already available in the programs run with the Transfer file, or amounted to no more than the obvious fact that the squirearchy and above were closely linked through their womenfolk.

Similarly, it was thought that the ID numbers of houses (which followed the numerical sequence of their UK National Grid references (from the British Ordnance Survey l″ = 1km maps) might prove useful in plotting maps of country houses at different dates. Once the maps had been designed, however, it was not at all clear what useful rather than ornamental purpose they could serve, except to help drive up the price of the book. This is a good, albeit modest, example of the kind of folly into which it is possible to be led by the computer's virtuosity.

ix. Conclusion

The initial net of questions cast with the aid of the computer was wide and far-ranging, and served to isolate problem areas, as well as to cover most demographic questions and all basic building problems. The tables produced in answer to questions posed, and the graphing of various parts of these tables, though frequently insufficiently explicit in themselves to warrant inclusion in the final analysis of the data, were nevertheless invaluable in narrowing down the study to those issues that were significant. In this respect, the computer was excellent at showing up false categories, and at correcting glib generalizations based on a few highly visible and well-documented examples which it showed to be exceptions rather than the norm. Without the corrective effect of many of these early computer runs, it would have been extremely tempting to give a very plausible account of major trends of one kind or another which, upon close inspection, turned out to be nothing of the sort.

There is little doubt that in dealing with data as sloppy as that provided by a variety of sources which are not uniform in their origin, arrangement, and degree of reliability, it is imprudent to rely entirely on the computer for more than fairly straightforward calculations. Devising a suitable code to deal honestly with this imprecision considerably heightens the historian's awareness of the relative reliability of the data used, even though this awareness is constantly in danger of being dulled by the aura of minute mathematical exactitude which the computer's *modus operandi* tends to impart to its output.

Cliometricians will certainly look askance at the way the computer was used, or misused, in this endeavour. The exciting possibilities it seemed to hold in store for the social sciences were the stimulus for the project in 1965, when it was originally put forward as an example of the type of historical problem which might perhaps benefit from the new technique. The suggestion was based on only the vaguest conception of how a computer might in fact function. In the long run, this ensured that the project would never be allowed to deviate from its primary historical purpose in order to conform to the needs of the machine, even though in the process the rapidly expanding possibilities of the computer were left largely unexplored.

TABLES

TABLE 2.1

County Endogamy of Gentry* and Titular Elite in 1640

| | Proportion of Wives from the Same County | | |
County	Gentry Only %	Knights and Barts. %	Both %
Hertfordshire[1]	37	31	36
Essex[1]	43	28	41
Dorset[2]			49
Suffolk[1]	69	43	67
Lancashire[3]			70
Norfolk[1]	72	44[6]	69
Cheshire[4]		48	75
Kent[5]	82	59	62

*It is by no means certain that the different compilers of these figures have used identical criteria for gentry. The gentry comparisons should therefore be treated with caution.

[1] C. A. Holmes, The Eastern Association (unpublished Cambridge Ph.D. Thesis, 1969), Appendix I. I owe this information to Professor Holmes.

[2] J. P. Ferns, 'Gentry of Dorset on the Eve of the Civil War', Genealogist's Magazine, 15, 1965, p. 108.

[3] B. G. Blackwood, 'Marriages of Lancashire Gentry on the Eve of the Civil War', Genealogist's Magazine, 16, 1970, p. 327. This breaks down into about 60% for the county gentry, and about 80% for the parish gentry.

[4] J. Morrill, Cheshire 1630-1660, Oxford, 1974, pp. 4 note 2, 16.

[5] A. Everitt, The Community of Kent and the Great Rebellion, London, 1966, p. 328.

[6] In 1660 and 1720 the figures for the 100-odd leading squires and above were 47% and 45% respectively, which closely matches Holmes's figures. I owe this information to Professor J. Rosenheim.

TABLE 2.2 (FIGS. 2.1 and 2.2)

County and Regional Endogamy[1]

(First Wives from Within the Same County or Region)

	Proportion of First Wives from the Same County or Region									
	Herts.				Northants.			Northumb.		
Period of Birth	Same County %	Same Region %	London %	N	Same County %	Same Region %	N	Same County %	Same Region %	N
-1549	28	42	7	43	44	74	69			
1550-99	30	55	15	73	30	55	97	57	90	19
1600-49	23	46	20	75	18	37	101	34	71	35
1650-99	17	47	23	71	19	34	67	38	62	55
1700-49	17	38	14	58	21	35	65	41	58	53
1750-99	23	46	17	48	14	29	63	28	55	67
1800-	16	40	15	58	25	36	56	21	47	57

[1]Owners born in the County only.

TABLE 2.3 (FIG. 2.3)

Density of Houses by Size in Seven Counties, c. 1662-1673[1]

Size of House by Number of Hearths	Thousands of Acres per House						
	Herts.	Northants.	Surrey	Suffolk	Warws.	Dorset	Derby.
20-24	23	32	11	32	38	53	55
25-34	25	71	28	56	72	90	132
35-44	81	64	61	157	113	211	-
45+	101	92	61	315	189	-	110
20-45+	10	14	5	17	18	29	29

[1]This evidence comes from the Hearth Tax Records for the various counties: Herts.: P.R.O., E179/248/23; 375/30; 375/31; Northants: P.R.O., E179/254/11, 14; 157/446; 'Surrey Hearth Tax, 1664', ed. C. A. F. Meekings, Surrey Record Society, xviii, 1940; 'Suffolk in 1674', Suffolk Green Books, xiii, 1905; Hearth Tax Assessment for 1670 in Warwickshire County Record Office (we owe this information to Dr. Judith Hurwich); Dorset Hearth Tax 1662-4, ed. C. A. F. Meekings, Dorset Record Society, 1951; 'Derbyshire Hearth Tax Assessments 1662-70', ed. D. G. Edwards, Derbyshire Record Society, vii, 1982.

TABLE 2.4 (FIG. 2.4)

Distribution of Private Estates by Size in 1873[1]

Size of Estates in Acres	Herts. %	Northants. %	Northumb. %
1 - 99	9	11	4
100 - 299	10	13	4
300 - 999	18	13	8
1,000 - 2,999	17	9	14
3,000 - 9,999	17	17	21
10,000+	23	30	50

[1]F.M.L. Thompson, English Landed Society in the Nineteenth Century, London, 1963, pp. 32, 114-15, 117.

These figures exclude both waste, and property corporately owned by the Crown, the Church, etc., which explains why they do not add up to 100% (letter of Professor F.M.L. Thompson, 6 Nov. 1979).

TABLE 2.5

Frequency Count of Owners by Date of Birth, According to Date Qualification

County	Qualification of date of birth[1]	Birth Cohorts							
		-1549 %	1550-99 %	1600-49 %	1650-99 %	1700-59 %	1750-99 %	1800+ %	Un-known N
Herts.	0 & 1	53	69	85	81	81	87	97	
	2	47	31	15	19	19	13	3	
	N	87	147	137	165	168	173	139	33
Northants.	0 & 1	55	76	85	84	86	86	99	
	2	45	24	15	16	14	13	1	
	N	95	135	134	119	125	110	92	11
Northumb.	0 & 1	50	63	85	84	86	96	96	
	2	50	37	15	16	14	4	4	
	N	2	19	39	63	72	97	83	1
All Three Counties	0 & 1	54	72	85	82	84	89	97	
	2	46	28	15	18	16	11	3	
	N	184	301	310	347	365	380	314	45

[1]For a definition of these qualifications, see above, p. x.

TABLE 2.6 (FIG. 2.5)

Correlation of Hearth Tax and Estimated House Size in 'Units',
c.1662–1673: Hertfordshire

House	Hearths	Units[1]
Moor Park	51	312
Hadham Hall	52	300
Gorhambury	51	250
Standon Lordship	48	220
Broxbournbury	36	160
Balls Park	31	142
Tyttenhanger	31	132
The Hoo	26	130
Aspenden Hall	27	130
North Mymms Place	24	117
Rothamstead	23	116
New Place	25	113
Aldenham Manor House	31	110
Aldenham House	23	105
Ware Park	26	100
Brocket Hall	20	90
Cokenhatch	22	90
Pishiobury	21	84
Wyddial Hall	21	80
Beechwood	14	80
Rawdon House	18	77
Bonningtons	15	70
Moor Place	22	68
Tewin Water	15	64
Bedwell Park	15	62
Brent Pelham Hall	12	60
Little Court	11	54
Temple Dinsley	10	50

[1]Estimated from evidence independent of the Hearth Tax.

TABLE 2.7 (FIG. 2.6)

Correlation of Hearth Tax and Estimated House Size in 'Units,'
c.1662–1673:   Northamptonshire

House	Hearths	Units[1]
Burghley House	70	463
Castle Ashby	64	418
Drayton House	60	335
Althorp	64	290
Kirby Hall	30	260
Apethorpe	48	236
Deene Park	45	228
Rushton Hall	44	220
Boughton House	42	180
Milton Hall	37	173
Thorpe Hall	35	173
Astwell Castle	32	170
Steane Manor House	33	170
Easton Maudit Hall	40	150
Lilford Hall	30	149
Rockingham Castle	26	140
Fawsley Hall	26	136
Barnwell Castle	37	125
Stoke Bruerne Park	18	124
Aynho Park	28	123
Canons Ashby Priory	23	120
Dingley Hall	24	110
Lamport Hall	23	100
Sywell Hall	20	92
Norton Hall	20	90
Winwick Manor House	21	85
East Carlton Hall	21	80
Stoke Doyle	18	75
Watford Court	18	74
Pytchley Hall	17	74
Edgecote House	16	71
Catesby Priory	20	70
Upton Manor House	17	70
Maidwell Hall	17	65
Eydon Hall	15	65
Southwick Hall	17	64
Kelmarsh Hall	17	62
Newton-in-the-Willows Hall	20	60

[1]Estimated from evidence independent of the Hearth Tax.

TABLE 3.1

Frequency Count of All Types of Transfer[1]

Period by Date of Transfer	Direct Inheritance[2] N	Indirect Inheritance[3] N	Total Inheritance N	%	Sales in Lifetime[4] N	Sales after Death[5] N	Total Sales N	Other Transfers[6] N	Total Transfers N
1540-59	37	14	51	88	2	1	3	4	58
1560-79	26	12	38	90	2	–	2	2	42
1580-99	58	18	76	88	5	2	7	3	86
1600-19	82	21	103	76	18	4	22	10	135
1620-39	84	19	103	82	17	6	23	–	126
1640-59	75	18	93	79	16	3	19	6	118
1660-79	100	25	125	75	20	9	29	12	166
1680-99	95	30	125	81	17	9	26	3	154
1700-19	76	45	121	80	18	8	26	5	152
1720-39	84	39	123	81	14	8	22	6	151
1740-59	75	51	126	81	6	15	21	9	156
1760-79	65	51	116	82	12	11	23	3	142
1780-99	72	43	115	70	23	19	42	7	164
1800-19	66	42	108	65	29	18	47	10	165
1820-39	76	45	121	76	18	13	31	7	159
1840-59	75	41	116	70	18	16	34	15	165
1860-79	94	34	128	74	18	15	33	12	173
	124	548	1,788		253	157	410	114	2,312

(NOTES TO TABLE 3.1)

[1] These figures differ from those in tables by date of acquisition or disposal (e.g. 6.1, 4.1) since they include transfers by insignificant owners (see p.   ) and exclude acquisition by entrants and Crown grantees.

[2] Direct transfers from father (or, if the latter predeceased his father, from paternal grandfather) to heir or an only heiress (whose husband became owner de jure uxoris).

[3] Transfers to younger sons, coheiresses, siblings, uncles and aunts, nephews and nieces, cousins, or persons related only by marriage.

[4] Fifty of these sales were made by insignificant owners, some of whom were selling long-neglected houses to purchasers who rebuilt them.

[5] Sales made by executors at owner's death or shortly after, and in four cases considerably later.

[6] Gifts, long leases, sales to existing leaseholders, and cases about which there is insufficient data.

TABLE 3.2 (FIG. 3.1)

Male Nuptiality

Period by Date of Birth	Proportion Never Married %	Proportion Married %	Proportion of Married Who Remarried %	Remarriages As Proportion of Marriages %	N
-1549	3	97	28	21	184
1550-99	6	94	26	20	301
1600-49	5	95	26	20	310
1650-99	15	85	16	13	347
1700-49	16	84	16	13	365
1750-99	13	87	16	13	380
1800-	13	87	15	13	314

TABLE 3.3 (FIGS. 3.2, 3.6, 3.7)

Age at, Duration, and Fertility of, First Marriages (Heirs Only)[1]

Period by Date of Birth[1]	Median Age of Husbands at First Marriage Years	Median Duration of First Marriage Years	Proportion of Child-less First Marriages %	Proportion of Child-less First Marriages Which Lasted %	N
-1549	21	30	10	100	39
1550-99	24	26	5	75	100
1600-49	24	22	9	55	134
1650-99	25	19	16	65	125
1700-49	26	22	19	58	148
1750-99	29	30	18	77	168
1800-	27	28	23	71	177

[1] By 'Heir' is meant eldest son and heir, including an eldest surviving son whose expectations at 20 were those of an heir.

[2] To convert these into dates of marriage, an extra 20 to 25 years should be added.

TABLE 3.4 (FIG. 3.3)

Male Life Expectation at Twenty-one (Heirs Only)

Period by Date of Birth	Life Expectation Years	N
-1549	63	75
1550-99	63	154
1600-49	64	191
1650-99	56	204
1700-49	62	206
1750-99	69	212
1800-	66	211

TABLE 3.5 (FIG. 3.4)

Termination of First Marriages
by Death of Husband or Wife

(Heirs Only)

Duration of Marriage Years	Terminated by Death of Wife %	Terminated by Death of Husband %	Total %	N
0-9	15	4	19	128
10-19	13	7	21	140
20-29	10	12	21	143
30-39	8	10	18	123
40-49	5	8	13	90
50 Plus	4	4	9	60
Total	54	46	100	684

TABLE 3.6 (FIG. 3.5)

Mean Number of Recorded Children Born[1]

Period by Date of Birth	Mean Number of Recorded Children by First Marriage	Mean Number of Recorded Children by All Marriages	Fathers N
-1549	4.1	4.9	179
1550-99	4.1	4.7	282
1600-49	4.0	4.8	295
1650-99	3.1	3.8	296
1700-49	3.3	3.8	308
1750-99	3.8	4.2	329
1800-	3.6	3.9	274

[1]This can only be an approximate estimate, especially in the earlier periods when a number of children who died in infancy failed to be recorded. But this merely reinforces the magnitude of the seventeenth-century decline.

TABLE 3.7 (FIG. 3.8)

Proportion of Owners Who Died without a Surviving Son

Period by Date of Birth of Owners	Unmarried Owners %	Owners Married but without a Surviving Son %	All Owners without a Surviving Son %	N
-1549	3	17	20	184
1550-99	6	19	25	301
1600-49	5	21	26	310
1650-99	15	26	41	347
1700-49	16	27	43	365
1750-99	13	26	39	380
1800-	13	24	37	314

TABLE 3.8 (FIG. 3.9)

Inheritances by Children as a Proportion of All Transfers by Inheritance[1]

Period of Transfer	Inheritances by Children			All Transfers by Inheritance N
	Male %	Female %	Total %	
1549–59	80	4	84	51
60–79	76	5	81	38
80–99	79	3	82	76
1600–19	79	2	81	103
20–39	78	5	83	103
40–59	82	4	86	93
60–79	78	6	83	125
80–99	75	5	80	125
1700–19	65	3	68	121
20–39	67	3	70	123
40–59	55	6	61	126
60–79	50	8	58	116
80–99	63	3	67	115
1800–19	63	3	66	108
20–39	61	5	66	121
40–59	65	2	68	116
60–79	73	4	77	128

[1] This includes all transfers of houses from parents to children, including children who were not heirs or heiresses, but excludes acquisitions by entrants.

TABLE 3.9 (FIG. 3.10)

Proportion of First Marriages of Heirs
after Their Father's Death[1]

Period of Inheritance[2]	First Marriages after Deaths of Fathers %	N
-1579	43	47
1580-1639	41	138
1649-99	47	157
1700-59	56	149
1760-1819	52	147
1829-79	38	183

[1]Known first marriages of eldest surviving sons.

[2]Since the periods are those of the sons' inheritance,
they are a rough approximation to the periods of the
marriages.

TABLE 3.10 (FIG. 3.11)

Median Age of Heirs at Their Father's Death[1]

Period by Date of Birth	Age	N
1550-99	29	103
1600-49	26	135
1650-99	19	143
1700-49	25	138
1750-99	28	127
1800-	29	128

[1]The pre-1549 numbers are too small, and too skewed to
those who survived until 1540, to be usable.

TABLE 4.1 (FIGS. 4.1 AND 4.2)

All Modes of Disposal

Period of Disposal	Direct Inheritance		Indirect Inheritance		All Disposals by Inheritance	Disposals by Sale	Other Disposals	Total Disposals
	% of Disposals by Inheritance %	% of all Disposals %	% of Disposals by Inheritance %	% of all Disposals %	% of all Disposals %	% of all Disposals %	% of all Disposals %	N
1540-59	82	78	18	18	96	4	-	51
1560-79	77	71	23	21	93	7	-	42
1580-99	82	79	18	17	96	3	1	77
1600-19	83	67	17	14	81	16	4	129
1629-39	85	68	15	12	80	18	2	126
1640-59	81	67	19	15	82	18	-	118
1660-79	86	68	14	11	79	15	6	149
1680-99	81	67	19	15	82	17	1	143
1700-19	72	59	28	23	82	15	3	150
1720-39	66	56	34	28	84	14	2	147
1740-59	66	56	34	29	85	12	3	145
1760-79	59	50	41	34	84	14	-	134
1780-99	68	51	32	24	75	24	1	157
1800-19	65	44	35	24	68	28	4	156
1820-39	65	52	35	28	80	16	5	143
1840-59	68	51	32	24	75	22	3	153
1860-79	69	55	31	25	82	18	-	165
								2,185

TABLE 4.2 (FIG. 4.3)

Transfers to or through Women as a Proportion
of all Transfers by Inheritance

Period of Transfer	Transfer to Women %	Transfer through Women %	Total Transfers to or through Women %	Total Transfers by Inheritance N
1540-59	8	6	14	51
60-79	8	5	13	38
80-99	4	5	9	76
1600-19	3	4	7	103
20-39	5	4	9	103
40-59	8	4	12	93
60-79	6	3	10	125
80-99	4	1	5	125
1700-19	11	6	17	121
20-39	8	2	10	123
40-59	13	9	22	126
60-79	17	12	29	116
80-99	9	8	17	115
1800-19	10	5	15	108
20-39	11	6	17	121
40-59	7	6	13	116
60-79	10	3	13	128

TABLE 4.3 (FIG. 4.4)

Proportion of all Marriages by Inheritors to
Heiresses or Widows

Period of Birth	Marriages to Heiresses %	Marriages to Widows %	All Marriages N
-1549	24	22	95
1550-99	22	11	237
1600-49	26	11	292
1650-99	29	8	278
1700-49	37	5	261
1750-99	24	6	265
1800-	13	3	231

TABLE 4.4 (FIG. 4.5)

Surname Changes in Britain, 1760-1899[1]

Period	Name Substitutions N	Name Additions by Hyphenation N	Total Changes N	Name Substitutions by Act of Parliament N	Name Additions by Prefix rather than Suffix N	% of Additions
1760-9	48	-	48	8		
70-9	132	-	132	6		
80-9	168	12	180	2		
90-9	248	60	308	2		
1800-9	256	96	352	1	16	17
10-9	236	124	360	2	20	16
20-9	168	176	344	1	28	16
30-9	188	156	344	1	32	20
40-9	116	124	240		20	16
50-9	136	192	328		32	17
60-9	252	308	560		84	27
70-9	396	476	872		192	40
80-9	456	552	1,008		284	51
90-9	376	472	848		240	51

[1]This is an estimate of the totals, based on a 25 percent sample (the
first 89 pages out of 357) taken from W.P.W. Phillimore and E. A. Fry,
An Index to Changes of Name, London, 1905.

TABLE 4.5

Surname Changes by Owners in Sample[1]

Date of Acquisition[2]	Sources of New Names			Total Name-Changes N	Total Owners in Sample N	Name-Changes Proportionate to Owners %
	Name of Wife N	Name of Mother N	Name of Other N			
-1579	-	-	-	-	183	-
1580-1639	-	-	1	1	356	-
1640-99	2	1	1	4	396	1
1700-59	2	8	7	17	425	4
1760-1819	3	10	20	33	416	8
1820-79	14	10	15	39	456	9

[1]This table 1) excludes surnames of donors which were given as first names to the eldest sons of the recipients; 2) includes both the substitution of one surname for another (which became a first name) and the addition of a surname as prefix or suffix by hyphenation.

[2]This is the date at which the owner inherited a seat and entered the sample. If it was the gift which led to the name-change that caused the owner to enter the sample, the two dates coincide.

TABLE 4.6 (FIG. 4.6)

Transfers by Inheritance by County as a Proportion of All Transfers

Period of Transfer	Herts.		Northants.		Northumb.	
	All Transfers N	Transfers by Inheritance %	All Transfers N	Transfers by Inheritance %	All Transfers N	Transfers by Inheritance %
1540-59	28	89	30	87		
1560-79	19	89	23	91		
1580-99	40	83	46	93		
1600-19	65	69	67	82	3	100
1620-39	55	78	62	93	9	100
1640-59	55	60	52	94	11	100
1660-79	82	66	68	84	16	94
1680-99	78	81	56	80	20	85
1700-19	69	73	57	86	26	85
1720-39	71	76	59	85	21	90
1740-59	75	76	54	81	27	93
1760-79	66	67	49	94	27	96
1780-99	85	61	48	77	31	84
1800-19	79	42	45	87	41	88
1820-39	82	70	48	83	29	83
1840-59	71	63	50	72	44	82
1860-79	88	61	41	88	44	86
1540-1879	1,108	68	855	85	349	88

TABLE 5.1 (Fig. 5.1)

All Owners and all Sellers by Mode of Acquisition[1]

Mode of Acquisition	All Disposals 1540-1879		All Sales 1540-1879	
	N	% of all Disposals	N	% of Disposals in the Category of Acquisition
Direct Inheritance[2]	871		102	12
Indirect Inheritance[2]	506		58	11
Total Inheritance[2]	1,377	63	160	12
Purchase	459		142	31
Inheritance from Purchaser	240		58	24
Total Purchase and Inheritance from Purchaser	699	32	200	29
Total Purchase and Inheritance	2,076	95	360	17
Mode of Acquisition Unknown	109	5	-	
Total Disposals 1540-1879	2,185		360	16

[1]Where the same owner acquired different houses by different modes he is counted more than once.

[2]Excluding heirs of purchasers.

TABLE 5.2 (FIG. 5.2)

Sales by Sellers' Mode of Acquisition and Motivation to Sell

Mode of Acquisition	All Sales	Sellers of Superfluous Houses[1]		Sellers without Heirs Male[1]		Unmarried Sellers		Sellers in Known Financial Difficulties[2]		Sellers with no Known Motive	
		N	% of Sales in that Category of Acquisition	N	% of Sales etc.	N	% of Sales etc.	N	% of Sales etc.	N	% of Sales etc.
Direct Inheritance[3]	102	17	17	45	44	20	20	35	34	17	17
Indirect Inheritance[3]	58	25	43	24	41	7	12	7	12	12	21
Total Inheritance[3]	160	42	26	69	43	27	17	42	26	29	18
Purchase	142	16	11	62	44	20	14	18	13	53	37
Inheritance from Purchaser	58	7	12	29	50	10	17	9	16	18	31
Total Purchase and Inheritance from Purchaser	200	23	12	91	46	30	15	27	14	71	36
Total Inheritance and Purchase	360	65	18	160	44	57	16	69	19	100	28

[1] Including 15 owners of superfluous houses who left no heirs male (8 of whom were inheritors and 7 purchasers or purchasers' heirs).

[2] Including 18 who also owned superfluous houses and/or had no heirs male (10 of whom were inheritors and 8 purchasers or purchasers' heirs).

[3] Excluding heirs of purchasers.

TABLE 5.3 (FIG. 5.6)

Sales by Sellers' Mode of Acquisition as a Proportion of
Sales and Disposals, by County

A. Herts.

Period of Disposal	Sales by Purchasers and Purchasers' Heirs			Sales by Inheritors[1]			All Sales		All Disposals
	N	% of Sales	% of Disposals	N	% of Sales	% of Disposals	N	% of Disposals	
1540–79	3	100	7	–			3	7	45
1580–1639	15	52	10	14	48	9	29	21	156
1640–99	33	66	16	17	34	8	50	24	202
1700–59	29	67	14	14	33	7	43	20	207
1760–1819	54	67	25	27	32	12	81	37	217
1820–79	38	68	18	18	32	9	56	27	209
Totals	172	65	16	90	35	9	262	25	1,036

B. Northants.

Period of Disposal	Sales by Purchasers and Purchasers' Heirs			Sales by Inheritors[1]			All Sales		All Disposals
	N	% of Sales	% of Disposals	N	% of Sales	% of Disposals	N	% of Disposals	
1540–79	1			1		2	2	4	48
1580–1639	3			13		8	16	10	164
1640–99	4			10		6	14	9	162
1700–59	5			8		6	13	8	163
1760–1819	4			8		6	12	9	131
1820–79	7			8		6	15	11	132
Totals	24	32	3	48	68	6	72	9	800

C. Northumb.

Period of Disposal	Sales by Purchasers and Purchasers' Heirs			Sales by Inheritors[1]			All Sales		All Disposals
	N	% of Sales	% of Disposals	N	% of Sales	% of Disposals	N	% of Disposals	All Disposals
1580–1639	–			–			–		12
1640–99	–			3		7	3		46
1700–59	1			3		4	4		72
1760–1819	2			4		5	6		99
1820–79	1			12		10	13		120
Totals	4	15	1	22	84	6	26	7	349

D. All Three Counties

	N	% of Sales	% of Disposals	N	% of Sales	% of Disposals	N	% of Disposals	All Disposals
Herts.	90	35	9	172	65	16	262	25	1,036
Northants.	48	68	6	24	32	3	72	9	800
Northumb.	22	84	6	4	15	1	26	7	349
Totals	160			200			360		2,185

[1]Less heirs of purchasers.

TABLE 5.4

Sales by Purchasers and Heirs of Purchasers in
Hertfordshire by Source of Wealth

Period of Acquisition	Government Officials N	London Lawyers N	London Business Men N	Landed (Magnates from Elsewhere) N	Total N
-1579	-	-	-	1	1
1580–1639	6	-	3	11	20
1640–99	5	7	14	12	38
1700–59	4	2	3	5	14
1760–1819	2	7	24	24	57
1820–79	2	4	24	12	42
Totals	19	20	68	65	172

TABLE 5.5 (FIG. 5.3)

Frequency of Sales Relative to the Size of Estates in 1873[1]

A. All Three Counties

Date of Last Sale	Total Estate under 2,999 Acres %	Total Estate over 3,000 Acres %	N
-1699	13	40	53
1700-1799	27	29	65
1800-79	60	31	117
N	153	82	235

B. Herts.[2]

Date of Last Sale	1-999 Acres %	1,000-1,999 Acres %	2,000-2,999 Acres %	3,000+ Acres %	N
-1699	8	21	29	50	20
1700-99	23	21	28	28	24
1800-79	69	58	43	22	56
N	48	24	14	14	120

[1] Acreages taken from Return of Owners of Land, London, 1873, and J. Bateman, The Great Landowners of Great Britain, London, 1879.

[2] This table replaces that in L. Stone and J.C.F. Stone, 'Country Houses and their Owners in Hertfordshire 1540-1879' in Dimensions in Quantitative Research in History, ed. W. O. Aydelotte et al., Princeton, 1972, p. 87, which was based on a more generous lower limit of what constituted a house in sample.

TABLE 5.6

Proportion of Houses ever sold, or sold Three Times or more

	Herts.		Northants.		Northumb.		Total	
	N	%	N	%	N	%	N	%
Ever Sold	89	60	48	39	17	19	151	43
Sold 3+ Times	23	15	1	1	–	–	24	7
Total N	151		123		88		362	

TABLE 5.7

Frequency Count of Houses which dropped out of Sample

	Houses N
Inherited by men not qualified for sample	15
Sold out of Sample: to Individuals	24
to Institutions	5
Reverted to Crown	4
Neglected, abandoned, or destroyed	83
	131

TABLE 5.8 (FIGS. 5.4 and 5.5)

Sales as a Proportion of all Disposals, by County

Periods of Disposal	Herts.		Northants.		Northumb.		Three Counties	
	Disposals N	Sales %	Disposals N	Sales %	Disposals N	Sales %	Disposals N	Sales %
1540–59	26	8	25	–			51	4
1560–79	19	5	23	9			42	7
1580–99	36	3	41	2			77	3
1600–19	62	23	64	9	3	–	129	16
1620–39	58	24	59	15	9	–	126	18
1640–59	56	36	51	2	11	–	118	18
1660–79	74	23	59	8	16	–	149	15
1680–99	72	18	52	15	19	16	143	17
1700–19	68	25	57	7	25	8	150	15
1720–39	74	20	53	8	20	5	147	14
1740–59	65	17	53	9	27	4	145	12
1760–79	63	25	45	2	26	4	134	13
1780–99	83	31	43	15	31	13	157	24
1800–19	71	55	43	7	42	2	156	28
1820–39	73	21	41	7	29	14	143	15
1840–59	63	35	46	17	44	7	153	22
1860–79	73	26	45	9	47	13	165	18
% N	1,036	25	800	9	349	7	2,185	16
Sales in each County as a Proportion of Sales in all Three Counties	73		20		7			

TABLE 6.1 (FIG. 6.1)

Entrants into Sample by Social Origins[1]

Period of Acquisition	Old Established Gentry Entrants[2]				Newcomer Entrants[3]				Total			
	Herts. N	Northants. N	Northumb. N	Total N	Herts. N	Northants. N	Northumb. N	Total N	Herts. N	Northants. N	Northumb. N	Total N
1540–79	4	7	–	11	33	27	–	60	37	34	–	71
1580–1639	–	8	8	16	30	14	2	46	30	22	10	62
1640–99	–	4	4	8	15	11	3	29	15	15	7	37
1700–59	2	1	12	15	12	8	11	31	14	9	23	46
1760–1819	1	2	9	12	18	3	15	36	19	5	24	48
1820–79	2	2	3	7	14	7	8	29	16	9	11	36
Total	9	24	36	69	122	70	39	231	131	94	75	300
Proportion of Total Entrants	7%	26%	48%	23%	93%	74%	52%	77%	44%	31%	25%	
Sellers	1	3	1	5	32	5	6	43				
Proportion of Sellers to Entrants	11%	13%	3%	7%	26%	7%	15%	19%				

[1] The number of entrants is smaller than the number of new houses since 19 houses were built on new sites by elite already in sample.

[2] Men who brought a house into the sample which (or the site of which) had been in their family for three or more generations.

[3] Purchaser-entrants who bought an estate either with a small house which they enlarged or on which they built anew. This category also includes entrants who were the sons or grandsons of purchasers of small houses or estates on which they built, rebuilt, or enlarged, as well as undocumented entrants.

TABLE 6.2

Purchasers and Purchaser Entrants by Personal Source of Wealth[1]

A. Herts.

Period of Acquisition	All Owners N	Purchasers and Purchaser Entrants N	% of Owners	Source of Wealth									
				Land		Office		Law		Business		Total Other than Land	
				N	% of Purchasers	N	% of Purchasers	N	% of Purchasers	N	% of Purchasers	N	% of Purchasers
-1579	86	28	33	7	25	13	46	2	7	6	21	21	75
1580–1639	167	48	29	19	40	11	23	6	13	12	25	29	60
1640–99	190	53	28	15	28	8	15	9	17	21	40	38	72
1700–59	196	44	22	10	23	8	18	11	25	15	34	34	77
1760–1819	192	86	45	28	33	6	7	9	10	43	50	58	67
1820–79	218	68	31	25	37	3	4	5	7	35	51	43	63
Total	1,049	327	31	104	32	49	15	42	13	132	40	223	68

B. Northants.

Period of Acquisition	All Owners N	Purchasers and Purchaser Entrants N	% of Owners	Land		Office		Law		Business		Total Other than Land	
				N	% of Purchasers	N	% of Purchasers	N	% of Purchasers	N	% of Purchasers	N	% of Purchasers
-1579	95	20	21	7	35	8	40	3	15	2	10	13	65
1580–1629	165	27	16	14	52	4	15	6	22	3	11	13	48
1640–99	159	19	12	10	53	2	11	3	16	4	21	9	47
1700–59	146	15	10	5	33	1	7	7	47	2	13	10	67
1760–1819	128	16	13	10	63	3	19	1	6	2	13	6	38
1820–79	128	18	14	11	61	3	16	1	6	3	17	7	39
Total	821	115	14	57	49	21	18	21	18	16	14	58	50

C. Northumb.

Period of Acquisition	All Owners N	Purchasers and Purchaser Entrants		Source of Wealth									
		N	% of Owners	Land		Office		Law		Business		Total Other than Land	
				N	% of Purchasers	N	% of Purchasers	N	% of Purchasers	N	% of Purchasers	N	% of Purchasers
-1579	3	-	-	-	-	-	-	-	-	-	-	-	-
1580-1639	27	2	7	2	100	-	-	-	-	-	-	-	-
1640-99	48	3	6	1	33	-	-	-	-	2	67	2	67
1700-59	85	8	9	3	38	1	38	3	38	1	13	5	63
1760-1819	99	11	11	8	73	-	-	2	18	1	9	3	27
1820-79	114	14	12	6	48	1	7	2	14	5	36	8	57
Total	376	38	10	20	53	2	5	7	18	9	24	18	47

D. All Three Counties

Period of Acquisition	All Owners N	Purchasers and Purchaser Entrants		Source of Wealth									
		N	% of Owners	Land		Office		Law		Business		Total Other than Land	
				N	% of Purchasers	N	% of Purchasers	N	% of Purchasers	N	% of Purchasers	N	% of Purchasers
-1579	184	48	26	14	29	21	44	5	10	8	17	34	71
1580-1639	359	77	22	35	45	15	19	12	16	15	19	42	55
1640-99	397	75	19	26	35	10	13	12	16	27	36	49	65
1700-59	427	67	16	18	27	10	15	21	31	18	27	49	73
1760-1819	419	113	27	46	41	9	8	12	11	46	41	67	59
1820-79	460	100	22	42	42	7	7	8	8	43	43	58	58
Total	2,246	480	21	181	38	72	15	70	15	157	33	299	62

[1]Multiple owners (and therefore purchasers) figure only once and those whose date of acquisition is not precisely known have been included. This table, as well as table 6.3, are the only tables of owners grouped by date of acquisition which include the latter.

TABLE 6.3

Purchaser and Purchaser Entrants by Family Source of Wealth

Date of Acquisition	Herts.			Northants.			Northumb.		
	Exclusively Land[1] N	All Purchasers N	Proportion %	Exclusively Land[1] N	All Purchasers N	Proportion %	Exclusively Land[1] N	All Purchasers N	Proportion %
1540–1639	7	76	9	10	47	21	2	2	100
1640–1759	2	97	2	1	34	3	4	11	36
1760–1879	9	154	6	15	34	44	12	25	34
Total	18	327	6	26	115	23	18	38	47

[1] Men whose parents, grandparents, and wives derived their fortunes exclusively from land, with no known addition of wealth from a non-landed source. The population of this table is the same as that of Table 6.2.

TABLE 7.1 (FIG. 7.1)

Owners by Personal Occupation or Source of Wealth[1]

Herts.	Period of birth						
	-1549	1550-99	1600-49	1650-99	1700-49	1750-99	1800+
	%	%	%	%	%	%	%
Land only	55	62	63	65	57	52	63
Office or Profession	38	25	22	21	23	23	14
Business	7	11	14	12	21	21	22
Unknown	-	2	1	2	-	4	1
N	87	147	137	165	168	173	139
Northants.							
Land only	83	81	88	87	83	75	75
Office or Profession	14	17	10	12	14	24	23
Business	2	3	1	1	2	2	2
Unknown	-	-	-	-	-	-	-
N	95	135	134	119	125	110	92
Northumb.							
Land only	-	95	90	79	79	73	75
Office or Profession	-	5	6	11	14	23	20
Business	-	-	5	10	7	3	5
Unknown	-	-	-	-	-	-	-
N	-	21	39	63	72	97	83

[1]Any owner with an office or profession as well as land is categorized 'Office or Profession'. Any owner with a business interest as well as an office or profession and land is categorized as 'Business'. This maximizes both occupational and business categories.

TABLE 7.2 (FIG. 7.2)

Inheritors by Personal Occupation or Source of Wealth[1]

	Period of birth							
Herts.	-1549 %	1550-99 %	1600-49 %	1650-99 %	1700-49 %	1750-99 %	1800+ %	1500-1879 %
Land only[2]	65	75	73	75	50	54	58	65
Office or Profession[3]	35	24	19	19	27	34	30	26
Business[4]	-	1	8	7	14	12	12	9
N	26	79	74	102	99	83	76	539
Northants.								
Land only[2]	90	94	92	80	78	72	70	82
Office or Profession[3]	10	6	7	19	21	28	28	17
Business[4]	-	-	1	1	1	-	1	1
N	31	82	101	95	109	86	67	571
Northumb.								
Land only[2]	-	80	83	84	72	59	57	68
Office or Profession[3]	-	-	7	8	11	29	40	22
Business[4]	-	20	10	8	17	12	3	10
N	-	5	30	38	46	69	65	253
All Three Counties								
Land only[2]	79	84	84	78	69	62	87	73
Office or Profession[3]	21	14	11	17	22	30	29	22
Business[4]	-	1	5	5	9	8	5	6
N	57	166	205	235	254	238	208	1,363

[1]Including those who acquired by marriage but excluding all entrants and purchasers' heirs.

[2]Excluding entrepreneurs on their own estates.

[3]Including courtiers.

[4]Including entrepreneurs on their own estates.

TABLE 7.3 (FIGS. 7.3 AND 7.4)

Owners by Family Occupation or Source of Wealth[1]

Herts.	Period of birth							Total
	-1549 %	1550-99 %	1600-49 %	1650-99 %	1700-49 %	1750-99 %	1800+ %	
Land only	11	18	18	24	20	18	18	
Office or Profession	51	39	31	30	32	30	42	
Business	21	28	42	36	40	40	34	
Unknown	17	14	10	10	8	12	6	
N	87	147	137	165	168	173	139	1,016
Northants.								
Land only	38	48	48	45	39	27	26	
Office or Profession	36	30	30	29	36	43	64	
Business	11	7	10	13	14	7	4	
Unknown	15	15	12	13	11	14	5	
N	95	135	134	119	125	110	92	810
Northumb.								
Land only	-	66	59	49	30	34	27	
Office or Profession	-	10	10	11	32	37	58	
Business	-	10	15	24	21	14	13	
Unknown	-	14	15	16	17	14	2	
N	-	21	39	63	72	97	83	375

[1]This table surveys the occupations--if any--of the owner himself, his father, and his father-in-law. If any of the three had an interest in an office or profession as well as land, the owner is categorized under 'office'. If any of the three had an interest in business as well as an office or profession, the owner is categorized under 'business'. The figures are therefore biased in the direction of professions and business.

TABLE 7.4 (FIG. 7.5)

Higher Education of Owners as Heirs or Younger Sons

Education Heirs[1]	Period of birth						
	-1549 %	1550-99 %	1600-49 %	1650-99 %	1700-49 %	1750-99 %	1800+ %
University	14	39	44	34	43	49	55
Inns of Court	23	28	31	20	16	10	15
Total Educated	26	48	55	42	48	50	56
N	109	210	220	241	245	231	222
Younger Sons[2]							
University	19	25	36	18	22	28	32
Inns of Court	20	29	40	19	14	15	8
Total Educated	25	37	56	29	30	33	33
N	75	91	90	106	120	149	92

[1]Future owners who were known to be heirs by age 20 and had been educated as such.

[2]Future owners who were still younger sons at age 20, and had been educated as such.

TABLE 7.5 (FIG. 7.6)

Proportion of Inheritors and Purchasers with Titles of Honour

Inheritors	Period of Birth						
	-1549 %	1550-99 %	1600-49 %	1650-99 %	1700-49 %	1750-99 %	1800+ %
Knights	38	37	12	4	3	1	1
Bts./Peers	11	24	39	34	33	32	31
N	125	227	248	293	292	290	251
Purchasers[1]							
Knights	35	40	26	12	4	1	-
Bts./Peers	12	17	31	18	20	14	19
N	57	70	58	50	69	86	59

[1]Including 32 Crown Grantees, all before 1649.

TABLE 7.6 (FIG. 7.7)

Higher Education of Owners by Father's Occupation

Father's occupation: Land	Owner's period of birth						
	-1549 %	1550-99 %	1600-49 %	1650-99 %	1700-49 %	1750-99 %	1800+ %
University	15	37	46	34	38	47	53
Inns of Court	19	16	32	19	8	11	13
Higher Education	23	43	56	42	41	50	54
N	103	187	210	230	214	218	186

Father's occupation: Office or Profession

University	26	28	44	28	53	45	41
Inns of Court	37	32	47	35	40	15	17
Higher Education	42	62	63	47	60	48	41
N	38	60	43	40	62	60	69

Father's occupation: Business

University	-	17	29	24	27	38	50
Inns of Court	-	21	24	15	21	15	13
Higher Education	-	21	41	28	33	38	53
N	-	24	41	46	52	53	32

TABLE 7.7

Membership of Parliament by Purchasers

Period of Acquisition	MP for County N	MP for Borough in County N	MP not in County N	Total MPs N	Total Purchasers N
Herts.					
1540–79	3	–	5	8	32
1580–1639	2	3	9	14	48
1640–99	2	4	4	10	54
1700–59	–	1	10	11	47
1760–1819	–	1	29	30	92
1820–79	1[1]	–	12	13	69
Totals	8	9	69	86 (25%)	342
Northants.					
1540–79	5	1	1	7	20
1580–1639	2	2	4	8	27
1640–99	2	3	4	9	19
1700–59	–	–	3	3	15
1760–1819	–	1	2	3	16
1820–79	1	–	3	4	18
Totals	10	7	17	34 (30%)	115
Northumb.					
1580–1639	1	–	–	1	2
1640–99	–	–	1	1	3
1700–59	–	2	–	2	11
1760–1819	–	–	–	–	11
1820–79	–	1	–	1	14
Totals	1	3	1	5 (12%)	41

[1]Heir of a Peer in sample.

TABLE 7.8

Local Office-holding by Inheritors and Purchasers

Period of Acquisition	Sheriff		JP			
	Inh. %	Purch. %	Inh. %	Purch. %	Inh. N	Purch. N
			Herts.			
1540–79	37	23	52	33	54	30
1580–1639	27	27	47	34	122	41
1640–99	22	20	59	38	135	50
1700–59	14	22	42	35	145	46
1760–1819	13	22	45	28	106	81
1820–79	17	22	60	63	144	67
			Northants.			
1540–79	39	20	45	45	74	20
1580–1639	27	15	46	42	139	26
1640–99	16	28	37	39	140	18
1700–59	18	14	8	14	131	14
1760–1819	31	13	7	7	111	15
1820–79	32	28	31	17	107	18
			Northumb.			
1540–1639	38	33	50	33	24	3
1640–99	20	–	11	–	46	2
1700–59	30	14	3	–	78	7
1760–1819	29	18	10	9	87	11
1820–79	28	27	48	33	99	15

TABLE 7.9 (FIG. 7.8)

Occupational Origin of Wives of Inheritors

Wife's Father's Occupation	Period of husband's birth						
	-1549 %	1550-99 %	1600-49 %	1650-99 %	1700-49 %	1750-99 %	1800+ %
A. Herts.							
Land	46	41	51	39	50	51	51
Office or Profession	14	16	8	18	13	18	26
Business	11	13	20	13	13	8	7
Unknown	29	30	21	30	24	23	16
N	35	87	89	106	92	86	74
B. Northants. and Northumb.							
Land	66	73	74	72	65	54	56
Office or Profession	20	11	5	6	7	23	31
Business	3	2	4	5	10	4	1
Unknown	11	14	17	17	18	19	12
N	35	101	135	131	130	138	128
C. All Three Counties							
Land	56	59	65	57	59	53	55
Office or Profession	17	13	6	11	10	21	29
Business	7	7	10	8	11	6	3
Unknown	20	21	19	23	20	20	13
N	70	188	224	237	222	224	202

TABLE 8.1 (FIG. 8.1)

Frequency Count of Owners in Sample

Date		Herts.	Northants.	Northumb.	Total
31 Dec.	1539	15	25	–	40
	1559	30	38	–	68
	1579	41	48	–	89
	1599	50	59	–	109
	1619	64	66	13	143
	1639	71	67	17	155
	1659	75	69	18	162
	1679	76	80	20	176
	1699	82	74	21	177
	1719	81	66	26	173
	1739	77	70	27	174
	1759	78	59	34	171
	1779	76	60	42	178
	1799	77	63	45	185
	1819	73	62	48	183
	1839	78	65	58	201
	1859	90	71	59	220
	1879	98	62	57	217

TABLE 8.2 (FIG. 8.2)

Proportion of Owners with Titles of Honour

Date		Hereditary titles				
		Knights and KBs %	Barts. %	Peers %	All %	N
31 Dec.	1539	18	–	8	8	40
	1559	24	–	6	6	68
	1579	15	–	8	8	89
	1599	13	–	5	5	109
	1619	37	4	7	11	143
	1639	15	8	10	18	155
	1659	12	12	12	24	162
	1679	11	19	12	31	176
	1699	8	16	15	31	177
	1719	4	15	16	31	173
	1739	2	12	16	28	174
	1759	2	12	13	26	171
	1779	2	13	16	29	178
	1799	1	9	14	23	185
	1819	1	10	13	23	183
	1839	2	8	12	20	201
	1859	–	7	11	17	220
	1879	–	8	11	19	217

TABLE 8.3 (FIG. 8.3)

Proportion of Owners with Higher Education[1]

	Period of Birth						
Education	-1549 %	1550-99 %	1600-49 %	1650-99 %	1700-49 %	1750-99 %	1800+ %
University	16	34	42	29	36	40	48
Inns of Court	22	28	34	20	15	12	12
Higher Education	25	44	55	38	42	43	49
N	184	301	310	347	365	380	314

[1]These percentages have not been adjusted for under-registration. Those for the sixteenth century, and to a lesser extent the seventeenth, are too low, ranging from about 25% or more of those born in the first half of the sixteenth century, to 20% for the second half, to 10% for the first half of the seventeenth century, to 5% for the second half.

TABLE 8.4 (FIG. 8.4)

Proportion of Owners holding Local Offices in the Three Counties

Period of Acquisition	Herts.				Northants.				Northumb.			
	Sheriff[1] %	JP[1] %	MP[1] %	N	Sheriff[2] %	JP[2] %	MP[2] %	N	Sheriff[3] %	JP[3] %	MP[3] %	N
1540–79	32	45	13	85	36	44	18	95	–	33	–	3
1580–1639	27	43	12	164	25	45	17	165	37	48	19	27
1640–99	21	52	8	189	17	36	23	159	19	10	10	48
1700–59	15	40	13	194	18	8	8	146	28	2	16	85
1760–1819	17	38	8	189	28	7	10	128	27	10	13	95
1820–79	19	60	6	214	30	29	23	128	28	46	13	114

[1] In Herts. only.
[2] In Northants. only.
[3] In Northumb. only.

TABLE 8.5 (FIGS. 8.5 AND 8.6)

Antiquity of Owners by Generation[1] as a Proportion of all Owners

| | Generations since Last Purchase | | | | | | | | | | | | | | | | | | |
| | Herts. | | | | | | Northants. | | | | | | Northumb. | | | | | |
Dates	1 %	2 %	3 %	4-5 %	6+ %	N	1 %	2 %	3 %	4-5 %	6+ %	N	1 %	2 %	3 %	4-5 %	6+ %	N
1659	36	20	11	19	14	82	8	15	14	27	34	72	–	11	5	21	63	19
1679	28	26	16	18	12	82	10	12	14	25	38	83	–	5	5	23	66	21
1699	18	28	17	19	18	83	16	8	13	27	36	76	13	4	4	17	60	23
1719	22	22	13	21	22	86	12	9	13	17	49	68	14	14	–	7	65	29
1739	16	22	15	23	24	81	11	10	14	14	51	72	10	10	3	13	63	30
1759	22	20	8	22	28	83	11	10	10	16	53	61	2	18	10	13	57	40
1779	23	16	14	17	30	81	10	11	10	8	61	61	–	19	10	16	54	48
1799	30	17	15	13	25	86	15	5	13	7	60	64	13	6	18	15	48	54
1819	38	12	14	10	26	79	11	8	14	14	54	65	12	5	14	22	47	56
1839	32	15	14	13	26	84	16	9	12	13	50	68	13	12	10	19	45	67
1859	33	18	14	9	26	92	22	10	10	10	48	74	8	14	10	23	45	63
1879	31	15	18	10	26	100	17	16	2	17	48	63	10	9	16	21	44	58

[1] Number of generations (i.e. owners) since the last purchase of the house, regardless of whether or not it was in sample. The purchaser is counted as the first generation.

TABLE 8.6

Duration of Tenure by Families of Purchasers and Purchaser Entrants

Period of Acquisition	Total Purchases N	Purchases Sold by Purchaser %	Purchases Sold within Next Two Generations %	Purchases in Family for 3+ Generations %
1540–79	53	2	38	60
1580–1639	80	18	30	52
1640–99	80	34	27	39
1700–59	70	20	27	53
1760–1819	119	50	26	24
1820–79	102	38	56	6
Totals	504	31	34	35

TABLE 11.1 (FIG. 11.1)

Frequency Count of Houses in Sample at Twenty-year Intervals

Date	Herts.	Northants.	Northumb.
31 Dec. 1539	14	24	
59	33	39	
79	49	52	
99	58	68	
1619	70	75	10
39	79	78	19
59	81	76	20
79	88	83	23
99	88	80	24
1719	92	76	27
39	92	75	30
59	94	70	37
79	95	69	47
99	102	69	52
1819	95	69	56
39	95	73	62
59	96	74	61
79	107	73	64

TABLE 11.2

Frequency Count of Houses entering and dropping out
of Sample at Twenty-year Intervals

	Herts.		Northants.		Northumb.	
Periods	In	Out	In	Out	In	Out
1540-59	20	1	15	-		
60-79	16	-	13	-		
80-99	10	1	17	1		
1600-19	13	1	10	3		
20-39	9	-	6	3	9	-
40-59	10	-	3	5	1	-
60-79	6	7	9	2	3	-
80-99	2	2	1	4	2	1
1700-19	8	4	4	8	6	3
20-39	6	6	3	4	4	1
40-59	5	3	2	7	8	1
60-79	7	6	2	3	12	2
80-99	12	5	2	2	8	3
1800-19	6	13	2	2	10	6
20-39	6	6	7	3	9	3
40-59	2	1	3	2	2	3
60-79	12	1	1	2	4	1
	150	57	100	51	78	24

TABLE 11.3

Frequency Count of Houses in Hertfordshire which
dropped out of Sample[1]

Period	Destroyed	Shrunk or Decayed	Leased	Urbanized	Passed to Owners Out of Sample	Total
1540-99	-	-	-	-		
1600-59	-	-	1	-	1	2
1660-1719	5	2	1	2	1	11
1720-89	5	5	3	-	2	15
1790-1829	13	2	6	-	2	23
1830-79	2	-	2	-	2	6
Total	25	9	13	2	8	57

[1]This table excludes 8 houses which remained intact but went into
abeyance by passing to owners who did not qualify for the sample.
If these 8 are added, the total amounts to the 57 in Table 11.2.

TABLE 11.4 (FIG. 11.2)

Median House Size in 'Units'

	Herts.	Northants.	Northumb.
1540	88	68	
60	90	77	
80	80	80	
1600	88	76	
20	89	80	68
40	85	78	66
60	90	78	52
80	90	78	52
1700	100	80	66
20	103	80	68
40	106	90	60
60	102	100	74
80	100	102	75
1800	106	102	75
20	110	120	88
40	118	113	100
60	120	112	110
80	122	116	115

TABLE 11.5 (FIG. 11.3)

Small Houses (50-79 Units) as a Proportion of the Sample

	Herts. %	Northants. %	Northumb. %
1540			
50			
60	41	51	
70	42	49	
80	47	46	
90	40	50	
1600	40	51	
10	41	55	
20	37	49	
30	39	48	71
40	40	50	66
50	38	49	68
60	38	49	75
70	40	51	71
80	39	51	69
90	36	52	69
1700	32	47	62
10	27	43	60
20	22	45	62
30	23	43	62
40	19	35	62
50	20	31	63
60	19	25	55
70	19	19	54
80	20	17	54
90	22	17	52
1800	20	19	51
10	18	14	48
20	14	15	40
30	11	22	36
40	10	21	29
50	10	22	28
60	12	23	27
70	7	21	23
80	8	15	18

TABLE 11.6 (FIG. 11.4)

Frequency Count of Large and Very Large Houses
(Over 150 and 250 Units)

	Herts.		Northants.		Northumb.	
	150+ Units	250+ Units	150+ Units	250+ Units	150+ Units	250+ Units
1540	1	–	4	–		
60	3	–	6	1		
80	7	2	11	4		
1600	10	3	12	5		
20	11	3	15	4	1	–
40	12	4	18	5	2	–
60	11	4	19	5	2	–
80	13	4	19	5	2	–
1700	13	3	19	5	3	–
20	14	3	20	5	4	–
40	14	4	21	5	4	–
60	13	4	22	6	6	–
80	19	4	21	8	6	–
1800	20	5	20	5	8	–
20	23	5	20	8	9	–
40	24	6	20	9	15	–
60	29	6	24	12	17	–
80	35	6	27	13	21	–

TABLE 11.7

Frequency Count of Wholly New Building[1]

	Herts.	Northants.	Northumb.	Total	Total on New Sites Only
1540–79	21	19	–	40	29 = 3/4
1580–1639	13	7	4	24	17 = 3/4
1640–99	10	4	5	19	12 = 3/4
1700–59	13	13	18	44	23 = 1/2
1760–1819	17	5	16	38	22 = 3/5
1820–79	11	2	8	21	10 = 1/2

[1] On new or old sites.

TABLE 11.8 (FIGS. 11.5, 11.6, AND 11.7)

House Size Profiles[1]

| | Units | | | | | |
| | Herts. | | | | | |
Dates	50–59 %	60–79 %	80–99 %	100–119 %	120–159 %	160+ %
1579	11	36	20	11	9	13
1679	9	30	14	14	18	15
1779	6	14	22	19	23	16
1879	–	8	11	23	34	25
	Northants.					
1579	10	36	10	8	14	20
1679	5	46	12	3	12	19
1779	–	17	25	17	17	23
1879	–	16	19	19	12	34
	Northumb.					
1679	53	16	5	16	5	5
1779	18	34	11	16	16	4
1879	2	16	16	18	26	21

[1]Proportion of all houses in sample in each unit group.

TABLE 11.9 (FIG. 11.8)

Total Building Activity in Units per Decade (Thirty-year Moving Averages)

	Herts. Units	Northants. Units	Northumb. Units
1550–9	1,062	414	
60–9	819	1,077	
70–9	804	1,056	
80–9	640	1,167	
90–9	746	524	
1600–9	654	428	
10–9	597	389	162
20–9	292	415	194
30–9	294	317	142
40–9	434	121	60
50–9	503	169	76
60–9	543	47	118
70–9	462	276	186
80–9	371	295	166
90–9	389	374	167
1700–9	386	331	204
10–9	458	401	226
20–9	488	425	245
30–9	374	511	239
40–9	309	436	329
50–9	243	333	402
60–9	665	260	493
70–9	513	218	460
80–9	655	223	453
90–9	808	262	445
1800–9	966	261	477
10–9	880	226	705
20–9	528	163	615
30–9	344	204	480
40–9	366	215	245
50–9	669	248	247
60–9	869	356	340

TABLE 11.10 (FIG. 11.9)

Builders and Major Builders as a Proportion of Owners

Date of Acquisition	Owners[1] N	Builders[2] N	%	Major Builders[3] N	%
−1579[4]	207		46		33
1580–1639	395		29		11
1640–99	426		29		10
1700–59	455		39		15
1760–1819	466		43		15
1820–79	478		35		10
Total	2,427	882	36	350	15

[1] As many times as they owned houses.

[2] All those responsible for any known improvement to house or grounds, whether or not it resulted in a change in the number of units.

[3] Those who were responsible for building events involving 50 units or more.

[4] Including those already in sample when it starts in 1540.

TABLE 11.11

Builders by Heir Status and Occupation

1. Expectations at Age 20	Occupation	Owners N	Builders[1] N	%	Major Builders[1] N	%
Younger Son	Yes	408		44		21
	No	416		37		15
Total		824		40	149	18
Heirs	Yes	294		43		19
	No	1,309		32		12
Total		1,603		34	211	13
2. Occupation						
	Yes	702		43	141	20
	No	1,725		33	209	12
Total		2,427	882	36	350	15

[1] See Table 11.10 for definitions of these categories.

TABLE 11.12

Builders by Occupational Category

Occupation	N	Builders[1] %
Officer	273	40
Law	182	40
Business	247	47
All Occupied	702	45
Unoccupied (Land Only)	1,725	33
	2,427	

[1]See Table 11.10 for a definition of this category.

TABLE 11.13

Builders by Mode of Acquisition

Mode of Acquisition		Total Owners N	Builders[1] N	Builders[1] %	Major Builders[1] N	Major Builders[1] %
Inheritors:	Direct	1,312		31		11
	Indirect	530		31		10
	Total	1,842		31	193	10
Purchasers and Grantees		552		51		24
Unknown		33		73		67
	Total	2,427	882	36	350	15

[1]See Table 11.10 for a definition of this category.

TABLE 11.14

Builders as a Proportion of Entrants

Entrants by Mode of Entry	Total Entrants[1] N	Builders[2] N	%	Major Builders[2] N	%
Inheritor Entrants	170	88		61	
Purchaser Entrants	130	99		80	
Total	300	278	93	207	69
Total Owners	2,747	882		360	
%	11	32		58	

[1]See above p.

[2]See Table 11.10 for definitions of these categories.

TABLE 11.15

Builders as a Proportion of Sellers

Sellers by Mode of Acquisition	Total Sellers[1] N	Builders[2] N	%	Major Builders[3] N	%
Inheritors	218	38	17	19[4]	9
Purchasers and Purchaser Entrants	142	88	62	87	61
Total	360	126	35	106	29

[1]See Table 5.2: total inheritance and inheritance from Purchasers.

[2]See Table 11.10 for definitions of these categories.

[3]Of whom 14 were entrants.

[4]Of whom 12 were entrants.

GENEALOGICAL CHARTS

Genealogical Chart 1

COCHILL OF ALDENHAM, HERTS.

(from J. E. Cussans, History of Hertfordshire, III, 1, p. 246)

Genealogical Chart 2

HUCKS/GIBBS OF ALDENHAM, HERTS.

(from J. E. Cussans, History of Hertfordshire, III, 1, p. 247)

Genealogical Chart 3

WILLES OF ASTROP, NORTHANTS., & HUNGERFORD PARK, BERKS.

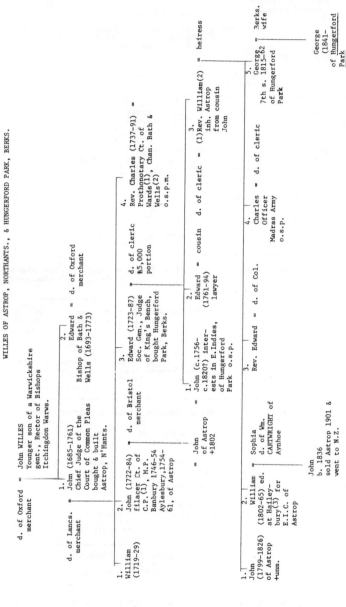

(From O. Barron, Northamptonshire Families, London, 1906, pp 341-53)

Genealogical Chart 4

LYTTON OF KNEBWORTH, HERTS.

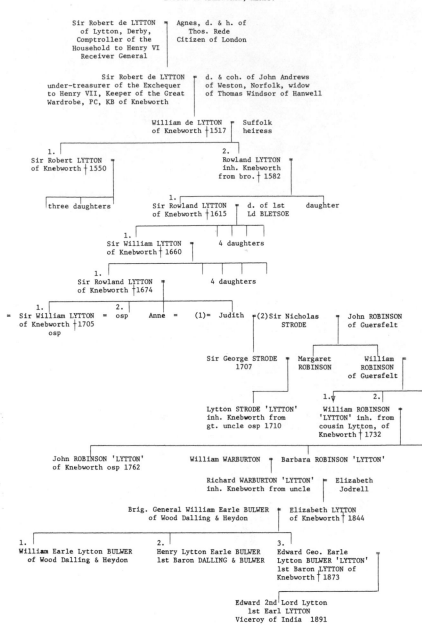

Sir Robert de LYTTON ┳ Agnes, d. & h. of
of Lytton, Derby,   Thos. Rede
Comptroller of the   Citizen of London
Household to Henry VI
Receiver General

Sir Robert de LYTTON ┳ d. & coh. of John Andrews
under-treasurer of the Exchequer   of Weston, Norfolk, widow
to Henry VII, Keeper of the Great   of Thomas Windsor of Hanwell
Wardrobe, PC, KB of Knebworth

William de LYTTON ┳ Suffolk
of Knebworth †1517   heiress

1.   2.
Sir Robert LYTTON ┳   Rowland LYTTON ┳
of Knebworth †1550   inh. Knebworth
                              from bro. † 1582

1.
three daughters   Sir Rowland LYTTON ┳ d. of 1st   daughter
                   of Knebworth †1615   Ld BLETSOE

1.
Sir William LYTTON ┳ 4 daughters
of Knebworth† 1660

1.
Sir Rowland LYTTON ┳ 4 daughters
of Knebworth †1674

1.   2.
= Sir William LYTTON = osp   Anne = (1)= Judith ┳(2)Sir Nicholas ┳ John ROBINSON
of Knebworth †1705   STRODE   of Guersfelt
osp

Sir George STRODE ┳ Margaret   William ┳
1707   ROBINSON   ROBINSON
                             of Guersfelt

1.   2.
Lytton STRODE 'LYTTON'   William ROBINSON ┳
inh. Knebworth from   'LYTTON' inh. from
gt. uncle osp 1710   cousin Lytton, of
                             Knebworth † 1732

John ROBINSON 'LYTTON'   William WARBURTON ┳ Barbara ROBINSON 'LYTTON'
of Knebworth osp 1762

Richard WARBURTON 'LYTTON' ┳ Elizabeth
inh. Knebworth from uncle   Jodrell

Brig. General William Earle BULWER ┳ Elizabeth LYTTON
of Wood Dalling & Heydon   of Knebworth† 1844

1.   2.   3.
William Earle Lytton BULWER   Henry Lytton Earle BULWER   Edward Geo. Earle
of Wood Dalling & Heydon   1st Baron DALLING & BULWER Lytton BULWER 'LYTTON'
                                                         1st Baron LYTTON of
                                                         Knebworth † 1873

Edward 2nd Lord Lytton
1st Earl LYTTON
Viceroy of India 1891

(from B. Burke, Peerage & Baronetage, London, 1902; Commoners of Great Britain,
1834, I, pp. 447-49; J. E. Cussans, History of Hertfordshire, III, iii, p. 113;
and D. Warrand, Hertfordshire Families, London, 1907, p. 201)

WAKE OF COURTEENHALL HOUSE, NORTHANTS.

```
                        = Sir Baldwin WAKE
                        | of Piddington,
                        | 1st Baronet
                        |                                                          |
          = Sir John WAKE          Sir Dru DRURY  = Susan JONES    Sir Samuel JONES
          | of Hartwell            of Riddlesworth |               of Courteenhall House &
          | 2nd Bt.                Norf. 2nd Bt.   |               Waltham Abbey, o.s.p.
          |                                        |
    Sir William WAKE  = Diana DRURY       Sir Robert DRURY
    of Piddington     |                   of Riddlesworth
    3rd Bt. 1632-98   |                   3rd Bt. +1712
      1. |_____|_____|_____
Sir John WAKE  = Sir Baldwin WAKE        = Robert WAKE           Samuel WAKE 'JONES'
4th Bt., 1661- | of Fritwell, Oxon       | Dean of               of Waltham Abbey
1714           | 5th Bt. 1701-40         | Bocking               1670-1713
         1. |_____| 2.      osp | osp |
         = Baldwin WAKE    Charles WAKE 'JONES'        William WAKE  =
         | 1695-1735       of Waltham Abbey            of Riddlesworth |
         |                 1701-40                     7th Bt. 1708-65 |
         |                                             inh. Courteenhall |
         |                                             House & Waltham   |
         |                                             Abbey from his     |
         |                                             cousin the 6th     |
         |                                             Bt.                V
    Sir Charles WAKE 'JONES'                               the WAKES of
    of Courteenhall House and                              Courteenhall House
    Waltham Abbey, 6th Bt.
    +1755
```

(From O. Barron, <u>Northamptonshire Families</u>, London, 1906, pp. 319-39)

Genealogical Chart 6

PLUNKETT-ERNLE-'ERLE-DRAX'

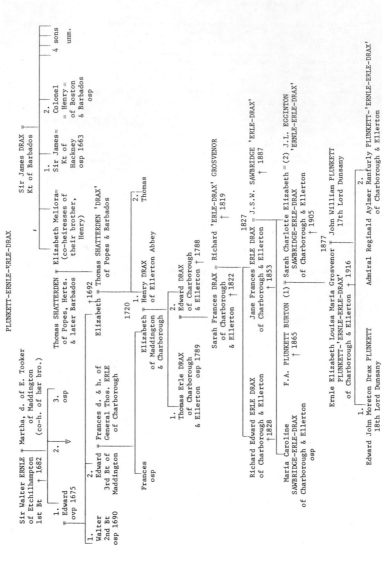

Burke's Landed Gentry, 1939, and Extinct Baronetage.

Genealogical Chart 7

PLUMER OF BLAKESWARE & NEW PLACE, HERTS.

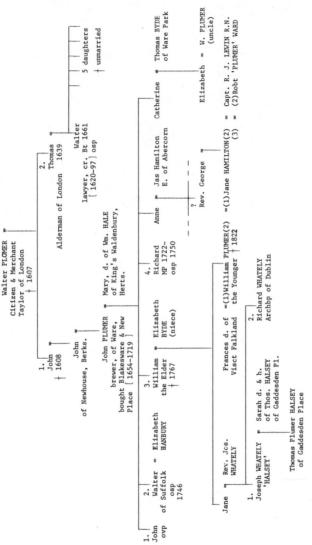

(from J. E. Cussans, History of Hertfordshire, I, ii, p. 128)

BIBLIOGRAPHY

BIBLIOGRAPHY

I. NON-PRINTED SOURCES

Bodleian Library, Oxford: Gough MSS, Herts. 13 vol. iii; Gough Herts. 4, 11, 13, 16, 17, 18; Gough Add. Herts. C. 5.

British Library: Add. MSS 9062-4; 32118-22; 32467; 32348-52, 33641, 36364-7, 36371.

College of Arms: Herts. Visitations 1669.

Glos. R. O., D.2002/F1.

Hatfield House: Private and Estate MSS, Accounts 168/2.

Herts. R.O.: Buckler Drawings, vols. i-iv; Cowper MSS A 18 and Box 20; Dimsdale Collection of Oldfield Drawings, vols. i-viii; Gerish Collection; Knowsley extra-illustrated Clutterbuck, vols. ii-ix; 80323b (Plan Case).

Huntington Library: Bridgwater MSS 8117.

Lambeth Palace: Court of Arches MSS, Process Books D. 601, 875, 1395, 1793; Lambeth Palace MSS 647/5.

Longleat, Bath MSS, Misc. Books, 179B.

Newcastle Central Library: extra-illustrated Mackenzie, *The County of Northumberland*, 1825.

Northants. R.O.: Clarke drawings; sale catalogues; quarter sessions attendance records.

Northumb. R.O.: Thomas Bell Collection of MS plans and drawings; sale catalogues.

Public Record Office: Chancery Proceedings, Series I, Jas. I, A 1/62; Libri Pacis in C 193 series; Hearth Tax Returns E 179/375/30 and 31.

R.I.B.A., British Architecture Library, Drawings Collection, C. R. Cockerell's Diary.

Society of Antiquaries of Newcastle-on-Tyne: Richardson Drawings; Swinburne Drawings.

II. PRINTED SOURCES

W. Marston Acres, 'The Directors of the Bank of England', *Notes and Queries*, 179, 1940.

J. Adams, *Index Villaris*, London, 1680.

After the Reformation, ed. B. C. Malament, Philadelphia, 1980.

D. C. A. Agnew, *Protestant Exiles from France in the Reign of Louis XIV*, London, 1886.

M. Airs, *The Making of the English Country House*, London, 1975.

K. J. Allison, ' "Hull gent. seeks a Country Residence", 1750-1850', *East Yorkshire Local History Society*, 36, 1981.

B. Allsopp and U. Clark, *Historic Architecture of Northumberland*, Newcastle-upon-Tyne, 1969.

Alumni Cantabrigienses, ed. J. and J. A. Venn, 10 vols., Cambridge, 1922-54.

[E. K. W.], *A Short History of Althorp and the Spencer Family*, 1949.

D. T. Andrew, 'The Code of Honour and its Critics: the Opposition to Duelling in England, 1799-1850', *Social History*, 5, 1980.

W. Angus, *Seats of the Nobility and Gentry*, 1787.

Archaeologia Aeliana, passim.

Archaeological Journal, passim.

P. C. Archer, *Historic Cheshunt*, Cheshunt, 1923.

Architecture of Sir Roger Pratt, ed. R. T. Gunther, Oxford, 1928.

W. Arnstein, 'The Survival of the Victorian Aristocracy' in *The Rich, the Well-Born, and the Powerful*, ed. F. C. Jaher, New York, 1973.

O. Ashmore, 'Household Inventories of the Lancashire Gentry, 1550-1700', *Lancs. and Chesh. Hist. Soc. Trans.*, 110, 1959.

R. Atkyns, *Ancient and Present State of Glostershire*, London, 1712.

J. Aubrey, *Wiltshire; the Topographical Collections of John Aubrey for the Natural and Topographical History of Wiltshire*, ed. J. E. Jackson, Devizes, 1862.

J. Austen, *Northanger Abbey* and *Persuasion*, ed. R. W. Chapman, Oxford, 1933.

G. E. Aylmer, *The King's Servants: The Civil Service of Charles I, 1625-42*, London, 1961.

F. Bacon, 'Of Building' in *Essays or Counsels Civil and Moral*, no. 45.

W. Bagehot, *The English Constitution* (World's Classics), London, 1958.

C. H. Collins Baker and M. Baker, *The Life and Circumstances of James Brydges, first Duke of Chandos*, Oxford, 1949.

G. Baker, *History and Antiquities of the County of Northamptonshire*, 2 vols., London, 1822-41.

S. G. R. Barratt, *A Short History of Totteridge*, London, 1934.

O. Barron, *Northamptonshire Families*, London, 1906.

J. Bassin, 'The English Landscape Garden in the Eighteenth Century: the Cultural Importance of an English Institution', *Albion*, 11, 1979.

J. Bateman, *The Great Landowners of Great Britain and Ireland*, London, 1879.

W. W. Bean, *Parliamentary Representation of the Six Northern Counties*, Hull, 1890.

G. Beard, *Georgian Craftsmen*, London, 1966.

A. B. Beaven, *The Aldermen of the City of London*, 2 vols., London, 1908-13.

A. Behn, 'The Younger Brother or the Amorous Jilt', in *Works*, ed. M. Summers, London, 1915.

T. Bell, *The Ruins of Livedon*, Peterborough, 1847.

T. Bernard, *Pleasure and Pain, 1780-1818*, ed. J. B. Baker, London, 1930.

W. Berry, *County Genealogies, Pedigrees of Hertfordshire Families*, London, 1844.

P. Bertie, *A Memoir of Peregrine Bertie, 11th Lord Willoughby de Eresby*, London, 1838.

W. Betham, *Baronetage of England*, 5 vols., London, 1801-15.

Biographia Britannica, London, 1747-66.

P. C. Birtchnell, *A Short History of Berkhamsted*, Berkhamsted, 1972.

[W. Blackett], *Memoirs of the Public Life of Sir Walter Blackett of Wallington, Baronet*, 1819.

B. G. Blackwood, 'Marriages of Lancashire Gentry on the Eve of the Civil War', *Genealogist's Magazine*, xvi. 1970.

F. Blomefield, *History of Norfolk*, 11 vols., London, 1805-10.

R. Blomfield, *History of Renaissance Architecture in England 1500-1800*, London, 1897.

[T. Blore], *A Guide to Burghley House*, 1815.

D. H. Boalch, *The Manor of Rothamstead*, Harpenden, 1953.

F. Boase, *Modern English Biography*, 6 vols., London, 1850-92.

A. T. Bolton, *The Architecture of Robert and James Adam, 1758-1794*, London, 1922.

L. Bonfield, 'Marriage Settlements and the Rise of Great Estates: the Demographic Aspect', *Economic History Review*, 2nd Ser., xxxii, 1979; comment and rejoinder in ibid., xxxiii, 1980; *Marriage Settlements, 1601-1740*, Cambridge, 1983.

W. Borlase, *Antiquities of the County of Cornwall*, Oxford, 1754.

P. Borsay, 'The English Urban Renaissance: the Development of Provincial Urban Culture, c.1680-c.1760', *Social History*, ii, 1977.

J. Boswell, *The Life of Samuel Johnson LL.D.* (Everyman ed.), London, 1906.

Boswell: the Applause of the Jury 1782-1785, ed. I. S. Lustig and F. A. Pottle, New York, 1981.

Boswell in Extremes 1776-78, ed. C. McC. Weiss and F. A. Pottle, New York, 1970.

Boswell: The Ominous Years 1774-76, ed. C. Ryscamp and F. A. Pottle, New York, 1963.

Private Papers of James Boswell, ed. G. Scott and F. A. Pottle, 18 vols., New York, 1928-34.

S. Botein, J. R. Censer, H. Ritvo, 'The Periodical Press in the Eighteenth Century English and French Society: a Cross-Cultural Approach', *Comparative Studies in Society and History*, 23, 1981.

528

BIBLIOGRAPHY

P. Bourdieu, 'Les stratégies matrimoniales dans le systême de reproduction', *Annales E.C.S.*, 27, 1972.

H. F. Bradfer-Lawrence, 'The Merchants of Lynn' in C. R. Ingleby, ed. *A Supplement to Blomefield's Norfolk*, London, 1861.

J. Brasbridge, *The Fruits of Experience*, London, 1824.

E. W. Brayley and J. Britton, *The Beauties of England and Wales*, 18 vols., London, 1801-15.

J. Brewer, 'English Radicalism in the Age of George III', in *Three British Revolutions*, ed. J. G. A. Pocock, Princeton, 1980.

J. Bridges, *History and Antiquities of Northamptonshire*, ed. P. Whalley, 2 vols., Oxford, 1791.

Bristol in the Eighteenth Century, ed. P. McGrath, Newton Abbot, 1972.

Britain and the Netherlands, ed. J. S. Bromley and E. H. Kossman, London, 1960.

J. Britton, *History and Description . . . of Cassiobury Park*, London, 1837.

G. C. Brodrick, *English Land and English Landowners*, London, 1881.

J. Brushe, 'Further Light on Cole Green House', *Architectural History*, 24, 1981.

D. Buckley and W. Le Hardy, *Wormley in Hertfordshire*, London, 1954.

J. Burke, *The Commoners of Great Britain*, 4 vols., London, 1833-8; *The Extinct and Dormant Baronetcies of England, Ireland and Scotland*, London, 1844; *Extinct and Dormant Peerages*, London, 1831; *Peerage and Baronetage of the British Empire*, London, 1839 etc.

J. B. Burke, *Genealogical and Heraldic Dictionary of the Landed Gentry of Great Britain and Ireland*, London, 1863, 1937; *Visitation of the Seats and Arms of Noblemen and Gentlemen of Great Britain and Ireland*, London, 1st Series, 2 vols.; 1852-3, 2nd ser., 2 vols.; 1854-5.

J. Byng, *The Torrington Diaries*, 4 vols., London, 1934-8.

Calendar of State Papers Domestic, 1547-80, ed. R. Lemon, London, 1856.

W. Camden, *Britannia*, London, 1610.

Camden Miscellany, x, *Camden Soc.*, 3rd Ser., iv, 1902; ibid., xxiii, *C.S.* 4th Ser., vii, 1969.

C. Campbell, *Vitruvius Britannicus*, 2 vols., London, 1715-17.

J. (Lord) Campbell, *Lives of the Chief Justices of England*, 4 vols., London, 1874; *Lives of the Lord Chancellors*, 8 vols., London, 1845-69.

D. Cannadine, 'Aristocratic Indebtedness in the Nineteenth Century: the Case reopened', *Economic History Review*, 2nd Series, xxx, 1977; 'The Landowner as Millionaire', *Agricultural History Review*, 25, 1977; *Lords and Landlords: the Aristocracy and the Towns 1774-1967*, Leicester, 1980; 'The Theory and Practice of the English Leisure Classes', *Historical Journal*, 21, 1978.

R. Carr, *English Foxhunting: a History*, London, 1976.

J. Carswell, *The South Sea Bubble*, London, 1960.

F. Cass, *East Barnet*, London and Middlesex Archaeological Society, London, 1885-92.

Catalogue of Publishers' Prospectuses in the John Johnson Collection, ed. J. P. Feather, Oxford Microfilm Publications, 1978.

'A Century of Land Values: England and Wales', in *Essays in Economic History*, ed. E. M. Carus-Wilson, London, iii, 1962.

E. Chamberlayn, *Angliae Notitia*, London, 1669.

C. K. Chambers, *Sir Henry Lee*, Oxford, 1936.

J. D. Chambers, *Nottinghamshire in the Eighteenth Century*, London, 1966.

B. Charlton, *The Recollections of a Northumbrian Lady*, ed. L. E. O. Charlton, London, 1949.

G. Chapman, B. Jonson, and J. Marston, *Eastward Ho*, London, 1605.

H. Chauncy, *The Historical Antiquities of Hertfordshire*, London, 1700.

D. Cherry, 'Sir Nicholas L'Estrange Non-Juror', *Norfolk Archaeology*, 34, 1968.

G. L. Cherry, *The Convention Parliament, 1689*, New York, 1966.

J. Child, *New Discourse of Trade*, London, 1693.

E. Churton, *The Railroad Book of England*, London, 1851.

A. W. Clapham and W. H. Godfrey, *Some Famous Buildings and their History*, London, 1913.

W. N. Clarke, *Memorials of his Family*, London, 1854.

C. Clay, 'Marriage, Inheritance and the Rise of Large Estates in England 1660-1815', *Economic History Review*, 2nd Series, xxi, 1968; 'Property Settlements, Financial Provision for the Family and the Sale of Land by the Greater Landowners, 1660-1790', *Journal of British Studies*, 21, 1981; *Public Finance and Private Wealth: the Career of Sir Stephen Fox, 1627-1716*, Oxford, 1978.

H. A. Clemenson, *English Country Houses and Landed Estates*, New York, 1982.

R. Clutterbuck, *History and Antiquities of the County of Hertford*, 3 vols., London, 1815-27.

G. E. Cockayne, *Complete Baronetage*, 6 vols., Exeter, 1900-9; *Complete Peerage*, 14 vols., London, 1910-65.

J. Cole, *History and Antiquities of Ecton*, Scarborough, 1825.

L. Colley, 'Eighteenth Century English Radicalism before Wilkes', *Transactions of the Royal Historical Society*, 5th Series, 31, 1981.

A. Collins, *The Peerage of England*, 8 vols., London, 1779.

J. Collinson, *History and Antiquities of Somersetshire*, Bath, 1791.

H. M. Colvin, *Biographical Dictionary of English Architects 1660-1840*, London, 1954; with M. Craig, eds., *Architectural Drawings in the Library of Elton Hall by Sir John Vanbrugh and Sir Edward Lovett Pearce*, Oxford (*Roxburghe Club*), 1964.

Commons Debates, 1621, ed. W. Notestein, F. H. Relf, and H. Simpson, New Haven, 1935.

W. M. B. Compton, Marquis of Northampton, *History of the Comptons of Compton Wynyates*, London, 1940.

W. H. Cooke, *Members admitted to the Inner Temple, 1547-1660*, London, 1878.

J. P. Cooper, 'Patterns of Inheritance' in J. Goody, J. Thirsk, and E. P. Thompson, eds., *Family and Inheritance*, Cambridge, 1976.

F. D. R. Copestick, *History of Cheshunt Great House*, (n.d.).

P. J. Corfield, 'Social and Economic History of Norwich 1650-1850: a study in urban growth', London Ph.D. Thesis, 1976.

J. Cornforth, 'Horton House, Northants.', in H. Colvin and J. Harris, *The Country Seat*, London, 1970.

Country Life, vols. xxix (1911), xxxv (1915), xli (1920), xlvii (1925), cxxxvii (1965), and passim.

W. Coxe, *Memoirs of Sir Robert Walpole*, London, 1798.

B. Cracroft, 'The Analysis of the House of Commons, or indirect Representation', *Essays on Reform*, London, 1867.

D. Cressy, 'Social Status and Literacy in North East England, 1560-1630', *Local Population Studies*, 21, 1978.

J. Mordaunt Crook, 'The Fate of Neo-Classical Houses', *Country Life*, London, cli, 1972, p. 1382.

J. E. Cussans, *History of Hertfordshire*, 3 vols., London, 1870-81.

Daily Advertiser, London, 1747-9.

L. Davidoff, *The Best Circles: Society, Etiquette and the Season*, London, 1973.

A. C. Fox Davies and P. W. Poole Carlyon Britton, *A Treatise on the Law Concerning Names and Changes of Names*, London, 1906.

R. Davis, *Aleppo and Devonshire Square*, London, 1967.

D. Defoe, *Moll Flanders*, ed. G. Aitken, 1895; *A Plan of the English Commerce* [London, 1728] and *The True-born Englishman* [London, 1701] in *Writings*, xiii and xiv, Oxford, 1927; *A Tour Through England and Wales* (Everyman Edition), London, 1928; *The Use and Abuse of the Marriage Bed*, London, 1727.

'Derbyshire Hearth Tax Assessments 1662-70', ed. D. G. Edwards, *Derbyshire Record Society*, vii, 1982.

T. M. Devine, 'Glasgow Colonial Merchants and Land, 1770-1815' in *Land and Industry*, ed. J. T. Ward and R. G. Wilson, Newton Abbot, 1971.

T. F. Dibdin, *Aedes Althorpianae*, 2 vols., London, 1822.

P. G. M. Dickson, *The Financial Revolution in England 1688-1756*, London, 1967.

Dictionary of National Biography, Oxford.

Dorset Hearth Tax 1662-64, ed. C. A. F. Meekings, *Dorset Record Society*, 1951.

K. Downes, *English Baroque Architecture*, London, 1966; *Hawksmoor*, London, 1959.

F. Drake, *Eboracum*, London, 1736.

W. Dugdale, *Antiquities of Warwickshire*, London, 1656.

A. D. Dyer, *The City of Worcester in the Sixteenth Century*, Leicester, 1973.

East Herts. Archaeological Soc. Trans., passim; *E.H.A.S. Newsletter*, passim.

W. A. Eden and B. B. Wragg, 'John Carr, Stone-cutter Extraordinary', *Transactions of the Ancient Monuments Society*, new series, 24, 1980.

N. W. Ellenberger, 'The Souls and London "Society" at the end of the Nineteenth Century', *Victorian Studies*, 25, 1982.

B. English and J. Saville, *Strict Settlement: a Guide for Historians*, University of Hull Occasional Papers on Economic and Social History, no. 10, 1982.

The English Matron, London, 1846.

Eton College Register, 1448-1889, ed. W. Sterry and R. A. Austen-Leigh, Eton, 1943, 1903-43.

European Society in the Eighteenth Century, ed. R. and E. Forster, New York, 1969.

E. J. Evans, 'Some Reasons for the Growth of English Rural Anticlericalism c.1750-1830', *Past and Present*, 66, 1975.

J. Evans, *Time and Chance*, London, 1943.

Diary of John Evelyn, ed. W. Bray, London, 1879.

A. Everitt, *Change in the Provinces in the Seventeenth Century*, Leicester, 1969; *The Community of Kent and the Great Rebellion*, London, 1966.

Memoirs of Lady Anne Fanshawe, 1600-1672, London, 1907.

J. Farthing, 'Matfen Estate', University of Newcastle thesis, 1964.

J. P. Ferns, 'Gentry of Dorset on the Eve of the Civil War', *Genealogist's Magazine*, xv, 1965.

H. Fielding, *An Enquiry into the Causes of the late Increase of Robbers*, London, 1751.

M. E. Finch. *The Wealth of Five Northamptonshire Families*, Northants. Record Soc., xix, 1955.

R. S. Fitton and A. P. Wadsworth, *The Strutts and the Arkwrights, 1758-1830*, Manchester, 1958.

S. Foote, *The Genuine Memoirs of the Life of Sir John Dinely Goodere, Bart.*, London, 1741.

T. Fordyce, *Historical Register*, 3 vols., Newcastle, 1867-76.

The Foreigner's Guide . . . to London, London, 1752.

R. Forster, *History of Corbridge*, 1881.

E. Foss, *Judges of England*, 9 vols., London, 1848-64.

J. Foster, *Alumni Oxonienses, 1500-1714*, 4 vols., Oxford, 1891-2; *1715-*

1886, 4 vols., Oxford, 1877-8; *Register of Admissions to Gray's Inn, 1521-1889*, London, 1889.

J. Franklin, *The Gentleman's Country House and its Plan, 1835-1914*, London, 1981.

J. A. Froude, *Short Studies on Great Subjects*, London, 1907.

T. Fuller, *The History of the Worthies of England*, ed. P. A. Nuttall, London, 1840; *The Holy State*, Cambridge, 1642.

T. Gage, *History of Hengrave*, London, 1822.

T. Garner and A. Stratton, *The Domestic Architecture of England during the Tudor Period*, London, 1911.

General View of Agriculture in the County of Hertfordshire, London, 1804.

'The Genius of Place': The English Landscape Garden 1620-1820, ed. J. D. Hunt and P. Willis, London, 1975.

Gentleman's Magazine Library: English Topography, 1731-1868, vols. v and viii, London, 1894 and 1896.

E. Gibbon, *Memoirs of my Life and Writings* [1788] in *An Eighteenth Century Miscellany*, ed. L. Kronenberger, New York, 1936.

M. Girouard, 'Elizabethan Architecture and the Gothic Tradition', *Architectural History*, 6, 1963; *Life in the English Country House*, New Haven, 1978; *Robert Smythson and the Architecture of the Elizabethan Era*, London, 1966; ed. 'The Smythson Collection of the Royal Institute of British Architects', *Architectural History*, 5, 1962; *The Victorian Country House*, Oxford, 1971.

T. Gisborne, *An Enquiry into the Duties of the Female Sex*, London, 1797.

L. K. J. Glassey, *Politics and the Appointment of Justices of the Peace, 1675-1720*, Oxford, 1979.

J. H. Gleason, *The Justices of the Peace in England, 1558-1640*, Oxford, 1969.

G. Goodman, *The Court of King James the First*, London, 1839.

J. Goody, 'Strategies of Heirship', *Comparative Studies in Society and History*, 15, 1973.

J. A. Gotch, *A Complete Account of the Buildings of Sir Thomas Tresham between the Years 1575 and 1605*, Northampton, 1883; *Country Houses of the Midlands: a review of the old halls and manor houses of Northamptonshire*, New York, 1936; 'Drawings and Letters of J. Webb', *J.R.I.B.A.*, 3rd series, xxviii, 1920-1.

R. Gough, *British Topography*, London, 1780; *History and Antiquities of the Parish of Myddle, County of Salop.*, London, 1875.

N. S. B. Gras, *Evolution of the English Corn Market from the Twelfth to the Eighteenth Century*, Cambridge, Mass., 1925.

R. Grassby, 'Social Mobility and Business in Seventeenth Century England', *Puritans and Revolutionaries*, ed. D. Pennington and K. Thomas, Oxford, 1978.

D. Green, *Blenheim Palace*, London, 1951.

A. Grey, *Debates of the House of Commons, 1667-1694*, London, 1763.

H. J. Habakkuk, 'The English Land Market in the Eighteenth Century', in *Britain and the Netherlands*, ed. J. S. Bromley and E. H. Kossman, London, 1960; 'English Landownership 1680-1740', *Economic History Review*, x, 1940; 'Landowners and the Civil War', loc. cit., 2nd Ser., xviii, 1965; 'Marriage Settlements in the Eighteenth Century', *Transactions of the Royal Historical Society*, 4th Ser., xxxii, 1950; 'The Rise and Fall of English Landed Families 1600-1800', loc. cit., 5th Ser., 29-31, 1979-81.

T. Habington, *Survey of Worcestershire*, ed. J. Amphlett, *Worcestershire Historical Society*, v (2 vols.), 1895-9.

A. Hakewell, *Thorpe Hall*, Peterborough, 1852.

H. J. Hanham, 'The Sale of Honours in Late Victorian England', *Victorian Studies*, 25, 1982.

J. Harris, *The Artist and the Country House*, London, 1979; *A Country-House Index*, Shalfleet Manor, 1971; *Georgian Country Houses*, Feltham, 1968.

The Harrow School Register, 1571-1800, ed. W. T. J. Gun, London, 1934; —*1800-1911*, ed. M. G. Danglish and P. K. Stephenson, London, 1911.

E. S. Hartshorne, *Memorials of Holdenby*, London, 1868.

E. Hasted, *A History of the County of Kent*, Canterbury, 1778-99 (2nd ed. 1797-1801).

D. Hay, 'Property, Authority and the Criminal Law' in D. Hay *et al.*, *Albion's Fatal Tree, Crime and Society in Eighteenth Century England*, London, 1975.

A. Heal, 'A Great Country House in 1623', *Burlington Magazine*, lxxxii, pp. 108-16.

M. E. W. Helms, 'The Convention Parliament of 1660' (Ph.D. Thesis, Bryn Mawr College, 1963), Ann Arbor, University Microfilms.

L. Henry, 'The Population of France in the Eighteenth Century' in *Population in History*, ed. D. V. Glass and D. E. C. Eversley, London, 1965.

Hertfordshire Genealogist and Antiquary, ed. W. Brigg, 3 vols., Harpenden, 1895-9.

Herts. County Records, Sessions Books, ed. W. Le Hardy, vols. v-ix, 1905-39.

O. Hill and J. Cornforth, *English Country Houses. Caroline 1625-1685*, London, 1966.

J. A. Hilton, 'Catholicism in Elizabethan Northumberland', *Northern History*, xiii, 1977.

R. L. Hine, *Hitchin Worthies*, London, 1932; *Relics of an Uncommon Attorney*, London, 1951.

Historical Manuscripts Commission, Hastings MSS.

Historical Manuscripts Commission, Salisbury MSS.

Historical Manuscripts Commission, Various MSS.

Historical Manuscripts Commission, Verulam MSS.

J. Hodgson and J. H. Hinde, *History of Northumberland*, 7 vols., Newcastle, 1827-58.

B. A. Holderness, 'The English Land Market in the Eighteenth Century: the Case of Lincs.', *Economic History Review*, 2nd Ser., xxvii, 1974.

T. H. Hollingsworth, *The Demography of the British Peerage*. Supplement to *Population Studies*, xviii, 1964; 'Mortality Among Peerage Families since 1600', *Population Studies*, 32, 1977.

C. Holmes, 'The County Community in Stuart Historiography', *Journal of British Studies*, xix, 1980.

C. A. Holmes, 'The Eastern Association', Cambridge University unpublished Ph.D. thesis, 1969.

G. Holmes, *Florentine Enlightenment*, London, 1969.

G. Holmes, *Augustan England: Professions, State and Society, 1680-1730*, London, 1982. 'The Professions and Social Change in England, 1680-1730', *Proceedings of the British Academy*, lxv, 1979.

T. J. Honeyman, *Patronage and Prejudice*, Glasgow, 1968.

[J. Horn], *A History of Burghley House*, Shrewsbury, 1797.

W. E. Houghton, 'The English Virtuoso in the Seventeenth Century', *Journal of the History of Ideas*, iii, 1942.

W. Howitt, *Visits to Remarkable Places . . . chiefly in the Counties of Durham and Northumberland*, London, 1842.

E. Hughes, *North Country Life in the Eighteenth Century*, 2 vols. Oxford, 1952-65.

C. Hussey, *English Country Houses: Early Georgian*, London, 1955;—*Late Georgian*, London, 1958; —*Mid Georgian*, London, 1956; *English Gardens and Landscapes 1700-1750*, London, 1967.

J. Hutchins, *History and Antiquities of the County of Dorset*, London, 1774.

W. Hutchinson, *A View of Northumberland*, Newcastle, 1778.

E. S. Hyams, *Capability Brown and Humphrey Repton*, London, 1971.

M. Hyde, *The Thrales of Streatham Park*, Cambridge, Mass., 1977.

R. Hyde, 'Mapping London's Landlords: The Ground Plan of London, 1892-1915', *Guildhall Studies in London History*, i, 1973.

An Irish Beauty of the Regency [Journal of the Hon. Mrs. Nicolson Calvert, *née* Frances Pery], ed. W. Blake, London, 1911.

G. Isham, 'Architectural History of Lamport', *Reports and Papers of the Northants. Arch. and Arch. Soc.*, lvii, 1953; 'Easton Maudit and the Parish Church of SS. Peter and Paul', *Northants. Record Society Pub-*

lications, 1969; 'George Clarke', *Northampton and County*, June, 1972; 'Thorpe Hall', *Northants. Antiquaries' Society*, lxii, 1958-9.

G. Jackson, *Hull in the Eighteenth Century*, Oxford, 1972.

M. R. James, *Family, Lineage and Civil Society*, Oxford, 1974.

F. Jenkins, *Architect and Patron*, Durham, 1961.

L. E. W. Jewitt and S. C. Hall, *The Stately Homes of England*, London, 1874-7.

G. P. Judd, *Members of Parliament, 1734-1832*, London, 1955.

M. F. Keeler, *The Long Parliament, 1640-41*, Philadelphia, 1954.

E. R. Kelly, *The Post Office Directory of the Six Home Counties*, London, 1845.

C. S. Kenny, *The History of the Law of Primogeniture in England and its Effect upon Landed Property*, Cambridge, 1878.

R. Kerr, *The Gentleman's House*, London, 1865.

A. Kingston, *History of Royston*, Royston, 1906.

J. Kip, *Brittania Illustrata*, 1708.

Memoirs of the 45 First Years of the Life of James Lackington, London, 1794.

Land and Industry, ed. J. T. Ward and R. G. Wilson, Newton Abbott, 1971.

R. G. Lang, 'Social Origins and Social Aspirations of Jacobean London Merchants', *Economic History Review*, 2nd Series, xxvii, 1974.

P. Laslett, *The World We Have Lost*, London, 1971.

J. Le Bras, 'Parents, Grands-parents, Bisaieux', *Population*, 28, 1973.

J. Lees-Milne, *The Age of Adam*, London, 1947; *The Age of Inigo Jones*, London, 1953.

E. Le Roy Ladurie, *Le Territoire de l'historien*, Paris, 1978.

Letters of John Chamberlain, ed. N. E. McClure, Philadelphia, 1939.

Letters and Papers, Foreign and Domestic, of the Reign of Henry VIII, ed. J. S. Brewer *et al.*, 1862-1910, vol. xiv, pt. 1.

D. Levine, ' "For their own Reasons": Individual Marriage Decisions and Family Life', *Journal of Family History*, 7, 1982.

J. Lewis, *Original Designs for Villas, Mansions and Town Houses*, 1780.

G. Lipscomb, *The History and Antiquities of the County of Buckingham*, 4 vols., London, 1831-47.

Literary Remains of Edward VI, ed. J. G. Nichols, *Roxburghe Club*, 2 vols., 1857.

J. Loftis, *Comedy and Society from Congreve to Fielding*, Stanford, 1959.

R. Lugar, *Plans and Views of Buildings*, London, 1823; *Villa Architecture*, London, 1828.

N. Luttrell, *A Brief Historical Relation of State Affairs from September 1678 to April 1714*, 6 vols., Oxford, 1857.

D. Lysons, *The Environs of London*, 4 vols., London, 1792-6.

M. E. Macartney, *English Houses and Gardens in the Seventeenth Century*, 1908.

M. W. McCahill, 'Peerage Creations and the Changing Character of the British Nobility, 1750-1830', *English Historical Review*, ccclxxix, 1981; 'Peers, Patronage and the Industrial Revolution, 1760-1800', *Journal of British Studies*, 16, 1976.

P. McGrath, 'Merchants and Merchandise in Seventeenth Century Bristol', *Bristol Record Society*, xix, 1955.

A. McInnes, *The English Town, 1660-1750*, Historical Association, London, 1980.

E. MacKenzie, *A Descriptive and Historical Account of the Town and County of Newcastle*, 2 vols., Newcastle-upon-Tyne, 1827; *An Historical, Topographical and Descriptive Account of the County of Northumberland*, 2 vols., Newcastle-upon-Tyne, 1825.

R. A. McKinley, *The Surnames of Oxfordshire*, Chichester, 1982.

J. Macky, *A Journey through England*, 1722.

F. N. MacNamara, *Memorials of the Danvers Family*, London, 1895.

Diary of John Manningham, Camden Soc., xcix, 1868.

G. Markham, 'George Clarke', *Northants. Notes and Queries*, NS, 1912-20.

G. W. Marshall, *Genealogist's Guide*, London, 1893.

W. Marshall, *On the Landed Property of England*, London, 1804.

Marx-Engels Selected Correspondence, 1846-95, London, 1936.

P. Mathias, *The Brewing Industry in England, 1700-1830*, Cambridge, 1959; *First Industrial Nation*, London, 1969.

L. Melville, *The South Sea Bubble*, London, 1921.

W. C. Metcalfe, *A Book of Knights*, London, 1885.

A. F. T. Michaelis, *Ancient Marbles in Great Britain*, Cambridge, 1882.

A. E. Middleton, *An Account of Belsay Castle in the County of Northumberland*, Newcastle-upon-Tyne, 1910.

C. Middleton, *Picturesque and Architectural Views of Cottages, Farm Houses and Country Villas*, London, 1793.

T. Middleton, *Michaelmas Term*, in *Works*, London, 1840, vol. i.

W. Minet, *Hadham Hall, the Manor of Bawdes*, Colchester, 1914.

G. E. Mingay, *English Landed Society in the Eighteenth Century*, London, 1963.

B. R. Mitchell and P. Deane, *Abstract of British Historical Statistics*, Cambridge, 1962.

R. Mitchell, *Plans and Views . . . of Buildings erected in England and Scotland*, London, 1801.

T. L. Moir, *The Addled Parliament of 1614*, Oxford, 1958.

The Montagu Musters Books, 1602-1623, ed. J. Wake, *Northants. Record Series*, vii, 1935.

R. Morden, *The New Description and State of England*, London, 1704.

J. Morley, *The Life of Richard Cobden*, London, 1903.

J. S. Morrill, *Cheshire, 1630-1660*, Oxford, 1974.

R. Morris, *Select Architecture*, London, 1755.

L. M. Munby, *The Hertfordshire Landscape*, London, 1977; 'Politics and Religion in Herts., 1660-1740' in his *East Anglian Studies*, Cambridge, 1969.

W. Musgrave, *Obituaries prior to 1800, Harleian Soc.*, 44-9, 1899-1901.

H. Muthesius, *The English House*, ed. D. Sharp, London, 1979.

L. B. Namier and J. Brooke, *History of Parliament, The House of Commons, 1754-1790*, London, 1964.

J. Nash, *The Mansions of England in the Olden Time*, 4 vols., London, 1839-49.

[T. R. Nash], *Index to Dr Nash's Collections for the History of Worcestershire*, ed. J. Amphlett, *Worcestershire Historical Society*, iii, 1894-5.

J. P. Neale, *Views of the Seats of Noblemen and Gentlemen of England, Wales, Scotland and Ireland*, 6 vols., London, 1818-23.

R. S. Neale, *Bath 1680-1850*, London, 1981.

J. Nelson, *Essays on the Government of Children*, London, 1768.

H. O. Nethercote, *The Pytchley Hunt, Past and Present*, London, 1888.

P. Newcome, *History of Saint Albans's Abbey*, London, 1795.

H. Nicholas, *Memoirs of the Life and Times of Sir Christopher Hatton*, London, 1847.

J. Nichols, *Progresses of James I*, 4 vols., London, 1828.

J. Norden, *Speculum Britanniae*, London, 1593-8; *Speculum Britanniae Pars Altera, or a Delineation of Northamptonshire in the Year 1610*, London, 1720.

Dudley Lord North, *Observations and Advices Oeconomical*, London, 1669.

R. North, *Autobiography of Roger North*, London, 1887; *Lives of the Norths*, London, 1826; *Of Building*, ed. H. Colvin and J. Newman, Oxford, 1981.

Northamptonshire Past and Present, passim.

History of Northumberland, 16 vols., Newcastle-upon-Tyne, 1893-1940.

L. S. O'Connell, 'The Elizabethan Bourgeois Hero Tale: Aspects of an Adolescent Social Consciousness', in *After the Reformation*, ed. B. C. Malament, Philadelphia, 1980.

V. L. Oliver, *History of the Island of Antigua*, 4 vols., London, 1894-9.

O. Ore, *Cardano the Gambling Scholar*, Princeton, 1953.

G. Paget, *The History of the Althorp and Pytchley Hunt, 1634-1920*, London, 1938.

W. and J. Pain, *British Palladio* [London, 1793], Farnborough, 1969.

J. Pain, *Plans . . . of Noblemen's and Gentlemen's Houses*, London, 1783.

Patterson's Roads, ed. E. Moggs, London, 1829.

R. Paulson, *Hogarth: His Life, Art and Times*, 2 vols., New Haven, 1971.

S. Peller, 'Births and Deaths among Europe's Ruling Families since 1500', in *Population in History*, ed. D. V. Glass and D. E. C. Eversley, London, 1965.

H. J. Perkin, *The Origins of Modern English Society, 1780-1880*, London, 1969.

N. Pevsner, *The Buildings of Britain, Hertfordshire*, 1958;—, *Northampton-shire*, 1961;—, *Northumberland*, 1975; and passim; *The Planning of the Elizabethan Country House*, Lincoln, 1960.

C. H. Philips, *The East India Company, 1784-1836*, Manchester, 1961.

H. Phillips, *The Grandeur of the Law*, London, 1684.

W. P. N. Phillimore, *The Law and Practice of Change of Name*, London, 1905; (with E. A. Fry), *An Index to Changes of Names 1760 to 1901*, London, 1905.

H. L. Piozzi, *Anecdotes of the late Samuel Johnson*, ed. S. C. Roberts, Cambridge, 1925.

W. Pitt, *General View of the Agriculture of the County of Northampton*, London, 1809.

J. H. Plumb, *Sir Robert Walpole: The King's Minister*, London, 1960; *Sir Robert Walpole: The Making of a Statesman*, London, 1956.

J. G. A. Pocock, 'Machiavelli, Harrington and English Political Ideologies in the Eighteenth Century', *William and Mary Quarterly*, 3rd Series, 22, 1965; ed., *Three British Revolutions*, Princeton, 1980.

Political and Social Letters, ed. E. F. D. Osborn, London, 1890.

R. Porter, *English Society in the Eighteenth Century*, London, 1982.

F. G. Hilton Price, *Handbook of London Bankers*, London, 1876.

H. Prince, 'The Changing Landscape of Panshanger', *East Herts., Arch. Soc. Trans.*, xiv, 1955-6.

Proceedings of the Society of Antiquaries of Newcastle, passim.

J. H. Pruett, *The Parish Clergy under the Later Stuarts*, Urbana, 1978.

[H. L. H. von Pückler-Muskau], *Tour of England, Ireland and France, in the years 1826, 1827, 1828 and 1829, by a German Prince*, Philadelphia, 1833.

R. E. Pumphret, 'The Introduction of Industrialists into the British Peerage', *American Historical Review*, lxv, 1959.

Quarter Session Records of the County of Northampton, ed. J. Wake, North-amptonshire Record Soc., i, 1924.

Quarterly Review, 101, 1857.

R. H. Quilici, 'Turmoil in City and Empire: Bristol Factions 1700-1775', University of New Hampshire Ph.D. thesis, 1976.

F. P. Delmé Radcliffe, *The Noble Science*, London, 1839.

J. Raine, *History and Antiquities of North Durham*, London, 1852.

P. Razzell, *The Conquest of Smallpox*, Firle, 1977; 'Social Origins of Officers in the Indian and the British Home Army, 1758-1962', *British Journal of Sociology*, 14, 1963, p. 253.

The Record of Old Westminsters, ed. G. F. R. Barker and A. H. Stern, 2 vols., London, 1928.

Records of Buckinghamshire, 16, 1953-60.

Records of Lincoln's Inn, ed. W. P. Baildon, 4 vols., London, 1897-1902.

The Red Books of Humphrey Repton, London, 1976.

Register of Admissions to the Middle Temple, ed. H. A. C. Sturgess, 3 vols., London, 1949.

H. Repton, *Sketches and Hints on Landscape Gardening*, London, 1794.

Return of Members of Parliament, 2 vols., London, 1878.

The Returns of Owners of Land, 1873, London, 1875.

C. J. Richardson, *Architectural Remains of the Reigns of Elizabeth and James I*, London, 1840.

G. Richardson, *New Designs in Architecture*, London, 1792; *The New Vitruvius Britannicus*, 2 vols., London, 1802-8.

D. Robert, *Paternalism in Early Victorian England*, London, 1979.

P. F. Robinson, *The Vitruvius Britannicus*, 5 parts in one volume, London, 1827-44.

J. Rocque, *Exact Survey of the City of London, Westminster, ye borough of Southwark and the Country 10 miles round London*, London, 1746.

J. C. Rogers, *The Manor and Houses of Gorhambury*, London, 1934.

N. Rogers, 'Money, Land and Lineage: the Big Bourgeoisie in Hanoverian London', *Social History*, iv, 1979.

P. E. Rossell, 'The Building of Wollaton Hall' (Sheffield University MA Thesis, 1957).

Royal Commission on the Ancient and Historical Monuments and Constructions of England, An Inventory of the Historical Monuments of Hertfordshire, London, 1911;—*of the County of Northampton*, London, 1975.

W. D. Rubinstein, *Men of Property*, New Brunswick, 1981; 'New Men of Wealth and the Purchase of Land in Nineteenth Century England', *Past and Present*, 92, 1981.

Lord William Russell and his Wife, ed. G. Blakiston, London, 1972.

N. V. Stopford Sackville, *Drayton House*, 1939.

St Alban's Architectural and Archaeological Soc. Trans., passim.

St James's Chronicle, London, 1788.

H. St John, Viscount Bolingbroke, *Works*, London, 1844.

N. Salmon, *History and Antiquities of Essex*, London, 1740; *The History of Hertfordshire*, London, 1728.

J. E. Saul, *Radlett Past and Present*, 1927.

C. de Saussure, *A Foreign View of England in the Reigns of George I and George II*, London, 1902.

R. Sedgwick and J. Brooke, *History of Parliament, The House of Commons, 1715-1754*, London, 1970.

W. A. Shaw, *The Knights of England*, 2 vols., London, 1906.

M. Shinagel, *Daniel Defoe and Middle Class Gentility*, Cambridge, Mass., 1968.

E. P. Shirley,*The Noble and Gentle Men of England*, Westminster, 1859; *Some Account of English Deer Parks*, London, 1867; *Stemmata Shirleiana*, 1841.

J. Simmons, *English County Historians*, East Ardsley, 1978.

A. W. P. Simpson, *An Introduction to the History of the Land Law*, Oxford, 1961.

[F. Skeet], *History of the Families of Skeet, Somerscales, Widdrington, Wilby, Murray, Blake, Grimshaw and Others* (privately printed), 1906.

Diary of Sir Henry Slingsby, ed. D. Parsons, London, 1836.

A. Smith, *The Wealth of Nations*, ed. E. Cannan, London, 1904.

D. B. Smith, *Inside the Great House, Planter Family Life in Eighteenth Century Chesapeake Society*, Ithaca, 1980.

T. Smith, *De Republica Anglorum*, ed. L. Alston, London, 1906.

J. Smyth, *The Berkeley MSS*, iii, *Bristol and Glos. Arch. Soc.*, Gloucester, 1885.

Some Designs of Mr Inigo Jones and Mr William Kent, London, 1744.

D. Spring, *European Landed Elites in the Nineteenth Century*, Baltimore, 1977.

C. D. Squibb, 'The End of the Name and Arms Clause', *Law Quarterly Review*, 60, 1953.

H. Heathcote Statham, *Modern Architecture*, London, 1892.

W. B. Stephens, 'Roger Mallock, Merchant and Royalist', *Trans. Devon Assoc.*, xcii, 1960.

L. Stone, 'The Building of Hatfield House', *Archaeological Journal*, cxii, 1956; 'Cole Green Park, Herts.' in *The Country Seat*, ed. H. Colvin and J. Harris, London, 1970; *The Crisis of the Aristocracy, 1558-1641*, Oxford, 1965; *Family and Fortune: Studies in Aristocratic Finance in the Sixteenth and Seventeenth Centuries*, Oxford, 1973; *The Family, Sex and Marriage in England 1500-1800*, London, 1977; 'The Original Endowment of Wadham College', *Wadham College Gazette*, cxlvi, 1959; 'Patriarchy and Paternalism in Tudor England . . .', *Journal of British Studies*, xiii, 1974; 'The Residential Development of the West End of London in the Seventeenth Century', in *After the Reformation*, ed. B. C. Malament, Philadelphia, 1980; 'The Size and Composition of the Student Body' in *The University in Society*, ed. Stone, Princeton, 1974; (with J. C. Fawtier Stone) 'Country Houses and their Owners in Hertfordshire 1540-1879' in *Dimensions of Quantitative Research in History*, ed. W. O. Aydelotte, A. G. Bogue, and R. W. Fogel, Princeton, 1972.

J. Stow, *Survey of London*, ed. C. L. Kingsford, Oxford, 1908.

R. Strong, *The Renaissance Garden in England*, London, 1979; (with M. Binney, and J. Harris), *The Destruction of the Country House, 1875-1975*, London, 1974.

D. Stroud, *The Architecture of Sir John Soane*, London, 1961; *Capability Brown*, London, 1957; *Henry Holland*, London, 1966; *Humphrey Repton*, London, 1962.

P. Styles, *Sir Simon Archer, Dugdale Soc. Occasional Papers*, 6, 1946.

'Suffolk in 1674', *Suffolk Green Books*, xiii, 1905.

J. Summerson, *Architecture in Britain, 1530 to 1830*, London, 1953; *The Book of Architecture of John Thorpe in Sir John Soane's Museum, Walpole Soc.*, xl, London, 1966; 'The Building of Theobalds, 1564-1585', *Archaeologia*, 97, 1959; 'The Classical Country House in Eighteenth Century England', *Journal of the Royal Society of Arts*, cvii, 1959; *Georgian London*, London, 1945; 'Theobalds', *The Listener*, 31 March 1955; 'John Thorpe and the Thorpes of Kingscliffe', *Architectural Review*, 106, 1949, pp. 291-300; 'Three Elizabethan Architects', *Bulletin of the John Rylands Library*, 40, 1957.

'Surrey Hearth Tax, 1664', ed. C. A. F. Meekings, *Surrey Record Society*, xviii, 1940.

J. Swift, *The Examiner*, London, 1710-11.

J. Sykes, *Local Records*, 2 vols., Newcastle-upon-Tyne, 1865-6.

The Tatler, ed. G. A. Aitken, London, 1899.

R. H. Tawney, 'Rise of the Gentry 1558-1640' in *Essays in Economic History*, ed. E. M. Carus-Wilson, i, 1954.

J. Taylor, *The Carriers' Cosmography*, London, 1637.

W. M. Thackeray, *The Book of Snobs*, London, 1848; *Pendennis*, London, 1879.

J. Thirsk, 'The Restoration Land Settlement', *Journal of Modern History*, xxvi, 1954; 'Younger Sons in the Seventeenth Century', *History*, 54, 1969.

D. Thomas, 'Social Origins of Marriage Partners of the British Peerage in the Eighteenth and Nineteenth Centuries', *Population Studies*, 26, 1972.

E. P. Thompson, *The Making of the English Working Class*, London, 1963; 'Patrician Society, Plebeian Culture', *Journal of Social History*, 7, 1974; *Whigs and Hunters*, New York, 1975.

F. M. L. Thompson, 'Britain' in *European Landed Elites in the Nineteenth Century*, ed. D. Spring, Baltimore, 1977; *English Landed Society in the*

Nineteenth Century, London, 1963; 'The Land Market in the Nineteenth Century', *Oxford Economic Papers*, 2nd Series, 9, 1957; 'The
Social Distribution of Landed Property in England since the Sixteenth Century', *Economic History Review*, 2nd Series, xix, 1956.

R. Thoroton, *Antiquities of Nottinghamshire*, London, 1677.

S. Thrupp, *The Merchant Class in Medieval London, 1300-1500*, London,
1948.

H. A. Tipping, *English Houses*, 9 vols., London, 1920-37.

H. J. Todd, *The History of the College of Bonshommes at Ashridge*, London,
1823.

R. M. Tomkins, *History of Hertford*, 1936.

W. W. Tomlinson, *Comprehensive Guide to Northumberland* [1888], Newton
Abbot, 1969; *Denton Hall and its Associations*, 1894.

E. Toms, *Story of St Albans*, London, 1962.

E. Topham, *Life of the late John Elwes, Esq.*, London, 1790.

D. L. W. Tough, *Last Years of a Frontier*, Oxford, 1928.

A Tour of Wales, London, 1806.

J. A. Tregelles, *A History of Hoddesdon*, Hertford, 1908.

The Trial of William Lord Byron for the Murder of William Chaworth, London, 1765.

A. Trollope, *The American Senator*, London, 1877; *The Last Chronicle of
Barset*, London, 1867; *Mr Scarborough's Family*, London, 1883; *Ralph
the Heir*, London, 1871.

T. A. Trollope, *What I Remember*, London, 1973.

R. Trumbach, *The Rise of the Egalitarian Family*, New York, 1978.

L. Turnor, *History of Hertford*, Hertford, 1830.

An Ungovernable People, ed. J. Brewer and J. Styles, New Brunswick,
1980.

A. F. Upton, *Sir Arthur Ingram*, Oxford, 1961.

The Complete Works of Sir John Vanbrugh, ed. B. Dobrée and G. Webb, 4
vols., London, 1927-8.

Victoria County History, Herts., 4 vols., London, 1902-14.

Victoria County History, Northants., 4 vols. (incomplete), London, 1902-
37.

Victoria County History, The City of York, London.

Memoirs of the Verney Family in the Seventeenth Century, ed. F. P. and
M. M. Verney, London, 1907.

Verney Letters of the Eighteenth Century, ed. M. M. Verney, London, 1930.

Vertue's Notebooks, IV, Walpole Soc., xxiv, 1935-6.

J. Viner, 'Possessive Individualism as Original Sin', *Canadian Journal of
Economics and Political Science*, 29, 1963.

The Visitation of Northumberland in 1615, ed. G. W. Marshall, London,
1878.

Visitations of Hertfordshire, 1572 and 1624, Harleian Soc., 22, 1886.

Visitations of the North, pt. iv, *Surtees Soc.*, 146, 1932.

Voltaire, *Lettres sur les Anglais*, Cambridge, 1961.

G. F. Waagen, *Treasures of Art in Great Britain*, 4 vols., London, 1854-7.

J. Wade, *The Black Book*, London, 1820.

J. Wake, *The Brudenells of Deene*, London, 1953.

E. Walford, *The County Families of the United Kingdom*, London, 1860, 1872.

Horace Walpole's Correspondence, ed. W. A. Lewis, New Haven, 1937-80.

Horace Walpole: Gardenist, ed. I. W. U. Chase, Princeton, 1943.

Horace Walpole's Journals of Visits to Country Seats, etc., ed. P. Toynbee, *Walpole Soc.*, 16, 1928.

D. Warrand, *Hertfordshire Families*, London, 1907.

E. Waterhouse, *The Gentleman's Monitor*, London, 1665.

M. Waterson, *The Servants' Hall*, New York, 1980.

W. Watts, *Seats of the Nobility and Gentry*, 1779-86.

J. Webb, *The Vindication of Stonehenge Restored*, London, 1665.

R. Welford, *Men of Mark 'twixt Tyne and Tweed*, London, 1895.

C. M. Westmacott, *British Galleries of Painting and Sculpture*, London, 1824.

W. Whellan, *History, Topography and Directory of Northamptonshire*, 1849; 2nd ed. by F. Whellan, 1874.

M. Whiffen, *T. Archer*, London, 1950.

J. Whitaker, *A Descriptive List of Deer Parks and Paddocks of England*, London, 1892.

J. B. Whitmore, *Genealogical Guide*, London, 1953.

M. J. Wiener, *English Culture and the Decline of the Industrial Spirit*, Cambridge, 1981.

R. S. Wilkinson, *The Church and Parish of Abbots Langley*, 1959.

T. S. Willan, *Muscovy Merchants of 1555*, Manchester, 1953; *Navigation of the River Weaver in the Eighteenth Century*, Manchester, 1951.

W. R. Williams, *Hereford MPs*, Brecknock, 1896; *Wales MPs*, Brecknock, 1895.

P. Willis, *Charles Bridgeman and the England Landscape Garden*, London, 1977.

J. Wilson, *Biographical Index to the House of Commons*, London, 1806.

R. G. Wilson, *Gentlemen Merchants 1730-1830*, Manchester, 1971.

F. Wood, 'Merchant and Class: A Social Identification of Merchants in Exeter 1680-1760' (MA Thesis, Monash University, 1977).

K. Woodbridge, *Landscape and Antiquity: Aspects of English Culture at Stourhead, 1718-1830*, Oxford, 1970.

J. R. Woodhead, 'The Rulers of London: the Composition of the Courts of Aldermen and of Common Council of the City of London 1660-1689' (London MA Thesis, 1961).

J. Woolfe and J. Gandon, *New Vitruvius Britannicus*, London, 1767-71.

H. Wotton, *Reliquiae Wottoniae*, London, 1651.

T. Wotton, *The English Baronetage*, 5 vols., London, 1741.

Wren Society, iv, vi, xii, xvii, xix, xxii, London, 1927-   .

J. Wright, *History and Antiquities of the County of Rutland*, London, 1684.

E. A. Wrigley, 'Fertility Strategy for the Individual and the Group' in *Historical Studies in Changing Fertility*, ed. C. Tilly, Princeton, 1978; (with R. S. Schofield), *The Population History of England, 1541-1871*, London, 1981.

Yorkshire Diaries and Autobiographies, Surtees Soc., 63, 1877.

A. Young, *A Six-Month Tour through the North of England*, London, 1771; *Travels in France and Italy, during the Years 1787, 1788 and 1789* (Everyman's Library), London, 1906.

J. Young, *The Country House in the 1980s*, London, 1982.

C. H. E. Zangerl, 'The Social Composition of County Magistrates in England and Wales, 1831-1887', *Journal of British Studies*, xi, 1971.

INDEX

* An asterisk indicates presence on the genealogical chart of that surname

Lane, William 155
Lane family 155
Langham, Sir James, 1st Bt. 156
Langham, Sir James, 2nd Bt. 209
Langham, Thomas 129
Langham family 106
Langleybury, Abbots Langley, Herts. 430, pl. VIIIB
Lascelles, Edwin 346-47
Latin 234, 245, 249, 262
Lauderdale, Duke of, *see* Maitland
Law, Edward, Lord Chief Justice Ellenborough 409
Lawes, John Bennet 160
Lawes, Sir John Bennet, Bt. 269
lawyers 55, 89, 114, 117, 134, 150, 161-68, 184, 189-91, 194, 197, 199-201, 209, 225-26, 228, 230-33, 237, 239-41, 243, 247, 256-57, 268, 277, 281, 289, 307, 317, 324-25, 358, 360, 363, 376-77, 389-90, 398-403, 419, 451-52, 481, 486-87, 510
Laxton Hall, Northants. 319, 433
Leach, William 352
the Leasowes, Halesowen, Worcs. 338
Lee, John [Fiott] 245
Lee, Sir Henry 349
Leeds, Yorks. WR 212-15, 217, 411; – Hunt 213
Leeds, Dukes of, *see* Osborne
Legh-Keck, George 137
Leghorn, Italy 151
Leicestershire 230, 267
Leigh, Sir Edward, Bt. 137
Leigh-Dryden, Sir Henry 111
Leman, Sir William 202
Lemmington Hall, Edlingham, Northumb. 434
Leoni, Giacomo 382
L'Estrange, Sir Nicholas 268
Levant Company 23, 202-03, 234-38, 289
Leventhorpe, Sir John, 1st Bt. 149
Leventhorpe, Sir Thomas, 4th Bt. 149-50
Leventhorpe family 149, 295
Leventhorpe Hall, Yorks. 149
Leveson, Sir John 136
Leveson-Gower, William 136
Leveson-Gower family 136
Lichfield, Staffs. 117
Liddell, George, Colonel 274
Lilford, Lord, *see* Powys

Lilbord Hall, Northants. 314, 330, 432, 465
Lilburn Towers, Eglingham, Northumb. 435
Lincolnshire 156
Linden House, Long Horsley, Northumb. 434
Lipscomb, George 55
Lipton, Sir Thomas, Bt. 289
Little Court, Layston, Herts. 162, 169, 381, 430, 464
Little Grove, East Barnet, Herts. 117, 166, 431
Little Harle Tower, Northumb. 240, 435
Little Houghton House, Northants. 433
Little Oakley Manor House, Northants. 432
Liverpool, Lancs. 36; –, Lord, *see* Jenkinson
Lloyd, Samuel, 1st Lord Overstone 220, 377
Locke, John 414-15
Lockleys, Welwyn, Herts. 330, 430
Lomax, Joshua I 190-91, 200
Lomax, Joshua II 191
Lomax, Thomas 191
London, 32, 34-48, 50, 52, 61, 113-16, 125, 133, 150, 156, 159, 162, 164, 166, 168, 170, 172-74, 178-79, 189, 191-94, 201, 204, 206, 209, 213, 215, 217-22, 228, 234-35, 237, 240, 248-49, 251-55, 267-68, 270, 272, 276, 280, 283, 285, 288, 290-91, 296-97, 299, 315-16, 323-27, 350, 361, 363, 365, 369, 384, 386, 390-91, 398, 404-05, 411, 413, 438, 481; Berkeley Square 325; Blackwell Hall 193; Bloomsbury 324; Cavendish Square 324; City of 16-8, 26, 165, 285, 289; Common Council of 219; Covent Garden 324; Fleet, Rules of 79; Grosvenor Square 255, 324-25; Guilds 233-34; Hanover Square 324; Holland House, Kensington 355, pl. XIIIB; Hyde Park 253; Lincoln's Inn Fields 324; Lord Mayor of 159, 168, 192, 201, 238, 252, 261, 287-88; Lothbury 267; Mayfair 252; Montagu House 355; Norfolk House 125; Pall Mall 34; Portland Place 308; Ranelagh House 354; St James's Park 216; St James's Square 252, 255, 289, 297, 324; St Paul's, Dean and Chapter

Date Due